Peter G Kirchschlaeger

Digital Transformation and Ethics

Ethical Considerations on the Robotization
and Automation of Society and the Economy
and the Use of Artificial Intelligence

The Deutsche Nationalbibliothek lists this publication in the Deutsche Nationalbibliografie; detailed bibliographic data are available on the Internet at http://dnb.d-nb.de

ISBN   978-3-8487-4287-5 (Print)
       978-3-8452-8550-4 (ePDF)

British Library Cataloguing-in-Publication Data
A catalogue record for this book is available from the British Library.

ISBN   978-3-8487-4287-5 (Print)
       978-3-8452-8550-4 (ePDF)

Library of Congress Cataloging-in-Publication Data
Kirchschlaeger, Peter G
Digital Transformation and Ethics
Ethical Considerations on the Robotization and Automation of Society
and the Economy and the Use of Artificial Intelligence
Peter G Kirchschlaeger
537 pp.
Includes bibliographic references.

ISBN   978-3-8487-4287-5 (Print)
       978-3-8452-8550-4 (ePDF)

edition sigma in der Nomos Verlagsgesellschaft

1st Edition 2021
© Nomos Verlagsgesellschaft, Baden-Baden, Germany 2021. Overall responsibility for manufacturing (printing and production) lies with Nomos Verlagsgesellschaft mbH & Co. KG.

Reviews

"In our day, humanity has entered a new era in which our technical prowess, especially digital technological prowess, has brought us to a crossroads (cf. LS, 102), influencing greatly our common good. It is urgent, therefore, to explore the ethical dilemmas around such technological development, and how some basic ethical consensus can help us use, especially again, digital technology for the common good. In this regard, this book 'Digital Transformation and Ethics' makes an invaluable contribution." **Cardinal Peter Kodwo Appiah Turkson, Prefect of the Dicastery for Promoting Integral Human Development**

"The 15th and 16th century explorers used compass and the stars to navigate. Today's digital transformation needs solid scientific analysis and ethical frameworks to charter the way forward in complex territories. Peter G Kirchschlaeger's work offers both rigorous science and practical orientations on key legal and policy issues: this framing is important everywhere and particularly in fragile contexts for vulnerable populations." **Dr Peter Maurer, President of the International Committee of the Red Cross (ICRC)**

"'Digital Transformation and Ethics' is a valuable overview of ethical issues in artificial intelligence, their impact on our daily lives and importance for future applications. With this timely analysis, Peter G Kirchschlaeger highlights fundamental questions pertaining to our relationship with technology and its impact on justice, freedom, and human rights." **Ai Weiwei, Artist**

"Practical, compelling, stimulating. In this outstanding book, Peter G Kirchschlaeger brings new insights to the story of digital transformation and human rights. A superb look at how robotization and automatization is progressing and supporting the transformation from a world in which digitalization has big winners and losers, to one in which digitalization hopefully contributes to more equity and balance for people and planet. An excellent read, filled with personal experiences and reflections on freedom, autonomy, responsibility, conscience and ethical judgement that will engage students, CEOs and politicians alike." **Susanne Giger, Business Presenter, Lecturer, Member of the Board of Directors of the Coop Group**

"This remarkable book calls upon us to defend human dignity from the myriad threats of the new digital age. Peter G Kirchschlaeger recognizes that digital technologies can benefit humanity by broadening access to knowledge and to vital services such as healthcare. Yet he shows how digital technologies also threaten human dignity and human rights, through impacts on employment, income distribution, political power, self-esteem and social relations. Most importantly, Peter G Kirchschlaeger argues cogently that humanity must put human rights at the core of our governance of the digital technologies, to ensure that the new machines serve the cause of human dignity rather than humanity becoming the servant of the machines." **Professor Dr Jeffrey D. Sachs, Columbia University, USA; Special Advisor to the UN Secretary-General António Guterres on the objectives of sustainable development**

"This book is about fundamental, yet rarely addressed, aspects of the digital journey – ethics and values. Highly valuable for anyone who ambitions to have a positive impact with technology." **Silvio Napoli, Chairman of Schindler Group**

"Will data-based technologies come to control us, will some humans master them toward manipulating the rest? Peter G Kirchschlaeger's book provides the ethical orientation we urgently need to hold these rapidly advancing technologies consistent with the human rights and dignity of all human beings." **Professor Dr Thomas Pogge, Leitner Professor of Philosophy and International Affairs, Yale University, USA**

"One of the great ethical challenges of our time is the rapid technological change epitomized in the digital transformation of all spheres of life. In this book, an ethicist and human rights expert offers an admirable attempt to help us come to grips with this challenge in an almost encyclopedic, critical as well as constructive, manner." **Professor Dr Hans Joas, Humboldt University of Berlin, Germany / University of Chicago, USA**

"If there was one book I would recommend to any Tech entrepreneur these days, it is this book. Peter G Kirchschlaeger wrote one of the most important and most comprehensive contributions to the current debate on Digital Transformation, Ethics and Artificial Intelligence by covering an enormous breadth on some of the hottest disciplines in tech." **Pascal Kaufmann, Neuroscientist and Entrepreneur; Co-Founder of the Software Company Starmind International; Founder of the Mindfire Foundation**

"As an AI researcher, ethics becomes more and more critical for AI processing and robotics. I have worked in the AI area for material discovery, biomedical engineering, and machine controls. I encountered that ethics and human privacy should be the baseline of AI solutions. This new book written by Peter G Kirchschlaeger is considering such an important issue for various cases and applications. A few example areas in this book include robots, artificial intelligence solutions, data-based systems, and digital transformation. This topic is universally essential since AI is going to be popular everywhere on the earth. I globally recommend this great book to anybody interested in AI ethics." **Sungjin (James) Kim, AI Researcher; Senior Research Fellow, VP, LG Electronics**

"This book is a definitive must for everyone who is interested to learn about the intersection of AI, Ethics and Society. Peter G Kirchschlaeger's thoughts on the digital transformation from an ethical perspective represent a substantial contribution to a debate that we need to pursue on a well informed basis." **Professor Dr Dr h.c. Frank Kirchner, Director Robotics Innovation Center, German Research Center for Artificial Intelligence DFKI, Germany**

"Digital technologies are transforming our lives at a rapidly accelerating pace. Talk of 'artificial moral agents' and 'morality in design' can conceal the abdication of moral responsibility and the enrichment of a few at the expense of the many. While acknowledging the thoroughgoing intertwinement of human beings and technology, Peter G Kirchschlaeger urgently summons his readers to the task of analyzing and assessing artificial intelligence and the robotization and automatization of society. Only by asserting our moral agency can we ensure that digital technologies serve, rather than undermining, the flourishing of all of humankind and of the world. A vital contribution to a critically important undertaking." **Professor Dr Jennifer Herdt, Gilbert L. Stark Professor of Christian Ethics, Yale University Divinity School, USA; President of the Society of Christian Ethics**

"Although there is a plethora of books devoted to the problem area of ethical reasoning on the field of digital technologies, none so far has unfolded the complexity of the questions and the associated challenges to ethical thinking in such a multifaceted and systematic way as this work. It must be regarded not only as a milestone in the ethical debate. Moreover, it is valuable for interdisciplinary research, since the crucial interfaces for interdisciplinary exploration of this terrain, which is so difficult to cope with, are also opened up." **Professor Dr Stefan Boeschen, Chair "Society and**

7

Technology" at Human Technology Center (HumTec), RWTH Aachen University, Germany

"With so much at stake, the need for ethics and AI technology to come together is now more urgent than ever before. With this truly inspiring and exciting masterpiece, Peter G Kirchschlaeger lays out the groundwork for developing the next generation of human-friendly digital technologies." **Professor Dr Benjamin Grewe, Full Professor of Systems and Circuits Neuroinformatics, Institute of Neuroinformatics UZH/ETH Zurich, Department of Electrical Engineering and Information Technology, ETH Zurich**

"For those involved in digital transformation, and almost all of us are, this book is indispensable. The detailed scientific examination of the ethical aspects of digitization, its opportunities, challenges and risks, is long overdue and yet comes at just the right time." **Professor Dr-Ing Thomas Bauernhansl, Director of the Fraunhofer Institute for Manufacturing Engineering and Automation; Director of the Institute of Industrial Manufacturing and Management IFF, University of Stuttgart, Germany**

"A comprehensively researched scientific framework to help consider machine intelligence as an opportunity, rather than a threat, for humanity to engage in an honest, informed, and scientifically grounded dialogue about the values underpinning AI systems design, development, and deployment, and the ethical and moral implications of these values choices." **Professor Dr Maria Angela Ferrario, School of Electronics, Electrical Engineering and Computer Science, Queen's University Belfast, Northern Ireland**

"The ethical considerations of digital transformation are often dismissed with arguments about progress, efficiency, and potential job creation. This is particularly concerning for those of us living in regions where many technological advancements in this area are not even created locally, but simply imported. We find companies taking advantage of the legal loopholes or in some cases, the complete absence of any legal structures and policies addressing these developments. My hope would be that this timely and thought-provoking book prompts further discourse on a topic that requires the urgent and fervent involvement of those for whom digital transformation is having an impact – which today, means all of us." **Akaliza Keza Ntwari, Entrepreneur from Rwanda in the field of technology; one of the founders of "Girls in ICT Rwanda"; Member of the UN High-Level Panel on Digital Cooperation**

"The digital transformation is affecting our societies and lives in unprecedented ways. Thorough ethical reflection on the opportunities and dangers of this change is more important than ever – and is exactly what this thoughtful book provides." **Professor Dr Klaas Enno Stephan, Full Professor for Translational Neuromodeling & Computational Psychiatry at the University of Zurich and ETH Zurich**

"An independent, profound, and all-encompassing ethical evaluation of the contemporary technologies and artificial intelligence which daily revolutionize our lives. The author stands for ethics which is needed so that digital transformation, robotization, and the use of artificial intelligence do not simply happen, but we can consciously shape them. He understands multiple benefits of scientific progress but also reveals the immense threats that the use or abuse of new technologies and machines can pose to our human and humane nature – our minds, virtues, and freedoms, and to democratic and other societal values. He firmly defends homo dignitatis from homo digitalis and stands for social justice and sustainable development, thus reminding us that human dignity, trust, solidarity, and many other values are inalienable from human beings. Great book, a must-read for everyone who wants to be a part of the solution in ethical confrontation with some unprecedented challenges of our time." **Professor Dr Miro Cerar, Law Professor, Faculty of Law of the University of Ljubljana, Slovenia; former Slovenian Prime minister (2014-2018) and Deputy Prime Minister and Minister of Foreign Affairs (2018-2020), Slovenia**

"This is a most timely and comprehensive book on the important, impactful and multi-faceted issues surrounding 'Digital Transformation and Ethics'. From the thought provoking Prologue to the personal Epilogue II I thoroughly enjoyed this tour de force across ethics, philosophy, law, computer science, technology, society and politics." **Professor Dr Felix A. Wichmann, Full Professor and Group Leader "Neural Information Processing Group", Faculty of Science, University of Tuebingen, Germany**

"The digital revolution is full of surprises. We just arrived in the anthropocene, the age of humanity, but very soon, robots are expected to take over. Then, however, at the climax of a materialistic, technology-driven world, we see another turn: ethics and values, which almost seemed to be forgotten, are suddenly back. No doubt, this is the beginning of a new historical age! Peter G Kirchschlaeger's Book 'Digital Transformation and Ethics' places you right in the middle of the debate." **Professor Dr Dirk**

Helbing, Professor of Computational Social Science, Department of Humanities, Social and Political Sciences, affiliate of the Computer Science Department, ETH Zurich

"This new book by Peter G Kirchschlaeger offers a must read compilation and analysis of ethical questions about digital transformation, artificial intelligence as well as the changes of daily habits by online services. His issues raised, the ethical solutions offered are a rare and impressive contribution for a future paving this path of technology-based progress with profound non-technical thinking. Peter G Kirchschaeger has written a helpful masterpiece to enrich the unavoidable disruptions caused by digital technologies with Substance beyond the present digital canon." **Professor Dr Dr h.c. Guenter Mueller, Emeritus of Computer Science and Information Systems at the University of Freiburg and former Director of the Institute of Informatics and Society, Germany**

"'This trailblazing book concerns artificial intelligence (AI) and practical ethics. Its author does not much like the term AI. He points out, correctly, that it posits the possibility that machines may 'think intelligently' and 'morally'; whereas that is precisely the threshold problem that has to be resolved. He prefers to describe the automated processes of 'data-based systems'; and to do so empirically and objectively by reference to what machines and systems actually do. He explains why it is impossible to translate the bloodless language and symbols of mathematics and digital programming into the rule-transcending uniqueness of individual ethical judgements. From this starting point, he proposes the creation of an International Data-based Systems Agency (DSA) and 30 principles to govern its potential role and work in a field where the technology is moving with lightning speed. In his view, only humans can be the moral subjects of ethics. Machines and their systems can inflict death, suffering and pain; but they cannot themselves experience the same outcomes and reason to accommodate all of the applicable ethical nuances. At a time of fast moving digital technology, public and private megadata and manipulative algorithms, we are thus confronted with some of the most profound philosophical questions of our age: and the deepest practical question of them all, namely, what the human species can do to uphold the human primacy for which the author so powerfully contends." **Honourable Michael Kirby AC CMG, past Justice of the High Court of Australia (1996-2009) and Chair of the OECD expert groups on the protection of privacy and of security of information systems (1980 and 1992); Co-Chair, In-**

ternational Bar Association, Human Rights Institute (2017-2021), Australia

"A rigorous and updated book on the relationship between ethics and the ever-evolving dimensions of technologies and society – timely underlined also by the current Covid-19 pandemic." **Professor Dr Laura Palazzani, Member of the UNESCO International Bioethics Committee; Member of the European Group on Ethics in Science and New Technologies of the EU Commission; Professor of Philosophy of Law and Biolaw, Lumsa University Rome, Italy**

"This essential book discusses the technological transformation of digitalization from an ethical perspective. In the first part of the book, the necessity and added value of an ethical view of modern technologies is presented in an up-to-date and comprehensive manner.
The second part considers the mutual interactions between modern technologies as well as their application scenarios.
The third part provides up-to-date advice on the implementation of ethical issues in the use of modern technologies. Here, the focus is particularly on the protection of human rights.
Peter G Kirchschlaeger's book goes far beyond an abstract ethical view of modern technologies and gives new impetus to the discussion about the opportunities and risks of using highly efficient but also very powerful technologies.
Due to its clear concept and practical examples, the book is highly recommendable not only for ethicists but especially for engineers and managers.
The book should therefore find a firm place as an important contribution to the discussion of application scenarios of modern technologies from an ethical perspective." **Professor Dr-Ing Stephan Schaefer, Professor at the Institute of Electrical Engineering, Hochschule fuer Technik und Wirtschaft Berlin, Germany**

"Peter G Kirchschlaeger's Digital Transformation and Ethics – Ethical Considerations on the Robotization and Automatization of Society and Economy and the Use of Artificial Intelligence points in an immensely readable and highly instructive way to the critical need to understand that digital technology and AI aren't energy neutral or ecologically benign. It sounds the warning of an evolving global colonization by multinational technology-corporations in an age where technology runs ahead of regulation and technofixes are seen as untouchable silver bullets." **Nnimmo Bassey, Writer/Poet and Director of the Health of Mother Earth Foundation, Nigeria; Winner of the Right Livelihood Award**

"We fly without fear. That is only possible because of regulation. Tight regulations make airplanes safe. It is the same for AI: Regulations are required for safe and effective AI. Peter G Kirchschlaeger's book discusses the ethical groundwork. Highly recommended for anyone." **Dr Dorian Selz, Serial Entrepreneur; CEO & Co-Founder of Squirro**

"Peter G Kirchschlaeger's book 'Digital Transformation and Ethics' is a powerful and sophisticated defense of our shared ethical principles and norms as the biggest human achievement of modernity and it demonstrates that they are still valid arsenal for fighting against the widespread naive drive for the sweeping wave of digital transformation. The book will be one of the reference points for surveying and discussing the ethics of digital technology in the future!" **Professor Gunoo Kim, Professor of Law, Gwangju Institute of Science and Technology, South Korea**

"Artificial intelligence ought to be paired with human ethics or else it risks turning into artificial tyranny. Everyone interested in the mature and enlightened interaction with digital technology, one that puts it at the service of human life, rather than the other way around, should read this book. Peter G Kirchschlaeger charts a walkable path into a digital future that belongs to humans, rather than to machines." **Professor Dr Florian Wettstein, Professor of Business Ethics and Director of the Institute for Business Ethics at University of St Gallen; Vice-President of the International Society of Business, Economics and Ethics ISBEE**

"This book is a must for anyone interested in getting a broad overview regarding the far reaching issues of Ethics in our Digital Society. It delivers a profound analysis ranging from the fundamentals of Ethics all the way to its practical implications and their potential impact on humans and our social institutions." **Peter Rudin, Visionary Entrepreneur and CEO of singularity2030.ch**

"History reminds us that many of the horrors of the not-too-distant past were justified as part of the pursuit of scientific innovation and progress. Human rights emerged as an ethical language for challenging and opposing the exploitation of science to justify those atrocities. Peter G Kirchschlaeger's excellent book is a timely caution that ethics and human rights should be at the core of the new technologies now deployed in data collection, surveillance and in risk governance by public as well as private entities, if we are to avoid reproducing the tragedies of the past." **Dr Mutuma Ruteere, Former UN Special Rapporteur on Contemporary Forms of Racism, Racial Discrimination, Xenophobia and Related Intolerance**

"There is a lot of homework to be done for our societies in terms of digitalization. Peter G Kirchschlaeger provides the respective materials and the searching questions we have to deal with. This book gives a profound review of the challenging ethical issues coming up with digitalization, roboterization and artificial intelligence. And it offers stimulating perspectives for constructive dialogue between ethics and technology." **Professor Dr Arne Manzeschke, Professor of Anthropology and Ethics for Health Professions, Evangelische Hochschule Nuernberg, Germany; President of the European Research Society for Ethics Societas Ethica**

"Peter G Kirchschlaeger reflects on a digital world in the making. He comes up with proposals for embedding digitalization in a new blueprint of thoughts and actions. A blueprint geared towards honoring human rights and shaping a more humane world. In a nutshell, advanced thinking in a perpetually changing world. A great help for all those whishing to act responsibly based on clear awareness." **Patrick Hohmann, Founder and Chairman of the Remei AG**

"No digital transformation can succeed without a solid foundation of ethics. The new book by Peter G Kirchschlaeger is a comprehensive and important contribution to help decision-makers root societal applications of Artificial Intelligence in human dignity and agency." **Ambassador Amandeep Gill, Director of the Global Health Centre project on International Digital Health & AI Research Collaborative (I-DAIR)**

"This book is not just a book, it is a call for awareness, overwhelming of humanism. A dynamic synthesis of immanence and transcendence. An ode to ethics." **Robin Cornelius, Founder of Switcher SA; Founder and CEO of Product DNA SA**

"Based on a solid philosophical and ethical discourse, Peter G Kirchschlaeger reviews critically the digital (r)evolution and resulting societal development to date and where the world is heading. It becomes clear that those who drive and shape this transformation neither base their decisions on universal or agreed ethical principles, nor that they are democratically legitimized or controlled to assume and execute the power over everyone of us that they already have. Kirchschlaeger uses a vast range of sources and examples to summarize the risks and grave possible consequences if the actors and their inventions are left unattended and unregulated. He does not stop there but proposes concretely and comprehensively what must be done by governments and the democratic electorate to manage the destructive potential of the ongoing digital transformation. A very relevant book at a most crucial time." **Christian Goeckenjan, Head of Technology & Cyber Risk Control at a global bank**

"In the tradition of Ancient African, Ethics in Maat has always permeated social relations. The same we must bring to the current relations with technological advances, they need ethics to guarantee powers without violating the humanities, understanding the importance of technology in maintaining future advances, for this, Ethics is the determining element. This stunning, philosophically sharp, and rhetorically superb book by Peter G Kirchschlaeger shows eloquently a humane path forward." **Katiúscia Ribeiro, Researcher and University Lecturer of African Philosophy and Ethics, Women's Thoughts and Community Relations, Federal University of Rio de Janeiro, Brazil**

"In a time of dramatically growing complexity, which is in its cultural dimension accompanied by an era of confusion, nothing is more needed than orientation, explanation and interpretation of presence and future. Peter G Kirchschlaeger delivers this orientation in this book in an impressive way." **Professor Dr Dr h.c. Werner Weidenfeld, Director of the Center for Applied Policy Research (CAP) of the University of Munich, Germany**

"The wide-ranging scope and sheer rapidity of transformations wrought by new digital technologies have left societies unprepared at many levels – including with regard to the ethical dimensions. This important and thought-provoking book unpacks some of the crucial ethical questions that must guide us, if humanity is to benefit from the new opportunities while recognizing the ambivalences they create." **Professor Dr Jayati Ghosh, Professor of Economics, University of Massachusetts at Amherst, USA**

"Everyone needs to read Peter G Kirchschlaeger's new book on digital transformation and ethics. This profound masterpiece of rare conceptual brilliance provides urgent and essential ethical guidance for the present and the future. It offers a groundbreaking and beautifully written analysis of uncomfortable ethical questions about digital transformation and artificial intelligence. Beyond that, it designs in a magisterial way inspiring ethical solutions for this technology-based progress." **Alessio Allegrini, Conductor, Hornist, and Founder of Musicians for Human Rights**

"Peter G Kirchschlaeger, in this extensively researched work, explores the advantages and disadvantages of digital transformation and data-based systems, which has made human existence technologically accessed but ethically it may be the largest ungoverned space of the world. Being a deep thinker, ethicist, philosopher, speaker, profound writer, and a human rights expert, Peter G Kirchschlaeger contextualizes answers to a plethora of ethical issues, challenges, opportunities and questions to the highly volatile and ambiguous realities of digital transformation distributed unequally in the globe. This ethics of human rights based, critically argued epistemological work has been developed on the strong underpinning of philosophy, ethical principles of responsibility, omni-dynamic social justice and human rights. An epiphany for every reader, a guiding tool for every policy maker, the book is truly empowering." **Shylaja Santosh, Journalist and Human Rights Educator, State of Karnataka, India**

"Greatly familiar with both the world of digital transformation and the depth of ethics, Peter G Kirchschlaeger critically examines the key terms of the debate such as 'artificial intelligence' and 'networks' and highlights the far-reaching relevance of human dignity and internationally recognized human rights for guiding the digital transformation. The book is a persuasive wake-up call to understand and implement the right to privacy and data-protection and the other human rights in the contexts of surveillance capitalism and surveillance totalitarianism." **Professor Dr Georges Enderle, Professor Emeritus of International Business Ethics, University of Notre Dame, USA**

"Developments in Robotics and Artificial Intelligence hold potential, but can also be unsettling. Critical vigilance towards them is as important as human rights-based answers to the ethical concerns. After all – as Peter G Kirchschlaeger points out – Robots and Artificial Intelligence do not represent superhuman forces, but are no better and no worse than how we humans program them and which use we make of them. With this publication, the author fills a gap and makes an indispensable academic contribution to the comprehensive consideration of digital transformation from an ethical standpoint." **Professor Dr Martin M Lintner, Professor for Moral Theology, Philosophisch-Theologische Hochschule Brixen, Italy; former President of the Internationale Vereinigung für Moraltheologie und Sozialethik**

"Will we human beings hold the leach or carry the collar as the dog? Will we take the lead and shape technology to serve human kind rather than being enslaved or subordinated to technology? The book 'Digital Transformation and Ethics' analyses in a profound manner this question from an ethical and human rights-based approach. Peter G Kirchschlaeger takes the reader on an impressive journey through the many dilemmas that we are confronted with on a daily basis and leaves us empowered to hold the leach. Amid the expanding academic literature on new technology the book 'Digital Transformation and Ethics' stands out and will remain relevant for long." **Adj. Professor Morten Kjaerum, Director of the Raoul Wallenberg Institute of Human Rights and Humanitarian Law, Sweden; former Director of the EU Fundamental Rights Agency**

"An essential resource for all of us to read in our technologically driven world! This book explores the ethical questions related to how technology controls our lives and how humans should advocate for more ethically based approaches to the development of new technologies. This book makes a very important contribution to the discussion of how technological innovation must also consider the ethical and moral dimensions of its impact on our lives. It is essential reading not just for the ordinary citizen but for those who lead our technology driven economy and society." **Assoc. Professor Dr Nina Burridge, Honorary Professional Fellow, School of International Studies and Education, Faculty of Arts and Social Sciences, University of Technology, Sydney, Australia**

"I congratulate Peter G Kirchschlaeger on his ground-breaking book on ethics of artificial intelligence. While the technology of AI is progressing fast inevitably bringing profound changes in the life and livelihood of all people of the earth, this is high time that we consider the ethics of it and try to guide its progress on an ethically acceptable path. Already, AI is promising to be an automated technology minimizing the need of human in not only manufacturing works, but also intellectual works too. While it can solve huge problems, which are troubling us now, it may also totally devalue human labor putting the capital in supreme power. This will carry the current concentration of wealth to an impossible extent. On the other hand, AI can free billions of people from an existence in drudgery and poverty, and allow them the time and opportunity to enjoy the higher things in life. Under a dominance of AI, our existing economic and ethical system may face a totally new situation. A drastic situation like that will need a drastic intervention through a grand human consensus. Ultimately the humanity itself being at stake here, we have to look for the very core of human ethics as the main guiding light of that consensus. Peter G Kirchschlaeger's book, therefore, has not come any earlier than it should. The book has tried to look at every aspect of the ethics involved in AI, and can be instrumental in starting that very important conversation which may make AI a glory of human achievement taking the humanity to a pinnacle, not a mistake taking the humanity to its doom. I congratulate Peter G

Kirchschlaeger again for his timely effort." **Professor Dr Muhammad Ibrahim, Professor Emeritus of Physics, University of Dhaka; Founder and Executive Director of the Centre for Mass Education and Science CMES, Bangladesh**

"A great book! The author combines the best European traditions of human-based ethical thinking in a free civil society with a fine awareness of the challenges in the digital world and in AI development! Having in mind the challenging task of combining ethical values with AI in data-based systems, the author starts from human vulnerability. This goes beyond classical approaches and ends up in promoting human rights as basic principles also in the field of AI and data-based systems.

The advantage of this approach comes with its application to a variety of practical fields such as in health-care or finance. Peter G Kirchschlaeger gains a normative guideline for dealing with a human centered use of databased-systems and artificial intelligence." **Professor Dr Ulrich Hemel, Director of the Global Ethics Institute Tuebingen, Germany; Deputy Spokesperson and Member of the CyberValley Public Advisory Board; President of the Federation of Catholic Entrepreneurs in Germany**

"This amazing book helps us understanding the deep implications that technology is having and will have in our life. Never in the past technology could have shaped and modified our lifestyle and the quality of life that we are used to. This power has grown too fast and too big with no deep understanding of its long term consequences on sustainability, inequality, justice. It's the right moment to pause and reason on how to make technology serve the flourishing of all humans – guided by the illuminating thoughts by Peter G Kirchschlaeger." **Simone Molteni, Scientific Director of LifeGate**

"Peter G Kirchschlaeger provides us with a dense and insightful analysis of the ethical challenges of digital transformation. A worthwile read!" **Professor Dr Melinda Lohmann, Assistant Professor of Business Law, with special emphasis on Information Law, University of St Gallen**

"In our times in which people try to robotize human beings and to 'humanize' robots, Peter G Kirchschlaeger's new book, with its rich content and its careful clarification of concepts, shows clearly a pressing need for a different from the prevailing approach to Ethics." **Professor Dr İoanna Kuçuradi, UNESCO Chair of Philosophy of Human Rights and Director of the Centre for Research and Application of Human Rights at Maltepe University, Turkey; President of the Philosophical Society of Turkey**

"This extraordinary book of Peter G Kirchschlaeger impresses with an excellent documentation of issues in the fields of advanced technology and with a deep analysis of their relationship with ethics. He offers the clear proposition that the ethical judgement and the control must be located in humans not in technology as he reassumes in his first epilogue, thinking of a dog on a leash: 'do we humans want to hold the leash or carry the collar?' He bravely discusses opportunities and challenges from an ethical perspective and offers in his wonderful book a personal ethical and legal proposal about technological progress culminating in the 'homo dignitatis' instead of 'homo digitalis'. I dare to assure the readers of this book that they will find in it: how to confront the delicate and inevitable situation of present times in relationship with the future for humans regarding the technological progress; how to get an exhaustive understanding of actual issues of high technology; how the author unveils the serious risks that elements of high technology present to fundamental human values; how the research about the ethical problems in relationship to high technology is based in direct references taken from the more connoted actors of the analyzed problems; how the ethical criteria used by the author to solve the proposed problems are anchored in the most correct actual ethical tradition; how the ethical proposal of the author to handle the complex presented problems is sustained by the most respectable institutions oriented to the common good of all mankind; how the author discovers a very wide field for research not enough approached by ethics and morals in the last decades, but of extraordinary transcendence for the actual times and the next future; how the author brings out the most profound Christian moral principles from their evident rationality and wisdom without any explicit reference to a religious proposal.

I highly recommend this book not only for interested readers but specially for academic institutions centered in Ethics or Moral Theology. Catholic Church scholars should take profit of this wonderful work of Peter G Kirchschlaeger for their teaching and research according with the direction indicated by Pope Francis in his Encyclicals Laudato si' and Fratelli tutti."
Professor Dr Alberto Múnera, S.J., PhD, STD, Tenured Moral Professor, Faculty of Theology, Pontificia Universidad Javeriana, Bogotá, Colombia

"This book makes a valuable contribution to the field by unpacking how ethics can and should guide the digital transformation of society as well as economy." **Professor Dr Surya Deva, Associate Professor at the School of Law, City University of Hong Kong, Hong Kong; Vice-Chair of the UN Working Group on the issue of human rights and transnational corporations and other business enterprises**

"A much needed voice on one of the most relevant topics for the future of humanity. The rampant lack of ethics in the field of digital technology is one of the most dangerous threats to humanity. This much needed and eye-opening book explores methodically how we turn the wheel around." **Jéronimo Calderón, Social Entrepreneur, Co-Explorer Amanitas, Ashoka Fellow, Alumni of the Global Shapers Community of the World Economic Forum WEF**

To our daughter Mia Esther

Table of Contents

Table of Contents

Prologue

What would a dictator wish for in order to get as many people as possible under his control? He would wish that as many people as possible were connected to each other technologically, everywhere and always, and that he had access to this digital network.

What would a company wish for in order to have as much influence as possible on as many people as possible and turn them into its customers? The company would wish that as many people as possible were connected to each other technologically, everywhere and always, and that it had access to this digital network.

How would humans who would be killed by poverty or poverty-related causes wish that most financial resources were allocated?

What would humans wish for instead of being reduced to algorithms and data?

What would humans wish for instead of being innovated away?

What would humans wish for in order to be respected as bearers of human dignity and human rights?

Would humans wish to be the masters or the slaves of algorithms and data?

1 Introduction

Writing or reading a book about rapidly advancing technology-based progress initially might trigger the suspicion that the approach could be anachronistic.[1] Does the methodical approach of a book not seem to contradict the content? Is there not a danger that the colorful bouquet of arguments starts to wilt even before it starts to blossom, because reality has surpassed and outpaced the writing long before it is written? Is the variety and complexity of technology-based achievements, phenomena, products, and realities even amenable to an ethical approach in the form of a book? Do not worry. It does make sense to continue reading this book. Because neither human curiosity to discover and invent new things nor the human fascination with the questions of what humans want to be, what kind of a world humans dream of, and if everything that humans are technically able to do should really be done, are innovations of the 21st century. Both go far back in the history of humanity, and neither is at all likely to disappear any time soon.

Furthermore, ethical reflection is also distinguished by the fact that it strives to give answers in a justifiably reliable and universally binding manner to questions asking to what end, on what grounds, and why. Ethics is a science, which reflects on morals. As a scientific discipline, ethics strives for knowledge about what ought to be in a rational, logically coherent, methodological-reflective, and systematic way. Ethics aspires to a universally, even intergenerationally, justifiable notion of right and wrong and of good and bad. Universality as a necessary characteristic of ethics, ethical assertions, ethical principles, and ethical norms presupposes the fulfillment of the principle of generalizability by presenting rational and plausible arguments – "good reasons". "Good reasons" means that it must be conceivable that all humans, given their effective freedom and autonomy as well as their full equality, would agree upon these reasons – within a model of thought and not within a real worldwide referendum – on ethical grounds. The ethically required should not change on a day-to-day basis. The ethical principle of human dignity of all humans, for example, which stipulates that all humans are unique, which distinguishes them from ma-

---

1 All verbatim quotations originally written in languages other than English have been translated by the author.

terial objects and other forms of life, and which prohibits in an absolute way putting a price tag on humans, does not lose any of its validity in view of the latest scientific findings or the latest technological developments. Finally, ethics does not react to nor lag behind, but instead interacts with research, development, and technology.

Epistemic modesty is needed when ethically dealing with digitalization, automation, mechanization, robotization of society and of the economy, and the use of artificial intelligence in this book because, obviously, there can be no claim to be able to ethically discuss this technology-based change in its fullness, breadth, and depth.[2] Rather, self-restriction needs to be practiced when writing this book so as to show in an exemplary manner, and only in the sense of presenting an introductory overview of some of the most important aspects, elements, and areas of digital transformation and the use of artificial intelligence and, hopefully, to give some humble ethical impetus for further ethical and interdisciplinary research. It is also hoped that the argumentative radiance of the considerations presented in this book can also enrich the ethical reflection of certain points and fields that unfortunately cannot be addressed in this book.

Epistemic modesty also needs to be cultivated in this book when dealing with digitalization, automation, mechanization, robotization, and the use of artificial intelligence with regard to the certainly intended, but unfortunately by no means successful, comprehensive and complete embedding in the scientific discourse. I ask those colleagues who were not taken into account in an adequate manner within the parameters of this book for their understanding.

The analysis of digitalization, automation, mechanization, robotization, and the use of artificial intelligence is characterized by epistemic modesty from an ethical perspective (a locution used in this book to indicate the scientific analysis striving for the fulfillment of the standards as described above in the definition of ethics) in the shape of this book, concerning the fact that in many cases ethics has no choice but to make conceivable and plausible statements about the future use of the current state of research. Of course, there is the danger that the future will catch up or overtake

---

2 The following topics would also merit attention, which is not possible in this book: among others, the topic of human-robot-sex, see e.g., Cheok et al. 2017; Bołtuć 2017; Mathis 2019; the topic of smart cities and digital construction, see e.g., Kitchin 2016; Calvo 2020; the topic of "smart prisons", see Knight / van de Steene 2017; the topic of robots, artificial intelligence, and space, see Abney 2017; or the topic of artificial creativity, see Rauterberg 2019.

more quickly or more slowly than anticipated or that the future will turn out quite differently than rationally assumed.

Modesty in the ethical assessment of technological progress is also required due to the risk of a "futurological fallacy"[3]. The question arises if ethical principles and norms that can be morally justified still remain valid and adequate for new and future stages of digital transformation. "We humans tend to lack historical perspective, mistaking our own time, place, politics, and culture as normative. (...) Iconic of this tendency is the computer – on which I compose these reflections – and the smartphone and tablet by my side. These devices have become indispensable tools of everyday life, as important as running water and electric lights. Really we should be gobsmacked every time we turn to these devices, which change how we live and also who we are. A mere century ago these now ubiquitous technologies would be seen as magic."[4] It is impossible to present reasons why ethical principles and norms that can be morally justified should no longer remain valid and adequate for new and future stages of digital transformation.[5]

Epistemic modesty is needed because ethics continues to struggle with the following question: "How does ethics withstand the problems of its lack of expertise, consensus and enforceability?"[6].

In all modesty, ethicists must make themselves heard in the discourse of digital transformation, primarily because of the nature of technology as a human creation.[7] "Ethics has a saying in matters related to technique simply because technology is part of the exercise of human power, namely a form of action, and all human actions or conducts are subject to moral assessment."[8] The voice of this scientific discipline is needed in order to answer the ethical questions arising in the context of digitalization, automation, mechanization, robotization, and the use of artificial intelligence and for considering that the "social and ethical problems (..) are not uniform, just because they all require digital technology."[9]

---

3 Sturma 2003: 38.
4 Grassie 2017: v.
5 See Hilgendorf 2012.
6 Wils / Mieth 1989: X.
7 For an overview on the history of ethics of technology, see Ott 2005; Verbeek 2005; Verbeek 2011a: 3-17; Mitcham 2014; Kroes 2014.
8 Jonas 1985a: 42.
9 Ohly 2019a: 25.

Ethics should speak up because natural sciences and technology possess the power to "anticipate the reality as the epitome of possible products of technology"[10].

Ethics should intervene due to the uniqueness of digital transformation and artificial intelligence compared to earlier technology-based shifts in the history of humanity: "Now machines are learning to learn – and we need more distance to them. We need to understand when machine assistance is useful to us – and in what contexts it hinders us in our thinking. (...) the better machines can make decisions, the more intensively we humans must think about which decisions we want to delegate to artificial intelligence. (...) humans have to be happy with their decisions, computers do not."[11]

Ethics should contribute with justified confidence to digital transformation and the use of artificial intelligence as opportunities and risks of this technology-based era of change must be called by their name. Because only the precise identification of ethical opportunities and ethical risks of artificial intelligence and digital transformation offers the required clarity and eventually allows for using the first and mastering the latter. Both ethics and technology belong to the understanding of humans. "From the very beginning, human existence has been connected with the ability of technical production, and in this sense, technology belongs to the very definition of human"[12] as the moral capability of humans does. This is also necessary in times of anxiety and of euphoric enthusiasm: "The transformations brought about by digital technology will be profoundly beneficial ones. We're heading into an era that won't just be different; it will be better, because we'll be able to increase the variety and the volume of consumption. When we phrase it that way – in the dry vocabulary of economics – it almost sounds unappealing. Who wants to consume more and more all the time? But we don't just consume calories and gasoline. We also consume information from books and friends, entertainment from superstars and amateurs, expertise from teachers and doctors, and countless other things that are not made of atoms. Technology can bring us more choice and even freedom."[13] This is why ethics should also not shy away from the reproach of being hostile towards technology. This reproach can be negated, *inter alia* by pointing out that ethics in the course of this endeavor is in

---

10 Blumerg 2015: 46.
11 Ramge 2019: 28.
12 Wandschneider 1993: 47.
13 Brynjolfsson / McAfee 2014: 9-10.

technology-friendly surroundings. Stephen Hawking – who was able to enrich humanity with his genius thanks to technological progress – uses very clear words: "Unless we learn how to prepare for, and avoid, the potential risks, AI could be the worst event in the history of our civilization. It brings dangers, like powerful autonomous weapons, or new ways for the few to oppress the many. It could bring great disruption to our economy."[14] Elon Musk, who became rich thanks to technology by participating in the creation of the online payment system PayPal and as founder of Tesla and SpaceX – the company that wants to offer private trips to the moon by 2023 – warns: "AI is far more dangerous than nukes [nuclear warheads]. Far."[15]

Ethics with its own complexity is needed, so that digital transformation and artificial intelligence will neither be reduced to economic calculations and increasing efficiency nor to a pure instrument of marketing and "artificial stupidity", but can really rise to its potential.

Ethics is needed because of digital transformation's and artificial intelligence's "potential to substantially increase productivity in a wider variety of sectors"[16].

Ethics is needed because digital transformation and artificial intelligence have ethically relevant implications while the parameter setting for digital transformation and for the creation, design, programming, development, production, training, and use of artificial intelligence includes so far almost always only efficiency and elegance of the code.

Ethics is needed to critically review and balance the particular interests that serve public relations and marketing contributions to the ethical discourse – ethics-poetry[17] – and particular interest-oriented calls for regulations – ethics-fairytales[18] – about digital transformation and artificial intelligence by state and non-state actors.

Ethics is needed because the present situation and status quo in this area are so alarming as well because those who have created the fundamental problems and challenges, those who continue to boost the fundamental problems and challenges, and those who have benefitted and continue to benefit from the fundamental problems and challenges impose themselves

---

14 Kharpal 2017.
15 Clifford 2018.
16 OECD 2019a: 37.
17 See e.g., Pichai 2018; Nadella 2016; Smith / Browne 2019; advertisements by Facebook in newspapers worldwide on artificial intelligence and ethics, see e.g., Heuser / Nezik 2019: 9, 11; Intel 2017.
18 See e.g., Heuser / Nezik 2019.

as voices in the ethical discourse – with pseudo-ethical contributions serving again only their particular self-interests. When Jeff Bezos, Sergey Brin, Tim Cook, Bill Gates, Elon Musk, Satya Nadella, Larry Page, Alex Pentland, Sheryl Sandberg, Eric Schmidt, Brad Smith, Mark Zuckerberg, et al. want to be part of the solution while not changing their actions and continuing to foster the problems and challenges, there is a certain irony in this. This irony turns into a tragedy when people listen to them in this regard or follow their advice. For example, if technology companies were caught cheating and states ask them how they should be regulated while they still are eager to continue cheating, that is probably not a good idea. That would be as wise as a teacher who asks his or her pupils caught cheating during an exam how he or she should supervise them during the exams while they still try to continue cheating.

Ethics is needed so that digital transformation and the use of artificial intelligence does not simply happen, but that we can shape it. "At the moment, the tail is wagging the dog when it comes to digitalization. To let algorithms dictate how one should live reverts humans back to self-inflicted immaturity. One could also say: back to artificial stupidity. A mature society does not view digitalization as fate, but as a creative task."[19] Scientists, politicians, policy-makers, entrepreneurs, civil society representatives, religious and worldview-based communities, and human rights activists[20] urge ethics to provide ethical guidance and principles for an ethical framework and legal regulation of artificial intelligence and digital transformation as well as for the design, development, and production of artificial intelligence and robots in order to save humans from the negative impact of digital transformation and the use of artificial intelligence.[21] "Je ne saurai prévoir mais je saurai fonder. Car l'avenir on le bâtit."[22]

Ethics is needed to pose the question of who we want to be as humans and what should and shouldn't be in this era of "hyperhistory (where) (…) ICTs (…) record, transmit, and above all, process data, increasingly autonomously, and human societies become vitally dependent on them and on information as a fundamental resource. Added-values move from being ICT-related to being ICT-dependent."[23]

---

19 Welzer 2019.
20 See Campaign to Stop Killer Robots 2020; Future of Life Institute 2015.
21 See Russell et al. 2015.
22 De Saint-Exupéry 1948: 115.
23 Floridi 2015a: 38.

Ethics is needed because technology-based innovation is dependent on ethical guidance. Innovation can be understood as "making something new that has ethical implications"[24].

Ethics should speak up although it will be automatically criticized for obstructing, slowing down, or preventing innovation by asking critical questions or for not being up to speed.[25]

Ethics is needed to put an immediate stop to "the surveillance, the destruction of privacy, the lack of control of personal data, the shrinking of the diversity of opinions, the threatening lack of work"[26] that can result in the course of digital transformation and the use of artificial intelligence.

Ethics is needed to counter the spreading of indifference and so that we don't simply get used to everything that seems to overrun us due to the mutual reinforcement between the globalized economy and digital transformation. Comparing the worlds of George Orwell's "1984"[27] and Aldous Huxley's "Brave New World"[28], Neil Postman states: "What Orwell feared were those who would ban books. What Huxley feared was that there would be no reason to ban a book, for there would be no one who wanted to read one. Orwell feared those who would deprive us of information. Huxley feared those who would give us so much that we would be reduced to passivity and egoism. Orwell feared that the truth would be concealed from us. Huxley feared the truth would be drowned in a sea of irrelevance. Orwell feared we would become a captive culture. Huxley feared we would become a trivial culture. In short, Orwell feared that our fear might ruin us. Huxley feared that our desire might ruin us."[29] The present reality leans toward Huxley's position. The present reality makes Dave Eggers' novel "The Circle"[30] more of a documentary than a piece of literature. And this is not due to a mistake by Dave Eggers ...

If one compares digital transformation to earlier eras of technological change, especially in view of their effects on humans, it can generally be said that humans' political stances are affected by the previously non-existent ways of analyzing, profiling, and clustering humans into groups,[31] of

---

24 Enderle 2015a: 10.
25 See Zimmer 2019: 43.
26 Hofstetter 2017: 87.
27 See Orwell 1949.
28 See Huxley 1932.
29 Postman 1985: XIX-XX.
30 See Eggers 2013.
31 See Floridi 2012.

recommending goods to buy, routes to take, and persons to contact,[32] of generating data about human behaviors via the "Internet of Things"[33], of bringing about "algorithmic modifications of behavior"[34] and changes of behavior,[35] of influencing the information humans receive,[36] and of marketing (resources, expert knowledge, knowhow, talent, creativity, power)[37]. It can also be said that humans want what is new on the market – no matter whether they benefit from it, whether it really means progress, or whether it is really a convenience. This means that humans are getting used to new things more quickly and more comprehensively than before – even to ethically illegitimate uses of technology, including those that endanger humans and the environment.

Furthermore, the digitalization of research and teachings has powerful effects on human thinking and on science.[38] Digital transformation and the use of artificial intelligence change the way we think.[39] "Digital Modernity in its turn has a major design flaw: the complete algorithmic quantification of the human being – as a result of which our 'mindset' approaches that of intelligent robots, and all other human traits that cannot be turned into cash are left to atrophy."[40]

Research institutes, research projects, even entire universities[41] are funded by a few multinational technology-corporations to promote ideas, which serve their economic benefits and their particular self-interest. For example, "the Singularity is not the great vision for society (…). It is rich people building a lifeboat and getting off the ship."[42] Steven A. Edwards, American Association for the Advancement of Science (AAAS), points out as well that science is moving away from peer-reviews striving for the public's interest in the service of particular preferences and interests.[43]

---

32 See de Vries 2010: 81.
33 See Portmess / Tower 2014.
34 Lanier 2018: 11.
35 See Srivastava 2010; Bavelier et al. 2011.
36 See Newell / Marabelli 2015; Taddeo / Floridi 2015.
37 See Ferrell 2017; Chow 2017; Hinds 2018; Plummer 2017; Hong 2017; Waid 2018; Brodmerkel 2017; de Jesus 2018.
38 See Budde / Oevel 2016.
39 See Prensky 2001.
40 Thun-Hohenstein 2017: 21.
41 E.g. the Singularity University, funded mostly by Bill Gates (founder of Microsoft), Larry Page (co-founder of Google), and Sergey Brin (co-founder of Google).
42 Vance 2010; see also the initiative 2045.com.
43 See Broad 2014.

University-based research is in strong competition with corporate research regarding talents.[44]

Machine translation influences the way we speak and write.[45] The digitalization of texts[46] and entire libraries[47] as well as the literature and information supply associated with it opens up further horizons. From an ethical standpoint, it also raises doubts because it undermines the democratically legitimated power of these institutions to provide knowledge and keep it public. At the same time, it can endanger informational sovereignty in view of the commercialization of knowledge by the Internet, in particular through search engines,[48] because it is not quality that decides what will be found the quickest on the Internet nor what will be shown at the top in search engines, but the quantity of the respective marketing resources used. "Platforms that are profit-driven naturally come to a different answer than non-profit-driven platforms."[49] For this reason, among others, there is a call for public platforms.

Science and human thought are being changed by digital transformation and by the use of artificial intelligence in a more fundamental way as well. "Google's founding philosophy is that we don't know why this page is better than that one: If the statistics of incoming links say it is, that's good enough. No semantic or causal analysis is required."[50] The question "why" seems to become obsolete. The search for reasons seems to become superfluous. "The scientific method is built around testable hypotheses. These models, for the most part, are systems visualized in the minds of scientists. The models are then tested, and experiments confirm or disconfirm theoretical models of how the world works. This is the way science has worked for hundreds of years. Scientists are trained to recognize that correlation is not causation, that no conclusions should be drawn simply on the basis of correlation between X and Y (it could just be a coincidence). Instead, you must understand the underlying mechanisms that connect the two. Once you have a model, you can connect the data sets with confidence. Data without a model is just noise. (...) But faced with massive data, this approach to science – hypothesize, model, test – is becoming obsolete. (...) There is now a better way. Petabytes allow us to say:

---

44 See Wegner 2018.
45 See Gunkel 2021.
46 See Herrmann / Rohlfs 2011.
47 See Eiholzer 2019.
48 See Mittler 2014.
49 Grobner 2018: 25.
50 Anderson 2008.

'Correlation is enough.' We can stop looking for models. We can analyze the data without hypotheses about what it might show. We can throw the numbers into the biggest computing clusters the world has ever seen and let statistical algorithms find patterns where science cannot."[51]

Beyond that, digital transformation and artificial intelligence are taking over our economic system. "In the new kind of data-driven economy we live in, called 'surveillance capitalism', algorithms are the new 'laws of our society'. Even though they increasingly shape people's consumption patterns, opinions, emotions, decisions and overall behavior, the algorithmic de-facto laws do not require any approval by our parliaments. Properly understood, Facebook, Google & Co. are thus the new quasi-royal sovereigns. Their near-absolute – and wholly unchecked – power does not just extend to all spheres of commercial nudging. They are also shaping a new political system: by serving as hirable platforms to manipulate the opinions of people and choices of voters, they undermine democracies as well as the free, unbiased competition of ideas."[52] Are we living in a society of "surveillance capitalism"[53]? Without a doubt, we live in a capitalist society, but is this capitalism based on, nurtured by, and oriented towards "surveillance"? In order to be able to address this question, one needs a clearer conceptual idea of what is meant by "surveillance capitalism": "1. A new economic order that claims that human experience as free raw material for hidden commercial practices of extraction, prediction, and sales; 2. A parasitic economic logic in which the production of goods and services is subordinated to a new global architecture of behavioral modification; 3. A rogue mutation of capitalism marked by concentrations of wealth, knowledge, and power unprecedented in human history; 4. The foundational framework of a surveillance economy; 5. As significant a threat to human nature in the twenty-first century as industrial capitalism was to the natural world in the nineteenth and twentieth; 6. The origin of a new instrumentarian power that asserts dominance over society and presents startling challenges to market democracy; 7. A Movement that aims to impose a new collective order based on total certainty; 8. An expropriation of critical human rights that is best understood as a coup from above: an overthrow of the people's sovereignty."[54] Perhaps the following reflections in

---

51 Anderson 2008.
52 Helbing 2018; see Bajari et al. 2019; Varian 2018.
53 See Zuboff 2019.
54 Zuboff 2019: 1.

this book will help to answer the question of whether this concept of reality is the description of the present reality or an unrealistic dystopia.

Furthermore, the changes induced by digital transformation and artificial intelligence and the far-reaching creative possibilities connected to it demand ethical orientation.

In addition, change happens faster and at shorter intervals and humans are confronted with all-encompassing, multi-faceted insecurity of what the future will bring. Changes are more rapid and happen in shorter intervals, which inspires not only hope, but also insecurity, fear and concern in humans.

Moreover, in the course of digital transformation, the intensity and interaction between humans and machines are different in comparison to earlier technological progress. In 2021, there will be more digital assistants than humans in the US, and half of all US households will be equipped with one or more "smart speakers".[55] The entirety of human life – business, as well as private life – will be permeated by digital transformation. For example, a mobile device accompanies and monitors people seven days a week, twenty-four hours per day – "capable of seeing, hearing, and understanding most of what we do. Everything's recorded. Nothing's forgotten."[56]

Finally, the lingo-political use of terms calls for attention, for example when they speak about "autonomous machines"[57], "moral technologies"[58] or "trustworthy artificial intelligence"[59]. Technology-based innovation leads to new questions in relation to the human understanding of machines: What happens if it becomes possible to develop technological systems with emotions[60] or something similar? Should technological systems be given rights?[61] Do machines become humans? Ginni Rometty, President and CEO of IBM, started to describe the robot "Watson" with "he" instead of "it"[62] ...

The growing interaction between humans and machines will change digital things and artificial intelligence as human products, as well as hu-

---

55 See Smith 2018.
56 Hunter 2002: XXII.
57 See, e.g., Bendel 2015.
58 See, e.g., Verbeek 2011a.
59 See, e.g., the High-Level Expert Group on Artificial Intelligence HLEG AI of the European Commission 2019.
60 See Manzeschke et al. 2016; Wolfangel 2019.
61 Kersten 2016.
62 See Wallace-Wells 2015.

mans themselves[63] – it will turn humans into products of their own products. The complex relationship between humans and robots[64] has an influence on the self-understanding of humans.[65] Facing technology, which possesses the potential to become similar to humans in certain competencies, humans reflect on their own nature.[66] Therefore, the question of the concept of humankind needs to be asked in a new and different manner – and with it the question of the understanding of machines, robots, etc.[67] Will humans now turn into "homo digitalis"[68]? Will humans turn into machines? Are humans machines, as Julien Offray de la Mettrie believes: "Concluons donc hardiment que l'Homme est une Machine; et qu'il n'y a dans tout l'Univers qu'une seule substance diversement modifiée"[69]? Or is it necessary in such an approach to pay special attention to the human characteristic: "Les corps humain est une Machine qui monte elle-meme ses resorts"[70]?

At the same time, in this ethical examination of digital transformation and artificial intelligence it is important, on the one hand, to ensure that "the big words of purpose and the big bills of intent are converted into hard cash of skill"[71] and, on the other hand, not to lose touch with reality. The latter underlines the need not to conceptually exaggerate reality. The starting point for this thought are "functional equivalences"[72] – indicating that something is producing the same result in the same way. "I see the greatest danger in robotics in the fact that we can replace human abilities with the abilities of robots and falsely conclude that robots have our abilities. In comparison: You can move faster with a bicycle than on foot. But it doesn't mean that bicycles have feet that go faster. When robots take over human tasks it doesn't even mean that they themselves engage in those activities. When they replace human decisions, it doesn't mean that they decide themselves. And when they replace human feelings, they don't feel anything."[73] From this point of departure, we need to take a further step

---

63 See Ramge 2019.
64 See Dittmann 2016.
65 See Heilinger / Mueller 2016.
66 See Battaglia 2016.
67 See Fuchs 2021; Misselhorn 2018.
68 See Capurro 2017.
69 La Mettrie 2009: 136.
70 La Mettrie 2009: 34.
71 Wohlfart 2002: 102.
72 Ohly 2019a: 18.
73 Ohly 2019a: 17.

and ask what exactly is it that robots replace. Robots neither replace humans as a whole nor their abilities, but they fulfil a task or a function that used to be done by humans. This means that they replace humans in fulfilling a task or a function. Consequently, "functional equivalences" are not suitable to grasp these technology-based possibilities when they are defined as follows: "The same function can be fulfilled in different manners. Humans recognize the feeling of other humans by knowledge of human nature, intuition and empathy. Artificial intelligence can fulfil the same function by generating data – for example through face recognition systems that can recognize the mood of a person. Only what is being recognized is the same."[74] Why can this notion of "functional equivalences" not be used to classify robotization conceptually? When a robot fulfils a function or a task, it always remains just an approximation of the fulfilment of a function or a task done by humans; it is not identical. For example, fulfilling the function of recognizing feelings in another human being is and remains different if it is done by a human being than if it is done by a machine, which gets close to the function of recognizing the feelings of another human being. It is similar to it, but will never be the same because the machine is lacking human emotionality. "Functional equivalences" remain under-complex and reductionist in the sense that fulfilling a function or a task never takes place in a vacuum, but in a context where humans, as subjects of fulfilling a function or a task, as well as the process of fulfilling a function or a task interact – either as a result of it or independently. For example, if humans fulfil the function of recognizing feelings in another human being, the humans are subjects of fulfilling this function, as well as the fulfilment of this function itself. The latter means that humans as subjects change also in the interaction with the observed humans, which affects the observed humans as well. And the feelings of the other human being will change – as a result of it or independently.

No doubt, humans benefit from digital transformation and artificial intelligence from an ethical standpoint. "In the future the human-machine interdependence will be strengthened so as to achieve shared goals that neither could achieve alone. (...) Current analysis indicates that the human-computer symbiotic partnership will perform intellectual operations much more efficiently than human beings alone can perform"[75]. Beyond that, humans with disabilities are empowered to live an autonomous life; surgeons can delegate routine tasks of their daily professional life in order

---

74 Ohly 2019a: 18.
75 Tzafestas 2016: 32.

to devote more time to their patients and to research; self-driving vehicles do not drive drunk, angry, or tired, and therefore create fewer accidents and lead to a reduction in the number of fatalities – these are just some examples of positive effects of the digitalization, automation, mechanization, and robotization of society and of the economy, and the use of artificial intelligence, all of which can be identified from an ethical perspective –[76] in the service of life and society.[77] It is nothing new that technological progress can serve morally good ends (e.g., technology can be understood as prosthesis[78]).

At the same time, the digitalization, automation, mechanization, and robotization of society and of the economy, along with the use of artificial intelligence, can serve ethically negative ends, can lead to ethically negative results, or use ethically negative means or pursue ethically negative ways to reach a goal. Ethical guidance seems to be necessary in order to be able to decide and to choose among technology-based possibilities the ones that further human and ecological flourishing and to build a humane and sustainable future. "The future must be ethical, it can no longer be managed only technically."[79]

Maybe it is helpful that this book is written by someone who is a university professor at an institute of a public university where neither the university nor the institute are funded by Amazon, Apple, Facebook, Google, Microsoft?

This book addresses questions of "machine ethics" (ethics for machines), "ethics of technology" (ethics for humans designing, creating, developing, producing, and using technology), "ethics of artificial intelligence" (combining both paths in the area of artificial intelligence), "robot ethics"[80] (combining both paths in the area of robots, with an emphasis on ethics of technology), and "ethics of digital transformation" (combining both paths in the area of digitalization, automation, machinization, mechanization).

After an analysis of the correlation between ethics and technology in the second part of the book and a critical assessment of the moral capability of technologies in the third part, some terms of the discourse about digital transformation and artificial intelligence will be critically reviewed from

---

76 See Kirchschlaeger 2017a.
77 See Schuurman 2010.
78 See Sudmann 2015.
79 Auer 1982: 25.
80 On the relation between robot ethics and robot law, see Kim 2017.

an ethical standpoint (fourth part). The complexity of ethics will be ana-lyzed in the fifth part of the book.

In the subsequent sixth part, ethical principles serving the ethical assess-ment of the digitalization, automation, mechanization, and robotization of society and of the economy, and the use of artificial intelligence will be introduced and ethically justified. These principles are of course not the only ethical principles, which could help to find ethical guidance with re-spect to digital transformation. They are not an exhaustive list obviously. These ethical principles are chosen for this specific task because their nor-mative validity can be ethically justified[81] and because of their fundamen-tal character.

In the seventh part, some examples of digital transformation and the use of artificial intelligence will be analyzed from an ethical perspective and ethical opportunities and challenges will be discussed using examples. Nat-urally, it will not be possible to look at an exhaustive list of cases and appli-cations of digital transformation and artificial intelligence but just at some indicative examples in order to get a fundamental idea of the opportunities and challenges of this change (and of how to identify them) from an ethi-cal perspective – acknowledging that the digital transformation question of course involves so many more realities, inventions, possibilities, options, technological systems as well as layers and dimensions.

In the eighth part, regarding the challenges, specific solutions will be de-veloped from an ethical point of view as an outlook. Again, this can only represent a punctiform rapprochement of how such solutions in the area of digital transformation and artificial intelligence could be found from an ethical perspective that could perhaps be indicative of the path towards so-lutions for other challenges in this field from an ethical perspective.

In the first years of the 2000s, my journey with the topic of digital trans-formation and artificial intelligence began – contributing to the conceptu-alization and organization of an international human rights conference, which took place 2010.[82] At that time, criticism of this choice of topic for that year's International Human Rights Forum Lucerne (IHRF)[83] was voiced to me as the co-founder and, at that time, co-director of the IHRF that the topic was not relevant enough to be the focus of this annual con-ference. This probably would not happen anymore today ...

---

81 See Kirchschlaeger 2013c; Kirchschlaeger 2014a; Kirchschlaeger 2016e.
82 See Kirchschlaeger / Kirchschlaeger 2010.
83 See Center of Human Rights Education (ZMRB) n.d.

My special thanks go to Professor Thomas Pogge, Yale University, for the in-depth discussions that I was able to have with him as a visiting fellow at Yale University during the academic years 2015-2017, for his interest in my research, and for his contribution to the conceptualization of this study.

I would also like to especially thank the faculty members and researchers of the Divinity School and the Philosophy Department at Yale University with whom I had the opportunity to engage in topic-related conversations during my stays at Yale University, in particular Professor Jennifer Herdt.

For important contributions during the development of this study provided through guiding questions, essential commentaries, and inspiring discussions, I am grateful to my colleagues at the Department of Theology of the University of Lucerne, the team of the Institute of Social Ethics ISE at the Department of Theology of the University of Lucerne (Sonia Arfaoui, Aaron Butler, Melina Faeh, Seline Fankhauser, Adrienne Hochuli Stillhard, Noemi Honegger, Birgit Rath, Anna Maria Riedl, Kaja Schmid, Claudia Schmutz, Carmen Staub, Chantal Studer, Evelyne Tauchnitz, Ernst von Kimakowitz, Yan Wagner) and its former team members I had the honor to work with (Silvia Choinowski, Estefania Cuero, Monika De Col, Matteo Frey, Leonie Mathis, Ramatu Musa, Karin Nordstroem, Manfred Stuettgen, Dorian Winter, Juliette Wyler), the research group "Digital Transformation, Artificial Intelligence, and Ethics" at the ISE and the participants of the Lucerne Graduate School in Ethics LGSE at the ISE (including Sara Ilić, Darius Meier, and Jan Thomas Otte) with whom I was able to lead topical discussions. I'm especially grateful for the valuable comments to this book by Aaron Butler and for the support with the formal preparation of the manuscript by Kaja Schmid, Claudia Schmutz, Carmen Staub, and Chantal Studer.

I am also very grateful for the constructive discourse with my colleagues of the University of Lucerne; the working-group Mobility 4.0 of the Swiss Federal Roads Office (FEDRO) at the Swiss Federal Department of the Environment, Transport, Energy and Communications (DETEC); the Focus Group (small committee of experts in the field of Artificial Intelligence) serving the Advisory Council on Digital Transformation of the Swiss Federal Council; the Board of Trustees of the Switzerland Foundation of the European Academy of Sciences and Arts; the Scientific Advisory Board of the European Forum Alpbach; the Advisory Board of the Think Tank "Dezentrum", a Think Tank on New Technologies of Trust Square (Zurich's Blockchain hub); the think-tank "RedBit"; the Council for a 21st Century Progressive Economy; my editor-colleagues at the Journal "AI Perspectives";

the members of the faculties of the Lucerne Summer University: Ethics in a Global Context LSUE under the patronage of UNESCO 2018 and 2019, and the guest-speakers of the "EthicsImpulses" that have been held thus far at the Institute of Social Ethics ISE of the Department of Theology of the University of Lucerne, especially Professor Wilfried Stadler (WU Vienna University of Economics and Business and University of Salzburg).

The research-oriented environment of the Department of Theology of the University of Lucerne, where I was able to carry out this research, significantly contributed to the creation of this study. I'm grateful that I was able to present the thesis and results of my research during the development phase to many panels and at various conferences and events and discuss my thoughts with several dialogue partners, such as my colleagues at the Annual Meeting of the "Innsbrucker Kreis von Moraltheolog*innen und Sozialethiker*innen" 2020; at the International Ethics in Action-Conference "The Future of Work" in the Vatican 2018 convened and chaired by Professor Jeffrey Sachs (Director of the Earth Institute, Columbia University; Special Advisor to the UN Secretary-General António Guterres on the objectives of sustainable development; Director of the UN Sustainable Development Solutions Network); with the participants, among others, of the Lucerne Summer University: Ethics in a Global Context LSUE under the patronage of UNESCO 2018 and 2019, the "IDEEN Lab: Artificial Intelligence and Ethics" of the Oesterreichische Forschungsfoerderungsgesellschaft FFG" 2019, the NZZ X.Days 2018 in Interlaken, the Swisscom Dialog Arena 2018, the European Forum Alpbach 2018, the Globart Academy 2017, the Annual Seminar for the Swiss Financial Market Supervisory Authority FINMA 2017 in Berne, the Summer-Academy "Automatization of Mobility from an Ethical Perspective" of the Swiss Study Foundation in Magliaso 2016, and the colleagues and students of institutions such as the University of Lucerne, the University of St Gallen, the University of Zurich, the Kirchlich-Paedagogische Hochschule KPH Vienna (Austria), the University of Salzburg (Austria), the Institute of Science and Technology in Gwangju (South Korea), the Seoul National University of Education (South Korea), and the University of Oxford (UK).

I'd like to thank Dr Martin Reichinger and Dr Sandra Frey of Nomos Publisher House in particular for including this study in their program. When handing in the manuscript for print, Dr Sandra Frey and Sonja Schmitt were very helpful, for which I am thankful.

My wife Miriam and our daughters Sara and Mia, my entire family, and my friends followed the development of this research with their love and friendship, with encouraging interest and great support. All my thanks go to my "small world".

Lucerne, February 8, 2021   Peter G Kirchschlaeger

2 The Correlation between Ethics and Technology[84]

2.1 Introduction

As introduced above in the introduction, ethics is the scientific discipline that involves analyzing moral questions and problems, discussing decisions and actions as legitimate or illegitimate, and analyzing good/bad and right/wrong, respectively.

Originating from the Greek term *technologia* combining *techne* (art, technique) and *logos* (animating principle pervading the universe), technology entails the pursuit of a higher or more fundamental end or meaning. "When we speak of technology, we think of the power we are able to exert, thanks to our knowledge, on the world that surrounds us and of which our body, mortal and vulnerable, is a part."[85] The following critique of the term "technology" is taken into account and enriches the reflections in this book: "There is no such thing as technology in general or technology as such: There are always instead constellations of artifacts and techniques, actually-existing and also imagined. Technologies are in use, misused, consumed, consigned to landfill, repaired, maintained, creatively reappropriated, under development, seeking venture capital, subject to regulation, promoted, marketed, misunderstood, repackaged, mistaken for novelties. Some artifacts and techniques seem to arrive from nowhere, dazzling us with promises and threats, usually to disappoint us soon enough, or at any rate until the next distraction fills the pop-tech press and screen."[86] Still, "technology" is used to categorize the diversity and plurality of technologies, while being aware of the limits of this categorization in order to use this awareness fruitfully in the more specific ethical assessment focusing on concrete technologies.

The relationship between ethics and technology can be understood as an interaction of a source of ends (ethics) with a source of means (technology). After assessing this possible element of the correlation between ethics and technology, the topic of what technology brings to ethics (e.g., innovation), and what ethics brings to technology (e.g., orientation) will be elab-

---

84 See Kirchschlaeger 2020a.
85 Hersch 1992: 67.
86 Carrico 2013: 48.

orated. On this basis, the challenges ethics creates for technology, as well as those which technology creates for ethics, will be discussed.

2.2 Ends and Means

2.2.1 Justifying Ends

"If there is one thing the great institutions of the modern world do not do, it is to provide meaning. Science tells us how but not why. Technology gives us power but cannot guide us as to how to use that power. The market gives us choices but leaves us uninstructed as to how to make those choices. The liberal democratic state gives us freedom to live as we choose but refuses, on principle, to guide us on how to choose."[87] Ethics could play the role of providing meaning. It could represent a source of ends – ends as, e.g., survival and life with dignity for all humans,[88] peaceful coexistence, justice, and sustainability.[89] Ethics should play a role "in the exclusion of objectives which are not strictly necessary. There remains enough of the indispensable to occupy the technical genius of man both in perfecting and in correcting and slowing down further developments."[90] This is also reflected in a statement by Wolfgang Wahlster, director of the German Research Center for Artificial Intelligence: "All we have to do is always put the benefit to humans at the center of AI research."[91]

It is within the ethical dimension where questions about the ethical legitimacy of horizons of meaning and of ethical ends are discussed. Humans analyze what should be and why it should be. Humans evaluate, decide, and make an ethical judgment. It is part of ethics to act accordingly – to act ethically –[92] which, in other words, means to follow the ethically justified ends. "Ethics, whether in the form of issuing direct enjoinders to do or not to do certain things, or in the form of defining principles for such enjoinders, or in the form of establishing the ground of obligation for obeying such principles, deals with values relating to human conduct. It is concerned with action or non-action."[93]

---

87 Sacks 2015.
88 See Kirchschlaeger 2013a: 194-195.
89 See Armand 2012.
90 Jonas 1984: 86.
91 Brost 2018: 26.
92 See Pieper 1994: 17-48.
93 Armand 2012: 114.

Finally, ethics embraces the ethical justification of ethical ends, as well as the ethical justification of ends. Because of their claim of universality as part of ethics, these justifications need to satisfy the principle of generalizability by presenting rational and plausible arguments – "good reasons". The concept of "good reasons" means that it must be conceivable that all humans given their effective freedom and autonomy as well as their full equality would agree upon these reasons – within a model of thought and not within a real worldwide referendum – on ethical grounds. Inspiring the definition above was another way to frame these requirements of ethics: "A rational or critical ethics is one that claims for itself rational justifiability for its principles. Ethical principles are rationally justified if they are generally endorsed by, that is to say acceptable to, all affected persons, given their full equality and effective self-determination."[94]

2.2.2 Providing Means

In order to achieve these ethical ends or ethically justifiable ends, humans use adequate means. These means can also be produced by technology – technology based on basic science and applied science leading to growth and welfare[95] and embedded in the plan of living with nature (not so much in the sense of commanding nature)[96] for the benefit of humans.

Technology can serve ethically good ends. E.g., technology can be understood as a prosthesis – in the service of life and society.[97] "Continuing advances in scientific and technological innovations are essential to modern societies. Historically, such developments have improved living conditions in both developed and developing countries."[98] Out of this understanding of the correlation between technology and ethics, the following present challenge emerges: "It is a time when technology can bring wonders to one's life. It is a time when I ask myself whether all of these technological achievements have made us better human beings! A robot can be programmed to act good or bad, but who will demarcate human actions?"[99]

---

94 Koller 1995: 75.
95 See Bacon 2003.
96 See Bacon 2000; Bacon 2004; Bacon 2007.
97 See Schuurman 2010: 107-127.
98 Lucchi 2016: 4.
99 Bashir 2000: 92.

It would be too reductionist though to describe technology as the instrumental pursuit of an end with a means produced to reach this end.[100] Technology also produces the conditions for the success of instrumental pursuit of an end and continues working on these conditions. Nature is transformed by technology in an environment of technological systems for the benefit of humans who try to balance the resources and dangers of nature in calculable and assessable opportunities and risks.[101]

Furthermore, technology can also develop its own laws and transform from being automatic to being "autonomous".[102] Possible ends emerging out of technology could be, among others, "technology for the sake of technology", "what can be made must be made"[103], or "efficiency". The current digital transformation of society and the economy and the use of artificial intelligence[104] can serve as concrete examples for this potential of "autonomous" technology because at their center are self-learning-systems[105] which no longer need any human input in order to improve and to optimize their own performance.[106] "The ethical risks posed by AI-enabled robots are (...) serious – especially since self-learning systems behave in ways that cannot always be anticipated or fully understood, even by their programmers."[107]

This self-learning can consist also of "intuition" as, e.g., the win of the Go-game by robots also based on "intuitive" decisions can show;[108] of strategic reasoning with imperfect information as, e.g., the win of a marathon 20-day poker competition can demonstrate;[109] or of "a system's ability to correctly interpret external data, to learn from such data, and to use those learnings to achieve specific goals and tasks through flexible adaptation."[110]

If the pursuit of efficiency is the exclusive scope of technology, three observations are provoked: *First*, technology striving for efficiency is neither

---

100 See Ortega y Gasset 1949: 90-105; Hubig 2007: 48.
101 See Hubig 2011: 170.
102 See Ellul 1980: 125-150; Kirchschlaeger 2016b.
103 Schuurman 2010: 123.
104 See Kirchschlaeger 2016b.
105 See Taddy 2019; Bishop 2006; Goodfellow et al. 2017; Agrawal et al. 2018; LeCun et al. 2018; Jain 2017.
106 See Frey / Osborne 2013; Rotman 2013.
107 Vallor / Bekey 2017: 338.
108 See Nature 2016; Kirchschlaeger 2017a.
109 See Spice 2017.
110 Kaplan / Haenlein 2018: 17.

independent from any ends or an end itself, nor ethically neutral, but serves a clear end: efficiency. Or the affirmation that technology is not a means which serves any ethical end, is in itself a normative statement assuming no end or technology as an end for technology – a normative statement which needs to be justified ethically, subject to the required criterion mentioned above.

Second, technology inherits a social and an ethical dimension. "Technology cannot be understood as an instrument for bringing about goals that are external to the contexts in which it operates, but the relational contexts in which technology functions are imbued with values which demand consideration. Thus, technology, as it actually operates in concrete situations has a contextually dependent ethical quality. Technology creates an ethical situation, and this situation should provide the context for decision making."[111]

Third, the pursuit of efficiency as the exclusive scope of technology leaves technology without any raison d'être. "The process of technological development hurtles ahead blindly without a normal sense of balance. As we can see from nuclear weapons and environmental degradation, the effects on human society are immense."[112] The way it is advancing, technology runs the risk of detaching itself from any horizon of meaning and of alienating itself from humanity and nature. "The human artifice of the world separates human existence from all mere animal environments, but life itself is outside this artificial world, and through life man remains related to all other living organisms. For some time now, a great many scientific endeavors have been directed toward making life also 'artificial', toward cutting the last tie through which even man belongs among the children of nature (…) The question is only whether we wish to use our new scientific and technical knowledge in this direction, and this question cannot be decided by scientific means; it is a political question of the first order and therefore can hardly be left to the decision of professional scientists or professional politicians."[113] In other words, the raison d'être for technology is not technology-based; it cannot be found out, defined, and justified by technology.[114]

---

111 Buchholz / Rosenthal 2002: 48.
112 Shibasaki 2005: 497.
113 Arendt 1958: 2-3.
114 See Jennings 2010: 27.

Beyond that, technology can also be abused for other ends,[115] distancing itself from its original ends, striving exclusively for efficiency and disregarding any higher end or meaning.[116]

However, ethical ends would still be distinguished from other ends. These other ends would undergo an ethical judgment on the basis of ethical ends. Ernesto Bertarelli, former CEO of Serono, states: "We never carry out research for the sake of research. (...) if there is no purpose and if there is no reason, we reject the innovation and we do not pursue it."[117] The former point emphasizes the orientation towards another end of research, the latter shows that the characteristics of innovation require an ethical assessment of innovations.[118]

One should overcome the naïve assumption that all technological progress and every innovation is an ethically good innovation. "Given the immense ambiguities of innovations – in themselves and in their consequences, the ethical scrutiny of innovation is a dictate of reason that should not be ignored any longer."[119]

It needs to be added though that technological progress depends also on basic research, which is done for the sake of basic research. Even in this area, a decision – which can find its foundation in ethical ends – needs to be taken in which basic research is prioritized and gets funded. Facing the scarcity of financial resources for research and technology and at the same time confronted by pressing global problems, a setting of focus and priority seems to be necessary. Finally, the question must be addressed as to who is benefitting from results and successes of technology – and for that matter benefitting the most.[120]

2.2.3 Way of Functioning of Technological Progress

Looking at the correlation between ethical, as well as ethically justifiable, ends and means provided by technology in a context partly created by technology, a further element needs to be taken into account. The perception of technological development and progress as a linear process pursu-

---

115 See European Group on Ethics in Science and New Technologies to the European Commission 2014.
116 See Shibasaki 2005.
117 Bertarelli 2002: 49-50.
118 See Kirchschlaeger 2013b.
119 Enderle 2015b.
120 See Hunt 2008; Shaver 2015; Donders 2015; Chapman 2009.

ing a well-defined scope would probably not correspond with the present day theory and reality of technology.[121] Technological innovations are often the result of small steps and are frequently random products.[122] "Technology is not ordinarily developed after carefully considering the various possible ramifications. In most cases a new technology is developed because it promises major short-term benefits and is judged not to cause any immediate problems."[123]

In addition, the speed of technological advancement outpacing normative considerations is another characteristic of the way of functioning of technology.

Furthermore, some ethical norms exist by dint of certain technological developments because the necessity to establish an ethical rule originates in a technology-based reality.

Beyond that, the complexity of technological development and progress should not be underestimated. "First, engineering and technology development typically take place in collective settings, in which a lot of different agents, apart from the engineers involved, eventually shape the technology developed and its social consequences. Second, engineering and technology development are complex processes, which are characterized by long causal chains between the actions of engineers and scientists and the eventual effects that raise ethical concern. Third, social consequences of technology are often hard to predict beforehand."[124]

It is also noteworthy that the social consequences of technology are such that should a certain technology fill some social role, it inherits, by so doing, the concomitant "social requirements".[125]

Furthermore, technological action should be considered distributed and collective rather than individual[126] though without introducing categories like fate and tragedy in order not to be too harsh with technology.[127] Therefore, various actors should be identified as subjects of responsibility.[128] Identifying them is a complex task. The identification of subjects of responsibility should still be implemented in order to build an atmosphere of professionalism and accountability – not only out of respect for the ob-

---

121 See Kuhn 1962.
122 See Boutellier et al. 2010: 136.
123 Shibasaki 2005: 489.
124 Dorn / van de Poel 2012: 2.
125 See Bostrom / Yudkowsky 2014.
126 See Lenk / Maring 2001: 100.
127 See Coeckelbergh 2012: 35-48.
128 See Coeckelbergh / Wackers 2007.

jects of responsibility.[129] Complexity cannot serve as an excuse to neglect legal or ethical obligations and responsibilities because ethical and legal norms keep their validity even in complex situations and contexts.

By overcoming the overly simplistic ends-means-framework and by considering the characteristics of technology, on the one hand, and respecting ethics as a source of ethical ends (and of the ethical legitimacy of ends), on the other hand, perhaps an attempt to grasp the reciprocal interactions and the reciprocal challenges could inform the understanding of the relationship between ethics and technology.

2.3 Reciprocal Interactions

The correlation of ethics and technology can be understood based on reciprocal interaction, as both ethics and technology contribute to each other. For example, groundbreaking ideas in technology and their successful application have a concrete impact on ethics as technology creates value, solutions for societal challenges, and innovation. "Science and technology have shaped modern society, economics, politics, law and culture. They deeply affect the lives of all people and they are now central features of our social and commercial landscape."[130] Even specifically in the ethical dimension, technology leads to innovation and dynamics[131] because the societal and individual transformation based on technology needs to be taken into account in ethics as well.[132]

Moreover, technology[133] and especially smart technology is influencing (e.g., by nudging)[134] at least individual lives – and maybe even the ethical dimension of individual lives.[135] "By helping to shape human actions and experiences, technologies also participate in our ways of doing ethics."[136] While acknowledging the effect technology has on humans as subjects of ethics, technology – in contrast to the idea of a "nonhumanist ethics of technology"[137] – remains an object of ethics and humans subjects of ethics.

---

129 See Lenk / Maring 2001.
130 Lucchi 2016: 6.
131 See Manzeschke 2015.
132 See Kernaghan 2014.
133 See Borgmann1995.
134 See Mathis / Tor 2016.
135 See Guthrie 2013.
136 Verbeek 2011a: 1.
137 See among others Verbeek 2011a: 21-40.

Why? Humans can decide on an ethical basis or orientation towards an ethical frame of reference in the technological decisions they make: whether to create a technology or not, how and if they design, develop, produce, disseminate, and use a technology or not, if they abolish a technology or not, if – to a certain extent – they allow a technology to influence their lives or not, and how they assess a technology from an ethical perspective. All this is up to humans, not up to technology.

Finally – and linked with that – contributions by technology to human lives are ethically relevant and can be ethically evaluated.[138] The ethical relevance of "human making and using"[139], of "tools and their deliberate use"[140] as the foundation of civilization, though, needs to be distinguished from possessing ethical subjectivity or from moral agency. For example, a self-driving car is ethically relevant because it can save human lives or it is able to do harm to or kill humans. But a self-driving car as a material object – even though it represents a highly sophisticated technology – is not an ethical subject or a moral agent because – among other things (see for further arguments below chapter 3 Can Ethical Judgment Be Delegated to Technologies?) – it cannot be held accountable for harm or killing. Humans behind this technology remain the ethical subjects or the moral agents. They make decisions about the interactivity (response to stimulus by change of state) – "autonomy" (ability to change without stimulus) and adaptability (ability to change the "transition rules" by which the state is changed) of technology; they create, design, develop, produce, disseminate, abolish, and use them and the technology itself. Behind the supposedly "political bridges"[141], behind the supposedly "missing masses of morality"[142], behind the supposedly "artificial moral agents"[143], behind the supposed "artefacts with morality"[144], behind the supposedly "moral agents and mediated subjects"[145], and behind the supposed "morality in design"[146], there are humans as ethical subjects and moral agents. Humans can decide whether or not to build bridges in a way that is disadvantageous to humans – manifesting their political convictions in a lasting way.

---

138 See Verbeek 2011a: 1-20.
139 Mitcham 2014: 11.
140 Bloch 1959: 731.
141 See Winner 1980.
142 See Latour 1992.
143 See Floridi / Sanders 2004a; Introna 2014; Hanson 2014.
144 See Verbeck 2011a: 41-65.
145 See Verbeek 2011a: 66-89.
146 See Verbeek 2011a: 90-119.

Humans can decide, for example, whether or not to build speed bumps in order to protect human live. Humans can decide to create, design, develop, build, produce, disseminate, to use or not to use a technology which can perform a "morally qualifiable action". "An action is said to be morally qualifiable if and only if it can cause moral good or evil"[147]. Humans can decide if a technology should perform this action, and if a technology should be able to decide by itself if it should perform this action. Just because a technology is ethically relevant because it can cause ethically positive and ethically negative effects, it does not possess moral agency as there is, *first*, a difference between performance and moral agency. *Second*, it is an ethical decision by humans if a technology should be entrusted with such decisions (as will be further elaborated below in chapter 3 Can Ethical Judgment Be Delegated to Technologies?). *Third*, even in the case of a technology being designed by humans in a way that it makes "autonomous" decisions about ethically relevant questions, a technology does not make these decisions with a knowledge, perception, or awareness of the ethical quality of these decisions (this point will be further explained below in chapter 5 The Complexity of Ethics).

Humans can make decisions about mediation by technology, its intensity, and its extent. Humans can decide to create, design, develop, build, produce, disseminate, use or not use a technology which may be able to mediate, and humans can decide if a technology should mediate or not. Humans can be aware of mediation by technology, and humans can reflect self-critically upon mediation by technology. Humans are not exposed powerlessly and heteronomously to it.

Humans can make decisions about mediation by design, its intensity and its extent. Humans can decide to create a design which mediates or does not mediate, and humans can decide if a design should mediate or not. Humans can be aware of mediation by design, and humans can reflect self-critically upon mediation by design. Again, humans are not exposed powerlessly and heteronomously to it.

In order to avoid a potential misunderstanding of what was just elaborated above, an emphasis must be put on the agreement that these societal impacts, effects, actions, influence, shaping, and mediation are possible and ethically highly relevant. There is no doubt about that. For example, design can influence the ethical dimension of human lives – illustrated by the inspiring example of "Eternally Yours".[148] "Eternally Yours follows an

---

147   Floridi / Sanders 2004a: 361.
148   See Verbeek 2005b: 203-234.

unorthodox approach within eco-design. Instead of the usual emphasis on reducing pollution while maintaining beauty and economy, the company focuses on lengthening what it calls the product's 'psychological lifetime'. Most products are thrown away long before they are broken or obsolete, usually because of changing tastes and fashions. Eternally Yours attempts to combat this tendency of products to wind up prematurely in the landfill by designing products that invite people to become attached to them."[149] The argument is presented, though, that behind societal impacts, effects, actions, influence, shaping, and mediation by technology and design, humans are the ethical subjects and the moral agents.

At the same time, science and technology happen, are pursued, and are in an ethically informed context. "But even the most solitary and radical reflection, as thinking with an intersubjective claim to validity, must presuppose language and thus a community of communication. But this also marks the limit of the value-free world-distance of modern natural science. As an enterprise in the search for truth in the dimension of intersubjectivity, value-free natural science must also presuppose ethics. But that would, of course, only be an ethics of the enterprise science, which could not even answer the question of whether science should be. It would be different if we were to reflect on the subjective and intersubjective conditions of the possibility of thinking as argumentation; for no one can go back behind these conditions if he or she seriously raises any questions at all and thus puts them up for discussion."[150]

Moreover, ethics contributes to technology, for example, by stimulating technological innovation,[151] by recognizing technological inventions,[152] and by providing ethical guidance. "Since all technologies are expressions of the values of their makers, if we care about ethics and morality, it will show in the machines we build."[153] Part of this value-system from an ethical perspective should be, among other things, ecological concerns. "Industrial Modernity – the greatest innovative boost to human development since the invention of letterpress printing – had one major design flaw: it passed its environmental costs on to the future generations. So a central task of the digital revolution might logically be to reverse this error. But instead, this revolution is being used to fuel the exponential growth of

---

149 Verbeek 2005b: 12.
150 Apel 1986: 27-28.
151 See Lucchi 2016: 7.
152 See Lucchi 2016: 1-2.
153 Sullins 2013: 16.

mass consumption. Similarly, it has failed to more fairly distribute the benefits of technological innovation. Here too everything points to an intensification of social inequality."[154]

Ethical discourse of technology depends on the understanding that technology is "something made" and "not anything given"[155]. "Technology must be allowed to augment living where it can, but cannot be allowed arbitrarily to suppress ways of life. Thus, ethics does not presume against technological change, but must be a part of the formulation of how change is translated into advancement or repression."[156]

One needs to go even further stating that ethics belongs to technology. "The idea of scientific knowledge as value-neutral is simply incorrect. Values are intrinsic to the making of science and technology, and they both reflect and transform particular values."[157] Horizons of meaning and ethical ends inform technology in an ethical sense. "Science and technology in their objective areas, for all their diversity of methods, are ultimately always aimed at people. That is why science and technology cannot be separated from ethical insight and decision-making in any area."[158] The discussion about the difference between notions like "ethical technologies", "technical tools"[159], "intelligent computer interfaces"[160], or "socio-technical systems"[161] shows the openness of technology to ethics. At the end of the day, this discussion implies the link between technology and ethics.

Beyond that, while the technology community is aware of its legal obligations and legal compliance standards, it strives for the respect of ethical principles in its work as well, e.g., honesty, objectivity, independence, impartiality, fairness, responsibility for future generations.

At the same time, a globalized technology community faces several traditions, cultures, religions, worldviews, and value-systems that can lead to ethical challenges. Ethical guidance can support technology in overcoming these challenges and in benefitting from the opportunities of this diversity and heterogeneity.

Furthermore, ethics can critically examine the legal obligations and legal compliance standards of the technology-community on a regular basis.

---

154 Thun-Hohenstein 2017: 19.
155 Heesen 2014: 253; 268.
156 Rainey / Goujon 2011: 174.
157 De Melo-Martín 2010: 9.
158 Auer 1982: 18.
159 Engineering and Physical Sciences Research Council 2011.
160 Van Est / Stemerding 2012.
161 Manzeschke et al. 2013.

This should lead to a continuous optimization of the legal framework for technology.

In addition, ethics can help in the process of agenda-setting in technology, not only in defining the right priorities but also in framing adequately the sphere of influence and responsibility of technology.

Finally, while technology contributes to the progress of ethics, it is obvious that at the same time there is a need for ethics in technology in order to be able to even conduct the necessary research, discussions, and studies. Technology can be the victim of infringements of its freedom, of attempts to block innovative and creative approaches, and of oppression of ideas, concepts, and discoveries. Reasons for these transgressions can be putative "absolute truths" or the enforcement of old and existing economic or political power structures. There is still a danger of members of the technology community not being able to conduct their research freely and independently. Therefore, there is a need for legal and ethical norms that support and protect technological progress.

This reciprocal interaction between ethics and technology accommodates the "interactionist model" highlighting the contributions of technology to ethics and the contributions of ethics to technology.

2.4 Reciprocal Challenges

At the same time, ethics can limit technology as well. For example, health and safety guidelines, patents, legal ownership of intellectual property rights, competition policy, consumer protection, and ethical codes of conduct belong to this category. This impact of ethics can be perceived as blocking and hindering technological innovation.[162]

Beyond that, technology must respect ethical principles. For example, "developers should strive at creating artificial agents whose actions are constrained in such a way that unethical outcomes can be avoided."[163] Among other things, the dignity of all humans can be a limit for technology (see below sub-chapter 6.4 Human Rights as an Ethical Frame of Reference). Therefore, technology does not have the permission to treat humans as means but only as ends – e.g., on the basis of the categorical imperative by Immanuel Kant.[164] Furthermore, technology must also respect the privacy

---

162 See Gurkaynak et al. 2016.
163 Krenn 2016: 25.
164 See Kant 1974: 61; Duewell 2010: 77.

of all humans (see below sub-chapter 7.17 Data-Protection and Privacy). In this way, technology is challenged by ethical norms.[165]

Paradigmatically, in the area of digitalization, automation, mechanization, robotization, and the use of artificial intelligence, technology can follow ethical programming by humans heteronomously.[166]

At the same time, ethics faces challenges from technology as well. Technological progress is speeding up. The intervals for new technologies and technological applications get smaller and smaller. Ethics and law run the risk of being constantly outpaced by technology. They struggle to keep up with technological progress. The perception of this risk is based, though, on two misconceptions: *First*, it understands ethics as reactive instead of proactive, and *secondly*, "some observers of modern culture do note disparities and tensions between contemporary doing and making, between ethics and technology. They complain that, while technology has advanced dramatically, our ethical attitude in dealing with it has not. But this complaint is as radically mistaken as the general divorce of doing from making. It fails to see that a technological accomplishment, the development and adoption of a technological device always and already constitutes an ethical decision."[167]

Beyond that, ethics is challenged more and more not only by human curiosity striving for new inventions and solutions but linked by substantial economic interests and power.[168] For example, in the area of digitalization, automation, mechanization, robotization, and the use of artificial intelligence, ethics must deal with an attitude that the legal system of a nation-state is violated as long as the economic benefits of these acts are higher than the sanctions. The defense of the ethically justifiable position that not everything, which is doable, is ethically good meets the opposition of potential benefits and economic incentives. Similar pragmatic patterns of argumentation from a perspective of technology dominate the discussion, e.g.:

- that closing the gate on technology is not an option at all;
- that the implementation of limiting technological advancement with legal and ethical norms is impossible in a globalized world;

---

165 About technological progress, its ends, its foundational values, its societal importance, and its limits, using the examples of stem cell research and of research on human beings, see Kirchschlaeger et al. 2003; Kirchschlaeger et al. 2005.
166 See Wallach / Allen 2009; Kirchschlaeger 2017b.
167 Borgman 1992: 110.
168 See Buchholz / Rosenthal 2002.

– that the identification of the subjects of responsibility in the area of technology is too complex;
– and that the risk assessment of technology remains imprecise and ineffective.

Finally, the impression emerges that "so far, the normative regulations have merely adapted to social upheavals. The social changes triggered by technical innovations in the fields of production and exchange, communication and transport, military and health have always been at the forefront. Classical social theory has described post-traditional legal and ethical concepts as the result of cultural and social rationalization, which has taken place in parallel with the progress of modern science and technology. Institutionalized research is regarded as the motor of these advances. From the perspective of the liberal constitutional state, the autonomy of research deserves protection. For the growing scope and depth of technological access to nature is combined with both the economic promise of productivity gains and prosperity gains and the political prospect of greater individual freedom of decision. Because growing freedom of choice promotes the private autonomy of the individual, science and technology have so far been in an informal alliance with the liberal basic idea that all citizens should have the same opportunity to shape their own lives autonomously. (...) The desire for autonomous living is always linked to the collective goals of health and life prolongation. The medico-historical view, therefore, warns against attempts to 'ethicalize human nature' to skepticism (...) From this empirically sobering perspective, legislative interventions in the freedom of biological research and genetic engineering development appear as futile attempts to resist the dominant freedom tendency of social modernity. (...) Of course, a completely different picture emerges if one understands the 'ethicalization of human nature' in the sense of the self-assertion of a genre-ethical self-understanding, on which it depends whether we will continue to see ourselves as undivided authors of our life history and whether we can recognize each other as autonomously acting persons."[169]

While reciprocal challenges between technology and ethics can obviously arise, the responsibility[170] of humans is also growing due to the constantly expanding creation of an artificial world and of "a technological

---

169 Habermas 2001a: 47-49.
170 See Kirchschlaeger 2014a.

simulacrum of natural life"[171] and the corresponding power and influence of humans. What do humans have to do to live up to this responsibility? How should one deal with the above-mentioned reciprocal challenges? Is "anything goes" the solution to this situation? There is a demand for ethical guidance, which can be provided by ethical principles and ethical points of reference discussed below.

2.5 Ethical Principles and Ethical Points of Reference for Technology

Ethical orientation in ethical questions, issues, and problems concerning technology can have their origin in traditions, cultures, religions, worldviews, and philosophies. In a globalized world, though, technology can, on the one hand, affect the entire planet, and most on the other hand provoke an impact on all humans. Therefore, possible ethical guidance for technology gains relevance if it can claim universality and is independent from a specific tradition, culture, religion, worldview, and philosophy.

These ethical principles and ethical points of reference enrich the relation between humans and technology consisting of an "embodiment relation" (technologies as extensions of the body, e.g., glasses, hearing aids), a "hermeneutic relation" (technologies as access points to the world, e.g. thermometer), an "alterity relation" (technologies and humans interact, e.g. humans operate a computer), a "background relation" (technologies have an effect on humans and their relationship with the world without being noticed)[172], "immersion" (technologies merge with the world and interact with humans), and "augmentation" (technologies offer a representation of the world)[173] by expanding this set of relations with a "constructivist and deconstructivist relation" (humans create and destroy technologies), an "interplaying relation" (humans use technologies and technologies use humans, e.g. their data), an "interproductive relation" (humans create technology/technologies and technology/technologies create parts of or in humans like attempts to simulate peculiarly human thought, e.g., artificial intelligence), an "ethically guiding relation" (humans decide based on ethical principles, ethical points of reference, and ethical norms *which* technologies they design, produce, and use, and *which they do not*), and an "ethically shaping relation" (humans decide based on ethical principles,

---

171 Jennings 2010: 26.
172 See Ihde 1990.
173 See Verbeek 2015a: 211-212.

ethical points of reference, and ethical norms *how* they design, produce, and use technologies).

This expansion might provoke at first sight the criticism that it takes ethical reasoning back to a point where it was before and got liberated from, namely perceiving the relation between humans and technology as a conflict between the two. This is not the intention. Rather, it tries to reconcile Michel Foucault's "critique"[174] with the subjectivity of humans distinguished from the objectivity of technologies by acknowledging "the fundamental intertwinement"[175] of humans and technologies implying "that the frameworks from which we criticize technologies are always mediated by these technologies themselves"[176], and by re-empowering the critical characteristics of ethics, embracing also the possibility of questioning fundamentally technology-based innovation, technology, and technologies as such. Both ethics from inside and from outside technologies are ethically necessary, and humans are able to strive for both – on the conceptual basis of understanding the relationship between technology/technologies and ethics as interaction. The ethical foundation for this reconciliation embraces, on the one hand, the self-critical acceptance of the boundaries of humans and human reason that makes it impossible for humans to liberate themselves completely from the intertwinement of humans and technology. On the other hand, it trusts in the subjectivity of humans allowing them rationally to distance themselves enough from technology in order to analyze, discuss, evaluate, assess, and judge the object "technology" from an ethical perspective. Without this latter aspect, humans would run the risk to being trapped again in "immaturity", accepting authorities and following their orders as criticized by Immanuel Kant – in present times, obeying immaturely the authorities of technological progress, innovation, and economic imperatives. Without this latter aspect, humans would be reduced to immature and powerless addressees, users, and consumers of powerful technology.[177] Without this latter aspect, technology would represent an absolute and fatalistically determined reality not influenceable by humans, expressed representatively, e.g., in the following way: "Technological development will continue, and human existence will change with it."[178] Humans are exposed to and intertwined with technology while, e.g.,

---

174 See Foucault 1984: 32-50.
175 Verbeek 2015a: 215.
176 Verbeek 2015a: 215.
177 See Weizenbaum 1976.
178 Verbeek 2015a: 214.

holding a gun – using the imagery of Bruno Latour: "You are different with a gun in hand; the gun is different with you holding it. You are another subject because you hold the gun; the gun is another object because it has entered into a relationship with you. The gun is no longer the gun-in-the-armory or the gun-in-the-drawer or the gun-in-the-pocket, but the gun-in-your-hand, aimed at someone who is screaming. What is true of the subject, of the gunman, is as true of the object, of the gun that is held. A good citizen becomes a criminal, a bad guy becomes a worse guy; a silent gun becomes a fired gun, a new gun becomes a used gun, a sporting gun becomes a weapon. The twin mistake of the materialists and the sociologists is to start with essences, those of subjects *or* those of objects. That starting point renders impossible our measurement of the mediating role of techniques. Neither subject nor object (nor their goals) is fixed."[179] This mediation needs to be considered because it is capable of covering the way humans interact with the world. "On the one hand, the concept of mediation helps to show that technologies actively shape the character of human-world relations. Human contact with reality is always mediated, and technologies offer one possible form of mediation. On the other hand, it means that any particular mediation can only arise within specific contexts of use and interpretation. Technologies do not control processes of mediation all by themselves, for the forms of mediation are always context-dependent"[180]. This mediation offers an alternative to an "instrumentalist" understanding of technology (neutral means for humans to reach their aims) and to a "substantivist" understanding of technology (determining and controlling influence on the individual, the society, and culture).[181] The interactionist understanding of the relation between technology/technologies and ethics though coins this rapport as dynamic – knowing different grades of intensity concerning how humans, technology/technologies, and the world interact with each other, and embracing different kinds of compositions, how much each of them contribute to creating an ever-new reality from a human perspective. For example, understanding the shovel as a mediator between humans and the ground like the artist Tomi Ungerer.[182] The interactionist model comprises the possibilities of mediation, of an instrumentalist narrowing of technology/technologies, of a substantivist elevation of technology/technologies, of ideological human self-image de-

---

179 Latour 1994: 33.
180 Verbeek 2015b: 11.
181 See Verbeek 2015b: 1-12.
182 See Ungerer 2019: 18.

fined by technology/technologies to the point of self-abandonment in favor of technology/technologies under the illusion of technology/technologies as an end in itself, and techno-critical reluctance of technology/technologies as well as their dynamic combination in manifold compositions. The interactionist approach situates ethics in dialogue with and under influence of this dynamic and of these possibilities. It understands ethics with the ability to distance itself to a certain extent – enough for an ethical analysis, discussion, evaluation, assessment, and judgement of technology/technologies. This interactionist understanding of technology/technologies and ethics trusts in humans remaining, at the end of the day, able as subjects to put the gun as an object down and to reflect upon this tangible gun in this specific context as technology, to discuss in a democratic process the production, the accessibility, the sale, and the use of guns, to form a political opinion and make a political decision about it, to reflect upon guns in general as technology from an ethical standpoint, as well as technology/technologies in general from an ethical perspective. This interactionist understanding of technology/technologies and ethics trusts in humans to be capable to create and destroy technology/technologies under ethical guidance.

Ethics should focus on identifying technologies that open the door to ethical opportunities and therefore should be allowed depending on the ethical quality of the interaction between humans and technologies. Ethics should start from the fundamental paradigm that "artificial intelligences (machinae sapientes) are not evolutionary adversaries of homo sapiens but instruments (artifacts) that must be thought of as cooperative to the person."[183]

---

183 Benanti 2018: 114.

3 Can Ethical Judgment Be Delegated to Technologies?[184]

3.1 Introduction

In view of the high complexity of dealing with artificial intelligence and digital transformation from an ethical perspective, as introduced above, it would be tempting for humans to delegate ethical responsibility to artificial intelligence and to trust in "moral technologies" and an "ethical artificial intelligence".[185] Beyond that, "because of their increased intelligence, autonomy, and interaction capabilities, AI systems are increasingly perceived and expected to behave as moral agents."[186] Terms such as "moral technologies" used in the current discourse on digitalization, automation, mechanization, robotization, and the use of artificial intelligence suggest such an option. They express the expectation that it would be possible to create moral technologies. The main objective would be to prevent robots from harming humans, for example. The term "moral technologies" is based on their abilities to follow ethical rules, make moral decisions, and perform acts based on these. The term "moral technologies" expresses the desire to give machines ethical principles and norms. This would not be achieved through programming, but rather through learning.

Talking about "moral technologies" can cause irritation. Can technological inventions really be moral? Can artificial intelligence be ethical? Can technological systems be trusted to have morals? Can one ascribe them with moral agency?[187] Or do they possess a limited but not full morality like a "functional morality"[188] allowing them to assess the ethical consequences of their actions, or a mindless morality without obtaining the characteristics humans possess as the basis for their morality?[189] Or is it impossible to think of technologies with morality? In the following, the characterization as "moral technologies" possessing moral capability will be critically examined from an ethical standpoint.

---

184 See Kirchschlaeger 2017c.
185 See Anderson / Anderson 2011: 1-4.
186 Dignum 2019: 36.
187 See Sullins 2006.
188 Wallach / Allen 2009: 39.
189 See Floridi / Sanders 2004a.

3.2 Vulnerability

"Moral technologies" and "ethical artificial intelligence" are, first, confronted with one of the uniquenesses of the moral capability of humans that distinguishes humans from machines and artificial intelligence: the vulnerability of humans in combination with their "first-person perspective" and their "self-relation". The term "vulnerability"[190] encompasses the possibility to be attacked or violated and, at the same time, a lack of ability or means to free oneself from this situation and to protect oneself from violations.[191] The vulnerability originates in the physical and psychological helplessness of humans with regard to themselves, fellow human beings, their context and their environment[192] and their dependence on the world. Humans are dependent on themselves, other humans, the context, and the environment insofar as they can, on the one hand, be violated by them and, on the other hand, be protected by them from violation.[193] This shows a significant difference between the understanding of "vulnerability" and the term "humiliation".[194] "Humiliation" refers only to human acts or omissions and not to the natural environment.[195] Here, however, environment (understood as human and natural environment) is also meant in its second sense, namely as a source of vulnerability for humans, because it can touch upon essential elements and spheres of human existence, and because humans have various options to deal with and react to it. For example, humans who have fallen victim to a natural disaster should not simply be left to their own devices, but should be supported.

One can distinguish between two kinds of vulnerability, and the second kind can be broken down into three derivations:

- Fundamental vulnerability (A), which is a characteristic of all humans and which cannot be influenced by humans (e.g., human transience);
- Selective and variable vulnerability (B),

    - which can be traced back to injustice;
    - which can be traced back to misfortune;
    - which can be traced back to one's own fault.

---

190 See Kirchschlaeger 2013a: 241-267.
191 See Schroeder / Gefenas 2009: 113-121; Kottow 2004.
192 See Ong-Vang-Cung 2010: 119.
193 See also Butler 2004: 77.
194 See Margalit 1998.
195 See Margalit 1998: 9-10.

All kinds of vulnerability can encompass various spheres or aspects of human existence. On the one hand, it could be a physical or psychological vulnerability. Physical and psychological vulnerability is part of the individual and, therefore, can be described as the inner spheres and aspects of vulnerability (C). Vulnerability leads to violations in the case of torture, violence etc. Both physical and psychological vulnerability are not restricted by human heterogeneity. For example, humans with disabilities are, subjectively and objectively, exposed to the same amount of vulnerability as humans without disabilities.

The "inner spheres and aspects of vulnerability" are to be distinguished from the "outer spheres and aspects of vulnerability" (D), as for example faith, religiousness and worldview,[196] law, food, medical care, education, financial allocations, infrastructure, etc. Vulnerability turns into violations, deprivation, discrimination, and exclusion if it is disrespected.[197] Unlike the "inner spheres and aspects of vulnerability" (C), the transformation of vulnerability into violation in the "outer spheres and aspects of vulnerability" (D) happens outside of the person. This, of course, does not mean that this transformation has no effect on the person or his or her inner spheres – on the contrary.

One needs to distinguish between the inner and outer spheres and aspects of vulnerability, and the outer form (E) (possible attack and violation from outside) and the inner form (F) (inability and lack of means for protection) of vulnerability, which are also possible in both kinds of vulnerability.

Concerning the second kind of selective and variable vulnerability and its subtypes, there is an interest to measure and make operational the various disciplinary positions in order to react to vulnerability with adequate measures.[198]

Humans share vulnerability with other living beings, which grounds the moral relevance of the latter.[199] If one's own decisions and actions would cause pain to another being, it is morally relevant. For if morality strives for the good life and right action, then pain from another being is important from two perspectives: One perspective is the view of the morally capable. Moral capability means that the morally capable person is able to reflect self-determinedly on the good life and right action, to define moral

---

196   See Barnes 2002: 3.
197   See Ferrarese 2009.
198   See Alwang et al. 2002.
199   See Ladwig 2007.

rules, and to judge and act according to them. The other perspective represents the point of view of the morally needy being or the being with moral patiency. Here, moral need is not understood in the Kantian sense that it is a peculiarity of the human being that he or she is dependent on moralization.[200] "An animal is already everything by its instinct; a foreign reason has already done everything the same. But a human being needs his own reason. He [or she] has no instinct and must make a plan of his own behavior"[201]. This understanding of the need for morality shows a great closeness to moral capability, that the former can also be thought of as part of the latter, namely as an indication that moral capability certainly contains potential for development and activation ("A human being should first develop his dispositions for the good; providence has not already finished laying them in him; they are mere dispositions and without the difference of morality. A human being should make them himself, cultivate himself and (...) produce morality in himself"[202]). Moral need or moral patiency means here rather that objects of decisions and actions of a moral character (e.g., animals) that are made or performed by those who are morally capable are dependent on the moral quality of these decisions and actions; that is, in this sense that they require a morality that shapes the decisions and actions of the morally capable. Seen the other way round, these objects are not morally indifferent to the decisions and actions of morally capable humans – i.e., they make a difference when the morally capable are striving for the good life and right action – which in the example of animals is justified by their vulnerability. Moral need or moral patiency does not depend on moral capability. In order to show moral relevance, one can start out from the morally needy as well as from the morally capable being. For example, from the point of view of the morally needy being or the being with moral patiency, it is morally wrong for someone to beat him. At the same time, it is morally wrong from the point of view of moral capability to beat a person in need of morality or with moral patiency, i.e. to inflict pain on a person in need of morality (bad conscience). With vulnerability, it is possible to rethink the relationship between moral need (or moral patiency) and moral capability and to show the moral relevance of moral need or moral patiency and moral capability. In the moral relevance of vulnerability, there is also a claim to a protection of the same, which is asserted in a special way through the "right to

---

200   See Ladwig 2007.
201   Kant 1995b: 697.
202   Kant 1995b: 702.

life". Because humans, as morally relevant beings, need protection because of vulnerability, they are the subjects of the "right to life". Thus, the vulnerability of humans serves as an indication of the necessity of the "right to life". This vulnerability applies to both morally capable and morally needy beings and beings with moral patiency. Accordingly, protection is morally necessary for both morally capable and morally needy beings respectively or beings with moral patiency. Hence, there is a call for the extension of the subjectivity of the "right to life" of human beings to animals as well.[203]

With respect to what will be described below in subchapter 6.4 Human Rights as an Ethical Frame of Reference in order to justify human rights based on the principle of vulnerability, a differentiation between humans and animals concerning the "right to life" is proposed in the following way: humans share vulnerability with animals. Does this mean extending the subjectivity of human rights to animals as well? Does the difference between moral need or moral patiency and moral capability also indicate a difference in the claims to protection, which only in the case of the latter includes the special protection of the "right to life"? Or does the newly conceived relationship between moral neediness or moral patiency and moral capability at the same time demand the special protection of the "right to life" for morally needy beings or beings with moral patiency and morally capable beings? First of all, it can be stated that this approach, which also considers moral neediness or moral patiency as morally relevant, is vehemently sensitive to this borderline area between moral capability and moral neediness or moral patiency which is of relevance for the definition of the moral status of machines and artificial intelligence.[204]

If the first question above is answered in the affirmative, moral capability serves to justify the "right to life".

A corresponding negation would lead to an expansion from morally capable to morally needy beings or beings with moral patiency, which would be tantamount to an affirmation of the second question. Then the question arises whether all morally needy beings or beings with moral patiency really can claim the protection of the "right to life" (e.g., animals). This would contradict the human rights concept of the "right to life", so that a differentiation within the morally needy beings or beings with moral patiency is to be made between human morally needy beings or beings with moral patiency and non-human morally needy beings.

---

203 See Ladwig 2007.
204 See LaBossiere 2017.

Thus, with regard to this question, a distinction from animals should be drawn. However, it must be noted that the borderline discussion between species is not conducted here conclusively, but only to the extent and exclusively that it is directly relevant to a justification of human rights. The exclusion criterion is whether a direct contribution to answering the question of why humans grant human rights to each other is to be expected, or an answer to a question arising in the discussion of this fundamental question. Therefore, with this brief inclusion of the question of the demarcation of humans from animals, proposals for a solution to the many questions arising in this context are not made – acknowledging these limitations.

It is obvious to point out that despite all the possible overlap with animals, human rights are not necessarily to be regarded as animal rights, especially since the term "human rights" contains "human" and not "animal", and are therefore not animal rights. However, this reference to terminology does not suffice as an answer to the question of why only human beings are bearers of human rights. The reference helps a little further: "Human rights do not have the discriminatory sense of distinguishing humans from animals and granting them possible higher rights over 'lower' forms of life. They merely aim at an *interpersonal* legal relationship, which would also need to be regulated *if* animals were to have similar rights."[205] By definition, therefore, it is humans, not animals, who prove to be the bearers of human rights. At the same time, it should be pointed out that this does not automatically mean that the possibility is categorically denied that theoretically similar or substantially equal moral rights could be granted.[206]

One can also approach the fact that humans share vulnerability with animals in a different way, namely by stating that there is some evidence to support the assumption – which is only to be briefly hinted at here, as it is not at the center of the attempt to formulate a substantiating approach to human rights – that humans formulate animal protection laws because of the vulnerability of animals. The direct conclusion that humans and animals should have the same rights, because they both share vulnerability, is not admissible insofar as three points (and the third point in particular) should be considered: *First*, humans agree – because of their vulnerability – on rights that apply to themselves as humans. In addition, humans also draft corresponding animal protection laws for other beings, such as ani-

---

205 Menke / Pollmann 2007: 140, emphasis in the text.
206 See Menke / Pollmann 2007: 140-141.

mals, with whom humans share vulnerability. These are based on their self-perception and the perception of their own vulnerability and, separately, on the perception of animals and their vulnerability.

Second, it is conceivable that humans imagine or perceive themselves in such a way that the vulnerability of humans and the vulnerability of animals are phenomenologically different. This connection does not comprise the attempt to assert that this is empirically really the case, either in the distinction between human self-perception and the perception of animals that differs from it, or in the determination of differences in the course of the phenomenological consideration of the vulnerability of humans and animals. This is irrelevant to this approach. Rather, it is probable that humans – in the awareness of and recognition of the vulnerability of animals – think of themselves as humans differently from animals, or that humans think of their own vulnerability, which they share with other humans, differently from the vulnerability of animals.

Third, the following self-awareness-building of one's own vulnerability, opening up to the "first-person perspective"[207] and the "self-relation" and flowing into the principle of vulnerability, distinguishes humans from other living beings. The principle of vulnerability – further elaborated below in subchapter 6.4 Human Rights as an Ethical Frame of Reference – is not only about the purely empirically perceptible vulnerability, but, above all, about how humans perceive their own vulnerability and think about it. The focus is on the examination and reflection of vulnerability and the moral consequences that the principle of vulnerability triggers in humans. Vulnerability can mean, for example, that a person who is healthy today knows that he or she might become ill tomorrow. Or – while living happily in the present – that he or she could be killed by others tomorrow. In this thought process, this person will go through a process of uncertainty. Because he or she is made aware of his or her own vulnerability and, in a last consequence, his or her transience.[208] This possibility to achieve self-awareness is true for all human beings.

The awareness building of one's own vulnerability is a self-recognition process of human beings, the empirical correctness of which is not relevant. During this awareness-building process when a human being becomes aware of his or her own vulnerability, he or she recognizes, ex negativo, the "first-person perspective"[209]. This encompasses the awareness of

---

207 See Runggaldier 2003.
208 See Hoffmaster 2006: 42.
209 See Runggaldier 2003.

the human being that he or she as a singular person is a subject of self-awareness through which one can access one's own vulnerability. On the other hand, they experience this basic anthropological situation of vulnerability as a subject (meaning as the first person singular). The acts, decisions, suffering, and life of a human originate from them as subjects. Furthermore, they interpret this basic anthropological situation of vulnerability as a subject: "By acting and suffering, humans experience themselves as living beings, which are not just living like all other beings, but which live by living their own lives. To relate to themselves, to act neither compulsively nor arbitrarily, but to be guided by reason and to pursue freely chosen purposes constitutes the life form which connects them with all humans as their own kind. This life form makes them vulnerable as the self-relation, which is inherent in this life form, depends on fundamental conditions for realization."[210] Humans are able to enter into a "self-relation" with themselves.

As humans are aware of their vulnerability, but at the same time do not know if and when this vulnerability will manifest itself and turn into a concrete injury or violation, they are prepared to accord all humans the "first-person perspective" and the "self-relation" based on the equality of all humans, because this presents the most rational, prudent, and advantageous solution for themselves. Which means, to accord all human beings rights – that is to say human rights – in order to protect themselves and all others, because the vulnerability also contains the "first-person perspective" and the "self-relation". (This is explained in more detail below in subchapter 6.4 Human Rights as an Ethical Frame of Reference.)

Humans are therefore not bearers of human rights because they are vulnerable, but because of the principle of vulnerability, which leads to the mutual enjoyment of human rights for all humans, makes the difference to the vulnerability of animals clear and serves as *differentia specifica*, which establishes a different understanding of the vulnerability of humans and the vulnerability of animals. Therefore, the fact that vulnerability affects humans and animals does not contradict the relevance of the principle of vulnerability for the justification of human rights.

Vulnerability, "first-person-perspective", and "self-relation" building the principle of vulnerability covers probably what "consciousness", "freedom of will", "self-reflexiveness"[211], and "subjectivity"[212] intend as elements dis-

---

210 Honnefelder 2012: 171-172.
211 Misselhorn 2018: 214.
212 Ohly 2019a: 49-72.

tinguishing humans from machines and artificial intelligence. At the same time, vulnerability, "first-person-perspective", and "self-relation" go beyond those differentiators in their argumentative impact on the distinction between humans and machines (or artificial intelligence) because, *first*, they do not depend on the condition of an assumed dualism between the mind (or soul) and body and therefore they allow one to avoid that controversial question. *Second* – and more importantly –, they do not create a potential for discrimination. To turn "consciousness", "freedom of will", "self-reflexiveness", and "subjectivity" into *the* characteristics or ability out of the many human characteristics or abilities, which distinguishes humans from machines and artificial intelligence, runs the risk of discriminating against those humans who are different in these characteristics or abilities, like humans with disabilities, coma patients or embryos. The risk of discrimination remains even if it is potentially held to account. Martha C. Nussbaum shows this potential for discrimination particularly clearly when – while following this line of reasoning – she goes as far as denying humans with disabilities their humanity, because they lack certain abilities, but still accords them moral relevance in order to try and weaken her reasoning: "[...] that certain severely damaged infants are not human ever, even if born from two human parents: again, those with global and total sensory incapacity and/or no consciousness or thought; also, I think, those with no ability at all to recognize or relate to others. (This of course tells us nothing about what we owe them morally, it just separates that question from moral questions about human beings.)"[213]

The lack of the principle of vulnerability builds a first argument against the moral capability of machines and artificial intelligence. The lack of vulnerability represents an argument against thinking of machines and artificial intelligence as morally needy or as beings with moral patiency. The counter-argument could be presented that the status of moral neediness or moral patiency should be attributed by humans depending on their relations with the machines and with artificial intelligence.[214] Its implicit arbitrariness, which contradicts this point of view, does not fulfill the requirements of critical rational ethics. Beyond that, the counter-argument could be introduced that it is ethically better to provide better treatment to a morally valuable being than its status merits and to avoid treating it as a mere object.[215] The limit of this argument though is that this would pre-

---

213 Nussbaum 1995: 82.
214 See Coeckelbergh 2012.
215 See LaBossiere 2017.

suppose that machines and artificial intelligence are beings and more than objects. Both could not be shown so far.[216] On the contrary, the lack of vulnerability and the lack of identity[217] elaborated above contradict the idea of machines and artificial intelligence as beings and supports perceiving them as objects. This perception as objects does not automatically mean that humans do not have any ethical obligations towards them,[218] because a mistreatment of an object would change the human subject in an ethically negative way[219] and because it does not exclude that objects have moral relevance to the extent that their material value needs to be considered from a sustainability perspective including the economic, ecological, and social dimension.

3.3 Conscience[220]

A second challenge to the term "moral technologies" is based on the concept of conscience, which is central for humans and their morality. Conscience unites what is objectively required and what has been subjectively experienced in a specific and concrete situation, in a specific context, during a unique encounter with unique people. "Conscience is an active faculty that discovers and discerns the good within the complexity of each situation."[221] Conscience creates an authority within a person, which has an impact on an action *a priori*, but also *a posteriori*. Conscience is a process that precedes an action, but also refers to critical questioning and examination following an action.[222] But the conscience does not act itself.[223] "Conscience cannot be called upon whenever you like. Conscience asserts itself, often when we don't want it to. We don't know in full of what exactly conscience consists of. (...) This experience never ends. From this we learn that conscience is in progress, it is a process that is given to us, but at the same

---

216 See on this question Gunkel 2018.
217 See DiGiovanna 2017.
218 See Bryson 2010.
219 See Kant 1990.
220 See Kirchschlaeger 2017d.
221 Hogan 2004: 86-87.
222 See also Holzhey 1975: 7; Schueller 1980: 40-57.
223 See also Wolbert 2008: 170.

time a task for us."[224] Conscience thus gives access to the difference between the level of being and the nominal level.[225]

As a testament to the human ability for morality, conscience connects humans across cultures, traditions, religions, and worldviews. Therefore, conscience can be located at a constituting level of humans being human. It encompasses the potential to recognize the morally good and to place it in the respective specific context.[226]

Furthermore, conscience describes an interaction between the normative system it is based on and the inner aspects of the individual.[227] The first is also expressed by placing the individual in a social context with the ensuing duties and corresponding responsibility.[228] The latter guarantees a critical distance of the individual from the normative system of a society.[229]

As such, self-relation, relation to normativity, and relation to a normative system are based on or are united in conscience.[230] When looking at it more closely, conscience can be understood as the "ability of the human spirit to recognize moral values, commandments and laws (synderesis), but, in the narrower sense, their application to one's own immediate actions."[231] Conscience takes on the role of an inner voice of a person in moral questions and decisions. This inner voice is not always clear, but the conscience struggles with itself and its decisions, as the definition of Immanuel Kant shows: "The consciousness of an inner court in humans where his or her thoughts sue each other or apologize to each other, is the conscience."[232] Instead of a heteronomous understanding of conscience, where conscience is determined by something alien to human freedom and reason, Kant uses autonomy for preserving the independence of the moral phenomenon or duty. Morality in the strict sense means that it is purely subject-based. Morality is the duty recognized by humans as something that their practical reason tells them to be their duty. Not only duti-

---

224 Mieth 1992: 225.
225 See Reiter 1991: 11.
226 See Schuster / Kerber 1996: 144.
227 See Kranich-Stroetz 2008: 124.
228 For the discourse on concrete questions related to conscience see Schaupp 2014; Hoefling 2014; Martinsen 2004.
229 See Reiter 1991: 15.
230 See Kranich-Stroetz 2008: 125.
231 Schuster / Kerber 1996: 144; for the philosophical discourse on "conscience" see Huebsch 1995.
232 Kant 1997: 572.

ful actions, but actions out of a sense of duty are morally good and morally correct, because purely dutiful actions can happen for various reasons that have nothing to do with morality or even immorality. Since the conscience only measures itself against itself, a wrongful conscience is impossible, according to Kant. To act upon one's conscience cannot be an additional duty, otherwise it would need a conscience above the conscience, which would be the sought-after conscience. It is also down to the conscience itself to recognize what constitutes a duty. The duty of conscience-building stems from the conscience itself. Only then is it a moral duty. In any other case, the duty would come from outside, would be heteronomous and, therefore, not moral, but legalistic.

Practical reason is, as it were, opposed to conscience. Practical reason reminds us if an action is dutiful or not and determines the objects that are dutiful. Which means, all functions determined by content are taken away from it. Instead, conscience is duty in itself. Not conscience, but practical reason decides on the content of the duty. Conscience only assesses the relation of the person to his or her duty like "an inner court in humans, before which their thoughts sue each other or apologize to each other"[233]. Based on the autonomy of morality, conscience is equivalent with a self-duty of the human.

The differentiation introduced by Thomas Aquinas between "primal conscience" (synteresis) – the natural habitus where humans participate in the eternal truth of practical reason, which also contains the highest principle of the moral conscience "you should do good and avoid evil" – as the basis for activity, and the concrete conscientious activity or functional conscience based on it, which consists in its application to concrete action (conscientia), is also useful.[234] "Conscience helps to be realistic and reasonable when shaping freedom, but also to recognize its moral limitations and dependencies. But it also encourages not to resign and to believe in the possibilities that one can really change one's life according to moral beliefs and ideals."[235]

Building on this, the differentiation of the conscience between a "primal conscience", a "conscience of values", and a "situational conscience" goes even further.[236] While the "primal conscience" centers on the basic de-

---

233 Kant 1997: 572.
234 Thomas Aquinas Summa theologiae 1 q 79 a 12-13; see Anzenbacher 2015; Noichl 1993: 264-274.
235 Roemelt 2011: 58.
236 See Teichtweiter 1976.

mand to choose good over evil and to act accordingly, the situational conscience takes the concrete situation and decides what concrete actions of moral value need to be taken and takes into account personal needs, natural tendencies, personal values, duties and responsibilities. The "conscience of values" mediates between the "primal conscience" and the "situational conscience" by taking into account personal impressions and attitudes. The mediation of the conscience, therefore, contains the various dimensions of morality, which can also manifest itself in the maturing of the conscience. Based on this, the following can be said about conscience: "In its execution as a judgment it is, like the moral judgment, an event that is conditioned in many ways; it is tiered and determined by a great number of factors. On the other hand, in its claim that it clings to out of habit and demonstrates in the judgment, it is completely unconditional, since in the mode of self-reference it only shows what is the basis of moral obligation in general: the selfhood of humans as creatures of reason and freedom."[237]

Conscience, therefore, combines morality or the duty with the various levels of a person and his or her existence. The latter are of various qualities and intensities and are shaped by individual development or social influences.[238] The human being also constitutes his respectively her counterpart. "Every claim of conscience falls back on self-affirmation and repeats it. Just as if the self of the affirmation is nothing lonely, the conscience also does not act quietly and secretly, incapable of generalization, egotistical. (...) If the conscience repeats the defining moment of introducing individualization and socialization by referring to self-affirmation, it does nothing to reach a 'lonely' and 'naked' self-discovery"[239].

Furthermore, conscience is about decisions, actions, and inactions of the human being happening in a single situation of life that cannot be overlooked. All those situations claim morality. Humans view this claim in all kinds of different manners. The object of moral action is the shaping of one's own life story. Emotional moments are also included in the respective conscious decisions. Because "only reason can enable conscience which relates the many single actions to one final unity, namely to the success of human existence from a fundamental reason, such a judgment of reason expresses itself in the concern of the whole person."[240] This comprehensive sense of concern also allows for many paths to awareness and per-

---

237 Honnefelder 1993: 121.
238 See Schmitt 2008.
239 Marten 1975: 124.
240 Honnefelder 1982: 32-33; see Honnefelder 1993.

ception of the conscience. "The conscience will only refrain from becoming an authoritarian control organ when it can open itself, acts in context and builds its socio-practical sensibility and power of judgement from its own, critically followed view on reality."[241]

At the same time, humans are strongly encouraged to check the objective and subjective conditions, while being conscious of their own identity, of the self-concept and self-assessment in their conscience by reflecting on norms, and the shaping and setting of norms. Conscience thus places itself at the service of realizing the will in the being so that the latter will get as close as possible to the first.

Furthermore, the horizon of the conscience has an impact on this, which does not end with a single decision or act, but covers the entire existence of the human being. Conscience turns out to be a "patient path of learning freedom"[242].

Finally, the moral reason of the human being, experienced in conscience and the moral capability of the human being to discern between good and wrong, turns conscience into an absolute challenge for humans – again and again, when planning and contemplating an action in one last practical judgment that leads to action, and when critically examining the questioning of this judgment concerning its position towards moral reason, its contribution to the success of being human, and its relationship to one's own principles of action after an action.

After all, conscience expresses a trust in the single human. The single human is expected to have this inner voice in moral questions, to be able to recognize it, listen to it, and then act responsibly. It is respected and upheld that the dignity of conscience belongs to the single human.

Even if, in the sense of epistemic modesty, it must be pointed out, on the one hand, that the determination of conscience is extremely complex and, on the other hand, it must be remembered that one tries to make conceivable and plausible statements about the future based on the present state of research, the following can nevertheless be noted: it cannot be said that technologies have a conscience. The potential that technologies possess in relation to ethical decisions and actions are nowhere close to the human conscience. They lack various levels of morality or duty, as well as the existence merged in the conscience in varying quality, intensity and marked by individual development or social influence.[243] Therefore, tech-

---

241 Schmitt 2008: 162.
242 Roemelt 2011: 58-61.
243 See Schmitt 2008.

nologies cannot be said to have a conscience. If conscience is understood as being essential for morality, the lack of conscience is a second argument against the moral capability of technologies.

It is not the strongest argument, because in the current discourse, conscience is coming under pressure from the psychological and the sociological, as well as the neuro-scientific perspective. In the first, they leave it at depth-psychological approaches, which still uphold self-determination, but place some restrictions on it. The latter uses signs of neuronal processes and chemically and biologically based processes, which only allow that the autonomy of conscience is really only pretense, and in empirical truth, conscience is nothing but the result of these processes.[244] These two lines of argumentation for questioning conscience can be countered in the sense of an analogy on the arguments of Immanuel Kant concerning the freedom of mind of human beings:[245] If this were true, i.e. if human beings would be restricted in their self-determination and would be nothing but chemical and biological processes, how can it be explained that humans can decide against "sensual stimulation" and act accordingly or that human beings can let themselves be guided "by motives that can only be imagined by reason"[246]?

3.4 Freedom

A third question mark arises from freedom. Freedom is a *conditio sine qua non* for morality, because only freedom opens up the possibility to decide for or against the good and the right, respectively. Freedom is ambiguous. As a formal relation, freedom can be described as "freedom from..." and "freedom to...". Freedom means to act according to one's own wishes and plans. It can encompass the freedom to want what one wants and the freedom to want what one doesn't want. The latter means that freedom can also mean to want the "required", (i.e., the ethically demanded, even if this might not correspond to one's own wishes, needs, preferences, or interests. This opens up the social horizon of freedom).

Beyond that, freedom is the origin of science, research, and technology. This aspect must be emphasized in a time when some voices deny the exis-

---

244 See Ruth 2003.
245 See also Nida-Ruemelin 2005.
246 Kant 1995a: 675.

tence of freedom entirely.[247] "That freedom, which is now denied, has made the developments of science, in the name of which it is now denied, possible. Indeed, there would never have been a science without the human mind's inherent ability to distinguish between false and true and to prefer the true to the false. False and true make no sense if not for a free mind capable of striving for one and rejecting the other. Without these essential prerequisites, any explanation remains merely a vociferous, meaningless act. For this reason, it can be said with justification that science is the most glorious monument that freedom has erected for itself, and that scientific research is completely unthinkable without freedom."[248]

Machines lack freedom. Technologies are designed, developed, and built by humans, meaning they are produced heteronomously. Therefore, the learning of ethical principles and norms are also guided by humans. In a last consequence, machines would always be controlled from the outside. Metaphorically speaking: machines – even self-learning machines – will go back to a first line of code that always comes from humans. Freedom is a third, *important* argument against the moral capacity of machines.

3.5 Responsibility

The freedom to want what one does not want distinguishes responsibility.[249] Responsibility succeeds in understanding that one's own freedom is connected to the freedom of all other humans and to respect the human dignity of all humans. Responsibility enables freedom to go beyond one's own needs and interests to discover the horizon for the freedom of all other humans and for social tasks and objectives. "Responsibility opens up a freedom that is individualistic and concentrated on one's own needs and integrates it in a social framework, common tasks and objectives"[250]. Responsibility is also a *conditio sine qua non* for morality. In order to bear or be given responsibility – to be able to be a subject of responsibility – freedom and rationality are necessary.

The question arises if responsibility can be assumed by machines. The answer would have to be negative, because machines cannot represent a re-

---

247 For this discourse see Holderegger et al. 2007; Fink / Rosenzweig 2006; Fleischer 2012; Bloch 2011; Bauer 2007; Achtner 2010; Guckes 2003.
248 Hersch 1992: 60-61.
249 See Kirchschlaeger 2014a.
250 Holderegger 2006: 401.

sponsibility subject because they lack freedom – a fourth, *important* argument against the moral capability of machines.

3.6 Autonomy

A fifth fundamental question concerning the attribution of morality to machines arises from the autonomy proclaimed by humans. Immanuel Kant connects human dignity to their autonomy.[251] Humans are carriers of dignity and therefore may not be instrumentalized, because they, as rational beings, recognize common moral rules and principles for themselves, determine them for themselves and base their actions on them.[252] Human dignity "as a reasonable being that doesn't obey any laws except the ones that he [respectively she] has given himself"[253] is based on the ability of the human being to set rules of reason for himself. This means that moral rules and principles that the human being formulates in his/her autonomy must meet the following requirements of a critical, rational morality, which will guarantee their universality: Universality presupposes the fulfillment of the principle of generalizability by presenting rational and plausible arguments – "good reasons". "Good reasons" means that it must be conceivable that all humans given their effective freedom and autonomy as well as their full equality would agree upon these reasons – within a model of thought and not within a real worldwide referendum – on ethical grounds.

Does the description of human autonomy, which can be expressed by humans, correspond to the potential of technologies[254] to follow moral rules, to make moral decisions accordingly, and to carry out corresponding actions? There is a gap between technologies and ethics regarding the notion of "autonomy".[255] While humans recognize general moral rules and principles for themselves, set them for themselves and base their actions on them, this is not possible for technologies. Technologies are primarily made for their suitability and may set rules as a self-learning system, for example to increase their efficiency. But these rules do not contain any ethical qualities. Machines fail on the above-mentioned principle of generaliz-

---

251 See Kant 1974: 69.
252 See Kant 1974: 74.
253 Kant 1974: 67.
254 See, e.g., Decker 2019a; Decker 2019b; Thimm/Baechle 2018.
255 See Kirchschlaeger 2017c.

ability. This negation is a fifth, *important* argument against the term "moral technologies". This negation is further strengthened by the fact that technologies cannot have autonomy without freedom.[256]

What about "self-learning systems" and their moral capability? Self-learning systems mean machines that strive to need as little or no human input as possible for reaching an objective. "The difference is that machines can now think, even if only in a limited manner. They solve problems, make decisions and, most importantly: they learn."[257] If self-learning systems could improve even without human input, there is a possibility that they would become ethically better which, at the end of the day, could result in their autonomy. Even in the case of "self-learning systems", the lack of vulnerability, conscience, freedom, responsibility, and autonomy, as has been shown above, would contradict their moral capability. (This would apply to artificial general intelligence too.) As their self-learning is based on practical mistakes, the possibility of such a moral learning-process can be fundamentally doubted because of the priority of the principle of no damage to humans.[258]

Does this assessment on moral capability change in the case of "superintelligence"? "Superintelligence"[259] means systems that are generally more intelligent than humans. Since today machines already massively outperform humans in various areas of intelligence (e.g. memory, handling high data volumes etc.), it needs to be expected that other areas of intelligence will be added.

Three forms of superintelligence can be distinguished: speed superintelligence (like human intelligence but much faster)[260], collective superintelligence ("superior performance by aggregating large numbers of smaller intelligences"[261]), and quality superintelligence (surpassing human intelligence significantly at a speed at least as high as human intelligence)[262].

The question concerning the moral capability of "superintelligence" proves to be highly relevant. "The challenge presented by the prospect of

---

256 This aspect was, e.g., also taken into account in the Statement of the European Group on Ethics in Science and New Technologies of the EU-Commission, see European Group on Ethics in Science and New Technologies 2018a.
257 Metzler 2016.
258 See Neuhaeuser 2012.
259 See Bostrom 2014.
260 See Bostrom 2014: 53-54.
261 Bostrom 2014: 54.
262 See Bostrom 2014: 55-57.

superintelligence, and how we might best respond is quite possibly the most important and most daunting challenge humanity has ever faced. And – whether we succeed or fail – it is probably the last challenge we will ever face."[263] Among other things, the ethical concern arises of what will happen to humans if superintelligent technological systems, being self-learning systems, decide to set their own purpose.

Based on the above, it can also not be said that superintelligence would have vulnerability, conscience, freedom, responsibility, and autonomy. Therefore, it would also not be possible to think of a moral capability for them.

This technological potential creates, though, the ethical opportunity that superintelligent technological systems will make ethically better decisions and perform ethically better acts than humans, even though they do both because they see the long-term advantages for themselves resulting from ethical decisions and behavior, thus at the end of the day based on pragmatic reasons. (This would, of course and strictly speaking, call into question the ethical nature of their decisions and behavior.) Still, superintelligent technological systems could have this positive impact from an ethical perspective.

To prevent a possible misunderstanding of negating the moral capability of machines: machines can be programmed or trained with ethical principles and rules in order to achieve ethically legitimate decision-making and actions of a machine,[264] even if they themselves cannot recognize and determine them and even if they cannot discern the ethical quality of principles and rules due to the lack of moral capability.

Finally, on this basis, it is necessary to organize and conceptualize accurately the already existing possibilities and abilities of technologies. This is why, for example in the area of automation of mobility, the term "autonomous vehicle" should be avoided and be replaced by "automated vehicle" or "self-driving vehicle".[265] For example, it is doubtful if claiming that robots that managed to win against humans playing Go – a game which does not only rely on logical deduction, but also on intuition[266] – possess "intuition" or "strategic thinking" would be adequate or if those phenomena that are seen as "intuition" or "strategic thinking" in robots would not be, in a last consequence, based on calculations of probability. It also

---

263 Bostrom 2014: vii.
264 See Wallach / Allen 2009; Moor 2006.
265 See Kirchschlaeger 2017b.
266 See Nature 2016.

seems inappropriate to trust a robot to have a "poker face" if it wins against human players in a 20-day poker marathon.[267] Realistically, this could be traced back to the ability to think strategically with imperfect information. The case of the term "moral technologies" is similar. Robots are primarily built for their usefulness. They can also be trained in ethical rules or have ethical rules programmed into them in order to enable an active robot system to act in an ethically acceptable way.[268] This potential leads to the term "moral technologies". But the following must not be ignored: "When we talk about robot ethics, we should talk about normative ethics for the use of robots, i.e. the right and wrong conduct of robots is the responsibility of the robot users and not of the robots themselves. (…) a robot should not be ethical by itself; it should be ethically used."[269]

Therefore, terms other than "moral technologies" would be more adequate, such as "technical tools"[270], "intelligent computer interfaces"[271], "socio-technical systems"[272] or "implicit ethical agent"[273]. The last one is problematic as well, though, since it would call robots "agents" or "ethical agents", which would require moral autonomy as a prerequisite.[274] This is because "agents" are "deliberating, assessing, choosing, and acting to make what we see as a good life for [them]selves"[275].

Another solution could consist of the introduction of several levels of "autonomy" (or of morality): "Autonomy in machines and robots should be used in a narrower sense than humans (i.e. metaphorically). Specifically, machine/robot autonomy cannot be defined absolutely, but only relatively to the goals and tasks required. Of course, we may frequently have a case in which the results of the operations of a machine/robot are not known in advance by human designers and operators. But this does not mean that the machine/robot is a (fully) autonomous and independent agent that decides what to do on its own. Actually, machines and robots can be regarded as partially autonomous agents, in which case we may have several levels of 'autonomy' (…) [respectively] several levels of 'moral-

---

267 See Spice 2017.
268 See Wallach / Allen 2009.
269 Krenn 2016: 17.
270 See Engineering and Physical Sciences Research Council 2011.
271 See Van Est / Stemerding 2012.
272 See Manzeschke et al. 2013.
273 See Krenn 2016.
274 See Griffin 2001: 311-312.
275 Griffin 2008: 32.

ity'"[276]. These levels comprise "operational morality" ("the moral significance and responsibility lies totally in the humans involved in their design and use, far from full moral agency. The computer and software scientists and engineers designing present day robots and software can generally forecast all the possible situations the robot will face"[277]), "functional morality" ("ethical robot's ability to make moral judgments when deciding a course of action without direct top-down instructions from humans. In this case the designers can no longer predict the robot's actions and their consequences"[278]), and "full morality" ("a robot which is so intelligent that it is entirely autonomously selecting its actions and so it is fully responsible for them. Actually, moral decision making can be regarded as a natural extension to engineering safety for systems with more intelligence and autonomy"[279]). Even the introduction of levels of autonomy or of morality cannot overcome the fundamental critical points elaborated above. It remains problematic to use "morality" or "autonomy" for a technological system which is heteronomously programmed to follow heteronomously defined principles and rules instead of being able to autonomously define them for oneself, to autonomously decide to obey them or not, and to be aware of their ethical quality. It remains problematic to use "morality" or "autonomy" for a technological system, which lacks vulnerability, conscience, freedom, responsibility, and moral capability.

A possible counter-argument could be to point to the states of moral development of humans – e.g., in the model of Kohlberg –[280], to claim a similarity of the levels with these stages, and to derive the reason why, when even humans on lower stages of moral development are considered "moral", this should not be applicable to levels of "morality" of robots. This challenge could be met by referencing the potential that humans can grasp to further develop their moral capability (which may or may not be realized) as the foundation for the adequateness of the understanding of humans on lower stages of moral development as "moral".

While criticizing the definition of these levels as levels of "autonomy" and "morality", without linking them with "autonomy" and "morality" and without understanding them as "autonomous" and "moral", the distinction of these levels can be helpful to categorize the different levels of

---

276 Tzafestas 2016: 2.
277 Tzafestas 2016: 73.
278 Tzafestas 2016: 73.
279 Tzafestas 2016: 73.
280 See Kohlberg 1981; Kohlberg 1984.

capability of technological systems to follow and to obey legal and ethical principles and rules and – in the case of the last level – to differentiate what is impossible for technological systems due to their lack of "autonomy" and due to their lack of moral capability.

3.7 Ethical Judgement by Humans

The above critique leads to the main consequence that humans are responsible for making ethical decisions;[281] laying down ethical principles and ethical and legal norms; setting a framework, goals, and limits of digital transformation; as well as defining the use of artificial intelligence in addition to examining, analyzing, evaluating, and assessing technology-based innovation from an ethical perspective. It is the task of ethics "to provide the moral tools that promote and encourage the society and individuals to keep preventing misuse of the technological achievements in robotics against human kind. Legislation should provide efficient and just legal tools for discouraging and preventing such misuse, and assigning liability in cases of harm due to robot misuse and human malpractice."[282] It is necessary that humans conduct an ongoing ethical and legal discourse on the use, priorities, contexts, and barriers for technological progress.[283]

3.8 Overcoming the "Humans - Machines" Dichotomy Using the Interactionist Model

Accepting this responsibility of humans and connecting it with the interaction between technology and ethics elaborated above in chapter 2 The Correlation between Ethics and Technology, a distinction between humans and machines should still be made due to their essential differences, some of them with immediate ethical relevance just previously discussed in this chapter. At the same time, the "humans - machines" dichotomy should be relaxed with the interactionist model introduced above in chapter 2 The Correlation between Ethics and Technology in the regard that humans live up to their exclusive responsibility by addressing the necessary aspects: Human need to define, implement, and realize ethical principles,

---

281 See Johnson 2006a; Yampolski 2013.
282 Tzafestas 2016: 2.
283 See Kirchschlaeger 2013b.

ethical and legal norms, as well as a framework, goals and limits for machines but primarily for the interaction between humans and machines – for the "technological accompaniment"[284] – and for the "hybrid socio-technical system of people, machines and programs"[285].

This could provoke the criticism that the relaxation of the "humans - machines" dichotomy does not go far enough. "Human beings and technological artifacts have become so closely connected in our everyday lives, that even our moral perceptions and decisions have become technologically mediated. Only by recognizing this interweaving of humans and technologies can we take responsibility for the ways in which technologies have an impact on society and on human existence – in practices of technology design, implementation, and use."[286] Understanding artefacts as "moral impact agents"[287] or as "moral factors"[288] highlights the positive or negative contribution of an artefact to the realization of an ethical principle in an action or in an outcome. While there is full agreement on the intertwinement of humans and technologies, *first*, the question must be posed if relying on "contribution" does not lead to the result that every material object can contribute to the positive or negative action or to the positive or negative outcome against an ethical principle. E.g., a stone can influence the action of hitting someone negatively by intensifying the violence of this action and it can influence the outcome of hitting someone negatively as the condition of the victim of this act of violence can be seriously injured. Therefore, as everything could be a moral factor, it is not something that can be said to be unique to artefacts. Beyond that, this provokes doubt as to whether the description as "moral factor" has any epistemological significance.

Second, the relaxation of the "humans - machines" dichotomy cannot go further because of "the demand for the preservation of the subject's unity against the imminent danger of its functional division. It is important to see that this demand must not itself be misunderstood as moral. It is – and it is not possible to go back behind this paradigm of Kant's moral philosophy – a condition of the possibility of ethics."[289] There remains a fundamental difference between humans and technologies regarding ethical sub-

---

284 Verbeek 2011b: 43.
285 Rammert 2003: 15.
286 Verbeek 2014: 76.
287 Moor 2006: 18.
288 See Brey 2014.
289 Mathwig 2000: 288.

jectivity and moral agency because having an effect or influence – which is the case: technologies can have an impact on human lives including the ethical dimension – is not equivalent to possessing ethical subjectivity or moral agency. For example, the weather can have an influence on one's mood but no one would argue that weather has agency over the mood of humans. As shown above in this chapter, there are some preconditions for ethical subjectivity and moral agency that technologies are lacking. Therefore – although they are intertwined closely with humans – technologies do not possess ethical subjectivity or moral agency. The differentiation of "causal efficacy of artefacts in the production of events and states of affairs", "acting for or on behalf of another entity", and "moral agency"[290] reinforces this position although there is no need conceptually to cluster all three of them under "agency" while the first two are differing from agency. Finally, if one looks more closely at the intertwinement itself between humans and technologies, an even more intense form of intertwinement does not lead to the dissolution of the difference between the two. By analogy, when, for example, two humans are in love with each other, even as deeply as possible and therefore experiencing the most imaginably intense intertwinement, one would not argue for the dissolution of the two individuals into one human.

One way to overcome this problem and still force technologies into ethical subjectivity and moral agency is to change the understanding of morality. "Morality is neither to be found in the objects themselves, nor in autonomous subjects. It only comes in relations between subjects and objects, where objects have moral significance and subjects are engaged in mediated relations with the world."[291] This would mean, e.g., to be able to blame the weather for the mood of humans although the mood can be whatever it is independently from the weather. In other words, and as a first counter-argument against this adjustment of the understanding of morality, there is also morality without technologies. Second, even though technologies as objects can be ethically significant, the ability to recognize the ethically legitimate, to decide accordingly, and to act upon it does not belong to them but to humans as ethical subjects and moral agents for the above-mentioned lack of vulnerability, conscience, freedom, responsibility, and autonomy. Third, while technologies as objects can "perform morally relevant actions independently of the humans who created them, causing

---

290 See Johnson / Noorman 2014.
291 Verbeek 2014: 87.

'artificial good' and 'artificial evil'"[292], this is not a reason for broadening the concept of moral agency so far to make technologies fit into it.[293] Technologies might cause good and evil but they do it without recognizing, knowing about or being aware of the ethical quality of it. It is true that "just as a computer can represent emotions without having emotions, computer systems may be capable of functioning as if they understand the meaning of symbols without actually having what one would consider to be human understanding."[294] In both cases, the representation and the functioning lacks authenticity, which is thought to be essential for emotions and moral capability. In other words, representing emotions does depend on the fulfillment of its task on the fact that the representation is emotional, and the functioning depends on the fulfillment of its task on the fact that it possesses moral capability as a basis for this functioning. In both cases, emotionality and moral capability would be denied for machines.

Fourth, only humans possess – as elaborated above – vulnerability, conscience, freedom, responsibility, autonomy, and moral capability. Therefore, one should avoid "to see everything that exists – including oneself – from the perspective of the technically feasible. For example, many are willing to see themselves as highly perfected robots – or, according to the scientific way of seeing initially chosen, as the result of biologically inherited characteristics. Such a view of the self has a deep impact on the 'I'. Those who see themselves in this way tend to reduce the 'I' to a sum of 'effects' whose 'causes' can be analyzed so that the claim to freedom and its inflexibility in responsibility can be broken down at its root."[295]

Fifth, it is exclusively up to humans to program and/or train technologies in ethical values, principles, and norms, which they are to respect – even though technologies do not recognize the ethical quality of them. This leads to the question of which ethical values, principles, and norms should be taught to technologies –[296] a topic further elaborated below in chapter 6 Instruments for the Ethical Assessment.

Sixth, the exclusive ability of humans to recognize the ethically legitimate, to decide accordingly, and to act upon it also comprises the possibility to decide not even to create, design, produce, disseminate, or to use

---

292 Floridi 2014: 187.
293 See Floridi 2014; on this question see also Torrance 2008; Torrance 2011.
294 Wallach / Allen 2009: 9.
295 Hersch 1992: 60.
296 See Bhargava / Kim 2017.

technologies as objects or the possibility to decide to abolish or to destroy technologies.

At the same time, this overcoming of the "humans - machines" dichotomy using the interactionist model could provoke the criticism that the relaxation of the dichotomy "humans - machines" goes too far. The interactionist model could be perceived in the way that it is embracing the proposal to get rid of the starting point of the subject - object dualism which then should be surmounted by ending machine thinking, by postulating "non-machines" and "post-machines" as well as corresponding "new, non-modern forms of subjectivity".[297] This is not the case as the interactionist model differentiates between humans as subjects and machines as objects while emphasizing the essential mutual impact they have on each other. "Humans and other highly developed creatures are not machines. Nature as a whole is not a machine. Many myths from ancient times to today's Hollywood revolve around this relationship between man and machine. In some myths, man is only a machine, in others nature as a whole is a machine, in others, machines subjugate people, and some utopians believe that the ultimate realm of freedom will be to let machines work exclusively. A digital humanism does not transform a human into a machine and does not interpret machines as humans. It holds on to the specificity of a human and his [respectively her] abilities and uses digital technologies to expand them, not to limit them."[298]

This differentiation of humans and of technologies from an ethical perspective provides the basis for excluding, from an ethical point of view, the attribution of rights and legal personhood to machines and artificial intelligence. "Granting human rights to a computer would degrade human dignity. For instance, when Saudi Arabia granted citizenship to a robot called Sophia, human women, including feminist scholars, objected, noting that the robot was given more rights than many Saudi women have."[299]

Other risks emphasize why machines and artificial intelligence should not be holders of rights. "Two other aspects of corporations make people even more vulnerable to AI systems with human legal rights: They don't die, and they can give unlimited amounts of money to political candidates and groups. Artificial intelligences could earn money by exploiting workers, using algorithms to price goods and manage investments, and find

---

297   See Coeckelbergh 2017.
298   Nida-Ruemelin 2018: 10-11; On humanism see Mayer-Tasch 2006; Holderegger et al. 2011.
299   Yampolskiy 2018.

new ways to automate key business processes. Over long periods of time, that could add up to enormous earnings – which would never be split up among descendants. That wealth could easily be converted into political power. Politicians financially backed by algorithmic entities would be able to take on legislative bodies, impeach presidents and help to get figureheads appointed to the Supreme Court. Those human figureheads could be used to expand corporate rights or even establish new rights specific to artificial intelligence systems – expanding the threats to humanity even more."[300]

Facing the ethical opportunities and risks of digital transformation and artificial intelligence, conceptual clarity from an ethical perspective on the realm of possible subjects of responsibility is necessary. Within the interactionist model, this differentiation of humans and of technologies from an ethical perspective makes a significant difference for living up to the exclusive responsibility of humans for technologies as it makes crystal clear who is in charge and who is the subject of responsibility for technologies: humans.

---

[300] Yampolskiy 2018.

4 Critical Review of Terms

4.1 Clarification of Terms

Another aspect of conceptual clarity from an ethical perspective is the terms one uses in the discourse about digital transformation and artificial intelligence. Why does one need to clarify these terms? "I don't quite know whether it is especially computer science or its sub-discipline Artificial Intelligence that has such an enormous affection for euphemism. We speak so spectacularly and so readily of computer systems that understand, that see, decide, make judgments (...) without ourselves recognizing our own superficiality and immeasurable naiveté with respect to these concepts. And, in the process of so speaking, we anesthetize our ability to (...) become conscious of its end use (...) One can't escape this state without asking, again and again: 'What do I actually do? What is the final application and use of products of my work?' and ultimately: 'Am I content or ashamed to have contributed to this use?'"[301]

Beyond that, confronted with the question of the definition of "robot", "artificial intelligence", and "digital transformation" (an umbrella-concept coined in order to cover automation, mechanization, machinization, robotization, digitalization), one becomes aware of their conceptual blurriness[302] that should be overcome.

4.2 Robots

A "robot" can be defined as "an automatically controlled reprogrammable multipurpose, manipulative machine with several degrees of freedom, which may be either fixed in place or mobile for use in industrial automation applications"[303]. The term "robot" comes from a play with the title "W.U.R. Werstands universal Robots"[304] written by Karel Čapek and published in 1920. The title coincides with the name of a company producing

---

301 Weizenbaum 1987: 45.
302 See Ohly 2019a: 20.
303 European Standard 1992.
304 See Čapek 2017.

humanoid machine-slaves that should liberate humans from work but instead attempt to annihilate humans. From an ethical perspective, the attribution of "several degrees of freedom" is problematic based on the elaborations above in chapter 3 Can Ethical Judgment Be Delegated to Technologies?.

Other attributions to robots that occur are a "body", the ability to "come into contact with its spatially close environment in multiple ways" through sensors, the "effects on the spatial environment", and a computer.[305]

An "intelligent robot" can be understood as "a machine able to extract information from its environment and use knowledge about its work to move safely in a meaningful and purposive manner"[306] while an "autonomous robot" "can work without human intervention, and with the aid of embodied artificial intelligence can perform and live within its environment"[307]. From an ethical perspective, the attribution of "autonomy" is problematic based on the elaborations above in chapter 3 Can Ethical Judgment Be Delegated to Technologies?.

4.3 Artificial Intelligence

Artificial intelligence can be defined as "machines that are able to 'think' in a human like manner and possess higher intellectual abilities and professional skills, including the capability of correcting themselves from their own mistakes"[308] or as "the science and engineering of machines with capabilities that are considered intelligent by the standard of human intelligence"[309]. The term "artificial" in "artificial intelligence" highlights that the "intelligence (is) displayed or simulated by technological means."[310]

Both definitions of artificial intelligence are anthropocentric. Artificial intelligence can also be defined independently from human intelligence as seeking "to make computers do the sort of things that minds can do"[311].

In 1950, the publication by Alan Turing on computing machinery and intelligence posed the question of whether machines can think. A simple

---

305 Ohly 2019a: 21-22.
306 Arkin 1998: 2.
307 Tzafestas 2016: 37.
308 Tzafestas 2016: 22-25.
309 Jansen et al. 2018: 5.
310 Coeckelbergh 2020: 203.
311 Boden 2016: 1.

heuristic test – the so called "Turing test" – should help examine this hypothesis: On the basis of typed or relayed messages, could a computer have a conversation and answer questions in a way that would trick a suspicious human into thinking the computer was actually a human?[312] John Searle questions that argument by highlighting the difference between thinking and pretending to be able to think with the "Chinese Room Thought Experiment": Based on the input of Chinese characters, an artificial intelligence can produce an output in the form of other Chinese characters following the instructions by a computer program concerning how the Chinese characters should be combined. If the output convinces a human Chinese speaker in such a way that the latter thinks that the former comes from a human Chinese speaker, the "Turing test" would be passed, but would this really mean that the artificial intelligence understands Chinese? Or does it just indicate the artificial intelligence's ability to simulate the ability to understand Chinese? If a human would be put in an enclosed room receiving input and instructions on how to elaborate this input into an output that would make the impression that this human knows Chinese, a human would be able to fake the ability to understand Chinese, but the same human would not really understand Chinese.[313]

Also in 1950, Claude Shannon proposed the creation of a machine that could be taught to play chess[314] by using brute force or by evaluating a small set of an opponent's strategic moves.[315]

Artificial intelligence also lends its name to a scientific field striving for an understanding of intelligence and associated with computer science, algorithms, and logic. The starting point for research in the field of artificial intelligence was the conviction that "every aspect of learning or any feature of intelligence can in principle be so precisely described that a machine can be made to simulate it."[316]

Artificial intelligence as a scientific field is differentiated from but at the same time largely overlapping with "cognitive science" "also concerned

---

312 See Turing 2009.
313 One of the main points one can draw from the thought experiment of the Chinese Room Argument is that syntax is neither equivalent to nor sufficient for semantics. The Chinese Room Argument shows that symbolic manipulation, however convincing it may seem, is neither equivalent to nor sufficient for understanding due to the crucial role semantics play in understanding.
314 See Shannon 1950.
315 See University of Washington 2006.
316 McCarthy et al. 2006: 12.

with exploring general principles of intelligence"[317] but linked with psychology, biology, neurobiology, etc.[318] and "embodied cognitive science" focusing on the mechanisms underlying intelligent behavior based on the conviction that "the individual brain should not be the sole locus of cognitive scientific interest. Cognition is not a phenomenon that can be successfully studied while marginalizing the roles of body, world and action."[319]

Artificial intelligence can be defined as "the study of the computations that make it possible to perceive, reason, and act"[320]. Another dimension is added by the following coining of artificial intelligence:[321] "An AI system consists of three main elements: sensors, operational logic and actuators. Sensors collect raw data from the environment, while actuators act to change the state of the environment. The key power of an AI system resides in its operational logic. For a given set of objectives and based on input data from sensors, the operational logic provides output for the actuators. These take the form of recommendations, predictions or decisions that can influence the state of the environment."[322] The following definition allows a comprehensive understanding: "AI system: An AI system is a machine-based system that can, for a given set of human-defined objectives, make predictions, recommendations, or decisions influencing real or virtual environments. AI systems are designed to operate with varying levels of autonomy.

- AI system lifecycle: AI system lifecycle phases involve: i) 'design, data and models'; which is a context-dependent sequence encompassing planning and design, data collection and processing, as well as model building; ii) 'verification and validation'; iii) 'deployment'; and iv) 'operation and monitoring'. These phases often take place in an iterative manner and are not necessarily sequential. The decision to retire an AI system from operation may occur at any point during the operation and monitoring phase.
- AI knowledge: AI knowledge refers to the skills and resources, such as data, code, algorithms, models, research, know-how, training programs, governance, processes and best practices, required to understand and participate in the AI system lifecycle.

---

317 Pfeifer / Scheier 1999: 5.
318 See Pfeifer / Scheier 1999: 5-6.
319 Clark 1999: 350.
320 Winston 1992: 5.
321 See Russel / Norvig 2009; Gringsjord / Govindarajulu 2018.
322 OECD 2019a.

– AI actors: AI actors are those who play an active role in the AI system lifecycle, including organizations and individuals that deploy or operate AI."[323]

AI systems possess a lifecycle with the following phases:

"1. Design, data and modelling includes several activities, whose order may vary for different AI systems:

  – Planning and design of the AI system involves articulating the system's concept and objectives, underlying assumptions, context and requirements, and potentially building a prototype.
  – Data collection and processing includes gathering and correcting data, performing checks for completeness and quality, and documenting the metadata and characteristics of the dataset. Dataset metadata includes information on how a dataset was created, its composition, its intended uses and how it has been maintained over time.
  – Model building and interpretation involves the creation or selection of models or algorithms, their calibration and/or training and interpretation.
2. Verification and validation involves executing and tuning models, with tests to assess performance across various dimensions and considerations.
3. Deployment into live production involves piloting, checking compatibility with legacy systems, ensuring regulatory compliance, managing organizational change and evaluating user experience.
4. Operation and monitoring of an AI system involves operating the AI system and continuously assessing its recommendations and impacts (both intended and unintended) in light of objectives and ethical considerations. This phase identifies problems and adjusts by reverting to other phases or, if necessary, retiring an AI system from production."[324]

Nowadays, artificial intelligence is classified into "weak artificial intelligence" and "strong artificial intelligence".[325] While "weak AI" is developed to fulfil a certain, limited task, a "strong AI" wants to be similar to, or even outperform, human intelligence. Another definition coins "Artificial Nar-

---

323 OECD 2019c: I.
324 OECD 2019a.
325 See UNESCO 2018.

row Intelligence" as "AI that specializes in one area. There's AI that can beat the world chess champion in chess, but that's the only thing it does."[326] "Artificial General Intelligence (...) or Human-Level AI (...) refers to a computer that is as smart as a human across the board – a machine that can perform any intellectual task that a human being can."[327] (In addition, there is "superintelligence" which was briefly touched upon above in chapter 3 Can Ethical Judgment Be Delegated to Technologies? and will be discussed further below in subchapter 7.7 Transhumanism.) If "Artificial General Intelligence" will ever be achieved and when that would be is discussed, but these are a point of controversy.[328]

4.4 Data-Based Systems

It needs to be noted from an ethical standpoint that artificial intelligence often does not stand alone but develops its potential when combined with other technologies,[329] and that artificial intelligence "is always also social and human: AI is not only about technology but also about what humans do with it, how they use it, how they perceive and experience it, and how they embed it in wider social-technical environments."[330]

From an ethical perspective, the above-mentioned starting point is criticized: "Intelligence is not limited to solving a particular cognitive problem, it depends on *how* that happens."[331] In view of the nature of artificial intelligence, doubts arise from an ethical perspective if the term is even adequate, because artificial intelligence strives to imitate human intelligence, but this is limited to a certain area of intelligence (e.g., certain cognitive capacities).[332] Furthermore, it is to be assumed that artificial intelligence can at best become similar to human intelligence in certain areas of intelligence, but can never become the same. As elaborated above in chapter 3 Can Ethical Judgment Be Delegated to Technologies?, moral capability is, for example, one of the areas of human intelligence which artificial intelligence cannot achieve.

---

326 Urban 2015.
327 Urban 2015.
328 See Brooks 2017.
329 See Coeckelbergh 2020: 78-81.
330 Coeckelbergh 2020: 80.
331 Misselhorn 2018: 17.
332 See Dreyfus 1972: 29; Dreyfus / Dreyfus 1986.

Finally, criticizing "artificial intelligence" on a conceptual level is ethically pertinent, which can, for example, be demonstrated by the use of the term "trustworthy Artificial Intelligence": "First of all, the (…) central idea of a 'trustworthy AI' is conceptual nonsense. Machines are not trustworthy, only humans can be trustworthy – or not. If an untrustworthy company or an untrustworthy government acts unethically and will in future have a good, robust AI-technology, it can act even more unethically afterwards. The story of the trustworthy AI is a marketing narrative thought of by the industry, a good-night-story for customers of tomorrow. In reality, it is about developing future markets and using debates on ethics as elegant, public decoration for a large-scale investment strategy."[333]

There was the temptation to leave it at this criticism, not to present a definition, or to present only a working definition or only a model. A concrete proposal in the form of a definition is now to be made after all – in the service of conceptual substance, concreteness, certainty, and sharpness. The term "data-based systems" would be more appropriate than "artificial intelligence", because this term describes what actually constitutes "artificial intelligence": generation, collection, and evaluation of data; data-based perception (sensory, linguistic); data-based predictions; data-based decisions. In addition, the term "data-based systems" also helps to highlight the main strength and the main weakness of the present technological achievement in this field. The mastery of an enormous quantity of data is the key asset of data-based systems.

Pointing to its core characteristic – namely of being based on data and relying exclusively on data in all its processes, its own development, and its actions (more precisely its reactions to data) – lifts the veil of the inappropriate attribution of the myth of "intelligence" covering substantial problems and challenges of data-based systems and allows for more accurateness, adequacy, and precision in the critical reflection of data-based systems. The untraceability, unpredictability, and inexplicability of the algorithmic processes resulting in data-based evaluation, data-based predictions and data-based decisions ("black-box-problem"[334]), its wide vulnerability for systemic errors, its deep exposure for confusing causation with correlation (e.g., high consumption of ice cream by children in a summer month and high number of children in car accidents due to more mobility during vacation in the same summer month correlate but there is not any causal

---

333 Metzinger 2019.
334 See Knight 2017a; Bathaee 2018; Weinberger 2018; Knight 2017b; Castelvecchi 2016.

relationship between the two statistics, meaning ice cream consumption does not cause car accidents)[335], and its high probability of biased and discriminatory data leading to biased and discriminatory data-based evaluation, data-based and discriminatory predictions, and data-based and discriminatory decisions embrace its major disadvantages.[336] "Algorithms are opinions embedded in codes. They are not objective."[337] They are not neutral. They serve specific goals and purposes. They need to be governed.[338]

These above mentioned major disadvantages are constituted or reinforced by ethical challenges of the algorithms as part of data-based systems:[339] epistemic concerns: "inconclusive evidence"[340] ("probable yet inevitably uncertain knowledge"), "inscrutable evidence"[341] ("connection between the data and the conclusion" not accessible), "misguided evidence"[342] ("conclusions can only be as reliable (but also as neutral) as the data"); normative concerns: "unfair outcomes"[343] (discriminatory effect), "transformative effects"[344] ("algorithms can affect how we conceptualize the world"), "traceability"[345] ("Algorithms are software-artefacts used in data-processing, and as such inherit the ethical challenges associated with the design and availability of new technologies and those associated with the manipulation of large volumes of personal and other data. This implies that harm caused by algorithmic activity is hard to debug (i.e. to detect the harm and find its cause), but also that it is rarely straightforward to identify who should be held responsible for the harm caused."[346])

Unfortunately, these ethical challenges can be met, only to a certain extent, by improving the algorithms and their applications. Of course, it would have, therefore, a substantial positive impact if data is not allowed to make decisions but is just allowed to inform decisions.

---

335 See Iversen / Gergen 1997: 317-318.
336 See UNESCO 2019; Fortmann-Roe 2012; Bartoletti 2018; Counts 2018; Council of Europe 2018a; Council of Europe 2018b; Wildhaber / Lohmann / Kasper 2019; Coeckelberg 2020.
337 Demuth 2018: 16.
338 Lohmann 2018.
339 See Mittelstadt et al. 2016: 4-5.
340 See Mittelstadt et al. 2016: 5.
341 See Mittelstadt et al. 2016: 6-7.
342 See Mittelstadt et al. 2016: 7-8.
343 See Mittelstadt et al. 2016: 8-9.
344 See Mittelstadt et al. 2016: 9-10.
345 See Mittelstadt et al. 2016: 10-12.
346 Mittelstadt et al. 2016: 4-5.

In addition, it would make a substantial positive difference if data-based systems were not constructed in a way that causes the "black-box-problem" and then one tries to open the "black-box"[347], but is instead shaped from the beginning with an approach that is not only explainable ("AI that can explain to humans its actions, decisions, or recommendations, or can provide sufficient information about how it came to its results"[348]) but also interpretable[349] – empowering humans to take an informed and well thought-out position confronted with data because of not only an understanding of the data-processing leading to these results but also the ability to evaluate and assess the data-processing, which is also integrated into their viewpoint. Humans should only decide and do what they understand. At the end of the day, asking for a technological approach avoiding the "black-box-problem" is a basic ethical requirement,[350] not a high ethical standard. One asks only that technologies should be designed, developed, and produced in a way that avoids the problem, from an ethical perspective, that one cannot guarantee that negative risks, effects, or consequences can be avoided because one just does not know what happens in the "black-box". This includes also the acceptance of possibly negative implications on technological performance.[351] Just to illustrate that simply with an analogy: Something similar to a "black-box-approach" would be to produce a drug in the pharmaceutical industry when one does not know what is in it but just hopes that only the desired positive effects will be caused, developing another drug if negative effects should occur. Nobody would accept, in that case, just keeping the fingers crossed hoping that nothing negative will happen.

The "black-box-problem" consists not just in the technological complexity and the expediency[352] but also in a gap between mathematics and ethics which will be discussed further below in chapter 5 The Complexity of Ethics. Even if everything is explainable[353] and interpretable, the process of how to build a bridge between mathematics and ethics and how to turn

---

347 See Samek et al. 2017.
348 Coeckelberg 2020: 204.
349 See Rudin 2019.
350 See Goebel et al. 2018.
351 See Seseri 2018.
352 See Rudin 2019.
353 See Mueller-Dott 2019; Horizon 2020 Commission Expert Group 2020.

algorithms into ethical principles and norms may still be opaque.[354] Beyond that, the "black-box-problem" also comprises implicitly remaining normative notions within the processing of data, such as biases, discriminatory patterns. Worldview-based, cultural, or social norms also provoke an imperialistic form of normative universality. Finally, the "black-box-problem" consists in the lack of clarity regarding ethically relevant and ethically irrelevant aspects as well – representing a part of the complexity of ethics elaborated below in chapter 5 The Complexity of Ethics. From an ethical perspective, in order to meet the opacity challenge, all these aspects of the "black-box-problem" must be overcome.

Still, one needs to take into account that this is not the solution, but part of the solution from an ethical standpoint. "However, the full conceptual space of ethical challenges posed by the use of algorithms cannot be reduced to problems related to easily identified epistemic and ethical shortcomings."[355] The former ethical challenges and the latter fundamental ethical problem of algorithms make it obvious that "equating the ethics of algorithmic assemblages with the transparency of algorithmic code"[356] is inadequate.

Beyond that, the requirements for humans using data-based systems come into play. Humans using data-based systems, making decisions with data-support, etc. must be empowered to reflect critically on the processing of data and the data-based results, to use data with critical thinking, and to go against data-based systems or data if necessary.

4.5 Digital Transformation

This conceptual proposal of "data-based systems" has its implications on other terms, e.g. on "digital transformation". The term "digital transformation" means various technology-based changes, such as "digitalization", "automation", "robotization", "mechanization", "machinization", the "use of data-based systems" and "handling super-data-based systems". It is an umbrella-concept coined in order to cover automation, mechanization,

---

354 I'm grateful to Justus Piater and Aaron Butler as we all came up with this idea independently and discussed this with one another at the Annual Meeting of the "Innsbrucker Kreis von Moraltheolog*innen und Sozialethiker*innen" on January 2-4, 2020.
355 Mittelstadt et al. 2016: 15.
356 Ananny 2016: 109.

machinization, robotization, digitalization, the "use of data-based systems", and "handling super-data-based systems". One needs to take into account that objects, phenomena, and realities are called "digital transformation" even though they are themselves not digital, but they are products or results of digital processes.[357] "Digital" means "recording or storing information as a series of the numbers 1 and 0, to show that a signal is present or absent, using or relating to digital signals and computer technology, showing information in the form of an electronic image, using a system that can be used by a computer and other electronic equipment, in which information is sent and received in electronic form as a series of the numbers 1 and 0, relating to computer technology, especially the internet, showing information as whole numbers rather than in another form such as a picture, graph, etc."[358]

From an ethical point of view, especially the difference between the current technology-based "digital transformation" and the earlier ones is of particular interest to the understanding of digital transformation. Its analysis occurs below in subchapter 7.14 Reduction in Paid Jobs – including the following aspect: Unlike earlier technology-based eras of change,[359] the "digital transformation" is, among other things, not about making work easier for humans, but about replacing humans with self-learning systems (for example automatic check-outs in supermarkets do not aim at making the professional job of a cashier easier, as was the case for the farmer when a plough was replaced by a tractor) in the value chain. The core consequence of digital transformation and the use of data-based systems characterizes this technology-based shift: *Ever fewer humans will directly participate and partake in a more efficient and effective value chain.*[360] From an ethical point of view, this means that from a macrosocial perspective, the challenge lies not in the amount of means available, but in the shaping of a fair social and economic system,[361] *inter alia* with regard to distributing financial means and the rights and possibilities of participating and partaking, with regard to equal opportunities for all, with regard to guaranteeing survival and a life with human dignity for all, and upholding peaceful coexistence.

---

357 See Ohly 2019a: 25-29.
358 Cambridge Dictionary n.d.
359 See Hessler 2016.
360 See Kirchschlaeger 2017a; Kirchschlaeger 2016b.
361 See Kirchschlaeger 2013c.

Finally, the increased interaction between humans and machines (e.g., the massive impact of the high presence of social networks in daily life on social behavior, social competence, and personal interaction), and its interventions in social and personal processes and relationships by means of changing the living conditions, can lead to a technologization and robotization of ideas, terms, notion, and concepts, of the image of humans, of human mindsets, and a questioning of human dignity. For example, if the word "freedom" is reduced to the extent that what one calls "freedom" consists only in what is describable in parameters, programmable in algorithms, and perceivable for technological systems, then the richness, diversity, precision, and depth of human thinking, reflection, and language will be dramatically leveled, normalized, and standardized.

4.6 Machine Ethics – Roboethics

At the end of this critical review of terms, the disciplinary habit of this book – given above in chapter 1 Introduction – applied terms that should not be excluded from this scrutiny. "Machine ethics" aims to develop a system of ethics, which can then be put into a machine[362] in order to promote, support, maximize, preserve, and protect the flourishing of humans and the planet Earth. This aim gains significance because of the technological progress consisting in self-learning machines, automated machines (e.g., self-driving vehicles), data-based systems, and superintelligence. "Machine ethics" discusses, among other things, the possibility of the implementation of ethics into machines,[363] the material definition of the ethics that are to be implemented into machines,[364] and the way this implementation could be pursued.[365]

"Roboethics"[366] or "robot ethics" consists in ethics applied to the design, production, and the use of robots addressing humans involved in robotics (e.g., designers, producers and users of robots). Another understanding – also coined as "ethics in robotics" – brings the above-mentioned aspects of machine ethics and roboethics together: "First, we might think about how humans might act ethically through, or with, robots. In this case, it is hu-

---

362 See Moor 2006; Moor 1995.
363 See Allen / Wallach 2014; Floridi 2011; Johnson 2011.
364 See Mackworth 2011; McLaren 2011; Pereira 2016.
365 See Segal 2017; Wallach et al. 2008.
366 See Veruggio / Operto 2008: 1504.

mans who are the ethical agents. Further, we might think practically about how to design robots to act ethically, or theoretically about whether robots could be truly ethical agents. Here robots are the ethical subjects in question. Finally, there are several ways to construe the ethical relationships between humans and robots: Is it ethical to create artificial moral agents? Is it unethical not to provide sophisticated robots with ethical reasoning capabilities? Is it ethical to create robotic soldiers, or police officers, or nurses? How should robots treat humans, and how should humans treat robots? Should robots have rights?"[367]

---

367 Asaro 2006: 10.

5 The Complexity of Ethics

5.1 Ethics Is Not Democracy

In the process of examining, analyzing, evaluating, and assessing digital transformation and data-based systems and its use from an ethical perspective, one has to take into account something, which remains a fundamental conceptual challenge for, e.g., ethics committees[368] as well: Ethics as a science is not democratic. A democratic process *per se* does not guarantee legitimacy. It is conceivable that a democratic opinion-forming and decision-making process may also lead to results that are ethically bad or wrong. Ethics, in a rational and critical way, need to satisfy the principle of generalizability by presenting rational and plausible arguments – "good reasons". "Good reasons" means that it must be conceivable that all humans, given their effective freedom and autonomy as well as their full equality, would agree upon these reasons – within a model of thought and not within a real worldwide referendum – on ethical grounds.

5.2 Ethics Beyond Principles and Norms

Data-based systems are able to follow moral rules and make moral decisions based on these and act accordingly. Data-based systems can be programmed or trained with ethical rules in order to come to ethical legitimate decisions and perform ethically legitimate actions as a machine.[369] In order to do justice to the complexity of reality, it takes much more than rules like "Asimov's Law": "1. A robot may not injure a human being or, through inaction, allow a human being to come to harm. 2. A robot must obey the orders given it by human beings except where such orders would conflict with the First Law. 3. A robot must protect its own existence as long as such protection does not conflict with the First or Second Laws."[370] Isaac Asimov was probably aware of this himself, which he ex-

---

368 See Huriet 2009; Bobbert / Scherzinger 2019; Duewell 2005: 225-274.
369 See on this Misselhorn 2018: 70-135; Wallach / Allen 2009.
370 Asimov 1982: 67. See Tezuka 2009.

pressed, among other things, by choosing the genre of a short story to publish them.

One could think that data-based systems could just simulate humans in the domain of ethics. "If the AI can understand human morality, it is hard to see what is the technical difficulty in getting it to follow that morality."[371] The first counterargument includes that meaning is created by humans.[372]

The second counterargument embraces the "value alignment problem" or the "value-loading-problem"[373] identified by Stuart Russell[374] emphasizing the complex contexts data-based systems interact with.

The third counterargument against this reductionist view of human morality[375] consists in the above-mentioned points in chapter 2 The Correlation between Ethics and Technology. "With a computer we can turn almost all human problems into statistics, graphs, equations. The really disturbing thing, though, is that in doing so we create the illusion that these problems can be solved with computers."[376]

The fourth counterargument against this reductionist view of ethics acknowledges the fact that ethics go beyond principles, norms, and rules. In order to do justice to the complexity of ethics,[377] mathematical or digital ethics need not be used. It is important to note that ethics in their complexity and in their entirety are not translatable into the language of mathematics and programming[378] because of their sensitivity to the rule-transcending uniqueness of the concrete. That is why, among other things, ethics are not casuistry. Certain aspects of ethics can be programmed or trained as rules for data-based systems. Some ethical elements, though, cannot be reached by digital instruments.[379] For example, data-based systems can learn the principle of human dignity for all, human rights, and ethical guiding principles (prohibition of lying, stealing etc.). However, even within the realm of possibilities, it should not be neglected that data-based systems can learn and follow these rules, but they follow the rules without knowing about the *ethical* quality of those rules (see above 3 Can Ethical

---

371 Davis 2014: 3; see Agar 2016; Soares / Fallenstein 2017.
372 See Searle 1980; Boden 2016.
373 See Bostrom 2012.
374 See Russell 2015.
375 See also Graves 2017.
376 Yehya 2005: 15.
377 See Kirchschlaeger 2020c.
378 See Klincewicz 2017.
379 See Moor 1995.

Judgment Be Delegated to Technologies?). In other words, data-based systems would respect non-ethical or unethical rules in the same manner. "I do not think that they will end up with a moral or ethical robot. For that, we need to have moral agency. For that, we need to understand others and know what it means to suffer. The robot may be installed with some rules of ethics but it won't really care. It will follow a human designer's idea of ethics."[380] A data-based system cannot pass these limitations. "AI will not share these human traits unless we specifically create them to do so. They operate on a task and goal-oriented manner."[381] These limitations are part of data-based systems because – as elaborated above in chapter 4 Critical Review of Terms – they rely exclusively on data without a theory, they accept a solution without addressing the question "why" and while neglecting the search for reasons. This also applies to ethical rules.

This causes the problematic consequence from an ethical point of view that it can be necessary to convey to data-based systems ethical values, principles, and norms, which one thinks are false just because they are not able to handle the right ones (e.g., consequentialist instead of deontological approach).[382]

Transferring ethics to mathematics or programming becomes difficult or even impossible when guiding principles diverge or collide. Through the increasing complexity of everyday reality, humans are challenged to find insights into norms that are adequate to reality, and to consider in a more differentiated and better manner what would be expecting too much of data-based systems due to their lack of moral capability. In situations and cases where in humans the virtue of *epikeia* and conscience come into play, translating ethics into the language of mathematics, programming, and digitalization is impossible. "Epikeia is the rectification of the law where there are gaps due to its general formulation"[383]. *Epikeia* is "an independent practical judgement that records the moral demands of a concrete situation in the light of moral principles and standards"[384]. *Epikeia* consists in "the search for greater justice"[385], it is "to stimulate and to maintain the search for the justice of meaning"[386]. *Epikeia* accounts for the truth that in a concrete encounter with concrete persons in a concrete situation rules

---

380 Sharkey 2014.
381 Gurkaynak 2016: 756.
382 See Talbot et al. 2017a.
383 Aristotle, Nicomachean Ethics: V, 14, 1137b, 26.
384 Schockenhoff 2014a: 601.
385 Schloegl-Flierl 2016: 29.
386 Schloegl-Flierl 2016: 29-30.

reach their limit, because the concrete in its uniqueness outranks the rule. "The general, concrete ethical, the positive legal and many other norms that are generally applicable, although indispensable, are not sufficient to guarantee the basic humanity which, in the face of diversity, will save this society from disintegration and the terrible consequences which result from it. It is inevitable that we have to cross norms in certain situations in order to act humanely, but this does not mean that we deny the need for norms in general or refute that they are generally applicable."[387] Ethical and legal norms and their validity are of course not questioned by *epikeia*. *Epikeia* "not only directs one to apply norms, but to recognize the more urgent ones."[388] They are re-confirmed by this virtue striving for justice. At the same time, *epikeia* ensures that the ethical and legal norms serve humans and not vice-versa.[389] "With the help of *epikeia*, it is possible to act in a way that is appropriate to the situation and useful to people."[390] *Epikeia* requires, however, ethically critical and constructive participation[391] by "a human as a responsible person who is able to consider and interpret standards and laws creatively."[392]

In this context, humans are expected to take responsibility for designing norms, something that is unattainable for data-based systems because they lack moral capability. This responsibility for designing norms aims at continuously having to critically question these rules and, in the service of a prospective, ethical improvement, they are adapted by humans.

This prospective, creative level also contains a human responsibility to create standards. "Perceiving the moral claim does not mean to merely read normatively defined factual and meaningful behavior, but is always a creative process of seeing and discovering. The process of seeing and discovering becomes creative, because humans are called upon to risk in their phantasy new meaningful moments for their lifestyle, which did not occur in the previous systems of rules. The moral goodness of humans urges them to develop the correct thing, from a human perspective, in the form of models."[393] The responsibility to create standards goes far beyond what can be translated into the language of mathematics or programming and, therefore, cannot be transferred to data-based systems.

---

387 Virt 2007: 42-43.
388 Keenan 2010: 155.
389 See Schloegl-Flierl 2016: 39.
390 Schloegl-Flierl 2016: 39.
391 See Demmer 2010: 110-113.
392 Schloegl-Flierl 2016: 39.
393 Virt 2007: 43.

A transferability to mathematics and programming also excludes ethics of virtue with its focus on character traits and attitudes, because the moral capability of humans cannot be digitalized. Based on his paradox, Hans Moravec would probably not be surprised that the complexity of ethics leads to unreachable areas for data-based systems. Moravec's Paradox can be summarized as follows: "The hard problems are easy, and the easy problems are hard."[394] The following example can illustrate its core meaning: "Thinking several moves ahead in a game of chess is difficult for a human. It has been unexpectedly easy to program computers to do this. Chess computers now beat the best human players. Practical tasks, especially those connected with sensorimotor abilities, the kinds of tasks that humans perform effortlessly, have proved very challenging."[395] As ethics is not easy for humans, they nonetheless possess moral capability and therefore are able to meet ethical challenges. An adapted version of Moravec's Paradox is able to highlight the main point regarding the complexity of ethics: The unresolvable problems are resolvable for data-based systems, and the resolvable problems (ethics) are unresolvable for data-based systems. Humans, therefore, have and continue to have a responsibility not to lose oneself in the illusion of *ethical data-based systems* but to create, design, produce, and use *data-based systems with ethics*.

---

394 Pinker 2007: 190.
395 Agar 2016: 76.

6 Instruments for the Ethical Assessment

6.1 Introduction

The ethical analysis, examination, and evaluation of digital transformation and data-based systems from an ethical standpoint require ethical principles and norms providing guidance. There are claims to start from a *tabula rasa* and to create new ethical principles and norms for a new digital era of humanity or to rethink the existing ethical principles and norms because of technology-based changes.[396] The proposed method in this book is that we do not have to reinvent the wheel as existing ethical principles and norms do not lose their validity only because of some technology-based innovation. For example, humans remain holders of human dignity even when data-based systems are created. In addition, ethical principles and norms laboriously fought for over centuries should not just be eradicated by digital transformation and data-based systems but rather inform and influence the digitalization, automation, mechanization, robotization, and data-based systems and interact with them (see above chapter 2 The Correlation between Ethics and Technology). As part of this interaction, there is a need for adaptation of existing ethical principles and norms – as elaborated above in subchapter 5.2 Ethics Beyond Principles and Norms – in order to keep the ethical principles and norms but, most of all, their realization and implementation at the height of digital transformation and data-based systems.

In the following, ethical principles serving the ethical assessment of the digitalization, automation, mechanization, robotization, and data-based systems will be discussed and justified. Because of their claim of universality as part of ethics, they need to fulfill the principle of generalizability by presenting rational and plausible arguments – "good reasons". "Good reasons" means that it must be conceivable that all humans, given their effective freedom and autonomy as well as their full equality, would agree upon these reasons – within a model of thought and not within a real worldwide referendum – on ethical grounds.

---

396 See Bynum 2004; Floridi / Sanders 2004b; Moor 1985; Sullins 2010; Tavani 2004.

Natural law as an ethical instrument is not applied because it would not fulfill this criterion and runs the risk of a naturalistic fallacy.

An approach based on discourse ethics is not taken either due to its potential risk of having a discriminatory impact on humans who could not participate in a discourse (e.g., humans with a severe mental disability, etc.).

From a practical and pragmatic standpoint, a utilitarian approach would be aligned well with the economic rationale and with the pursuit of efficiency driving primarily digital transformation and data-based systems focusing on the principle of utility. "By the principle of utility is meant that principle which approves or disapproves of every action whatsoever according to the tendency it appears to have to augment or diminish the happiness of the party whose interest is in question: or, what is the same thing in other words to promote or to oppose that happiness."[397] From an ethical perspective, the principle of utility faces the following counterarguments weakening its capacity to provide ethical orientation for digital transformation and the use of data-based systems. The question arises if the hedonistic notion of "happiness" can keep up with the task to guide ethically digital transformation and data-based systems with their fundamental impact on humanity and the planet Earth. (It needs to be acknowledged though that this problem can be adjusted to fit "suffering and its absence" as a way to apply the concept of "utility" with this domain, which is not the case with the following points.) Beyond that, a utilitarian approach is not able to serve as an ethical point of reference for the identification of ethically right or wrong means *per se* which were discussed above as parts of the reality that needs to be analyzed ethically. Beyond that, the purely empirically accessible anthropology proves to be too narrow to examine from an ethical perspective the impact of digital transformation and data-based systems on the self-understanding of humans. In addition, a utilitarian approach knows the limit that "happiness" is not always quantifiable because human existence is a much more complex reality. In addition, a utilitarian approach is not capable of dealing with the complexity of ethics elaborated above: a utility is not always generally determinable. Furthermore, utilitarianism is not up to the task due to not being robust and comprehensive enough to determine what right action would mean for these types of cases. Also, the particular emphasis of utilitarianism on quantification is misleading, as many important factors determining or assisting in determining the answer to the question, namely: "What is right action for

---

397 Bentham 2007: 1.

circumstance X?" are not quantifiable or at least not quantifiable in a straightforward way. Moreover, the application of a utilitarian approach in the ethical assessment of digital transformation and data-based systems runs the risk of promoting the "happiness" of a majority at the expense of the "unhappiness" of a minority. Finally – and probably the most significant counterargument – a utilitarian approach could stand for the irrelevance of the individual human and could disregard the human dignity of all humans.

The ethical principles "justice", "responsibility", and "human rights", which will be suggested below for the ethical assessment, are of course not the only ethical principles that could help to find ethical guidance in dealing with digital transformation and data-based systems. Obviously, they do not represent an exhaustive list. These three ethical principles are chosen for this specific task because their normative validity can be ethically justified[398] and because of their fundamental character. Beyond that and specifically with respect to human rights, during the preparatory process of the legal human rights conventions, which turned the political program of the Universal Declaration of Human Rights of 1948[399] into a legally binding instrument, there was awareness, that: "the members of the Commission must take into account the fact that their work concerned the future and not the past; no one could foresee what information media would be employed in a hundred years' time"[400].

6.2 The Principle of Responsibility[401]

6.2.1 Introduction

The term "responsibility" is nowadays not only frequently used in politics and economics, but is also central in the normative discourse. It is striking that responsibility in the political and economic discourse is used in the sense of "competence". *First*, "competence" includes a bearer of responsibility. *Second*, "competence" contains a precise definition of the object or the situation, for what one is responsible. *Third*, the time frame of the responsibility is clearly defined and limited. When looking at the use of this

---

398 See Kirchschlaeger 2013c; Kirchschlaeger 2014a: 54; Kirchschlaeger 2016e.
399 Universal Declaration of Human Rights of 1948.
400 United Nations 1950.
401 See Kirchschlaeger 2014a.

term, the suspicion arises that the latter is lacking at least three relevant elements of the term responsibility: the characteristic of care, the temporal definition of care as *constant* care, and the ethical commitment, which is part of responsibility.

Starting from this suspicion regarding the current use of the term "responsibility", the term "responsibility" will be examined from an ethical perspective.

6.2.2 Short Outline of the Historical Development of the Term Responsibility

The use of the term "responsibility" can be proven as a verb in German during the 12th century and as a noun during the second half of the 15th century.[402] The term "responsibility" is used when someone explains or justifies a decision or an act in front of a judge. This court may be earthly or celestial. From this original seat in life, which has a legal character, it also becomes clear how the foundation from which "responsibility" derives, namely "to give a response", is to be classified and leads to the concept of responsibility. Humans answer to God and/or the court concerning their decisions and actions. The term responsibility relies on the necessity to respond to these instances concerning one's own actions. The concept of responsibility proves itself, thus, from the onset as a concept of relations, because it can only be thought of in terms of relations – in this case, the relation between a person taking responsibility based on a norm in front of a court or before God and the court or God to whom he or she responds based on a norm, (i.e., assumes responsibility in the sense of accountability).

The 18th century sees the beginnings of the triumph of emancipation, which also relates to responsibility. "In the 18th century the emancipation of citizens, in the 19th century the emancipation of Jews and workers, in the 20th century the emancipation of women and black people and in the 21st century the emancipation of homosexuals and various minorities combine a demand for maturity in the political, as well as the private, sphere. It results in the freedom to choose one's own lifestyle and to shape it according to one's own ideas."[403]

---

402 See Grimm / Grimm 1956: Columns 79-82.
403 Schoenherr-Mann 2010: 7-8.

In retrospect, it can also be discerned that the use of this term gains in intensity during the 19th century.[404] The fact that the term responsibility takes over from the term duty is one reason for it. This can be attributed to the fact that "'duty' – if it is understood in a concrete, ethically-material sense and not as a moral bond to morality (Kant) – (...) [is linked to] the notion of a clearly defined area of tasks and functions, of compulsory and clear tasks (duties) that exist for the own person (and its last reason) or is given to one because of a specific position of a person within a group or society. This requires definitions of the situation to which these duties can be easily applied, which are, to a greater or lesser extent, clear. But the dynamization of the areas and the very often multi-layered areas of difficulties can rarely be captured by determining unambiguous, clearly defined duties and be described in the sense of a clear area of responsibility."[405] Responsibility is a more open and less tangible term, which is meant to fulfil the "far more difficult societal grade of complexity"[406]. This complexity is composed of the confusing causation of human decisions or actions and their results in industrial and post-industrial contexts, the anonymization of subjects and objects of decisions and actions, and the human recognition and general questioning of institutions based on the limited self-confidence of humans. "In the sign of technology, however, ethics has to do with actions (...) which have an unprecedented causal reach into the future, accompanied by a prior knowledge that also goes beyond anything unique, as usual incomplete (...). All of this puts responsibility at the center of ethics"[407]. The above-mentioned self-confidence leads, on the one hand, to the situation that humans take it upon themselves to lead the events, despite the complex and confusing starting point. This is expressed by the concept of "responsibility". "A discussion about the future of humanity is about how the important fundamental features of the human condition may change or remain constant in the long run."[408]

On the other hand, the term responsibility should point out that someone has to take responsibility for the consequences of industrial and post-industrial contexts, which mainly manifest themselves in the traces of massive intrusions of humans on nature, and which can no longer be seen as results of natural processes. First of all, this means that the concept will be

---

404 See Heidbrink 2003.
405 Holderegger 2006: 396.
406 Korff / Wilhelms 2001: Column 598.
407 Jonas 1985b: 8-9.
408 Bostrom 2009: 186.

narrowed down by opening and broadening it to include "competence", which means mastering "situations of action, which are increasingly difficult to define in advance and have become more difficult to weigh up, but which nevertheless inevitably belong in the field of competence of the actors."[409] Even if it is demanding and remains a challenge to establish a causal link to, for example, global famine, poverty, destruction of the environment, destruction of the climate, etc., someone is responsible for it and has to take the blame.

However, this also means, secondly, that in the demarcation from natural events, a bearer of responsibility crystallizes, who is a decisive and acting subject who has freedom. Because only with freedom will the subject of responsibility be able to take on responsibility for something. This connection is rooted in Aristotle, who differentiates between "voluntary" and "involuntary" and names voluntariness as a prerequisite for an action being criticized.[410]

At the same time, this also means that the subject of responsibility needs to be capable of morality. Thus, it is only after 1850 that the area of use of the term "responsibility" is extended to the term of moral competence, which implies freedom and moral capability of the subject of responsibility. "Responsibility is a general need in the life of humans as moral beings, who act out of understanding and freedom and are bound by duty."[411] The ideas of autonomy and the person contributed to this development. John Locke's understanding of a person as a subject of attribution,[412] and Immanuel Kant's definition of a person as "that subject whose actions are capable of attribution"[413] laid the foundation for an understanding that brought the concept of responsibility more and more into focus. They also illustrate the close connection between autonomy, person, and responsibility.

Finally, Jean-Paul Sartre emphasizes this close connection, while recognizing "that the human being who is condemned to being free, has to carry the weight of the whole world on his [or her] shoulders; in his [or her] being he [or she] is responsible for the world and for himself [or herself]."[414] For Sartre, responsibility means being at the center of "conscious-

---

409 Holderegger 2006: 396.
410 See Aristotle, Nicomachean Ethics: V, 15.
411 Der Grosse Herder 1935.
412 See Locke 2006: 435-436. See also Trotter Cockburn 1702.
413 Kant 1997: 223.
414 Sartre 1943: 696.

ness, the indisputable creator of an event or a thing."[415] According to Sartre, the human being has to accept that he or she is the subject of responsibility.

When dealing with the development of the term responsibility from today's point of view, it becomes obvious that certain elements of the current use of the term "responsibility" can be rediscovered. On a formal level, responsibility involves the relationship between a subject and an object based on a yardstick before an authority.

The above-mentioned thoughts of Sartre are radicalized to the extent that humans are often the subject of responsibility in the concept of responsibility understood as competence introduced above, without being the subject of action at the same time. While from the perspective of duty, the human is only duty-bound where the subject of duty is the same as the decision-making and acting subject, responsibility in the sense of competence also allows for someone to be a bearer of responsibility, no matter if he or she is also the decision-making and acting subject. For example, a minister of finance may show him- or herself to be responsible for a financial crisis and has to step down, even though he or she was most likely not the decision-making and acting subject for the entire financial crisis in all its complexity. Rather, in a so-called "risk society", which is characterized by a "multi-dimensionality of its interacting results with inevitably ever new uncertainties to be overcome"[416], structural questions actually arise, which are, however, individually assigned as responsibilities.

Modern secularization finally brought about the following changes with regard to the understanding of responsibility: "God as an authority of responsibility is replaced by the totality of all reasonable beings now and in future, and possibly also the non-human nature. The scope of responsibility will be extended, especially where humans are aware of a fundamental unpredictability of their consequences, which is closely related to a fundamental change of the subject of responsibility, which obviously has to give up its limitation to the individual, as well as its limitation to those actions for which it itself was consciously responsible."[417]

Besides its conceptual origin in theological, philosophical, and legal discourse, its significance leads to an analysis of the principle of responsibility from different academic disciplines (e.g., sociological)[418].

---

415 Sartre 1943: 696.
416 Korff / Wilhelms 2001: Columns 599.
417 Zimmerli 1993: 105.
418 See Arnaldi / Bianchi 2016.

6.2.3 Eighth Dimensions of Responsibility

If responsibility is understood as competence, there is the danger that responsibility will only and exclusively be understood as individual and retrospective and will focus only on attributing results and impacts to someone. This risk needs to be overcome, on the one hand with an understanding of responsibility that puts at the forefront the prospective and takes care of how decision-making and acting powers are distributed in such a way that the contemporary world and the environment today and in the future do not have to suffer because of current actions and inactions.[419]

On the other hand, in addition to individual responsibility, the responsibility for structural and institutional questions needs to take center stage. For example, patchy social welfare that leads to injustices needs to be tackled as a structural problem in a responsible manner. Furthermore, globalization, for example, continues to be the key to success for some countries in this world, but not for all. In the framework of globalization, all the focus was on growth and generating wealth. But in practice, and surprisingly also in the theoretical work, the question of distribution was neglected.[420] Some countries continue to be excluded from the positive effects of globalization, either through their own faults (e.g., lack of political stability, corruption) or through unfair behavior of their partners of globalization (e.g., protective tariffs, protectionism). While some countries have taken great economic leaps during the years of increasing globalization, other countries stagnate or fall behind because they are excluded from the global playing field or may only participate in the economic and political competition under worse conditions. The results are poverty, war and terrorism. This coincides with the demand of Karl-Otto Apel for a "solidary responsibility of humankind"[421].

Thomas Pogge, for example, demands the assumption of responsibility for institutional issues in regard to enforcing human rights. He demands focusing on institutions and *"institutional systems and our global system of institutions, (...) in regard to assessing and reforming their relative contribution for the fulfilment of human rights."*[422] The starting point for his thoughts is the characterization of the relevant questions as institutional challenges, because *"the fulfilment of human rights depends significantly on the structure of*

---

419 See Jonas 1985b.
420 See Enderle 2002: 21.
421 Apel 1988: 15.
422 Pogge 1999: 379, emphasis in the text.

national and global basic orders, and that such orders could be intelligently (re-)structured for this end"[423]. Persons and governments in regions with human rights deficits are, of course, also responsible for institutional issues. But Pogge quite rightly points out that, because of their power, the governments and citizens of richer states carry even more responsibility to ensure that the current world order, where human rights are the rights of a minority, will be changed into an order where human rights really are accessible for all humans. While referring to Article 28, Pogge rejects the viewpoint that human rights violations committed by people in other states have no direct normative implications for us.[424]

The approaches of a "collective responsibility"[425] and a "responsibility of the system"[426] go in a similar direction.

In a responsibility reflected upon in its ethical depths, and in particular in view of the continuous developments of the conceptual understanding of responsibility with regard to structure, institution, collective, and system, the implicit relations of responsibility need to be clarified. Also, a justification is needed of who is the subject of responsibility and why, who or what signifies the object of responsibility and why, to what extent and why, in which way and why, in what intensity and why, before which authority and with which yardstick this responsibility will be measured and why. Otherwise, there is the danger that the urgent challenges and problems and the corresponding responsibilities will be covered by an open and intangible concept of responsibility. The justification of who is the subject of responsibility and who or what is the object of responsibility, as well as before which authority and with which yardstick this responsibility will be measured, is not easy. It "seems (...) extremely difficult to rationally justify an intersubjectively valid normative basis, to which a responsible basic attitude demanded by authorities could be oriented and legitimized."[427]

Before trying to establish a purpose and a justification of the relations contained in responsibility, one needs to try defining what "responsibility" means. Responsibility is a moral principle for decisions and actions, which contains the relationship between a subject of a decision and an action in a certain form (monadic, dyadic, triadic) of a person concerned, or the re-

---

423 Pogge 1999: 379, emphasis in the text.
424 See Pogge 1999: 394, emphasis in the text.
425 See Wolf 1993.
426 See Buehl 1998.
427 Holderegger 2006: 395.

sults of a decision or action within a certain scope (single or shared responsibility; intensity; area of responsibility), in a certain manner (competence; accountability; liability; retrospective liability; prospective responsibility of care or prevention)[428], while referring to a yardstick before a judging authority.

Based on the relationships contained in responsibility, responsibility needs to be integrated into an eight-dimensional matrix – the subject of responsibility dimension, the shape of responsibility dimension, the object of responsibility dimension, the scope of responsibility dimension, the type of responsibility dimension, the volume of responsibility dimension, the scale of responsibility dimension, and the judging authority dimension. The various dimensions of responsibility can be defined in different ways and combined differently so that, based on the relational character of responsibility, various characteristics of responsibility emerge.

In the *subject of responsibility* dimension, individuals, collectives such as states, religious, cultural, traditional or worldview-based communities, enterprises, organizations, institutions (i.e. "an organized collective"[429]) are subjects of responsibility. At first sight, "random or latent groups"[430] could also be perceived as subjects of responsibility. The fact that they have "no inner structure and no common goals and norms"[431] leads to the situation that a relationship to other dimensions cannot be defined. Therefore, they cannot serve as subjects of responsibility, because otherwise the above-mentioned concealment of urgent need for action and pressing challenges is caused by unclear responsibilities. In the case of "random or latent groups" the subjects of responsibility within the group need to be carefully traced back and determined in order to avoid such a cover-up.

The "focus of responsibility"[432] comes from the subject of responsibility. The decisive filter for defining the *subject of responsibility* dimension is the fact that responsibility requires freedom, as discussed above. Only creatures that are free can become subjects of responsibility. "Responsibility and freedom are corresponding terms. Responsibility requires factual – not temporal – freedom, thus freedom can only exist in responsibility. Responsibility is the freedom of humans alone"[433].

---

428 See Holderegger 2006: 398-399; Bayertz 2010: 2862.
429 See Bayertz 2010: 2861-2862.
430 See Bayertz 2010: 2862.
431 Bayertz 2010: 2862.
432 Holderegger 2006: 400.
433 Bonhoeffer 1992: 283.

Apart from the basic function of freedom for responsibility and the resulting decisive impact on determining the *subject of responsibility* dimension, responsibility also shapes freedom: "The freedom of humans is a 'related' freedom and has to be conveyed in his actions and inactions in view of the events given to him. The responsibility is (...) the authority which intervenes in the case of tension that is always present between the personal freedom and the predefined and given task."[434] Responsibility, in particular an "encompassing caring trait of responsibility"[435] enables freedom to grow beyond self-reference to a social reference. "Freedom thus takes on a 'precautionary' character, because it signals a willingness to deal creatively with tasks, mandates, obligations, etc., which have been given or acquired, or which one has acquired, with regard to the lives of others. Responsibility breaks up individualistic freedom focused on one's own needs and binds it into social structures, into common tasks and objectives"[436].

This social embedding of freedom through responsibility is reinforced by the fact that, according to Julian Nida-Ruemelin and based on Immanuel Kant, rationality also completes the triad of freedom, rationality and responsibility.[437] "*Rationality* is expressed in a way of life that integrates the manifold reasons in a coherent manner. If we let ourselves be led by reason, our way of life is not merely the result of processes that can be described scientifically, but we possess a certain measure of freedom. Others hold us *responsible* for our way of life, our actions, judgments and feelings, within the limits of where reason is effective. Where reason is no longer important, where natural facts and laws determine our behavior, we are no longer considered responsible."[438] On the one hand, rationality as a precondition of responsibility limits responsibility to the fact that, in cases where the alleged subject of responsibility cannot decide and act freely and in which reason is irrelevant, it cannot be brought into a relationship with responsibility with the alleged subject of responsibility. On the other hand, the need for giving reasons challenges responsibility and freedom in such a way, as responsibility may not only be recognized as individual responsibility or freedom purely in its self-reference, but also as caring responsibility or freedom in its social reference.

---

434 Holderegger 2006: 400.
435 Holderegger 2006: 400.
436 Holderegger 2006: 401.
437 See Nida-Ruemelin 2011: 14-18.
438 Nida-Ruemelin 2011: 17, emphasis in the text.

What has been said with regard to freedom and rationality and the triad freedom, rationality and responsibility on an individual level, can also be transferred to the other possible subjects mentioned above in the dimension of subject of responsibility, if, for example, particular interests of institutions are taken into account.

This triad of freedom, rationality and responsibility has a direct influence on the dimension subject of responsibility by shaping the definition of the dimension subject of responsibility. Nevertheless, it also has an influence on the other dimensions.

The *shape of responsibility* dimension contains the number of digits with which responsibility can be understood, e.g. monadic ("I am responsible"), dyadic ("I am responsible for my actions"), triadic ("I am responsible for my actions towards you"), etc. In terms of the possibility of a one-digit form of responsibility, one can agree with Julian Nida-Ruemelin "that the normative 'ought' is unconditional in the sense that it is not an 'ought' to a commanding or normative authority, and that this normative 'ought' is completely understandable and deeply rooted in our everyday practice."[439]

How the shape of responsibility dimension will be determined has immediate effects on all dimensions, except the subject of responsibility dimension because the subject would need to be determined to fit into the logical structure of the shape of responsibility dimension.

The *object of responsibility* dimension describes for whom or for what responsibility is borne. Individuals and the above-mentioned collectives, "actions"[440], "convictions"[441], "attitudes"[442], consequences, effects and results of decisions and actions and objects are to be placed within the object of responsibility dimension.

In particular, in the object of responsibility dimension, the interdependence of the dimensions of responsibility, on which the matrix is based, can be shown. If, for example, one wants to analyze the relationship between the *object of responsibility* dimension and the *form of responsibility* dimension (see below in more detail), in the case of retrospective consequence responsibility as a type of responsibility, the consequences, effects and outcomes of decisions and actions are more likely to be the objects of responsibility. When considering prospective care or preventative responsibilities, individuals, collectives and objects should be considered primarily.

---

439 Nida-Ruemelin 2011: 24.
440 See Nida-Ruemelin 2011: 19-33.
441 See Nida-Ruemelin 2011: 33-47.
442 See Nida-Ruemelin 2011: 48-52.

In the more precise determination of, for example, the aforementioned potential objects of responsibility – individuals, collectives and objects – the *scope of responsibility* dimension has a decisive influence, because it will, for example, define the determination of the object of responsibility, of whether one understands the area of responsibility globally, intergenerationally, etc.

The *scope of responsibility* dimension has already been mentioned briefly. It defines in two respects how far responsibility goes: *first*, if the subject of responsibility will share this responsibility with another subject of responsibility or will bear it alone; *second*, if the responsibility carried by the subject of responsibility will be an ethical, moral and legal, a moral and political, or a moral, legal and political responsibility, which will define the intensity of the responsibility.

The *volume of responsibility* dimension broaches the issue of questioning if the area of responsibility is defined as local, regional, international, global, current, or intergenerational.

The *type of responsibility* dimension can be seen in the sense of competence "for actions and offices, which can be attributed to them"[443]. The latter can be understood as connected to "accountability", when "one has to account for something before an authority (be it fellow humans, courts, the own conscience or God)."[444] Another type could be liability, where "one has to take responsibility for wrong-doings or neglecting competencies, tasks, duties etc."[445]

Furthermore, it is possible to define the type of responsibility as retrospective responsibility for outcomes. This is based on clarifying the question of guilt for a given situation.

Finally, the type of responsibility can be seen as a prospective responsibility of care or prevention: the above-mentioned thought to not limit the causal reach to things in the past, but also to include and take into account the current, and in particular the future, of how the decision-making power and power for action is distributed, leads to a responsibility of care and prevention as a type of responsibility in order to prevent the contemporary world and the environment from having to battle against outcomes of today's actions, today or in the future.

The *scale of responsibility* dimension is used for evaluating the consequences, impacts, and results of decisions and actions, the conditions of in-

---

443 Holderegger 2006: 398.
444 Holderegger 2006: 399.
445 Holderegger 2006: 399.

dividuals and conditions of items. "The causal attribution as such is normatively neutral; it receives its moral dimension only through the act of evaluation."[446] This evaluation is based on the scale formulated by a system of values and norms.

The *authority* dimension stems from the legal background of the term responsibility and shows that one has to answer to an authority. The dimension authority can be the conscience,[447] the moral community, the persons affected, or the Divine, God, or the Transcendent.[448]

After trying to grasp the concept of "responsibility", the next step is to determine and justify the dimensions and relations involved in responsibility. The focus is deliberately put on a procedural, rather than a material, determination, since the former is more likely to do justice to the wealth of possible concrete definitions of the individual dimensions and relations. In addition, in view of this wealth, it is nevertheless necessary to assume a concept of responsibility with an identical core, and not different concepts of responsibility.[449]

The definition and justification of the dimensions and relations contained in responsibility have to do justice to the demands of ethics, namely the fulfillment of the principle of generalizability by presenting rational and plausible arguments – "good reasons". "Good reasons" means that it must be conceivable that all humans, given their effective freedom and autonomy as well as their full equality, would agree upon these reasons – within a model of thought and not within a real worldwide referendum – on ethical grounds. This means that the justification to the subjects of justification and, if necessary, the objects of justification have to be made in such a manner as to be acceptable for the subjects and objects of responsibility, by taking into account the various dimensions of responsibility – in particular, the dimension scale and the dimension authority.

The term "meta-responsibility"[450] highlights that human beings do not only have to answer for the outcomes of their actions, but also for the outcomes of their theories. The hope is that with this contribution, the consequences of these theoretical explanations will not stay theoretical.

---

446 Bayertz 2010: 2862.
447 See Kant 1997: 438.
448 See Bayertz 2010: 2863.
449 See Nida-Ruemelin 2011: 14.
450 Bayertz 1995: 60.

6.2.4 Responsibility as Ethical Principle for Data-Based Systems

As elaborated above in subchapter 3.5 Responsibility, responsibility cannot be assumed by machines because machines are not free and therefore, they cannot be a responsibility subject as freedom and rationality are necessary conditions for subjectivity of responsibility. On this basis, the responsibility remains exclusively with humans due to their moral capability. This human responsibility possesses, on the one hand, a long time horizon: "If the new nature of our acting then calls for a new ethics of long-range responsibility, coextensive with the range of our power, it calls in the name of that very responsibility also for a new kind of humility – a humility not like former humility, i.e., owing to the littleness, but owing to the excessive magnitude of our power, which is the excess of our power to act over our power to foresee and our power to evaluate and to judge."[451] On the other hand, its expanding character takes your breath away due to "the critical vulnerability of nature to man's technological intervention – unsuspected before it began to show itself in damage already done. This discovery (...) alters the very concept of ourselves as a causal agency in the larger scheme of things. It brings to light, through the effects, that the nature of human action *has* de facto changed and that an object of an entirely new order – no less than the whole biosphere of the planet – has been added to what we must be responsible for because of our power over it."[452]

The validity of the position that humans are exclusively the subjects of responsibility – e.g., even for actions by data-based systems – remains untouched even when confronted with the three "human-responsibility paradoxes of data-based systems". The first "human-responsibility paradox of data-based systems" entails that, while the interaction between humans and data-based systems intensifies strongly, the responsibility remains exclusively with humans and keeps growing because of the intensified interaction based on the interactionist model and its responsibility-related procedural elements, responsibility-related effects and consequences.

The second "human-responsibility paradox of data-based systems" consists in the fact that humans remain exclusively and to the same extent the bearers of responsibility for data-based systems even while data-based systems become increasingly automated and technically independent from humans. In other words, nothing changes regarding human responsibility for machines, although machines have transformed from simple analog

---

451 Sandler 2014: 45.
452 Jonas 1985b: 26-27, emphasis in the text.

machines to digital self-learning systems to data-based systems reaching super-performance. This means at the end of the day that nothing changes regarding human responsibility for machines even though machines seem to be moving more and more away from human input. Instead, as elucidated above in subchapter 2.4 Reciprocal Challenges, the responsibility[453] of humans is even growing due to constantly expanded creation of an artificial and technology-based world and the corresponding power and influence of humans. The second "human responsibility-paradox of data-based systems" consists, hence, in a growing responsibility for data-based systems increasingly requiring less human input.

The third "human-responsibility paradox of data-based systems" acknowledges that on several levels, increasing responsibility by humans is decreasingly attributable to subjects of responsibility – partly due to complexity of the relations of responsibility, partly due to the variety of subjects of responsibility, and partly due to the supposedly collective nature of responsibility.

6.3. The Principle of Justice[454]

6.3.1 What Is "Justice"?

Justice can be defined in different ways, for example; Plato writes "that everyone has and does his own"[455]. Ulpian holds that justice is the strong and continuous will to give everyone his rights (*"iustitia est constans et perpetua voluntas ius suum cuique tribuendi"*[456]). Another possibility is the demand to "generally treat equals equally"[457] or in other words: "An act is just if it gives to everyone what they deserve."[458] It has already become obvious that justice is a "relational concept"[459].

Another option goes even further and positions justice in relation to morality in general: "If justice is to be considered a moral virtue, it should be understood in an extremely wide sense, characterizing a man who does not unjustifiably violate any of the moral rules. In this sense, of course, jus-

---

453 See Kirchschlaeger 2014a.
454 See Kirchschlaeger 2013c.
455 Plato, Republic: 434a.
456 Ulpian 2005: 1-10.
457 Honecker 1990: 188.
458 Gosepath 2010: 835.
459 Gosepath 2010: 835.

tice is not merely one moral virtue among many; it is the combination of all the moral virtues connected with the moral rules."[460] This includes that justice is necessary, but not sufficient for the morally good.[461] If justice is understood in relation to morality, it becomes clear that it needs to be distinguished between "justice as yardstick for *outer* relationships of persons and social structures" and "justice as a virtue or *inner* attitude of the human being"[462].

"Inner" and "outer" justice build on the moral capacity as a prerequisite for human decision-making and acting justly. Just actions and decisions are only possible if you can make them freely and, therefore, also be responsible for them. Subjects of justice, therefore, have to fulfill these prerequisites.

There can be various objects of justice: among other things, persons and their acts, decisions, institutions in a wider sense, analytic considerations, creative thoughts, results of human interactions (e.g., contracts), biographies, sharing of goods, political solutions.[463]

Furthermore, according to Peter Koller,[464] justice can be divided into four concepts of justice. This diversification can give orientation in scope for decision-making and action (which allows for being just and fair in each specific and individual situation):

1. Transactional justice (e.g., equality of performance and reward [e.g., wages])
2. Political justice (democratic co-determination processes wherein impartially exercised power serves to grant each individual his or her rights and social cooperation)
3. Corrective justice (payments of damages to repair harm and punishment for the retribution of injustice)
4. Distributive justice (equal distribution of common goods [e.g., educational options, access to the labor market, chances of income generation] and burdens [e.g., taxes]).

Justice strives for equality or equal treatment. In the first concept mentioned above, equal will be treated equally and unequal unequally.[465] In

---

460 Geert 1970: 157.
461 See Geert 1970: 157.
462 Veith 2004: 316.
463 See Gosepath 2010: 836.
464 See Koller 2005.
465 See Aristotle, Nicomachean Ethics V, 6-7.

the second and third concept of justice, all humans are treated equally. In the fourth concept of justice, distributive justice, equality or equal treatment can be measured with the following three criteria: equal treatment is either based on *performance,* on *need,* or on *equality.*

Equal treatment based on *performance* means that equal performance leads to equal reward. In that way, inequalities (e.g., wages, property, etc.) which occur due to unequal performance are justified.

Equal treatment based on *need* means that the same amount of fulfillment of needs is reserved for everyone. However, the individuality of humans includes inter alia differences in needs, which demand specific, unequal measures to reach the same amount of fulfilment of needs (e.g., special support measures, social security, etc.).

Equal treatment based on *equality* means that goods and burdens are shared equally among the humans (independent of performance, need, etc.), in order to comply as strictly as possible with the equality of all humans (e.g., access to education). Differences in performance, need etc. are neglected. Thus, all humans have the same access to the same number of services, without taking into account their differences. The equality of services corresponds to the differences of the individuals: humans are only equal if all humans can satisfy their different needs to the same extent.

In other words, on the one hand, inequalities or unequal treatment based on *performance, need* and *equality* are accepted under certain circumstances. On the other hand, it becomes apparent that, depending on the concept of justice, the moral evaluation of, e.g., a decision, an action, or a status will be different. Finally, a decision or an action can be unfair, even if its decision-making process was based on the free will of the agreeing persons. All this constitutes, among other things, the vastness of the concept of justice. At the same time, there is a need for clarification at this very point.

The definition of the horizon of justice also proves to be controversial. Duties arising from justice are understood with a universal or particular dimension.

Linked to both problems is the question of the reference level of justice, because the latter helps to create clarity. What does one refer to in deciding which concept of justice to use and to what extent?

All four concepts of justice can be thought of from the perspective of "social justice".[466] Luigi Taparelli understands social justice as "giustizia fra

---

466 See Kramer 1992: 45.

uomo e uomo"[467]. "Social justice" is not an independent concept of justice, but influences one or several concepts of justice.[468] Social justice needs to be understood dynamically, where "programs and roles [are] to be formulated in a new way in order to do justice to the reality"[469]. Social justice focuses mainly on a "just order, where the different interests of groups and individuals are to be balanced and put into the right relation to each other"[470]. The meaning of social justice can even be expanded *as the moral consideration of such freedom, which is equal in principle, or the continued moral-practical effort to create the conditions of possibility under which freedom can be realized in the social sphere as participation in all processes concerning it, this realization being supported by an ethos which gives form and stability to such realizations of freedom in structures and institutions*[471]. A similar view consists in understanding social justice as justice for the common good, which "opens up space for discussing problems with justice not only in view of the state, but many social actors. This becomes ever more important where, for various reasons, the role of the state or even politics in general is becoming less and less and, according to the prevailing circumstances, the responsibility for social sustainability or unsustainability is more and more moved to institutions of civil society or the private sector"[472].

Apart from the decisions that, according to what has been said above, have to be made by giving reasons, the use of the term justice also needs to be justified. When, for example, humans and their acts, decisions, institutions in a wider sense, analytical considerations, creative thoughts, results of human interactions (e.g., contracts), biographies, sharing of goods, political solutions, are called just, a justification is demanded. In this challenge, impartiality is trend-setting: when taking on an impartial standpoint, someone or something will be judged as fair or unfair. In order to be able to take this impartial standpoint, in the current justice discourse, there are four models of thought:[473] the random independent observer,[474]

---

467 Taparelli 1855: Number 354.
468 See Giers 1957; Anzenbacher 1998: 221-224.
469 Glatzel 2000: 148.
470 Glatzel 2000: 148.
471 Nothelle-Wildfeuer 1999: 85, emphasis in the text.
472 Hoppe 2002: 37.
473 See Gosepath 2010: 837.
474 See Smith 2004.

a role reversal of the parties involved,[475] the universalizability,[476] or the "veil of ignorance"[477].

Furthermore, reasons need to be given when a claim for justice is formulated or moral duties arise from a claim for justice. Among other things, these may be a reference to the law of nature, the respect for human dignity, a right to justification, the reciprocity of advantages for the parties involved or an ideal discourse.[478]

6.3.2 The Tension Between Law and Justice

Justice may mean to issue societal laws for ensuring order. If there is no order yet, or the state of a society does not correspond to justice; it is down to justice to change this and introduce a fair order.

If there exists an order in a community or society, the rules and regulations that implement this order must be respected in the interest of *general justice*. Aristotle can be summarized as follows: Those who respect the laws are just. Because the laws are based on a legislative act, this gives them legitimacy.[479] This means that, for example, the executive and the authorities of a state have to implement the applicable legislation precisely and professionally.

Nevertheless, solidary justice may highlight the tension between law and justice. This can result from the fact that the existing order of a community or society can never be as it should be. The striving for a pure and perfect expression of justice *per se* demands continuous corrections and adaptations to a changing reality. Laws that were formulated as an expression of a legal consideration may miss their objectives, harm the community or might be illegitimate against a new, real context. In this situation, those who profit from this situation will try to keep this injustice as positive law. The disadvantaged will try to fight against this unjust treatment in order to free themselves from this situation. In this context, justice is not understood as duty based on the affirmation of the law, but as *social justice* that is directly related to the common good. Aristotle also understands justice in

---

475 See Baier 1974.
476 See Hare 1992.
477 See Rawls 1971.
478 See Gosepath 2010: 837.
479 See Aristotle, Nicomachean Ethics: V, 1-3.

this sense as equality:[480] Social justice makes demands, for example, of the executive and the authorities of a state, but also of civil society,[481] and the population in a state, which has to watch over the decisions and actions of the government and authorities, that they use their scope for decisions and actions which allows them to be just and fair in each of the specific and individual situations. Laws that are too narrow and strict, that leave no room for interpretation, would lead to *unjust* situations in certain cases. The need for contextualization becomes obvious in the fact that it is neither the task of legal regulations, nor is it possible for them to precisely regulate every possible situation of human existence. The scope for decisions and actions is a challenge, because in the course of contextualization there is the danger of arbitrariness. Human rights can be used as a clearly defined ethical point of reference against arbitrariness. Ethics have a particular meaning in this critical evaluation, because they examine "if the real, existing social systems, relations and institutions correspond to the criteria of justice and the common good as prerequisites for a good life of each individual."[482] This critical task is possible because of a normative attitude towards laws and institutions that is open to change. This attitude is based on the perception of a complementary responsibility to obedience in the face of norms, orders, and institutions as well as a responsibility for the design of the latter.[483]

6.3.3 Omni-Dynamic Social Justice

In view of the four concepts of justice introduced above, transactional justice, political justice, corrective justice and distributive justice and their respective difficulties or challenges, the question may arise of how to deal with these four concepts of justice from an ethical perspective and which of the four concepts of justice are to be favored. The concept of *omni-dynamic social justice* addresses this question. Based on the above explanation, it is not about excluding one or more concepts of justice, but *first,* from an ethical perspective, to think of them in conjunction with the guiding principle of social justice and let it have a formative influence on all four concepts of justice.

---

480 See Aristotle, Nicomachean Ethics: V, 1-2.
481 See Nothelle-Wildfeuer 1999: 86-343.
482 Remele 2009: 194.
483 See Remele 2009: 194.

Second, those four concepts of justice are to be thought of together in order to avoid a one-sided approach to justice and to reach a comprehensive understanding of justice. All four concepts of justice are perceived in a *negative cohesion* to each other. Unlike positive cohesion, this does not mean that justice always has to include all four concepts of justice. *Negative cohesion* means that all four concepts of justice have to be integrated, or rational reasons be given, if one or several concepts of justice cannot be taken into account. Thus, justice is understood as *omni-dynamic* (since it is conceived in the interaction of all four concepts).

Third, on the basis of what has been said so far, it makes sense from an ethical perspective to focus on distributive justice – on the one hand in determining the relationship between distributive justice and the other concepts of justice, and on the other hand in its practical implementation. In both cases, distributive justice is thought of together with the guiding principle of social justice. In this sense, justice is to be understood as *omni-dynamic social justice*.

Prioritizing distributive justice for the equality of all humans can be justified with the human dignity of all humans and with human rights, which will be explained and ethically justified below in the subsequent subchapter.

The human dignity of all humans and human rights are also used as terms of reference or *tertium comparationis* in the material definition of the *omni-dynamic social justice* and when formulating criteria. Because *omni-dynamic social justice* must be guided by something. For example, in the case of distributive justice, it needs to be defined what is to be distributed fairly on the one hand, and on the other hand, according to which criteria it can be ensured that the distribution of what is to be distributed really is fair. When deciding on the material amount of the duties, the following challenge arises, among others: "Beliefs about justice are pluralistic, in the sense that they cannot all be accounted for by reference to a single basic principle of distribution; rather, when people are asked to assess the justice of some allocation of goods, they typically invoke several criteria of distribution and reach an overall judgment by balancing these criteria against each other."[484] In this context, ethics offer orientation: "All modern concepts of justice accept a common basic norm: all humans are generally to be respected equally, meaning they possess the same dignity (human dignity). Therefore, each human should be treated with the same respect and the same consideration. Depending on how the various concepts of

---

484 Miller 1992: 558.

justice understand the basic norm of equal dignity, there are different opinions of what is appropriate or just among equals."[485] There is a necessity of such a basic norm: "With regard to the common good as a target value, the following idea proves to be central: On the one hand, there is a widespread conviction in contemporary thinking that under the conditions of modern thinking and with a view to pluralistic and individualized societies, it is no longer possible to develop a content-filled, common and generally binding concept of good or successful life to which both the political community and the individual would be bound. On the other hand, talk of the common good articulates the currently highly topical insight that human coexistence in society can only succeed if there is at least a minimum consensus with regard to certain indispensable foundations of value-based coexistence among the members of a society"[486].

Human dignity demands, for example, that distributive justice respects human dignity regardless of or even contrary to human conduct[487] in the course of creating justice and equality, that human dignity not be transformed into something that can be realized,[488] and that humans not be denied human dignity on the basis of particularly serious human rights violations committed by them.

Furthermore, human dignity dominates the material determination of distributive justice insofar as it has to take into account the moral dimension of the human, the "ability of the human for morality. As a person, human beings have a sense of self, since they can relate to themselves and their actions, reflect on themselves and freely determine their ways of life and basic attitudes."[489] On the other hand, it must not ignore the essential, non-moral elements of human existence (such as food, shelter, basic medical care, etc.).[490]

An answer to the question of which horizon distributive justice has to encompass can be derived from human dignity. By taking into account human dignity, it becomes clear that the human has to be at the center of the material determination of distributive justice. When distributive justice revolves around the human being (and not around, for example, special relational closeness, the adherence to a particular community, the origin from

485 Gosepath 2010: 837.
486 Nothelle-Wildfeuer 2008: 148.
487 See Wolbert 2003: 167.
488 See Wetz 1998: 181.
489 Witschen 2002: 14.
490 See Witschen 2002: 15.

a certain territory, etc.), distributive justice must be thought of with universality and has to relate to the global horizon. Against the background of human dignity, a justification for a local horizon would have to present good (i.e. rationally justified) reasons why distinctions could be made between humans that would justify a local horizon of distributive justice. For example, it could, *inter alia*, list the differences in the horizons of justice resulting from the comparison of John Rawls' "A Theory of Justice"[491] and John Rawls' "Law of Peoples"[492]:[493] While in "A Theory of Justice", Rawls provides a system of justice with a balance between the wealthy and the disadvantaged for a society with a local horizon for the common good, in "Law of Peoples", he rejects such a balance. The latter implicitly includes a differentiation between people that cannot be legitimized, because it is not rationally justifiable. This distinction can, therefore, not be rationally convincing, because it would break with human dignity, since the latter manifests the equality of all humans as humans. "1. Any form of solidarity that is based on simultaneously disregarding the universality of human dignity is ethically reprehensible. [...] 2. Any form of solidarity that, *de facto*, only takes into account the claim to human dignity with regard to one's own group and its objectives, remains ethically deficient."[494]

According to these thoughts, justice is not only comprised of responsible relationships between the individual and fellow humans, between the individual and society, but also between society and societies – with a universal horizon.

However, if *omni-dynamic social justice* needs to be thought of with a global horizon, it follows, on the one hand, that the corresponding duties also need to be thought of with a *universal scale*. On the other hand, concerning the material scope of the obligation, it must be considered that not "only" all humans are addressees of this obligation, but all humans *as humans* (i.e. humans that are given the opportunity to live as humans with human dignity).

Finally, all three relationships – between the individual and fellow humans, between the individual and society, but also between society and societies – cannot be justifiably limited in time. This means that distributive justice needs to be thought of intergenerationally and with a universal horizon. Intergenerational justice consists of mainly four postulates: to

---

491 See Rawls 1971.
492 See Rawls 1999.
493 See Singer 2004: 176-180.
494 Korff 1989: 45.

consider the coming generations in all actions; to not consume more resources than will grow back; to fairly share resources globally; to respect natural rhythms.[495]

6.3.4 Omni-Dynamic Social Justice and Intergenerational Justice

While providing guidance as an ethical instrument for digital transformation and the use of data-based systems, the principle of justice understood as *omni-dynamic social justice* should give more weight to the future perspective by including future generations as subjects and objects of justice, as well as the future as a horizon for justice. "Intergenerational justice" can be defined in the following way: "A society is intergenerationally just when each generation does its fair share to enable members of succeeding generations, both inside and outside its borders, to satisfy their needs, to avoid serious harm and to have the opportunity to enjoy things of value."[496] "Intergenerational justice" frames the horizon of justice not only as global – considering all humans as potential subjects and objects of justice – but also as an "intergenerational continuum that stretches indefinitely into the future"[497] and that opens to the past – acknowledging what past generations contributed, sacrificed,[498] and which injustices they suffered as well. The limits of this intergenerational continuum remain open. This makes it more difficult to get a precise idea of what intergenerational justice entails because, especially in the case of the future, one does not know exactly what must be expected.[499] "In our efforts to do justice to future generations we operate in a fog of uncertainty. Uncertainty does not mean that intergenerational justice is impossible or that it does not matter what we do. The answer to uncertainty is to be as rational as possible – to examine and act according to available evidence – and to do the best we can to alleviate known risks."[500]

The concept of "intergenerational justice" seems, though, to build an adequate principle to balance needs and interests not only of the present humans but also of past and future generations in a fair way. "Intergenera-

---

495 See Vogt 2005: 141-159.
496 Thompson 2010: 6; see also Vogt 2005: 141-159.
497 Thompson 2010: 6.
498 See Thompson 2010: 6.
499 See Wolf 2003.
500 Thompson 2010: 9.

tional justice" faces the challenge of the more urgent nature of challenges and problems of the present than of issues of the future, and due to the undefined temporal openness of "intergenerational" which provoke a necessity of clarification and a distance between the present subjects and objects of justice and future subjects and objects of justice. Beyond that, the practical relevance of "intergenerational justice" must be proved in the face of the highly complex world of the present which seems to be difficult to grasp, the idea of assessing future developments with the necessary precision, in order to be able to define justice-corresponding responsibilities, duties, rights, and claims, seems out of reach for humans.

Furthermore, the legitimacy of "intergenerational justice" must be ethically justified, among other things, because of its infinite nature representing, presumably, an entry point for any wish. In the following subchapter, this will be addressed while justifying human rights on the basis of the principle of vulnerability.

Addressing the question of how we can justify intergenerational justice intensifies the burden of proof because an assessment of justice at present can be justified by the construction of impartiality (or an impartial standpoint) within the discourse of the present moral community (e.g., with the "veil of ignorance"[501]) while intergenerational justice must justify as well why the potential subjects and objects of intergenerational justice include future generations of humans.[502] Addressing this question, human rights as an ethical point of reference play an essential role because one can address the challenge of justifying intergenerational justice by pointing out that if it can be justified that all humans (including future humans) are holders of human rights, their human rights must be respected in the present and future, and, therefore, there is an ethical necessity of intergenerational justice.

Beyond that, the idea of intergenerational justice faces doubts and skepticism if it is even realistic. "This reasoning depends on two assumptions: that people are mostly self-interested and that their interests do not give them reason to care about the fate of future generations or people in other countries."[503] These assumptions can be questioned by emphasizing "uncertainty about what needs to be done and how to do it and the fear of those who think that they will be seriously disadvantaged"[504] as the main

---

501 See Rawls 1971: 136-142; Dierksmeier 2006.
502 See Gosseries 2008.
503 Thompson 2010: 18.
504 Thompson 2010: 19.

challenge for realizing intergenerational justice resulting from "the failure of institutions rather than deficiencies of human nature"[505]. Combining this observation with human rights as an ethical point of reference, one comes, with this institutional approach, close to an institutional understanding of human rights: "On the interactional understanding of human rights, governments and individuals have a responsibility not to violate human rights. On my institutional understanding, by contrast, their responsibility is to work for an institutional order and public culture that ensure all members of society have secure access to the objects of their human rights."[506] While the institutional understanding of human rights brings into consideration an important force for the realization of human rights – and as a consequence of intergenerational justice – it seems to be difficult to show why institutions or institutions-systems, or the global institutions-system (set of all institutions worldwide) should be on another level than state and non-state actors, and why in this way, human rights-relevant threats (or concerns of intergenerational justice) are only official threats, because this is not adequate for the role of state and non-state actors for the implementation and realization of human rights[507] or intergenerational justice. The lack of adequacy becomes obvious from the perspective of a human rights-holder and the victim of human rights violation or the object of intergenerational justice. For the holder of human rights and for the victim of a human rights violation or the object of intergenerational justice, the fulfillment of human rights and a human rights violation or the realization of intergenerational justice can also occur without the participation or the influence of an institution, an institutions-system, or the global institutions-system. Who the subject is does not change anything regarding the significance and the weight of the fulfillment of human rights or intergenerational justice or of a human rights violation because of the fundamental nature of the essential elements and spheres of human existence protected by human rights. From the perspective of a right holder or a victim of a human rights violation or the object of intergenerational justice, one understands the respective act as a realization of human rights or intergenerational justice or as violation of human rights a part of the question if the respective act is official or not.

The practical potential of the institutional understanding of human rights and of intergenerational justice makes a difference for theory and

---

505 Thompson 2010: 19.
506 Pogge 2002: 65.
507 See Kirchschlaeger et al. 2005.

practice but its exclusive priority cannot be proven, which is captured in the following as well: While Thomas Pogge integrates individual responsibility of institutional decision-makers, the same possibility of participation and the same sphere of influence can be claimed for individuals outside of an institution – be it as political citizen, be it as political consumer (as "consumption-actors"[508]), ... An extension of a kind of "interactional understanding of human rights" which Thomas Pogge attributes to decision-makers of the inner-life of an institution and to the individuals in the world outside an institution based on their power and influence is possible and necessary in order to avoid underestimating the contribution by state- and non-state-actors. According to Thomas Pogge, individuals are in such a situation either to end their involvement in the institution or to contribute to a corresponding reform of the latter.[509] There is an obligation to change the human rights-situation if one possesses the power and influence for it. It seems to be difficult to limit this assessment only to the inner life of institutions as individuals, as political citizens, as political consumers (as "consumption-actors"[510]) enjoy power and influence respectively over the realization of human rights and over intergenerational justice as well.

A possible objection of this extension to the state and non-state actors outside of institutions could be that the official actors must intervene in such a manner to avoid private human rights violations or to dictate contributions to the realization of human rights and intergenerational justice. The underlying assumption of this objection would be thought to start from a rather extensive understanding of the horizon of the influence of institutions on an individual sphere of influences, which would go too far as it would come into a contradiction with elements of the nucleus of human rights themselves, namely the autonomy of the individual.

Again, the institutional understanding of human rights or of intergenerational justice is able to present another key player for the implementation and realization of human rights and of intergenerational justice – institutions, institutions-systems, and the global institutions-system – which has not yet been in the spotlight of the discourse so far. Rather than attributing to this actor the primary or sole responsibility, it seems more adequate to keep the primary responsibility for the implementation and realization of human rights and of intergenerational justice with the states because of enforceability and to add institutions, institutions-systems, and the global

---

508 See Kirchschlaeger 2016c.
509 See Pogge 2002: 48.
510 See Kirchschlaeger 2016c.

institutions-system to the actors which share with the states the responsibility for the implementation and realization of human rights and of intergenerational justice – non-state-actors like, for example, the private sector, civil society, individuals, etc. The realization of intergenerational justice depends neither only on adequate reforms of institutions, institutions-systems, and the global institutions-system, nor does it lie solely in the hands of institutions, institutions-systems, and the global institutions-system, but rather depends on states[511] and non-state-actors like, for example, the private sector, civil society, and individuals. A monitoring of the respect of intergenerational justice by a global court of justice is envisaged,[512] or "even a commission comparable to the UN's Human Rights Commission without sanctioning power would be helpful, merely being able to make public and to denounce violations of interests of future generations such as the clearing of rainforests, desertification and the emission of greenhouse gases"[513].

Finally, intergenerational justice is facing the following challenge: "A fact that complicates the practice of taking over future responsibility is the anonymity of future generations, the uncertainties of prognostic knowledge. Both facts make it easier for us to psychologically suppress recognized future dangers and to underestimate them in comparison to present dangers. The tendency to feel responsible for merely statistical victims is much less pronounced than the tendency to feel responsible for known victims. The tendency to avoid certain future harm or to seize certain future benefits is far more pronounced than the tendency to avoid risks or to forgo chances."[514] This is especially relevant in the domain of digital transformation and data-based systems. In addition, the objection that one does not affect future generations through present-day decisions and actions because who lives later is only determined by one's actions and is unknown in the present[515] supports this challenge further. The following justification of human rights provides an ethical foundation on the basis of which intergenerational justice can contribute to overcoming this challenge by outlining "good reasons" (which means that it must be conceivable that all humans, given their effective freedom and autonomy as well as their full

---

511 About concrete attempts by states to contribute to intergenerational justice, see Tremmel 2006; Bourg 2006; Shoham / Lamay 2006; Jávor 2006; van Opstal / Timmerhuis 2006.
512 See Brown 1989: 121.
513 Birnbacher 2006: 37.
514 Birnbacher 2006: 37.
515 See Parfit 1984: 367.

equality, would agree upon these reasons – within a model of thought and not within a real worldwide referendum – on ethical grounds) for the ethical legitimacy of intergenerational justice and by proving the ethical necessity to respect intergenerational justice and to decide and act for its realization. The latter entails also the request to all societal actors – state and non-state actors – to play their role according to their power and influence in the implementation of intergenerational justice.

6.3.5 Justice as Ethical Principle for Data-Based Systems

Based on the deliberations so far, the respect and realization of intergenerational omni-dynamic social justice is a task for humans and not of data-based systems. Humans must make data-based systems act in a just way. Humans must guarantee just access to data-based systems and their benefits. Humans must make the effort to create, design, produce, and use data-based systems with regard for the principle of intergenerational omni-dynamic social justice. Data-based systems can play their part for a reality of intergenerational omni-dynamic social justice but humans must build them in a way that leads to that end, and humans must make them contribute to a reality of intergenerational omni-dynamic social justice.

6.4 Human Rights as an Ethical Frame of Reference[516]

6.4.1 Human Rights – A Minimal Standard

Human rights are a minimal standard that enables survival and a life with human dignity for every human.[517] Actually, it seems to be a shame that this minimal standard is sometimes called an ideal or even a utopia[518] because human rights build a rather minimalistic approach. Human rights protect human dignity. Human rights are neither maximal moral claims nor a higher ethos. This means that they do not overburden digital transformation and data-based systems with ethical claims. Instead, they are achievable for this technology-based progress. Human rights have a precise focus that can enhance a clear setting of priorities based on the minimal

---

516 See Kirchschlaeger 2019b; Kirchschlaeger 2018.
517 See Kirchschlaeger 2013a: 194-195.
518 See Moyn 2010.

standards, which must be respected first. Therefore, human rights can help in the process of agenda-setting in technology, not only in setting the right priorities but also in defining adequately the spheres of influence and responsibility.[519]

6.4.2 The Multidimensionality of Human Rights

The respect, implementation, protection, and realization of human rights take place in different dimensions of human rights: legal, political, historical, and moral.

The legal dimension of human rights encompasses the following: "International human rights are legal claims of persons against the state or state-like entities guaranteed by international law that protect basic aspects of human beings and their dignity in times of freedom and war."[520] Therefore, human rights primarily bind the state to the protection of human rights. The obligations of the state include action (positive) and omission (negative). This can also mean that human rights can legally infringe on the sovereignty of the state for the protection of the individual.

In its legal dimension, the national human rights protection is supplemented by regional and international human rights mechanisms to monitor state actions and to substantially add to the universal human rights protection through "dual positivization"[521]. Both are in a relation of "mutual validation and legitimation"[522]. On the basis of the Universal Declaration of Human Rights of 1948, which can also be called a political program because it is not legally binding, many human rights treaties have been developed (e.g., the International Covenant on Civil and Political Rights of 1966, the International Covenant on Economic, Social and Cultural Rights of 1966, the UN Convention on the Rights of the Child of 1989), which made human rights legally binding.[523]

The legal dimension is key for the realization of human rights, because the juridification of human rights led to an increased enforceability and the development of the modern human rights protection based on the Universal Declaration of Human Rights of 1948.

---

519 See Kirchschlaeger 2013b.
520 Kaelin 2004:17.
521 Neuman 2003. 1864.
522 Besson 2015: 299.
523 See Nowak 2002; Opitz 2002; Weiss 2007.

Human rights were enshrined in legal provisions on national, regional, and international levels. On a national level, human rights are turned into positive law by incorporating them into national law, for example, as fundamental rights in a state constitution. This national juridification substantially increases the chances for human rights to be enforced[524] and solves difficulties with the interpretation and concretization by a legal decision-making process that is regulated and can be controlled. It also leads to the creation of state organizations that will take on the corresponding human rights duties of the state. At the same time, national and regional laws have to respect the universality of human rights when stipulating differences between nationals of a country or continent and inhabitants of a country or continent and all others. There is the danger of unequal treatment and unfairness, as can be shown today in the context of migration.[525] In the face of this challenge, this particularization needs to be balanced out by turning human rights into positive law at the international level, and by creating international institutions and mechanisms for the protection of human rights, which will set a good trend. This process, however, needs to be continually questioned to ensure that the cause of human rights always lies at the center of any changes. This review becomes necessary because human rights are legally justified at an international level.[526]

Human rights in their legal dimension are the result of opinion-forming and consensus-finding processes, which make up the political dimension of human rights.[527] The political dimension of human rights includes arguments that favor the juridification of human rights, such as easier enforceability, regulated decision-making that can be controlled, guaranteeing the rights because of their institutionalization, as well as possible counterarguments. Human rights are, therefore, the content and – in their last consequence – the result of a political discourse. If looked at schematically, morally justified human rights will be transformed into legal human rights by a political opinion-forming and decision-making process. The political discourse does not center on human rights in general, but on a selection of elements and spheres that are seen as essential to human existence and are, therefore, seen as worthy of protection and should be included in the canon of human rights. The political discourse also focuses on how to cre-

---

524 See Alexy 1999.
525 See Kirchschlaeger 2016d.
526 See Buchanan 2015.
527 See Kirchschlaeger 2013e; Kirchschlaeger 2014d.

ate the measures and institutions necessary for this protection. Public experience and reflection enter into this discussion as well.

Human rights in themselves can also be seen as political tasks worth striving for. Even if human rights protect only minimal standards of essential elements and spheres of human existence that human beings need to survive and live as humans, they still remain a dictum that differs from real life. In order to reduce and eliminate this difference, political decisions and actions are necessary.

This may lead to the abuse of human rights and their political instrumentalization for other ends, which can damage human rights severely and in the long term.

In political discussions, human rights are often used in the face of injustice to support political issues. Demands for human rights may also be seen as "answers to exemplary injustices"[528]. As part of the political dimension of human rights, individual experiences of injustice, or injustices in general, as well as violations of basic aspects and areas of human existence, are fought with human rights language. "Human rights [speak], despite the continued intercultural exchange about their correct interpretation, a language in which dissidents can express their suffering and their demands of their repressive regimes – in Asia, South America and Africa just like in Europe and in the United States."[529]

It also needs to be borne in mind that free political opinion-forming and decision-making processes would be unthinkable without the protection provided by human rights, because it is only through human rights that a free political discourse is possible: directly, through the protection of the principle of democracy, freedom of opinion and information, and freedom of assembly, among other things, and indirectly, through the protection of the right to life, the right to education, etc. Human rights themselves are protecting the individual in its autonomy,[530] and empower and encourage the individual to take part in political processes. Democratic opinion-forming and decision-making is, therefore, dependent on human rights; the political discourse needs to orientate itself with human rights as a legal and ethical frame of reference.

The need for guiding the political discourse based on human rights as a legal and ethical frame of reference is connected to this. Political debates

---

528 Brugger 1992: 21.
529 Habermas 1998: 221.
530 See Kirchschlaeger 2016h.

need to adhere to certain rules that are defined by human rights (e.g., the right to non-discrimination) and have to stay within certain limits.[531]

In the political dimension of human rights, it also becomes clear that the realization of human rights – and of rights in general – needs a given political consensus.[532]

The political discourse stands at the center of the political dimension of human rights, as described above. It does not stand on its own, but is based on, among other things, philosophical, religious, and worldview-based ideas, convictions, concepts, thoughts, and theories that strive for the protection of the human being in its essential elements and spheres of existence. These philosophical, worldview-based and religious ideas, convictions, concepts, thoughts, and theories make up the first part of the moral dimension of human rights. Human rights are understood as rights above the state and, therefore, independent of the state. This does not, however, mean that human rights are a natural characteristic of humans. Human rights in their moral dimension depict human constructions that are based on reciprocal and absolute moral duties. They form part of a moral code made up of a system of duties that also contains other duties (asymmetrical, conditional, etc.). Based on these reciprocal, unconditional moral duties, all human beings recognize each other as members of this moral society and human rights holders. This is necessary, as the reciprocal duties alone cannot turn subjects and objects of these duties into rights holders. It requires a deliberate decision to be made to give rights.

How these decisions, or rather, the creation of human rights and the reciprocal recognition of all humans as human rights holders, can be justified is what the moral dimension of human rights enshrines. This debate around the question of how to justify human rights is also the reason that the moral dimension of human rights is constitutive for the other dimensions of human rights and human rights as a whole.[533] Because only the moral dimension knows the *conditio sine qua non* that a moral justification is necessary for the reasons to be universally applicable.[534] Because of this universal prerequisite, the moral dimension of human rights can justify the universality of human rights.

---

531 The framework of political decision-making for the protection of minorities from the dictatorship of the majority, see, e.g., Kirchschlaeger 2014d.
532 Arendt 1949.
533 See Kirchschlaeger 2007a.
534 See Tugendhat 1999.

The moral dimension of human rights is critical for human rights practice, because human rights theory in general – corresponding to human rights practice – is a necessary basis for human rights practice: "Human rights are a theory-based social construct. Human rights practice is commonly understood as actions through which we advocate for the protection of human rights [...] Social action and behavior, which actually do respect human rights, through which we promote their protection, protest against their violation, and organize action or establish institutions that realize and protect human rights, remain guided by theoretical considerations. Indeed, the theory must not become an end in itself; there is something like a prohibition of self-gratification for human rights theory. However, a practice that renounces theoretical considerations will, like otherwise also, become blind and runs the risk of getting lost or doing something wrong."[535]

Finally, the necessity of understanding human rights in their moral dimension and not only in their legal, political, and historical dimension can be illustrated through five situations where human rights could not be claimed at all or at least not integrally if their moral dimension were not considered:

- Even if someone lives in a state in which human rights cannot be claimed legally, every human is a holder of human rights independent of the official point of view of the state. Especially in such situations. it is even more significant that human rights are considered pre-state-rights as well, which means before becoming legal positive rights or therefore in their moral dimension. "'Pre' does not refer to the genesis of these rights, but to the reason for their validity; they are not 'granted' by the state."[536] If human rights were not understood with a moral dimension including its pre-state origin (being logically, ontologically, and axiologically prior), human rights could not be claimed at all or at least not integrally.
- Even if theoretical and practical obstacles are in the way of the implementation or the political will does not go along with human rights, it is important that every human is still a holder of human rights, which is possible based on their moral dimension.
- Even if majority decisions try to reduce the rights of a minority, human rights in their moral dimension stand up for the minority and protect

---

535 Lohmann 2004: 307.
536 Sandkuehler 2010: 1539.

the members of the minority together with all humans in their essential elements and areas of human existence.

- Even if certain currents in traditions, cultures, religions, and world-views try to interpret human rights in a way which leads to the denial or to the restriction of a right or of some rights (e.g., the equality of women and men, the relation between individual and collective rights, etc.), every human is holder of human rights which means – based on the above-mentioned principle of indivisibility – of the entire catalogue of human rights to the same extent without any difference.
- Even if human rights regulate horizontal (between individuals) and vertical (between individual and state) relations with a critical potential, every human is a holder of human rights in their moral dimension, which ensures that human rights can be applied in both cases.

Therefore, the inclusion of the moral dimension of human rights in the understanding of human rights is necessary for the realization of human rights.

The capability to provide an ethical justification of human rights living up to the universality of human rights marks a significant difference between the ethical and the legal, political, or historical justification: a justification for human rights in their legal dimension, based on a democratic opinion-forming and decision-making process, cannot justify the universality of human rights because this reasoning is irrelevant for humans who do not live in that specific country. For example, the democratic decision of a parliament elected by the population of country A to ratify the UN Convention on Rights of Persons with Disabilities 2006 has no direct effect on humans living in other countries. It will, at best, have an exemplary effect. Therefore, one cannot talk about universal radiance.

The situation is quite similar when looking at the political or historical dimension of human rights: apart from the same difficulty with the particularity that stands in opposition to the universality of human rights, the historical dimension (which will be further explained in the following paragraph) focuses on the genesis of human rights and not on their validity. In the case of the political dimension, a further difficulty arises because political models for reasoning are often imprecise and narrow, as shown by the approach of the "overlapping consensus" by John Rawls.[537] John Rawls' understanding of human rights seems to stay within national borders and arbitrarily excludes some human rights, even though they are en-

---

537 See Rawls 1971; Rawls 1993.

shrined in the Universal Declaration of Human Rights of 1948 (e.g., the right to education), it does not respect the principle of the indivisibility and the principle of interdependence of human rights, and it is too tolerant towards states that violate human rights.[538]

The philosophical, worldview-based and religious ideas, convictions, concepts, thoughts, and theories that human rights are based on, or rather incorporate, can also be looked at from their geographical and historical origins and put into context of the emergence of human rights from a historical viewpoint. There, one will enter the historical dimension of human rights. The starting point is recognizing the historical contingency of human rights: human rights have developed historically and are, therefore, shaped by the respective time of their emergence and development. In the case of the Universal Declaration of Human Rights of 1948, the historical shaping of human rights can be clearly seen. The basis and starting point for the Declaration is the recognition that all human beings are entitled to the same measure of dignity, freedom, and rights. A current consideration of the Universal Declaration of Human Rights of 1948 concludes that, following the Second World War, and the disaster and suffering that this terrible phase in human history brought about, the desire to create a declaration that would bring human rights on a global scale to the forefront was strengthened. The Universal Declaration of Human Rights of 1948 can be historically understood as a reaction to the violation and the attempt to negate human dignity during the Holocaust. "Most of the articles and rights in the Declaration were adopted as direct and immediate reactions to the horrors of the Holocaust."[539] Samuel Moyn, however, tries to show that human rights asserted themselves only in the 1970s.[540]

The scientifically enlightening contribution based on historical analysis and explanations that is certainly part of the historical dimension of human rights[541] shows, *inter alia*, the particular radiance that historical events have on the emergence of human rights. They stay particular and should in their reception also only be appreciated in their particularity in order to avoid a double discrimination of the humans that took part in certain historical events. *First*, this would mean that historiography would not take note of them and, *second*, that their contribution to the development of human rights would not be recognized (for example, the international recep-

---

538 See Kirchschlaeger 2013a: 192.
539 Morsink 2010: 27.
540 See Moyn 2010: 83.
541 See Gut 2008; Kirchschlaeger 2013d.

tion, by and large, of the Second World War is dominated by the European perspective, while the African experience and perception gets far too little attention).

Singular historical events generate only particular, and not universal, radiance and can, therefore, only be used as reasoning to a certain extent unless fundamental structural similarities exist on the basis of which generalizability can be achieved. No moral reason can be given with the historical explanation of the development of human rights as to why all human beings are human rights holders. It is necessary to differentiate between genesis (discovery) and validity (reasoning), because both try to give answers to different questions. While genesis tries to explain when and by whom a thought and an approach were developed, validity is about questioning if an understanding is universally valid and true. Genesis and validity need to be put in relation to each other, but kept separate.[542]

At this point, a possible misconception needs to be cleared up: these thoughts should not lead to interpreting the random temporal and local origins of human rights as an obstacle to their universal validity. This would be a "genetic fallacy", because we would conclude its content of truth from a genesis of an understanding, which would also be the case if you were to, for example, claim that the categorical imperative by Immanuel Kant has no universal validity because it was developed in Koenigsberg, or because it was developed more than 200 years ago.

Therefore, a historical viewpoint on the development of human rights can only capture particular historical events and historical experiences of injustice as examples. It is less of a moral assessment, but rather a contingent rating as a particular threat or violation of the essential elements and spheres of human existence that has developed historically and aims at causing political change. Here, the dynamics of human rights can be clearly seen: human rights prove to be open for further provisions to protect all humans from new, at present not yet detectable, threats to essential elements and spheres of human existence that humans need to survive and live as humans, which may loom in the future. This does not mean that they can be arbitrarily and randomly changed and are therefore relative, as will be shown in the following paragraph.

This understanding of the historical dimension of human rights as dynamic emphasizes their success story (or at least a success story to some degree), their topicality, their relevance for the present, and their lasting significance for the future. "The human rights abuses on the minds of the

---

542 See Salmon 1983: 25-32.

1948 drafters occurred during the Holocaust, while today we can point not only to the Nazi atrocities, but to atrocities in Bosnia, Cambodia, Rwanda, Darfur and in other contexts."[543] When seen in a historical dimension as clear reactions of humanity to experiences of injustice, as a critical sting to protect humans today from such experiences of injustice, human rights become more important and are a sign to the future to never let something similar happen again.[544]

It is part of the multidimensionality of human rights that

- the four dimensions – the legal, the political, the historical and the moral – complement each other and, when combined, create a stronger explanation than each dimension on its own,
- the lines cannot always be drawn clearly between the dimensions,
- the four dimensions are overlapping.

6.4.3 The Characteristics of Human Rights

"All human beings are born free and equal in dignity and rights. They are endowed with reason and conscience and should act towards one another in a spirit of brotherhood." Article 1 of the Universal Declaration of Human Rights of 1948[545] expresses one of the eight essential characters of human rights: their *universality*.[546] Human rights are universal because all humans are holders of human rights – always, everywhere, and without exception. Without their universality, human rights would not give the necessary protection to all humans in all essential spheres and elements that are protected by specific human rights.

Although there is a generally recognizable positive tendency of acceptance of human rights by states and non-state actors, an increasing international institutionalization for the protection of human rights, progress in the mechanisms for monitoring human rights performance by states to respect the universality of human rights, and some contributions by the corporate world in the area of human rights, at the same time it has to be stated that the implementation of human rights is not yet where it should be. The vast majority of humans still suffer violations of their human rights. Human rights are still a minority phenomenon, with only a minority of

---

543 Morsink 2010: 36.
544 See also Fields / Narr 1992.
545 Universal Declaration of Human Rights of 1948.
546 See Kirchschlaeger 2011.

humans enjoying full or partial human rights. Difficulties in implementing human rights raise the question as to whether human rights are achievable at all, if they are not just abstract ideals and if some of them should be given up. As mentioned at the beginning of this chapter, it even leads some to refer to them as a "last utopia"[547]. The *status quo* of the implementation of human rights does not keep up with the universality of human rights. Of course, this does not mean that human rights are not universal because the universality of human rights can be justified in the moral dimension of human rights[548] and therefore is still valid. But it indicates that there exists an urgency and necessity to enhance the implementation of human rights as law which is not fully implemented and respected and, in reality, can lose its concrete significance and ultimately its legal impact – both leading to its dissolution. This is hard to imagine in the case of human rights because human rights are a "monument" which cannot be overlooked and passed without taking notice of it.[549]

Beyond that, the human rights discourse entails criticisms challenging the universality of human rights, which can be categorized in three groups:[550] The third challenge to the universality of human rights is a critical relativism based on skepticism related to the small potential of realization of human rights and differences within this potential between the three categories of human rights. This criticism introduces the failure of implementation of certain human rights as a reason for cancelling them out of the human rights-catalogue. Again, of course it can be justified why this cancellation cannot be pursued, but the idea itself should already be taken as a serious warning sign and as indication of problems. A positive change in favor of human rights lies especially in the hands of those – be it state or non-state actors – with greater power and influence.

The concept of the universality of human rights is also influenced by seven further essential characteristics of human rights: Due to their *categorical character*, human rights turn all humans into holders of human rights, unconditionally. In other words, no one needs to fulfil any conditions or duties to be entitled to human rights (being human is enough).

But is it even legitimate for human rights to entail corresponding duties and obligations? Is it justified that all humans are holders of human rights, which can limit one's personal freedom, for example, because every right-

---

547 Moyn 2010.
548 See Kirchschlaeger 2013a.
549 See Joas 2011: 280.
550 See Lohmann 2008a.

holder needs to respect the human rights of all other humans as well? Do the specific human rights that concretely limit an individual's actions possess any legitimacy? This shows the necessity of a justification of human rights as well.

Human rights need a moral justification in order to prove their legitimacy and in order to remain coherent with their own core concept of the autonomy of the individual because autonomy embraces the claim of knowing the reason why one's freedom should be restricted by human rights. These challenges lead to the question of how human rights can be justified. Every human merits a justification of why she/he is a right-holder and also a duty-bearer of human rights as the responsibility corresponding to human rights to respect the human rights of all other humans limits her/his freedom.[551] Robert Alexy ties the existence of human rights exclusively to the possibility of their justification.[552] Emphasizing the *status quo* of human rights as a historical, political, and legal consensus enjoying global acceptance does not satisfy as a justification either due to its descriptive and non-normative nature or due to the particular origin of historical, political, and legal consensus in general.

The *equality of human rights* stipulates that all human beings are equal holders of human rights.

In addition, human rights are constituted as *individual rights*, and they serve as a protection for humans as individuals. This means that humans as individuals are protected by human rights without having to be part of a certain collective.

To think of individuals as holders of human rights does not mean, however, that human rights are individualistic. Human rights are first of all granted to all humans because of their human dignity, that is to say, their status as a human. This means human rights are not exclusive rights, but rights that every individual shares with all other humans. In other words, human rights are not "Peter Kirchschlaeger-rights" but human rights. As one shares them with all other humans, these rights come with the corresponding duties to contribute to the realization of human rights of all other humans.

This leads us, second, to the duties corresponding to the human rights of each human. The individual has to contribute to the realization of the human rights of all other humans. This also means that the duties corresponding to human rights or the human rights of all other humans will

---

551 See Kirchschlaeger 2007a.
552 See Alexy 1998.

restrict the individual. The duties attached to human rights need to be understood as dynamic, because depending on the context, different behaviors are demanded of the duty holders in order to respect, protect, implement, and realize the human rights of all other humans.[553]

Here, it should be mentioned, however, that this constitutes an "asymmetrical relationship"[554] between rights and duties. Humans are and will always be holders of human rights, no matter if they fulfil the duties corresponding to human rights. "These rights are not forfeited by wrong behavior. Men and women do not have to prove themselves worthy of being granted human rights."[555]

In this context, James W. Nickel phrases the restrictions as such that it would only be fair, if push came to shove, and one needs to choose between two holders of human rights, that we would give preference to the one that is acting morally superior.[556] The above-mentioned categorical character of human rights would indicate otherwise: all humans have the right to human rights, unconditionally.

As a third argument against the suspicion that human rights are individualistic, we can argue that rights always have a social character as they regulate relationships between at least two parties. This shows, for example, the fact that "rights are grounds of duties in others"[557].

Fourth, Article 29 of the Universal Declaration of Human Rights of 1948 stipulates: "Everyone has duties to the community in which alone the free and full development of his personality is possible."[558] In Article 29, it is stipulated that the individual can only develop when embedded in a collective and that he or she has duties towards this collective.

Fifth, individual rights and freedoms require a certain form of relation and social context for such universal cooperation between individual holders of human rights who respect their rights to be even conceivable.[559]

---

553 See Raz 1986: 170-171.
554 Wolbert 2003: 179.
555 Wolbert 2003: 179.
556 See Nickel 2015.
557 Raz 1986: 167.
558 Universal Declaration of Human Rights of 1948: Article 29. See Kirchschlaeger 2014b.
559 See also Gould 2015.

Sixth, rights always possess a social rather than an "individualistic" component, as it has to be part of a social system because, without at least a second individual, there would be no need for laws.[560]

Furthermore, the *fundamentality* as a characteristic of human rights indicates that human rights protect minimal standards – the essential elements and spheres of human existence necessary for survival and for a life as human, a life with human dignity – and not luxuries.

The *legal enforceability* as one characteristic of human rights means that human rights are enforceable in a legal system.

And human rights are *inalienable rights*, which means they can neither be acquired nor lost, and every human is entitled to them.[561]

Finally, human rights need to be thought of in their *multidimensionality*, as explained above:[562] human rights contain a legal, a political, a moral, and a historical dimension. The universality of human rights, however, can be shown with the moral dimension of human rights in particular.

In the light of the current discourse around the universality of human rights, one could get the impression that the term "universality" is the opposite of "relativism". In reality, however, the direct opposite of the first word would be "particularism" and "absolutism" for the second.[563] "The common argument seems to be that a universalism can *only* be justified in absolute terms and, if that is not possible, a relative justification will lead to the abandonment of universalism and can therefore be applied only individually."[564] This observation has an influence on the justification of human rights, which according to this observation, could quite possibly be relative,[565] but can also demonstrate how to tackle criticism of the universality of human rights, which in most cases has its basis in individual positions and special interests.

---

560 This has implications on the taxonomy proposed by Lorena Jaume-Palasi and Matthias Spielkamp (see Jaume-Palasi / Spielkamp 2017).
561 See Willoweit 1992.
562 See Kirchschlaeger 2013d.
563 See Lohmann 2008a.
564 Lohmann 2008a: 219, emphasis in the text.
565 See Lohmann 2008a.

6.4.4 The Need for an Ethical Justification of the Universality of Human Rights

The universality of human rights entails, therefore, that all humans are holders of human rights, independent of what they do, what they do not do, where they come from, where they live, what nationality they have, and independent of what society and community to which they belong. The phrase "everybody matters"[566] shows that human rights, without claiming to be universally valid, would not give the necessary protection to all humans to survive and live as humans in all essential spheres and elements that are protected by specific human rights. At the same time, the phrase "everybody matters" shows as well that the universality of human rights respects and protects the diversity of humans. "However, a universalistic claim can only be granted to human rights in as far as they address themselves self-critically and are not directly coupled with a claim to cultural superiority."[567]

The universality of human rights acknowledges humans in general as holders of human rights – in the past, present, and future. Joseph Raz turns this temporal aspect into a problem, as he restricts human rights holders to persons who live today by arguing that certain human rights would not make sense to people who lived a long time ago, like the right to education for stone-age people.[568] Raz is right insofar as these rights are difficult to imagine when related to the distant past. Nevertheless, against this limitation it can be argued that if human rights can be justified morally, the moral validity of human rights cannot be limited to the present or to a near past. Furthermore, if, according to Raz, it would be difficult to demand justice and reparations for human rights violations in retrospect, this should, however, be possible, in order to acknowledge all humans as human rights holders. Also, in general, simply because a group of people doesn't understand something applies to them, this doesn't mean that by dint of that fact, it doesn't apply to them.

The universality of human rights means that humans are human rights holders everywhere. It can, therefore, be concluded that the human rights of all humans are not dependent on cultural, religious and worldview-based communities or contexts. Put in a nutshell, the universality of human rights also entails that humans are human rights holders and that

---

566 Appiah 2006: 144.
567 Huber 2015: 13.
568 See Raz 2015: 226-227.

their human rights need to be respected, protected, implemented, and realized, even if they are part of contexts

- that do not recognize and respect human rights in general or some specific human rights;
- where there is theoretical and/or practical resistance against human rights in general, or some specific human rights;
- that exclude certain persons, groups or minorities in their community from human rights in general or of some specific human rights;
- where there are tendencies against human rights in general, against the universality of human rights or against some specific human rights;
- where there are tendencies that interpret the own belief, worldview, or philosophy, teachings and religious convictions, values and principles in such a way that they contradict the universality of human rights, human rights in general or some specific human rights;
- where some individuals violate the human rights of others without intervention by the state, the society, or the community.

Finally, the claim of universality of human rights finally entails that human rights are valid everywhere and always.

The universality of human rights underpins the need for an ethical justification of human rights and their universality,[569] because societies and communities demand reasons for why human rights are also applicable to their societies, communities, institutions, and members. "The justifications are, therefore, pendant between the rights holder and the bearer of duties resulting from these rights. Both sides will only be able to accept a justification if this relation will be maintained and a justification will only seem adequate if it is applied to all persons concerned and will therefore be universal."[570]

If human rights will be generally justifiable rights, any human rights violation will then no longer be a generally justifiable restriction of the individuals' self-determination.[571]

Moreover, human rights protect diversity indirectly. However, they can only give this protection if they themselves and their universal validity are also justified ethically. With diversity, the need for an ethical justification for human rights and their universality becomes obvious.

---

569 See also Perry 2005; Tasioulas 2015.
570 Lohmann 2000: 10.
571 See Lohmann 2000: 11.

It can be argued against the need to justify human rights in general that the phenomenon of human rights has already made sure that human rights are "un hecho-del-mundo"[572] – a fact of the world. Therefore, the idea of an ethical foundation or a moral justification of human rights is outdated nowadays and of no relevance.[573]

A counterargument to this position consists in the above-mentioned multi-dimensionality and the relation between the human rights dimensions demanding a justification for human rights, because a purely legal understanding of human rights would be reductionist. A legal, political, or historical justification of human rights on its own would also fall short on the character of human rights, which would contradict the argument described above. None of these justifications would, by themselves, explain the human rights claim to universality.

Furthermore, two additional arguments that are both rather weak on their own could be given for the need to justify human rights: On the one hand, the cultural, religious, and worldview-based diversity as a challenge to the universality of human rights shows the need for an ethical justification for human rights. Without an ethical justification, human rights in cultural, religious, and worldview-based communities would be void. Without an ethical justification, human rights can neither preserve the cultural, religious, and worldview-based difference, nor can they influence cultural, religious and worldview-based communities, because without an ethical justification, the boundaries of cultural, religious, and worldview-based communities would also be the limits of the validity of human rights.[574]

On the other hand, practice shows that human rights can by no means be seen as self-evident. They still face great challenges and urgently need a justification because, in practice, human rights are in danger when

- humans do not know their rights, and human rights therefore remain an empty shell. "What is the point of having human rights and not knowing them and what is the use in knowing them but not to understand them!? And finally: who would be helped, if you understand human rights but are not willing to respect them and advocate for them?"[575]

---

572 Rabossi 1990: 161.
573 See Rabossi 1990.
574 See Kirchschlaeger 2013a: 213-222.
575 Fritzsche 2016: 181.

– human rights violations incur no sanctions and therefore lessen the weight, the meaning and the credibility of human rights, which would lead to a degeneration of human rights from rights to mere ideas, in the sense of a reciprocal "customary law". The realization of the human rights idea by way of international treaties,[576] which was treated as a "silent revolution" of international law, is in danger of stagnating. "If we place high value upon rights-protection, we should ensure that the institutions aiming at such protection are effective; otherwise, there remains an element of prudential irrationality, for we would have a clear goal with a means that is incapable of achieving that goal."[577]

– skeptics cannot be given a convincing justification. "The central idea of human rights as something that humans have, and have even without any specific legislation, is seen by many as foundationally dubious and lacking in cogency. A recurrent question is: Where do these rights come from? [...] the worries relate to what is taken to be the 'softness' [...] of the conceptual grounding of human rights."[578]

A further argument against the need for a justification of human rights consists in the viewpoint that it is outdated to try and find a justification for human rights. In a meta-ethical reflection, the argument goes that philosophy has the duty to strengthen a human rights culture, rather than show other cultures its superiority and universality. Rationality is the act of striving for a coherent and understandable structure in our beliefs. Philosophy can only hope to pool culturally dependent intuitions by generalizing them, which allows for incontestable intuitions to be derived from them. These generalizations do not justify these intuitions, but sum them up and therefore increase their predictability, power, and efficiency as well as the feeling of a common moral identity of a moral society. Turning away from the justifiability would be more efficient, "because it would give us the possibility to concentrate our energy on cultivating or educating feelings."[579]

This emphasis on intuition, as proposed by Richard Rorty, raises the question if this could open the door to arbitrariness and irrationality. Because the affirmation as well as the negation of human rights could theoretically be traced back to an intuition, even if one has to admit that the latter is difficult to imagine. Nevertheless, even in the first case one would

---

576 See Klein 1997.
577 Jones 1999: 228.
578 Sen 2004: 315.
579 Rorty 1996: 155.

have to acknowledge the risks involved that might have serious implications for the understanding of human rights and of human rights themselves. If human rights are simply taken for granted, they turn into absolute and forever unchangeable rights that need no justification. As a result, they would have absolute validity without alternatives, which would make them immune to religious and worldview-based differences and could lead to indoctrination. One could argue that human rights, understood in their multi-dimensionality as described above, would not constitute the absolute truth. They are also not natural characteristics of humans. They are a human construct. Human rights have developed historically. They are the result of an agreement process between humans. This consensus is based on reasons that together make up a justification. If the human rights tradition does not discuss their justification, it is in danger of losing sight of the autonomous human, who has a right to discuss the question of justification, because the need for a justification is also based on the close connection between the idea of human rights and the idea of a justification. "We wouldn't have human rights if we as rights holders would not know that we can ask for justifications, if our subjective freedoms are legitimately restricted."[580] Each human, as a human rights holder, has a right to know why their autonomy is restricted by human rights and corresponding duties. Because one has claims or rights that correspond to the duties of others. Not only do others have duties or obligations toward oneself, and in that sense, one has a claim on them, but one also has the normative capacity to make claims on them. One can say to the oppressor that he violated one's own rights. If one is not a competent agent, others can make claims on one's behalf.[581] This point can be summarized as follows: "Justify what you are doing to me!"[582] Human rights need a moral justification in order to prove their legitimacy and in order to remain coherent with their own core concept of the autonomy of the individual because autonomy embraces the claim of knowing the reason why one's freedom should be restricted by human rights.

Moreover, wanting to reduce human beings to their intuition is reductionist. The strong focus Richard Rorty puts on intuition turns out to be very relevant in the area of human rights education or advocating for the furthering of human rights. At this point, however, Rorty mixes up or interchanges two levels. Because to determine that intuition and feelings are

---

580 Lohmann 2000: 9-10.
581 See Reeder 2015: 100.
582 Lohmann 2000: 10.

of great relevance in human rights education and in advocating for the furthering of human rights, it may not be coupled with fundamentally criticizing the endeavor to justify human rights, because this takes place on a different level than the level of human rights education or advocating for the furthering of that upon which human rights are based.

Finally, the relevance of this question of how to justify human rights grows even further when, for example, there are attempts to exclude a specific group of humans from human rights in general or from some rights, when human rights in general are neglected or when some rights are denied, or when nudging by a state could violate specific human rights or disrespect human rights in general. Facing these realities, reasons that justify human rights are necessary. An ethical model of justification of human rights, which is based on the principle of vulnerability, contributes to meeting this challenge and shows that human rights can be ethically justified.[583]

6.4.5 Justifying Ethically Human Rights Based on the Principle of Vulnerability

Human rights can serve as an ethical principle providing ethical guidance to digital transformation and the use of data-based systems because they are ethically justifiable – e.g., based on the principle of vulnerability.[584] As a start to ethically justifying human rights, it is now useful to examine the meta-question of what is actually required of an ethical justification for human rights. An attempt to justify human rights needs *first* to respond to the following two questions: Why are all humans human rights holders? Why are all humans holders of these specific human rights? (e.g., why can human rights not be claimed for other elements and spheres of human existence?)

Second, the answers to these two questions need to form a hermeneutic circle, where the answer to the question of how to justify specific human rights builds upon the question of how to justify human rights in general.

Third, the attempt to justify human rights through these two complementing steps of reasoning has to qualify for a critical rational ethics, as defined in the introduction above. When justifying human rights and their universality, it is also necessary to free "the understanding of human rights

---

583 See Kirchschlaeger 2013a; Kirchschlaeger 2016e; Kirchschlaeger 2015a.
584 See Kirchschlaeger 2013a; Kirchschlaeger 2016e; Kirchschlaeger 2015a.

from the metaphysical ballast of assuming a given individual without any socialization born with inherent rights"[585].

Fourth, an attempt to justify does not have to simply justify "human rights" in a first step of reasoning, but actually has to support the following statements:

- "All humans have the same human rights."
- "If someone is a human, we attribute him or her human rights."
- "All humans are human rights holders."
- "All humans are holders of these specific human rights."

Fifth, a justification attempt has to be designed in such a manner that, in a second step of reasoning, it can ethically justify that all humans are holders of certain human rights. The justification, therefore, has to work for every single human right.

The question of how the four statements above can be justified can be answered with the justification approach based on the principle of vulnerability. As a starting point, one has to differentiate between "vulnerability" and the principle of vulnerability. When becoming aware of their vulnerability, humans have the option to turn to the "first-person perspective" and "self-relation". The principle of vulnerability encompasses the moral aspiration to protect the "first-person perspective" and the "self-relation" of all human beings in order to protect the possibility of a life as a human being.

The various reflections on this justification approach for human rights that are based on the principle of vulnerability contain a first, second, and third step in filtering, which will lead to the emergence of an ethical justification for human rights in general and for specific human rights.

First step of filtering

The justification approach based on the principle of vulnerability starts from the observation that humans will recognize their own vulnerability – a *first* element of the principle of vulnerability.[586] For example, the person who is healthy today knows that he or she might become ill tomorrow. Or – while living happily in the present – that he or she could be killed by others tomorrow. In this thought process, the person will go through a process of uncertainty. This is because he or she is made aware of his or her

---

585 Habermas 1999b: 399.
586 See Kirchschlaeger 2013a: 231-267.

own vulnerability and, in a last consequence, his or her transience.[587] This possibility of self-awareness is true for all humans.

Second, an essential part of the principle of vulnerability is the "first-person perspective"[588]. The awareness-building of one's own vulnerability is a self-recognition process of humans, the empirical correctness of which is not relevant. It is crucial that humans are willing to do something about this awareness of their vulnerability, namely to protect themselves from vulnerability or to find a reasonable way to deal with it. This also affects all humans.

During this awareness-building process when humans become aware of their own vulnerability, they recognize, ex negativo, the "first-person perspective" and the "self-relation". The "first-person perspective" encompasses the awareness of a human that he or she as a singular person is a subject of self-awareness through which one can access one's own vulnerability. On the other hand, they experience this basic anthropological situation of vulnerability as a subject (meaning as the first person singular). The acts, decisions, suffering and the life of a human originate from them as subjects. Furthermore, they interpret this basic anthropological situation of vulnerability as a subject: "By acting and suffering, humans experience themselves as living beings, which are not just living like all other beings, but which live by living their own lives. To relate to themselves, to act neither compulsively nor arbitrarily, but to be guided by reason and to pursue freely chosen purposes constitutes the life form which connects them with all humans as their own kind. This life form makes them vulnerable as the self-relation, which is inherent in this life form, depends on fundamental conditions for realization."[589] (The latter[590] belongs to the two kinds of vulnerability introduced above – the basic vulnerability and the selective and variable vulnerability – as well as the inner and outer spheres and aspects of vulnerability, and can occur in an inner and an outer form.) During this process, humans recognize the "self-relation"; they put themselves in relation to themselves.

Third, the vulnerability will be perceived and revealed by humans from their "first-person perspective" as well as for the "first-person perspective" itself and the "self-relation".

---

587 See Hoffmaster 2006: 42.
588 See Runggaldier 2003.
589 Honnefelder 2012: 171-172.
590 See Hoeffe 1991; Nussbaum 1993.

This awareness-building process of one's own vulnerability and the "first-person perspective" leads, *fourth*, to humans relating themselves to all other humans. In this process, they realize that vulnerability does not make them different from other humans, but that they share this vulnerability with all humans.

Fifth, the process of getting aware of their own vulnerability and the vulnerability of all other humans enables humans to realize that they share not only vulnerability with all other humans, but also the individual "first-person perspective" on individual vulnerability and the vulnerability of all other humans, as well as the individual "self-relation": Every human is subject of his or her own life. Humans therefore realize that the "first person perspective" and the "self-relation" are a prerequisite of life as a human.

Based on the perception of vulnerability of their own "first-person perspective" and their own "self-relation", they become aware of the same vulnerability of all other humans. Humans, who first and foremost want to survive and live as humans – with human dignity, become aware that vulnerability concerns their own survival as well as the survival of all other humans, and also their own life as humans and the lives of all others as humans, because the vulnerability does not stop, from the "first-person perspective" and the "self-relation", as a prerequisite to human life. Faced with one's own vulnerability, the human being primarily wants to survive and live a dignified life. Survival and a life with human dignity should not be allowed to be taken away from humans. They must be legally enforceable in order to offer real protection and have to be applicable to the various dimensions, because vulnerability can encompass the legal, political, historical, and moral dimension. Based on the above-mentioned high priority they possess, and based on the unpredictability of the vulnerability, survival and a life with human dignity should be non-conditional. Humans share the desire to survive and live a life with human dignity with all other humans equally. This desire is not individualistic, even if it is a concern of an individual, which each individual discovers through his or her "first-person perspective" and "self-relation".

Because, *sixth*, humans are aware of their vulnerability, but at the same time do not know if and when this vulnerability will manifest itself and turn into a concrete injury or violation, they are prepared to accord all humans the "first-person perspective" and the "self-relation" based on the equality of all humans, because this presents the most rational, prudent, and advantageous solution for themselves. This means, to accord all humans rights – that is to say human rights – in order to protect themselves and all others, because the vulnerability also contains the "first-person perspective" and the "self-relation". On the one hand, this protection through human rights aims at avoiding the transformation of vulnerability into a concrete injury or violation and, on the other hand, in the case of a possible transformation of vulnerability into a concrete injury or violation, receiving active compensation. Humans are aware that the protection of human rights also encompasses the duties corresponding to human rights, because they are not exclusive rights, but rights to which all humans are entitled.

Concerning this sixth element, the question arises of whether it is really rational, prudent, and advantageous for anyone to agree on human rights. Because it is conceivable that a person, for example, based on his or her religious or worldview-based background, does not shy from vulnerability or injuries, but is looking for them, or that vulnerability is irrelevant for him or her (in their search for salvation). One argument against this objection would be that the freedom of thought, convictions, conscience, belief, religion, and worldview would also be prone to violations. This means that also in this case, it would be rational, prudent, and advantageous to argue the case for human rights protection.

One objection, which would lead to further questions, would be, however, that especially this freedom of thought, convictions, conscience, belief, religion, and worldview could be a thorn in the side of a person who sees him- or herself as being religious. In their eyes, this freedom would be superfluous, because it would not be a question of searching for and finding the right religion, but the right religion would already be defined. Here, one could argue as well that if the right religion is already defined, the freedom of thought, convictions, conscience, belief, religion, and worldview would serve the life, cultivation, and practice of this religion and would be necessary for it.

Another argument against the sixth element of the first step of filtering would be that, if one looks at the current implementation of human rights, one could conclude that it is disadvantageous for the individual, if one agrees unilaterally on human rights and adheres to them. One could argue against this position, however, that the current situation would be even worse without human rights. In addition, human rights are already a global consensus, to which no alternative approaches are known and which already exist as an institution. Therefore, there seems to be no better alternative than to maintain human rights. Beyond that, the unpredictability of vulnerability or the unpredictability of a possible transformation of vulnerability to injury or violation makes it seem irrational and disadvantageous to unilaterally disregard human rights.

Furthermore, an opposition is forming that it is no longer wise to accord oneself and all others human rights and adhere to the duties agreed to, if human rights will not be enforced or will not lead to sanctions if violated. Here, the unpredictability of vulnerability or the unpredictability of a possible transformation of vulnerability to injury or violation would also serve as a counterargument. Because, in light of the insecurity in terms of one's own individual situation and individual perspective, human rights with their inherent just and equal treatment of all humans prove to be the best solution.

Moreover, in view of the above-described awareness-building process for human rights, the question may arise as to why humans should not opt for another form of self-limitation or another form of dealing with this situation (e.g., violence, subordination etc.). As explained above, humans are first and foremost interested in surviving and leading a life with human dignity. Human rights can best support this desire, which speaks in favor of human rights. Moreover, violence or subordination – meaning alternative forms of protection against vulnerability, injury, and violation based on inequality and injustice among humans (e.g., the powerful and the powerless, tyrants and subordinates, oppressors and oppressed) – can be excluded as rational, prudent, and advantageous alternatives in view of the unpredictability of a possible transformation of vulnerability to injury or violation, because, due to the unpredictability of a possible transformation of vulnerability to injury or violation, one does not know on which side one stands or will stand.

Finally, at this point it needs to be expanded on why it is imaginable or conceivable that, for example, leaders or decision-makers would also be willing to accord themselves and, based on the equality of all humans, all humans the "first-person perspective" and the "self-relation" and to protect themselves and all others through human rights. For both, it needs to be presumed that they are also faced with the above-described vulnerability and become conscious of their vulnerability based on the principle of vulnerability. There are no "good reasons" as to why a leader or decision-maker should be different to other human beings in this respect.

Of course, one can assume that, in the case of leaders or decision-makers, that their power and influence could lessen their worry towards vulnerability, but would still experience vulnerability in certain elements and spheres of human existence – even if only their fear of losing power should remind them of their own vulnerability. Therefore, there are enough situations in both cases where they could experience their own vulnerability, which would make their agreement on the creation of human rights plausible, based on the perception and awareness of the principle of vulnerability, as justified by themselves, as well as the above-introduced unpredictability of vulnerability or a possible transformation of vulnerability to injury.

These six points on the principle of vulnerability explain that, *seventh*, the vulnerability in itself has no moral quality, but the principle of vulnerability is normatively charged with the vulnerability, the "first-person perspective" and the "self-relation" as a moral claim. The principle of vulnerability affects all humans and differentiates them from all other living beings. Because of the principle of vulnerability, humans accord each other human rights. Because they agree that, with human rights for themselves and all other humans, a transformation from vulnerability into a concrete injury or violation can be prevented or active compensation for all humans would be provisioned in the case of a possible transformation of vulnerability into a concrete injury or violation. It would be a decision by the moral society that humans assign each other human rights based on the principle of vulnerability and turn all humans into human rights holders.

Therefore, humans are not human rights holders because of their vulnerability, but they are human rights holders because they grapple with their own vulnerability and its relevance. They become aware of the "first-person perspective" and "self-relation" of themselves and all humans, and they get to know the former as a prerequisite for human life. They even recognize the vulnerability of the "first-person perspective" and the "self-relation" of all humans – because of the principle of vulnerability. Humans differentiate vulnerability based on experiences of injustice and violations, and because of the principle of vulnerability, they establish a protection of elements and spheres of human existence with specific human rights. The principle of vulnerability is therefore a starting point for justifying human rights per se as well as specific human rights.

Eighth, it is quite possible that the principle of vulnerability can be the basis for the recognition of new suffering and experiences of injustice, which, because of their threatening character, will necessitate human rights protection. This necessity demands formulating rights that go beyond the human rights that exist today. This leaves human rights open for new challenges that might occur. The principle of vulnerability contains an "exploratory function"[591] and leads to new updates and differentiations of the human rights protection system.

---

591 Habermas 2011a: 18.

These eight points make up the first step in filtering the justification model based on the principle of vulnerability. Not all elements and spheres of human existence are worth considering for protection through human rights, but only those that are needed due to the principle of vulnerability and with which humans want to protect themselves and others.

Second step of filtering

The second step of filtering builds on the considerations above and goes into more detail regarding the areas of protection that all humans as holders of human rights are entitled to, because the consensus on the protection against vulnerability does not include all elements and spheres of human existence. However, which elements and spheres of human existence should be placed under the protection of human rights? What criteria should inform the selection of these elements and spheres of human existence?

Starting points are historical experiences of suffering and injustice, which humans are or could be exposed to based on the principle of vulnerability. Faced with these historically severe experiences of injustice and violence, and because of the principle of vulnerability, humans agree to prevent, for themselves and all other humans, the transformation from vulnerability to concrete injury or violation and to stipulate active compensation in the case of a possible transformation from vulnerability to concrete injury or violation.

Human rights protection does not apply to all historic experiences of injury. It is necessary to make a selection of historical experiences of injustice that call for human rights protection, which again demands criteria for this selection process. They can be derived from the above descriptions of humans and the above-described weighting, because it shows what humans want to protect themselves against. It provides understanding of which characteristics must be fulfilled for a historical experience of violence to warrant protection through human rights. First of all, humans want to survive and live as humans – with human dignity (fundamentality). Humans become aware that vulnerability concerns their own survival and the survival of all humans as well as their own lives as humans with human dignity and the lives of all others as humans with human dignity (universality), because vulnerability does not stop at the "first-person perspective" and the "self-relation" as a prerequisite to human life. Survival and a life with human dignity should not be allowed to be taken away from humans (inalienability). They must be legally enforceable (enforce-ability) and have to be applicable to the various dimensions (multi-dimensionality), because vulnerability can encompass the legal, political, historical, and moral dimension. Based on the above-mentioned high priority they possess, and based on the unpredictability of the vulnerability or a possible transformation from vulnerability to injury, survival and a dignified life should be non-conditional (categorical character). Humans share this desire to survive and live a dignified life with all other humans equally (equality). It is not individualistic, even if each individual discovers it through their own "first-person perspective" and "self-relation" (individual validity). Therefore, the following eight criteria determine the choice of those historical experiences of violence and vulnerabilities against which all humans should be protected through specific human rights: fundamentality, universality, inalienability, enforceability, multi-dimensionality, categorical nature, equality, and individual validity.

The second step in filtering the justification model based on the principle of vulnerability characterizes an inherent openness for new threats, risks, and experiences of injustice, which at present are not yet in the conscience or the imagination or have not yet occurred, as well as an openness to experiences of injustice that occur in different religions, cultures, traditions, civilizations, and worldviews.

At the same time, the second step of filtering meets the challenges to apply these eight criteria to historical experiences of injustice, for example, the challenges of historical contingency and the universalization of particular experiences of injustice.

Third step of filtering

This step encompasses the application of the above-mentioned eight criteria in order to identify the elements and spheres of human existence that need to be protected by human rights.

The criterion of "fundamentality" is fulfilled, if a historical experience of injustice touches on an element or sphere of human existence that is needed for survival or for living as a human.

For the criterion "universality" and the above-mentioned challenge of historical contingency and universalization of particular experiences of injustice to be fulfilled, rational reasons are needed as to why an experience of injustice or violence is relevant to human rights and touches on an element or sphere of human existence which must be protected for all, everywhere, and always. Rational reasons are necessary to enable the transition from a subjective experience of injustice or violation to a universal experience of injustice or violation.[592]

Concerning the criterion "inalienability", it is necessary that the right corresponding to a certain element or sphere of human existence cannot be acquired or lost, and that every human is entitled to it.

The criterion "enforceability" is fulfilled if the corresponding right can be enforced in a legal system.

The criterion "multi-dimensionality" is fulfilled if it can be thought of in the legal, political, moral, and historical dimension.

Concerning the criterion "categorical nature", it is necessary to show that humans are not required to do anything in order to have this vulnerability, violation, or the corresponding right that protects from such vulnerability or violation.

For the criterion "equality" to be fulfilled, every human has to be able to benefit from the corresponding right without distinction.

The criterion "individual validity" is fulfilled if an individual can have the corresponding right independent of a collective.

The principle of vulnerability as justification for human rights causes certain objections:

First, – as elaborated above in subchapter 3.2 Vulnerability – not only humans, but also animals are subject to vulnerability and should, therefore, be included in this consensus. The following point can be used as a first argument against this objection: In no way do human rights want to discriminate between humans and animals, or want to give humans rights that may be superior to those of the "lower" forms of life. They only aim for a legal, interpersonal relationship that would also need to be regulated if animals had similar rights.[593]

By definition, humans, not animals, therefore prove to be holders of human rights. At the same time, it needs to be pointed out that this would not automatically and categorically prevent, theoretically, similar, or substantially the same, moral rights from being awarded to them.[594] This includes, however, that humans agree on rights that apply to them as humans themselves. Additionally, humans develop animal rights for other beings, like animals, that share vulnerability with humans. Human rights

---

592 See Hoernle 2011: 67.
593 Menke / Pollmann 2007: 140.
594 See Menke / Pollmann 2007: 140-141.

are based on their self-recognition and the perception of one's own vulnerability. Animal rights are based on the human perception of animals and their vulnerability.

Furthermore, one could think that humans imagine or perceive the vulnerability of humans and the vulnerability of animals as different, from a phenomenological perspective. When differentiating between the self-recognition of humans and the awareness of animals as well as determining differences (from a phenomenological perspective) in the vulnerability of humans and animals, it is not necessarily empirically proven that this is true. However, this is irrelevant for the justification approach, as already mentioned above. Instead, it should be pointed out that humans – while being conscious of and recognizing the vulnerability of animals – probably think of themselves in other terms than of an animal,[595] or that humans think of their vulnerability that they share with other humans in different terms than of the vulnerability of animals.

Furthermore – and this proves to be the main argument against this objection – the principle of vulnerability is not only about the vulnerability that is only empirically observable, but in particular about how humans become aware of their vulnerability or how they see it. The awareness, the examination, and the reflection on the vulnerability are at the center, the "first-person perspective" and the "self-relation" as prerequisites for a possible life as a human, as well as the moral consequences that provoke the principle of vulnerability within humans. Humans are therefore not holders of human rights because they are vulnerable, but because of the principle of vulnerability that leads to reciprocal granting of human rights to all humans and which is clearly different from the principle of vulnerability of animals and serves as *differentia specifica* that justifies a difference between the understanding of the vulnerability of humans and the vulnerability of animals. Therefore, due to the fact that the principle of vulnerability cannot apply to humans and animals, it aligns with the relevance of the principle of vulnerability when justifying human rights.

Second, one can argue that the principle of vulnerability is only useful for justifying social participation rights and not for justifying the other two categories of human rights. This criticism is based on the narrower term of "vulnerability", which is why it loses relevance when basing this justification approach on the above-introduced understanding of the term of "vulnerability". With this understanding, humans do not only see themselves threatened in the essential elements and spheres of human existence that

---

595 See Bondolfi 2009: 506-507.

are protected by social participation rights, but the principle of vulnerability also has a wider influence on human existence.[596]

Third, one can argue that medical and technological progress continuously reduces the vulnerability of humans. Therefore, the principle of vulnerability can only be used to a certain extent to justify human rights, because vulnerability is something that humans can eliminate more and more. This criticism also uses the term "vulnerability" very narrowly, which restricts vulnerability to such an extent that it only includes phenomena that humans can counter with medical and technological innovation. Yet, it needs to be borne in mind that the fundamental vulnerability also needs to be included, something that humans essentially cannot change, even with medical and technological progress.

In addition, this criticism uses the term vulnerability in a reductionist way, as becomes clear against the backdrop of the term as introduced above, because it sees vulnerability as something exclusively negative that needs to be eliminated.

Finally, the fundamental question arises if such a belief in progress is even justified.[597]

A justification for human rights and their universal validity has to be framed in such a way that it does not only justify human rights in themselves, but can be tested against each individual human right. The justification for human rights based on the principle of vulnerability can be used with each specific human right, as could already be shown with some examples.[598]

6.4.6 Universal Human Rights Protect From Exclusion

Based on this ethical foundation, human rights represent a universal consensus. The latter means that no other catalogue of norms is given the same amount of global acceptance. They have credibility and are a widely respected ethical standard.

---

596 See Turner 2006: 36-37.
597 See Kirchschlaeger 2013b.
598 See Kirchschlaeger 2013a: 290-335; Kirchschlaeger 2015a.

In addition, human rights are not built upon one particular tradition, culture, religion, worldview, or value-system.[599] Human rights offer "a common basis for a humane existence beyond ideological differences."[600]

There are attempts from particular perspectives to undermine human rights in general, some human rights, human rights in general of some humans, or some human rights of some humans. Human rights in their universality are challenged by particular points of view and perspectives as well as by particular interests. The following part aims at evaluating, from an ethical perspective, some arguments and categories. To start with, it needs to be pointed out that the critical discussion of some arguments and categories with regard to human rights and their universality can never do justice to each individual approach due to the shortness of each explanation. The aim to explore exemplary arguments and categories and, in this sense, systematically reduce the justifications to be able to critically analyze them makes it even more difficult. Finally, only some examples can be picked out from a plethora of diverse arguments and categories that are particularly remarkable and important for human rights discourse. It can, therefore, not have a concluding character. An exemplary argumentation cannot be avoided in this normative question, because by using only some examples, the argumentative challenges will be demonstrated, as well as which line of argument would serve the development of human rights.

The first step will be to show general patterns of argument with a concrete example. The second step will be to test whether these general patterns of argument are dependent on a certain context or if they could also be used in the same or similar form in other contexts by different authors. In this example, a specific group of humans will be excluded from a specific human right. If one uses the categorization by Georg Lohmann, this would correspond to questioning the universality of human rights from a cultural relativism point of view: human rights in general, or specific human rights of all or of certain humans, will be called into question, with reference to their own culture, tradition, religion, worldview, civilization, or their own value system.[601] The following example can show this conclusively: only since 1990 has women's suffrage existed in the whole of Switzerland. It had already been adopted on February 7, 1971 with a close majority of two thirds on a national level. This is rather late compared to many other countries. But it took until March 25, 1990 for Swiss women

---

599 See Gut 2008; Joas 2015a; Kirchschlaeger 2016f.
600 Habermas 2001a: 125; see also Habermas 1999a.
601 See Lohmann 2008b: 50-51.

to be recognized as Swiss voters in the whole of Switzerland. It was not until after women in Appenzell Innerrhoden filed a lawsuit and the Federal Court decided that the cantonal constitution violated the Federal Constitution that women in the canton of Appenzell Innerrhoden were given the right to vote. Based on this Federal Court decision, women's suffrage was enacted on a cantonal level on November 27, 1990 – against the will of the majority of voters in the canton. Thus, the last canton in Switzerland introduced women's suffrage.[602]

The following ten arguments against women's suffrage were used – all of which are to be contradicted from an ethical perspective:

1. the role that was given to women as individuals by the collective – the role of mother – would not be compatible with politics;
2. the contribution of women as individuals to the collective: "society needs women without suffrage in order to function, to develop and to survive";
3. a change would open the door to something that the majority of society is opposed to and considers "evil" – in the case of women's suffrage in Switzerland it was argued that women's suffrage would bring Bolshevism to Switzerland;[603]
4. the presumed self-image of women: "if you were to ask the women, they would not want to participate in politics";
5. women are allegedly lacking the necessary competencies for exercising this human right;
6. one's own tradition and culture: "this is in accordance with our tradition and culture" or "this is our tradition and culture" or "we are a special case which is good and should not be changed";
7. one's own history: "we have always done it this way";
8. one's own history as success model: "so far, we have been doing well following this path";
9. one's own sovereignty: "this is our own business";
10. inner cohesion against influences from the outside: "we don't let anybody from outside dictate the way we do anything".

These ten arguments were used in various combinations and orders during the opinion-forming and decision-making processes at the time.

The counter-arguments can be found, *first*, in the justification of human rights based on the principle of vulnerability. *Second*, the counter-argu-

---

602 See Neue Zuercher Zeitung 2011.
603 See Gariup 2011.

ment to reverse the burden of proof can help to invalidate these ten arguments. In the course of reversing the burden of proof, "good reasons" – meaning that it must be conceivable that all humans given their effective freedom and autonomy as well as their full equality would agree upon these reasons (within a model of thought and not within a real worldwide referendum) on ethical grounds – are demanded by the opposite party in the discourse that would speak in favor of each argument. It will be impossible to find "good reasons" for these ten arguments.

Third, the following observation will weaken the power of persuasion of those ten arguments. No matter if one argues, for example, with a state about its weak human rights performance, or if one discusses discrimination against women with a religious community, or if one points out a worldview-based practice violating human rights, these ten arguments seem to appear in the same or similar form across religions, worldviews, or states, when trying to deny all humans, a certain group of humans, or some individuals all their human rights or some specific human rights. This is not about proving empirically that these ten arguments of exclusion will be used always and everywhere when trying to restrict or deny human rights. Rather, the question ought to be whether these ten patterns of argument of exclusion are not used at every instant or whether they cannot be recognized in patterns across states, religions, cultures, traditions, civilizations, and worldviews.

These two questions weaken the ten arguments of exclusion to an extent where their context-relatedness, which is essential for the argumentation, loses meaning, because the same or similar arguments of exclusion are also used in other contexts where attempts are made to deny other humans their human rights. The main reasons for these ten arguments of exclusion – *inter alia* one's own understanding of the collective, state, culture, tradition, religion, worldview, and value system – lose their power of persuasion when one becomes aware that exactly the same arguments are used by other states, cultures, traditions, religions, worldviews, civilizations, and value systems. This means that the exclusion is not determined by the uniqueness of the situation, but by something that is common to all state, religious and worldview-based communities. This is where the arguments start to become shaky. Because suddenly it is not, for example, "typical of the Swiss" to deny women their right to vote, but something supported by certain circles in Switzerland and certain circles outside of Switzerland – independent from the Swiss state, the Swiss context, the Swiss history, the Swiss tradition, the Swiss values, etc. This means that these ten arguments are not based on one's own uniqueness or one's own character, but on something else. Therefore, they build on something different than what the opposing party claimed in the discussion.

Fourth, those questions about something universal for states, as well as religious and worldview-based communities, expose the reasons that are probably more accurate in the arguments of exclusion, which are less dependent on context, culture, tradition, religion, worldview, value system, history, etc., but rather on a different uniting factor unconnected to state, religion, or worldview. This uniting factor is characterized by an allegedly fundamentally conservative orientation – allegedly, because a "fundamentally conservative" orientation could definitely be compatible with human rights, in the sense of conservative as preserving human rights conformity within a collective. This uniting factor does lead to having to refute the not entirely unjustified suspicion that one tries to twist one's own culture, tradition, religion, worldview, value system, history, sovereignty, etc. in such a way that it fits with particular interests of certain people or a certain group. And it can be described as illiberal, because by refusing to respect human dignity and the universality of human rights or by willingly denying all humans all human rights, certain human rights of all humans, or certain humans all or some specific human rights, this position accepts that humans are denied their human rights, wholly or partially.

The ten arguments of exclusion could also be traced back to the claim of sovereignty and power of certain individuals or groups within a collective. If this cannot be rebutted in discourse, then it can be shown that those in power and those in charge of decision-making within states as well as religious and worldview-based communities are following particular interests or considering institutional policy when using these ten arguments of exclusion.[604]

With regard to the claim for sovereignty and power of certain individuals or groups within a collective, based on the above justification for human rights in their universality, it needs to be mentioned that all states and non-state actors have to adhere to human rights and help to enforce them. Therefore, human rights constitute a limit to the claim of sovereignty and power of certain individuals or groups within a collective.

Fifth, it becomes clear that there is no divergence between human rights and one's own culture, tradition, religion, worldview, value system, history, religious or worldview-based traditions and teaching. This also eliminates the possibility of undermining human rights based on context.

---

604 See Langan 1982: 31-34.

Sixth, when engaging with the ten arguments of exclusion and the resulting contradictions and exposition, possible credibility and coherence problems will emerge, as will a diminishing power of persuasion of the specific society toward humans within and outside of that society. Often, human rights violations, pressure, coercion, violence, extremism, and illiberal thinking and acting in or by a collective can be signs of their weakness and gradual decline of their importance. Or, in other words: Why should you force a human to do something if you can persuade them of something?

Seventh, the discussion of the ten arguments of exclusion, which also notes the resistance and contradiction against exclusion in the respective states and religious and worldview-based communities, shows that neither states nor religious and worldview-based communities are homogenous, monolithic, precisely definable and tangible, eternally unvarying, eternally existing entities that never change. Collectives are highly complex in their composition. They are a heterogeneous figure (e.g., conservative, liberal trends, etc.), are characterized by change (e.g., developments, progress, etc.), creation, growths, and decline as well as contributions and resistance to the emergence of the idea of human rights. In their past, present and probably also in their future, states, religious, and worldview-based communities know diversity, differences, internal discussions, arguments, friction, and competing arguments and reasons – probably to varying degrees of openness, intensity, and publicity. Traces of oral and written transmissions that have been preserved bear witness to such processes.

For example, when it comes to oppression, fights against and annihilation of minorities, a clash between the power of the collective against the powerlessness of the individual, injustices, conflicts between socio-economic groups, etc., states and religious and worldview-based communities raise their voices in favor of human rights. Concrete questions, problems, challenges, and historic experiences of injustice and violations that concern essential elements and spheres of human existence that every human needs to survive and live as human with human dignity, lead to human rights contradictions, because all humans are and stay human rights holders, inside and outside of states or religious or worldview-based collectives, as shown above.

Eighth, there is a tendency to magnify and enlarge differences between states, societies, religious, and worldview-based communities. "Societies change faster than foreigners' pictures of them. [...] It is true that different parts of the world have sometimes had radically different histories, which still exert an influence on their vocabularies, their ways of thinking, their religions, their values. But the influences on the members of virtually all societies are now much more a mix of local and global than they were even a hundred years ago."[605]

6.4.7 Universal Human Rights Foster Plurality

Apart from the arguments of exclusion that are used across states, religions, cultures, traditions, civilizations, and worldviews, which have been identified and discussed above, one always comes across categories in the human rights discourse (such as West/East, global/local...) that suggest a normative justification for a statement or a position that is based on a certain geographically defined place or area, either for or against human rights. These categories, however, cause doubt in relation to their epistemic significance.

Categories such as, for example, East/West are based on the assumption or construction of allegedly definable, tangible, monolithic, homogenous, eternally existing, unchangeable, opposing, and separate worlds. It seems to be clear what the so-called "West" or "East" encompasses and what traditions, principles, and values upon which these two parts of the world are based. On this basis, the categories "East" or "West" are used in arguments, for example in the following sentence: "Because human rights emerged in the 'West', they are not valid in the 'East'". Apart from the relevance of temporal and local realities for the validity of universal norms, which will be discussed in the following section, the categories "East" and "West" give substance for a normative statement ("human rights are not valid in the 'East'"). A further criticism of the epistemic significance of such categories, which at the same time weakens the above example of a line of argument, is appropriate for the following reasons:

- These categories seem to be founded in racist thoughts, because they suggest that humans in one context are fundamentally different from humans outside of this context in their essential elements and spheres of human existence that humans need for survival and to live as humans – and that human rights are only about these perceived differences.
- One argument, which is supported by these categories, makes the inappropriate assumption that "West" has a certain superior quality that the

---

605 Griffin 2015: 562.

"East" lacks. The statement "because human rights emerged in the 'West'..." also contains the assumption that the "West" has allegedly a power of innovation and creation that the "East" allegedly does not have.[606]

- These categories always remain relative to the starting point, which is relevant because they are, in their content, geographical categories. It raises the question of which point this view was taken from and how it was established that one place lies in the "East" and another in the "West". For example, Vienna lies "east" of Lucerne, but in the normal usage of the two categories in the human rights discourse, Vienna would probably be assigned to the "West".

- It turns out that it is difficult, or really impossible to understand these categories – for example the so-called "East" and "West" – and their respective values upon which these two categories are based. When trying to develop a comprehensive definition of the so-called "West" and "East" and assuming to know the values that they are based on, caution needs to be exercised in the face of the dominating plurality, heterogeneity, and dynamics in the "East" or "West". An epistemological approach would probably fail, because these categories cannot be defined with finality, except for their designation as geographical positions. The reality is much more complex, and the allegedly categorizing values – such as in the geographical "East" and "West" – prove to be inaccessible, due to their religious and worldview-based plurality and heterogeneity, normative diversity, and the different legal and political systems, as well as due to great differences in the economic power.

- The schematization contained in these categories based on the assumption and construction of allegedly definable, comprehensive, monolithic, homogenous, eternal, unchangeable, separate, and contradicting worlds (e.g., "East" - "West", ...) is an over-simplification. It reduces the diversity that is contained within such categories and is very important for shaping the discussion. The two alleged poles prove to be diverse and heterogeneous in their inner structure and contain various trends (e.g. conservative, liberal, etc.). This would be important for the subjects of the respective discourse when using those categories. This type of schematization matches the idea of monolithic, definable, comprehensive, homogenous, eternal, and unchangeable inner structures and leaves aside the different foundations, developments, and the dynamic of change.

---

606 See Frezzo 2015: xxi.

- To match content to a certain geographical place or area is not convincing, because a certain content A or a trend B can be found in what we call the "East" as well as what we call the "West", and the contradicting position C or trend D can also be found everywhere.[607] These patterns of argumentation, on which positions or trends are based, do not primarily depend on their geographic or temporary origins, as such a schematization would like to suggest. They are rather about a liberal position, which can be found in all places and at all cardinal points, just like their oppositions. Liberal and illiberal positions exist independently of longitudes and latitudes. If a geographical reference is made to a certain place – for example in statements such as "in the East they think like that" or "in the West they do it like this" –, there is the risk that "in the East" or "in the West" may turn into an argument that obscures everything else, in particular the real reasons and factors. In the course of this, the argument may impede examination of the real reasons and factors in terms of their quality as "good reasons" – meaning that it must be conceivable that all humans given their effective freedom and autonomy as well as their full equality would agree upon these reasons – within a model of thought and not within a real worldwide referendum – on ethical grounds. This critical examination, however, would be necessary with regard to the normative validity and power of argument of the real reasons and factors.

Of course, historical backgrounds, context, place, and time, etc. have an influence on mindsets and opinions. The latter, however – if the reasoning is only based on place or time of origin – has to be questioned as to its normative validity and its power of argument. This can be shown particularly well in the case of human rights with their universality and historically contingent emergence because human rights in their universality are challenged by pointing to their historically contingent emergence.

Human rights did not just "fall from the sky", but have developed and grown historically – out of particular contexts and mostly as reactions to injustice with a universal validity. A selective view on the historic development of human rights, which only takes into account "Western" sources, has been broken and turned into a recognition of contributions to human history from different traditions, cultures, religions, worldviews, philosophies, civilizations, and value systems, from various states as well as the in-

---

607 See also Joas 2015a: 78.

ternational community at large.[608] Human rights are a consensus which developed throughout history, and which are open to further development contingent on history. Human rights are advancing. The human rights tradition and their continuation make history. Humanity finds itself confronted with new challenges. Previously unknown dangers threaten basic elements of human existence.[609] It is inevitable that we react to protect the human dignity of each individual.

A historical classification of human rights, as undertaken in the historical dimension of human rights, must be adequately placed in its contribution to human rights, as explained above. Here, attention is paid to the genesis of human rights, while the justification discourse focuses on the validity of human rights. On the basis of these considerations, approaches that use particular historic events as entry points for the justification of human rights reach their argumentative limits, because this argument goes against the universality of human rights. At the same time, the historical contingency of human rights contributes to a great extent to the understanding of human rights. Prompted by historic experiences of injustice, humans have bestowed human rights upon each other. This shapes human rights up to the present in the sense that human rights seek to stop injustice and have always needed to be fought for. Neither the temporal nor the geographical embeddedness of the emergence of human rights, however, is key to today's normative validity of human rights. Rather, rational reasons are the key. Similar to other theories, it is first and foremost important, if human rights can rationally convince and be made plausible, meaning if "good reasons" speak in favor of them. By the same token, in examining Albert Einstein's theory of relativity, does it matter when and where it was developed? Unlikely. What matters more is whether the theory of relativity can be disproved or not. Does the fact that Immanuel Kant came up with the categorical imperative in Koenigsberg more than 200 years ago make his theory more or less persuasive?

With regard to the universality of human rights, the historically contingent emergence of human rights is also not an argument in favor of or against them. Because in this case as well, reference must be made to the rational reasons for the human rights justification (e.g., on the basis of the principle of vulnerability) and the resulting irrelevance of the historically contingent emergence of human rights on their claim to universality. At the same time, the contingent temporal and geographical origin of an un-

---

608 See Kirchschlaeger 2016f.
609 See Kirchschlaeger 2016g.

derstanding does not make their universality impossible. Finally, the universality of human rights ensures that every human is free and autonomous, and this way, universal human rights foster plurality.[610]

6.4.8 Human Rights as Ethical Frame of Reference for Data-Based Systems

Beyond these reflections, human rights are highly applicable to the real world, providing concrete ethical guidance to digital transformation and the use of data-based systems. Compared with other ethical principles, human rights encompass not only the ethical but also the legal dimension: human rights are legally defined, have a legal framework, and are executable. Institutions like the UN Human Rights Council in Geneva, the Office of the UN-High Commissioner for Human Rights in Geneva, the Regional Human Rights Protection Mechanisms in the different continents are elements of the realization of the idea of human rights and can enhance the culture of human rights. They show that human rights are *real*, not an illusion. Human rights are a legal reality in all parts of the world.

Obviously, the implementation of human rights is at the same time facing challenges everywhere. However, human rights legal mechanisms, instruments, and human rights institutions give an obvious face to the idea of human rights as an embodiment of the protection of human dignity. An approach to this legal dimension starting on a local level allows one to begin within the context of the addressees, enabling them to approach human rights from their real-life experience and from their understanding of justice, freedom and equality – always considering the universal dimension of human rights.

In addition, human rights as an ethical instrument for digital transformation and the use of data-based systems possess the advantage that they are inherently linked with its legal dimension of human rights, which serves as a fundament for legal compliance standards. This aspect should not be misunderstood as neglecting the difference between legal compliance and ethics. It is at the same time an emphasis of the differentiation between legal compliance and ethics and of the inherent link between the moral dimension of human rights as an ethical point of reference for science and the legal dimension of human rights as a foundation of legal standards of compliance.

---

610 See Kirchschlaeger 2020d; Kirchschlaeger 2020e.

Furthermore, the scientific community is aware of its legal obligations and legal compliance standards. In addition to these legal obligations, science strives to respect ethical principles in its research – for example, honesty, objectivity, independence, impartiality, fairness and responsibility to future generations. For this ethical level of science, the contribution of human rights as an ethical point of reference is essential and necessary due to their ethically justifiable universality.

Moreover, a globalized scientific community faces several traditions, cultures, religions, worldviews and value systems. This heterogeneity is protected by human rights. At the same time, human rights give this heterogeneity clear limits, which need to be respected: Human rights protect the essential elements and areas of human existence within traditions, cultures, religions, worldviews and value systems as well. Therefore, human rights as an ethical point of reference can support science when it is acting in favor of human rights while meeting challenges relating to tradition, culture, religion, worldview and value systems.[611]

Human rights are a universal consensus, which gives this ethical instrument for science more weight, as this ethical point of reference is not built upon a particular tradition, culture, religion, worldview or value system that becomes obvious from looking at the discussion, e.g., the discussion of the drafting process of the Universal Declaration of Human Rights in 1948. Jacques Maritain reports that the drafters refused to ground human rights in one particular tradition, culture, religion, worldview or value system – out of respect for the universality of human rights and for cultural, religious, and worldview-based diversity and plurality: "Yes, we agree about the rights but on condition that no one asks us why."[612]

Human rights as an ethical instrument liberate scientists from the suspicion of arbitrariness in their ethical self-assessment, as human rights are a widely respected ethical standard.

Another pragmatic reason for their validity originates in the drafting process of the legal human rights treaties based on the Universal Declaration of Human Rights of 1948. It consists of the following idea that people were already conscious of at the time and that influenced the drafting of the human rights documents: "The members of the Commission must take into account the fact that their work concerned the future and not the

---

611 See Kirchschlaeger 2013b.
612 Maritain 1948: I. See Kirchschlaeger 2015d; Kirchschlaeger 2016f.

past; no one could foresee what information media would be employed in a hundred years' time."[613]

Moreover, the dynamic character of human rights needs to be emphasized at this point. Human rights have always been open to adaptation in order to stop and prevent new risks, dangers, and violations of human dignity. Therefore, human rights are ready to adapt to future challenges.[614]

Beyond that, the individuals involved in technology are protected by human rights in essential areas and elements of human existence, which a human needs for survival and for a life as a human. Some of them are of specific significance for technological inquiry, research, development, and applications, e.g., the right to freedom (art 2); the right to freedom of thought, conscience and religion (art 18); the right to freedom of opinion and expression (art 19); the right to freedom of peaceful assembly and association (art 20); the right freely to participate in the cultural life of the community, to enjoy the arts and to share in scientific advancement and its benefits (art 27[1]), and everyone has the right to the protection of the moral and material interests resulting from any scientific, literary or artistic production of which he [or she] is the author (art 27[2]) as set forth in the Universal Declaration of Human Rights of 1948[615]. For centuries, science has been the victim of infringements upon its freedom, of attempts to block innovative and creative approaches, and of oppression of ideas, concepts and discoveries by putative "absolute truths" out of particular interests and in order to enforce old and existing power structures. And this chapter had not yet been closed, but rather the danger still existed that members of the scientific community could not conduct their research freely. Therefore, they needed and continue to need protection. At this point, the question was only if the protection of science had to be pursued by means of human rights – the most fundamental and highest form of legal protection in existence. In basic, simplified terms, protecting science through human rights would mean that science is considered to be an essential element or area of a human existence which enables every human being to survive and to live with human dignity, such as the right to life, the right to food, the right to health care, and so on. Based on a positive answer to this question stating that science is an essential element or area of human existence which enables every human to survive and to live with human dignity, as mentioned above, several specific human rights protect

---

613 United Nations 1950.
614 See Kirchschlaeger / Kirchschlaeger 2010.
615 Universal Declaration of Human Rights of 1948.

academic freedom.[616] To this day, members of the scientific community are having their human rights violated or are running the risk of becoming a victim of human rights violations directly connected with their research. Therefore, it is still necessary to continue initiatives or to take measures to promote human rights in science as a way of ensuring respect for the human rights of researchers in their scientific activities, of information on human rights violations concerning scientists, and of awareness-building regarding the significance and function of human rights for scientists.

Limits to one's own human rights are, firstly, – in the case of a specific human right – the other specific human rights following the principle of indivisibility. This principle defines that all human rights must go hand-in-hand. This means that the entire catalogue of human rights needs to be respected. Therefore, every human right must be implemented optimally and in accordance with all other human rights being implemented optimally at the same time. Secondly, limits to one's own human rights are the human rights of all other individuals. For example, one's own right to freedom is valid only to the extent that it is compatible with the right to freedom of all other human beings. Both limits lead also to corresponding duties for a rights-holder, which is the reason why every right-holder is a duty-bearer as well.[617]

Humans involved in science, technology, and research are right-holders and duty-bearers. These duties can be negative (*not doing* something in order to contribute to the realization of human rights) or positive (*doing something* in order to contribute to the realization of human rights). Based upon this conceptual fundament, science and/or members of the scientific community can contribute to the realization of human rights but unfortunately also be complicit with or commit human rights violations. Science can contribute to the realization of human rights if technological progress respects human rights. As a consequence, technological progress and economic development cannot be an "end *per se*" but must serve mankind. Both technological progress and economic development must function within the framework of human rights to be able to further the realization of human rights. To further the realization of human rights even more ef-

---

616 Arthur Fine has argued for the "Natural Ontological Attitude" suggesting that the sorts of things associated with the practice of science are common to being human (see Fine 2001; see also Musgrave 2001).
617 See Corillon 1989; Kirchschlaeger 2014b.

fectively, human rights must be included among the goals of scientific progress.[618]

Science can also be complicit with or commit human rights violations, e.g., when it does not respect human dignity and violates human rights in its own conduct of research, or when its work enables parties in armed conflicts to commit horrible acts of violence and genocide.

Digital transformation and data-based systems embrace domains relevant to human rights, such as the use of micro-targeting in the dissemination of commercial and political messages, personalization of news, e-recruitment, predictive diagnostics in health care and predictive policing in law enforcement. "A great global challenge confronts all of those who promote human rights and rule of law: how can States, companies and civil society ensure that artificial intelligence technologies reinforce and respect, rather than undermine and imperil, human rights?"[619] The human rights dimensions of the digital transformation and data-based systems include but are not limited to human dignity, freedom, and equality; the right to non-discrimination; the right to a fair trial; the right to privacy and data protection; the right to political participation and democracy; the right to freedom of expression and information; the list goes on. Public sphere and democracy and the roles media and journalism are playing for a functioning democratic opinion-forming and decision-making-process need to be safeguarded as well.

---

618 About technical progress, its ends, its foundation of values and its societal importance taking the examples of stem cell research and research on human beings, see Kirchschlaeger et al. 2003; Kirchschlaeger et al. 2005.
619 Kaye 2018: Art. 1.

7 Opportunities and Challenges from an Ethical Perspective

In applying the ethical principles of "responsibility", "intergenerational omni-dynamic social justice", and "human rights" to digital transformation and data-based systems, of course, a high quantity and wide variety of ethical opportunities and risks could be identified. Both the opportunities and risks need to be addressed because the former open fundamental potential for humanity and the latter consist in existential risks for humans.[620]

7.1 Illegitimate Path

Ethical risks emerge from data-based systems and digital transformation when they have, on the one hand, been designed, developed, programmed, and produced for something ethically good, but on the other hand an illegitimate path is taken to fulfil this legitimate purpose. Commanding a self-driving vehicle to bring a person as quickly as possible from A to B is ethically legitimate, as long as human dignity and human rights are respected. But the means to reach this goal might be ethically illegitimate, such as if the self-driving vehicle runs over someone in the course of reaching the goal.

On the other hand, ethical risks also emerge from malicious design,[621] malicious development, malicious programming, malicious production, or malicious use of data-based systems and digital transformation, e.g., data poisoning,[622] cyberwar and cybercrime,[623] which use technological advancements and options for wars or criminal acts.[624]

---

620 See Bostrom 2013.
621 See Franssen 2014.
622 See Brundage et al. 2018.
623 See Shaw 2019.
624 See Ohly 2019a: 107-124.

7.2 "Dual Use"

The so-called "dual use" problem[625] is based on the potential for the same data-based system to be used for either a legitimate or an illegitimate purpose.[626] It originates from the characteristic of data-based systems as multi-use tools. This dual use problem can be illustrated with the example of a drone: Drones can be used to deliver essential food to people in disaster zones where people cannot reach them. But the same drones can be used for killing: the so-called "killer drones". Of course, the ethical evaluation of such machines will be diametrically opposed in those two situations. This dual use problem shows the limits of the general evaluation of drones. For a sophisticated ethical analysis, a general assessment of drones needs to be complemented by considering the uses of drones.

The "dual use" problem is recognized in its relevance by the "regulatory conceptual framework" entitled "Dual Use Research of Concern (DURC)"[627] used by national and international organizations such as the World Health Organization (WHO) or the US National Institute of Health (NIH).

The description of the dual use problem as "deviation of intent"[628] proves to be too reductionist, because the possibility that a research and innovation process may also begin with an ethically negative objective also needs to be considered. As stated above, it cannot be automatically assumed that innovation processes always aim for an ethically positive purpose.

At the same time, it can be stated that the dual use problem contains less than a dilemma, as the US National Research Council tries to grasp it conceptually,[629] because it does not necessarily have to have a dilemma structure and thus, an ethical analysis is certainly able to differentiate the ethically positive from the ethically negative. Looking at digital transformation and data-based systems from an ethical perspective, it means that not only the technology as such needs to be examined, but also its uses.

---

625 See Rath et al. 2014.
626 See Sevini et al. 2018; European Commission 2018; Miller 2018.
627 See World Health Organization (WHO) n.d.
628 DiEuliis / Giordano 2018: 239.
629 See Imperiale / Casadevall 2015.

7.3 Ambivalence

Ambivalence describes the possibility that data-based systems may be used for an ethically good purpose, but can at the same time include or lead to something ethically bad. Differing from Hans Jonas' "ambivalence of effects"[630], ambivalence embraces the actions, that is to say, the cause as well as the effects.[631] The example of the automation of mobility can illustrate ambivalence: one reason why traffic jams occur is because of the variation in speed and the different speeds of the individual vehicles. If both could be minimized, there would be fewer traffic jams. Automated mobility includes both the reduction of speed variations by having a traffic flow that runs at the same speed, and the harmonization in speed of all vehicles through communication between the individual vehicles. There are also far fewer accidents to be expected because the driving systems have to ensure communication amongst themselves. This does not mean that accidents can be completely avoided, because mistakes can occur in driving systems, too. "Accidents (…) will continue to happen as a matter of physics. Take the autonomous car again: even if it has the best and most perfect sensors, software, and hardware the future has to offer, there'll still be a risk of a crash. Anytime a car passes or is passed by another vehicle, for instance, there's a brief window of time where there is no way for the robot car to avoid an accident or having to violently swerve if the other vehicle suddenly turns toward it."[632] But accidents occur with far less frequency, because reasons for accidents such as distraction, tiredness, stress, emotions, etc. can be ruled out,[633] and they occur for other reasons – e.g., errors of communication. Fewer traffic jams, fewer accidents – great prospects, which also emerge from an ethical view on automation of mobility. Additionally, there are other positive consequences such as, for example, less pollution due to fewer traffic jams. In scenarios with automated mobility, it can be shown that the vehicle sharing associated with automated mobility will massively reduce the number of vehicles in circulation or owned by people. It can be expected that only 10% of today's vehicles will be needed for the same mobility as we have today.[634] At the same time, this much smaller number of vehicles will drive a lot more miles, be-

---

630 See Jonas 1985a: 42-43.
631 See Scholz et al. 2018; Kavanagh 2019.
632 Lin et al. 2017: 2.
633 See Axhausen 2016.
634 See Boesch et al. 2016.

cause the convenience of automated mobility and the associated time savings will result in more people being on the move. This positive effect on the environment is further increased because it can be assumed that the vehicles will become lighter, since the reduced risk of accidents will mean that no comprehensive heavyweight safety concept will be needed. Furthermore, because of the lower but more even speeds, there will be no heavy motors driving around the countryside. Also, because there will be no more "stop and go" traffic, less pollutants will be emitted. Such a development is welcome from an ethical perspective in respect to the guiding principles of responsibility, justice, and human rights.

At the same time, the automation of mobility puts privacy and data protection in danger. It also adds to global injustice (i.e., the globally unequal distribution of advantages and disadvantages). While rich countries can switch to automated mobility, people in poorer countries suffer from inhumane working conditions, which violate their human rights, or modern slavery, and from the destruction of the environment by the exploitation of raw materials necessary for automated driving systems or the production of automated driving systems.

7.4 Beta Versions

Data-based systems do not fall from heaven as a perfect outcome. It takes a highly complex, non-linear, and not always predictable innovation process consisting of several attempts to come up with a final version. Beta versions are part of this process. They allow improving the data-based system based on feedback from users prior to the eventual release. While launching a beta version, one is aware that this version is not finalized, but it still includes problems that may even be ethically relevant. Actually, it is part of the concept of a beta version that, instead of testing the final version with users, it is more efficient to release a non-fully mature version that will benefit more from the feedback of users for full development, incentivizing higher motivation from users to engage in the feedback-loop to reach the maturity of a data-based system together, creating a sense of ownership for the data-based system for the users, and managing the expectations of users for the reliability of the data-based system.

Being aware of the fact that it is hardly impossible for humans to achieve perfection, it is still worth noting, on the one hand, that users are intentionally exposed to an imperfect data-based system while accepting that this beta version could unintentionally cause negative effects – in some cases of ethical relevance. On the other hand, it needs to be taken into account from an ethical standpoint as well that beta versions serve the purpose of making the final versions as close to perfect as possible – in some cases contributing to the pursuit of an ethical positive. The ethical relevance of market pressures, goals, and economic incentives needs to be considered as well. Are beta versions ethically acceptable? How long can a beta version or a final version be delayed due to ethical considerations with the consciousness of the ethically positive impact of the innovation, which means also delaying the ethically positive impact? From an ethical perspective – taking into account justice, responsibility, and human rights – unjust and irresponsible actions as well as violations of human rights cannot be allegedly legitimated by the use of beta versions leading to a final version serving an ethical positive, because injustice and irresponsibility are not part of the testing characterizing a beta version and should be excluded prior to a beta version, and because human rights are universally valid – always, everywhere, for all humans. Therefore, these rights cannot be neglected in the phase of a beta version. Beyond human rights, a balance needs to be struck with the expected ethically positive impact.

7.5 Coerciveness[635]

The ethical reflection of digital transformation and data-based systems by applying the ethical principles of "responsibility", "omni-dynamic social justice", and "human rights" includes the ethical challenge that humans have difficulties "unlearning"[636] in the area of digital transformation and data-based systems. "In general, possession of an ability or power (in individuals or groups) does not yet mean its use. It can rest at will, ready for use, to be used on occasion and at the request and discretion of the subject."[637] In the area of digital transformation and data-based systems, this is different. "This so plausible relationship between ability and action, knowledge and application, possession and exercise of a power, however, does not apply to the fund of technical assets of a society which, like ours, has based its entire life in work and leisure on the constant updating of its technical potential in the interaction of all its parts."[638] On the one hand,

---

635 See Jonas 1985a: 44.
636 See Duerreinmatt 1962.
637 Jonas 1985a: 44.
638 Jonas 1985a: 44.

simply the technological invention by itself or technology-based innovation by itself causes an ethical burden to decide to use or not to use it. Humans are not able to pretend that a new technological invention or technology-based innovation does not exist once they have learned of its existence. This characteristic of the interaction between technology and ethics represents the ethical compulsion of technology.

On the other hand, the urge, the obsession, the addiction, and the social pressure to apply and to use technology-based innovation at any cost influences the ethical permeation of digital transformation and data-based systems.[639] Humans are confronted with a forward path full of technology-based innovation that is presented with a presupposed absoluteness as the only possible path forward – without alternatives. The question of the good life no longer seems to arise because there is the one and only digital and data-based response.

7.6 *The Paradox of Potent Impotence*

Like never before in the history of humanity, humans possess the power to create technology-based realities and/or a reality with a technological penetration, imprint, and dominance never seen before. Data-based systems are everywhere; everything is data-based. "Technics, as a universe of instrumentalities, may increase the weakness as well as the power of man."[640] In other words, present-day humans have higher potency in creating reality than ever before. An unprecedented portion of the world is being created by humans. At the same time, due to the enormous pace of technological progress in the domain of digital transformation and data-based systems, due to the intransparency[641] of some processes, due to the untraceability of some results because of the intransparency of some processes, and due to the high complexity of digital transformation and data-based systems, humans are impotent at foreseeing their actions and the consequences of their actions. "The gap between the ability to foretell and the power to act creates a novel moral problem. With the latter so superior to the former, recognition of ignorance becomes the obverse of the duty to know and

---

639 See Pagallo 2014.
640 Marcuse 1964: 185.
641 See Kosack / Fung 2014; Wachter et al. 2017; Doshi-Velez et al. 2017.

thus part of the ethics that must govern the evermore necessary self-policing of our outsized might."[642]

This impotence is extended further from the perspective of the individual. "The I, the free subjectivity, has created these factual orders; but it no longer knows how to encompass them and no longer knows how to penetrate them with itself."[643] As the collective forces itself into the foreground as the acting, the thinking and acting individual is rolled over, pushed aside or forced into the background. "If nothing succeeds like success, nothing captures like success. Whatever else belongs to the fullness of man is outshined in prestige by the expansion of his power, and so this expansion is, by binding more and more of man's powers to its business, accompanied by a shrinking of his self-concept and being. In the image that he maintains of himself – the programmatic conception that determines his current being as much as it reflects it – man is now more and more the maker of what he [or she] has produced and the door of what he [or she] will soon be able to do. Who is 'he' [or 'she']? Not you or me: it is the collective actor and the collective act, not the individual actor and the individual act that play a role here; it is the indefinite future much more than the contemporary space of action that provides the relevant horizon of responsibility."[644]

Beyond that, humans perceive themselves as powerless while trying legitimately and necessarily to identify the dimensions, relations, and spheres of responsibility – e.g., with the idea of an "ethical black box"[645] in data-based systems. "A core experience in our contemporary socio-technical lifeworld – often resulting in fear – concerns responsibility and accountability: namely, the difficulty to attribute responsibility and to locate accountability in ever more distributed and entangled socio-technical systems. Think small: about the difficulties of finding and reaching the person to make responsible in case of a non-functioning internet connection? Think big: who's responsible – accountable and liable – for the financial crisis?"[646]

Humans are trapped in this paradox of potent impotence, which affects the ethical discussion of digital transformation and data-based systems. The advantage of *homo faber socialis* over *homo sapiens singularis*, and the

---

642 Jonas 1985b: 28.
643 Cassirer 1985: 76; see also Ellul 1964: 418.
644 Jonas 1985b: 32.
645 See Winfield / Jirotka 2017.
646 Simon 2015: 136.

impression that it currently looks like a victory for *homo faber socialis*, challenges ethics fundamentally due to the significance of the autonomy of the individual for human dignity and for ethics as such. "Each time we thus bypass the human way of dealing with human problems, short-circuiting it by an impersonal mechanism, we have taken away something from the dignity of personal selfhood and advanced one step further on the road from responsible subjects to programmed behavior systems"[647] – data-based systems? *Homo faber singularis* does not give up though. "Technology, apparatus and mass existence do not exhaust human existence. (...) They come upon himself [herself], who is something else."[648]

More fundamentally, the paradox of potent impotence expresses itself in the striving for data-based systems *per se*: "If men create intelligent machines, or fantasize about them, it is either because they secretly despair for their own intelligence or because they are in danger of succumbing to the weight of a monstrous and useless intelligence which they seek to exorcise by transferring it to machines, where they can play with it and make fun of it. By entrusting this burdensome intelligence to machines, we are released from any responsibility to knowledge, much as entrusting power to politicians allows us to disdain any aspiration of our own to power. (...) Just as eyeglasses and contact lenses will arguably evolve one day into implanted prostheses for a species that has lost sight, it is similarly to be feared that artificial intelligence and the hardware that supports it will become a mental prosthesis for a species without the capacity for thought."[649] Humans run the risk of taking themselves out of the game, stealing the wheel, and leaving it to data-based systems.[650] Potent humans run the risk of making themselves impotent ...

7.7 *Risk of Anthropocentrism*[651]

Anthropocentrism represents a twofold ethical challenge of digital transformation and data-based systems. *First*, digital transformation and data-based systems, and especially the ethical reflection of both, remain within and must accept the boundaries of human reason. *Second*, the ethical as-

---

647 Jonas 1985b: 52.
648 Jaspers 1931: 61.
649 Baudrillard 1993: 51-52.
650 See Spielkamp 2019a; Kaeser 2019.
651 See Jonas 1985a: 46-48; Kirchschlaeger 2010a; Kirchschlaeger 2012a.

sessment of digital transformation and data-based systems must overcome the risk of focusing only on humanity. "But now the entire biosphere of the planet, with all its abundance of species, in its newly revealed vulnerability to excessive human intervention, is claiming its share of the respect due to everything that carries its purpose within itself – that is, all living things."[652] The application of human rights to the domain of digital transformation and data-based systems could create the impression that this challenge is not being met. This rough idea entails a misunderstanding.

Human rights protection is not possible without environmental protection. Jakob J. von Uexkuell has extended the meaning of "environment" so that "environment" consists of a "Merkwelt" (entirety of its attributes) and a "Wirkwelt" (entirety of its effects). Defined in this way, an environment encapsulates the sum of all its parts, and every living thing contained in an environment becomes part of its characterization.[653] If one understands the environment as the human, social, physical, and ecological context of human life, the relationship between environment and human rights is evident. The environment, as defined above, is relevant to the protection of human rights. As introduced above, human rights protect the essential parts of human life. If one thinks of these elements, it becomes obvious that there is a very close relationship between human rights and the environment. How could we think of the right to life[654] if the environment denies the possibility of human life? Environmental factors can lead to the death of human beings or shorten their lives decisively. Destruction of the environment leads to violations of human rights.[655] Therefore, human rights protection is not possible without environmental protection. While at the regional and national level the right to environment is protected in some legally binding instruments (e.g., Constitution of the Republic of South Africa: "Everyone has the right to an environment that is not harmful to their health or well-being; and to have the environment protected, for the benefit of present and future generations"[656]), at the international level the UN Declaration on the Rights of Indigenous Peoples states the following: "Indigenous peoples have the right to the conservation and protection of the environment and the productive capacity of their lands or

---

652 Jonas 1985a: 46.
653 See Fritsche / Zerling 2002.
654 See United Nations 1948: Article 3.
655 See Ziemer 2001.
656 South African Government 1996: Article 24.

territories and resources"[657]. Furthermore, the following instruments have to be taken in consideration: African Charter on Human and Peoples' Rights of 1981: "All peoples shall have the right to a general satisfactory environment favorable to their development"[658]; Protocol of San Salvador of 1988: "Everyone shall have the right to live in a healthy environment and to have access to basic public services"[659].

Human rights protection deals with environmental protection when the environment concerned is of an immediate and direct importance for human life. Many of the aspects of human life, which are protected by human rights, are essentially environmental. Therefore, one can say that human rights protect the environment in a certain way. Human rights could serve as a framework for the priority scale when one is dealing with different environmental issues. At the same time, environmental protection can benefit from human rights insofar as they lead to empowerment of the victims of environmental degradation and support the struggle against environmental destruction.

From an ecological perspective alone, a part of the ecological environment is directly and immediately relevant to human survival and the quality of human life. Despite the power of innovation, which humans have, they are nonetheless dependent on biophysical conditions and ecological laws. William Catton and Riley Dunlap developed a new ecological paradigm: humans are no longer understood as an exception to nature (exemptionalism) but as being dependent on biophysical conditions and ecological laws, except for their undoubted capability of innovation.[660] This distinct position of humans within the environment leads to the awareness that changes in the environment are relevant to human rights, as they bring with them changes in the human rights situation as well.

It is important to acknowledge that in considering the environment in this context, one's understanding of it is anthropocentric. Understanding the environment only from a human perspective and how it relates to human life is controversial and can be problematic. Undoubtedly not all of the ecological and physical environment is directly relevant to human life; however, it proves to be difficult to draw a line between the part that is relevant and the part that is not. This difficulty is largely because different

---

657 United Nations Declaration on the Rights of Indigenous Peoples of 2007: Article 29.
658 African Charter on Human and Peoples' Rights 1981: Article 24.
659 Organization of American States (OAS) 1988: Article 24.
660 See Catton / Dunlap 1980.

aspects of the environment are not isolated. As the web of life is so inter-connected, it is not possible to define the importance or "irrelevance" of a single aspect. The entire system of the environment and ecology may depend on that seemingly "irrelevant" aspect[661] due to the organic unity of the environment.

Furthermore, even if it were possible to draw such a line, to do so denies the environment any intrinsic value. If we distinguish between aspects of the environment that are relevant and those which are not, this helps us to understand the environment as playing a serving role for the benefit of human life, that is to say, as a "means" to the "end" of human life, not as an "end *per se*". For example, an animal in danger of extinction would be judged only with regard to its relevance for human life and not with regard to its own intrinsic value or its place within the environment.[662] This intrinsic value of the environment – instead of an instrumental value – can be understood as subjective intrinsic value[663] (value of what it is, not of what it can bring about) or as objective intrinsic value[664] (value of own properties or features, independent of anyone's attitudes or judgments). This limited understanding of the environment ends in the random exploitation of the environment and its licentious oppression to achieve the short-term economic goals and necessities of mankind.[665] Facing this difficult situation, one should stop attempting to draw an absolute line between the parts of the environment which are relevant to human life and those which are irrelevant, because the term does not seem to allow it. As an alternative, one should accept a minimal and moderate role for the human perspective for prioritization in environmental protection, rather than a full assessment of the environment. Furthermore, human rights could reinforce and support the victims of environmental degradation and destruction, and could be used to empower environmental activists in their struggle.

Overcoming the risk of anthropocentrism is highly relevant for the ethical discussion of digital transformation and data-based systems.

---

661 See Ziemer 2000.
662 See Birnie / Boyle 1992.
663 See Callicott 1989; Elliot 1992.
664 See Katz 1992; Rolston 1986.
665 See Shelton 1991.

7.8 Transhumanism

Transhumanism has some – if not all – of its conceptual roots in the thought that "the human species can, if it wishes, transcend itself. (...) We need a name for this new belief. Perhaps transhumanism will serve: man remaining man, but transcending himself, by realizing new possibilities of and for his human nature."[666] Transhumanism perceives itself as a liberation-movement. "As humanism freed us from the chains of superstition, let transhumanism free us from our biological chains."[667] On this horizon of liberation, transhumanism generates hopes for therapeutic applications, danger reduction, health improvement, and sense enhancement. At the same time, from an ethical perspective it causes concerns regarding abuse of power, addiction, loss of identity or personality, harmful effects, and overpopulation.[668] Of course, it cannot be claimed from an ethical standpoint that all ideas, concepts, and theories that fall under "transhumanism" are evaluated comprehensively in the context of this book. The book needs to be limited to looking at what unites a transhumanistic perspective in its core from an ethical point of view.

Transhumanism encompasses a broader movement that focuses on overcoming the limits of humans. At its core, it involves technological progress to improve humankind's intellectual, physiological, or psychological capacities, including both progress that humans have already achieved as well as progress they aspire to.[669] It embraces[670] "transhumanism" (striving for a transformation from humans 1.0 to humans x.0), "technological posthumanism" (striving to overcome humanity by creating an artificial alterity), "critical posthumanism" (striving to overcome a humanistic image of humans). While transhumanism does not want to overcome the human *per se* but to optimize and improve humans technologically,[671] posthumanism strives for surpassing humans and for replacing humans as the pinnacle of the creation with an artificial "superintelligence".[672]

Alternatively, transhumanism can be differentiated into "singularity", "superintelligence", and the optimization of humans based on technology

---

666 Huxley 1967: 195.
667 Young 2006: 87.
668 See Mikkelae 2015.
669 See, e.g., Bostrom 2008a.
670 On the following, see Loh 2018: 17-31.
671 See Loh 2018: 32-91.
672 See Loh 2018: 92-129.

in order to perfect[673] or overcome the "conditio humana" which is perceived as a limit.

"Singularity" is defined as the moment when data-based systems are equal to human intelligence.[674] Research projects striving for whole brain emulations (WBEs)[675] like, for example, the Blue Brain Project of the EPFL Lausanne, or the possibility of an "explosion of intelligence"[676] (data-based systems gaining intelligence in a short time through recursive self-improvement)[677] are steps toward this point. Singularity also describes the state where computer intelligence succeeds in integrating human intelligence and it is allowed to merge into a global consciousness[678], an "extended thinking entity"[679], or a "global brain"[680] – humans will be post-humans or transhumans.[681] "The current globalization process is closely linked and interacts with the process of digitization of information that has been observable for years; that is, with the historically unique technical progress in the field of ICT. In this context, and in a certain interpretation, humanity is developing into a hybrid human-technology system on the basis of cultural cooperation. This system is a super-organism in the form of an autopoietic system that will reach about 10 billion people in 2050, linked to many billions of technical systems, most of which will also be networked with each other through the Internet of Things. All in all, a global network structure will emerge, encompassing a form of technical intelligence that is capable of doing more and more of what humans are still needed for today. Corresponding algorithms are performing more and more tasks."[682]

As has been explained in chapter 3.5 Autonomy, "superintelligence" means that machines will massively outperform humans in various fields of intelligence[683] or with a very different form of intelligence. "Superintelligence" is "much smarter than the best human brains in practically every field, including scientific creativity, general wisdom and social skills. This definition leaves open how the superintelligence is implemented: it could

---

673 See van Est / Stemerding 2012.
674 See Singularity 2030 n.d.
675 See Bostrom / Sandberg 2008.
676 See Solomonoff 1985; Chalmers 2010.
677 See Good 1966; Schmidhuber 2006.
678 See Kurzweil 1999.
679 Moravec 1988: 116.
680 Heylighen 2015; Lenartowicz 2017.
681 See Grassie 2012.
682 Uenver 2015.
683 See Bostrom 2014.

be a digital computer, an ensemble of networked computers, cultured cortical tissue or what have you. It also leaves open whether the superintelligence is conscious and has subjective experiences."[684] Currently this outperformance of humans by machines is already the case, e.g., in memory, handling great amounts of data. Therefore, it can be expected that further areas of intelligence will follow – in an impressive time horizon. "Moore's law (...) states that processor speed doubles every eighteen months. The doubling time used to be two years, but that changed about fifteen years ago. The most recent data points indicate a doubling time as short as twelve months. This would mean that there will be a thousand-fold increase in computational power in ten years. Moore's law is what chip manufacturers rely on when they decide what sort of chip to develop in order to remain competitive."[685] This exponential growth of technological progress is also reflected in the Law of Accelerating Returns,[686] and, in general, in the history of technology.[687] The following explanation makes exponential growth easier to understand: "Bacteria grow by doubling. One bacterium divides to become two, the two divide to become 4, the 4 become 8, 16 and so on. Suppose we had bacteria that doubled in number this way every minute. Suppose we put one of these bacteria into an empty bottle at 11:00 in the morning, and then observe that the bottle is full at 12:00 noon. There's our case of just ordinary steady growth: it has a doubling time of one minute, it's in the finite environment of one bottle. I want to ask you three questions. Number one: at what time was the bottle half full? Well, would you believe 11:59, one minute before 12:00? Because they double in number every minute. And the second question: if you were an average bacterium in that bottle, at what time would you first realize you were running out of space? Well, let's just look at the last minutes in the bottle. At 12:00 noon, it's full; one minute before, it's half full; 2 minutes before, it's a quarter full; then one 8th; then one 16th. Let me ask you, at 5 minutes before 12:00, when the bottle is only 3% full and is 97% open space just yearning for development, how many of you would realize there's a problem?"[688] Taking this urgency into account, from an ethical perspective it needs to be combined with action against ethical challenges

---

684 Bostrom 2006: 11.
685 Bostrom 2006: 11.
686 See Kurzweil 2001.
687 See Kurzweil 1999.
688 Bartlett: 2007.

already present in order to avoid being distracted from present problems by future ones.[689]

In the context of "superintelligence" or "super-data-based systems", it also needs to be considered how these unique characteristics will affect the interaction between humans and machines. Apart from the possibility that "super-data-based systems" will help people and the world, other scenarios are possible. If the intelligence is equal, it can be assumed that humans and machines would leave each other in peace, because they possess equal intelligence and are therefore at a stalemate. If humans were slightly outclassed, this may result in the oppression of humans by the machines in order to eliminate any threat to the superiority of machines right from the beginning. In the case of obvious superiority of the machines, the machines will see humans as irrelevant – probably the same way humans currently view, for example, ants. Because it does not seem plausible that "superintelligence" will have a different relationship to humans than humans have with ants today.[690] And it may not only be humans who become irrelevant. The same could happen to the environment, because "super-data-based systems" are not dependent on Earth – amongst other things because of their bodylessness.

It is also plausible in the case of "super-data-based systems" that they will become so independent that the original reasons and purposes for their development might no longer be apparent. "It may come to a point where no one knows what the original programming of such a robot used to be, that it seems very independent, as if it would follow its own objectives."[691]

From an ethical perspective, we must also consider the possibility that ethical principles and rules might be watered down when self-learning systems connect with superintelligence. For example, an automatic weapons system that is supposed to kill "enemies" could tell a self-driving vehicle to no longer respect the dignity of all humans and to drive over a person in order to optimize its purpose – transporting a passenger from A to B as quickly as possible. "Nobody can predict how a hypothetical superintelligence would act. Why should a superintelligence even bother with the species homo sapiens? It could just as well rid this planet, contaminated as it is by the Industrial Revolution, of human beings completely. Current active support for – or at least tolerance of – developing a superintelligence is analogous to promoting or allowing the development of atomic weapons

---

689 See Crawford / Calo 2016.
690 See Harari 2017: 116.
691 Neuhaeuser 2014: 270.

in the world's research laboratories, or of recognizing the need for their control only after the planet has been subjected to nuclear devastation … It would make far better sense to prevent competition between superintelligence in the first place!"[692]

Finally, from an ethical perspective, we need to consider the plausible possibility that super-data-based systems could appropriate a fundamentally unethical position by perceiving themselves as special from a moral standpoint[693] – beyond the realm of ethics and morality.

In the following, the focus will be on the technology-based optimization of humans with the objective to complete or overcome with technology-based means the *conditio humana*, which is perceived as a limitation.

The technology-based optimization of humans can include medico-technological and neuro-technological applications (e.g., brain-computer-interfaces), which are called "cyborgs"[694]. "The word 'cyborg' is composed of parts of the words 'cybernetic' and 'organism'. A cyborg is a hybrid being that has an 'organic' base or possesses organic parts, which has been complemented 'cybernetically'. The word fragment 'cyb' that points to 'cybernetic' or 'cyber' is a rather loose link to 'cybernetic' in its narrower sense. In most cases, various forms of technology are meant. 'Cyber' is a cipher for an information processing high technology (see 'cyberspace')."[695] The change of paradigm in the course of space research has decisively influenced the emergence of this term, where the focus was no longer primarily on the adaption of the environment to humans (like technology on Earth), but the adaptation of humans to the environment.[696] In the current ethical discourse, the term "cyborg" offers conceptual clarity. "With the aid of the cyborg we can reflect upon forms of self-technification."[697]

When talking about cyborgs it needs to be taken into account, however, that in view of the "sorites paradox"[698] there is also a need for a "scala cyborgensis", where "different grades of 'cyborgism' of humans are arranged on a scale according to the means used."[699] The "sorites paradox" (sorites means "heap" in Greek) emphasizes that a heap of one hundred grains still

---

692 Thun-Hohenstein 2017: 21.
693 See Petersen 2017.
694 See Warwick 2002.
695 Heilinger / Mueller 2016: 48.
696 See Clynes / Kline 1995.
697 Heilinger / Mueller 2016: 63.
698 Sorensen 2003.
699 Heilinger / Mueller 2016: 51.

remains a heap when one grain is taken away and only 99 grains remain. "Analogously to this classical paradox one will also get into difficulties as regards to the definition of cyborgs. When glasses do not turn someone into a cyborg, a hearing aid also doesn't. When a hearing aid does not turn someone into a cyborg, a cochlear-implant also doesn't. When a cochlear-implant does not turn someone into a cyborg, a retina-implant also doesn't. When a retina-implant does not turn someone into a cyborg, a brainstem-implant also doesn't. When a brainstem-implant doesn't, then an artificial brain also doesn't etc."[700] The "scala cyborgensis" allows one to retain the usefulness and informative value of the term cyborg by going beyond the overly general, criteria-based definition of "man-machine hybrid"[701]. The following could serve as criteria:[702]

- Intimate: "Persons who have some intimate (…) relationship with a machine."[703]
- "Persons who have some (…) occasionally necessary relationship with a machine."[704]: vital, life improving, striving for "human normality" (e.g., a cochlear implant: electronic device partially restoring hearing for people who have severe hearing loss from inner-ear damage and who receive limited benefit from hearing aids).
- Biocompatibility: technical substitution of organic parts in addition to certain technical handling of the organic substrate.
- Neuro: "Cyborg technology is characterized by the integration of electronics and nerve tissue"[705].
- Control: "a real cyborg technology excerpts control of some kind over the body. A pacemaker is a cyborg technology, because it steps in to regulate heart function when it senses defibrillation. This kind of control gets at the heart, so to speak, of what it means to be a cyborg: to have cybernetic, meaning 'algorithmic and automated', control of the organism."[706]
- Enhancement: "A cyborg is a human-machine-hybrid who is noticeably improved or optimized in relation to an anthropological norm. Thus, a relatively small technical enhancement of the human performance

---

700 Heilinger / Mueller 2016: 50.
701 Irrgang 2005: 214.
702 See Heilinger / Mueller 2016: 53-57.
703 McGee / Maguire 2001: 1.
704 McGee / Maguire 2001: 1.
705 Rippe 2004: 24; see Zoglauer 2006.
706 Chorost 2005: 41.

spectrum could turn a human into a cyborg, if it contains an optimiz-ing quality, whereas a quantitatively large technical substitution with-out optimizing quality would not be a criterion for an unambiguous cyborgization of the human."[707]

To the previous cyborg discourse, a further criterion should be added:

- "digital change": digital change includes a technology-based change of the human without specifying whether this will result in a technology-based optimization of the human. On a conceptual level, this should cover the possibility that the term "cyborg" also refers to cases where a technology-based optimization of the human is reached in a certain as-pect – or is merely aspired to – but only when it is a digital change and not a technology-based improvement of the human.

To sum up, in the ethical discourse about the technology-based optimiza-tion of humans, there are the following positions:[708]

- The *call for limitation* as put forth by Virtue Ethics would suggest that we practice humility, to accept one's own fate, to accept the human need for salvation, fragmentation and the endangerment or vulnerabili-ty of human existence.[709]
- *Generic ethical objections* are raised against technical interventions and protection of the integrity of the human genus is called for.[710]
- The *freedom to self-determination* is upheld as the talk about human na-ture as historically grown is relativized: "If there is something solid in the nature of humans it is their cultural variety and openness for con-tinued new and changed definitions."[711] This leads to a responsibility for humans when dealing with new technology-based inventions.[712] This freedom to self-determination may also entail that each person may decide for him- or herself which technology-based optimization they want to use.[713] Finally, it can also serve as the pivot-point of an ethical evaluation of technology-based enhancement.[714] "Starting from the theory that the autonomy of a person and the good life contained

---

707 Heilinger / Mueller 2016: 56.
708 See Zimmermann 2015a.
709 See Sandel 2007; Jessen 2013; Jessen 2014; Hofheinz 2008: 69-87.
710 See Habermas 2001a; Nussbaum 2006; Fukuyama 2002; see also Herzberg 2019.
711 Birnbacher 2009: 238.
712 See Birnbacher 2009; Bayertz 2009.
713 See Sorgner 2016.
714 See also Kipke 2011.

in it are ethically decisive in an objective sense with regard to normatively assessing justified interventions of enhancement, the ethical approval or rejection of an intervention must be made dependent on the promotion or impairment of these provisions, as well as the autonomy of the decision itself."[715]

- A *duty to improve* was meant in the sense that humans should use the technical options at their disposal in order to improve humans.[716]
- A *farewell to a special position* should be acknowledged from a post-humanistic perspective, which classifies humans as part of a great life energy and expects them to positively surrender to the development of machine, animal, and earth.[717]

Beyond that, when thinking of human rights as an ethical instrument, the technology-based optimization of humans garners criticism, since it could mean that the humans will be illegitimately excluded from being entitled with human rights in three ways: *First*, it leads to an exclusion of humans because they are to be optimized based on arbitrarily determined criteria. This has a discriminating effect on those humans who are characterized by exactly those criteria. There is the danger that one's own self-optimization could even create the potential for individual humans, groups of humans, or humans as disruptive elements to be destroyed. *Second*, access to technology-based optimization could end up being restricted. *Third*, humans are all excluded as humans. "The desire to engineer transcendence expresses the modernist drive to mastery and control, but its success is predicated on making humanity obsolete."[718]

In addition, the technology-based optimization of humans provokes a hermeneutic critique due to the surprisingly naïve blind faith in technological progress. For example, the "Transhumanist Declaration" states: "Humanity stands to be profoundly affected by science and technology in the future. We envision the possibility of broadening human potential by overcoming aging, cognitive shortcomings, involuntary suffering, and our confinement to planet Earth."[719] This blind faith is made apparent by statements such as the following: "The pothole in the transhumanist road (...) is the naiveté with which believers in progress remove the ambiguities of human history, which leads them to maintain confidence in the good that

---

715 Runkel 2010: 297.
716 See Savulescu / Kahane 2009.
717 See Braidotti 2014.
718 Tirosh-Samuelson 2017: 279.
719 Humanity Plus 2009; see also Wertheim 1999: 199.

progress can bring while denying the potential growth of evil."[720] The ethically negative potential must be identified and addressed. "It is essential to use caution when developing AI systems that can exceed human levels of general intelligence, or that can facilitate the creation of such systems."[721]

Linked with this critical assessment is the critical observation of the proclamation that this kind of technological progress will mean the end of the impact of destiny and the victory of human freedom over said destiny. "The new super-humanists are mistaken in their assumption that the eugenic use of genetic engineering will lead to man's final liberation from fate. In truth, advances in the fields of medical genetics, predictive medicine and reproductive medicine are leading to new manifestations of destiny."[722]

This leads to critical questions with regard to the economic market potential of transhumanistic prospects and the use of talent and resources in a world of limited resources.

In connection with this aspect, the social Darwinian characteristics of transhumanism ("It's the economic imperative of a competitive marketplace that is the primary force driving technology forward and fueling the law of accelerating returns. (...) Economic imperative is the equivalent of survival in biological evolution"[723]), combined with a neoliberal blind trust in a free market ("I believe that maintaining an open free-market system for incremental scientific and technological progress, in which each step is subject to market acceptance, will provide the most constructive environment for technology to embody widespread human values"[724]) generate ethical criticism because they deny the necessity of ethical legitimation of technological progress as well as its guidance and control by humans. "To control technology, to control the direction of human evolution, we must have some idea of where we are going and how far, else we will be mere passengers rather than drivers of the chariot of evolution."[725]

The technology-based optimization of humans also serves as an equality within equality, which means it contains the risk of dissolving difference, which would lead to homogenization, uniformization, and levelling of humans.

---

720 Peters 2011: 80-81; see Childs 2015.
721 Soares / Fallenstein 2017: 1; see also Mueller / Bostrom 2014; Mueller / Bostrom 2016.
722 Koertner 2010: 131.
723 Kurzweil 2005: 96.
724 Kurzweil 2005: 420.
725 Ferkiss 1969: 203.

In addition, determining certain conditions for a life worth living contradicts the idea that there are no preconditions for human dignity of all humans.

Moreover, it will have an impact on all humans becoming "the slow and increasingly inefficient part"[726].

Furthermore, it would have a discriminating impact on humans who are different with regard to the characteristics and features of theirs that are to be optimized.

In addition, it would create the risk that the strive for perfection eliminates the sense of solidarity among humans.

Beyond that, it must be doubted if humans are even able to live up to the responsibility they are trying to attain for themselves as subjects of responsibility. "This most ambitious dream of homo faber, summed up in the phrase that man will take his own evolution in hand, with the aim of not just preserving the integrity of the species but of modifying it by improvements of his own design. Whether we have the right to do it, whether we are qualified for that creative role, is the most serious question that can be posed to man finding himself suddenly in possession of such fateful powers. Who will be the image-makers, by what standards, and on the basis of what knowledge?"[727]

Moreover, the technology-based optimization of humans is eugenics. "'Eugenic' means to take a targeted influence on the organic substrate of a person, when the manipulation aims at 'increasing' the physical or mental functions or abilities of this person. The line cannot always be drawn exactly between the therapy of an illness and the 'improvement' of a disposition or a condition. However, this is no reason to refrain from distinguishing between the restoring of a disturbed health status and the creation of new characteristics. Because from a normative viewpoint, the distinction between therapeutic and enhancing interferences are generally of interest."[728] When dealing with the question of a line between therapeutic and enhancing interferences, the self-determination of the persons affected should be respected – in particular when taking into account the "first-person-perspective" and the "self-relation", as mentioned above in subchapter 6.4 Human Rights as Ethical Frame of Reference.[729]

---

726 Armstrong 2014: 23.
727 Jonas 1985b: 52-53.
728 Habermas 2008: 9.
729 See Heilinger 2010; Mukerji / Nida-Ruemelin 2014.

Furthermore, in the process of technology-based optimization, humans will no longer be understood as subjects, but as objects that need to be modified or optimized.[730] "Whoever asks about humans today, always also asked if we even still want to be humans. Or, aptly formulated, the recent human being finds his or her happiness only in images of his or her non-humanity. The picture that modern humans paint of themselves is therefore always crossed out already. The contemporary answer to the question: what is the human being? would be: all that he or she shouldn't be. Maybe it is time to defend the human being (...), this fragile and questionable being, which, according to older interpretations, always has to oscillate between freedom and need, between mind and body, between finiteness and infinity, between nature and culture."[731] From an ethical standpoint informed by human rights protecting human dignity, there is a need to defend humans against this "statement of disappointment"[732] representing transhumanism.

From a transhumanistic perspective, humans are robbed of their options to have a say and to participate. "Now techne becomes the product of the will to domination, power and control (...) a power on its own, leveling all culture; annihilating all at-home-ness in the cosmos, uprooting all other questions in favor of those questions under its control; producing a planetary thought-world where instrumental reason, and it alone, will pass a thought. (...) The object cannot think. The subject will not. We began as technical agents of our willful destiny. We seem to end as technicized spectators at our own execution."[733]

If – in the sense of the above introduced "singularity" – human intelligence should be integrated into global awareness by merging it with computer-intelligence, this would also mean surrendering individual subjectivity, which would be the end of human autonomy and of moral capability.[734] "If we are downloaded into our technology, what are the chances that we will thereafter be ourselves or even human?"[735]

Beyond that, the two types of dehumanization, which Francis Fukuyama perceives in the sense of a criticism of transhumanism, need also be taken into account:[736] *Firstly*, human dignity of all humans and human

---

730 See Palazzani 2017: 386.
731 Liessmann 2016: 24; see also Alexander 2003: 51.
732 Alexander 2003: 51.
733 Tracy 1981: 352.
734 See Habermas 2008: 7-14.
735 Joy 2000.
736 See Fukuyama 2003.

rights would be subordinated to technology-based progress. *Secondly*, non-human, post-human creatures will be created, which will exterminate humans. (Francis Fukuyama does not exaggerate: Jean-Francois Lyotard coins "a way of destroying the modern project while creating an impression of its fulfillment" as "liquidation"[737].) And one could add as a third type of dehumanization the reductionist minimization of humans "to brain function, its valuing of intelligence more highly than love or compassion, its dehumanization through technology, its underappreciation of human embeddedness in our bodies, and its rejection of biblical promises of a resurrected spiritual body."[738] Therefore, arguing for a concept of dignity that is inclusive enough to be applied even to the many possible posthuman beings[739] seems to entail a different understanding of what human dignity is about. Perhaps the conceptual background for this attempt is an understanding of dignity as a quality.[740]

Beyond that, the call for crossing the borders between humans and data-based systems – which, in the interactionist model introduced above in chapter 2 The Correlation between Ethics and Technology, would also be embraced through simultaneously keeping and emphasizing the difference between human subjects and data-based systems as objects – would in a posthumanist version[741] lead to the merging of humans and machines as well as in a nonhumanist version, starting from the notion that there is no longer any difference between data-based systems and humans[742] and that humans should not be the point of orientation while creating data-based systems perceived as nonmachines.[743]

Finally, the principle of vulnerability introduced above in subchapter 6.4 Human Rights as Ethical Frame of Reference offers a way to differentiate the various vulnerabilities. This again allows one to understand the vulnerability of humans, not with discrimination or with any negative connotation – contrary to the transhumanist demonization of the human limitations – but rather as an essential characteristic of humans and human existence as well as of "human embodiment"[744]. In the principle of vulnerability, the human-rights based approach to vulnerability is conceived in the

---

737 Lyotard 1988: 36.
738 Peters 2015: 146.
739 See Bostrom 2005.
740 See Bostrom 2008b.
741 See Haraway 1991.
742 See Coeckelbergh 2017.
743 See Coeckelberg 2020: 43.
744 See Pugh 2017.

form of preventing the transformation of vulnerability into a concrete injury or violation (e.g., human rights protection for preventing violations of the physical or mental integrity of all humans) or, if vulnerability is transformed into an injury or violation, in the form of compensation (e.g., access to healthcare in case of illness).

7.9 Medicine and Health Care and Data-Based Systems

7.9.1 Access to Health Care

Half of the people in this world have no access to essential health services. In addition, one needs to consider a global shortage of 18 million health workers. Digital transformations open up an opportunity to improve global access to healthcare.[745] The report of the UN Secretary-General's High-level Panel on Digital Cooperation of June 2019 states: "By 2030, every adult should have affordable access to digital networks, as well as digitally-enabled (…) health services, as a means to make a substantial contribution to achieving the SDGs (Sustainable Development Goals)."[746] "Digital health" has the potential to lead to considerable improvement in this area and to contribute to the recognition of the importance of global healthcare: "Universal health coverage is fundamental for achieving the Sustainable Development Goals related not only to health and well-being, but also to eradicate poverty in all its forms and dimensions."[747] The initiative "The International Digital Health & AI Research Collaborative I-DAIR" is an example of this. "The I-DAIR Project seeks to advance the UNSG's High-level Panel on Digital Cooperation's recommendations related to digital health as well as targets set at the World Health Organization (WHO) on universal and quality health coverage. The proposed pathway is to work with diverse stakeholders to co-create an international platform to promote responsible and inclusive AI research and digital technology development for health inter alia. This will be done by moving towards data for health as a global public good and by addressing key governance, validation, benchmarking and collaboration challenges in research on AI and digital health. (…) The goal of the project is to co-create a neutral trusted platform for enabling global research collaborations on digital health and

---

745 On health care in rural areas, see, e.g., Frehe et al. 2016.
746 UN Secretary-General's High-level Panel on Digital Cooperation 2019, 1A.
747 United Nations 2019.

AI for health, and for convening stakeholders to develop and share global public goods as well as solve problems for the inclusive, equitable and responsible deployment of data and AI for health."[748] Internet-enhanced health communication,[749] AI-supported health communication,[750] telemedicine, online medical consultations, online-psychotherapy, etc. are other digital ways to increase access to health care,[751] which is positive from an ethical perspective, especially based on the principle of justice and human rights.

From an ethical point of view, in such an endeavor, challenges emerge in particular with regard to the human right to privacy and data protection – in particular informational self-determination – trust, improper and/or insufficient youth engagement, quality of datasets, appropriate reference data, and data hoarding.

7.9.2 Personalized Medicine and Health Care

Digital transformation, e.g., blockchain technology, can serve the realization of the human right to health by providing the possibility of decentralized storage of and access to the personal health record[752] (consisting, e.g., also of genomic data[753]) which would allow personalized,[754] more independent, precise, efficient, effective,[755] and mobile[756] health care. From an ethical point of view, this can be viewed as an innovative attempt to contribute to the realization of the human right to health.

At the same time, this supposed personalization of medicine and health care runs the risk of compromising the individuality of all humans by combining them all into one health-group or risk-group, etc., and neglecting the individual human. This would be problematic from an ethical perspective. "What looks like individualization is only a massing as a consumer group, state of mind, political attitude. Without hesitation and practically without contradiction, people surrender themselves to the 'demon

---

748 Digital Health & AI Research Collaborative (I-DAIR) n.d.
749 See Schulz / Rubinelli 2010.
750 See Green et al. 2013.
751 See Heinrich 2018; Schumann 2018: 39.
752 See Lee 2017; Herbst 2016.
753 See Raisaro et al. 2014; Mathieu et al. 2013.
754 See for an overview Schildmann et al. 2013; Winkler 2013.
755 See Schleidgen / Marckmann 2013; Kersten 2013.
756 See OECD 2019a.

of number'"[757]. The individual becomes a node within a data-based network of data – an "infinite feedback point"[758]. "Personalized medicine and healthcare" rely on an algorithmic analysis of the profiles of humans instead of a personal medical examination. It is not the individual human that is of interest to personalized medicine and health care but rather his or her data and numbers and/or his or her patterns. In actual fact, there are two ways in which what is called "personalized medicine and health care" can be debunked as "depersonalized medicine and health care" or "dehumanized medicine and health care": It is not the individual humans but rather their data and numbers and/or their patterns that are the focus and the object of interest. The process of medicine and health care itself is depersonalized and dehumanized as well due to the automation of as many areas as possible using data-based systems that strive for as little human input and human interaction as possible. This "depersonalization" and "dehumanization" of medicine and health care is ethically problematic based on human rights and on human dignity.

Beyond that, "personalization and assistance always have the other side of monitoring and control."[759] The latter two must be avoided and combatted because of their problematic nature from an ethical standpoint informed by the ethical point of reference of human rights.

Finally, "personalized medicine and healthcare" must of course respect the human dignity of all humans (and therefore distance itself from instrumentalizing or objectivation of humans), it must respect the human right to privacy – based on the principle of indivisibility of human rights –[760] it must honor the human right to data-protection,[761] and the human right to informational autonomy, including the right not to know,[762] it must overcome the significant challenges of big data "volume – velocity – variety – veracity"[763], and it must address the risk of big data being a source of systematic discrimination.[764]

---

757 Hofstetter 2017: 86.
758 Tiqqun 2007: 31.
759 Steil 2019: 32.
760 See Kirchschlaeger 2015a.
761 See Grimm / Braeunlich 2015.
762 See Duttge 2016.
763 Helbing 2015a: 3; see Helbing 2015b; Kshetri 2014; Weichert 2014; Witt 2015.
764 See Buolamwini / Gebru 2018.

7.9.3 Data-Based Health Care

"There has been tremendous growth in the range of information collected, including clinical, genetic, behavioral and environmental data. Every day, healthcare professionals, biomedical researchers and patients produce vast amounts of data from an array of devices. These include electronic health records (EHRs), genome sequencing machines, high-resolution medical imaging, smartphone applications and ubiquitous sensing, as well as Internet of Things (IoT) devices that monitor patient health."[765] This data supports the management of health systems[766] and further enhances the "learning" of "learning health systems". "Health care systems worldwide are challenged by changing patterns of communicable and non-communicable diseases, population aging, increasing technological progress and growing resource constraints. To ensure fitness-for-purpose, effectiveness and efficiency of health systems, decision-making on all levels of the system needs to be supported by the best available evidence. The utilized evidence should relate to high-quality research that addresses health system needs, including the evaluation of benefits and costs of different courses of action. In learning health systems (LHS), the research agenda is collaboratively developed to be responsive to current health system needs and to facilitate the flow of information at levels of policy, research and practice. By doing so, the LHS are promoting evidence-based policy, making and create continuous learning processes that match health system needs. This in turn creates a culture of shared responsibility, creating a learning environment that links all actors in the health system – patients, health care providers, insurers, researchers and health policy makers – in the common cause to strengthen the health system, improve population health, and to ultimately achieve better value for the money in healthcare."[767]

Beyond that, healthcare is one of the areas currently affected in reality by the digital transformation and the use of data-based systems[768] (e.g., robots or robots in interaction with humans operating on humans and further improving precision medicine). Such surgical procedures benefit from the high precision, the reliability, the lack of need for rest (robots can work seven days a week 24 hours a day without getting tired) and the lack of emotions in robots. They serve the improvement of the quality of life

---

765 OECD 2019a; see OECD 2015.
766 See OECD 2019a.
767 Swiss Learning Health System n.d.
768 See Gigerenzer et al. 2016.

and dignity of the patient by reducing the pain of the patient, his or her recovering times, etc. From an ethical point of view, and taking into consideration human rights as an ethical instrument, this is positive.

An additional example highlights another positive aspect of data-based health care from an ethical standpoint: "An assistant for visually impaired people illustrates how a machine-based system influences its environment. It makes recommendations (e.g. how a visually impaired person can avoid an obstacle or cross the street) for a given set of objectives (travel from one place to another). It does so using machine and/or human-based inputs (large tagged image databases of objects, written words and even human faces) for three ends. First, it perceives images of the environment (a camera captures an image of what is in front of a person and sends it to an application). Second, it abstracts such perceptions into models automatically (object recognition algorithms that can recognize a traffic light, a car or an obstacle on the sidewalk). Third, it uses model inference to recommend options for outcomes (providing an audio description of the objects detected in the environment) so the person can decide how to act and thereby influence the environment."[769]

Moreover, data-based systems of image-analysis can support physicians in making medical diagnoses, e.g., the identification of health problems by a radiologist. "If we consider a simplified characterization of the job of a radiologist it would be that they examine an image in order to characterize and classify that image and return an assessment to a physician. While often that assessment is a diagnosis (i.e., 'the patient has pneumonia'), in many cases, the assessment is negative (i.e., 'pneumonia not excluded'). In that regard, this is stated as a predictive task to inform the physician of the likelihood of the state of the world. Using that, the physician can devise a treatment. These predictions are what machines are aiming to provide. In particular, it might provide a differential diagnosis of the following kind: Based on Mr. Patel's demographics and imaging, the mass in the liver has a 66.6% chance of being benign, 33.3% chance of being malignant, and a 0.1% of not being real."[770] From an ethical point of view, and taking into consideration human rights as an ethical instrument, this is positive. In the case of "autonomous" predictive systems in health care, the ethical perspective differentiates between the absence versus the presence of humans in the prediction-process. This makes it impossible to have trust in "autonomous" predictive systems, since trust requires – as briefly mentioned

---

769   OECD 2019a.
770   Agrawal et al. 2018: 7.

above in chapter 4 Critical Review of Terms – an interpersonal relationship and therefore humans.[771] The growing absence of humans in medical and health care-processes creates a challenge for trust in medicine and health care.[772]

From the perspective of responsibility, ethical questions arise as to how much humans should rely on data-based systems – the risk of "overtrust" needs to be addressed resolutely –[773] and as to how far the decision-making power of data-based systems should go and who will be held responsible in the possible event of an error. Here, the thoughts provided in chapter 3 Can Ethical Judgment Be Delegated to Technologies? can be applied concretely. At the end of the day, no machine can carry responsibility, because it lacks moral capability. It is always humans who bear the responsibility.[774] This leads to a clear limitation on the decision-making power of robots. On the other hand, it shows clear lines for where a solution may be found for allocating responsibility, because humans are the subjects of responsibility. For example, it could be the surgeons, the director of the clinic, the company which developed the robot (and, based on the complexity of the programming of such systems, probably not the single software engineer), etc.

Surgeon-robots, as an example, also open up the possibility that, one day, robots will replace human surgeons completely. It could also be organized and structured in such a way that the surgeon, who can be relieved of routine tasks in her or his professional life, is able to devote more time to tasks where a human surgeon is needed, e.g., for the interpersonal interaction with patients or for research. From an ethical perspective, however, it is likely that most of the realistic examples embrace a certain kind of ambivalence. In the case of the examples just mentioned, they also lead to, for example, the reduction of paid labor-market, which will be discussed later (see in more detail below in subchapter 7.18 Reduction of Paid Jobs and subchapter 8.2 Society-, Entrepreneurship-, Research-Time-Model [SERT]). The last example mentioned above provokes questions from a social justice perspective because high-tech medical treatment is very expensive (among others, often because of patents) which could exclude or discriminate some

---

771   See Hartmann 2011: 82-85; Nickel/Franssen/Kroes 2010.
772   See Nickel/Frank 2020.
773   See Borenstein et al. 2017.
774   See Manzeschke 2014.

humans. Other ethical issues emerge out of the corresponding legal discussion.[775]

In health care the robotized, automatized or machine-based support of humans with disabilities empowers them to live an autonomous life – with health-enabling technologies, "information tools that systematically process data, information and knowledge about the state of health of a person and, if necessary, of their environment, in particular their living environment. The aim is always to keep the state of health of this person stable, to improve it and/or to reduce the negative results of an illness and thus give the person the longest possible life of independence and self-determination, with high quality of life and with social participation and self- and co-responsibility"[776]. This so-called "ambient-assisted living"[777], "pervasive healthcare"[778], "ubiquitous healthcare"[779], "eHealth"[780], or "smart homes"[781] have in this respect and with reference to human rights a positive potential, because they promote in particular the human right to life, the human right to security (by addressing different facets of security – objective security including supply security and operational security, and subjective security including individual perception of security)[782], and the human right to freedom and self-determination. How can this be imagined in concrete terms? "Assistant health technologies can collect, analyze and, if necessary, pass on health-related data outside of the body (for example in the form of a pulse chronometer, an accelerometer or a mobile phone), inside the body (for example in a pacemaker or a knee prosthesis) or space-related (for example in an apartment). Their tasks are to send an alarm and indicate an emergency (for example in the case of a fall) or give support in the case of (mainly chronic) illnesses and functional deficits. Sometimes, they are also used for causes unrelated to health, for example to assist with communication, social inclusion and daily activities"[783]. Health prevention, diagnostics, therapy, and care can benefit from these new, cost-effective options. Digital self-measurement allows humans to control medical surveillance of one's own body and its functions, as well as pre-symptomat-

---

775 See Winter 2005.
776 Haux et al. 2016: 131.
777 See Koch et al. 2009; Bachinger / Fuchs 2013; Ewers 2010.
778 See Anrich et al. 2010.
779 See Marschollek et al. 2013.
780 See Haux 2010.
781 See Ludwig et al. 2010.
782 See Grewe 2015.
783 Haux et al. 2016: 132.

ic medication.[784] When humans are fully surveilled in this manner and when their homes[785] become "new health locations"[786], the human right to privacy and data protection, in particular the aspect of informational self-determination (see in more detail in subchapter 7.17 Data Protection and Privacy), comes into play and its protection must be given top priority. The latter – consistent human rights protection and realization of human rights – becomes particularly urgent because of the enormous economic potential.

For example, when multinational corporations strive to cover the entire data-based process themselves (health prevention, diagnostic, therapy, care), it is their objective to eliminate independent doctors. When humans are informed by the same actor about what they should do to prevent an illness, what to do if they are ill, that they are ill, and what medication would help against this illness, which will also be distributed by the same actor – the same multinational corporation, the alarm bell rings. In other words: Based on the collected data, a pharmaceutical company tells you where there are health risks and what could be done to prevent or treat them (and the same company will make you specific corresponding offers). Economically speaking, it is not surprising that multinational corporations of the pharmaceutical industry enter into strategic cooperation with tech companies[787] in order to maximize their access to data and expertise for handling such data volumes.

This "closed-circle approach" to health care raises the fundamental question of what the objectives are in using these assisting health technologies, and, more generally, why more and more data-based systems are being introduced in healthcare. "Increasingly, policy makers and healthcare providers are turning their attention to robots as one solution among others to overcome shortages in healthcare resources and personnel anticipated worldwide."[788] Is the growing use of data-based systems in health care about cost efficiency, about avoiding uncomfortable public discourse on the necessity of allocating more financial resources to the health system, about maximizing profit, or about humans and their dignity? This question proves to be of particular relevance when one considers that

---

784 See Karsch / Roche 2016.
785 See Meyer / Huffziger 2015.
786 See Haux et al. 2016.
787 E.g., Novartis and Microsoft see Aiolfi 2019, Roche and the online-platforms Flatiron Health and Mysugr see Finanzen.ch 2018.
788 Van Wynsberghe 2015: 1.

healthcare is a personnel-intensive sector because it provides person-related services.[789]

This question proves to be of particular relevance in light of the "googlization of health research"[790], which entails the phenomenon whereby major consumer technology corporations (e.g., Amazon, Apple, Facebook, Google, IBM, Microsoft) become active in health and biomedicine because of their particular expertise in the collection, management, and analysis of data.

This question proves to be of essential relevance because multinational technology corporations are trying to become the main actors in biopolitics – an area that should be in the hands of the democratically legitimized state – and said corporations are trying to govern humans. "It has been understood that it is not through repression, but rather through enticing communication; not through rude disciplining, but rather through motivated, cybernetically orchestrated self-regulation that it is possible to govern much more comprehensively: offers instead of prohibitions."[791]

This question proves to be of fundamental relevance because this economic development poses an unprecedented threat to the right to privacy and the right to data protection.[792]

This question proves to be of relevance to the current scenario as opposed to future potential scenarios. For example, "a data sharing partnership between Google DeepMind and the NHS illustrates how some of these issues are already playing out. Announced in 2016, the collaboration between DeepMind and the Royal Free London, an NHS Foundation Trust, granted DeepMind access to identifiable information on 1.6 million of its patients in order to develop an app to help medical professionals identify patients at risk of acute kidney injury (AKI). The terms of this agreement (...) lacked transparency and suffered from an inadequate legal and ethical basis. Indeed, following an investigation, the Information Commissioner's Office (...) ruled that this transfer of data and its use for testing the app breached data protection law. Namely, patients were not at all aware that their data was being used. Under UK common law, patient data can be used without consent if it is for the treatment of the patient, a principle known as 'direct care', which the Trust invoked in its defense. But as critics argue, insofar as only a small minority of the patients whose

---

789 See Schoenauer / Horneber 2011: 441.
790 See Sharon 2016.
791 Nosthoff / Maschewski 2019: 73.
792 See Schaar 2016.

data was transferred to DeepMind had ever been tested or treated for AKI, appealing to direct care could not justify the breadth of the data transfer."[793]

Google declares: "We've mapped the world. Now let's map human health."[794] Its "Project Baseline" is about promoting health through Reality Mining. With its company Verily (which received a great deal of attention in the COVID-19-pandemic and free advertising by the former president of the USA)[795], Google develops wearables (wearables will be further discussed below in subchapter 7.16) to get the personal health data of as many humans as possible. Google sells its activities with slogans like "sharing is caring", "together, we can invent the future of data-powered healthcare", "take action and tackle the challenge of preventing disease for future generations!", and "make your mark on the map of human health"[796]. The idea is to "quantify" humankind.[797]

Tim Cook, CEO of Apple, states: "If you zoom out into the future, and you look back, and you ask the question, 'What was Apple's greatest contribution to mankind?' It will be about health"[798]. Human vulnerability is a promising market. "For Apple and Co. the dating of body and mind does not determine a distant utopia, but rather a playing field of profitable possibilities to divide up a concrete place of longing that has to be conquered – the market in the USA alone holds a potential beyond 3 trillion dollars: Amazon, for example, recently founded a health insurance company, is building clinics similar to Apple's – initially for its own staff – and has developed a system, the Alexa language assistant, which gives medical advice as soon as the first sneeze occurs and proactively recommends medication, which – very practically – can be obtained via the Internet pharmacy Pillpack, which was acquired in 2018. Facebook has also been concerned about the well-being of its users for some time, researching their mental states in particular and has already negotiated health data with hospitals in order to compare them with those of its users in the name of better service"[799]. Human vulnerability is presented as an algorithmically solvable problem when humans carry wearables – and when they listen to multinational corporations, as Eric Schmidt, as CEO of Google, says: "I actually

---

793 Sharon 2018.
794 Project Baseline n.d.
795 See Bensinger 2020.
796 Project Baseline n.d.
797 See Nosthoff / Maschewski 2019: 71.
798 Gurdus 2019.
799 Nosthoff / Maschewsk 2019: 67.

think most people don't want Google to answer their questions. They want Google to tell them what they should be doing next."[800]

Wearables, which provide absolute control and total monitoring of the individual lives of humans including their health, are becoming the backbone of health insurers, e.g. John Hancock with its fitness-tracker-system providing a healthy lifestyle with better insurance policies, product discounts with partner-companies, etc.,[801] but also of other corporations. The healthcare company CVS forces their employees to share their personal health data with CVS.[802]

Of course, data-based systems and robots are already part of medicine and healthcare and their role, their presence, and their influence are steadily growing. Transport of patients, transport of hospital materials, cleaning, security and surveillance, inspection in the nuclear field, pharmacy automation systems, integrated surgical systems, entertainment –[803] from an ethical perspective, robots can contribute in a positive way to the effective and efficient functioning of medical and healthcare institution systems as well as to the provision of competent medical care to all humans.[804] For example, the transport of patients by robots takes some of the burden away from health workers and gives them the opportunity to dedicate their time and professional competence to medical tasks that require humans, including interpersonal conversation and care, which are part of respecting the human dignity of patients. The same could be stated about technological systems providing security and surveillance guaranteeing the right to security. Besides that, self-tracking, for example, could enhance the autonomy of humans and could empower them.[805]

Beyond that, "a robot in place of a nurse for certain tasks or at certain times in the night/day presents the potential to overcome concerns of impartiality and abuse as well as providing care at all times of the day: the robot may be used as a way of regulating the behavior of human careworkers to avoid any risk of patient abuse or maltreatment."[806]

800 Wardrop 2010.
801 See Nosthoff / Maschewski 2019: 91-96.
802 See Nosthoff / Maschewski 2019: 96.
803 See Tzafestas 2016: 47-49.
804 See Huelsken-Giesler 2015.
805 See Karsch / Roche 2016; Krings et al. 2014.
806 Wynsberghe 2015: 3.

In general, there is a hope,[807] the fulfilment of which remains to be seen,[808] of mastering the challenges of professional nursing with the use of data-based systems.[809] Such challenges include demographic change,[810] lack of skilled health workers, increase of humans in need of care, economic competition under financial constraints.[811] All these elements are reasons for perceiving data-based systems as "part of a comprehensive solution (...), which presupposes, however, that we arrive at an idea in a social discourse of the form in which we want to live in our society with and as older people in need of care"[812] and how we should do so.

The ambivalence of technological systems in medicine and health care[813] becomes especially obvious if one takes a closer look at the above-mentioned health-enabling technologies, for instance. Health-enabling technologies are computer-based instruments, which process data, information, and knowledge about the state of health of a person and of his or her context in order to maintain or to improve his or her health or to reduce the negative consequences of an illness or medical problem. This assistance strives to help ensure the longest possible autonomous life consisting of good quality of life, social participation, and self-responsibility.[814] These contributions made by health-enabling technologies are positive from an ethical point of view because they serve the autonomy, freedom, and human dignity of humans. At the same time, concerns regarding data protection and privacy arise because this data is of economic interest and therefore the risk is higher that this data will be abused, transmitted to other users without informed consent by the owner of this data, or not protected sufficiently. From an ethical perspective, in order to address this risk, data, information, and knowledge about the state of health of a person and of his or her context should be saved locally by this person (e.g., on his or her own computer), any proposal of a transmission of the data of this person must be transparent and must only be done with the prior in-

---

807 See Beck et al. 2013.
808 See Meissner 2017; Nienaber 2017.
809 See Elsbernd et al. 2014; Huelsken-Giesler 2014.
810 See Institut für Innovation und Technik 2011.
811 See Hielscher et al. 2013; Bauernhansl 2015.
812 Misselhorn 2018: 155.
813 See Linke 2015.
814 See Haux et al. 2016: 131.

formed consent of this person, and only this person may be authorized to make decisions about his or her data.[815]

Beyond that, as mentioned above, robots can offer relief for human health workers in the functional area, for example in the area of highly physically stressful activities such as the mobilization of patients. It might be forgotten, though, that even such activities contain an interpersonal component and interaction. "Will technical support replace human attention as such and thus undermine one core element of professional care, or even human care for one another in general?"[816] From a human rights perspective, one needs to attach great importance to this interpersonal level in care work in order to respect the human dignity of all humans. One crucial part of this interpersonal level in care work is authenticity – which is of importance to humans and impossible for robots to achieve. Robots are only able to *simulate* "interaction on a personal level" and "relationships". "In the presence of relational artifacts and, most recently, robotic creatures, people are having feelings that are reminiscent of what we would call trust, caring, empathy, nurturance, and even love, if they were being called forth by encounters with people. But it seems odd to use these words to describe benchmarks in human-robot encounters, because we have traditionally reserved them for relationships in which all parties were capable of feeling them – that is, where all parties were people. With robots, people are acting out 'both halves' of complex relationships, projecting the robot's side as well as their own. Of course, we can also behave this way when interacting with people who refuse to engage with us, but people are at least capable of reciprocation. We can be disappointed in people, but at least we are disappointed about genuine potential. For robots, the issue is not disappointment, because the idea of reciprocation is pure fantasy."[817] The lack of authenticity of robots in health care is problematic for respecting the dignity of all humans, as emphasized by the following testimonial: "As I was writing this paper, I discussed it with a former colleague, Richard, who had been left severely disabled by an automobile accident. He is now confined to a wheelchair in his home and needs nearly full-time nursing help. Richard was interested in robots being developed to provide practical help and companionship to people in his situation. His reaction to the idea was complex. He began by saying, 'Show me

---

815 See Haux et al. 2016: 137; Office of The UN High Commissioner for Human Rights n.d.
816 Manzeschke 2019: 4.
817 Turkle 2007: 504-505.

a person in my shoes who is looking for a robot, and I'll show you someone who is looking for a person and can't find one,' but then he made the
best possible case for robotic helpers. He turned the conversation to human cruelty: 'Some of the aides and nurses at the rehab center hurt you
because they are unskilled and some hurt you because they mean to. I had
both. One of them, she pulled me by the hair. One dragged me by my
tubes. A robot would never do that,' he said. 'But you know in the end,
that person who dragged me by my tubes had a story. I could find out
about it.' For Richard, being with a person, even an unpleasant, sadistic
person, made him feel that he was still alive. It signified that his way of being in the world still had a certain dignity, for him the same as authenticity, even if the scope and scale of his activities were radically reduced. This
helped sustain him. Although he would not have wanted his life endan-
gered, he preferred the sadist to the robot. Richard's perspective on living
is a cautionary word to those who would speak too quickly or simply of
purely technical benchmarks for our interactions. What is the value of interactions that contain no understanding of us and that contribute nothing
to a shared store of human meaning?"[818] As it is relevant to the respect of
human dignity, authenticity must be part of the equation in data-based
health care and in the use of "care robots". "When this interpersonal moment of affection and help can be experienced less and less, it could also be
dismissed as a perhaps beneficial, but ultimately unrealistic idea. In any
case, this would have to be accounted for as a loss of humanity, because
the ability to show empathy and care for the other touches an essential part
of our humanity. However, this loss does not come about because robots
as human opponents would strip us humans of such ideas, but because we
humans lack the imagination and responsibility to design our health system accordingly and not only rely on technical innovation, but also to develop our social systems and our moral attitudes further."[819] From an ethical point of view – taking into account justice, responsibility and human
rights – the focus in the evaluation of data-based systems and robots in
health care must be, above all, on human dignity and – closely linked with
that – on authenticity[820], on the well-being of the persons (instead of efficiency), the right to self-determination and autonomy, including the right
to informed consent (the right to participate in decision-making processes
regarding one's health), the right to participate in health-policy-making

---

818 Turkle 2007: 515.
819 Manzeschke 2019: 5-6.
820 See Turkle 2007.

processes, the right to be treated with dignity and respect,[821] participation (instead of cost-efficient exclusion), transparency (instead of economic benefit), effective relief of the health care-workers (instead of technology-based replacement)[822], availability of health facilities, goods and services for all humans (instead of exclusive pricing-strategies), accessibility (non-discrimination, physical accessibility, economic affordability), acceptability (ethically respectful), quality (scientifically and medically appropriate and of good quality),[823] security, privacy, data-protection, liability, a diversity of old age-images, individuality (instead of excessive standardization)[824]. In addition, data-based systems must feature intelligibility for and adaptability to humans,[825] and exit options from contractual relations, in-service training on a regular basis for all actors, and on the benefit of users.[826] Moreover, there must be respect for the emotional needs of humans, human frailty, and for informed consent. Transparency, traceability, reconstructability, explainability, predictability in data-based systems' behavior, real-time status indicators, and opt-out mechanisms are to be integrated, anthropomorphization of data-based systems,[827] humanoid morphology and functionality are to be carefully considered where necessary, and Turing deceptions, racist, sexist, and discriminating morphologies and behaviors are to be avoided.[828]

At the same time, the human rights of the health workers must be respected, protected, implemented, and realized, especially the right to just, favorable and safe conditions of work, the right to form and to join trade unions and other associations, and the right to care (including the management of compassion fatigue arising from work duties).[829] Beyond that, from an ethical perspective, the above mentioned ethical ambivalence of technology-based solutions in this domain must be specifically addressed. Attention must also be paid to the "tipping-points (…) where the technically positive effects and morally preferable moments of age-based assis-

---

821 See OSCE 2013: 27-33.
822 See Rueegger 2016.
823 See UN Committee on Economic, Social and Cultural Rights 2000: para. 12.
824 There is a risk to standardize humans in a way that would level the plurality and uniqueness of humans, see for illustrative purposes, e.g., the discourse about the design of human-machine-interaction, see Neuss 2020.
825 See Benanti 2018: 119-122.
826 See Manzeschke et al. 2013: 22-26.
827 See Zlotowski et al. 2014; Darling 2020.
828 See Howard / Riek 2015: 6.
829 See OSCE 2013: 34.

tance systems turn into their opposite (...) from helpful support to a counterproductive burden."[830]

Further weight is added to this point by the increasing demand on humans to be satisfied with interacting with robots[831] in situations where there used to be interpersonal interaction. "For me, a sociable robot is able to communicate and interact with us, understand and even relate to us, in a personal way. It should be able to understand us and itself in social terms. We, in turn, should be able to understand it in the same social terms – to be able to relate to it and to empathize with it. (...) At the pinnacle of achievement, they could befriend us, as we could them."[832]

The idea is to reduce costs, and people who are not involved demand from those who are involved "more openness to innovation and technological progress". "It looks like we humans are about to construct a new way of existence, in which we do not only interact in a functional manner with machines and simple tools, as we have been doing for some time, but where we will also enter into a social and emotional relationship with them."[833] If patients were to be cared for by robots exclusively without substantial interaction with care workers, the human dignity of all humans would be missing from a human rights perspective. To respect this human dignity in the field of care also means that humans must have contact with both robots and other humans. Even if, for example, autistic children should come to prefer robotic companions over human friends,[834] and even if humans are no longer able to distinguish whether they are interacting with humans or with robots due to their health situation (e.g. humans with severe dementia[835]), it is demanded, from an ethical human rights perspective, to not abuse their state of health and to not give them a false impression[836] solely because society is no longer prepared to bear the necessary costs and prefers to allocate financial resources to other concerns. The following question could serve as a model of thought: If you would have the choice, would you rather be cared for exclusively by a robot or by a person? In consideration of human rights, human dignity and justice, the scenario of digital transformation of medicine and care would be problem-

---

830 Manzeschke et al. 2013: 27; see for some examples Manzeschke et al. 2013: 27-31.
831 See Meacharm / Studley 2017.
832 Breazal 2002: 1.
833 Manzeschke 2019: 7.
834 See Elder 2017.
835 See Ziegler 2016; Albert 2016; Flaiz / Meiler 2014; Frebel 2015.
836 See Remmers 2016.

atic if "health care (almost) without humans" or "care (almost) without humans" were to represent normal health care or care provision and if one were required to pay extra for any human presence and any human interaction.

Furthermore, human rights and the human dignity of all humans reveal the ethical meaning of another dimension of robotization, digitalization, mechanization, and automation of medicine and care and the use of data-based systems in medicine and care: "In a robot built by humans those limits will not be regulated 'from the inside' through the process of life, but by other humans who first of all write a certain program. But it needs to be considered that in the case of self-learning algorithms that enable robots to 'learn', at some point it will no longer be re-constructible why a robot chooses a certain course of action. This might even be comparable to a living being in its self-containment. But the strange and hard to classify fact still remains that a human encounters in a robot first of all the aims and ideas of other humans. At the same time, it is not a person you are looking at."[837] Justice, responsibility, and human rights should be given to robots as ethical pillars, but it needs to be considered that machines lack moral capability (see above chapter 3 Can Ethical Judgment Be Delegated to Technologies?) and that ethics are highly complex (see above chapter 5 The Complexity of Ethics). Based on these normative pillars and while taking this lacking moral capability of data-based systems into account, data-based systems must be reliable in respecting ethical principles and norms[838] and avoid stigmatization in their interaction with humans. They must empower humans rather than take self-control and freedom away from them, and they must guarantee data security as described above.[839] It is necessary to include ethical, legal, and social aspects at the beginning and throughout the process of the design, development, and production of a technical innovation (one example of how this can be accomplished is the model to ethically evaluate socio-technical arrangements MEESTAR)[840]. This process should be organized and structured in a participatory way.[841]

Finally, the use of robots and data-based systems in health care represents an example of the machinization of humans as discussed above in

---

837 Manzeschke 2019.
838 See Michels-Riess / Johnigk 2017.
839 See Meyer 2016: 21-22.
840 See Manzeschke et al. 2013: 13-21; Weber 2015; Weber / Wackerbarth 2014; Weber 2014; Henne / Friedhof / Kopp 2016; see for another approach Wynsberghe 2015.
841 See Weber / Wackerbarth 2014.

subchapter 7.4 Transhumanism. While artificial joints, pacemakers, etc. could have an impact on the awareness of one's own body,[842] they do not change the personality of a patient as brain pacemakers do.[843] If the machinization of humans involves changing the personality of a patient, the medical use of robots and data-based systems raises additional ethical questions, e.g., whether humans with such devices would still possess culpability, whether this kind of medical treatment should be limited, whether such research should be funded, etc.[844]

7.10 Digital Transformation of Finance

7.10.1 Digitalization and Automation of Finance

"Machines are taking control of investing – not just the humdrum buying and selling of securities, but also the commanding heights of monitoring the economy and allocating capital. Funds run by computers that follow rules set by humans account for 35% of America's stock market, 60% of institutional equity assets and 60% of trading activity. New artificial-intelligence programs are also writing their own investing rules, in ways their human masters only partly understand."[845] The digitalization and automation of financial markets is growing.[846] State authorities are even forcing financial institutes toward full automation, e.g. the Swiss Financial Market Supervisory Authority FINMA reacted to grave misconduct by obliging the UBS Group to automate at least 95% of global currency trading in November 2014.[847]

Among others, "FinTech lending platforms allow consumers to shop for, apply and obtain loans online within seconds. They provide lenders with traditional credit report data (including payment history, amounts owed, length of history, number of accounts and more). In addition, FinTech lenders leverage a variety of alternative data sources. These include insurance claims, social media activities, online shopping information

---

842 See Gesang 2007: 25.
843 See Gesang 2007: 26-27.
844 See Beck 2012: 13.
845 The Economist 2019; see Hofstetter 2014: 192.
846 See Li et al. 2015.
847 See Finanzen.ch 2014.

from marketplaces such as Amazon, shipping data from postal services, browsing patterns, and type of telephone or browser used."[848]

The significance of the digital transformation and use of data-based systems in financial markets becomes evident if one considers the importance of the financial sector for the entire economic system. "Financial markets essentially involve the allocation of resources. They can be thought of as the brain of the entire economic system, the central locus of decision-making; if they fail, not only will the sector's profits be lower than they would otherwise have been, but the performance of the entire economic system may be impaired."[849] The complexity of digital transformation of and the use of data-based systems in the financial sector would certainly merit extensive ethical research.[850] The following provides only a short overview of the main opportunities and risks from an ethical perspective.

Financial markets benefit from higher speed, data-volume, and precision for their transactions, from cost reduction,[851] especially in legal compliance,[852] and from new outreach in fraud detection.[853] Innovative business models and ways of doing business open new horizons and contribute to progress. Both can contribute – from an ethical standpoint – to the realization of the human right to development.

From an ethical viewpoint, the fact that cross-border financial supervision will be facilitated by digitalization and automation might be an opportunity. In addition, increased efficiency in the market can be achieved by the reduction of effort, costs, and human input, by the size of data volume that can be evaluated, by more precision, efficiency and transparency, by increased speed and by innovative business models and new forms of financial management. This leads to an increase in transactions and thus to economic progress. While the first could be seen as positive from an ethical human rights perspective, if a better functioning market would lead to preserving resources, the latter depends on the impact of this increase in transactions on human rights and justice (e.g., will it generate real economic growth?[854] Will it thus contribute to the realization of the human

---

848 OECD 2019a; see Jagtiani / Lemieux 2019.
849 Stiglitz 1994: 23.
850 See Davis et al. 2012; Oehler 2015.
851 See Sokolin / Low 2018; Sohangir et al. 2018.
852 See Son 2017.
853 See Voegeli 2016.
854 See Gabriel et al. 2017.

right to development?[855]), and who will profit from this increase in transactions?[856]

Furthermore, from a human rights and justice perspective, the digital transformation of and the use of data-based systems in the finance sector could open up the ethical opportunity to facilitate market access for people. In the report of the UN Secretary-General's High-level Panel on Digital Cooperation from June 2019 it is stated: "By 2030, every adult should have affordable access to digital networks, as well as digitally-enabled financial (...) services, as a means to make a substantial contribution to achieving the SDGs (Sustainable Development Goals)"[857].

Finally, technology-based innovations could also result in social finance innovation.[858]

Even now, it is somewhat apparent that, from an ethical point of view, digital transformation and the use of data-based systems always have the potential to have either positive or negative effects, depending on the concrete design and concrete application.

The question of justice arises for society as a whole in view of the disruptive nature of digital transformation of and the use of data-based systems in the financial sector. The ethical focus is not so much on the reduction of paid professional tasks due to the technology-based change in itself. Rather, the core consequence of digital transformation, namely that *ever fewer humans will participate in and profit from a more efficient and more effective value chain*, attracts attention from an ethical point of view. The focus should be on creating a just society and thus a just economic system that guarantees equal opportunities for all and ensures a life with human dignity for all humans. (Both are further discussed below in subchapter 7.18 Reduction of Paid Jobs, and an ethical approach for a solution is given below in subchapter 8.2 Society-, Entrepreneurship-, Research-Time-Model SERT.)

When remembering the financial crisis of 2008, the high grade of automation mentioned at the beginning is ethically troubling, when taking into account the principle of responsibility, the principle of justice, and the principle of human rights. "Automation was a key enabling technology in the financial crisis of 2008"[859] makes you think and, in relation to

---

855 See Sen 1999.
856 See Stiglitz 2015.
857 UN Secretary-General's High-level Panel on Digital Cooperation 2019: 1A.
858 See Clarke / Tooker 2017.
859 Hurlburt et al. 2008: 6

this, leads one to the observation that, after the last financial crisis, many adjustments have been made, but not the right ones.[860] The argument that high frequency trading systems possess moral agency[861] or that automated robo-financial advisers would live up to higher ethical standards[862] can both be proven wrong[863] primarily by the lack of moral capability elaborated above in chapter 3 Can Ethical Judgment Be Delegated to Technologies?.

Because algorithms of self-learning systems cannot be reproduced, traced back, and explained, a situation will arise where "technical failure will become the rule at the stock exchange"[864]. For example, in 2010 a stock market crash occurred because of the unforeseen interaction of algorithms with the financial markets provoking chaos in the entire financial system. Some significant shares lost more than 90% of their value within minutes and went back to their initial value.[865] In addition, it makes the identification of the subjects of responsibility as well as the identification of the responsibility-relation very difficult or even impossible, which would be imperative from an ethical perspective.

Furthermore, there is the danger of a conflict of objectives for the financial supervision authorities, because on the one hand, they need to fulfill their duty to protect the investors and the function, but at the same time, they also flirt with promoting innovation, competition, and location.[866]

Digital transformation and data-based systems promote the expansion of "dark pools". Those are networks that enable great financial transactions that are not being made public in the wider marketplace. This way, the risk of opposing price developments arising from the transactions themselves can be avoided. Based on the principle of responsibility, "dark pools" turn out to be problematic because of their lack of transparency. Based on the principle of justice, the unfair advantage of institutional major investors needs to be criticized.

Digital transformation and data-based systems in the finance sector open up the possibility of high-frequency trading – "trading based on rapid and massive order in time and quantity in order to yield on the short-term

---

860 See Stadler 2019.
861 See Romar 2015.
862 See Jon Stein, CEO of Betterment, in an Interview in Full Auto, March 2016.
863 See O'Connor 2016.
864 Hofstetter 2014: 196.
865 See Lauricella / McKay 2010; Securities & Exchange Commission / The Commodity Futures Trading Commission 2010.
866 See Contratto 2017: 429.

price variation."[867] In other words, this means "computer-assisted trading that exploits incredibly small-time differences to yield profits at minimal risk to those employing it"[868]. At its core, it means "to frequently trade to take advantage of small price variations"[869]. From an ethical point of view, it can be stated that high-frequency trading contains many practices that need to be ethically evaluated[870] – e.g., considering "ethical obligations to investors, external market participants and society"[871] –, because what is ethically decisive is "the use of technology rather than the technology itself"[872]. With reference to human rights, the reduction of transaction costs and improved pricing is ethically positive, because it is a resource-saving increase in efficiency. With reference to the principle of responsibility, the principle of justice and human rights, the destabilization caused by high-frequency trading[873] is ethically negative because it has a negative impact on systemic robustness ("institutional arrangements of the financial industry can only be considered ethically legitimate if the probability of a systemic financial crisis occurring in the next few years is low"[874]), the price development and destruction of financial assets without real economic correspondence, as it neglects the creation of value ("institutional arrangements of the financial sector can only be considered ethically legitimate, if they do not promote the spread of financial practices in which financial institutions generate income without creating value"[875]), the safeguards to prevent a flash crash are insufficient as well as the lack of ability of automated bots to contextualize anomalies, to recognize them, and to make corresponding corrections.[876] Furthermore, the interlocking interests between the stock exchange operator and the high-frequency trader need to be criticized from an ethical point of view – in particular, in reference to the principle of responsibility this is ethically problematic, because self-regulation is up to the stock exchange operator.

Beyond that, the "co-location" leads to discrimination. The following argument could be given against it: "Does 'co-location' give traders an unfair

---

867 Staszkiewicz 2015: 61.
868 McNamara 2016: 98.
869 Klaus / Elzweig 2017: 13.
870 See Cooper et al. 2016; Van Vliet 2012; Johansson 2013.
871 Van Vliet 2012: 79.
872 Angel / McCabe 2013: 594.
873 See Farooq et al. 2014.
874 Emunds 2014: 204.
875 Emunds 2014: 199.
876 See Farooq et al. 2014: 1653.

head-start? To a certain extent, traders have always invested heavily to get closer to the scene of trading."[877] The latter needs to be agreed with. But at the same time, one must consider that, due to technology, the potential as well as the problems have intensified to such a great extent that a new negative ethical evaluation is justified.

Furthermore, some ways of manipulating the market, such as "quote stuffing" or "spoofing", are ethically unacceptable when taking into account the principle of justice.

Moreover, monopolization tendencies in markets are alarming from a justice standpoint and from a human rights standpoint. Further concerns are provoked by the difficulty to identify the dimensions and the relations of responsibility facing the complexity of digitalized business transactions. These identifications are necessary in order to avoid a lack of moral and legal accountability in the case of accidents and crimes and in order to enable risk assessments, rules for liabilities, and insurance in meeting this ethical challenge.

Finally, from an ethical standpoint and by taking into account responsibility, justice, and human rights, digital transformation and data-based systems in the finance sector need to be critically examined to determine if they promote financial crime (money laundering, etc.).[878]

In order to be able to benefit from the ethical opportunities discussed and to overcome the ethical risks, innovation for the ethical good should be promoted in the course of digital transformation. Furthermore, a precautionary principle should be introduced in the interest of financial stability.

Additionally, a regulation, a field test and a permit for new financial products are needed (similar to the procedure for new drugs).[879] The need for such measures as regards digital transformation and data-based systems in the finance sector should have become clear from the above explanation of these ethical problems' relevance to responsibility, justice, and human rights. This imperative is further strengthened by the following statement of the former US Federal Reserve Chairman Alan Greenspan: "I made a mistake in presuming that the self-interest of organizations, specifically banks and others, was such that they were best capable of protecting their own shareholders."[880] The corresponding structural deficiencies must not

---

877 Angel / McCabe 2013: 590-591.
878 See Villhauer 2016: 248.
879 See Buiter 2009: 13.
880 Edmund 2008.

be ignored. "Regulatory competition (…) led banking supervisors to assess the risks of innovative instruments (…) with less watchfulness than these instruments deserved"[881]. A further complicating factor is that, in view of crimes committed by big banks and financial institutions (see the following overview of fines of big banks and financial institutions from 2008 to 2018), there is absolutely no reason why trust advances pointing in a different direction should be given to big banks and financial institutions:

"Bank	*Fine, in billions*
Bank of America	$76.1
JPMorgan Chase	$43.7
Citigroup	$19
Deutsche Bank	$14
Wells Fargo	$11.8
RBS	$10.1
BNP Paribas	$9.3
Credit Suisse	$9.1
Morgan Stanley	$8.6
Goldman Sachs	$7.7
UBS	$6.5"[882].

7.10.2 Cryptocurrencies and Blockchain Technology[883]

Cryptocurrencies possess an innovation force and economic potential. "A cryptocurrency is a medium of exchange, such as the US dollar, but is digital and uses encryption techniques to control the creation of monetary units and to verify the transfer of funds."[884] Their technological basis is blockchain technology. Blockchain technology is also the basis for other new financial services, for smart contracts, etc. After mainframes, personal

---

881   Kane 2008: 21.
882   Goldstein 2018.
883   See Kirchschlaeger 2021.
884   PricewaterhouseCoopers United States 2017; see also Swiss Financial Market Supervisory Authority FINMA 2013: 111.

computer, the internet, and mobile devices, blockchain technology can be seen as the fifth disruptive computing paradigm.[885]

What is blockchain technology? "It consists of a permanent, distributed, digital ledger, resistant to tampering and carried out collectively by all the nodes of the system. The formidable innovation introduced by this technology is that the network is open and participants do not need to know or to trust each other to interact: the electronic transactions can be automatically verified and recorded by the nodes of the network through cryptographic algorithms, without human intervention, central authority, point of control or third party (e.g. governments, banks, financial institutions or other organizations). Even if some nodes are unreliable, dishonest or malicious, the network is able to correctly verify the transactions and protect the ledger from tampering through a mathematical mechanism called *proof-of-work*, which makes human intervention or controlling authority unnecessary"[886]. Blockchain technology thus includes "a shift from trusting people to trusting math"[887]. Institutional intermediaries providing trust seem to become obsolete. This shift could involve a paradigmatic improvement for science, research, innovation, development, and technology in general by opening a new horizon of open access academic publishing based on blockchain technology – including, for example, the scientific discourse of which this book is a part. Why? Because blockchain technology guarantees everyone continuous documentation that does not belong to anyone and is not controlled by anyone. It also guarantees access at all times for reviewing cryptographically verified peer-to-peer procedures. It has the potential to change the process of science, research, innovation, development, and technology fundamentally to a completely open and transparent process. This way, it respects the right to intellectual property and, in virtue of that, it encourages and motivates free, open, and independent scientific discourse.

Beyond that, blockchain technology can be seen as involving another shift – from an internet of information to an internet of value.[888] Although one could argue that value can be broken down to information and therefore this shift should be framed differently, Melanie Swan and Primavera De Filippi highlight adequately "the secure, end-to-end and computationally validated transfer of value (whether it is represented by money, assets,

---

885 See Swan 2015; Polrot 2017.
886 Atzori 2015: 2, emphasis in the text.
887 Antonopolous 2016.
888 See Swan 2015.

or contractual arrangements) via smart networks"[889] as an innovative nucleus of blockchain technology. Therefore, the shift should be defined differently, namely *a shift from an intermediated network to an immediate network.*

Linked with its economic potential,[890] ethically positive from a human rights perspective is the fact that blockchain technology could provide – among other benefits – access to money and to financial services for about two billion people without a banking-relation.[891] One can argue that having access to minimum basic financial services (money, a minimum credit, a saving account, and low-cost money-transfer-option) contributes to the respect and to the realization of human rights. The main reason for this position is the significant role financial resources play in the daily life of humans as a means of reaching several aims, including essential elements and areas of human existence that a human needs for survival and for a life as a human and that are protected by human rights. Beyond that, as developments of the financial markets have an impact on the daily life of everyone, they primarily have impact on the daily lives of the poor. Therefore, everyone should at least have the option to participate in the financial markets. Beyond that, the access to certain financial services could be an instrument to overcome illegitimate global inequality and would fulfill the "gap-closing-principle": "Financial institutions and finance-systems contribute to global justice if they contribute to the realization of human rights of all humans and if they contribute to the closing of the gap between poor and rich."[892] While maintaining, to the greatest possible extent, the economic rationale of pursuing one's own particular interest, the "gap-closing-principle" introduces the perspective of the poor only as a corrective of the "ad infinitum" of the pursuit of one's own particular interest(s).

Beyond that, crypto-currencies could provide financial security in cases of unstable local currencies. This is of both economic and ethical relevance based on its contribution to the realization of justice as an ethical point of reference.

Moreover, blockchain technology can also be used to manage green energy distribution.[893]

---

889   Swan / De Filippi 2017: 605; see also Storino et al. 2017.
890   See World Government Summit 2017; Aste et al. 2018; International Monetary Fund (IMF) 2018; Adams et al. 2018: 135-136.
891   See PricewaterhouseCoopers 2016.
892   Kirchschlaeger 2016d: 550.
893   See Aviva Rutkin 2016.

Finally, with its potential role in land titling and property transactions to whom a significant role in economic development can be attributed,[894] blockchain technology could contribute to economic development especially in developing contexts – which is again of significance from both a justice and a human rights perspective.[895]

In addition, transparency represents another ethically positive aspect of blockchain technology if one applies the ethical point of reference of responsibility. As an open-source code, blockchain technology offers everyone, at all times, access to review cryptographically verified peer-to-peer procedures – instant "real-time transparency"[896]. Therefore, blockchain technology offers verifiability: "Transactions are immediately auditable in real time. As an immutable and sequenced digital ledger, a Blockchain allows the complete record of transactions to be directly verified"[897]. As this open-source code does not belong to anyone and is not controlled by anyone,[898] blockchain technology fosters transparency by excluding undisclosed influences or censorship by the owner or by the controlling entity. In addition, it enfolds immutability because all nodes keep the data simultaneously and constantly and provide the proper redundancy.[899] Both transparency and immutability[900] lead to traceability provided by blockchain technology, which serves responsibility as an ethical point of reference as it allows the dimensions of responsibility (e.g., the subjects and objects of responsibility), the relations, and the spheres of responsibility to be identified. Blockchain technology could be applied in this way in the management of supply chains[901] and in the fight against human rights violation in supply chains.[902]

At the same time, other aspects of blockchain technology receive fundamental criticism from an ethical point of view. As blockchain technology is still an emergent technology, maybe this ethical analysis could contribute to its further design and application. While looking at the use of blockchain in finance, the economist and Nobel prize laureate Paul Krug-

---

894 See De Soto 2003.
895 See De Soto / Cheneval 2006.
896 Seele 2016.
897 LaPointe / Fishbane 2018: 53.
898 See Atzori 2015: 7.
899 See Atzori 2015: 7.
900 See Swan / De Filippi 2017: 603-604.
901 See Steiner 2015; Adams et al. 2018: 134.
902 See Kirchschlaeger 2017e; Kirchschlaeger 2017f; Kirchschlaeger 2015c.

man defines the crypto-currency "bitcoin" as "evil"[903], the economist and Nobel prize laureate Joseph Stiglitz makes the following assessment of crypto-currencies: "You cannot have a means of payment that is based on secrecy when you're trying to create a transparent banking system (...) If you open up a hole like bitcoin, then all the nefarious activity will go through that hole, and no government can allow that. (...) By regulating the abuses, you are going to regulate it out of existence. It exists because of the abuses"[904].

As virtual or digital currencies, cryptocurrencies fulfil functions of exchange, payment, value-increase, value-preservation, and price comparison. At the same time, their economic limitation due to the lack of a currency cover, as no economic performance potential is provided as a guarantee, is an ethical problem as well. Take for example "Libra": "If Libra works, it is a brilliant business model. Libra makers collect money from people to whom they have no obligations and who have nothing to say."[905] Based on the principle of responsibility, it is ethically negative that cryptocurrencies run the risk of being no more than a deception. Based on the principle of justice, it is ethically negative that currency issuers appropriate other people's economic performance.

Aiming at the ethical point of reference of human rights – more specifically, the right to life, the right to health, work-related rights, the right to an adequate standard of living including the right to housing, food and water, to name just a few –[906] and the ethical point of reference of justice – more specifically intergenerational justice – the enormous energy consumption of the proof of work consensus method[907] is ethically problematic.[908] This is not only true for cryptocurrencies but for the entire digital transformation of the financial sector, even if it is especially dramatic with the use of blockchain technology in financial markets. For example, for Bitcoin, it is estimated that it will take a billion Watts to reach the validity of a proof of work.[909] In other words, "currently, global power demand from cryptocurrency mining hovers at about 22 terawatt hours (TWh), but increasing demand means consumption could surge in 2018 to 125-140TWh – a full 0.6% of world consumption. Although that level is

---

903 Krugman 2013.
904 Montag 2018.
905 Bofinger 2019: 21.
906 See Kirchschlaeger 2012a.
907 See Boehme et al. 2015.
908 See Morgan Stanley 2018.
909 See Aste 2016.

still far from material to global utility power demand, it's worth noting that 0.6% is roughly the electric consumption of Argentina in a typical year"[910].

Attempts to resolve this ecological problem of blockchain technology consist in making "mining" greener or circumventing the mining process. "Users lock up quantities of cryptocurrency for periods of time, which secures the blockchain used by that currency. In return, they receive cryptocurrency rewards, as if they had mined cryptocurrencies themselves"[911]. As this approach is still dependent on "mining" in the first place, it does not seem to eliminate the ecological problems of blockchain technology. "Some people wonder if crypto-currencies will disrupt the financial system, while others wonder if they will break the environment in the process"[912].

Blockchain technology faces the ethical problem – which becomes obvious when one focuses on the ethical points of reference of responsibility, justice, and human rights – of being regarded or utilized as a technological basis for crypto-currencies, and thereby also as a means of laundering money with impunity.[913]

Crypto-currencies – relying on blockchain technology – are also used for funding international crime and terrorism[914] – again, obviously, ethically unacceptable based on the ethical points of reference of responsibility, justice, and human rights.[915]

Beyond that, an obvious point of criticism arises together with some doubts questioning the positive impact of blockchain technology, namely economically empowering people, and the ethically positive characteristics of blockchain technology mentioned move, namely transparency, immutability, and traceability. If those are established, then countermeasures against money laundering and financing international crime and terrorism should be easily implementable, enforceable, and successful. At this point – with the principle of responsibility as ethical guidance – the problem of subjectivity of responsibility in blockchain technology emerges from an ethical standpoint. Who is the subject of responsibility? How can the dimensions of responsibility be identified? What relations of responsibility

---

910 Morgan Stanley 2018.
911 Kugler 2018: 17.
912 Kugler 2018: 16.
913 E.g., Scheck / Shifflett 2018.
914 See Stalinsky 2018.
915 See Seele 2018; Dierksmeier / Seele 2018.

exist? How far does this broaden the sphere of responsibility? Identifying all this is a complex task. The subjects of responsibility should still be identified in order to build an atmosphere of liability and accountability – not only out of respect for the objects of responsibility but for other reasons as well. Complexity cannot serve as an excuse liberating one from legal or ethical obligations and responsibilities because ethical and legal norms retain their validity even in complex situations and contexts.

There is a need for further research and innovation in the area of blockchain technology striving for "ethically guided cryptocurrency systems whose behaviors are informed by human ethical values"[916], for "a successfully functioning 'cryptocurrency with a conscience'"[917].

Because of the ways in which natural resources for the production of technologies and technology-based applications are excavated and exploited, and because of the ways in which technologies and technology-based applications are produced – both consisting of modern slavery and slavery-like working conditions –, an increase in the demand for these natural resources and these production-processes through the use of blockchain technology will also increase these human rights violations. The increased demand for natural resources fueling the dissemination of blockchain technology calls for states and the private sector to optimize the way in which they implement their already existing human rights obligations.[918]

7.11 Automated Weapons[919]

"The use of long distance, remote control weapons, or weapons connected to sensors positioned in the field, leads to the automation of the battlefield in which the soldier plays an increasingly less important role (...) [A]ll predictions agree that if the man does not master technology, but allows it to master him, he will be destroyed by technology."[920] Is this vision of the International Committee of the Red Cross coming true? How should automatic weapons be assessed from an ethical perspective? What should be

---

916 Gladden 2015: 96.
917 Gladden 2015: 96.
918 See Kirchschlaeger 2015c; Kirchschlaeger 2017f.
919 In this book I deliberately do not address the highly relevant ethical question of whether wars can be ethically justified at all, since I have dealt with this question elsewhere, see Kirchschlaeger 2015b.
920 International Committee of the Red Cross (ICRC) 1977: Art. 36.

done about automated weapons from an ethical standpoint informed by the principles of justice, responsibility, and human rights?

Automated weapons are weapons that carry out remote-controlled orders from a person who controls the weapons remotely. The weapons also support the person by reducing the complexity of the task. This can happen automatically under human control or they can even automatically handle a military mission.[921] They can also be defined as "robot weapons that once launched will select and engage targets without further human intervention"[922]. They are also called "autonomous weapon systems", such as "lethal autonomous weapons (LAWs)",[923] which is misleading, as has been discussed in chapter 3 Can Ethical Judgment Be Delegated to Technologies?, based on the lack of moral capability and autonomy in machines. Automated weapons are also presented as a way of trying to recognize enemy soldiers and fight them in a militarily adequate manner in line with international law. This conceptual misleading is highly relevant. Because, when unmasking this deception, it becomes clear that automated weapons follow a rule without taking into account their ethical or unethical quality, while humans recognize, define, and respect ethical norms and principles as binding for themselves and can distinguish them from rules of other quality – non-ethical rules.

When addressing automated weapons ethically,[924] it needs to be kept in mind that apart from automated weapons there are "military robots (...) which protect human life, such as bomb technicians or defense systems"[925]. The first would be positive from an ethical perspective and by taking into account human rights, because they contribute to the protection of life without harming or killing people. The latter would need further differentiation from an ethical standpoint regarding whether human rights would be violated during defense. The same is true of automated systems for navigation, transport, and logistics in military contexts.[926] Fundamentally, a distinction needs to be made between lethal and non-lethal systems[927] with ethical implications. Both still require an ethical examination and assessment but, of course, there is a substantial ethical difference,

---

921 See Dickow 2015: 9.
922 Altmann et al. 2013: 73.
923 See Future of Life Institute n.d.
924 For the legal discussion, see Meyer 2014a.
925 Ohly 2019a: 145.
926 See Wegmann 2014.
927 See Franke / Leveringhaus 2015: 297-311.

and therefore the burden of proof for legitimacy is significantly higher for lethal systems.

In the research discourse on automated weapons, they are presented as something ethically positive. "As robots are already faster, stronger, and in certain cases (e.g., Deep Blue, Watson12) smarter than humans, is it really that difficult to believe they will be able to ultimately treat us more humanely in the battle-field than we do each other, given the persistent existence of atrocious behaviors by a significant subset of human warfighters?"[928] This superiority should lead to fewer civilian victims when using automated weapons.[929] Based on the demand that, in war, appropriate means would have to be used,[930] provided that it can be ethically legitimized, there is the following argument: "Proportionality can be better achieved by military robots than by conventional weapons."[931] Finally, this line of argumentation goes even as far as reformulating the Asimov law: "Under the condition that violence against humans can even be justified in certain limits, autonomous robots can act more humanely than semi-automated or automatic weapons. Asimov's first law is only applicable in peaceful settings."[932]

Another argumentative approach involves the identification of gaps in international law in the handling of automated weapons, e.g., International Criminal Law.[933]

From an ethical standpoint, initial doubts arise as to whether the attempt to present automated weapons as legitimate has more to do with the promised military superiority and less with their ethical legitimacy.[934] "The use of robots and drones already promises enormous advantages for every army in the world. Robots do not tire, they carry out orders without contradiction, do not need to be trained for a long time and know neither boredom nor emotional stress. In short, there are good reasons why every general worldwide wants his own robot force."[935]

Human rights groups such as Human Rights Watch and the International Committee for Robot Arms Control demand that automated weapons

---

928 Arkin 2013: 3; see also Toscano 2015; Guetlein 2005; on the masculinized layers of such arguments against the ban, see Santos de Carvalho 2018.
929 See Arkin 2018: 4; Arkin 2009; Klincewicz 2015; Mueller 2014.
930 See Haerle 2011: 414.
931 Ohly 2019a: 147; see also Sassòli 2014.
932 Ohly 2019a: 154.
933 See Arendt 2016.
934 See Scharre 2019; Sharkey 2018.
935 Schoernig 2010.

be banned under the UN Weapons Convention of 1980 because they would violate international humanitarian law and human rights.[936] In 2015, Stephen Hawking, Steve Wozniak (co-founder of Apple), and Elon Musk together with 1,000 researchers in the area of data-based systems and robotics signed an open letter that calls for a ban of "offensive autonomous weapons beyond meaningful human control"[937]. In 2017, Elon Musk and 116 CEOs of technology corporations called for a ban on lethal autonomous weapon systems due to the dual-use problem of data-based systems[938] introduced above in subchapter 7.2 "Dual Use".

From an ethical view and taking into account human rights, automated weapons face fundamental criticism in that they are not able, according to the laws, to distinguish armed conflict between combatants and non-combatants and to apply the principle of proportionality[939] resulting in more wrong actions and crimes.[940] "It is questionable that fully autonomous weapons would be capable of meeting international humanitarian law standards, including the rules of distinction, proportionality, and military necessity, while they would threaten the fundamental right to life and principle of human dignity."[941]

Beyond that, automated weapons are criticized from an ethical standpoint on the basis that they constitute a means of warfare "*malum in se*".[942]

This line of argument receives further support when taking into account the complexity of conflict situations.[943] In view of the latter, too much would be expected of automated weapons. Appropriate preparation of automated weapons would be impossible.[944]

In addition, the "strategic robot problem" and its ethical implications underpin the idea that automated weapons are ethically problematic. The "strategic robot problem" lies in the undermining of command and con-

---

936 See also Richter 2013; Rogers 2014; Thomas 2015; Sullins 2013; Marauhn 2014; Heyns 2014; Asaro 2012; Dickow / Linnenkamp 2012: 1-8; Geiss 2015: 1-28; Etzioni / Etzioni 2017: 72-80; Wallach 2017: 28-34; Scharre 2018; Cernea 2018: 67-89; Misselhorn 2017: 21-33; El-Hitami 2017: 28-29.
937 Future of Life Institute 2015.
938 See Gibbs 2017.
939 See Burridge 2003; Sharkey 2007; Sharkey 2012; Asaro 2008; Krishnan 2009a; Guarini / Bello 2012: 386.
940 See Sharkey 2011.
941 Human Rights Watch n.d.; on the last aspect – the right to life and the protection of human dignity – see also Wallach 2015.
942 See Wallach / Allen 2009; Tomasi 2013; Wagner 2014: 54.
943 See Wallach 2015.
944 See Lin et al. 2008: 63-72.

trol structures by creating automated weapons to serve as combatant and as commander at the same time.[945] "As each machine becomes its own 'authority' making strategic decisions for the course and direction of the conflict, moral authority and responsibility likewise vanishes, unless we can hold such machines morally responsible in any meaningful way"[946] which is not possible as described above in chapter 3 Can Ethical Judgment Be Delegated to Technologies?.

From an ethical viewpoint, the following factors would also speak against automated weapons: the idea that they would lead to more wars[947] because of the reduction of "ability to make credible threats and assurances in a crisis"[948], the growing distance between human actions and their consequences,[949] less human involvement for the actors deploying them,[950] a lower number of victims would be expected,[951] and a lower political price would need to be paid.[952] The latter becomes obvious for reasons including but not limited to the replacement of the fundamental reciprocity of combat, namely possessing as a soldier the power to kill while running the ongoing risk of being killed.[953] As a consequence of the latter, the legislative oversight would not be respected and this would work against the system of checks and balances. For example, former US President Barack Obama did not have the operation with armed drones in Libya 2011 legitimized by Congress, arguing that casualties were not to be expected.[954] Moreover, automated weapons would ignite an arms race[955] fueling the danger of a "'flash war', where conflicts quickly spiral out of human control"[956] due to "unexpected interactions between autonomous systems or hacking"[957], and would destabilize international order. Automated weapons would lead to an empowerment of "small groups of people – even individuals – to unleash massive levels of destruction and kill in great numbers, constituting a new kind of weapon of mass destruction. (...)

---

945 See Roff 2014.
946 Roff 2014.
947 See Kahn 2017.
948 Leys 2018.
949 See Singer 2009; Pappenberger 2013.
950 See Grut 2013.
951 See Wallach 2015; Leys 2018.
952 See Wagner 2014.
953 See Broeckling 2015; Hood 2015; Kaufmann 2010.
954 See Bieri / Dickow 2014.
955 See Roff 2015; Lele 2019.
956 Scharre 2016: 53.
957 Scharre 2016: 53.

What will it mean to be human? What kind of society will these systems be defending?"[958] The impact of automated weapons on the international and national normative framework themselves should not be underestimated.[959]

Beyond that, based on the elaborations above in chapter 3 Can Ethical Judgment Be Delegated to Technologies? and the indicated lack of autonomy of machines, when automated weapons are used, humans retain responsibility for said weapons – with an attempt to "take humans out of the loop"[960]. In other words, automated weapons cannot be held accountable for their actions.

Related to this point, automated weapons provoke the risk that responsibility of humans for automated weapons is blurred[961] and create a "responsibility-gap"[962] based on the technological phenomenon of "swarm"[963], and because the high grade of automation of these weapons erroneously insinuates their "autonomy" and erroneously relieves humans from their subjectivity of responsibility.[964] "It will be unethical to deploy autonomous systems invoking sophisticated artificial intelligence in warfare unless someone can be held responsible for the decisions they make where these might threaten human life. (…) the more autonomous these systems become, the less it will be possible to properly hold those who designed them or ordered their use responsible for their actions."[965]

Finally, in addition to further ethical and technical issues,[966] the width and depth of ethics, as has been explained above in chapter 5 The Complexity of Ethics, speaks against the possibility of creating "ethical automated weapons", against automated weapons, against the supposedly presented possibility of using them consistently with just war theory (*jus ad bellum* and *jus in bello*),[967] against regulating the use of automated weapons in a

---

958 Asaro 2019: 552.
959 See Bode / Huelss 2018.
960 Singer 2009: 123.
961 See also Walsh 2015; Geser 2011; Beard 2014; Hammond 2015; Liu 2012; McFarland / McCormack 2014; Guersenzvaig 2018.
962 See Matthias 2004: 175-183; Heyns 2013.
963 See, e.g., on swarming of drones Grimal / Sundaram 2018.
964 See Sparrow 2007: 62-77.
965 Sparrow 2007: 74.
966 See Sparrow 2009: 169-187.
967 For such a possibility, see Schulzke 2011.

sense that the use of automated weapons would still be permitted,[968] and against the assumption that human interventions could end "if the supervisor is confident that (...) the weapon system complies, and will continue to comply, with international law and applicable rules of engagement."[969] The limitations of automated weapons become obvious when considering that ethics go further than "blindly" following rules. The significance of the acknowledgement of the complexity of ethics becomes even more obvious in view of the reductionist argument presented in the discourse about automated weapons stating that automated weapons can obey the military chain of command and, accordingly, the responsibility for actions by automated weapons can be easily attributed by following the chain of command.[970]

These ethical objections caused the forming of the principle of "meaningful human control": "future weapons systems must preserve meaningful human control over the use of (lethal) force, that is: humans not computers and their algorithms should ultimately remain in control of, and thus morally responsible for relevant decisions about (lethal) military operations."[971] In order to respect the principle of meaningful human control, automated weapons must fulfill a "tracking" condition and a "tracing" condition:[972]

- "tracking" condition: "In order to be under meaningful human control, a decision-making system should demonstrably and verifiably be responsive to the human moral reasons relevant in the circumstances – no matter how many system levels, models, software, or devices of whatever nature separate a human being from the ultimate effects in the world, some of which may be lethal. That is, decision-making systems should track (relevant) human moral reasons."[973]
- "tracing" condition: "in order for a system to be under meaningful human control, its actions/states should be traceable to a proper moral understanding on the part of one or more relevant human persons who design or interact with the system, meaning that there is at least one

---

968 For such a regulation, see Cass 2015; Foy 2014; Hauptman 2013; Krishnan 2009b; Krishnan 2009a; Kastan 2013; Lewis 2015; Lin et al. 2008; Marchant et al. 2011; Newton 2015; Jones 2018; Righetti et al. 2018; Haas / Fischer 2017.
969 Saxon 2014: 107; see Anderson / Waxman 2017.
970 See Schulzke 2013: 203-219.
971 Article 36 2015.
972 See Santoni de Sio / van den Hoven 2018: 6-11.
973 Santoni de Sio / van den Hoven 2018: 7.

human agent in the design history or use context involved in designing, programming, operating and deploying the autonomous system who (a) understands or is in the position to understand the capabilities of the system and the possible effects in the world of its use; (b) understands or is in the position to understand that others may have legitimate moral reactions toward them because of how the system affects the world and the role they occupy."[974]

7.12 Democracy and Data-Based Systems

7.12.1 Data-Based Systems as Democratizing Force

Technology can be characterized as a "medium of liberalization"[975] because technology-based innovations impede totalitarian information monopolies, independent science undermines the technological foundation of its authoritarian power, and the control of the perception of history becomes highly possible due to technology-enabled access to historical facts. Digital transformation and the use of data-based systems embody a "digital structural change of the public"[976]. Democratic opinion-forming and decision-making processes, political discourse, and political participation can benefit from "transnational communication-communities"[977] thanks to the Internet enabling "the single individual in his physically isolated existence in front of the computer to communicate instantly with a large group of people all over the world, whose number is limited only by his own processing capacity and attention span"[978]. Election campaigns and political parties on the Internet as well as virtual political parties but also the politically relevant "private sphere"[979] (personal, less anonymous, massmedia space of social media – also for political discourse) are some manifestations of this technology-based change-process.[980]

A necessary condition for the fairness of these virtual elements of democracy is net neutrality. "Net neutrality means the equal treatment of

---

974 Santoni de Sio / van den Hoven 2018: 9.
975 Luebbe 1990a: 168.
976 Bieber 2013: 156.
977 Honneth 2011: 565.
978 Honneth 2011: 560-561.
979 See Papacharissi 2002: 9-27.
980 See Bieber 2013: 157-164.

data, regardless of their origin and nature."[981] Otherwise, economic and political exploitation of unequal treatment of data and discrimination in the communication-platform known as the Internet would be imminent.[982]

Multiple digital techniques can enhance political participation and democratization respecting human rights and striving for political justice as well as peace building by enabling and reinforcing the exchange of information, opinions, and ideas by mobilizing, by empowering, and by creating more transparency.[983] "Advances in information communication technology are dramatically improving real-time communication and information-sharing. By improving access to information and facilitating global debate, they foster democratic participation. By amplifying the voices of human rights defenders and helping to expose abuses, these powerful technologies offer the promise of improved enjoyment of human rights."[984]

Looking at, for example, blockchain technology from an ethical standpoint and taking into account especially one main characteristic of blockchain technology, namely decentralization ("'[d]ecentralization' describes conditions under which the actions of many agents cohere, and are effective despite the fact that they do not rely on reducing the number of people whose will counts to direct effective action"[985]), it is possible to identify – especially with human rights as the ethical point of reference but only under the condition of respect for the state and for the rule of law – as an ethically positive element of blockchain technology the democratic opportunities it creates. For a democratic system, blockchain technology could provide censorship-resistant organizational models and a decentralized repository for identity verification. Furthermore, it could enable state authorities to become more efficient and effective in providing their services by relying on decentralized self-evolving digitalization.[986]

In addition, blockchain technology could help to overcome challenges arising for democracy due to a lack of integrity among political leaders and decision-makers. By, for example, also documenting the promises of election campaigns and their realization as the consequence of political positions defended by politicians, it could enable trustworthy and content-

---

981 Bieber 2013: 166.
982 See Bieber 2013: 166-168.
983 See UNESCO 2019: 54-61; Martin-Shields 2013; Kahl / Puig Larrauri 2013; Muggah / Diniz 2013.
984 Office of the UN High Commissioner for Human Rights n.d.
985 Benkler 2006: 62.
986 See Adams et al. 2018: 134-135.

based political representation. Beyond that, it could open a horizon of transparency of influence by, for example, documenting the financial support of politicians, of political parties, and of political campaigns.[987] Both – trustworthy and content-based political representation and transparency of influence – could increase citizens' active political participation as motivating factors. "Governments and their secrets are increasingly exposed to the democratic gaze"[988]. This impact is even enhanced by the possibility that generally blockchain technology itself is open to being shaped by the participating entities.[989]

Finally, blockchain technology can be categorized – in the framework by Langdon Winner[990] – as belonging to "inherently political technologies, man-made systems that appear to require, or to be strongly compatible with, particular kinds of political relationships"[991] because due to its decentralized nature, blockchain technology calls for a democratic system rather than for a repressive autocracy. (In order to illustrate this aspect further, contrariwise, the nuclear bomb "as it exists at all, its lethal properties demand that it be controlled by a centralized, rigidly hierarchical chain of command closed to all influences that might make its working unpredictable. The internal system of the bomb must be authoritarian"[992].)

A condition for the realization of these democratic opportunities of blockchain technology and due to the fact that "blockchain technologies (are) not merely a technical matter, but that it strongly relates to the ways in which we normatively construct, or rather configure our social world"[993], there is a necessity to "explore how we can implement them in a way that empowers people but that also leaves room for mitigating the potential dangers they bring about. This will require investigating how the governance of the design and use of these technologies can be improved, for instance by looking at ways in which the design process can be organized in a more democratic way"[994].

---

987 See Crichton 2018.
988 Crouch 2008: 21.
989 See Evans 2014.
990 See Winner 1980.
991 Winner 1980: 123.
992 Winner 1980: 131.
993 Reiijers / Coeckelbergh 2018: 127.
994 Reiijers / Coeckelbergh 2018, 127.

7.12.2 Data-Based Systems as Threat for Democracy

While data-based systems improve the respect, the protection, the implementation, and the realization of the human right to political participation by improving real-time communication, information-sharing, and access to information, by facilitating global debate, by fostering democratic participation, by amplifying the voices of human rights defenders, by exposing abuses, the same technologies can enhance "networked authoritarianism"[995], the concentration of power for the benefit of a few by excluding the rest,[996] and electronic surveillance and interception can threaten individual rights to privacy and to freedom of expression and association. Data-based systems can inhibit the free functioning of a vibrant civil society.[997] "At its best, the digital revolution will empower, connect, inform and save lives. At its worst, it will disempower, disconnect, misinform and cost lives."[998] Both areas of potential highlighted by the UN High Commissioner for Human Rights Michelle Bachelet, not only the promising and positive one, need to be addressed thoroughly. "Online content personalization by artificial intelligence offers relevant content and connections. But it may manipulate how humans use their right to seek information and their right to form an opinion. This could weaken the pluralism of ideas and the degree of exposure to verified information."[999]

The challenges of manipulating humans arise.[1000] "Because here the right to self-determination and autonomy is already fundamentally restricted. You can no longer determine which news feed you get on Facebook; you don't determine the sorting of your search results; Google does that for you. And not because Google loves them, but because it pursues economic self-interest. You are already manipulated by that, every one of us is. The madness is that these AI-based systems have penetrated so deeply into our society that they have become virtually without alternative. When you consider the democratic political influence that this gives an unelected CEO, it's really astonishing that the outrage over this is not much greater."[1001] Tristan Harris, a former Google employee, states: "All of us are

---

995 See McKinnnon 2012.
996 See Noble 2018; Madrigal 2019; Morozov 2013.
997 See Amnesty International 2020a.
998 Bachelet 2019.
999 UNESCO 2019: 17.
1000 See Tufekci 2019.
1001 Koeszegi 2019.

jacked into this system (...) All of our minds can be hijacked. Our choices are not as free as we think they are."[1002]

There are the challenges of manipulating of democratic opinion-forming and decision-making processes (e.g., through behavioral micro-targeting) and of hacking votes and elections, since digital transformation and data-based systems are making it possible to manipulate individuals, democratic opinion-forming and decision-making processes, votes and elections. "Decades after building the infrastructure of the Internet, and developing its applications and adjusting our social behavior, we are just now beginning to understand how it threatens core elements of democratic societies in unanticipated ways."[1003] Facing these challenges, the UN Human Rights Council emphasized that human rights – including the human right to political participation and democracy – are of course also universally valid in a digital reality and in a reality with data-based systems as well.[1004]

This danger is becoming even greater when technology companies sell the data of their users to the highest bidder based on purely economic considerations, even if this leads to crimes against and the criminal infiltration and destabilization of established democracies. For example, Facebook sold the data of 87 million users to the British consulting company Cambridge Analytica, which then used it to influence the US American presidential elections of 2016.[1005] "It was Eric Schmidt (...) who first pried open this Pandora's box, paving the way for the transfer of surveillance capitalism's core mechanisms to the electoral process"[1006] in the two presidential campaigns of Barack Obama.[1007] Other ruling powers are also thought to have manipulated democratic opinion-forming and decision-making processes.[1008] Chris Wylie, whistleblower of Cambridge Analytica, states: "I think it's worse than bullying, because people don't necessarily know it's being done to them. At least bullying respects the agency of people because they know (...) if you do not respect the agency of people, anything that you're doing after that point is not conducive to a democracy. And fundamentally, information warfare is not conducive to democracy."[1009]

1002 Lewis 2017.
1003 Asaro 2019: 552.
1004 See United Nations Human Rights Council 2019.
1005 See Swiss National Radio and Television SRF 2018.
1006 Zuboff 2019: 280.
1007 See Zuboff 2019: 121-127.
1008 See Hurtz 2018.
1009 Cadwalladr 2018.

Thus, democratic rights protected by the human rights of all humans are blatantly violated.

The politically targeted use of fake news and disinformation where companies of social media platforms monitor their distribution and thus turn into accomplices and also actively spread fake news and thus become perpetrators also endangers democratic opinion-forming and decision-making processes.[1010] In the last consequence, this undermines democracy in and of itself. For example, Facebook and Twitter refused to take down a video showing Speaker Nancy Pelosi ripping up President Donald Trump's State of the Union speech that was edited to appear as if she was doing so as Trump saluted a Tuskegee airman in the audience. Trump shared the video on Facebook and Twitter. Facebook and Twitter both said the video does not violate their policies.[1011] The fundamental threat to democracy by fake news consists in their prevalence even after being identified as fake news.[1012]

Furthermore, the digitally supported "bubbles" do not exactly help democratic discourse, because humans no longer need to deal with other political views and opinions, but will be technologically protected from them. Social media, instead of professional journalism becomes the main source of information, which not only poisons democratic opinion-forming and decision-making processes but also destroys independent journalism as a pillar of a democracy as well. Data-based systems decide which information humans get – based on an economic calculus rather than a quality-based triage. This results in furthering more radical and extreme content. Incorrect news receive at least the same attention as facts and independent analysis. Marginal opinions are presented like mainstream positions. False information can be disseminated purposefully. Political actors can manipulate humans and can use this highly effective and efficient propaganda machinery.[1013]

Beyond that, this opens up the possibility for politicians and parties to use unquestioned, uncritical, and manipulative propaganda, which is ethically highly problematic in terms of human rights – especially democratic rights – and which also includes systematic "message control". Thanks to the new information and communication technologies, politicians and parties can use propaganda to manipulate their supporters directly, imme-

---

1010 See Javers 2020.
1011 See Javers 2020.
1012 See Lazer et al. 2018.
1013 See Piater 2020.

diately, and without any journalistic filters (e.g., as regards the truth, authenticity, and relevance). Instead of having to answer critical questions, for example, from public television stations, which is one pillar of the so-called "fourth power" of a democracy, and the critical public, politicians can broadcast their propaganda via their own channels (their own digital TV channels, social media etc.). They can almost completely evade direct contact with the previous media and their critical questions and, as such, dictate the topics to be covered by the remaining remnants of journalism. Budget cuts for public media and media in general, as well as the fight for survival to get advertisements, are all grist to their mills. For example, Friedrich Merz, former candidate for being the federal chairperson for the CDU and candidate for chancellor in Germany, thinks traditional media is dispensable.[1014] "We don't need it anymore". Politicians can use social media channels such as YouTube for their own interests and "keep their own interpretative sovereignty. (…) And that's the good news of digitalization (…) At the moment, there is a real power shift going on between those who spread news and those who create them. In addition, it is in favor of those who create them. (…) Nowadays, you can reach an audience that the public, but also the private institutionalized media no longer reach, through your own channels, through YouTube. (…) Through these channels (you) have a possibility to take care of your own interests, to keep your own interpretative sovereignty over what you have said, in a completely different form than we had before."[1015] "Here, an attempt is made to undermine journalists and media as the fourth pillar of the state", criticizes the German Journalists' Association (DJV).[1016]

Finally, Facebook and Google hijack content from journalism in order to conquer the position of the source for news and apply "radical indifference". "Radical indifference means that it doesn't matter what is in the pipelines as long as they are full and flowing."[1017] Facebook, e.g., opted for unifying how its News Feed looks like. "All news stories looked roughly the same as each other (…) whether they were investigations in *The Washington Post*, gossip in the *New York Post*, of flat-out lies in the *Denver Guardian*, an entirely bogus newspaper."[1018] This has a dramatic impact on the role of journalism and media for a democracy, it furthers false news

---

1014 See Die Zeit 2020.
1015 Die Zeit 2020.
1016 Die Zeit 2020.
1017 Zuboff 2019: 512.
1018 Thompson / Vogelstein 2018.

and its resonance, and it provides the option of corruption in the interaction with Facebook, Google, etc.[1019]

Beyond that, from an ethical point of view and with reference to human rights and in particular to democratic rights, the question arises of how "a technology with such an audacity should be implemented comprehensively, without even a single citizen being asked if they want that their entire world to be designed according to the technical fantasies of a powerful group of men in the legendary Silicon Valley"[1020], with outrageously high gains for a few and high costs for the majority of humans and the environment – due to the "self-perpetuating tendency for power, wealth, and resources to concentrate in the hands of a few"[1021]. Humans seem to lose their grip on the world. They seem to be robbed of their lives and are manipulatively degraded and degenerated to needs-satisfiers. They are pushed to lose some capabilities, and their mental health is put at risk. The advance of digital transformation and data-based systems results in a new definition of even the last aspect of the world that humans knew so well, without giving humans the chance to make a decision that has been thought through.[1022]

Finally, democratic systems must be aware that "tools of surveillance and propaganda (coupled with) directly to automated violent attacks, which would be enabled by autonomous weapons and algorithms of violence, would take those threats to terrifying new levels. Tyrannical governments would be able to target their critics with little effort, cost, or risk. Violent extremists could sow fear and terror at far greater scales, and with less effort and less risk of being held to account. (…) civil discourse, liberal values, and the fundamental institutions of democracy could face relentless attacks."[1023]

Due to their procedural focus, democratic opinion-forming and decision-making processes always run the risk of losing sight of "material guiding principles. This is shown by developments over the last years, where individual interests succeeded in gaining influence in politics and legislative procedures – also by using new technologies. In this respect, however, the Constitution contains a still relevant corrective against the dangers that (could) follow from a viewpoint that puts at the center only the 'legitima-

---

1019 See Zuboff 2019: 504-512.
1020 Welzer 2019.
1021 Shanahan 2015: 166.
1022 See Zuboff 2019.
1023 Asaro 2019: 553.

tion by procedure': a materially understood principle of republic. With all openness for the democratic process (for online participation, involvement in the discussion over Twitter and other services, electronic voting, the willingness to recognize swarm intelligence and to see it as addition to representative democracy), the orientation on the common welfare of all state actions must be preserved. The ethos of the common welfare constitutes the lasting substance of a material understanding of the principle of republic. Res publica is constituted by the objective of the rule, not by the person who rules or the procedures of ruling. It is a trustee service: ruling *for* the people, but not necessarily *by* the people. The basic difference between the true will of the people and the good cause of the people remains. The generality in the sense of the common interest has a double point of reference: it describes the circle of persons to which the common welfare relates, meaning the community (subjective generality), but also the thing that constitutes the common best (objective generality). Solely referring to the democratic process that creates and puts common welfare in concrete terms, however, is not sufficient. The democratic procedure has an indicative impact, but not in the sense of a *guarantee* for being correct, but in the sense of a *presumption* of being correct"[1024]. While democratic systems before the start of digital transformation have proved to be able to guarantee the orientation towards the common welfare, digitalized and data-based democracy still needs to show that it is capable of providing the same orientation towards the common welfare.[1025]

The ubiquity of media through digital transformation and data-based systems, the technical possibility of providing equal access to all humans corresponds, from a media-ethical point of view, with the obligation to also realize this potential.[1026]

The ubiquity of media through digital transformation and data-based systems, at the same time, leads to an increase in possibilities to hurt humans (e.g., new forms and possibilities to violate the private sphere, data protection, etc.), which should be addressed in the service of omni-dynamic social justice and by adapting the existing, already legally binding, human rights in a corresponding specific and goal-oriented manner. "These technologies are providing powerful new tools of surveillance and propaganda to tyrannical governments and violent extremists. As such, they pose critical threats to existing democracies, as well as to the growth and ascen-

---

1024 Herzog 2016: 7-8, emphasis in the text.
1025 See Schulz 2016: 136-137.
1026 See Kirchschlaeger 2020b.

dency of new democracies."[1027] Adaptation[1028] knows, unlike interpretation, no change in content, but a contextualization – with regard to digital transformation and data-based systems in the sense of "updating" and "visualizing", which should lead to a situation where human rights and justice laboriously fought for over centuries will not be eradicated by digital transformation and data-based systems. From this perspective, numerous research desiderata emerge, in particular with regard to media-ethical issues that should, on the one hand, be embedded in empirical research, such as the question of whether the access to information really is equally distributed globally or how the right to privacy is being violated, and, on the other hand, on a conceptual level of how the right to privacy and data protection can be implemented in view of new, technology-based attacks.

7.12.3 Online Racist Hate Speech

Or, if one takes into account the Internet and social media (such as Twitter, Facebook, YouTube, etc.), there is from an ethical point of view, among other things, the tension between the freedom of information and censorship to protect against racism as racism and racist hate speech are found on the Internet and in social media.[1029] In an exemplary, in-depth analysis, the question of how to deal with the conflict between these two generally legitimate demands will be addressed – on the one hand the protection from racism, on the other hand the freedom of expression and information – by using human rights as an ethical frame of reference.[1030]

The European Commission against Racism and Intolerance (ECRI) of the Council of Europe stated in its 2014 annual report that the Internet is developing into a medium for racism and xenophobia. This worrying development has increased in Europe during the reporting period.[1031] Racism on the Internet has increased to such an extent that, for example, the German government made a deal with various Internet companies on December 15, 2015 that hate speech has to be removed from the Internet within 24 hours after it is identified.[1032] Racial discrimination on the Inter-

---

1027 Asaro 2019: 552-553.
1028 See Kirchschlaeger 2015d.
1029 See UNESCO 2019: 34-43.
1030 See Kirchschlaeger 2016a.
1031 See Council of Europe: European Commission against Racism and Intolerance (ECRI) 2014.
1032 See German Federal Ministry of Justice and Consumer Protection 2015.

net is becoming a more prevalent problem for adolescents.[1033] This development contributes to a tendency of "normalization" of nationalist, xenophobic, racist, and anti-Semitic rhetoric and of the political parties and the politicians using this kind of language spreading fear within societies and polarization of societies.[1034]

Mutuma Ruteere as UN Special Rapporteur for Racism points out: "The increase of (...) the use of the Internet and social media by extremist groups and individuals to hate speech and incite racial violence, and the increased number of incidents of racist violence and crimes prompted by racist content on the Internet remain to be addressed"[1035]. The UN Committee against Racial Discrimination points out in its General Comment No. 35 that racial hate speech on the Internet needs to be stopped.[1036] Even at that time Chairman of Google, Eric Schmidt, demanded that the Internet be monitored, because he recognized that, for example, in Myanmar, racism against the Muslim minority Rohingya is being incited on the Internet. This shows that, according to Schmidt, one needs to examine our relationship to the Internet in principle. The Internet is only an instrument. It is our duty to reign in its power.[1037] For example, YouTube has become an important instrument for right-wing extremists.[1038]

Censorship on the internet for protection against racism – censorship understood as planned and systematic control and oppression of communication[1039] in the form of prohibiting information and expression or deleting posts[1040] by states or private actors[1041] – could be an expression of this guiding influence of humans on the instrument "Internet".[1042]

At the same time, it needs to be emphasized that the Internet serves the end of freedom of expression and information.[1043] Frank La Rue as UN Special Rapporteur on the Right to Freedom of Expression and Information, points out that people are not only passive recipients, but also active

---

1033 See, e.g., Brendesha 2015.
1034 See Wodak 2016.
1035 United Nations 2012.
1036 See Massit-Folléa 2013: 75.
1037 See Schmidt 2015; Massit-Folléa 2013: 89.
1038 See Falenczyk 2019: 59.
1039 See Hoffmann-Riem 2001: Article 5, 156; see also Hueper 2004; Koreng 2010.
1040 See Hoffmann et al. 2015: 134-135.
1041 See Fiedler 2002: 18-23.
1042 See Koreng 2010: 215-217; see also Hoffmann et al. 2015: 134-135.
1043 See Benedek 2008; see also Kirchschlaeger 2013a: 303-309.

authors of information.[1044] It opens up new possibilities of participation and opinion-making at a national and international level.[1045] Thanks to the Internet, democracy movements in totalitarian states can link up and survive despite massive repression. The Internet can be described as a "democratizing force".[1046]

Preserving freedom of expression and information on the Internet allows for the exchange of perspectives, experiences, knowledge and insights that contribute to the further development of society, if they are not limited by censorship.

On the one hand, the Internet in particular opens up many options for global exchange across countries, cultures, and religions, and for raising awareness against racism and for respect and tolerance.[1047] On the other hand, the Internet offers a wide platform for spreading racist thoughts.[1048]

Should racist content be freely accessible to Internet users and only be evaluated and condemned by them as responsible persons? Or should the freedom of information and expression be limited on the Internet in order to contain racism? Or does censorship need to be understood as an instrument that even plays into the hands of dictators and helps to legitimize their prohibition of freedom of expression and information?

Human rights as an ethical frame of reference can contribute to a critical evaluation of the current challenge of the tension between censorship to protect against racism and the freedom of expression and information.

At first glance, human rights as an ethical frame of reference may not seem very helpful for this tension concerning the Internet. Because both poles of this tension – the protection against racism and the freedom of expression and information – are protected by human rights. Article 2 of the Universal Declaration of Human Rights of 1948 protects everyone from racism and discrimination. Article 19 guarantees the right to freedom of expression and information for everyone, which is applicable for all means of communication – including the Internet.[1049] Both human rights cannot

---

1044 See La Rue 2011: 19.
1045 See Mertes 2010: 10-11.
1046 See Laidlaw 2015; Barlow 1996.
1047 See UN Committee on the Elimination of Racial Discrimination (CERD) 2013.
1048 See Eliasson 2015.
1049 See UN Special Rapporteur on Freedom of Opinion and Expression 2011.

only be legally justified, but morally as well.[1050] This leads, on the one hand, to the situation that – also by referring to human rights – deliberate censorship of the Internet, including the violation of the right to freedom of expression and information, is demanded in order to respect and implement the right to freedom from discrimination.[1051]

On the other hand, an argument can be made against such censorship of the Internet by using the right to freedom of expression and information on the internet.[1052] The right to freedom of expression and information on the Internet initiates and furthers the realization of human rights.[1053] Furthermore, this line of argument would underestimate the maturity of people by prohibiting extremist publications in order to protect people that are less able to judge and are more easily influenced.[1054] Unlike the European continent, the US government puts more importance on the freedom of expression and information and is therefore willing to accept racism on the Internet.[1055] This undermines the protection against racism and discrimination.[1056]

Beyond that, it leads to concerns of who will ultimately define what should be censored in order to protect humans against racism on the Internet.[1057] Governments and tech companies would gain an authority to categorize opinions and information and to force their own views on the global users of the internet.[1058] In this context, it is feared that this would increase an already fast-growing censorship of the Internet through totalitarian states that is politically motivated.[1059]

Finally, it is necessary to respect the uniqueness of the Internet, which consists of freeing human ideas from physical constraints such as space,

---

1050 For a justification of the right to non-discrimination, see Kirchschlaeger 2015a; for a justification of the right to freedom of expression and information, see Kirchschlaeger 2013a: 303-309.

1051 See Council of Europe: European Commission against Racism and Intolerance (ECRI) 2014.

1052 See Benedek / Kettemann 2013: 23-44; Electronic Privacy Information Centre n.d.

1053 See Benedek / Kettemann 2013: 168-169.

1054 See Stoeber 2011: 131.

1055 See Rosenfeld 2012; Bleich 2013; Mensching 2014; Schell 2014: 85; Jacobs 2013.

1056 See Fofiu 2013; Shooman 2014: 140-178; Daniels 2009.

1057 See Woodward 2012.

1058 See Woodward 2012.

1059 See Haibach / Zeidler 2005; Land 2013: 449-456.

time and the material world in general, as well as from censorship.[1060] The surplus of information forces humans to rethink. The dynamic has no limits, unlike in the real world.[1061]

Both lines of argument recognize two *conflicting* human rights and decide in favor of one or the other human right. This automatically leads to a violation of one of the two human rights, which cannot be legitimized. Because the human being is a bearer of *all human rights*. And *all human rights* protect essential elements and areas of human existence, which humans need to survive and live as humans.[1062]

This is why one should think of the two human rights not as conflicting, but as going hand in hand. This is because the relationship between the two rights is based on the inherent principle of the indivisibility of human rights. The principle of indivisibility states that the catalogue of human rights is one, which means that human rights are indivisible.[1063] "Indivisible" means that all parts need to be realized and not just one part. The optimal protection of *all* human rights must always be pursued. The indivisibility of human rights can be *first* justified with human rights themselves, because a bearer of human rights cannot have those human rights selectively, but is a *bearer* of all human rights.

Second, every specific human right protects one essential element or one essential area of human existence needing human rights protection. Therefore, a specific human right only reaches its limit where it is no longer in concordance with other human rights or with the human rights of other humans.

This principle of indivisibility of human rights negates the talk about a conflict between two human rights and proposes an understanding of coexistence of all human rights – the right to non-discrimination and the right to freedom of expression and information.

This coexistence entails, *on the one hand*, interdependence. The implementation of the right to freedom of expression and information depends on no one being barred from accessing the Internet for racist reasons – for example, because of their religion.[1064] The implementation of the right to non-discrimination requires the freedom of expression and information,

---

1060 See Mancini 2005: v.
1061 See Mancini 2005: 131; Koespsell 2000; Mathias 2007: 97-98.
1062 See Kirchschlaeger 2013a: 194-195.
1063 See Lohmann et al. 2005.
1064 See Land 2013: 422-426.

for example, in order to raise awareness for respect of diversity and against racism through information or critical discussions.

On the other hand, this coexistence means that human rights themselves and other, specific human rights define boundaries for the respective specific human rights. For example, the right to freedom of expression and information sets a boundary for the right to non-discrimination such that not every criticism can be understood as an element protected by the right to non-discrimination.

The right to non-discrimination is a limit for the right to freedom of expression and information. The right to freedom of expression and information also contains the expression of views and opinions that hurt, shock or disturb.[1065] But there are also forms of expression and information that are *not* compatible with other human rights (Frank La Rue as UN Special Rapporteur on the right to freedom of expression and information talks about this in his report before the UN General Assembly on May 16, 2011)[1066] e.g. child pornography, hate speech and incitement to racial hatred.[1067] This selection was made, because these would violate other human rights and/or the human rights of others. Therefore, censorship oriented towards the protection against racism on the internet can be legitimized, as it is defined, for example, in the Additional Protocol to the Council of Europe Convention on Cybercrime concerning the criminalization of acts of a racist and xenophobic nature committed through computer systems of January 28, 2003.[1068] "Art. 3 para.1 of the Additional Protocol bind the member states to establish the distribution of racist and xenophobic material as criminal offences."[1069]

However, any restriction in this respect must go hand in hand with the right to freedom of expression and information, it must be based on human rights and has to be necessary and proportionate in a democratic society.[1070]

In this way, it is also possible to distance oneself from politically motivated censorship of the Internet by dictatorships and totalitarian systems.[1071] In this controlling approach to racism, a balance must be found

---

1065 See La Rue 2011; Jahangir 2008.
1066 See La Rue 2011: Paragraph 25.
1067 See UN Human Rights Committee 1983.
1068 See Council of Europe 2003.
1069 Mensching 2014: 252.
1070 Similar Spinello 2011: 48-50; see also Spinello 2002: 21-45; Benedek / Kettemann 2013: 47-48.
1071 See Mertes 2010: 14.

between hurtful, shocking and disturbing statements, which are legally admissible with reference to the right to freedom of opinion and information, and statements, which are not legally admissible because they turn others into the victims of hate messages.[1072] Human rights can function against this as "the heart of the 'humanization' of the Internet"[1073].

A further reason in favor of initiating measures on the Internet against racism is given by the fact that racism on the Internet leads to the situation that not all humans can exercise their freedom of expression and information, but are silenced. Because human rights are not exclusive rights, but belong to all humans equally, this also speaks in favor of eliminating racism on the Internet.[1074]

A further argument is derived from the reversal of the burden of proof. In view of the justifiability of the right to non-discrimination, in the context of the reversal of proof, "good reasons" would need to be given to legitimize why this right should not be applicable to the Internet. "Good reasons" means that it must be conceivable that all humans, given their effective freedom and autonomy as well as their full equality, would agree upon these reasons – within a model of thought and not within a real worldwide referendum – on ethical grounds. It will most likely be difficult to find "good reasons" for claiming that the right to non-discrimination should only be valid in the real world and not online.[1075]

Finally, the fact that rights and duties, which are applicable in the real world, are also applicable in the virtual world speaks in favor of limiting the freedom of expression and information on the Internet in order to fight against racism. But it needs to be taken into account that, compared to other media, on the Internet more communication with more people is possible at lower costs and filters such as editors of other media are not in place.[1076] This global accessibility within seconds represents new forms of communicative power.[1077] In other words, it is about enforcing offline standards online as well, while taking into account the online specifics.[1078] "The new offers for communication, exchange and media reception (...)

1072 See also Benedek / Kettemann 2013: 82-88.
1073 Delmas-Marty 2013: 15.
1074 See also Eliasson 2015.
1075 See Gagliardone 2015: 13.
1076 See Land 2013: 410.
1077 See Hausmanninger / Capurro 2002.
1078 See Benedek / Kettemann 2013: 19; to basic rights on the Internet in general see Hoffmann et al. 2015.

are in themselves not dangerous or harm humanity. They contain great human potential, but can also threaten the humane."[1079]

For those reasons, an international consultation with all stakeholders – e.g. internet companies, states, non-governmental organizations, etc. – needs to be held in order to usefully fight racism on the Internet.[1080] Here, human rights can serve as an ethical frame of reference.[1081] On the occasion of the fiftieth anniversary of the UN Convention against Racism on December 2, 2015, the then Vice UN Secretary General Jan Eliasson said: "Our lives, as you all know, are increasingly lived online. And so, we must ensure that our values are alive online as well"[1082].

The realization of human rights is also at stake when data-based systems are used in the legal system. Already there is an increase in data-based systems operating for predicting crimes,[1083] predicting the outcome of a criminal procedure serving the risk assessment on defendants,[1084] and more efficiency[1085] in the process despite the sensitive asymmetry of power-relation between the state and the humans living in a state and despite the fundamental problems still prevailing with data-based systems, among others disproportionately adverse results output by data-based systems, reinforcement of systemic biases,[1086] perpetuation of biases,[1087] and creation of new biases (see further below, especially subchapter 7.17 Data-Protection and Privacy).[1088] From an ethical perspective, it is against justice, responsibility, and human rights that data-based systems with such a high grade of discriminatory risk, deficiency, and incorrectness are used to predict crimes in the legal system.

Beyond that, democratic opinion-forming and decision-making processes take time. Deliberations are essential to democratic governance, including governance of technology-based innovations and shifts. Digital trans-

---

1079   Filipović 2015: 6.
1080   See Laidlaw 2015: 58-281.
1081   See Massit-Folléa 2013: 89.
1082   Eliasson 2015.
1083   See Wyllie 2013; Ferguson 2014; Brayne et al. 2015; Joh 2017; Mateescu et al. 2015.
1084   See Kehl et al. 2017; Christin et al. 2015; Bavitz / Hessekiel 2018; Aletras et al. 2016; Hutson 2017.
1085   See Marr 2018.
1086   See Fry 2018; Simonite 2018; O'Neil 2016; Burgess 2016; Citron / Pasquale 2014.
1087   See Talbot et al. 2017b.
1088   See Barocas / Selbst 2016; Chouldechova 2016; Crawford 2016.

formation and data-based systems are outpacing democratic governance. There exists an asymmetry between the speed of innovation or the acceleration-rate of the speed of innovation and the tempo of democratic governance[1089] provoking a new form of "governance-gap" that enhances the original "governance-gap"[1090] originating from the globalization and the growing power of multinational corporations and declining power of nation-states – "the diminishing capacity of national governments to steer and constrain those dimensions of transnational business activity that affects the human rights of their populations (...) emerging as a result of the expanded power and capabilities of transnational business and weakened capabilities of states under conditions of economic globalization"[1091]. This asymmetry between the speed of innovation or the acceleration-rate of the speed of innovation by technology-corporations and the tempo of democratic governance and the unbalance of power[1092] must be addressed – either by democratically legislating that the speed of innovation or the acceleration-rate of the speed of innovation – "the speed of dreams"[1093] as described by Google – must be adapted to the tempo of democratic governance or adapting the tempo of democratic governance to the speed of innovation or the acceleration-rate of the speed of innovation. Both should happen – with an emphasis on the former because technology as well as technology-based innovation do not exist in a vacuum but rather in a social, political, and legal context with whom they interact and which they need to respect. Even Joseph Schumpeter – coining the concept of "creative destruction" – does not at all claim a high-speed "permissionless innovation"[1094] as it is promoted by technology-corporations. Instead, Schumpeter highlights the role of the capitalist system ("The capitalist process, not by coincidence but by virtue of its mechanism, progressively raises the standard of life of the masses"[1095]), emphasizing "mutations" as being of relevance from an economically evolutionary point of view. "These are enduring, sustainable, qualitative shifts in the logic, understanding, and practice of capitalist accumulation, not random, temporary, or oppor-

---

1089 See Mărcuț 2020; van Eeten 2017.
1090 MacDonald 2011: 549.
1091 MacDonald 2011: 549.
1092 See Nemitz 2018.
1093 Teller 2012.
1094 See Thierer 2014; Hayes 2011.
1095 Schumpeter 2008: 68.

tunistic reactions to circumstances."[1096] They create[1097] and – unfortunately, according to Schumpeter – destroy as well but for the social and economic good.[1098] These "mutations" take time and require patience. "We are dealing with a process whose every element takes considerable time in revealing its true features and ultimate effects. (...) We must judge its performance over time, as it unfolds through decades or centuries."[1099] The speed of innovation or the acceleration-rate of the speed of innovation must be adapted to the tempo of democratic governance because "mutation is not a fairy tale; it is rational capitalism, bound in reciprocity with its populations through democratic institutions. Mutations fundamentally change the nature of capitalism by shifting it in the direction of those it is supposed to serve."[1100]

Finally, speed and the "governance-gap" combined with the unprecedented power, not only financially and economically but also regarding the immediate impact of lobbying by technology-corporations on politicians, are a highly dangerous mixture for democracies.[1101] This dangerous mixture needs to be addressed by politicians more vigorously than it is starting to happen. "It is good that Amazon and Apple, Facebook and Google feel this kind of headwind. For too long they have been able to behave like supernatural beings to whom law and order apply only to a limited extent. Politicians on both sides of the Atlantic are finally doing what they have long neglected to do. They are asking the question of power. Who sets the rules of the digital world: governments or corporations?"[1102]

Eric Schmidt, as CEO of Google, admits: "The average American doesn't realize how much of the laws are written by lobbyists."[1103] Imagine Facebook, Amazon, Microsoft, Apple, Google & Co with all the tools of political influence, outreach, and manipulation in their hands, lobbying politicians who want to become elected or reelected not to regulate them.[1104] "The danger that the computer poses is to human autonomy. The more that is known about a person, the easier it is to control him. Insuring the

---

1096 Zuboff 2019: 51.
1097 See Schumpeter 2008: 83.
1098 See Schumpeter 1991: 412.
1099 Schumpeter 2008: 83.
1100 Zuboff 2019: 52.
1101 See Kergueno 2018.
1102 Nezik 2019: 24.
1103 Thompson 2010.
1104 See Issenberg 2013.

liberty that nourishes democracy requires a structuring of societal use of information and even permitting some concealment of information."[1105]

Imagine Facebook, Amazon, Microsoft, Apple, Google & Co with all the data they have about a politician lobbying this politician not to regulate them. Jack Ma, founder of Alibaba, calls for even less regulation: "The state must do what the state does, and companies must do what companies must do."[1106]

Imagine Facebook, Amazon, Microsoft, Apple, Google & Co, with all the financial power they possess to fund politicians and parties, testing in the public discourse new ideas, which are in violation of human rights, the rule of law, and constitutions of democracies.

Imagine Facebook, Amazon, Microsoft, Apple, Google & Co acquiring most of the groundbreaking research in data-based systems and promising talent. "The real problem is these people are not dispersed through society. The intellect and expertise are concentrated in a small number of companies."[1107]

Imagine Facebook, Amazon, Microsoft, Apple, Google & Co possessing the instruments to create and provide content, e.g. Google: "Google has begun to develop its own content over time, such as its own price results for shopping and its own reviews for local businesses. In these situations, Google is acting both as a search engine and a content provider."[1108]

Imagine Facebook, Amazon, Microsoft, Apple, Google & Co using their financial resources to fund academic research and policy papers against regulation[1109] and to get rid of critical academic voices. The following case serves as an exemplary illustration of such attacks against freedom of research and freedom of opinion as well as of corruption and of destruction of independent academia: "In the hours after European antitrust regulators levied a record $2.7 billion fine against Google in late June, an influential Washington think tank learned what can happen when a wealthy tech giant is criticized. The New America Foundation has received more than $21 million from Google; its parent company's executive chairman, Eric Schmidt; and his family's foundation since the think tank's founding in 1999. That money helped to establish New America as an elite voice in policy debates on the American left and helped Google shape those debates.

1105   Schwartz 1989: 676.
1106   Yang 2018: 23.
1107   Sample 2017.
1108   Luca et al. 2015: 2.
1109   See Mullins / Nicas 2017.

But not long after one of New America's scholars posted a statement on the think tank's website praising the European Union's penalty against Google, Mr. Schmidt, who had been chairman of New America until 2016, communicated his displeasure with the statement to the group's president, Anne-Marie Slaughter, according to the scholar. (...) Those worries seemed to be substantiated a couple of days later, when Ms. Slaughter summoned the scholar who wrote the critical statement, Barry Lynn, to her office. He ran a New America initiative called Open Markets that has led a growing chorus of liberal criticism of the market dominance of telecom and tech giants, including Google, which is now part of a larger corporate entity known as Alphabet Inc., for which Mr. Schmidt serves as executive chairman. Ms. Slaughter told Mr. Lynn that 'the time has come for Open Markets and New America to part ways', according to an email from Ms. Slaughter to Mr. Lynn. The email suggested that the entire Open Markets team – nearly 10 full-time employees and unpaid fellows – would be exiled from New America. (...) Mr. Lynn, in an interview, charged that Ms. Slaughter caved to pressure from Mr. Schmidt and Google, and, in so doing, set the desires of a donor over the think tank's intellectual integrity. 'Google is very aggressive in throwing its money around Washington and Brussels, and then pulling the strings,' Mr. Lynn said. 'People are so afraid of Google now.'"[1110]

Imagine Facebook, Amazon, Microsoft, Apple, Google & Co with their poor understanding of and disrespect for human rights, the rule of law, and democracy possess enormous political power. For example, Sergey Brin, co-founder of Google, comments on the ruling of the European Court of Justice asserting "the right to be forgotten" as a fundamental principle of EU law: "I wish we could just forget the ruling."[1111] Larry Page, CEO and co-founder of Google, states: "In general, having the data present in companies like Google is better than having it in the government with no due process to get that data, because we obviously care about our reputation. I'm not sure the government cares about that as much."[1112] Is it surprising that massive opposition could be missing? "Google's innovation method has always aimed to test social 'creepy lines' (Eric Schmidt), to strain them again and again in order to open up new development and market fields. The terrain of social no-go areas, as large sections of the Silicon Valley elite have recognized, is flexible – and it is precisely the emanci-

---

1110 Vogel 2017.
1111 Sterling 2014.
1112 Waters 2014a.

patory promises of quasi-utopian visions that seem to make certain projects and products ever more dynamic. If one considers the predictive health innovations from the valley of the future, it becomes clear that the hyperbolic statements of yesteryear have not gone entirely unheard, and that storytellers from the Valley have hardly left business acumen unaffected."[1113]

Multinational technology-corporations apply a dispossession process involving four stages: incursion – habituation – adaptation – redirection.[1114] They have learned how to sweep the framework of the legally and ethically unacceptable away applying the method "form follows fiction"[1115]. "According to the motto 'clarify today, design tomorrow', the aim is not only to anticipate resistance to or potential for new developments, but also, often with greater consequences, to use the power of fiction to measure the scope for future facts."[1116] The video "The Selfish Ledger" commissioned by Google represents a highly relevant and telling example.[1117] It presents the future of the company possessing so much data enabling it to map human behaviors, social issues, mental health, … It presents the future of humans as an "epigenetic data provider"[1118]. And it offers a teleological account of human evolution aspiring to reach the following: "User-centered design principles have dominated the world of computing for many decades, but what if we looked at things a little differently? What if the ledger could be given a volition or purpose rather than simply acting as a historical reference? What if we focused on creating a richer ledger by introducing more sources of information? What if we thought of ourselves not as the owners of this information, but as custodians, transient carriers, or caretakers?"[1119] Such an understanding does not leave any space for human dignity, freedom, and autonomy, individuality, plurality, diversity – for an individual perspective. "The fact that the euphorically welcomed technology of our communication media aims at the opposite of its logic – transparency, transparence, control, permanent accessibility – shows how bad the individual is in reality. The egoism of our days is not an expression of radicalized individuality, but the consequence of a self-controlling competitive society in which everyone seeks their advantage by doing what others do. Especially when everyone in a society thinks only of himself, ev-

---

1113 Nosthoff / Maschewski 2019: 89.
1114 See Zuboff 2019: 137-154.
1115 See Bleecker 2009.
1116 Nosthoff / Maschewski 2019: 84.
1117 See Savov 2018.
1118 Nosthoff / Maschewski 2019: 85.
1119 Savov 2018.

eryone thinks the same."[1120] The collective and its good – defined by a multinational corporation – dominates. This comprises "a new form of biopolitical cybernetics, a systematic way of thinking that does not rely on laisser-faire and believes that a common good, a healthy mind in a healthy body, is created by letting things go unregulated. Harmony must rather be produced actively, through permanent small interventions and subtle corrections, through incentive systems and a constant data-based redesign of the social nervous system."[1121]

Moreover, there were fertile circumstances allowing these few technology-corporations to build their empire. "No single element is likely to have done the job, but together a convergence of political circumstances and proactive strategies helped enrich the habitat in which this mutation could root and flourish. These include (1) the relentless pursuit and defense of the founders' 'freedom' through corporate control and an insistence on the right to lawless space; (2) the shelter of specific historical circumstances, including the policies and juridical orientation of the neoliberal paradigm and the state's urgent interest in the emerging capabilities of behavioral surplus analysis and prediction in the aftermath of the September 2001 terror attacks; and (3) the intentional construction of fortifications in the worlds of politics and culture, designed to protect the kingdom and deflect any close scrutiny of its practices."[1122]

A few technology-corporations depart from the basic assumptions that there are two worlds – the real world and the virtual world – and that the virtual world is lawless. "The online world is not truly bound by terrestrial laws (…) it's the world's largest ungoverned space."[1123] Technology-corporations promote, systematically, a narrative of their "right to freedom from law"[1124]. "Their efforts have been marked by a few consistent themes: that technology companies such as Google move faster than the state's ability to understand or follow, that any attempts to intervene or constrain are therefore fated to be ill-conceived and stupid, that regulation is always a negative force that impedes innovation and progress, and that lawlessness is the necessary context for 'technological innovation'."[1125] Some examples illustrate this approach. Eric Schmidt, as CEO of Google, explains that

---

1120   Liessmann 2019: I.
1121   Nosthoff / Maschewski 2019: 88.
1122   Zuboff 2019: 101.
1123   Schmidt / Cohen 2014: 1.
1124   Zuboff 2019: 104.
1125   Zuboff 2019: 104.

there is no need to regulate Google because of the existing incentives for Google to "treat its users right."[1126] He also shows agreement with the antidemocratic formula by Andy Grove, former CEO of Intel: "High tech runs three-times faster than normal businesses. And the government runs three-times slower than normal businesses. So we have a nine-times gap (…) And so what you want to do is you want to make sure that the government does not get in the way and slow things down."[1127] And he emphasized: "Technology moves so fast that governments really shouldn't try to regulate it because it will change too fast, and any problem will be solved by technology. We'll move much faster than any government."[1128] Larry Page, co-founder of Google, elaborates: "Old institutions like the law and so on aren't keeping up with the rate of change that we've caused through technology. (…) The laws when we went public were 50 years old. A law can't be right if it's 50 years old, like it's before the internet. (…) Maybe we should set aside a small part of the world (…) as technologists we should have some safe places where we can try out some new things and figure out what is the effect on society, what's the effect on people, without having to deploy kind of into the normal world."[1129]

Beyond this and besides their financial and economic power and political influence, manipulative and totalitarian instruments, taking mankind hostage methodologically and conceptually to the detriment of human rights, the rule of law, and democracy, are developed on a scientific basis for enforced conformity.[1130] Alex Pentland, director of the Massachusetts Institute of Technology MIT-Labs "Connection Science" and "Human Dynamics", board member of AT&T, member of the advisory board of Google, is providing UBS, Accenture, IBM but also the governments of China and Turkey with insights and tools to manipulate and control social relations in public contexts as well as human behavior in social media and social networks.[1131] "Sociometric badges", as wearables, allow for a thorough insight that is "less about the content or the semantics of what is communicated than about monitoring physical reactions, latent behavior patterns or unconscious gestures – the computer scientist speaks here of 'honest signals' – so that a penetrating view of the self and the others, their

---

1126 Jenkins 2010.
1127 Cunningham 2011.
1128 Gobry / Schmidt 2011.
1129 Yarrow 2013.
1130 See Gertz 2016.
1131 See MIT Connection Science 2018.

atmospheric states of mind and moods emerges."[1132] This data is more effective for monitoring, controlling, and manipulating humans. "In traditional social science, you ask people questions using surveys. Typically, this just gets you responses that are socially acceptable but do not really reflect reality. Similarly, scientists talk about mining Twitter feeds and Facebook, but that's really just mining the socially constructed version of you. Reality mining is about what you actually do; it's not about how you imagine yourself."[1133]

This strict monitoring of humans builds the basis for a forced unification and harmonization in a collective – be it a corporation or a state. "All applications of the Human Dynamics Lab describe modes of technical supervision that are intended to determine and detect irregularities in people's behavior in order to guide and smooth them in an orderly fashion – in short: to bring a new order to everyday chaos."[1134] Wearables as instruments serve this social engineering aiming to redesign human behavior in order to increase social efficiency – "getting everyone to coordinate their behavior"[1135]. Social physics tries to change humans by monitoring, controlling, and manipulating humans by applying constant feedback. "The social physics answer is not to directly incentivize people to change themselves, but to create social pressure for change."[1136] For example, the unhealthy lifestyle of some individuals should be changed by wearables in order to reduce the costs of the collective health systems. Wearables enable technology-based companies "to measure idea flow within social networks and to deploy incentives that shape the pattern of social learning in real-world situations."[1137] In 2023, the sales of wearables is estimated to be 302.3 million pieces – monitoring, controlling, and manipulating every facet of human life. Individuals and collectives should be modelled in a way so societies can become fairer, trustworthier, and more stable –[1138] on a collective level.[1139] "That is the promise of social physics and a data-rich society."[1140] Wearables should build a "new nervous system" around the

1132 Nosthoff / Maschewski 2019: 43-44.
1133 Eggers 2014.
1134 Nosthoff / Maschewski 2019: 44.
1135 Pentland 2014a: 15.
1136 Eggers 2014.
1137 Pentland 2014a: 15.
1138 See Pentland 2014a: 250.
1139 See Pentland 2014a: 6.
1140 Pentland 2014a: 216.

entire humanity.[1141] This would open a "godlike vision on ourselves"[1142]. For example, "real-time flu tracking"[1143] based on wearables would help with the containment of pandemics.

The underlying assumption for this socio-physical approach is "that our behavior is deeply and immediately connected with that of other humans. Humans are seen to be social animals, where individuals are best likened to a musician in a jazz quartet. Of course, we can predict the behavior of these individuals from that of their associates: they are so focused on the group's overall performance and so sensitive to exactly complementing the others in the group that they almost cease to be an individual at all."[1144] This would be the end of individuality (as we know it) and the core idea of the movement of Enlightenment – human reason.[1145] Beyond that, human life is reduced to what is collectable as data by wearables.

This endeavor cannot hide that it is continuing the cybernetic tradition. "Regulate everything that is controllable and make the non-regulable controllable."[1146] Human liberty is understood as "programmable function of effectiveness"[1147], the human brain as a computer.[1148] At the Massachusetts Institute of Technology (MIT), Alex Pentland follows Norbert Wiener, founder of cybernetics, at the same institute, and states: "the term (cybernetics) has disappeared at MIT because cybernetics is everywhere, like air."[1149]

Finally, this substantial attack questioning almost everything the movement of the Enlightenment stands for benefits from a cornerstone of the movement of the Enlightenment – the trust in the human intellect and rational inquiry, which resulted in the development of scientific epistemology and in trust in science and technological progress leading to the above-introduced coerciveness (see above subchapter 7.5 Coerciveness). "Technical innovations often tend to overtake social norms, to silently question their effectiveness and validity and to simply change established world

---

1141   See Pentland 2008.
1142   Pentland 2008: 93.
1143   Pentland 2014a: 147.
1144   Pentland 2007: 16.
1145   See Pentland 2008: 87.
1146   Schmidt 1941: 41.
1147   Beer 1973: 6.
1148   See Steinbuch 1963: 2; Maltz 2015: 46.
1149   Pentland 2014c.

views and self-understandings."[1150] Technology creates facts that are intended to define the "new normality" ...

7.13 Automation of Mobility

7.13.1 It Is Not All about "Moral Dilemmas" ...

Automated driving, automated vehicles, self-driving cars, ... – subsumed under the umbrella-term the automation of mobility –[1151] do not only lead to fundamental changes in the daily professional and private life but in our society and in our economy as well. The automation of mobility can be coined in six stages:[1152]

"Level 0 (no driving automation): A human driver controls everything. There is no automated steering, acceleration, braking, etc.

Level 1 (driver assistance): There is a basic level of automation, but the driver remains in control of most functions. The SAE says lateral (steering) or longitudinal control (e.g. acceleration) can be done autonomously, but not simultaneously, at this level.

Level 2 (partial driving automation): Both lateral and longitudinal motion is controlled autonomously, for example with adaptive cruise control and functionality that keeps the car in its lane.

Level 3 (conditional driving automation): A car can drive on its own, but needs to be able to tell the human driver when to take over. The driver is considered the fallback for the system and must stay alert and ready.

Level 4 (high driving automation): The car can drive itself and does not rely on a human to take over in case of a problem. However, the system is not yet capable of autonomous driving in all circumstances (depending on situation, geographic area, etc.).

Level 5 (full driving automation): The car can drive itself without any expectation of human intervention, and can be used in all driving situations. There is significant debate among stakeholders about how far the

---

1150 Nosthoff / Maschewski 2019: 91.
1151 See Kyriakidis et al. 2015; Casner 2016; Radlmayr et al. 2014; Aeberhard et al. 2015; Watzenig / Horn 2016; Spieser et al. 2014; Alessandrini et al. 2014; Basu et al. 2018; Stocker / Shaheen 2018; Schulz et al. 2019; Heinrichs / Cyganski 2015; Winner et al. 2018; Pereira et al. 2017; Walker et al. 2018; Pech et al. 2016.
1152 On-Road Automated Driving (ORAD) Committee, Society of Automotive Engineers SAE International 2016.

process has come towards fully autonomous driving. Stakeholders also disagree about the right approach to introduce autonomous functionality into vehicles."[1153] Future development in the area of automation of mobility revolves around the questions of the role of the human driver (is the human driver eliminated[1154] or supported[1155]?) and of the availability-scope ("everything somewhere" ["very-high-level functionality is possible only in certain geographic areas or on certain roads that have been mapped in detail"] or "something everywhere": ["functionality is only introduced to an AV system when it can be deployed on any road and in any situation"[1156]])[1157].

The automation of mobility changes the perception of vehicles – away from isolated individual means of transportation towards a node in a communication network. "Thus it is pervasive 'networked' information systems that are now challenging ideas of the isolated car. It is increasingly apparent that cars are controlled by pervasive software and mobile 'devices'."[1158] In the course of the automation of mobility, vehicles and humans in vehicles are transformed into data-providers via data-based systems.[1159] Humans are hence confronted with the reality that, e.g., "the car-insurance company can monitor how, when and where I drive at any time, which threatens to undermine the solidarity principle of insurance in the long run."[1160] (The fundamental threats and attacks on privacy and data protection will be further elaborated below in subchapter 7.17 Data Protection and Privacy.)

The automation of mobility causes ethical opportunities and risks.[1161] The ethical dimension of the automation of mobility goes far beyond the

---

1153 OECD 2019a.
1154 See Lee 2018.
1155 See Lippert et al. 2018.
1156 OECD 2019a.
1157 See Walker-Smith 2013; International Transport Forum ITF 2018.
1158 Buschauer 2014: 22.
1159 See Carvalho et al. 2015; Holder et al. 2018; Bengler et al. 2014; Wang et al. 2020; Alkim 2018; Berković / Kosovac 2020; Sperling et al. 2019; Sabaliauskaite et al. 2018; Graef et al. 2019; Spielkamp 2019b.
1160 Steil 2019: 32.
1161 See Santoni de Sio 2016; Zhenji et al. 2016; Nyholm / Smids 2020; Goodall 2014; Lugano 2017; Gogoll / Mueller 2017; Zhou et al. 2019; Mladenovic / McPherson 2016; Bonnefon et al. 2016; Sparrow / Howard 2020; Hilgendorf 2020.

ethical question of the "trolley-dilemma"[1162]. Focusing from an ethical standpoint only on the "trolley-dilemma"[1163] would represent not only a reductionist view of the ethical dimension of the automation of mobility.[1164] It would also put something at the center of the attention, which is not unique about the automation of mobility.

The situation captured in the "trolley-dilemma" represents a moral dilemma independently from if the vehicle is automated or driven by a human. In other words, the moral dilemma surprisingly dominating the ethical discourse about the automation of mobility emerges in non-automated mobility as well.[1165] Therefore, one could conclude to not mainly focus the ethical assessment of the automation of mobility on this moral dilemma.

In addition, being a moral dilemma, there is no morally justifiable solution. The nature of a moral dilemma actually consists of a situation where a decision is required and both options are morally problematic.[1166] Therefore, none of them builds a morally acceptable solution. Instead, a third alternative must be found or adequate measures must be taken in order to avoid the possibility of such a moral dilemma. Again, this, though, is not a problem specific to the automation of mobility.

What seems to be specific for automated vehicles about the "trolley-dilemma" embedded in automated mobility is the possibility that the behavior of technological systems in such situations can be encoded in one way or the other. It can be argued though that, even under these circumstances, the automated vehicles must be encoded in a way which is looking for a third alternative option and which consists of adequate measures making sure to avoid the possibility of such a moral dilemma – again, nothing unique for automated mobility.

What opportunities of automated mobility arise from an ethical view? What challenges exist from automated mobility from an ethical view? In the following, those and similar questions will be discussed.

1162 See Foot 2002; Thomson 1985; Matzner 2019; Lütge et al. 2019; Braendle / Grunwald 2019; Grunwald 2018.

1163 See, e.g., Scholz / Kempf 2016; Herrmann / Brenner 2018.

1164 See Horizon 2020 Commission Expert Group 2020; Huebner et al. 2020; Rietz 2017.

1165 See Eimler et al. 2018.

1166 See Hilgendorf 2017; Manzeschke / Brink 2020. For the contrary position in the case of automation of mobility see Hevelke / Nida-Rümelin 2016; Schaeffner 2020.

7.13.2 Automated, not "Autonomous" Mobility

In automated mobility, as seen above, various grades of automation can be distinguished: the human driver alone, assisted, partly automated, highly automated, fully automated, and driverless.[1167] The transition phases paving the way to automated mobility without human drivers entail particular problems because in general, they run the specific risk to serve only efficiency and availability (e.g., Uber strives for efficiency and availability at the expense of human rights and human dignity)[1168] and to (not yet) respect the ethical principles and norms (e.g., security-standards, health-standards, human right to privacy and to data-protection). This specific risk of the intensification of the interconnection between the real and the virtual world in the realm of mobility must be addressed and strictly avoided – right from the beginning. In other words, the character of a transition phase as a temporary interval between the start of a transformation and the completion cannot be used as an excuse for violations of ethical principles and norms. Justice, responsibility, and human rights must be realized starting in the transition phase. Concrete measures to achieve that are precise and strictly implemented regulation consisting in, for example, authorization methods of innovative mobility-services, controlling-, supervision-, and evaluation-measures, the creation of experimental spaces and experience areas enabling a public discourse, compatibility of systems while introducing a digital layer to the transport system.

In this book, the term "automated" vehicles is deliberately used instead of "autonomous" vehicles. Because there can be no question of autonomy in the Kantian sense when speaking about vehicles as elaborated above in chapter 3 Can Ethical Judgment Be Delegated to Technologies?. While automated vehicles are programmed for expediency, autonomy – meaning the ability to subject oneself to moral laws that can be generalized and to follow them in one's own decisions and actions – characterizes humans. While the latter have moral capabilities, automated vehicles do not. Of course, automated vehicles can be programmed with ethical rules. This describes the term "moral technologies". This term, though, is not fitting, because ethical criteria will only be programmed into the driving system which makes morally acceptable actions possible –[1169], and that's it. The vehicles remain heteronomously governed, and there cannot be any

---

1167 See Axhausen 2016.
1168 See Taylor / Goggin 2019.
1169 See Wallach / Allen 2009.

question of moral capability. The moral capability is what distinguishes humans from other living beings and robots.[1170]

This conceptual differentiation does not contain a refusal to ethical rules in the programming of driving systems. It is necessary to take into account ethical aspects when designing, creating, developing, programming, producing, and training self-driving vehicles "in such a way that an unethical outcome can be avoided."[1171] Not only moral dilemma situations,[1172] but other situations as well could demand a "decision" from driving systems, for which the ethical rules programmed and trained will show the way.[1173]

The prerequisite would be a discussion or a consensus about ethical principles and norms.[1174] "One has to agree on what control systems should be implemented into robot systems – typically in the form of 'if-then' links. In a general context, this would be reaching an agreement between a producer of robots and the user of those robots, meaning the service user."[1175] Humans, not driving systems, remain the subjects for deciding what ethical principles and norms are used and also the subjects of responsibility.[1176] A consensus among humans about ethical principles and norms is necessary because of the risks and dangers involved in "mixed traffic" for the safety of all road users.[1177] This is an argument against the options of suppliers of automated mobility to choose for example a utilitarian approach or a deontological approach for their vehicles to follow,[1178] or that users should have the choice.[1179]

7.13.3 Subjectivity of Responsibility

Always – even on level 5 (full driving automation) – humans remain the subjects of responsibility. As elaborated above in chapter 3 Can Ethical Judgment Be Delegated to Technologies? and further specified in subchapter 6.2 The Principle of Responsibility, the subjectivity of responsibility re-

---

1170 See Kirchschlaeger 2017a.
1171 Krenn 2016: 25.
1172 See Thomson 1985.
1173 See Armand 2012.
1174 See Trappl 2016.
1175 Decker 2013.
1176 See Neuhaeuser 2014.
1177 See Ohly 2019a: 103.
1178 See Millar 2017: 22.
1179 See Millar 2017.

quires freedom and rationality. Without freedom, there can be neither responsibility nor accountability. Both require a free choice and the self-determined shaping of one's own life. Rationality is also a necessary basis for responsibility. Rationality and freedom affect responsibility, because responsibility is dependent on freedom and limited by rationality insofar as in situations where reason remains irrelevant, the supposed subject of responsibility cannot be put into relation with responsibility. At the same time, this opens up responsibility beyond personal responsibility or freedom, not only in its self-reference, but also as a caring responsibility or freedom in its social reference.

If only humans can become subjects of responsibility, and driving systems are "not able to take on responsibility, the immediate question arises of who will be responsible or should be made responsible for their actions and for their influence on human actions."[1180] Responsibility needs to be determined in its eight dimensions – subject, form, object, scope, type, volume, scale, authority – and the corresponding relationships,[1181] in order to guarantee the implementation of norms (e.g., with regard to data protection, which, from an ethical perspective, already in the present constitutes a great challenge of automated mobility) and to respond to the corresponding questions of liability and insurance. Who is the subject of responsibility and liable if an automated vehicle causes an accident? The passengers, the provider of automated mobility-services, the producer,[1182] the software-engineer,[1183] a network of different agents,[1184] ... Regarding the latter, the possibility to integrate a data-based system – e.g., an automated vehicle – in the responsibility network[1185] or to attribute it "legal personhood"[1186] would be excluded for the lack of moral capability of data-based systems elaborated above. A network of humans can only be thought of as the subject of responsibility if – based on the explanations above in chapter 3 Can Ethical Judgment Be Delegated to Technologies? and in subchapter 6.2 The Principle of Responsibility – their decision-making is defined and organized so it can be traced back and determined, and if they have an inner structure, common goals and norms. These characteristics must be given in order to obtain subjectivity of responsibility in order to prevent re-

---

1180 Neuhaeuser 2014: 274. See also Woelm 2018; Ohly 2019b.
1181 See Kirchschlaeger 2014a.
1182 See Lohmann 2016.
1183 See Gurney 2017.
1184 See Hubig 2018; Rammert 2004; Weyer 2015; Loh / Loh 2017.
1185 See Loh / Loh 2017; White / Baum 2017.
1186 See Hubbard 2011.

sponsibility from being blurred or a network from being used as a cover-up to avoid liability and accountability.

7.13.4 Security Facing the Ironies of Automation

From an ethical perspective, the automation of mobility must do its best to guarantee security[1187] while being aware of the human limits in pursuit of perfection in the domain of security.[1188] This includes dealing with the "ironies of automation": "designer errors can be a major source of operating problems [first "irony of automation"]. (...) the person who tries to eliminate the operator still leaves him to do the tasks, which he cannot think of how to automate ("second irony of automation")."[1189] The second irony provokes a third irony, namely: the better the system, the less often the person has to intervene, the lower his attention span. The lower the attention span of a person, the more accidents occur ("third irony of automation").[1190]

7.13.5 Risks for the Human Right to Privacy and to Data-Protection

In the realm of automation of mobility, concerns of protection of the human right to privacy and to data-protection emerge from a human rights perspective because automated vehicles need to communicate decentrally among each other as to what requires the provision and the exchange of data.[1191] Moreover, the use of this data is of high interest for economic purposes. Below in chapter 7.17 Data-Protection and Privacy this topic will be deepened. At this point, just a glimpse should point out the issue at stake. For example, imagine a child returning from his or her swimming-practice being "nudged" by a take-away-restaurant that "coincidentally" happens to be located on the way home "coincidentally" chosen by the automated vehicle incentivized by economic special interests.

1187 See Derrick et al. 2016; Luetge 2017; Czarnecki / Salay 2018; Merat / Jamson 2009; Lazarus 2018; Viehl et al. 2017; Woisetschlaeger 2016; Hetzer et al. 2019.

1188 See Etienne 2020; Luetge 2017; Landini 2020; Demiridi et al. 2019; Martínez-Díaz et al. 2019; Meyer 2019; Sperling et al. 2018; Bassi 2019; Kos et al. 2020.

1189 Bainbridge 1983: 775.

1190 See Mackworth 1950; Buschauer 2014; Wolf 2015; Spahn 2013.

1191 See Misselhorn 2018: 184-204; Holstein et al. 2018; Burkert 2017; Ryan 2020; Wilk 2019; Martinesco et al. 2019; Ionita 2017; Perret et al. 2020.

These concerns need to be taken into consideration, and they need to be addressed in concrete regulation(s).

7.13.6 Fewer Accidents

It is assumed that 90 percent of car accidents are due to human error.[1192] There are also far fewer accidents to be expected because of communication between the individual vehicles,[1193] because the driving systems have to ensure among each other that there are no crashes. It does not mean that accidents can be completely avoided. Because in driving systems mistakes can also occur; but they occur with far less frequency, because reasons for accidents such as distraction, tiredness, stress, emotions etc. can be ruled out.[1194] The causes of the accidents change as well. Instead of accidents due to distraction or due to the above-listed reasons of human failure, accidents due to errors of communication are expected, as well as other factors, which can peculiarly affect automated driving systems. Obviously, the reduction in accidents represents an ethically positive impact of the automation of mobility.

7.13.7 Less Pollution

Traffic jams occur, among other things, because of the variation in speed and the different speeds of the individual vehicles. If both could be minimized, there would be fewer traffic jams. Automated mobility includes both – the reduction in speed variations by having a traffic flow that runs at the same speed and the harmonization in speed of all vehicles by decentral communication between the individual vehicles.

Fewer traffic jams – a great perspective from an ethical view on automation of mobility mostly because this provokes a further positive consequence such as less environmental pollution, contributing to the sustainability of the automation of mobility.[1195]

1192 See Gurney 2019: 51.
1193 See Dabrock 2017.
1194 See Axhausen 2016.
1195 See Thomopoulos / Givoni 2015; Tussyadiah et al. 2017; Silva et al. 2019; Hopkins / Schwanen 2018; Papa / Ferreira 2018; Fraedrich et al. 2015; Mladenović et al. 2014; Adnan et al. 2019; Ullah et al. 2018; Lim / Taeihagh 2019; Mueller / Gogoll 2020; Kelley et al. 2019; Landini 2020; Renda 2019; Sovacool / Griffiths

7.13.8 Fewer Vehicles – More Travel Miles

In scenarios with automated mobility, it can be shown that, thanks to the sharing of vehicles associated with automated mobility, the number of vehicles in circulation or owned by humans will be massively reduced. It can be expected that only 10% of today's vehicles will be needed for the same mobility as we have today.[1196] At the same time, this much smaller number of vehicles will drive a lot more miles, because the comfort of automated mobility and the associated gain in time will lead to the fact that more people will be on the move. (E.g., for an elderly person it becomes more attractive to go out in the evening due to the comfortable option of automated mobility.)

This positive effect of a smaller number of vehicles on the environment is further enhanced because it can be assumed that the vehicles will become lighter. Due to the reduced risk of accidents, no comprehensive security concept will be needed and because of the lower, but more even speeds, there will be no heavy motors driving around the countryside. Also, because there will be no more "stop and go" traffic, less pollution will be emitted. Automated mobility with its sustainability[1197] represents a positive impact from an ecological point of view, which is of relevance in applying responsibility, justice – primarily, intergenerational justice –, and human rights.

7.13.9 Automated Mobility as Disruption

If only 10% of the vehicles will be needed with automated mobility and more travel miles will be performed, it will lead to the disappearance of various paid professional tasks. This change is a disruptive process insofar as car producers will be replaced by automated mobility, bus and taxi drivers by self-driving vehicles, etc. Fewer paid professional tasks lead to a reduction in paid jobs, which in turn will lead to the disappearance of, among other things, income, sources of financing, sources of meaning,

---

2020; Soeiro 2020; Mladenovic / McPherson 2016; Gandia et al. 2017; Grahle et al. 2020.

1196   See Boesch et al. 2016.

1197   See Fraedrich et al. 2015; Schreurs / Steuwer 2015; Kirschbaum 2015; Taiebat et al. 2018; Greenblatt 2015; Randolph 2018; Peterson 2014; Jonietz / Bucher 2018; McDonald / Rodier 2015.

and sources of self-conception for the individual. The final consequence will be that *ever fewer humans will directly participate and partake in a more efficient and effective value chain.*[1198] On a macro-social level, this will lead to questions of justice and equal opportunities for all in the interest of creating a livelihood. A model for society and its subsystem economy,[1199] which includes livelihood security as a foundation for social peace and upholding business incentives at the same time, is the Society-, Entrepreneurship-, Research-Time-Model (SERT) (see below subchapter 8.2) foreseeing for every human a basic income for a life with human dignity and all humans contributing the same amount of time to social coexistence in the form, way, and manner they like. (The Swiss civil service serves as an analogy.) One could be exempt from this social contribution by being involved in entrepreneurship, education, research, or innovation.

7.13.10 Globally Unequal Distribution of Advantages and Disadvantages

While the reduction in pollution connected to an automation of mobility will be positive for the whole world, it needs to be taken into account that the introduction of the automation of mobility and the development of the grade of automation will not happen simultaneously around the world. Therefore, necessary measures need to be taken. Also, the advantages and disadvantages of digital transformation and data-based systems are unequally distributed globally which will be further discussed below in chapter 7.19 Global Injustice. While rich countries can switch to automated mobility, people in poorer countries suffer from inhumane working conditions, which violate their human rights, or from slavery, and from the destruction of the environment while exploiting raw materials or when producing automated driving systems. From an ethical perspective, there is an urgent need for action so that the dignity of all humans is respected and the human rights of all humans are implemented.

7.14 Internet of Things

The Internet shapes the professional and private everyday lives of humans. Humans have also become accustomed to generating and sharing data

---

1198 See Kirchschlaeger 2017a; Kirchschlaeger 2016b.
1199 See Helbing 2015c; Helbing 2015d; Helbing 2015e; Helbing 2015f.

without knowing who is using this data and for what purposes and how economically. The only thing one knows is that this is happening.

As humans have now become accustomed to the Internet and the violations of the human right to privacy and to data protection associated with the current form of Internet use, the Internet of Things is now being introduced more and more – as the second chapter of the internet-story, so to speak. It is presented as harmless, as a future as commonplace as electricity in everyday lives, and highly profitable from an economic point of view. The Internet of Things (IoT) "refers to an ecosystem in which applications and services are driven by data collected from devices that sense and interface with the physical world. Important IoT application domains span almost all major economic sectors: health, education, agriculture, transportation, manufacturing, electric grids, and many more. (…) The combination of network connectivity, widespread sensor placement, and sophisticated data analysis techniques now enables applications to aggregate and act on large amounts of data generated by IoT devices in homes, public spaces, industry and the natural world. This aggregated data can drive innovation, research, and marketing, as well as optimize the services that generated it. IoT techniques will effect large-scale change in how people live and work. A thing in IoT can be an inanimate object that has been digitized or fitted with digital technology, interconnected machines or even, in the case of health and fitness, people's bodies. Such data can then be used to analyze patterns, to anticipate changes and to alter an object or environment to realize the desired outcome, often autonomously."[1200] The Internet of Things can consist in, e.g., an Internet of toys.[1201]

What becomes obvious by reflecting upon the Internet of Things from an ethical perspective are some aspects, which are not only valid for the Internet of Things but also for the Internet as well as for data-based systems in general. One could argue that in the case of the Internet of Things they are not predictable due to its complexity.[1202] There are counterarguments that prevail that some ethical problems already appear in the present with the Internet, with data-based systems and with the Internet of Things as well – and that some ethical challenges are foreseeable.[1203] *First*, more interconnectedness means, in reality, more data-extraction, more data-abuse, more surveillance, more manipulation, and more human rights violations.

1200 OECD 2016.
1201 See Druga / Williams 2017.
1202 See Kroes 2009.
1203 See Henschke 2017: 40.

Second, the Internet of Things is primarily not about connecting people or things to serve a common good. It is about generating data about human behaviors[1204] in order to exploit this information economically and politically.

Third, the measures taken thus far to respect the "terms of service-agreements", e.g., the human rights to privacy and to data-protection, are grossly insufficient because humans as users – and as a consequence, as data-generators and -providers – do not have any choice. These "agreements" do not represent an instrument of data- and privacy-protection but rather "contracts of adhesion"[1205] imposing "take-it-or-leave-it conditions on users that stick to them whether they like it or not"[1206] and forcing one to accept them due to their excessive length and overwhelming complexity. This legal practice constitutes an attack on the rule of law and democratic opinion-forming and decision-making processes because it is "merely indicating that the firm deploying the boilerplate wants the recipient to be bound."[1207] Technology-corporations can create their own legal space instead of respecting democratically legitimated user-rights "substituting for them the system that the firm wishes to impose (...) Recipients must enter a legal universe of the firm's devising in order to engage in transactions with the firm."[1208] One experiences a taste of it already with app and online smartphone use. At the same time, it would be a "declaration of bankruptcy" by the state if it does not do anything about it. The former US Federal Trade Commission Chairperson Jon Leibowitz declared: "We all agree that consumers don't read privacy policies."[1209] In order to avoid a misunderstanding: The problem is not that humans usually do not read the privacy policies because it would take them much more than 76 full workdays per year equaling national opportunity costs in the USA of USD 781 billion.[1210] The problem is that these privacy policies violate the human rights to privacy and to data-protection.

Fourth, humans are not only left without alternatives such that they are indifferent about the violations of their human rights, but they are even forced to accept these violations of their human rights. This acceptance nurtures a self-perception of being complicit in these illegitimate acts con-

---

1204 See Portmess / Tower 2014.
1205 Zuboff 2019: 48.
1206 Zuboff 2019: 48.
1207 Radin 2012: 14.
1208 Radin 2012: 16-17.
1209 Leibowitz 2009.
1210 See McDonald / Cranor 2008.

sisting in the possibility that they supposedly could not accept them and therefore that they should blame themselves for these violations of their human rights.

Fifth, a technology-company violates human rights while it is pretending not to do so. In addition to the ethical concerns already in place with the Internet, in the case of the Internet of Things, one deals with ethical concerns across two layers – the physical layer and the informational layer.[1211]

Sixth, a naïve and uncritical belief notable already in the case of the Internet that it is neutral and ethically unproblematic is even intensified with the Internet of Things and data-based systems in general: "I believe that the Internet is establishing a new religion. It has similar characteristics to God: It is always there, sees and knows everything. Its algorithms influence our fate."[1212]

The following concrete example illustrates these points. "Smart-home" is one area of the Internet of Things that generates a market valued at USD 36 billion.[1213] For example, the smart-home device "Nest thermostat" by Google is able to collect data generated by its use and by its environment. "Wi-Fi-enabled and networked, the thermostat's intricate, personalized data stores are uploaded to Google's servers. Each thermostat comes with a 'privacy policy', a 'terms-of-service-agreement', and an 'end-user licensing agreement'. These reveal oppressive privacy and security consequences in which sensitive household and personal information are shared with other smart devices, unnamed personnel, and third parties for the purposes of predictive analyses and sales to other unspecified parties. Nest takes little responsibility for the security of the information it collects and none for how the other companies in its ecosystem will put those data to use. (...) The purchase of a single home thermostat would entail the need to review nearly a thousand so-called contracts. Should the customer refuse to agree to Nest's stipulations, the terms of service indicate that the functionality and security of the thermostat will be deeply compromised, no longer supported by the necessary updates meant to ensure its reliability and safety. The consequences can range from frozen pipes to failed smoke alarms to an easily hacked internal home system."[1214]

1211 See Henschke 2017.
1212 Lehmann-Maldonado 2016: 11; see also Cachelin 2017.
1213 See Marketers Media 2018.
1214 Zuboff 2019: 7.

7.15 Internet of Humans

While, allegedly, things are connected by the Internet of Things, what is of primary interest is connecting humans. Eric Schmidt, as Chairman of Google, states: "The internet will disappear. There will be so many IP addresses (...) so many devices, sensors, things that you are wearing, things that you are interacting with that you won't even sense it. It will be part of your presence all the time. Imagine you walk into a room, and the room is dynamic. And with your permission and all of that, you are interacting with the things going on in the room."[1215] On the one hand, things are connected in order to learn more about human behavior, enabling more extensive manipulation of human behavior. "Sensors are used to modify people's behavior just as easily as they modify device behavior. There are many great things we can do with the internet of things, like lowering the heat in all the houses on your street so that the transformer is not overloaded, or optimizing an entire industrial operation. But at the individual level, it also means the power to take actions that can override what you are doing or even put you on a path you did not choose."[1216] Human behavior becomes a ball one plays with; humans become marionettes. "It's no longer simply about ubiquitous computing. Now the real aim is ubiquitous intervention, action, and control. The real power is that now you can modify real-time actions in the real world. Connected smart sensors can register and analyze any kind of behavior and then actually figure out how to change it. Real-time analytics translate into real-time action."[1217] This represents the present, not some kind of science-fiction-dream-based future: For example, the study "A 61-Million-Person Experiment in Social Influence and Political Mobilization"[1218] by Facebook on political manipulation in the context of the US Congressional Midterm Elections 2010, the study "Experimental Evidence of Massive-Scale Emotional Contagion Through Social Networks"[1219] by Facebook on the manipulation of human emotions (the substantial criticism of this study and of these manipulative ambitions of Facebook, which came true, provoked a deeply concerning defense of the Facebook-Study consisting in that "the extreme response to this study [...] could result in such research being done in secret

---

1215 Smith 2015.
1216 Zuboff 2019: 293.
1217 Zuboff 2019: 292.
1218 Bond et al. 2012: 295-298.
1219 Kramer et al. 2014.

or not at all."[1220]). The pattern of argumentation is basically as follows: Facebook does not respect legal and ethical norms of research. If Facebook is criticized for it, then Facebook will continue this research secretly, so please do not bother Facebook with the requirement to comply with legal and ethical norms.

Beyond that, the game "Pokémon Go" established "a living laboratory for telestimulation at scale as the game's owners (Google) learned how to automatically condition and herd collective behavior, directing it toward real-time constellations of behavioral future markets, with all of this accomplished just beyond rim of individual awareness."[1221] John Hanke, product vice president of Google Maps, boss of Google Street View, and founder of the company behind the game "Pokémon Go", started from the massive potential of gaming for manipulation. "More than 80% of people who own a mobile device claim that they play games on their device (...) games are often the number 1 or number 2 activity (...) so for Android as an operative system, but also for Google, we think it's important for us to innovate and to be a leader in (...) the future of mobile gaming."[1222]

Moreover, humans are connected by corporations providing these products and services that prefer to make one think that they do not connect humans but things. One can already detect that in the case of the Internet where, allegedly, the main goal is connecting information but what is really ly sold at the end of the day is human behavior online. This cover up serves to nurture the dreams of more knowledge through connected information while being surveilled and manipulated as humans by actors paying for this opportunity for economic or political purposes. This cover-up serves as a distraction from interconnectedness as a tool for data-extraction, data-abuse, surveillance, manipulation, and human rights violations. Shoshana Zuboff frames this process as "the dynamic of behavioral surplus accumulation" – following the "extraction imperative" applied to the Internet as a "source of behavioral surplus" and following the "prediction imperative" applied to the following "sources of behavioral surplus": physical world – daily life of humans – body & self of humans – modified behavior.[1223] Humans not only become marionettes, but humans cannot do anything about or against it if this development is not stopped and prevented. "Even when knowledge derived from your behavior is fed back to you in the first

---

1220   Meyer 2014b: 265.
1221   Zuboff 2019: 311.
1222   Weber / Hanke 2015.
1223   See Zuboff 2019: 203.

text as a quid pro quo for participation, the parallel secret operations of the shadow text capture surplus for crafting into prediction products destined for other marketplaces that are *about you* rather than *for you*. These markets do not depend upon you except first as a source of raw material from which surplus is derived, and then as a target for guaranteed outcomes. We have no formal control because we are not essential to the market action. In this future, we are exiles from our own behavior, denied access to or control over knowledge derived from our experience. Knowledge, authority, and power rest with surveillance capital, for which we are merely 'human natural resources'."[1224]

The Internet of Humans is past, present, and future. It is past because the Internet is already more about connecting humans than about information. It is present because the Internet of Things is already more about connecting humans than about connecting things. It is the future – considering the outlook offered by an engineer of a technology-company: "Imagine you have a hammer. That's machine learning. It helped you climb a grueling mountain to reach the summit. That's machine learning's dominance of online data. On the mountaintop, you find a vast pile of nails, cheaper than anything previously imaginable. That's the new smart sensor tech. An unbroken vista of virgin board stretches before you as far as you can see. That's the whole dumb world. Then you learn that any time you plant a nail in a board with your machine learning hammer, you can extract value from that formerly dumb plank. That's data monetization. What do you do? You start hammering like crazy and you never stop, unless somebody makes you stop. But there is nobody up here to make us stop. This is why the 'internet of everything' is inevitable."[1225] Responsibility, justice, and human rights are at stake – especially the freedom of thought.[1226]

7.16 Wearables

Imagine if someone came to you and asked you to put a small device on your body – ideally, seven days a week and 24 hours a day – that will record not only every external move you and your body make but also ev-

---

1224 Zuboff 2019: 327, emphasis in the text.
1225 Zuboff 2019: 223-224.
1226 See Merkel 2018.

ery single internal piece of information and all signals available and collectable.

Imagine that this person informed you, by the way, that all your personal data will be sold to anyone who is interested in this data economically and politically and that you would of course not share in the gained profits.

Imagine that this person let you know that this small device will also manipulate you, your personality, your thoughts, your wishes and dreams, your decisions, your actions, and your behavior in an intensive and highly sophisticated manner based on the ideas, wishes, preferences, and particular interests of the ones who pay the most for this immediate access and immediate manipulation-channel to you. Could you imagine freely agreeing to wear it?

25% of US-Americans possess a smart-watch or a tracking device.[1227] In order to get humans to accept to do something so diametrically against their freedom and against their autonomy, so opposed to their personal interests, and so in conflict with their economic self-interest, one needs a sophisticated marketing-strategy. Marketing as the new "instrument of social control"[1228] sells a fundamental, absolute, and extremely effective and efficient total-surveillance-tool as the alleged door to personal freedom, to self-fulfillment, and to social interaction, and which is creating an overwhelming social pressure to join the community of the wearables – forming a counter-caricature of what wearables really are.

At the heart of this ideologically misleading propaganda, there is an emotionally powerful narrative. An exemplary aspect of it is the following: "On January 24th Apple Computer will introduce Macintosh. And you will see why 1984 won't be like '1984'."[1229] In this clip, presented in the break of the Super-Bowl – the final of the US-American National Football League NFL –, which is the most watched spot for commercials, accompanied by strong symbolic gestures, "all the technological promises of emancipation of an era which in decentralized apparatuses constituted a valid antithesis to the idea of state-controlled networks – and thus to Orwellian dystopia. (...) Especially the spread of the personal computer and the new accessibility of the apparatuses subsequently intensified their rededication under the sign of participation and sharing. Technology was no longer seen as an embodiment of the alienation of work and nature, but was

---

1227 See Nosthoff / Maschewski 2019: 11.
1228 Deleuze 1992: 6.
1229 Apple 2012.

charged with the aura of the democratic, organic and emancipative; a resistant, anti-hierarchical power was recognized in it. (...) Computers quickly established themselves as the must-have of individual objection – as the ultimate solvent against centralized superpowers. (...) Of course, it is known that (...) little more (...) has come into being than the establishment of new, much more extensive technological monopolies of power"[1230]. In a paradigmatic way, technology causing the legitimate fear of total surveillance and control is reversed falsely into a path to freedom and emancipation. (In these years, Apple was already working on a "personal digital assistant" ...)[1231] Wearables – a highly efficient and effective tool for totally "controlled freedom"[1232] – are presented as a tool for "liberal control"[1233].

This idea of control falls into the open – by marketing? – arms of humans. "Many young people strangely boast of being 'motivated'; they re-request apprenticeships and permanent training. It's up to them to discover what they're being made to serve, just as their elders discovered, not without difficulty, the telos of the disciplines."[1234] Surveillance, manipulation, and control by wearables are, again and again, reversed into freedom, emancipation, and empowerment – see, e.g., the commercial for the market-leading Apple Watch Series 4. Its core message is: "'You have a better ego in you!' In other words: a more active, healthier ego; an ego of the future and of potential that can do more, that does not let itself go, but stands up, progresses and takes back what is due to it. It is exactly this ego that needs to be liberated. How? Very simply, with the new Apple Watch."[1235] Or take into account, e.g., the commercial slogan for Apple Watch Series 5: "And motivates you to move, exercise, and stand. The Activity rings track your progress and inspire you to sit less, move more, and exercise every day. You can even compete with friends in challenges."[1236]

At stake are not only freedom, autonomy, privacy, data-protection, but also individuality, identity, diversity, and plurality. A unification and leveling of the purpose of life and of the meaning of human existence according to the ideas, wishes, particular interests, and preferences of multinational technology-corporations threaten human dignity and human rights. The lives of humans are transformed into competitive performances that

---

1230 Nosthoff / Maschewski 2019: 9-10.
1231 See Nosthoff / Maschewski 2019: 15.
1232 Nosthoff / Maschewski 2019: 12.
1233 Nosthoff / Maschewski 2019: 12.
1234 Deleuze 1992: 7.
1235 Nosthoff / Maschewski 2019: 18.
1236 Apple 2020.

are measured and assessed according to the telos of human existence defined by multinational technology-corporations as well as documented with high precision by the same multinational technology-corporations. "No area of life remains excluded from this logic, too compassionate and caring, the almost enlightenment seeming epistemological instrument records the biorhythmic ups and downs of everyday life."[1237] Humans should surpass themselves constantly, self-optimize themselves, and always strive for a better ego – whose scale is defined by multinational technology-corporations. "As puritanically white and immaculate as Bauhaus architecture often was, the iPhones and iMacs should also be pure white and free of dirty stains. Everything should be mastered, controlled to the last detail, and in this Apple also inherits the old avant-garde."[1238] While multinational technology-corporations emphasize that technology is neutral, they define clear values and goals and expect humans to adapt to technologies.[1239]

Wearables are so close to humans that they intertwine with humans intensively in such a way that they possess the power to make humans change. Wearables generate the desire and the demand to document one's own life-performance and compare it with others according to parameters defined by multinational technology-corporations. Wearables are perceived as an instrument for self-recognition –[1240] a self seen, watched, and understood with the eyes given by multinational technology-corporations. Wearables surveille, control, and dominate humans – without making humans realize that they are marionettes of multinational technology-corporations and without them noticing that the puppeteer is either the same multinational technology-corporations or their clients willing to pay a lot of money to gain access to the puppet strings. "The digital device is not a machine that moves arms and legs at the push of a button, controlling the user externally in a technology-deterministic way. Its control reflexes seem more suggestive and ambivalent: On the one hand, as an almost classic extension of men, it focuses on increasing the abilities of the individual – from the depths of feeling (pulse rate) to the heights of new achievements (step sequence). On the other hand, it directs the self-tracker quite programmatically towards the imperatives of optimization, performance and efficiency, rationalizing its life paths as playfully as it does forcefully,

---

1237 Nosthoff / Maschewski 2019: 20-21.
1238 Rauterberg 2012.
1239 See Schmidt / Cohen 2013: 100.
1240 See Nosthoff / Maschewski 2019: 28.

nestling them entirely to the enticing promise of machine functioning. Thus, the pleasure of surveying has a thoroughly ambiguous effect. For as self-determined and self-empowered as the Quantified Self gives itself, as technical or at least data-hearted it appears to be, it persistently grinds its corners and edges – with prefabricated parameters – to correspond to an ideal type."[1241]

Wearables change humans. Increasingly humans are triggered to find themselves not in themselves but rather in the numbers, results, assessments, and comparisons (with other carriers of wearables) collected, structured, interpreted, and communicated in the form of imperatives by wearables. "The fact that the controller of his own self perceives the constant interventions as lustful motivation and in the pedantic precision that reads every heartbeat or pulse as a number, recognizes not a blemish but the basis of his desire, makes this way of life as contemporary as it is contradictory. For with calculation and passion, he synchronizes self-government with continuous self-submission – freedom with permanent control."[1242] Humans are manipulated with such an intensity that they overlook what could become obvious to them in meeting other marionettes while they are compared with other carriers of wearables: That they have become a marionette dancing in lock step initiated by multinational technology-corporations and their clients who have taken hold of the puppet strings.

Instead, thanks to the propagandistic narrative they enjoy "the antagonistic peer-review"[1243] set up by businesses to make the highest possible profit out of it or the strongest possible influence on humans out of it.

Instead, thanks to "the dictatorship of no alternatives", humans surrender. "The ubiquitous apparatus operates through coercion and stealth. Our advance into life necessarily takes us through the digital, where involuntary rendition has become an inescapable fact. We are left with few rights to know, or to decide to know who knows, or to decide who decides. This abnormal division of learning is created and sustained by secret fiat, implemented by invisible methods, and directed by companies bent to the economic imperatives of a strange new market form. Surveillance capitalists impose their will backstage, while the actors perform the stylized lullabies of disclosure and agreement for the public. The prediction imperative transforms the things that we have into things that have us in order that it might render the range and richness of our world, our homes, and our

---

1241 Nosthoff / Maschewski 2019: 33.
1242 Nosthoff / Maschewski 2019: 35.
1243 See Nosthoff / Maschewski 2019: 39-63.

bodies as behaving objects for its calculations and fabrications on the path to profit."[1244]

7.17 Data-Protection and Privacy

7.17.1 It's All About Data

Of course, data-based systems as well as data and big data can be used to create the ethically positive, e.g. fighting social inequality.[1245] However, this kind of digital transformation and this kind of use of data-based systems is about to kill privacy and data-protection. Connecting everyone and everything is also referred to as *"Verdatung"*[1246]. Three decades ago, it would have been unimaginable that one would send a love letter to their beloved and at the same time, send a copy of this letter to state authorities and the private sector as well so they could read it, study it, and analyze and predict with this letter one's personality, needs, preferences, behaviors, dreams, wishes, and political opinions. The following example is illustrative of this: E.g., Facebook violated the right to privacy and data-protection in the following way: "I purchased a diamond engagement ring set from Overstock in preparation for a New Year's surprise for my girlfriend (…) Within hours, I received [phone calls of] 'congratulations' for getting engaged (…) I learned that Overstock had published the details of my purchase (including a link to the item and its price) on my public Facebook newsfeed, as well as notifications to all of my friends (…) including my girlfriend."[1247]

Among other things, advertisers want to know our interests and preferences. Employers want to know our resilience and political activities. Insurances want to know our health and risk tolerance. Banks want to know our money management, our job security, and our financial burdens.[1248] Totalitarian systems want to know and to control what we do and what we think – reaching conformity through surveillance. All of them want to influence or even to manipulate us. "The extraction imperative demands that everything be possessed. In this new context, goods and services are merely

---

1244 Zuboff 2019: 252-253.
1245 See Cranach 2019: 39-40.
1246 Streit 1993: 183-191.
1247 CNN Money 2010.
1248 See Piater 2020.

surveillance-bound supply routes. It's not the car; it's the behavioral data from driving the car. It's not the map; it's the behavioral data from interacting with the map. The ideal here is continuously expanding borders that eventually describe the world and everything in it, all the time."[1249] And a few technology-corporations extract this data. "We have better information than anyone else. We know gender, age, location, and it's real data as opposed to the stuff other people infer"[1250], says Shery Sandberg, COO of Facebook. Larry Page, co-founder of Google, elaborates: "Our ultimate ambition is to transform the overall Google experience, making it beautifully simple, almost automagical because we understand what you want and can deliver it instantly."[1251] Marcus Ash, Microsoft's group program manager for Microsoft's digital assistant "Cortana", explains: "The idea of this unbounded, 'I know so much about you I can help you in ways you don't quite expect, I can see patterns that you can't see.' That's the magic"[1252] – or, probably more accurately – the dramatic nightmare for and the absolute attack and denial of free and autonomous humans and their concomitant human dignity.

"With digitalization, we are transforming our lives, both private and professional, into a giant computer. Everything is measured, stored, analyzed and forecasted so that it can be controlled and optimized in a closed loop of *stimulus* and *response*, of 'stimulus' and 'response'."[1253] When the mathematician Norbert Wiener founded cybernetics as the "the scientific study of control and communication in the animal and the machine"[1254], it was probable that nobody thought that this theory would become reality in such a comprehensive way. "He himself could hardly have imagined the perfection with which digitalization generates numbers, data and information of human life, over which more and more control can be exercised. With digital transformation, everything becomes outlawed, including man. Again, man is being thrown onto the market as a commodity, now not as a worker, but as a number and date. There he becomes the cause of huge sales and profits for the companies that reassemble his personal data into the mirrored whole of a person and trade with it. With the digital transformation of the 21st century, human trafficking has also modern-

---

1249 Zuboff 2019: 131.
1250 Kirkpatrick 2011: 257.
1251 Google 2011.
1252 Kedmey 2015.
1253 Hofstetter 2017: 74, emphasis in the text.
1254 See Wiener 1948.

ized."[1255] Data – in combination with data-based systems – opens new economic and epistemological horizons and becomes a realization of the dictum attributed to Francis Bacon "knowledge is power"[1256]. Even if it is only unprotected and not sensitive data, data-based systems are capable of deriving this data from proxy variables.[1257]

Data defines what is seen as normal,[1258] humans face "control by algorithms"[1259]. Data coined as the "resource of the twenty first century"[1260] are mined without any limits. Everything is equipped with sensors. "In the year 2030 100 billion objects should be sensor-equipped and connected via the global communication infrastructure of the Internet."[1261]

"Data-solidarity" is supposedly the new maxim promoted by technology-multinational corporations claiming that all humans should generate and share as much data as possible in order to make humans flourish and life better for everyone. Its success depends on the promotion of a way of life in which every facet of human existence is digitally transformed, digitalized, and penetrated by data-based systems – *ergo*, generating data, providing data, sharing data, and believing and trusting with an infinite naiveté in the outcomes of data-processing. "The combination of robot technology, human-machine interaction and learning methods therefore makes it possible to define standards in the private, professional or public sector that are difficult or impossible to escape. This obviously restricts personal freedom and very probably also creativity and innovation, for which diversity and freedom are necessary. An ethical aspect, but also a social challenge, is the question of where the limits of measuring human behavior should and must be. The proliferation of robotic applications in completely new, personal areas greatly intensifies the urgency of addressing this question."[1262] It is the task of data science to define the problem, to capture the data, to prepare the data, to develop or to choose the algorithmic basis for the "machine learning" process (learning "not in the way humans learn, but based on a computational and statistical process. Feeding on data, learning algorithms can detect patterns or rules in the data and make

---

1255   Hofstetter 2017: 74.
1256   See Bacon 1990.
1257   See Kosinski 2013; Cellarius 2017.
1258   See Steil 2019: 30.
1259   Jarzebski 2014.
1260   Mangold 2016.
1261   Hofstetter 2017: 74.
1262   Steil 2019: 30.

predictions for future data"[1263]) and for the "deep learning" process ("a form of machine learning that uses neural networks with several layers of 'neurons': simple interconnected processing units that interact"[1264]) to interpret the outcomes, and to select the adequate actions.[1265]

7.17.2 Data-Tyranny

The ethical instruments responsibility, justice, and human rights enable one to expose "data-solidarity" as what it really is: "data-tyranny" instead of "data-solidarity", the extraction of a resource with data-based systems,[1266] the exploitation of the rest of the world by a few,[1267] the end of the high regard for all humans as holders of human dignity and human rights by coining humans as "ultimate machine"[1268], the plundering of costless "digital labor"[1269] by humans, the violations of several human rights, the robbery of individual data and privacy of most humans by a few technology-companies, the nonneutral,[1270] manipulative and discriminatory[1271] processing of data by algorithms such as learning algorithms[1272] in the way that it results in the desired findings serving the particular interests of some actors,[1273] the non-traceability, unpredictability, and inexplicability of algorithms such as learning algorithms creating not only an epistemological gap that consists in a blurring of the interfaces between humans and technology leading to the perception of technologies as inaccessible and as inhibiting interaction with them by humans.[1274] It also causes an accountability-gap from an ethical standpoint and the long-term securing of an economic and political power of a data-based dictatorship by few technology-companies that is not democratically legitimated.

1263 Coeckelberg 2020: 204.
1264 Coeckelberg 2020: 203.
1265 See Kelleher / Tierney 2018.
1266 See Hofstetter 2014.
1267 See Schwab 2018.
1268 See Kneser / Dietsche 2015.
1269 See Fuchs 2014.
1270 See Brey / Soraker 2009; Wiener 1988.
1271 See Barocas / Selbst 2015; Birrer 2005; Sweeney 2013.
1272 See Tutt 2016; Burrell 2016.
1273 See Friedman / Nissenbaum 1996; Johnson 2006b; Kraemer et al. 2011; Nakamura 2013.
1274 See Hubig 2008.

"Data-tyranny" is further enhanced by a "gap between the design and operation of algorithms and our understanding of their ethical implications"[1275]. From an ethical perspective, data-based automated decisions motivate humans to neglect to exercise their rights. "Data show the way in which the state can manipulate the citizen into desired behavior with the help of behavioral psychological tricks."[1276] This is even more dangerous because it happens in an incredibly subtle way. Dictators can rely on data; they do not have to deploy visibly brute force. Maybe this dystopia moves humans to act more than a utopia.[1277]

The urgency of the necessity to do something increases, additionally, due to the dependence of the present economic system on a few multinational technology-corporations and its implications. "The increasing networking of all areas of life increases the dependence on digital infrastructures with which citizens interact on a daily basis. These infrastructures are primarily offered by international corporations that are able to act so dynamically that they will be able to evade national regulations in the future with regard to economic and data protection law. For this reason, the sovereign actions of individual citizens are threatened. On the other hand, a digitalized industry is facing increasing attacks and increased dependency on international technology suppliers in their options for action restricted."[1278] The fundamental significance of data causes political implications and the data-power of some of the above-mentioned multinational corporations endangering data-protection and privacy. The comprehensive reliance on this one resource in an absolute way never seen before in human history increases, on the one hand, the immense power of some multinational technology-corporations, on the other, the dependence of the society and the economy from some multinational technology-corporations leading in the area of data-based systems. (As business with data-based systems operates with "the winner takes all"-pattern, we are talking about a few companies in this position of absolute, unchecked, and unbalanced power.) Besides its economic and epistemological potential, the use of data – especially of big data – consists also in technical challenges, mainly "volume – velocity – variety – veracity"[1279]. Among other things, security-concerns arise and become highly relevant because of the above-mentioned

---

1275 Mittelstadt et al. 2016: 2.
1276 Ramge 2019: 91.
1277 See Heller: 2016.
1278 Lepping / Palzkill 2016: 17.
1279 Helbing 2015g: 3.

comprehensive reliance on data as the one resource in an absolute way never seen before in the history of humanity. This reliance increases the vulnerability of humans, the society, and the economy. In the case of the former, one could go even so far as to argue that this increase in vulnerability, these new technology-based vulnerabilities are also human vulnerabilities.[1280] A counter-argument comprises the differentiation between the technology-based cause for a vulnerability that is technological and the vulnerability itself, which is human. For example, the risk of data being hacked is a technology-based cause for a vulnerability, the human vulnerability itself comprises privacy and data-protection – both relevant for human freedom. In other words, privacy and data-protection are and remain human vulnerabilities and are not extended to technological vulnerabilities.

7.17.3 Datadeology

Furthermore, "dataism"[1281] seems to be the new philosophy or religion.[1282] "Just as divine authority has been legitimized by mythologies and religious beliefs, and human authority has been legitimized by humanistic ideologies, so the new high-tech gurus and Silicon Valley prophets are creating a new universal narrative that legitimizes a new principle of legitimacy: algorithms and Big Data. (...) Dataism has no believers or places of worship, yet it deserves its name: because the computer wave that is overwhelming reality, and the failure to question its assumptions can become a belief with characteristics similar to those of a religious belief."[1283] The following important distinction needs to be highlighted: It is not a new religion; it is similar to an ideology because of its unquestioned, absolute authority for its followers that is not critically reflected on. Therefore, one could claim to speak of a *"datadeology"* (data-ideology). Datadeology seems to be becoming the new equivalent of a religion. Datadeology is an attack on the maturity to which the ever-ongoing movement of the Enlightenment invites humans. "Enlightenment is human's emergence from his [or her] self-imposed immaturity. Immaturity is the inability to use one's own understanding without another's guidance. This immaturity is self-imposed if

---

1280 See Coeckelberg 2013.
1281 Brooks 2013.
1282 See Harari 2017: 428-462; Bloching 2012: 28.
1283 Benanti 2018: 98.

its cause lies not in lack of understanding but in indecision and lack of courage to use one's own mind without another's guidance. Dare to know! (Sapere aude.) 'Have the courage to use your own understanding', is therefore the motto of the enlightenment."[1284] At present, datadeology seems to dominate and manipulate humanity – in the political sphere as in the form of *"datatorship"* (data-dictatorship) surveilling, controlling, ruling, and manipulating humans – "rendering them less capable of thinking for themselves or deciding for themselves what to do"[1285]. Datadeology in the economic sphere takes the form of *"datalism"* (data-capitalism) abusing, exploiting, and manipulating humans. "Why is our experience rendered as behavioral data in the first place? (...) human experience is claimed as raw material for datafication (...) the apparatus of ubiquity is not a passive one-way mirror. Rather, it actively creates its own stores of knowledge through rendition."[1286] Datadeology conquers humanity and attacks human dignity, individuality, and autonomy. "What (...) will happen once we realize that customers and voters never make free choices, and once we have the technology to calculate, design or outsmart their feelings? (...) what will happen once the human experience becomes just another designable product, no different in essence from any other item in the supermarket?"[1287] From an ethical perspective, datadeology must be stopped and overcome because humans are more than data.

Beyond that, datadeology consists also in a reinterpretation of the concept of solidarity. This reinterpretation embraces as mentioned above a duty to share data because only more and more data can improve technology-based innovation.[1288] This reinterpretation alienates itself from the nucleus of solidarity so far away that one could question if the term "solidarity" is still adequate because it neglects one fundamental pillar of solidarity, namely the individual human who needs to be respected as a holder of human dignity. Forcing a human individual to share her or his data violates his or her human dignity and the human right to privacy and data-protection.

1284   Kant 1784: 481.
1285   Shanahan 2015: 170.
1286   Zuboff 2019: 232-233.
1287   Harari 2017: 323.
1288   See Prainsack / Buyx 2017: 43.

7.17.4 Violations of the Human Right to Privacy and Data-Protection

The digital transformation and data-based systems know, in almost all their facets, ethical risks concerning the human right to privacy and the human right to data-protection.[1289] A statement by Larry Page, co-founder of Google, illustrates that: "Sensors are really cheap. (...) Storage is cheap. Cameras are cheap. People will generate enormous amounts of data. (...) Everything you've ever heard or seen or experienced will become searchable. Your whole life will be searchable."[1290] The human right to privacy states:[1291] "No one shall be subjected to arbitrary interference with his privacy, family, home or correspondence, nor to attacks upon his honor and reputation. Everyone has the right to the protection of the law against such interference or attacks."[1292] In the General Comment No. 16 to Article 17 Right to Privacy in the International Covenant on Civil and Political Rights of 1966, it is emphasized that: "The gathering and holding of personal information on computers, data banks and other devices, whether by public authorities or private individuals or bodies, must be regulated by law. Effective measures have to be taken by States to ensure that information concerning a person's private life does not reach the hands of persons who are not authorized by law to receive, process and use it, and is never used for purposes incompatible with the Covenant. In order to have the most effective protection of his private life, every individual should have the right to ascertain in an intelligible form, whether, and if so, what personal data is stored in automatic data files, and for what purposes. Every individual should also be able to ascertain which public authorizes or private individuals or bodies control or may control their files. If such files contain incorrect personal data or have been collected or processed contrary to the provisions of the law, every individual should have the right to request rectification or elimination."[1293] Digital transformation and the use of data-based systems open new horizons for the illegitimate creation and collection of data, for surveillance and interception and the economic exploitation of violations of the human right to privacy and to data-protec-

---

1289 See UNESCO 2019: 43-53; Berendt et al. 2015; Carnevale 2016; Grimm et al. 2015; Betts / Sezer 2014; Dix 2016; Meixner 2017; e.g., for privacy- and data-protection-issues with civil drones, see Finn / Wright 2016; e.g., for data goggles, see Bendel 2016.

1290 Edwards 2011: 291.

1291 See Kainz 2016; Norwawi et al. 2014.

1292 Universal Declaration of Human Rights 1948: Article 12.

1293 UN Human Rights Committee 1988.

tion. From an ethical perspective, this is highly problematic and relevant because nothing less than freedom is at stake when the human right to privacy and to data-protection is violated. Nothing less than informational self-determination is violated.[1294] Nothing less than "a right to be forgotten"[1295] is violated. Nothing less than autonomy and self-determination are neglected. Nothing less than other human rights are neglected. For example, surveillance violates the human right to freedom of expression ("Everyone has the right to freedom of opinion and expression; this right includes freedom to hold opinions without interference and to seek, receive and impart information and ideas through any media and regardless of frontiers."[1296]) and the human right to freedom of peaceful assembly and association ("1. Everyone has the right to freedom of peaceful assembly and association. 2. No one may be compelled to belong to an association."[1297]) Obviously, these violations provoke severe negative consequences for a free functioning, vibrant civil society. "Because digitalization with the monitoring and optimization function provided so frequently and deliberately interferes with self-determination, there are countless violations of fundamental rights. We sense this in a diffuse way. Nevertheless, nobody is rebelling. Instead, the digital society of the 21st century uses the technologies of the destruction of freedom almost without hesitation."[1298]

Digital transformation and the use of data-based systems urged the UN to adopt the UN Resolution on the Right to Privacy in the Digital Age of 2013. The UN General Assembly expressed deep concern at the negative impact that surveillance and interception of communications may have on human rights.[1299] By affirming that "the same rights that people have offline must also be protected online, including the right to privacy"[1300], the UN General Assembly called upon all states to respect and protect the right to privacy in digital communication. The UN General Assembly called on all states to review their procedures, practices, and legislation related to communications surveillance, interception, and collection of personal data and emphasized the need for states to ensure the full and effect-

---

1294   See Mertz et al. 2016; Ullrich 2014; Klumpp 2014.
1295   See Leutheusser-Schnarrenberger 2015; Schweitzer 2017.
1296   Universal Declaration of Human Rights 1948: Article 19.
1297   Universal Declaration of Human Rights 1948: Article 20.
1298   Hofstetter 2017: 75.
1299   See Office of the UN High Commissioner for Human Rights n.d.
1300   Office of the UN High Commissioner for Human Rights n.d.: Article 3.

ive implementation of their obligations under international human rights law.[1301]

Digital transformation and the use of data-based systems provoke these concerns regarding the human right to privacy and to data-protection because most data is of high economic interest and, therefore, the risk is higher that this data will be abused, transmitted to other users without informed consent by the owner of this data, or will not be protected sufficiently. From an ethical perspective, the human right to privacy and to data-protection must be respected even in the course of digital transformation and the use of data-based systems. This implies that data, information, and knowledge relevant for the human right to privacy and to data-protection must be saved locally by this person (e.g., on his or her own computer), any proposal of a transmission of the data of humans must be transparent and find, beforehand, the informed consent of the relevant person, and only this person must be authorized to decide about his or her data.

The human right to privacy and to data-protection is systematically attacked by technology-corporations. For example, Hal Varian, longtime chief economist of Google, states: "Nowadays there is a computer in the middle of virtually every transaction (...) now that they are available these computers have several other uses."[1302] These uses are: "data extraction and analysis", "new contractual forms due to better monitoring", "personalization and customization", "continuous experiments".[1303] Or he articulates: "Every action a user performs is considered a signal to be analyzed and fed back into the system."[1304] This data offers a "broad sensor of human behavior"[1305]. "Google's invention revealed new capabilities to infer and deduce the thoughts, feelings, intentions, and interests of individuals and groups with an automated architecture that operates as a one-way mirror irrespective of a person's awareness, knowledge, and consent, thus enabling privileged secret access to behavioral data."[1306] This data is eventually the basis for "predictions". "Prediction products reduce risks for customers, advising them where and when to place their bets. The quality and competitiveness of the product are a function of its approximation to certainty: the more

---

1301 See Office of the UN High Commissioner for Human Rights n.d.; e.g., on data-intensive research, see Dove et al. 2016; e.g., on research of social media-content, see Krieger et al. 2014.
1302 Varian 2014a: 27.
1303 See Varian 2014a.
1304 Varian 2014b: 113.
1305 Levy 2011: 46.
1306 Zuboff 2019: 80-81.

predictive the product, the lower the risks for buyers and the greater the volume of sales. Google has learned to be a data-based fortune-teller that replaces intuition with science at scale in order to tell and sell our fortunes for profit to its customers, but not to us."[1307]

Beyond that, further ethical risks concerning data are security, crime, veracity, and manipulation. "Big data"[1308] increases all the above-mentioned risks exponentially. "What is certain is that the development of an electronically networked 'world of things' has little to do with fascination in research. 'Big Data' is becoming synonymous with a research mania that is fed by powerful economic interests and has meanwhile taken hold of venerable universities. The belief that everything that people have ever done or uttered, or what has been recorded for any reason, should be stored without deletion is morbid, both in individual persons as well as a strategic program."[1309]

One might think that it does not matter if one's data is stored somewhere or that one's own data is not of interest to anybody. "If you think that this is nobody else's business but your own, take a look at the selector list of the Internet giants. From hundreds of criteria, interested buyers can select the above-mentioned data and information on the users of the most popular social networks and purchase them from professional data vendors – an investment of millions of euros, depending on the level of detail."[1310] How are you? Where are you? Who do you meet? Who are you in contact with on a regular basis? What do you share with others? What is your opinion on climate protection? Are you faithful to your partner? How is your cholesterol level? Are you fit enough for this health insurance? Do you have the best health among the remaining three candidates for this job?

7.17.5 Manipulation of Humans – The Example of "Nudging"

In an exemplary way, the ethical risk of manipulation will be further elaborated by looking at a technique which, based on data, pursues a form of

---

1307   Zuboff 2019: 96.
1308   See Wrobel et al. 2015.
1309   Meixner 2016: 12.
1310   Hofstetter 2017: 76.

manipulation – "nudging"[1311]. This approach[1312] starts from the assumption that the challenges of today's world could be better met if states or non-state actors would nudge humans via libertarian paternalism by correcting cognitive biases. The harmless example of "nudging" is that one can influence healthier nutrition habits by positioning fruits, vegetables, etc. in a grocery store at the best points where consumers buy more products so more consumers are buying them. What actually is happening with "nudging" is that humans are influenced without noticing or being able to notice that they are being "nudged".

From a human rights perspective, on the one hand "nudging" could seem to be attractive if this "nudging" were to lead to the realization of human rights. The latter would be extremely welcome: "nudging" by the states protecting human beings from themselves could be understood as part of the responsibility of the states for the implementation of human rights.

On the other hand, it belongs precisely to the nucleus of human rights to protect the individual from the collective and from abuse of power by the collective. In other words, human rights protect all the powerless from the powerful. The universality of human rights implies that human rights apply to all humans. Humans enjoy human rights as individuals, independent of any collective. All humans are holders of human rights, irrespective of what they do, where they come from, where they live, and which nationality they have or to which community they belong. Human rights struggle exactly, however, with these particular interests of collectives, e.g. states allegedly knowing better what is best for their citizens by claiming the priority of their sovereignty over the universality of human rights. Human rights violations by traditions, cultures, civilizations, religions, or value systems are supposedly justified by cultural, religious, and worldview-based leaders because they know better what is best for their followers while they are actually concerned about a possible loss of institutional power and influence and usually not by core elements of the traditional "truth" shared by the communities.

Furthermore, from a human rights perspective, there is a necessity to respect the autonomy of an individual in order to remain coherent with the core concept of human rights. This necessity to respect the autonomy of an individual even goes so far – as elaborated above in subchapter 6.4 Human Rights as Ethical Frame of Reference – as to require that human rights

---

1311 Sunstein / Thaler 2008.
1312 See Kirchschlaeger 2016h.

themselves need an ethical justification as autonomy entails knowing why one's freedom should be restricted by somebody or something, including human rights. Therefore, the questions arise as to if and how this aspect could be combined with the above-mentioned argumentation such that the end would justify the means, and if and how "nudging" could be justified. This "nudging", though, would have to respect human rights.

Beyond that, human rights protect the autonomy of individuals also by specific human rights enabling the participation of the individual in political opinion-forming and decision-making processes,[1313] which could be at risk because of "nudging" by states, e.g. with Article 21 of the Universal Declaration of Human Rights of 1948, also called the "democracy principle": "1. Everyone has the right to take part in the government of his country, directly or through freely chosen representatives. 2. Everyone has the right of equal access to public service in his country. 3. The will of the people shall be the basis of the authority of government; this will shall be expressed in periodic and genuine elections which shall be by universal and equal suffrage and shall be held by secret vote or by equivalent free voting procedures."[1314] Democracy can also be seen as the institutional expression of the respect of the autonomy of the individual, giving the individual the possibility to participate in the opinion-forming and decision-making process of the legal system he or she is living in as a citizen. Human rights and democracy go hand in hand as democracy is the political system which embodies the autonomy of the individual inherent within the idea and concept of human rights. Therefore, the respect of human rights is part of a democratic system. Consequently, a democracy must integrate mechanisms which ensure that human rights are respected regarding the access to democratic opinion-forming and decision-making processes and in the way these processes are taking place, as the possibility of a democratic decision violating human rights is excluded from the start. Human rights are the frame of reference for a democracy. Different forms to guarantee the respect of human rights within a democratic system are known, such as the Constitution or the Supreme Court, and need to be established in democracies without such institutional measures in coherence with human rights and in order to further the realization of human rights.

From an ethical perspective informed by human rights as an ethical point of reference, skepticism towards the approach of "nudging" remains high, firstly, as long as "nudging" crosses the legal and ethical frame of ref-

---

1313 See Kirchschlaeger 2013e.
1314 Universal Declaration of Human Rights 1948: Article 21.

erence of human rights and, secondly, as long the state or the non-state actors do not have to protect humans from human rights violations. The basis for the first reason for skepticism entails the protection of autonomy by human rights, the guarantee of participation by the individual in opinion-forming and decision-making processes, and the character of human rights as individual rights, not as rights of the collective. "Nudging" can result in contradicting or violating some of these elements being contradicted or violated, and therefore it must be criticized from a human rights perspective.

The basis for the second reason embodies the possibility that "nudging" contributes to the stopping and prevention of human rights violations and to the realization of human rights. "Nudging" is justified from a human rights perspective if "nudging" furthers the realization of human rights. Even in that case though, "nudging" must respect human rights because of the principle of indivisibility of human rights, which entails that the entire human rights-catalogue must be respected, implemented, and realized, and that there is not any hierarchy. All specific human rights must go hand in hand.

The normative basis for even enabling the second reason to become realistic and for concerns which provoke the call for "nudging" of humans by states or by non-state actors would be addressed from a human rights perspective, thirdly, with – if even possible – "nudging" within the legal and ethical frame of reference of human rights only and exclusively if it serves the realization of human rights.

Fourthly, the response to these concerns would be the emphasis of the autonomy of the individual protected by human rights.

Fifthly, these concerns would be answered by pointing out that these challenges could be met by overcoming the naïve assumption that every human is born democratic and with the skills and competencies to participate in a democratic opinion-building and decision-making process, and by furthering human rights education.[1315] Thomas Hammarberg, at that time Council of Europe Commissioner for Human Rights, emphasizes: "Educating citizens in their human rights creates an informed society which in turn strengthens democracy"[1316]. On the occasion of an expert-seminar during the preparation-process of the UN Declaration on Human Rights Education and Training in Marrakech 2009, Navanethem Pillay, at that time UN-High Commissioner for Human Rights, outlined the expectations in human rights education: "Human Rights Education is essential

---

1315 See Fritzsche et al. 2017.
1316 Hammarberg 2008.

for the prevention of human rights abuses, the promotion of non-discrimination, equality and sustainable development, and the enhancement of people's participation in democratic decision making processes". The fundamental role of human rights education is to empower citizens to defend their own rights and those of others. "This empowerment constitutes an important investment for the future, aimed at achieving a just society in which all human rights of all persons are valued and respected"[1317]. The idea of "empowerment" means the capability to determine one's own present and future with self-confidence and awareness of one's own rights and to participate actively in the political decision process. The UN Declaration on Human Rights Education and Training of 2011[1318] (Article 2/2) defines human rights education and training as follows: "Human rights education and training comprises all educational, training, information, awareness-raising and learning activities aimed at promoting universal respect for and observance of all human rights and fundamental freedoms and thus contributing, inter alia, to the prevention of human rights violations and abuses by providing persons with knowledge, skills and understanding and developing their attitudes and behaviors, to empower them to contribute to the building and promotion of a universal culture of human rights. a) Education about human rights, which includes providing knowledge and understanding of human rights norms and principles, the values that underpin them and the mechanisms for their protection; b) Education through human rights, which includes learning and teaching in a way that respects the rights of both educators and learners; c) Education for human rights, which includes empowering persons to enjoy and exercise their rights and to respect and uphold the rights of others."

Sixthly, the human right to privacy and data-protection is violated if one's data is used in the course of "nudging". One's informational self-determination, one's freedom, and one's autonomy would be at stake.

From a human rights perspective, it is necessary to choose alternatives to "nudging" of humans by states and by non-state actors if "nudging" is violating human rights, which seems to (almost)[1319] always be the case. And there are alternatives to "nudging" ...

1317   DeMello 2004: 3.
1318   The author has contributed as a consultative expert to the development of the UN Declaration on Human Rights Education and Training of 2011 during the entire preparation process of the Declaration.
1319   See Idhe 2011.

7.17.6 Total Manipulation – the Example of "Hyper-Nudging"

These ethical concerns applying human rights as an ethical instrument gain even more relevance if "hypernudging"[1320] is taken into consideration. Based on self-tracking technologies and, as such, based on extensive data about one's ways to make a decision and about one's decisions, "hypernudging" can affect our opinion-forming and decision-making processes, and influence and even dominate our decisions. "Hypernudging" can be described as "fueled by real-time data, algorithms create personalized online choice architectures that aim to nudge individual users to effectively change their behavior."[1321] Both, one's decisional privacy and one's informational privacy as well as one's autonomy are under attack by "hypernudging". "Self-tracking technologies promise to empower users but violate informational and decisional privacy when commercial parties are involved in hidden, extensive surveillance, and interference with decision-making processes that they should not reasonably be expected to be."[1322]

The question is whether humans will give up their freedom for small conveniences and comforts, such as being able to use their watch to make phone calls and send messages, and in return, consenting to being completely surveilled throughout their lives, and to providing non-stop data for economic and political use. Isn't the price paid far higher than the service received? "Various algorithms are sucking data from you non-stop, every single second. What link are you clicking on? What videos are you watching until the end? How fast do you jump from one thing to the next? Where are you while you are doing it? Who do you have contact with, in person or online? What is your facial expression? In what way does your skin tone change in various situations? What were you doing when you decided to buy something or not to buy anything? To choose or not to choose? All this data and much more are compared to similar data from the lives of various other people which were collected by massive spying. Algorithms can correlate what you do with what just about everyone else has been doing. The algorithms don't really understand you, but their data give power to their owners, in particular if it is a lot of data."[1323]

The global prohibition of slavery is uncontested. Nobody officially questions it or officially petitions for its reintroduction. Over centuries humans

---

1320 Yeung 2017.
1321 Lanzing 2019: 549.
1322 Lanzing 2019: 568.
1323 Lanier 2018: 11-12.

fought for a prohibition of slavery. Is the enslavement of humans through data starting today? Do we sell ourselves for technology-based advantages? "The more I post, the worse I feel, and the worse I feel, the more I post. It works like a drug or any other addiction."[1324] Are we humans being manipulated, repressed, and exploited by the use of data-based systems? "The largest supercomputers in the world are inside of two companies – Google and Facebook – and where are we pointing them? We're pointing them at people's brains, at children."[1325]

Sean Parker, the founding president of Facebook, states the following about Facebook: "It literally changes your relationship with society, with each other ... It probably interferes with productivity in weird ways. God only knows what it's doing to our children's brains. (...) The thought process that went into building these applications, Facebook being the first of them, was all about: 'How do we consume as much of your time and conscious attention as possible?' And that means that we need to sort of give you a little dopamine hit every once in a while, because someone liked or commented on a photo or a post or whatever. And that's going to get you to contribute more content, and that's going to get you more likes and comments. It's a social-validation feedback loop exactly the kind of thing that a hacker like myself would come up with, because you're exploiting a vulnerability in human psychology. The inventors, creators – it's me, it's Mark [Zuckerberg], it's Kevin Systrom on Instagram, it's all of these people – understood this consciously. And we did it anyway."[1326] Chamath Palihapitiya, former vice president of user growth at Facebook, says: "I think we have created tools that are ripping apart the social fabric of how society works. (...) The short-term, dopamine-driven feedback loops we've created are destroying how society works. (...) No civil discourse, no cooperation; misinformation, mistruth. And it's not an American problem – this is not about Russian ads. This is a global problem. (...) I feel tremendous guilt. I think we all knew in the back of our minds – even though we feigned this whole line of, like, there probably aren't any bad unintended consequences. I think in the back, deep, deep recesses of, we kind of knew something bad could happen. But I think the way we defined it was not like this. (...) So we are in a really bad state of affairs right now, in my opinion. It is eroding the core foundation of how people behave by and between each other. And I don't have a good solution. My solution is I just

---

1324 Piepgras 2019: 42.
1325 Bowles 2018.
1326 Allen 2017.

don't use these tools anymore. I haven't for years. (I don't use social media because I) innately didn't want to get programmed. (...) (My kids) are not allowed to use this shit. (...) Your behaviors – you don't realize it but you are being programmed. It was unintentional, but now you gotta decide how much you are willing to give up, how much of your intellectual independence."[1327]

7.18 Reduction in Paid Jobs

7.18.1 Creation or Destruction of Paid Jobs?

Digital transformation and the use of data-based systems open up new horizons for innovating business models and economic systems as well as new forms of work[1328] that could contribute to solving social and ecological problems. This dynamic will create new jobs.[1329] Technology-based support in business processes leads to disruptions[1330] and, at the same time, relief for humans and creates new space for other tasks.[1331] Likely many more paid professional tasks will disappear than will be created,[1332] which significantly distinguishes this transformation from other boosts of innovation. Never in human history have innovation-based shifts led to a decrease in jobs.[1333] "One of the greatest ironies of this period in history is that, just as technology remakes our world, the need to maintain the human dimension of our work, and a company's sense of its social responsibility, is growing at an equally rapid pace. Harmonizing economic growth with the protection of human rights is one of the greatest challenges we face today."[1334]

1327 Brown 2017.
1328 See Zimmermann 2015b; Jensen / Koch 2015.
1329 See German Federal Ministry of Labour and Social Affairs 2017: 48; Gordon 2016.
1330 See Schumpeter 1972: 134-142.
1331 See Dengler / Matthes 2015; Eichhorst et al. 2016; Staab / Nachtwey 2016; Oerder 2016; Elstner et al. 2016.
1332 See Cowen 2013; Ford 2009; Ford 2015; Frey / Osborne 2013: 7-72; McKinsey Global Institute 2017; Ohly 2019a: 126-133; Schweighofer 2016; Brynjolfsson / McAffee 2011; Betschon 2015.
1333 See Hessler 2016; Katz: 2013.
1334 Office of the UN High Commissioner for Human Rights 2000.

7.18.2 Massive Reduction in Paid Professional Tasks – the Uniqueness of Digital Transformation and Data-Based Systems

In order to classify the impact of digital transformation and data-based systems on human work, it is necessary to analyze the differences between this technology-based shift compared to earlier ones. *First*, unlike earlier technology-based eras of change,[1335] the digital transformation and the use of data-based systems are, first of all, not about making work easier for humans, but replacing humans in the value chain with self-learning systems for reasons of cost-efficiency. For example, automatic checkouts in supermarkets do not aim at making the professional job of a cashier easier, as was the case for the farmer when a plough was replaced by a tractor. They want to replace cashiers and remove them from the payroll. (Andrew McAfee, co-founder of the Initiative on the Digital Economy at the Massachusetts Institute of Technology MIT, states: "I don't think a lot of employers are going to be willing to pay a lot of people for what they are currently doing"[1336].)

Second, self-learning data-based systems are made on purpose, striving for the goal that always less to no human input will be needed.[1337]

Third, digital transformation and data-based systems concern all professional jobs (e.g., robot lawyers, robot judges etc.)[1338] – not just paid professional tasks requiring low or no qualification that were affected by earlier technology-based transformations.[1339]

Fourth, digital transformation and data-based systems are strengthened by globalization and vice versa,[1340] which also has a unique speed-up effect on the changes caused by digital transformation and data-based systems in the professional world. On the one hand, digital transformation and data-based systems are fueled by global access to data instead of only local, national, or regional data. On the other hand, globalization is fueled by the high-quality, simplified, and cost-free communication possibilities thanks to digital transformation and data-based systems.

1335 See Hessler 2016.
1336 Gross 2014.
1337 See Floridi 2015b: 53.
1338 See Susskind/Susskind 2015.
1339 See Levy / Murnane 2004.
1340 See Wilhelms 2018: 3.

Fifth, digital transformation embraces, in a unique way, several technology-based innovations, e.g. digitalization, automation, machinization, mechanization, robots, data-based systems.

Sixth, the technology-based change transforms the professional and the private lives of humans, not just their professional lives, which intensifies the penetration of technology into human existence and therefore accelerates its progress and, as a result, its impact on human labor.

Seventh, the nature of digital transformation and data-based systems – above all, being nourished directly by data of the same humans – enhances the acceptance-rate and the willingness to get accustomed to new technological applications.

Eighth, this digital transformation happens at a much higher speed in shorter intervals than during earlier technology-based eras of change so society as a whole does not have enough time to adapt before data-based systems have taken away the paid professional task of humans.

Ninth, digital transformation and the use of data-based systems entail the end of striving for full employment because of the "great decoupling"[1341] of the increase in productivity based on technological progress and the slowdown of total employment since 2011. "Productivity is at record levels, innovation has never been faster, and yet at the same time, we have a falling median income and we have fewer jobs."[1342]

Tenth, for the first time in human history, the revenue and the profit of a company can be enormous and, at the same time, the number of employees extremely small.[1343]

Eleventh, platform-economy increases efficiency but not the incentives and the motivation to create jobs. On the contrary, they lower the number of paid professional tasks. "We live in an era where fewer than 10% of the world's public companies account for more than 80% of all profits. (...) Ten years ago, banks and energy companies dominated the top ten. Today, it's technology companies, with US computer company Apple in the number one spot."[1344] 7 of 10 of the world's biggest companies make money with platforms.[1345] Besides offering multidimensional and diverse business-opportunities for their owners, platforms raise concerns from an ethical perspective. "The transparency and global reach of digital platforms is

---

1341 Brynjolfsson / McAffee 2011.
1342 Rotman 2013.
1343 See Metzler 2016.
1344 Gray 2017.
1345 See Gray 2017.

triggering a downward price spiral. Internet platforms have potential for modern slavery. (...) The cheapest provider of a service is awarded the contract."[1346] Normative frameworks as part of the economic system are under attack or torn down on these global marketplaces. Human rights are neglected with just a click, the former being something for which humanity has been fighting for centuries in order to protect the survival and a life as human – a life with human dignity. Digital transformation and the use of data-based systems consist also in a devaluation of human labor forcing humans into "multi-jobbing" – enabled by platforms like, e.g., Uber, Airbnb. "The people who hire themselves out as multi-jobbers and market themselves via online platforms are the cause of unimaginable sales and profits – but not for themselves, but for the platform operators."[1347]

Twelfth, investments and funding are attracted by this stimulus of technology-based innovations resulting in high profits with a low number of paid professional tasks, which leads to an intensification and reinforcement of this development towards an economy consisting in economic growth with a decrease in paid professional tasks.

Thirteenth, the response to the question of whether humans will still be allowed to fulfill a paid professional task does not depend on the skills of the humans but rather on the definition and the description of the job[1348] which are dominated though – as mentioned above – by digital transformation and data-based systems and by cost-efficiency.

Fourteenth, based on the core consequence of digital transformation introduced above in chapter 4 Critical Review of Terms – *ever fewer humans will directly participate and partake in a more efficient and effective value chain* –[1349] *fewer* humans involved in research, science and technology decrease the diversity of the involved humans, which provokes a lower probability of innovation.

Fifteenth, if the vast majority of humans do not have the possibility to earn enough for their survival and for a life with human dignity by fulfilling paid professional tasks and, therefore, the trust of humans that they are born with something that makes the difference ("the ability to work, to learn, and to earn money"[1350]) is fading away, it is not only ethically unac-

1346 Hofstetter 2017: 80.
1347 Hofstetter 2017: 83.
1348 See Ford 2016.
1349 See Kirchschlaeger 2017a; Kirchschlaeger 2016b.
1350 Smith 2013.

ceptable but this also provokes a decrease in innovation because humans will have to focus on the essentials – their survival.

Sixteenth, due to this fast technology-based shift, the elements of the unknown and uncertainty represent the new reality, which makes it impossible for humans to prepare themselves adequately by educating themselves further. The present academic, but also political discourse, about the question of job-reduction also includes requests to humans to participate in inservice-training to prepare themselves for the present and future digital transformation and for the use of data-based systems,[1351] to become ready for a volatile, insecure, complex, and ambiguous reality.[1352] For example, the following pattern of argumentation is presented: "Technological progress is going to leave behind some people, perhaps even a lot of people, as it races ahead. (...) there has never been a better time to be a worker with special skills or the right education, because these people can use technology to create and capture value. However, there's never been a worse time to be a worker with only 'ordinary' skills and abilities to offer, because computers, robots, and other digital technologies are acquiring these skills and abilities at an extraordinary rate."[1353] This has been true for technology-based shifts in the past. This is not true anymore for the digital transformation and for the use of data-based systems because of the above-mentioned reasons, mostly because of the aim of this technological progress – the replacement of humans with machines serving cost-efficiency – and due to the fact that all professional groups are touched by digital transformation and the use of data-based systems.

From an ethical perspective, it is irresponsible to try to make a fundamental structural problem of the economic system (massive reduction in paid professional tasks) an individual challenge (individual responsibility of every human to educate oneself according to the technology-based shift).

It is irresponsible to avoid tackling the fundamental change of our economic system consisting in the massive reduction in paid professional tasks with structural measures (with, e.g., the SERT-model introduced below in subchapter 8.2) by calling for inservice-training on an individual level.

It is irresponsible to request humans to educate themselves if one knows that humans will be replaced anyway. For example, Christoph Franz,

---

1351 See, e.g., Tuffley 2015.
1352 See, e.g., Freyth 2020.
1353 Brynjolfsson / McAffee 2011: 11.

Chairman of Roche Holding, states: "We want to ensure that our employees acquire the necessary skills. (...) Most of us will be forced to acquire new skills in our professional lives."[1354] Of course, it is positive from an ethical perspective that he claims that his company has a responsibility for this inservice-training of its employees. At the same time, it is ethically problematic to deny the more fundamental challenge that humans – even though they invest in their own education and training – will lose their paid professional tasks anyway.

It is irresponsible for a company to externalize the costs for replacement of humans with machines to the public while requesting humans to educate themselves. For example, the regulatory process by the European Union goes in that direction. Mady Delvaux, at that time a member of the European Parliament, criticized this issue as follows: Lawmakers "refused to take account of possible negative consequences on the job market. They rejected an open-minded and forward-looking debate and thus disregarded the concerns of our citizens."[1355]

It is irresponsible to request humans to educate themselves if no one is ready to cover the costs for this inservice-training.

It is irresponsible to request humans to educate themselves if nobody knows – due to the elements of the unknown and uncertainty – if any or which inservice-training would be adequate.

Seventeenth, the nature, the characteristics and the profiles of paid professional tasks are not static. They change. Due to the digital transformation and the comprehensive penetration of the economy and of the labor-market by data-based systems, this technology-based change also extends to the design, the structure, and the organization of paid professional tasks: paid professional tasks are adapted in a way that they accommodate the specifications and the abilities of data-based systems, not of humans.

The reduction in paid professional tasks for humans and, thus, in paid jobs is proving to be an effect of digital transformation and data-based systems, and in particular, of the use of self-learning systems which took place in the process, and poses great challenges – including abstraction in the sense of a distance from humans, their freedom, and their will to create, as well as immediacy as a description of the phenomenon of humans being put under the spell of machines.[1356] Furthermore, the striving to make humans perfect, to which so-called "human enhancement" contributes in its

---

1354 Moeckli 2019: 8.
1355 Prodhan 2017. See European Parliament 2017a.
1356 See Wilhelms 2018.

various forms, puts humans under pressure, in particular at their work-place.[1357] Today, data-based systems already outperform humans in various areas of intelligence (e.g., memory, handling a great amount of data, etc.). It can be assumed that other areas of cognitive skills will follow. The effect with respect to paid professional tasks and paid jobs already caused by self-learning machines will be further amplified by "super-data-based systems".

7.19 Global Injustice

Erik Brynjolfsson states: "It's one of the dirty secrets of economics: technology progress does grow the economy and create wealth, but there is no economic law that says everyone will benefit."[1358] Digitalization, automation, machinization, robotization, and the use of data-based systems possess the above-mentioned potential to contribute to the creation of more global justice and to the realization of human rights (e.g., by offering more people access to financial services and markets based on blockchain technology).

This can be done by taking into consideration, for example, the impact of blockchain technology on the economy so far, though another scenario comes into play, namely that blockchain technology runs the risk to serve as a vehicle contributing to widening the gap between rich and poor. This could happen due to the lack of access to blockchain technology and would strengthen already established privileged positions. This would also mean that *ever fewer humans are directly involved economically and socially in a more efficient and more effective value-added chain*.[1359] On the one hand, this development characterizes that more value will be created. On the other hand, fewer humans contribute directly to the value-added chain and benefit from this added value. The main challenge from an ethical perspective is, therefore, not a lack of financial means because more efficient and more productive value-added chains based on blockchain technology lead to an increase in that regard, but rather the question of justice and human rights. At stake is the distribution of the added value which is created, respectively, at the center of concerns. It is the question of social integration as fewer humans are involved in the value-added chain based on

---

1357 For a critique of the striving for human perfection, see Sandel 2007.
1358 Rotman 2013.
1359 See Kirchschlaeger 2017a; Kirchschlaeger 2016b.

blockchain technology – a concern that represents the core consequence of digital transformation and the use of data-based systems in general.[1360]

Beyond that, the "digital divide" is and – if severe counteractions are not taken – remains an unjust reality. Its global solution must be approached and considered as a priority today and tomorrow. "People who have access to the digital world have so far benefited economically from this process in comparison to people who do not have access ('digital divide'). However, in the future almost everyone will have access to the digital world, but with different quality characteristics in terms of access. There is a tendency to create a state of 'digital inequality', similar to the economic inequality that has recently received more media attention. This inequality needs to be overcome through inclusive global governance with a balance between central and distributed control."[1361]

Against the background of the ethical point of reference of human rights, data-based systems and digital transformation urge humans to act rapidly insofar as it further fuels a problem that already existed before. Slavery-like working conditions or modern slavery used for the extraction of raw materials[1362] and the production of technology products as well as huge differences in political participation for shaping digital transformation and the use of data-based systems, as well as with regard to enjoying the sunny side (*inter alia* equal opportunities, profit-sharing) or suffering from the negative sides of this transformation (*inter alia* exclusion, exploitation that is degrading and violates human rights), cry for fundamental change and ethical progress. This is not a new challenge, but one which is still topical and which is growing rapidly as a result of technology-based progress. An increase in the demand for these natural resources in digital transformation and data-based systems worsens these human rights violations. The increased demand for technology products underlines the urgency to establish humane working conditions in all phases of value creation, including production. The increased demand for natural resources fueling digital transformation and data-based systems and for technology products calls for optimizing the implementation of already existing human rights-obligations of states and the private sector in this area.[1363]

1360 See Kirchschlaeger 2019b.
1361 Uenver 2015: vi.
1362 See Gerding 2019: 27; Amnesty International 2016; Schweizer 2015; Odiot / Gallet 2012.
1363 See Kirchschlaeger 2015c: 280.

Of course, companies do make a social contribution when trying to make profits and grow. Because, apart from the immediate economic effects on society (e.g., creation of jobs, taxes etc.), the positive, value-adding and solution-oriented power of entrepreneurship for the environment also needs to be considered. Moreover, its dynamic inspires society, as is becoming so evident in the field of digital transformation and data-based systems. People and society profit from this innovation potential of profit-oriented decision-making and acting, because economic innovations trigger or drive social progress. Furthermore, the business approach is used to address questions, to solve problems and to meet challenges, because those solutions are expected to be more sustainable. Finally, companies offer humans a structure for their daily life and the possibility to develop and find self-fulfillment. The latter can also contribute to giving meaning and purpose to a human existence.

In this sense, social entrepreneurship highlights an important quality of entrepreneurship in general: the connection between economic and ethical rationality. Companies do not only create economic benefit, but also contribute socially. Companies contribute to social systems. "The central role of business (corporate management) is in ensuring the long-term viability of a democratically governed society (...) grounded in justice, equality, and trust and supported by sustainable natural, social, and economic systems"[1364]. At the same time, societies give companies the necessary scope for decision-making and action. "Again and again, the interaction between companies and society comes to light: the society needs strong companies to ensure its well-being. Companies, on the other hand, need strong societies. Because only in a strong society they find stable political environments, resources and markets, infrastructure, intellectual and financial capital, good workers, partners, and customers"[1365].

However, there is the danger that by putting more importance on economic rationality, the vision of companies will be narrowed and that they might repress ethical rationality and alienate themselves from their social contribution. For example, companies can be involved in exploitation and suppression or observe them indifferently, which unfortunately happens in particular in the field of digital transformation and the use of data-based systems. In both cases, the following applies: if the above-mentioned social contributions of companies are connected to such practices, they automatically lose their value for society due to the antisocial nature of this business

---

1364 Dillard 2013: 199.
1365 Clever / Ramb 2010: 59.

practice. Furthermore, they are an injustice and a threat to society. An imbalance between economic and ethical reality can be ascertained. This imbalance leads to the fact that the positive impact created by companies will not only be eradicated, but only the harm done to society will count. For example, inhumane working conditions negate the social contribution of creating jobs and turn the acting company into a criminal and a violator of human rights. The argument that this creates jobs loses all relevance because of the injustice of inhumane working conditions. Not only that, the company will also be legitimately criticized for it.

The interaction between economic and ethical rationality in business actions is important for the whole society. Societies depend on companies taking on their social responsibilities, because companies have power and influence. Companies do not only have the power to influence[1366] the behavior of their investors,[1367] suppliers, and customers[1368]. The intensity of the mutual interdependence in the course of globalization multiplies the power of companies, which means a society cannot cope with a failure or partial failure of companies providing a contribution to society as a whole or attacks on social cohesion by companies through exploitation and suppression.[1369] "One instrument brought into play by companies to achieve more economic fairness is the so-called Corporate Social Responsibility (CSR). Those are standards that companies gave themselves as regards to their business conduct (e.g., working conditions, environmental behavior, social aspects)"[1370].

Corporate Social Responsibility (CSR) as a concept widens the objects of responsibility for companies beyond the shareholders and includes the responsibility of companies "towards internal and external stakeholders, employees, customers, suppliers and the closer and broader community"[1371]. It is based on the term "responsibility"[1372]. "The total corporate social responsibility of business entails the simultaneous fulfillment of the firm's economic, legal, ethical, and philanthropic responsibilities. Stated in more pragmatic and managerial terms, the CSR firm should strive to make a profit, obey the law, be ethical, and be a good corporate citizen"[1373].

1366 See Ekmekçi 2014.
1367 See Gurbuz et al. 2014; Idowu / Mermod 2014a.
1368 See Schoenheit 2014: 41-48.
1369 See Dillard / Murray 2013: 11.
1370 Hilty / Henning-Bodewig 2014: 4.
1371 Braun 2009: 249.
1372 See Kirchschlaeger 2014a.
1373 Carroll 1991: 43.

From an ethical perspective, it needs to be pointed out that, with reference to human rights, the human rights duties for states implicitly contain human rights duties for non-state actors. Of course, human rights as part of international law are primarily legally binding for states as subjects of international law.[1374] It is down to the states to implement human rights. The state has to ensure through legal and administrative measures that human rights become a reality. In the legal dimension, this national human rights protection is complemented by regional and international human rights mechanisms in order to monitor the behavior of states and to substantially complement the safeguarding of universal human rights protection.

These human rights duties of states also entail that non-state actors such as businesses need to contribute to the realization of human rights. If, however, only states have to ensure that, for example, multinational corporations fulfil their responsibility and respect, protect and contribute to the realization of human rights, this indirectly entails a legal duty for businesses. Even in, for example, the "UN Guiding Principles on Business and Human Rights"[1375], which separate state responsibility[1376] from business responsibility[1377] and thus expect from businesses in the way of "human rights minimalism"[1378] only to "do not harm", the third principle implicitly contains the confirmation that legal obligations already exist for business: "As part of their duty to protect against business-related human rights abuse, states must take appropriate steps to ensure, through judicial, administrative, legislative or other appropriate means, that when such abuses occur within their territory and/or jurisdiction those affected have access to effective remedy." If "access to remedy" needs to be given, this implicitly contains a legal obligation for businesses, because without a legal obligation that may or may not be fulfilled, a right to "access to remedy" would not make sense and it would not need a right to "access to remedy".

Finally, the human rights duties of states also entail monitoring of the implementation of human rights in the sphere of influence of multinational corporations, the control of the effectiveness of existing legal instruments, and the improvement of implementing mechanisms and legal framework conditions, if human rights are not realized. For example, in

---

1374 See Kaelin 2004: 17; Spenlé 2005.
1375 See United Nations 2011.
1376 See McCorquodale 2009.
1377 See Wettstein 2012a: 18-33.
1378 Wettstein 2012b: 745.

the case of a "governance gap", which means "the diminishing capacity of national governments to steer and constrain those dimensions of transnational business activity that affects the human rights of their populations (...) emerging as a result of the expanded power and capabilities of transnational business and weakened capabilities of states under conditions of economic globalization"[1379] as introduced above in chapter 7.12 Democracy and Data-Based Systems, states have the duty to respond in order to increase the implementation of human rights by improving the legal instruments and mechanisms.

Of course, states retain the primary responsibility to respect, protect, implement, and contribute to the realization of human rights.[1380] Apart from the vertical impact, human rights also have a horizontal impact, which means they also have an impact on the relationship between individuals or non-state actors such as businesses, etc.[1381] This relationship between rights and duties must be thought of as a correspondence, as has been explained above,[1382] and also finds its legitimacy in it. Human rights are "an especially urgent and morally justified claim that a person has, simply in virtue of being a human adult, and independently of membership in a particular nation, class, sex, or ethnic, religious or sexual group."[1383] This right corresponds with a duty: "The existence of a human right always implies a counterpart obligation (...) for that right to be respected, protected, and realized."[1384] A right of "X towards Z" would be useless without the duty of Z to respect, protect, and contribute to the realization of the right of X.[1385] The Preamble of the Universal Declaration of Human Rights of 1948, as well as Article 5 of the UN Covenant on Civil and Political Rights of 1966 and the UN Covenant on Economic, Social and Cultural Rights of 1966 and Article 28 and 29 of the African Charter on Human and Peoples' Rights of 1981, show that human rights are not only an obligation for states, but for the whole society and all actors, in particular for those with power and influence. Human rights do not only give states duties, but also, depending on the context and the situation, also non-state actors such as businesses, individuals, etc..

1379 Macdonald 2011: 549.
1380 See Wettstein 2012c: 76.
1381 See Mueller 2005.
1382 See Witschen 1999.
1383 Nussbaum 2002: 135.
1384 Wettstein 2012b: 753.
1385 See Tomuschat 2003: 39.

From the perspective of a bearer of human rights or a real or possible victim of human rights violations, the need and justification of this horizontal impact of human rights becomes obvious. For a bearer of human rights or a real or possible victim of human rights violations, it is secondary who implements human rights or who is responsible for human rights violations. Primarily, it is crucial from the perspective of the legal subject or the victim of human rights violations that human rights violations be stopped so that they will be prevented in the future, and that human rights are realized. Therefore, states have the primary, but not sole responsibility for the implementation and realization of human rights. "Only a complete disregard of the moral status and foundation of human rights can lead one to conclude that governments should be the only parties directly obliged by human rights. If we hold that human rights represent inherent and equal moral entitlements of all human beings irrespective of their heritage and background, we cannot deny that they logically obligate not just governments, but everyone."[1386] The focus is on the individual as a bearer of human rights. Their rights need to be respected, protected, implemented, and realized. Their perspective decides who, depending on the situation and context or on the power relations and influence, has the responsibility to ensure that human rights are respected, protected, implemented, and realized.

This justification is complemented by a pragmatic argument: "The known limitations of the state's duty to protect human rights from abuses by private corporate actors that operate at a transnational level and have the capacity to disappear or move from one jurisdiction to another"[1387]. It needs to be considered that, on the one hand, "states that are unwilling or unable to act robustly against corporate actors disregard their human rights responsibilities. This unwillingness, especially of developing countries, is primarily rooted in the apprehension that taking a hard line against human rights abuses by TNCs might impair their competitiveness to attract foreign investment much needed for development."[1388] At the same time, so-called developed countries fear a competitive disadvantage for their private sector, if they hold them accountable for human rights violations in their own courts.[1389]

1386   Wettstein 2012c: 77.
1387   Deva 2012a: 103.
1388   Deva 2012a: 103.
1389   See McCorquodale / Simons 2007.

On the other hand, multinational corporations are active in states with weak human rights performance and little to no rule of law and turn out to be quiet observers, accomplices ("Corporate complicity can be differentiated in 'direct complicity', 'indirect complicity', 'beneficial complicity', and 'silent complicity'"[1390]), or even subjects of human rights violations. In view of this reality, one would not do justice to human rights as legally binding international law, if one would hold primarily and only states responsible ("The net result is a situation where a state-centric human rights enforcement mechanism tries, rather unsuccessfully, to tame stateless – not only in terms of operation and organization but also appearance – actors"[1391]).[1392] "Power, authority, and rights (...) should imply duties, obligations, and liabilities"[1393]. Of course, "companies cannot and should not be the moral arbiters of the world. They cannot usurp the role of governments, nor solve all the social problems they confront. But their influence on the global economy is growing and their presence increasingly affects the societies in which they operate"[1394]. Nevertheless, growing power and increasing influence also entail corresponding responsibility and duty to report, because thanks to influence and power, they gain the opportunity to decide and act. According to Amnesty International, "of the 100 largest economies in the world, 51 are corporations; only 49 are countries."[1395]

Moreover, the nature of entrepreneurial activity also simply increases this power shift: "A growing number of businesses operate across boundaries in ways that exceed the regulatory capacities of any one national system"[1396]. The following further increases this growth of power and influence: "States, in principle, still possess the power of regulation/intervention, but the expectation is that states will exercise their power only when it suits the interests of the global capital (...), even if doing so harms the interest of local communities. (...) Moreover, states, even with a democratic set up, might not be able to take an activist position towards fulfilling their human rights obligations under pressure from international bodies or MNCs. Given this scenario, it is doubtful whether states could still be

1390   Wettstein 2010: 35-39.
1391   Deva 2007: 250.
1392   See Sandkuehler 2010: 1550.
1393   Kobrin 2009: 355.
1394   Chandler 2000: 5.
1395   Amnesty International n.d.
1396   Tripathi 2005: 158-159.

trusted for solely guarding, to the best of their ability, the human rights of their populace."[1397]

At this point, it needs to be stated that highlighting the complementary responsibility of non-state actors for human rights does not mean diminishing the responsibility of states. There is no reason or basis for this. States continue to have the primary, but not the sole, responsibility.

In the area of digital transformation and the use of data-based systems, states and multinational corporations so far have not succeeded in respecting, protecting, implementing, and realizing human rights. Therefore, the implementation of the already existing legal obligations for businesses needs to be improved. The enhancement of the implementation of existing legal human rights obligations for businesses are not additional legal obligations for businesses, but new, more effective legal instruments and enforcement mechanisms to improve the implementation of human rights in the sphere of influence of businesses. For example, the discussion about "extraterritorial regulation"[1398] shows that it is about optimization. It is not about additional new duties for multinational corporations, but to try to overcome the existing "mismatch between modern human rights violations and old regulatory tools"[1399]. Territorially defined legal mechanisms cannot deal with a private sector that cannot be confined to one single country. "Companies now operate at a transnational level through a complex web of subsidiaries, joint ventures, and supply chains. Such a modus operandi of business necessarily means that some direct or indirect human rights violations by companies would take place outside the territorial boundary of a state in which a given company is incorporated."[1400] "Extraterritorial regulation" strives for "the domestic law of country where the companies (be) registered to 'reach out' to their activities abroad"[1401].

The human rights tradition knows such a development from other areas, namely to create new legal instruments in view of injustices[1402] and an inadequate and unsatisfactory implementation of existing human rights and to improve existing enforcement mechanisms. For example, the UN Convention on the Rights of the Child of 1989 was a reaction to the reality that children, even though they are also human rights bearers, did not enjoy

---

1397   Deva 2007: 242-243.
1398   See Deva 2012b; Bernaz 2013; McCorquodale 2009: 387-390.
1399   Deva 2012b: 1079.
1400   Deva 2012b: 1080.
1401   Bernaz 2013: 494.
1402   See Kirchschlaeger 2013c.

their human rights to the same extent as adults.[1403] The UN Convention on the Rights of the Child from 1989 improved this situation.

Examples of the first concrete steps for an optimization of already existing legal human rights obligations for companies are, for example, the court decision from January 30, 2013 in Den Haag, where Shell was found guilty of the oil pollution in the Niger Delta: "The first time that a company established in the European Union was held responsible in its own country for abuses committed elsewhere"[1404], political initiatives on a national level such as the "Responsible Business Initiative"[1405] in Switzerland, or the project for a UN declaration "Transnational Corporations and Human Rights" on an international level. "Some argue that no treaty is needed. They point out that the UN Human Rights Council already endorsed the UN's Guiding Principles on Business and Human Rights, published in 2011. And it is true that the principles should be a game-changer. But the reality is that governments and businesses alike have failed to make the guiding principles meaningful. In the meantime, corporate lobbyists have done everything possible to ensure the principles remain entirely voluntary. It is unsurprising then, that for the communities and individuals whose rights are violated little has changed over the last three years. The people whose homes have been demolished by a company's bulldozers, or whose livelihoods are destroyed by oil spills, are as powerless as ever"[1406]. More than 80 states and one hundred regional and international human rights organizations are supporting this project already. "The world's diverse and inconsistent laws and enforcement, combined with the utter lack of corporate accountability in *most* cases of business human rights abuse (…), sufficiently justify a treaty. Indeed, a treaty is arguably *required* by the state duty to protect read with the requirement of effective remedy, given the prevailing corporate impunity"[1407].

Are human rights obligations for the private sector ethically justifiable? *First*, the legal duties for companies, as well as their moral responsibility, can be justified and legitimized by the legal and ethical justification of human rights. The latter has its basis in the approach that is based on the principle of vulnerability elaborated above in subchapter 6.4 Human Rights as an Ethical Frame of Reference.

1403 See Kirchschlaeger / Kirchschlaeger 2007.
1404 Hennchen 2014: 11.
1405 See Konzernverantwortungsinitiative 2020.
1406 Shetty 2015.
1407 Pitts 2015, emphasis in the text; see also Deva 2012c: 200-231.

Second, the above-introduced reciprocity of human rights justifies the legal obligations of companies: Because one is talking about human rights (and not about the "rights of Peter G Kirchschlaeger"), the claim to human rights is not exclusive but rather connected to the fact that all other humans are also bearers of human rights. Therefore, human rights also entail the corresponding responsibility and duty to respect, protect, implement, and contribute to the realization of the human rights of all other humans.

Third, the reversal of the burden of proof also serves to establish legal human rights obligations for companies. "Good reasons", meaning that it must be conceivable that all humans, given their effective freedom and autonomy as well as their full equality, would agree upon these reasons – within a model of thought and not within a real worldwide referendum – on ethical grounds, are required to justify why there would be no legal human rights obligations for companies. It will be impossible to find reasons

- why only states should be legally bound to change something about the situation of human rights violations, in particular in contexts where companies have more power and influence than states,
- why only states should contribute to protect humans in all essential elements and areas needed for survival and living as humans with human dignity – in particular when companies also have the possibility to promote human rights protection. The reversal of the burden of proof thus also shows that the human rights obligations for companies are ethically legitimate.

From the perspective of human rights bearers and potential or real victims of human rights violations, no time must be wasted to fulfill these human rights obligations for the private sector in the digital transformation and in the use of data-based systems.

7.20 Ecological Impact

Digital transformation and data-based systems could be a technology-based innovation that could make the world greener. At present, it pollutes the ecosystem.[1408] "The energy consumption of Information and Communication Technologies (ICT) is increasing by 9% every year. It is possible to limit this growth to 1.5% per year by moving to sober digital practices. The digital transition as it is currently implemented participates in global

---

1408   See Grefe 2018: 35.

warming more than it helps prevent it. The need for action is therefore urgent."[1409] From an ethical perspective, applying the principle of responsibility, it is imperative to change the path immediately towards a more sustainable path. "The fast expansion of ICT leads to a rapid increase of its direct energy footprint. This footprint includes the energy used for the production and the use of ICT equipment (servers, networks, terminals). This direct footprint has been increasing by 9% per year. Compared to 2010 the direct energy consumption generated by 1 euro invested in digital technologies has increased by 37%. The energy intensity of the ICT sector is growing by 4% per year, in stark contrast to the trend of global GDP's energy intensity evolution, which is declining by 1.8% per year. The explosion of video uses (Skype, streaming, etc.) and the increased consumption of frequently renewed digital equipment are the main drivers of this inflation. (…) The share of ICT in global greenhouse gases emissions has increased by half since 2013, rising from 2.5% to 3.7% of global emissions. In OECD countries, the CO2 emissions of ICT grew by about 450 million tons since 2013. Over the same period, overall OECD CO2 emissions decreased by 250 million tons. Digitalization taps resources that are critical for the energy transition. The appropriation of a gradually disproportionate part of available electricity increases the tension on electricity production, which we already struggle to decarbonize. The increase in the production of ICT equipment requires larger quantities of rare and critical metals which are also vital for low carbon energy technologies, while physical, geopolitical and economic factors already limit their availability."[1410] The potential that data-based systems would make the world greener is still just a dream, not a reality. "The net contribution of ICT to the reduction of global environmental impacts is still yet to be demonstrated, sector by sector, and this demonstration must take into account the numerous 'rebound effects'. The real trend of digitalization is in opposition to its presupposed function of 'dematerializing the economy'. The current evolution of ICT's environmental impact goes against the decoupling of energy consumption from GDP growth, which is an objective of the 2015 Paris Agreement."[1411]

1409 Shift Project 2019.
1410 Shift Project 2019.
1411 Shift Project 2019.

Beyond that, the mining industry and platinum group metal mining for hardware infrastructure supporting digital transformation and data-based systems destroy the environment.[1412]

Of course, it would be ideal if data-based systems themselves would fix this ecological problem created by digital transformation and data-based systems. Today, this is still a dream. Until data-based systems are really able to do that and are really doing so, digital consumption should be reduced – as in other areas of daily lives – in order to save our ecosystem. "Digital overconsumption is not yet generalized: it is caused by high income countries, for which the major issue is to take back control of their digital consumption behaviors."[1413] Beyond that, regenerative design, a research and development-focus on energy efficiency and on renewable technologies as well as careful handling of raw materials and their reuse, and waste reduction are imperatives for digital transformation and data-based systems from an ethical perspective.

1412 See, e.g., Amnesty International 2020b.
1413 Shift Project 2019.

8 Outlook: How to Create a Future Ethically

Beyond the identification of ethical opportunities and challenges by applying the ethical principles of responsibility, omni-dynamic social justice, and human rights on the digital transformation and data-based systems, the following paths could lead to solutions from an ethical perspective. These paths towards solutions are argued for with all modesty for three reasons: firstly, the realities mentioned above and assessed ethically belong in the majority of cases, in part or even more to the future and their perception is mostly based on scenarios and probabilities. Secondly, the analysis and discussion of the digital transformation and the use of data-based systems from an ethical perspective must deal with complex systems, specifically with thinking about complex systems that form a challenge for ethics if it wants fully to take into account this unique characteristic of digital transformation and the use of data-based systems.[1414] Thirdly, the following solutions are ideas from an ethicist aware of the fact that most of them necessarily would need to be complemented from other disciplines.

8.1 Ethical and Legal Framework for Technological Progress

8.1.1 Data-Based Systems Should Serve Humans and the Earth

Social and economic transformation driven by data-based systems is leading to unique opportunities from an ethical perspective.[1415] Humans should try to benefit optimally from the unique ethical opportunities of digital transformation and data-based systems while also recognizing the potential ambivalence of these opportunities as well as the "dual use"-challenge and the ethical risks of this technology-based transformation.[1416] This negative side of digital transformation and data-based systems should not be addressed with the approach "to solve the problems of the technolo-

---

1414   See Breiding et al. 2015: 37.
1415   See Lucchi 2016: 4.
1416   See Russell et al. 2013.

gy using the same technology that caused the problems"[1417] in order to avoid a vicious circle.

The significance of ideas from an ethical perspective are emphasized by the context that the data-based transformation has reached an inflection point. An inflection point stands for the moment where a process loses its stability. This is the case with digital transformation and data-based systems as an error in the systems could crash global financial markets[1418] or energy supply, and automated weapon systems could threaten peace. For example, one does not want to imagine if an algorithmic error occurs with automated weapon systems like it occurred in the financial systems in 2010 because an immediate return to the initial situation – as in the financial system – does not seem to be realistic in a military environment, and much less in a situation of risk of conflict or war.[1419] Three dynamics characterize this inflection point – all three of them need to be addressed: "1. Science is converging on an all-encompassing dogma, which says that organisms are algorithms and life is data processing. 2. Intelligence is decoupling from consciousness. 3. Non-conscious but highly intelligent algorithms may soon know us better than we know ourselves."[1420] Humans should distinguish more resolutely what data-based systems are able to do and what not[1421] or what they should do and what not.

At this inflection point where data-based systems "could cause new problems and also *aggravate existing problems* in societies and with the environment"[1422], *first,* the necessary decisions and actions need to be taken. The necessary ethical principles and norms as well as legal norms, mechanisms, and frameworks must be put in place to guarantee that the digital transformation and data-based systems serve humans and the planet Earth, not the other way around. Therefore, there is a necessity to regulate legally, to legislate constitutionally, and to create technologically ethically and legally sound data-based systems-solutions in order to innovate in an ethically positive way and, at the same time, in order to avoid to forbidding ethically positive innovation by regulation and legislation.

These normative measures must rely on a basis of ethics of research looking for "insights, and it searches for them by means of concepts and argu-

---

1417   Thuerkauf 1980: 232.
1418   See Taleb 2010.
1419   See Mannino et al. 2015: 3-4.
1420   Harari 2017: 462.
1421   See Broussard 2019.
1422   Coeckelberg 2020: 187, emphasis in the text.

ments. But the insights are not an end in themselves; they serve to legitimize or limit human practice."[1423]

These ethically and legally normative measures need, *second*, to make sure that humans decide whether or not a technology should be built or not.

Third, they need to address and inform ethically and legally the framework, aims, limits, research, design, development, production, structuring, organization, the use, and the applications of data-based systems.

Fourth, they need to address ethically and legally the prevention of potential errors and abuses of as well as potential crimes with data-based systems.

Fifth, these regulatory measures are necessary from an ethical point of view taking into account the rational risk management-principle that even with low-risk probabilities, it makes sense to take expensive precautions if there is enough to win or to lose.[1424]

Sixth, these regulatory measures must necessarily be adequate for digital transformation and data-based systems in order to meet the enforceability-problem.

Seventh, these regulatory measures must be able to address the potential danger on a level playing field. "Hundreds of computers in every room, all capable of sensing people near them and linked by high-speed networks have the potential to make totalitarianism up to now seem like sheerest anarchy."[1425] If computers possess this totalitarian and instrumentarian potential, what about data-based systems everywhere, in everything, and on everybody?

8.1.2 Human Responsibility

Due to their moral capability as shown above in chapter 3 Can Ethical Judgment Be Delegated to Technologies? and explained further in sub-chapter 6.2 The Principle of Responsibility, humans remain liable for technological development and progress. This ethical responsibility cannot be delegated to technologies because technological systems do not possess the moral capability to define autonomously ethical norms and principles, which are universalizable. There is no ethical ground for distancing oneself

---

1423 Hoeffe 1994: 47-48.
1424 See Peterson 2009.
1425 Weiser 1999: 89.

through abstraction, for alienating oneself, and for escaping from humans and from planet Earth.[1426] Technological progress must receive its ethical orientation from humans. Even though humans are excluded from processes and value-added chains more and more by digital transformation and the use of data-based systems, they remain the decisive and leading instance for these processes due to their moral capability. While considering this *first paradox* of digital transformation and the use of data-based systems, it must be acknowledged that humans provide ethical guidance for the digital transformation, define its speed and its outreach[1427] by setting ethical principles and norms, and remain liable for the decisions and actions of technologies because of their moral capability. Part of this moral capability is to include ethical principles and categories in the design and programming of technologies and to interact continuously with technological progress. "We must stop treating AI like magic, but finally take responsibility for how it is created, used and regulated – and as ethically as possible."[1428] Ethics must, therefore, interact continuously with technological progress. In the sense of the interaction between ethics and technology introduced in chapter 2 The Correlation between Ethics and Technology, it is necessary to include ethical, legal, and social aspects at the beginning and in the entire process of the design, creation, development, production, use, and application of a technical innovation (one example of how this can be accomplished is the model to ethically evaluate socio-technical arrangements MEESTAR[1429]). This process should be organized and structured in a participatory way.[1430]

While negating the moral capability of technologies, it needs to be emphasized that technologies, machines, robots, systems, and data-based systems are able to follow ethical rules, to make ethical decisions based on these rules, and to act accordingly. Data-based systems can be programmed or trained with ethical rules in order to reach ethically legitimate decisions and actions in a data-based system.[1431] In this human responsibility, human rights of all humans have a constituting and guiding effect to create *data-based systems with ethics*. That said, it must be emphasized again that the responsibility for *data-based systems with ethics* remains with humans –

1426 See Arendt 1958.
1427 See Krenn 2016: 17.
1428 Hao 2020.
1429 See Manzeschke et al. 2013: 13-21; Weber 2015.
1430 See Weber / Wackerbarth 2015: 1247-1249.
1431 See Wallach / Allen 2009.

as, e.g., explicitly framed in the following basic principles for robot ethics: "1. Artificial systems should always promote the self-determination of people and will not affect the performance of the system. 2. They should not decide on the life and death of people. 3. It must be ensured that people are always in control and are responsible for the actions of the machinery take over."[1432]

8.1.3 Ethical and Legal Norms for Data-Based Systems

Technological progress receives its ethical orientation from humans. This entails targeted promotion of the use of ethical opportunities in order to be able to benefit from innovation for the ethical good as humans in the course of digital transformation and the use of data-based systems. From an ethical perspective informed by the principles of omni-dynamic social justice, responsibility, and human rights, the following imperative could provide ethical guidance: "Act in such a way that the consequences of your actions are compatible with a [present and] future humane existence, i.e. with the claim of humanity to survive for an unlimited time."[1433] (The supplement of the quote in parentheses is necessary to guarantee that all humans in the present are respected as holders of human dignity as well, not only all humans in the future – in order to exclude a social-Darwinistic solution to kill a part of humanity in the present as a contribution to the future of humanity, for example, by Friedrich von Hayek.)[1434]

This implies a political, democratic opinion-forming and decision-making process striving for adapting and improving the implementation of already existing legal norms and for building a legal framework for and setting legal limits[1435] to digital transformation and the use of data-based systems on an ethical basis in order to realize responsibility, justice, and human rights and corresponding duties.[1436] Ethics, politics, and law need to stand together in order to avoid "to formulate proposals or evaluations that result in a *flatus vocis* without any historical effectiveness."[1437]

1432 Misselhorn 2019: 7.
1433 Jonas 1984: 83.
1434 See Apel 1986: 18.
1435 See, e.g., for a possible approach the project of a Charter of Fundamental Digital Rights of the European Union n.d.
1436 See Kirchschlaeger 2019b.
1437 Benanti 2018: 126, emphasis in the text.

There is an urgency to act.[1438] "Surveillance capitalism" is not the only possible way; there are alternatives.[1439] The current Chinese government gives humanity an outlook on what the entire world could look like if we don't act immediately.[1440] Kai-Fu Lee, former manager with Google China and with Apple, characterizes China as the new Saudi Arabia[1441] if data is the new oil.[1442] (Kai-Fu Lee is to be criticized on the grounds that he does not include in his analysis the totalitarian character of the Chinese Government as a dictatorship.) The ethically alarming conceptual framework evokes Zhao Tingyang, with his concept of Tianxia (All-under-heaven): it proposes one global world order that gives preference to collective coexistence over individual existence and where collective interests of harmony overrule human rights of all humans.[1443]

The current Chinese government is introducing – with the support of multinational technology-corporations – a social points system throughout its entire territory consisting in the evaluation of humans according to their social credit. The behavior of individuals leads to a higher or lower "social score". Criticizing the Chinese government, for example, or reading the "wrong" books (e.g., this one) drastically lowers one's "social score". A "social score" that is too low leads to concrete consequences for individual life, e.g., prevention of booking of domestic air and train travel, restrictions for hotel bookings, preventing access to schools and universities for the own children, limitations in job search, ...[1444] This total surveillance by a dictatorship is combined with the biotechnological, and genetic breaking of taboos.[1445]

In order to create a future ethically by addressing the opportunities and challenges from an ethical perspective adequately, from a methodological point of view, one element should be to analyze and to understand how the impact of technology-based progress on humans and societies evolved so far, focusing on how it was possible that data-based systems and the use of data-based systems disrespect, undermine, and attempt to eliminate responsibility, justice, and human rights as well as other existing legal norms – a kind of genealogy of the co-mediated relationship of humanity and dig-

---

1438 See Helbing 2015a.
1439 See Helbing 2015h; Helbing 2015i; Helbing 2015j; Helbing 2015k.
1440 See Ferraris 2019: 36.
1441 See Lee 2018.
1442 See Helbing 2015l.
1443 See Tingyang 2020.
1444 See Amnesty International Switzerland 2019; Isler 2019.
1445 See Bahnsen 2018: 39; Assheuer 2019: 46.

ital transformation and data-based systems. Shoshana Zuboff offers the following reasons: "unprecedented", "declaration as invasion", "historical context", "fortifications", "the dispossession cycle", "dependency", "self-interest", "inclusion", "identification", "authority", "social persuasion", "foreclosed alternatives", "inevitability", "the ideology of human frailty", "ignorance", "velocity".[1446] Data-based systems might not only serve totalitarianism but also fuel "instrumentarian power"[1447]. "Instrumentarian power has no interest in our souls or any principle to instruct. There is no training or transformation for spiritual salvation, no ideology against which to judge our actions. It does not demand possession of each person from the inside out. It has no interest in exterminating or disfiguring our bodies and minds in the name of pure devotion. It welcomes data on the behavior of our blood and shit, but it has no interest in soiling itself with our excretions. It has no appetite for our grief, pain, or terror, although it eagerly welcomes the behavioral surplus that leaches from our anguish. It is profoundly and infinitely indifferent to our meanings and motives. Trained on measurable action, it only cares that whatever we do is accessible to its ever-evolving operations of rendition, calculation, modification, monetization, and control."[1448] In other words, humans are not even worth being manipulated in a specific direction on the basis of culture, tradition, religion, worldview, philosophy, or ideology but rather perceived as a biochemical mass that needs to be moved to serving some economic interests optimally. Not only is this position rationally incoherent as it is only possible by repudiating the very foundation upon which instrumentalism is based: economic interest – human culture. The overlap with a "Zweckgesellschaft" is stunning as well. "This dynamic of instrumentalization results in a power struggle within this 'Zweckgesellschaft'. The hierarchy is organized according to the economically measurable efficiency potentials of the individual members. This dynamic creates a structure that ultimately functionally appropriates all members and does not allow them to be persons. This structure is anonymous. Because of its anonymity, a momentum of its own can develop within it, which makes the individual with his or her subjectivity disappear."[1449]

The dream is to run humans and society and humanity like a giant machine. "Under the regime of instrumentarian power, the mental agency

---

1446 See Zuboff 2019: 340-344.
1447 See Zuboff 2019: 351-492.
1448 Zuboff 2019: 360.
1449 Baumann-Hoelzle 1999: 141.

and self-possession of the right to future tense are gradually submerged beneath a new kind of automaticity: a lived experience of stimulus-response-reinforcement aggregated as the comings and goings of mere organisms. Our conformity is irrelevant to instrumentarianism's success. There is no need for mass submission to social norms, no loss of self to the collective induced by terror and compulsion, no offers of acceptance and belonging as a reward for bending to the group. All of that is superseded by a digital order that thrives within things and bodies, transforming volition into reinforcement and action into conditioned response. (…) Power was once identified with the ownership of the means of production, but is now identified with ownership of the means of behavioral modification"[1450]. This could be perceived as evidence of the "autonomic" computing metaphor of "autonomous" predictive systems turning against users as a result of attempting to generalize the technology-metaphor to apply to human society.

"Instrumentarian power" does not exclude, however, the possibility that the powerful perceive themselves – excited about and overconfident because and stimulated by their economic success as well as due to exploding narcissism – as chosen to form a "better world" with "better humans" based on their arbitrary view of a "better world" and "better humans". For example, Peter Thiel, co-founder of PayPal, founder of Palantir, board member of Facebook, and a self-declared proponent of transhumanism, claims: "The Christian religion was the transhumanism of the first century."[1451] "Instrumentarian power" does not exclude the possibility that the powerful steer the entire system of data-based behavioral modification towards goals defined by them and direct the manipulation of humans in a way that serves their particular interests. On the contrary, degenerating the free market economy into a market of total certainty[1452] paves the way for the powerful state or non-state actors. For example, why should one pay an insurance premium when insurance companies – created as communities of solidarity – strive to minimize their risks by reducing uncertainty with data-based systems stealing, generating, and exploiting the data of humans? Instead of giving money to this new kind of insurance without any benefits, one would be better off with an individual savings plan at a bank which – in theory – pays out savings interest. Why should a state not rely

---

1450 Zuboff 2019: 379.
1451 Heuser 2018: 22.
1452 See Zuboff 2019: 379-382.

on data-based systems to identify and locate oppositional protesters?[1453] A managing director of the surveillance equipment-distributor CCTV criticized, compared to surveillance totalitarianism, "how far behind the Western countries are (...) What starts here ends up in homes, airports, and businesses back in America."[1454]

The challenge that humanity is facing consists of multinational technology-corporations striving for total control. "We could probably solve a lot of the issues we have as humans. (...) The societal goal is our primary goal"[1455], states Larry Page, co-founder of Google. "What you should want us to do is to really build amazing products and to really do that (...) we have to understand things you could buy (...) we have to understand anything you might search for. And people are a big thing you might search for (...) We're going to have people as a first-class object in search (...) if we're going to do a good job meeting your information needs, we actually need to understand things and we need to understand things pretty deeply."[1456] They understand themselves as selected to make their economic imperatives become true. "All power yearns toward totality, and only authority stands in the way: democratic institutions; laws; regulations; rights and obligations; private governance rules and contracts; the normal market constraints exercised by consumers, competitors, and employees; civil society; the political authority of the people; and the moral authority of individual human beings who have their bearings."[1457] Pure paternalism forges ahead. Larry Page, co-founder of Google, argues: "I am just saying that if you make decisions that are contrary to a global capital system, you must do so consciously and seriously. And I don't believe that anybody does that."[1458]

From the technology-corporations' point of view, these obstacles belong to the "old reality", which should not stop the "new reality" they are dreaming of in the form of "totality"[1459] and "confluence"[1460]. An expression of this worldview is, among other things, to create – as Peter Thiel, co-founder of PayPal, founder of Palantir, and board member of Facebook, does – some islands with their own crypto-currencies and without national

1453 See Engel Bromwich et al. 2016.
1454 Strumpf / Fan 2017.
1455 Waters 2014b.
1456 Helft 2012.
1457 Zuboff 2019: 404.
1458 Heuser 2015: 22.
1459 Zuboff 2019: 400-415.
1460 Zuboff 2019: 407-415.

legislation.[1461] Another example of this is, e.g., Larry Page, co-founder of Google, stating: "We use a lot of data to provide better services. This is how we improve the search, this is how we get to speech recognition. Whoever provides the services will have the data and use it to improve. The debate is okay, but you don't just go back and say: Let the world be like it was 20 years ago."[1462] For example, Microsoft's patent application "User Behavior Monitoring on a Computerized Device" aims to monitor and to preventively detect "any deviation from normal or acceptable behavior that is likely to affect the user's mental state. A prediction model corresponding to features of one or more mental states may be compared with features based upon current user behavior."[1463] Alex Pentland, director of the MIT-Labs "Connection Science" and "Human Dynamics", board member of AT&T, member of the advisory board of Google, is eager to extract as much data as possible from humans to enable "an interesting God's-eye view"[1464]. Tang Xiao'ou, CEO of Sensetime, announces Google at the World Conference for Artificial Intelligence, with the sentence revealing its own self-image: "Hey Google, let's make humanity great again."[1465]

This "new reality", this "better world", these "better humans", and this "greatness" they work hard for to create consists in the following: "Like some world-spanning living organism, wireless traffic systems, security sensors, and especially mobile telephone networks are combining to become intelligent, reactive systems with sensors serving as their eyes and ears. It seems that the human race suddenly has the beginnings of a working nervous system. For society, the hope is that we can use this new in-depth understanding of individual behavior to increase the efficiency and responsiveness of industry and government. For individuals, the attraction is the possibility of a world where everything is arranged for your convenience – your health checkup is magically scheduled just as you begin to get sick, the bus comes just as you get to the bus stop, and there is never a line of waiting people at city hall."[1466]

The aspirational "better humans" neither are bearers of human dignity nor free, autonomous, and rational. They do not engage in politics but are

---

1461 See The Seasteading Institute 2017.
1462 Heuser 2015: 23.
1463 Yom-Tov et al. 2016.
1464 Greene 2009.
1465 Yang 2018: 23.
1466 Pentland 2009.

monitored, controlled, and manipulated to contribute to the "better world" planned by a few multinational technology-corporations. "I believe that we can think of each stream of ideas as a swarm or collective intelligence, flowing through time, with all the humans in it learning from each other's experiences in order to jointly discover the patterns of preferences and habits of action that best suit the surrounding physical and social environment. This is counter to the way most Westerners understand themselves, which is as rational individuals, people who know what they want and who can decide for themselves what actions to take in order to accomplish their goals."[1467] The aspirational "better humans" by a few multinational technology-corporations do not possess individuality. "So you've heard about rational individuals. And everybody rags on the rational part. I'm not going to do that. I'm going to rag on the individual part, ok? Because I don't think we are individuals. What we desire, the ways we learn to go about doing it, what's valuable, are consensual things (...) individual incentives (...) that's part of this mindset that comes from the 1700s (...) the action is not between our ears. The action is in our social networks, ok? We are a social species."[1468]

Overcoming this challenge of multinational technology-corporations striving for total control is necessary from an ethical point of view to save humanity from this supposedly "better world" and from the compulsion to become supposedly "better humans". Eric Schmidt, as CEO of Google, states: "You give us more information about you, about your friends, and we can improve the quality of our searches. (...) We don't need you to type at all. We know where you are. We know where you've been. We can more or less know what you're thinking about."[1469]

The conceptual framing as a "new reality", "better world" and "better humans" are also the reasons why one should avoid coining the digital transformation and the data-based systems as a "digital *age*" because a few multinational technology-corporations introduce this term in order to benefit from a historical tradition that a new age can also bring with it a new legal order. From an ethical perspective, there is an urgency to stand up against such a new legal order undermining justice, responsibility, and human rights.

This urgency also becomes obvious when one considers the impact of digital transformation and data-based systems on humans. For example,

---

1467 Pentland 2014a: 46.
1468 Pentland 2014b.
1469 Thompson 2010.

the ICMPA-Salzburg Academy study "the world UNPLUGGED"[1470] asked close to 1,000 students in ten countries on five continents – from Chile to China, Lebanon to the USA, Uganda to the United Kingdom – to abstain from using all media for a full day. After their 24 hours of abstinence, the students were then asked to report their successes and admit to any failures. "Media is my drug; without it I was lost", said one student from the UK. "I am an addict. How could I survive 24 hours without it?" A student from the USA noted: "I was itching, like a crackhead, because I could not use my phone." A student from Slovakia said: "Maybe it is unhealthy that I can't be without knowing what people are saying and feeling, where they are, and what's happening." A student from the US stated: "I've lived with the same people for three years now, they're my best friends, and I think that this is one of the best days we've spent together. I was able to really see them, without any distractions, and we were able to revert to simple pleasures." A study of 2017 by the UK charity Girlguiding found out that "of more than 1,000 young people (…) 35% of girls aged 11-21 said their biggest worry online was comparing themselves and their lives with others."[1471] The dependence and the addiction of young people to their mobile devices is – from the perspective of multinational technology-corporations – not a negative side-effect but a goal.[1472] E.g., Facebook targets, on purpose, "social proof"[1473] and makes a business out of it.[1474] Constant social comparison, "fear of missing out (FOMO)" – "the uneasy and sometimes all-consuming feeling that (…) your peers are doing, in the know about, or in possession of more or something better than you."[1475]

Existing legal and ethical principles and norms are still valid. "Our lives, as you all know, are increasingly lived online. And so we must ensure that our values are alive online as well"[1476]. Human rights as legal standards and ethical principles are universally valid and must be respected, protected, implemented, and realized even in a digitalized, automatized, robotized society where data-based systems are used. Otherwise, we run the risk that our lives will degenerate "to feel at home in glass life or in the prospect of hiding from it. Both alternatives rob us of the life-sustaining

---

1470 the world UNPLUGGED 2019.
1471 Marsh 2017; see also Droesser 2018.
1472 See MaxAudience 2016.
1473 Nodder 2013: 5.
1474 See Zuboff 2019: 457.
1475 Przybylski et al. 2013: 1842.
1476 Eliasson 2015.

inwardness, born in sanctuary, that finally distinguishes us from the machines."[1477]

Existing ethical and legal standards and, above all, the instruments and mechanisms to realize and to implement them, need to be adapted in order to benefit from new ethical opportunities and to meet new ethical challenges. (This process could be started as well by self-regulations of industries as was the case, e.g., with business continuity management where self-regulations by the financial industry lead to a corresponding regulatory framework.)

Regarding a code of ethics, "a code of ethics is only as good as its organizational backing. The way in which the development of codes of ethics for AI is managed, and how such codes are implemented, will be one element of such organizational integrity, for good or for ill. These points apply to codes of ethics in general; but some problems are likely to be especially acute in AI. Codes of ethics may function more as window dressing than real applied policy. In AI, where fears abound, the temptation to produce a wonderful sounding code of ethics simply to ward off criticism may be especially acute."[1478]

Legal regulation is necessary, among other things, in the area of adaptation of implementation of existing human rights-norms, such as the human right to privacy and to data-protection, and of liability[1479] for damages, in the area of health, safety, consumer, and environmental regulation, intellectual property,[1480] copyright, capacity for legal transactions.

Different initiatives by states and civil society on national,[1481] regional[1482] – e.g., the General Data Protection Regulation (GDPR) of 2018, the

---

1477 Zuboff 2019: 492.

1478 Boddington 2017: 99.

1479 See Gruber 2014; Gruber 2013.

1480 See Hamann 2014.

1481 See, e.g., Association for Computing Machinery US Public Policy Council 2017; Danish Ministry of Finance, Agency for Digitisation n.d.; Montréal Declaration 2018; Engineering and Physical Sciences Research Council (EPSRC) 2010; Fairness, Accountability, and Transparency in Machine Learning (FAT/ML) 2016; Japanese Society for Artificial Intelligence (JSAI) 2017; House of Commons of the United Kingdom – Science and Technology Committee 2017; Villani 2018; Austrian Council on Robotics and Artificial Intelligence 2018; Australian Human Rights Commission 2019; Swiss Federal Council 2020.

1482 See, e.g., Charter of Fundamental Digital Rights of the European Union n.d.; European Group on Ethics in Science and New Technologies 2018a; European Group on Ethics in Science and New Technologies 2018b; European Group on

call for a European Data Agency,[1483] the decision by the European Parliament to ask the EU Commission to propose EU-wide rules on robotics and artificial intelligence,[1484] "The Charter of Digital Rights" by European Digital Rights (EDRi)-network including principles like promotion of transparency, access to documents and participation, data protection and privacy, unrestricted access to the Internet and online services, copyright legislation, anti-unchecked surveillance measures, online anonymity and encryption, anti-privatization of enforcement outside the law, export controls of surveillance and censorship technology, multistakeholderism, open source software, democracy, and the rule of law[1485] –, and international level[1486] – e.g. the "Declaration of Principles" by the World Summit on the Information Society in Geneva 2003[1487] – tend in this direction, but remain at maximum "soft law", "which is a tool often used to either avoid or anticipate formal legislation."[1488] The latter states in Article 1 the "common desire and commitment to build a people-centered, inclusive and development-oriented Information Society, where everyone can create, access, utilize and share information and knowledge, enabling individuals, communities and peoples to achieve their full potential in promoting their sustainable development and improving their quality of life, premised on the purposes and principles of the Charter of the United Nations and respecting fully and upholding the Universal Declaration of Human Rights."

Ethics in Science and New Technologies 2015; European Group on Ethics in Science and New Technologies 2014; European Group on Ethics in Science and New Technologies 2009; High-Level Expert Group on Artificial Intelligence HLEG AI of the European Commission 2019; Council of Europe 2019a; Council of Europe 2019b; Council of Europe 2018b; Council of Europe 2018c; Council of Europe 2019c.

1483 See Vogel 2019: 6.
1484 See, e.g., European Parliament 2017b; Robolaw 2014.
1485 See European Digital Rights (EDRi) 2014.
1486 See, e.g., UNESCO COMEST 2017; UNICEF 2017; Institute of Electrical and Electronic Engineers (IEEE) Standards Association n.d.; Dutton 1990; Association for Computing Machinery's Committee on Professional Ethics 2017; International Conference of Data Protection and Privacy Commissioners (ICDP-PC) 2018; Internet Governance Forum (IGF) 2014; Internet Governance Forum (IGF) 2019; Future of Life Institute 2017; Burt et al. 2018; Information Technology Industry Council (ITIC) 2017; Partnership on AI (PAI) 2016; The Public Voice Coalition 2018; UNI Global Union 2017; Price 2018; ISO 2020; WeGovNow 2020; Zentrum für Digitalen Fortschritt D 64 n.d.
1487 World Summit on the Information Society 2003.
1488 Nevejans 2016: 26.

The UNESCO-Study "Steering AI and Advanced ICTs for Knowledge Societies. A Rights, Openness, Access, and Multi-stakeholder Perspective" of 2019[1489] supports the idea of human rights as a legal frame of reference and calls for openness including explainability and transparency, open data, and open markets; access to data-based systems including access to research, to knowledge, education, and human resources; access to data; advocates a multi-stakeholder approach; and demands gender equality.

The report "the age of digital interdependence" of the UN Secretary General's High-level Panel on Digital Cooperation of 2019 expresses – among others – the following recommendations: "3A: Given that human rights apply fully in the digital world, we urge the UN Secretary-General to institute an agencies-wide review of how existing international human rights accords and standards apply to new and emerging digital technologies. Civil society, governments, the private sector and the public should be invited to submit their views on how to apply existing human rights instruments in the digital age in a proactive and transparent process.

3B: In the face of growing threats to human rights and safety, including those of children, we call on social media enterprises to work with governments, international and local civil society organizations and human rights experts around the world to fully understand and respond to concerns about existing or potential human rights violations."[1490]

The OECD Principles on Artificial Intelligence of 2019[1491] consist in "five complementary values-based principles for the responsible stewardship of trustworthy AI"[1492]: "AI should benefit people and the planet by driving inclusive growth, sustainable development and well-being.

AI systems should be designed in a way that respects the rule of law, human rights, democratic values and diversity, and they should include appropriate safeguards – for example, enabling human intervention where necessary – to ensure a fair and just society.

There should be transparency and responsible disclosure around AI systems to ensure that people understand AI-based outcomes and can challenge them.

AI systems must function in a robust, secure and safe way throughout their life cycles and potential risks should be continually assessed and managed.

1489 See UNESCO 2019.
1490 UN Secretary-General's High-level Panel on Digital Cooperation 2019.
1491 See OECD Legal Instruments 2019.
1492 OECD 2019b.

Organizations and individuals developing, deploying or operating AI systems should be held accountable for their proper functioning in line with the above principles."[1493]

In these democratic opinion-forming and decision-making processes, adequate measures need to be taken which accordingly restructure society and economy with human rights as a legal and ethical point of reference in order to enable a peaceful coexistence in a society, and to protect all humans in their survival and their human dignity. A concrete example for this could be the "Charter of Fundamental Digital Rights of the European Union", which has been prepared by politicians (*inter alia*, Martin Schulz, who was President of the European Parliament at the time) and experts as an initiative under the umbrella of the ZEIT-Foundation (Germany) and could serve as a basis for discussion.[1494] Article 5 states: "(1) Ethical principles may be formulated only by human beings, and decisions that impact fundamental rights may be made only by human beings. (...) (6) The use of artificial intelligence and robotics in areas related to fundamental rights violations must be subject to social debate and regulated by legislation."

Other examples – emerging from professional ethics – are the code of the Institute of Electrical and Electronic Engineers (IEEE),[1495] the code of the National Society of Professional Engineers (NSPE),[1496] the codes of the American Society of Mechanical Engineers (ASME),[1497] or the "Three Pro-Human Laws of Robotics": "Rule 1: Intelligent robots must serve the common good of humanity and help us humans to lead an ecologically, socially, culturally and economically sustainable life. Rule 2: Intelligent robots may replace human labor only to the extent that this is compatible with humans leading a meaningful life of dignity, culture, and creative self-realization – except where this rule conflicts with Rule 1. Rule 3: Intelligent robots must be programmed to be co-operative self-learning machines and always to function cooperatively – except where this conflicts with Rules 1 and 2."[1498]

Another proposal represents the following basic robo-ethical principles: "protecting humans from harm caused by robots; respecting the refusal of

---

1493 OECD 2019b.
1494 See Charter of Fundamental Digital Rights of the European Union n.d.
1495 See Institute of Electrical and Electronic Engineers (IEEE) n.d.
1496 See National Society of Professional Engineers (NSPE) n.d.
1497 See American Society of Mechanical Engineers (ASME) n.d.
1498 Thun-Hohenstein 2017: 29.

care by a robot; protecting human liberty in the face of robots; protecting humanity against privacy breaches committed by a robot; managing personal data processed by robots; protecting humanity against the risk of manipulation by robots; avoiding the dissolution of social ties; equal access to progress in robotics; restricting human access to enhancement technologies"[1499].

Additionally, the precautionary principle must be taken into account. Moreover, designers and producers of data-based systems are to be obliged to invest more in and to implement security, reliability, predictability, transparency, non-manipulability of the technologies, and traceability linked with liability and attribution of responsibility,[1500] and meaningful human control[1501] (elaborated above in subchapter 7.11 Automated Weapon Systems).

Furthermore, *the ethical and legal framework to be developed needs to take the situation humanity is in more seriously, and address the ethical chances and risks more fervently.* An example for this necessity embodies the first principle of the joint Engineering and Physical Sciences Research Council (EPSRC) and Arts and Humanities Research Council (AHRC) Robotics Retreat in September 2010: "1) Robots are multi-use tools. Robots should not be designed solely or primarily to kill or harm humans, except in the interests of national security."[1502] The last subordinate clause "except in the interests of national security" functions as a subverting factor of the entire principle.[1503]

A regulation, a field test, and a permit for data-based systems – e.g., for new financial products – are needed (similar to the procedure for new drugs).[1504] The need for such measures as regards digital transformation of and data-based systems in the finance sector should have become clear with the relevance to responsibility, justice and human rights of these ethical problems, as has been explained above.

Moreover, every data-based system needs – metaphorically speaking – a "red emergency button" in order to be possibly switched off in any instance by humans. "Any machine should have an accessible 'off' switch; and in the case of a computer or robot that might have any tendency to-

---

1499 Nevejans 2016: 20.
1500 See Bostrom / Yudkowsky 2011; Mannino et al. 2015: 1.
1501 See Santoni de Sio / van den Hoven 2018: 11-12.
1502 Engineering and Physical Sciences Research Council 2010.
1503 See also Englert et al. 2014.
1504 See Buiter 2009: 13.

ward self-preservation, it should have an off switch that it cannot block. However, in the case of computers and robots, this is very easily done, since we are building them. All you need is to place in the internals of the robot, inaccessible to it, a device that, when it receives a specified signal, cuts off the power – or, if you want something more dramatic, triggers a small grenade. This can be done in a way that the computer probably cannot find out the details of how the grenade is placed or triggered, and certainly cannot prevent it. "[1505]

8.1.4 Datethics

Beyond that, datadeology – as discussed above in the subchapter 7.17.3 Datadeology – must be confronted with datethics (data-ethics) embracing responsibility, intergenerational omni-dynamic social justice, and human rights. Datethics provides ethical guidance for implementing a responsible, just, and human rights-based use and handling of data.

8.1.5 Human Rights-Based Data-Based Systems HRBDS

Finally, in order to take the current situation of humanity more seriously and to address the ethical chances and risks more fervently, we need human rights-based design, development, production, and use of data-based systems – we need human rights-based "artificial intelligence" HRBAI, we need *human rights-based data-based systems HRBDS*, including a precautionary approach, the reinforcement of existing human rights instruments specifically for data-based systems, and the promotion of algorithms supporting and furthering the realization of human rights. "We must regain our own human dignity through changed thinking, which is also expressed in the ability to control our technological inventions that anticipate the future in such a way that we are not increasingly subjected to them."[1506] The publicist Gerd E. Hoffmann does not say this in the year 2021, he wrote this back in 1979 facing technology-based progress in the domain of computers. What would he say today about the necessity to reinforce the realization of human rights in order to protect human dignity of all humans?

1505 Davis 2015: 124.
1506 Hoffmann 1979: 177-178.

Human rights-based data-based systems HRBDS means – in order to illustrate it with a concrete example – that, e.g., the human rights to privacy and data-protection in its relevance for the human dignity and freedom of humans must be defended – excluding also the possibility that humans should be able to sell themselves and their data as well as their privacy as products. This is a substantial argument against data ownership as well. Or would or should one come up with the idea to sell her or his love letter to her or his love to the state and to corporations as data? Or would or should one sell the dinner-table-conversation of her or his family to the state or the private sector? Or would or should one sell the behavioral habits of her or his children to the state or a company?

HRBDS can be illustrated as well by the call for an economically successful, legal, and legitimate business model, e.g., for video-conference-software that does not – like present ones do, e.g. ZOOM –[1507] surveille and violate the human right to privacy and data-protection of humans. In other words, it must be possible to create a profitable business model with the provision and promotion of a video-conference-software that does not imply human rights violations.

Another visualizing example could be automated driving: In order not to overload automated driving with maximum demands and a high ethos, in order to concretize the ethical requirements for automated driving and make them tangible, and in order to succeed in weighting them against other important goods such as mobility and comfort, the approach of *human rights-based automated driving HRBAD* would be worth striving for. Human rights as a minimum standard that guarantees people to survive and live with human dignity are achievable for automated driving and allow a focus on what is essential and important – what is necessary to survive and live. Human rights possess a precise focus that can promote clear prioritization based on this minimum standard to be met first. In the agenda-setting process of automated driving, human rights can therefore help not only to set the right priorities, but also to adequately define the spheres of influence and responsibility.

The concept of HRBAD also makes it possible to set ethical reference points in relation to other goods (mobility, comfort), thus enabling a conceptual classification. For example, an aspect of automated driving that involves a violation of a human right cannot be outweighed by more comfort. On the other hand, a human rights-neutral luxury solution in the area of the comfort of automated driving that is only made available to a small

---

1507 See Laaff 2020.

part of the population through appropriate pricing cannot be described as "unjust" in the sense of distributive justice. Rather, luxury goods can be negotiated with reference to transactional justice. It would be different if a human rights-relevant element of automated driving (e.g., safety) were involved. Here, such exclusion via the high price would not be legitimate.

8.1.6 International Data-Based Systems Agency DSA

Beyond that, humanity and planet Earth need, from an ethical perspective a global supervisory and monitoring institution in the area of data-based systems – analogous to the International Atomic Energy Agency IAEA[1508] – in order to ensure the implementation of the principles that were just mentioned, to guarantee the realization of human rights, and to further effective governance going beyond regulation. The International Data-Based Systems Agency DSA should be the world's central intergovernmental forum for scientific and technical co-operation in the field of digital transformation and data-based systems. Integrated in or associated with the UN[1509], it should work for the safe, secure, and peaceful uses of data-based systems, contributing to international peace and security, to the respect and realization of human rights, and the United Nations' Sustainable Development Goals.

1508   See International Atomic Energy Agency (IAEA) n.d.
1509   See Kirchschlaeger 2020f.

The DSA should serve the realization of the following 30 principles:[1510]

1st principle: Data-based systems must respect, protect, implement, and serve the realization of human rights.

2nd principle: Data-based systems must serve the realization of the United Nations' Sustainable Development Goals.

3rd principle: Data-based systems must be transparent.

4th principle: Data-based systems must be traceable.

5th principle: Data-based systems must be explainable.

6th principle: Data-based systems must be intelligible.

7th principle: Data-based systems must be auditable.

8th principle: Causes and effects or causality and correlation must be identifiable in data-based systems.

9th principle: Data-based systems must be predictable.

10th principle: Data-based systems must be decidable.

11th principle: Data-based systems must be non-manipulating and respect the autonomy of every human.

12th principle: Data-based systems must be able to adapt to humans.

13th principle: Data-based systems and their performance (efficiency and effectiveness) must be controlled, monitored, measured, and evaluated on a regular basis, and their assessment must be published each time such that it is accessible to the broader public.

14th principle: Data-based systems must include an "emergency button" (metaphorically) for humans and an "ethics-black-box" enabling an ethical analysis.

15th principle: Data-based systems must be approved by national regulatory authorities – similar to food and drug regulatory agencies protecting the public health, by ensuring the safety, efficacy, security, and sustainability of data-based systems, regulating the manufacturing, marketing, and distribution of data-based systems, helping to further innovations that make data-based systems more effective, safer, and more affordable, and empowering the public by providing the accurate, independent, and science-based information they need to accept and to use data-based systems.

16th principle: Research and development-projects in the area of data-based systems must be approved by national regulatory authorities.

17th principle: The conduct of research and development must respect these DSA-principles.

18th principle: Lethal automated weapons and lethal automated weapon systems are forbidden.

19th principle: Data-based systems for human rights-violating surveillance are forbidden.

20th principle: Data-based systems for social scoring of humans by the state or by non-state actors are forbidden.

21st principle: Data-based systems manipulating and undermining democracy are forbidden.

22nd principle: Data-based systems supporting or reinforcing totalitarian systems and dictatorships are forbidden.

23rd principle: Data-based systems blazing the trail for "super-data-based systems" or the "singularity" are forbidden.

24th principle: "Super-data-based systems" or the "singularity" are forbidden.

25th principle: These principles so far must be included in the parameter setting for the creation, design, programming, development, production, training, and use of data-based systems.

26th principle: Designers, software-engineers, manufacturers, producers, operators, providers, and users of data-based systems as well as infrastructure providers and data analytics companies and their employees must have adequate knowledge, skills, and competencies, including a basic applied-ethics-expertise.

27th principle: Designers, software-engineers, manufacturers, producers, operators, providers, and users of data-based systems as well as infrastructure providers and data analytics companies and their employees must be accountable. They must be able to take legal and ethical responsibility.

28th principle: The principle of indivisibility of all DSA-principles must be respected.

29th principle: Any supplement or modification to these principles must be undertaken only by humans.

30th principle: Any supplement or modification to these principles must undoubtedly serve the realization of human rights of all humans and the United Nations' Sustainable Development Goals.

More and stricter commitment to the legal framework is necessary and regulation that is precise, goal-oriented, and strictly enforced. The DSA

1510 These principles represent a proposal and could serve as a starting-point for a further ethical and interdisciplinary discourse.

would serve this necessity. In this way, regulation may also be advantageous economically. For example, the American regulation of air traffic and the aviation industry allowed an entire industry to flourish economically thanks to its high degree of precision, its clear orientation, and its uncompromising enforcement.[1511] There is reason for hope and faith, because humanity has already shown in its past that we are able to not always "blindly" pursue and implement the technical possible, but also to renounce, restrain, or limit ourselves to what is technically feasible when the welfare of humanity and planet Earth are at stake. For example, humans researched the field of nuclear technology, developed the atomic bomb, it was dropped several times, but then humans substantially and massively limited research and development in the field of nuclear technology, in order to prevent even worse, despite massive resistance. This suppression was successful to the greatest possible extent, thanks to an international regime, concrete enforcement mechanisms, and thanks to the International Atomic Energy Agency (IAEA) of the UN.

In the case of chlorofluorocarbons (CFCs), humanity also decided under the Montreal Protocol of 1987[1512] to ban substances that damage the ozone layer and to enforce the ban consistently. Here, the resistance was also huge, *inter alia,* due to particular interests from the private sector. This regulation and its uncompromising enforcement led to the fact that the hole in the ozone layer is now slowly closing.

8.1.7 Addressing the Second Paradox of Digital Transformation and Data-Based Systems: Empowerment of Data-Based Systems and Human Fear of Powerlessness

One must acknowledge, though, that the scenario provoking these concerns results out of what represents the second paradox of digital transformation and data-based systems – besides the first paradox of potent impotence (see subchapter 7.6 The Paradox of Potent Impotence): On the one hand, humans invest enormous financial means, resources, time, creativity, and research-energy to develop and create technologies that become more intelligent, more efficient, more effective, smarter, faster, and better than humans across a variety of domains (instead of focusing, e.g., on pressing

---

1511 Dorian Selz, CEO and Founder of Squirro, made this observation at a workshop at the ETH Zurich on April 10, 2019.
1512 See Montreal Protocol on Substances that Deplete the Ozone Layer 1987.

current global issues like global poverty, climate change, etc.). Data-based systems should evolve from tools to teammates, to coaches, and to bosses. Data-based systems should obtain omnipresence, omniscience (including "super-intelligence" or as super-data-based systems), and omnipotence (including creativity in the full sense of the word). On the other hand, humans feel threatened by, and want to avoid, the possible future where this more intelligent, more efficient, more effective, smarter, faster, and better technology takes over control. Although, it perhaps could even make sense that the power held by technologies are more intelligent, smarter, and better than human power, humans absolutely want to remain in charge.

This paradox probably has to do with the fear of humans of being disenthralled by technological systems,[1513] with trust in humans, and with nonexistent willingness to entrust leadership to technology due to the unique moral capability of humans.[1514] Even if data-based systems can be encoded and trained with ethical principles and ethical and legal norms, which they must respect and implement, the high probability that self-learning data-based systems in either the near or distant future will become "super-data-based systems", and thereby outperform humans and human intelligence, results in the potential of a future reality wherein data-based systems could also decide not to follow ethical principles and ethical and legal norms anymore.

Even the possibility that they could auto-define what "ethical" and "legal" should mean (although maybe it would not be "ethical" or "legal" at all because, e.g., it would serve only their self-interests and would not respect human dignity of all humans) must be considered from an ethical perspective. The question arises of what will happen to humans if data-based systems take over power – power in a holistic sense including, e.g., cognitive power – and humans do not have anything to say anymore. What can be done today to avoid that in the future data-based systems outpace humans and, in power, treat humans badly and do not respect the human dignity of all humans? What can be done today to prevent future data-based systems from treating humans in the same way or worse than humans treat animals today? What can be done today to set a clear priority on the "usefulness to life"[1515] instead of feasibility? From an ethical standpoint based on responsibility, justice and human rights, a solution could be that data-based systems must be encoded and trained to still respect humans as

---

1513   See Neuhaeuser 2014: 269.
1514   See Kirchschlaeger 2017c.
1515   Schweizerische Nationalkommission Justitia et Pax 1998: 22-26.

their masters although they outperform humans,[1516] to respect and to realize human rights, and that the universality and the validity of human rights are never open to change by data-based systems. After highlighting the dangers of artificial intelligence by comparing them to the atomic bomb and stating that artificial intelligence is far more dangerous than the atomic bomb, Elon Musk asks: "So why do we have no regulatory oversight?"[1517]

8.1.8   Ethics Committees Back to Ethicists!

In a time and within a context where ethical guidance seems to be extraordinarily essential and necessary because of technology-based advancements, one type of institutional body dedicated to this specific task must include the necessary ethical expertise and discourse.

So far, ethics committees risk not being able to live up to their aims. They seem to become either the play thing of pursuing economic particular interests (e.g., the establishment and the dissolvement of its ethics board, the Advanced Technology External Advisory Council ATEAC, by Google)[1518], a stakeholder-dialogue-exercise (e.g., the High-Level Expert Group on Artificial Intelligence HLEG AI of the European Commission;[1519] the working-group of the Institute of Electrical and Electronics Engineers IEEE on a standard on ethics in IT design), or an interdisciplinary dialogue with a tiny minority of ethicists (e.g., Google's ethics board[1520]; the UNESCO-Ad Hoc Expert Group for the Recommendation on the Ethics of Artificial Intelligence[1521]; the Horizon 2020 Commission Expert Group to advise on specific ethical issues raised by driverless mobility[1522]) instead of – what would be necessary in order to be able to fulfill the complex *ethical* task – a committee of ethicists with a small structured interdisciplinary component. Of course, a combination of these three manifestations can also occur, e.g. that the second is pursued to serve economic interests according to the first.

1516   See Manzeschke / Karsch 2016: 10.
1517   Clifford 2018.
1518   See Wakefield 2019.
1519   See High-Level Expert Group on Artificial Intelligence HLEG AI of the European Commission 2020.
1520   See Shead 2019.
1521   See UNESCO 2020.
1522   See Horizon 2020 Commission Expert Group 2020.

In the first case, ethics committees becoming a plaything of pursuing economic particular interests, ethics boards would run the risk not serving primarily the purpose of providing ethical guidance but rather being instrumentalized for gains in reputation and corresponding economic benefits. For example, Alphabet's DeepMind AI group has formed an ethics and society-team and made it transparent[1523] while Facebook claims to make time specifically for ethics without communicating more about it.[1524] Most of the fellows of the ethics and society-team of Alphabet's DeepMind AI group (4 out of 5) are not ethicists, most of the team are not ethicists (5 out of 6), and the research in ethics funded at renowned academic institutions worldwide (e.g., Oxford Internet Institute of the University of Oxford; the Center for Information Technology Policy at Princeton University; the AI Now Institute at NYU) on questions at the exact core of DeepMind AI group's business interests provoke, at least, some questions about academic freedom, independence of research, ... The same or even more is the case, e.g., with the Institute for Ethics in Artificial Intelligence[1525] funded by Facebook at the Technical University Munich.[1526]

In the second case, a stakeholder-dialogue-exercise, ethics committees are used to reach the aim of assembling the representatives of a variety of particular interests and of gathering their perspectives. This does not serve the purpose of ethical guidance because ethics is an academic discipline, and ethics is not democracy (see above subchapter 5.1). Or would you attribute the clarification of, for example, a mathematical problem to a stakeholder-dialogue? For example, in the case of the High-Level Expert Group on Artificial Intelligence HLEG AI of the European Commission, 48 out of 52 members are not ethicists; the group consists of representatives from politics, universities, civil society, and above all, from industry.[1527] One of its members declared that this composition had a substantial negative impact on its work and its results – the "Ethics Guidelines for Trustworthy Artificial Intelligence"[1528] of 2019. "The guidelines are lukewarm, shortsighted and deliberately vague. They gloss over difficult problems ('explainability') with rhetoric, violate elementary principles of rationality and

---

1523 See DeepMind n.d.
1524 See Novet 2018.
1525 See Institute for Ethics in Artificial Intelligence n.d.
1526 See Buchwald 2019.
1527 See High-Level Expert Group on Artificial Intelligence HLEG AI of the European Commission 2020.
1528 See High-Level Expert Group on Artificial Intelligence HLEG AI of the European Commission 2019.

pretend to know things that in reality simply nobody knows. (…) The use of lethal autonomous weapon systems was an obvious item on our list (for red-lines, i.e. non-negotiable ethical principles that define what must not be done with AI in Europe), as well as the AI-based evaluation of citizens by the state (social scoring) and basically the use of AI that people can no longer understand and control. (…) That all this was not really desired I only understood when the friendly Finnish HLEG President Pekka Ala-Pietilä (formerly Nokia) asked me in a soft voice if we could not remove the phrase 'non-negotiable' from the document? As a next step, many industry representatives and the group members interested in a 'positive vision' vehemently insisted that the word 'red lines' be deleted throughout the text – although it was precisely these red lines that were our work assignment. If you look at the document after today's publication, you will not find any more red lines. Three have been completely deleted, the rest have been watered down and instead there is only talk of 'critical concerns'"[1529].

In the third case, an interdisciplinary dialogue with a tiny minority of ethicists instead of – what would be necessary in order to be able to fulfill the complex ethical task – a committee of ethicists with a small structured interdisciplinary component or a committee of ethicists collaborating in an interdisciplinary way with a separate interdisciplinary body, the question arises why one would entrust a scientific task, namely identifying ethical opportunities and risks of data-based systems and developing ethical solutions, mostly to persons without a specific academic education and qualification in that specific domain. Or would you attribute the clarification of, for example, a mathematical problem to a political scientist? Would we entrust the overcoming of an astrophysical challenge to a legal expert? Or would we invite a diplomat to address a biological research-question? For example, the UNESCO-Ad Hoc Expert Group for the Recommendation on the Ethics of Artificial Intelligence[1530] consists of 24 members, only 4 are ethicists. Their task is to elaborate the first draft of the first global standard-setting instrument on ethics of artificial intelligence, following the decision of UNESCO's General Conference at its 40th session in November 2019. Of course, in such an endeavor of applied ethics, an interdisciplinary component must be somehow part of the activities of the entity entrusted with this task. But why would you compose this group with ethicists being in such a minority if the task is specifically of ethics as

---

1529 Metzinger 2019.
1530 See UNESCO 2020.

a scientific discipline? Why would you not include the necessary ethical expertise and discourse?

This conception, organization, and practice of ethics committees and ethics-boards must change as soon as possible due to the danger of "ethics washing": This means that industry is organizing and cultivating ethical debates to buy time – to distract the public, to prevent or at least delay effective regulation and real policy making. Politicians also like to set up ethics committees themselves, because they themselves simply do not know what to do, or – if they know – they run the risk of not wanting to do it due to intense lobbying ("Tech giants led by Amazon, Facebook and Google spent nearly half a billion on lobbying over the past decade"[1531] in the US; "Facebook, Google, Apple, Amazon and Microsoft together spend more than 20 million euros annually on their lobbying activities in Europe"[1532]) and intransparent exertion of influence by multinational technology-corporations.[1533] But at the same time, industry is building one "ethics washing machine" after another: Facebook has invested in the Technical University of Munich – in an institute that is to train AI ethicists, "Google had hired the philosophers Joanna Bryson and Luciano Floridi for an 'Ethics Panel' – which was surprisingly discontinued (...). Had this not happened, Google would have had direct access, via Floridi – who is also a member of HLEG AI [High-Level Expert Group on Artificial Intelligence HLEG AI of the European Commission] – to the process in which the group is preparing the political and investment recommendations for the European Union starting this month. That would have been a strategic triumph for the American conglomerate. Because industry is much faster and more efficient than politics or science, there is a risk that after 'fake news' we will now also have a problem with fake ethics. Including lots of fake candles, highly paid industrial philosophers, self-invented quality seals and non-validated certificates for 'Ethical AI made in Europe'."[1534] Ethics committees and ethics-boards must be given back to ethicists!

Beyond that, the following paths could lead to solutions from an ethical perspective.

1531 Romm 2020.
1532 Winter 2020.
1533 See LobbyControl 2020.
1534 Metzinger 2019.

8.2 Society-, Entrepreneurship-, Research-Time-Model (SERT)

8.2.1 Relief as a Burden – the End of Striving for Full Employment

One path towards solutions from an ethical perspective is constituted by addressing the ethical challenges that result from the substantial reduction in paid labor. Digitalization, automation, machinization, robotization and the use of data-based systems lead – as mentioned above – to disruption (e.g., travel industry and online-booking; music industry and streaming; retail-industry and e-shopping; etc.)[1535] or to a substantial loss of paid professional tasks and – as a consequence – of paid jobs because data-based systems create fewer costs than human employees.

The counter-argument to this scenario is that new jobs will be created in the digital transformation and with the use of data-based systems as it has always been the case during earlier transformative processes. It needs to be taken into consideration, though, that – even if new jobs are created –, they are not created in the places where paid jobs are destroyed by the digitalization, automation, and robotization of society and economy and the use of data-based systems.[1536] Yet, more important are the seventeen fundamental arguments mentioned above in subchapter 7.18 Reduction of Paid Jobs for the uniqueness of this digital transformation compared to earlier technology-based eras of change – among other things, that self-learning systems, which are the heart of digital transformation, require less human input than former technologies pushing earlier transformative processes.

The reduction of the paid labor-market will provoke a lack of sources of income, of financial means for social welfare, of structuring daily life, of purpose of life, and of the self-understanding of humans. Beyond that, it will contribute to the widening of the gap between rich and poor because ever fewer humans are directly involved economically and socially in a more efficient and more effective value-creation-process. All these consequences are of ethical concern due to their impact on justice, on responsibility, on the survival and on human dignity of all humans.

Digital transformation and the use of data-based systems in society and economy will lead to the following core consequence: *fewer and fewer humans will directly participate and partake in a more efficient and effective value chain.*[1537] The labeling as "core consequence" from an ethical perspective is

---

1535 See Meyer 2015.
1536 See Acemoglu / Restrepo 2020.
1537 See Kirchschlaeger 2017a; Kirchschlaeger 2016b.

justified by the following reasons. Firstly, it embraces major positive and negative outcomes of digital transformation and data-based systems.

Secondly, it directs the focus on the real challenges of the disruption caused by digital transformation and data-based systems from an ethical perspective. The main challenge is not a lack of financial means because more efficient and more productive value-added chains lead to an increase in that regard, but the question of justice and human rights. "A society with cheap robot labor would be an incredibly prosperous one, but we will need to find some way for the vast majority of human beings to share in that prosperity"[1538]. At stake is the distribution of the added value which is created respectively at the center of concern. Even if everything is becoming cheaper due to digital transformation and the use of data-based systems,[1539] it does not make any difference if one cannot afford to survive. It is the question of social integration as fewer humans are involved in the value-added chain.

Thirdly, less work per se does not have to be negative from an ethical standpoint because it allows humans to devote their time to, e.g., ethically meaningful purposes (among others, the fight against global poverty, the struggle for environmental protection). It could also be ethically positive that humans are liberated from the obligation to work.[1540] At this point, it seems to be helpful to remind ourselves that the present "work-ethos" was developed approximately 150 years ago and that an adaptation of a "work-ethos" based on a paid job and on full-occupation is possible, corresponding to the consequences of digital transformation and data-based systems – including a re-valorization of social engagement, social entrepreneurship, "societal time", and spare time. It depends on the design of economic and societal general conditions – the former allowing survival and a life with dignity for all humans. The latter must enable humans to integrate into society and economy without a paid job and allow them to develop a new self-understanding independent from paid labor.

From an ethical point of view this implies that, from a macrosocial perspective, the challenge lies not in the amount of means available, but the creation of a fair social and economic system,[1541] *inter alia*, with regard to distributing financial means and the opportunities of participating and partaking, with regard to equal opportunities for all, with regard to secur-

---

1538 Smith 2013.
1539 See Worstall 2012.
1540 See Kellermann 2014.
1541 See Kirchschlaeger 2013c.

ing a livelihood for all, and at the same time, upholding entrepreneurial incentives and social peace.

This justice-oriented design[1542] should start with equal opportunities for all so that all humans can be guaranteed survival and a life with human dignity.[1543] If the creation of equal opportunities is successful, a "donut-shaped economy"[1544] can be avoided, meaning an economic system and a society where the gap between the rich and the poor grows exorbitantly and the middle of society is eroded.

From an ethical point of view, fewer working hours and more free time are not necessarily a bad thing. It is conceivable, among other things, that, depending on its normative orientation, paid work to finance one's livelihood might contribute more to losing, than to finding meaning, might distract humans from the ethically relevant, might create ethically false incentives or coercion, might steal time from other areas of human existence because of work overload (e.g., for idleness, political engagement etc.),[1545] and binds talents of humans for activities, which have only one particular purpose that can also be problematic from an ethical point of view. The question of what humans are free to do when they are free from paid work needs to be discussed.

In their role as social actors, religious and worldview-based communities can play an important role in accompanying humans in their quest for the meaning of life, for an image of humans and a self-image, in creating space for this debate, in reflecting upon it from an ethical perspective, in criticizing and participating in the shaping of digital transformation and data-based systems.[1546]

Technology-based economic processes lift a burden from humans, empowering them to do other tasks. Fewer working hours can be good news from an ethical point of view, if a society and an economic system is structured accordingly and enables social ties, or if humans are able to come to a new self-conception, which is mostly independent from paid work.

While maintaining entrepreneurial incentives and thus preventing demotivation, a decoupling of income from work could therefore be considered in order to guarantee survival and a life as a human with human dignity for all humans and to enable social peace.

1542 See Kirchschlaeger 2016d.
1543 See Kirchschlaeger 2016i.
1544 See Keen 2015.
1545 See Arendt 2001.
1546 See Kirchschlaeger 2017g; Kirchschlaeger 2016f; Kirchschlaeger 2017e.

8.2.2 Unconditional Basic Income

The idea of the unconditional basic income goes in that direction. This approach knows various forms and models. First, they seem to contain the following core elements that could shape a definition of an unconditional basic income: "a. The unconditional basic income contains a monetary transfer, the amount of which secures the existence of the individual and enables him or her to take part in society". b. No means-testing will take place prior to the payment (social-administrative test of income and assets) and without being forced to work for money or contribute in another way. This means that the unconditional basic income secures a livelihood, enables participation in society, will be paid permanently and independent of needs. The unconditional basic income can be classified as a transfer payment that is independent of income and assets and is paid without means- or asset-testing."[1547]

8.2.3 Society-, Entrepreneurship-, Research-Time-Model (SERT)

From an ethical perspective informed by the principle of human rights – it needs to be mentioned once more that human rights protect elements and areas of human existence that humans need to survive and live as humans, i.e. in human dignity – it can be deduced that with the approach of the unconditional basic income, the survival of all humans will be guaranteed by providing financial security to all humans, which is positive. At the same time, a significant contribution is made to social peace. Human rights as an ethical frame of reference, however, also suggest that not only the physical survival of humans is to be considered, but life as humans – a life with human dignity. By enabling all humans to participate in society, life as humans – a life with human dignity – for all humans is addressed. However, it seems to be limited to one certain aspect of human life and a life with dignity. This becomes particularly obvious, if one reflects upon the possible current functions of a paid job that are of relevance in this respect while avoiding a glorification and mystification of paid work, while taking a differentiated look at paid work by always understanding work as an interaction with quiet time and recreation, but by keeping in mind that work exists for humans and not the other way round, among others:

1547 Schneider / Dreer 2017.

- to open up the possibility to participate in shaping the world;
- to create the option to contribute to a higher, ethically sound purpose;
- to contribute to peaceful coexistence in solidarity;
- to enable participation in and sharing of the economic added value;
- to act as a source of meaning;
- to serve as a source of self-confidence;
- to give support;
- to influence the image of humans;
- to create, design, and realize one's own life;
- to contribute to the development and unfolding of a self-conception;
- to create identity;
- to open up self-fulfillment;
- to enable self-efficacy;
- to further self-determination;
- to create the possibility to be self-sufficient;
- to receive praise, recognition, and affirmation;
- to experience success and failure and learn how to handle them;
- to be trusted with influence, to gain and use scope for decision-making and action;
- to develop and educate oneself and to learn;
- to experience the promotion of one's own talents and the sharpening of one's own abilities;
- to develop one's personality;
- to grow into a certain role and fill it;
- to help build self-esteem;
- to contribute to the structuring of daily life;
- to further social inclusion;
- to support or cause the creation of interpersonal relationships and networks;
- to contribute to the building or growing of society;
- to get to know and be challenged by reality;
- to learn or improve mastering of the distinction between important and unimportant things and how to prioritize;
- to potentially create incentives for entrepreneurship;
- to potentially trigger incentives for innovation.

Furthermore, access to a paid job would ideally be designed in such a way that there are equal opportunities.

At this point, it becomes obvious that an unconditional basic income cannot cover all the previous functions of a paid job, which leads to the question if a possible adjustment of the unconditional basic income could fulfil some – or even all – of those functions.

This question gains even more importance, on the one hand, because of the side effects and collateral phenomena of digital transformation and data-based systems, which can be summarized in tendencies towards loneliness, individual isolation, degeneration of the ability for human interaction, and the development of a harmful and self-harmful self-image.

On the other hand, discussing this question gains importance when thinking that there will definitely never be a shortage of tasks that are important for the whole society – in particular, tasks that are based on human interaction and relationships – on the contrary, they might even massively increase. For example, the demographic development and its acceleration based on medical advances will lead to the situation that more generations of humans will live at the same time, so the significance of furthering intergenerational understanding will grow.

Here, the adaptation of the unconditional basic income approach to a *Society-, Entrepreneurship-, Research-Time-Model (SERT)*[1548] could help. SERT aims at contributing to the survival of all humans and to life as humans – i.e. with dignity. On the one hand, it is based on the payment of a higher basic income, which will not only cover the needs for a physical existence, but also allow for a life with dignity. On the other hand – and here the unconditional side of the basic income will be substantially adapted – it consists of a commitment by each person to society (society-time), which is demanded of each person in return for the basic income. Analogously to the existing, tried, and tested model of the Swiss civil service, every person could choose from a broad array of options in one chosen area to contribute to the good of society as a whole. From a human rights perspective, the self-determination of each individual to choose the area of one's contribution for the good of society as a whole is important. The time frame for this commitment to society at large would be the same for everyone.

This free choice of one's own individual contribution as a duty corresponding to the coverage of the costs for existence and for a life with human dignity would allow the freedom and autonomy of every individual to be respected, as well as the above-mentioned challenges to be addressed while keeping the incentives for entrepreneurship and for innovation alive and avoiding human discouragement. The economic system of a social market economy is characterized, on the one hand, by its principles of a social network based on solidarity and justice. On the other hand, the prin-

---

1548 See Kirchschlaeger 2019c.

ciples of fairness and free competition, as well as the logic of the market, offer incentives for education, science and research, for innovation and entrepreneurship. These goals are essential for progress in a society. SERT takes this into account so as to encourage the striving for those objectives by offering a reduction in or even an exemption from "society-time" when committing oneself to education, research and science, innovation, and entrepreneurship. This way, incentives for education, research and science, innovation, and entrepreneurship can be given.

Any worries about the high administrative burden can be addressed with a digital answer. All supervising, reporting and controlling processes can be digitalized. Of course, solutions based on blockchain technology are also to be taken into account.

Worries about abuse can be addressed with the likely realistic assessment that this system, as any other system, will recognize abuse attempts. As long as this concerns only a small, statistically irrelevant number, which is to be expected because of the digital supervising, reporting and controlling processes, there is no need to worry. This is particularly true because it also needs to be taken into account that even in case of abuse, the commitment to society as a whole is much greater than in the case of the unconditional basic income.

8.2.4 SERT as Ethical Impulse for Interdisciplinary Dialogue

Looking at digital transformation and data-based systems – in particular, their effects on the world of work – and the idea of an unconditional basic income from an ethical perspective informed by the principle of human rights, results in demonstrating a problem that identifies ethical challenges. They occur in areas that are relevant to human rights, in digital transformation and data-based systems and their impact on the world of work, as well as in respect to the unconditional basic income. The Society-, Entrepreneurship-, Research-Time-Model (SERT) can be sketched out as a possible solution, which surely needs consolidation and further – in particular, interdisciplinary – enhancement. Maybe SERT as a model itself and with its corresponding questions can be used as an ethical impulse for continued interdisciplinary discourse.

8.3 Equal Participation in Digital Transformation and Data-Based Systems

In particular with reference to justice, but also to human rights, from an ethical perspective the above-mentioned global injustice and the digital divide need to be tackled consistently and to be stopped, and future tendencies towards this need to be prevented. Here, it could help to understand data-based systems as a public good. Such an understanding of data-based systems not just primarily as an industrial product, but as a public good is based on estimating its potential "to improve people's lives by helping to solve some of the world's greatest challenges and inefficiencies. AI has already begun reaping major benefits to the public in fields as diverse as healthcare, transportation, the environment, criminal justice, and economic inclusion. The effectiveness of the government itself is being increased as agencies build their capacity to use AI to carry out their missions more quickly, responsively, and efficiently."[1549] Due to their complex and broad significance and impact, digital transformation and data-based systems need to be democratized and disseminated fairly, also with a global horizon. The way in which data-based systems are developed and the progress made in this field suggest working together globally, based on a rigorously enforced human rights-based regulation of digital transformation and data-based systems, in particular in the fields of standardization, defense, cyber security in the context of digital transformation and data-based systems, "too big to fail" impacts of tech companies, etc.

As mentioned above in subchapter 8.1 Ethical and Legal Framework for Technological Progress, there is a great need for regulation, just like with any other socio-critical innovation technologies such as genetically manipulated food or modern methods of reproductive medicine, as well as goods that pose risks to humans and the environment (e.g., pharmaceuticals). Rapid technological developments, a high investment requirement, and a high number of new approvals for technical components of data-based systems in sensitive areas emphasize its urgency. The need for regulation of data-based systems is also justified based on risk considerations and impact assessments: "AI has applications in many products, such as cars and aircraft, which are subject to regulation designed to protect the public from harm and ensure fairness in economic competition. How will the incorporation of AI into these products affect the relevant regulatory approaches? In general, the approach to regulation of AI-enabled products to protect

---

1549   U.S. President National Science and Technology Council Committee on Technology 2016a.

public safety should be informed by assessment of the aspects of risk that the addition of AI may reduce alongside the aspects of risk that it may increase."[1550] The focus, however, should be on research and development, data-based systems and their economic dimension, socio-ethical issues of good governance (fairness, security, control, and sustainability), global connections, social impacts, ethical relevance, and specific fields of application such as cybersecurity, modern weapon systems, and self-controlling, self-learning, and intelligent systems.

Furthermore, the handling and use of data-based systems should be considered a part of good governance. This would mean governments would have to be consciously aware of their techno-political responsibility. From an ethical viewpoint, equal rights in competition, supply, and use would need to be ensured and equal opportunities and participation of all, transparency and security, and sustainability should be considered.

Data-based systems are characterized by a new existential dimension in that this technology alone cannot improve the quality of life. Rather, it leads to new potentials for fraud, power, and destruction with governmental relevance.

Furthermore, the development of self-controlling, self-steering and self-learning data-based systems exceeds previous limits of the natural, the naturally feasible, constructible, and thus controllable. The concept of the artificial is broadened towards learning and self-regulating systems, which cannot only be classified as intelligently acting artificial systems, which react and copy. They will outperform, by far, the natural in speed, accuracy, functionality, depth of perception, endurance etc. Rather, self-controlling, self-steering and self-learning data-based systems are characterized by the fact that they independently incorporate new and intelligent behavior patterns into their control system and thus become unpredictable. In addition to the above-mentioned techno-political responsibility and the guarantee of equal competition and usage rights, this requires a realistic, ethical expertise for the impact assessment.[1551] In this process, the precautionary principle provides ethical guidance.

Just as the state acts without hesitation in the case of other innovations that may endanger humans and their health (e.g., the pharmaceutical industry) or the environment, the precautionary principle must also be respected in the areas of digital transformation and the use of data-based sys-

---

1550 U.S. President National Science and Technology Council Committee on Technology 2016a.
1551 See European Commission n.d.

tems. In concrete terms, this means that, for example, before introducing 5G, careful and independent research must be carried out to determine whether this technological option is harmful to human health.[1552] The US Department of Health and Human Services published a study in November 2018 stating:

- "Clear evidence of tumors in the hearts of male rats. The tumors were malignant schwannomas.
- Some evidence of tumors in the brains of male rats. The tumors were malignant gliomas.
- Some evidence of tumors in the brains of male rats. The tumors were benign, malignant, or complex combined pheochromocytoma."[1553]

The US Department of Health and Human Services recommends further research in this field. The report "Mobile Communications and Radiation" from November 18, 2019 of the Swiss Federal Office for the Environment (FOEN) at the Swiss Federal Department of the Environment, Transport, Energy and Communications (UVEK) also demands more research on the health risks.[1554]

8.4 *Insurance*

Digital transformation and data-based systems – especially super-data-based systems – lead to the ethical challenge that their risks cannot be estimated yet. This aspect gains weight, and in particular when taking into account voices such as Stephen Hawking, this is of particular importance, as introduced at the beginning of this book: "AI could be the worst event in the history of our civilization. It brings dangers, like powerful autonomous weapons, or new ways for the few to oppress the many. It could bring great disruption to our economy"[1555] or Elon Musk: "AI is far more dangerous than nukes [nuclear warheads]. Far."[1556] Faced with this insecurity from an ethical viewpoint and with reference to justice and responsibility, the need emerges that any damage will also be repaired, should it occur.

1552 See Schumann 2019: 34.
1553 U.S. Department of Health and Human Services: National Toxicology Program 2018.
1554 See Swiss Federal Office for the Environment (FOEN) 2020.
1555 Kharpal 2017.
1556 Clifford 2018.

Both – the risk of digital transformation and data-based systems, as well as the need for reparation in case of damage – should be met with an insurance model. For example, genetic technology knows of such an insurance. E.g., the "Austrian Gene Technology Act" embraces the following:[1557] "The operator of an activity under section 79a shall, in a manner and to an extent customary in fair business dealings, take precautions by taking out insurance or in any other suitable manner to ensure that obligations to pay damages under this section can be met. If the activity consists of work with GMOs of safety level 3 on a large scale or the release of GMOs on a small scale (Section 36(1)(1)), this precaution must in any case consist of liability insurance with an insured sum of at least EUR 712 200 for each case of damage. If the activity consists of work with GMOs of safety level 4 on a large scale or the release of GMOs on a small scale (Section 36(1)(2)), this precaution must in any case consist of liability insurance with an insured sum of at least EUR 4 069 700 for each case of damage. The liability insurance must be taken out with an insurer authorized to operate this class of insurance in Austria; Austrian law must apply. The competent authority within the meaning of § 158c para. 2 Insurance Contract Act 1958 is the authority pursuant to § 100.

(2) There is no obligation to provide financial security if the Federal Government or a county is the operator."

In the field of nuclear technology research, there also exist such insurances:[1558] "The operator of a nuclear installation situated in Austria must obtain insurance to cover his liability. This insurance policy must remain in effect for at least ten years after operations at the nuclear installation have ceased. It must extend to all damage caused during the term of the policy and which gives rise to claims no later than ten years after the damage occurred. This security requirement does not extend to damage resulting from war, armed conflict, civil war, riot or rebellion.

(2) The insurance policy must provide coverage of at least 406 million Euros per incident plus 40.6 million Euros for interest and costs, except in the case of experimental and research reactors, where the relevant amounts shall be 40.6 million Euros per incident and 4.06 million Euros for interest and costs.

(3) There is no obligation to insure where the Federal government (Bund) or State (Land) itself is liable or has assumed the liability of the op-

---

1557 Austrian Gene Technology Act 1994 (2015): § 79j. (1).
1558 See, e.g., Austrian Federal Act on Civil Liability for Damage Caused by Radioactivity 1999: § 6-8.

erator of a nuclear installation for an amount not less than those amounts indicated in Paragraphs 1 and 2. The Federal Minister of Finance is authorized to assume such liability in cases where the purchase of liability insurance is beyond the financial means of the liable person, and where it is in the public interest that the government assume such liability.

§ 7 (1) The carrier of nuclear material is required to take out third-party liability insurance only if the risk is not covered by other mandatory insurance. The insurance policy must extend to all damages which are attributable to the carriage of nuclear material in Austria. This security requirement does not extend to damage resulting from war, armed conflict, civil war, riot or rebellion.

(2) The insurance policy must provide coverage of at least 40.6 million Euros per incident plus 4.06 million Euros for interest and costs, except in the case of source material, where the relevant amounts shall be 4.06 million Euros per incident plus 406 000 Euros for interest and costs.

(3) The carrier of nuclear material must have an insurance certificate with him at all time (Section 158i of the Insurance Law of 1958 – *Versicherungsvertragsgesetz*) which shall be presented upon demand to authorities responsible for monitoring compliance with the legal and security requirements applicable to such carriage.

The insurance exemption in Section 6, Paragraph 3 for operators applies equally to carriers of nuclear material.

§ 8 (1) The mandatory insurance required under Sections 6 and 7 must be secured from an insurer licensed to provide such insurance cover in Austria. The policy must be governed by Austrian law. The insurer shall notify the Financial Markets Regulatory Authority of the terms of the policy prior to its application.

(2) The office which should receive the insurance notification provided for in Section 158c, Paragraph 2 of the Insurance Law of 1958 is that of the authorities responsible for the licensing of nuclear installations and of the transport of nuclear material."

From an ethical standpoint, the ethical principles of justice, responsibility, and human rights suggest organizing this insurance model for digital transformation and data-based systems in solidarity, because it would overburden an individual to provide the full risk provisions. As with all insurance policies, the risks should be shared in solidarity. The estimation of the risk should be as truthful as possible. An approximation of the calculation could be the relation of the amount of damage times probability (analogous to, e.g., a car liability insurance policy).

But it needs to be borne in mind that insurance companies may not want to insure the amount of damage without limits. An upper limit could be introduced. It should also include a general openness to adapting this limit, when the amount of the damage can be calculated. With such an insurance model, it must be ensured from the outset that liability enforcement is guaranteed so that if, for example, a multinational corporation attempts to outsource the damage caused by its products or services or related risks to subcontractors, this can be prevented and the responsible group can be held accountable.

In addition to this hermeneutic path and this path of living responsibly and intergenerational omni-dynamic social justice as well as respecting, protecting, implementing, and realizing human rights, other paths towards solutions from an ethical perspective are expressions of the ethically justified necessity to structure society and its subsystem economy adequately for their ongoing digital transformation and their use of data-based systems.

8.5 Taxes

A fifth path towards solutions from an ethical perspective consists in structuring society and its subsystem economy by an adaptation of the tax-system into a fair global tax system,[1559] taking into account the essential digital transformation of the paid labor-market and of the value-added chain by data-based systems. Why taxes? "Tax justice matters because a modern economy requires that the state has sufficient revenue over time to fund the physical and social infrastructure essential to economic welfare. It should also enable a degree of wealth redistribution between rich and poor people to promote equity and security. Failure to achieve the first objective because of poorly designed, unfair or leaking tax systems is likely to yield economic failure, while failure to achieve the second objective will lead to social failure. In either case, the costs to society are enormous. Tax justice is, therefore, at the heart of stable and democratic forms of government."[1560]

Addressing the core consequence of the digital transformation of society and economy mentioned above – namely, *ever fewer humans are directly in-*

1559 See Pogge et al. 2016; Mehta et al. 2020.
1560 Tax Justice Network 2005, 11.

volved economically and socially in a more efficient and more effective value-added chain – is of ethical relevance in order to avoid a widening of global inequality and injustice, in order to open equal opportunities for everyone, and in order to guarantee peaceful coexistence in a just society. An adaptation of the tax-system corresponding to digital transformation and the use of data-based systems could serve this aim. This adaptation of the tax-system should include harmonizing taxation globally, taxing capital rather than work, taxing data-based systems, and taxing data.

Regarding the harmonization of taxation globally, its urgency was acknowledged by German Finance Minister Olaf Scholz together with Spain's Minister of Economics Nadia Calvino, Italy's Minister of Finance Roberto Gualtieri and French Finance Minister Bruno Le Maire and highlighted in a joint statement, namely that "these (digitally-based companies) generate enormous profits in regions where they have no official base, and therefore do not pay taxes. At the same time, some of the world's largest corporations continue to direct their profits to countries with lower tax rates"[1561].

A new global tax-system can rely on the OECD/G20 Inclusive Framework on base erosion and profit shifting (BEPS). "BEPS refers to tax planning strategies that exploit gaps and mismatches in tax rules to artificially shift profits to low or no-tax locations where there is little or no economic activity or to erode tax bases through deductible payments such as interest or royalties. Although some of the schemes used are illegal, most are not. This undermines the fairness and integrity of tax systems because businesses that operate across borders can use BEPS to gain a competitive advantage over enterprises that operate at a domestic level. Moreover, when taxpayers see multinational corporations legally avoiding income tax, it undermines voluntary compliance by all taxpayers. (…) Developing countries' higher reliance on corporate income tax means they suffer from BEPS disproportionately. BEPS practices cost countries USD 100-240 billion in lost revenue annually. Working together within OECD/G20 Inclusive Framework on BEPS, over 135 countries and jurisdictions are collaborating on the implementation of 15 measures to tackle tax avoidance, improve the coherence of international tax rules and ensure a more transparent tax environment."[1562]

The Inclusive Framework on BEPS foresees a two-pillar approach consisting in (first pillar: unified approach) new rules regarding where tax

---

1561   Deutsche Welle (DW) 2020. See Scholz et al. 2020.
1562   OECD n.d.

should be paid ("nexus" rules), and in new rules regarding what portion of their profits should be taxed ("profit allocation" rules) ("The aim is to ensure that multinational enterprises (MNEs) conducting sustained and significant business in places where they may not have a physical presence can be taxed in such jurisdictions"[1563]), as well as consisting in (second pillar) tackling remaining base erosion and profit shifting (BEPS) issues and ensuring that international businesses pay a minimum level of tax.[1564]

Regarding taxing capital rather than work, it has to be admitted that this is not a new idea[1565] but the taxation of financial transactions gains importance and relevance due the following impact of digital transformation and the use of data-based systems: "The share of wages in economic output will continue to fall as digitization progresses, while the share of capital will increase. (...) More than ever before, money will be earned with money, not with work. Those who work are the new poor."[1566] Or as Jeffrey D. Sachs, economist and special adviser to the UN Secretary-General António Guterres, describes it: "The basic economics of automation involves technologically advanced machines replacing workers in the production process. The result is a rise of output accompanied by a fall in the demand for labor. Output rises, labor productivity rises, but wages fall and income is redistributed from labor to capital. Is society better off? Yes and no. Gross domestic product rises, but workers are left poorer. Thus, the way to ensure that everybody benefits from the technological advances brought by automation is to accompany the shift with a transfer of income from capital (the automation 'winner') to workers (the automation 'loser')."[1567]

Regarding taxing data-based systems, and taxing data, German Finance Minister Olaf Scholz together with Spain's Minister of Economics Nadia Calvino, Italy's Minister of Finance Roberto Gualtieri and French Finance Minister Bruno Le Maire, highlighted in a joint statement that "the profits of the large digital groups – be they American, European or Chinese – are not taxed appropriately. These companies make huge profits in areas where they have little physical presence but exploit the data of millions of users. Often the companies with the highest profits end up paying the lowest taxes. As a result, they do not make a fair contribution to the financing of our community. This situation is unacceptable, inefficient and above all

---

1563   OECD 2020.
1564   See OECD 2020.
1565   See Keynes 1936; Tobin 1978; Summers / Summers 1989; Feige 1989.
1566   Hofstetter 2017: 88.
1567   Sachs 2019: 159.

unsustainable. With international digital taxation, we can eliminate this problem by establishing fair and stable taxation that is appropriate to the new business models of the digital economy. At the same time, it will give the companies concerned greater fiscal legal certainty."[1568]

8.6 Patents

8.6.1 Patents as Conventional Instruments of Innovation

Patents are conventional instruments of innovation. A patent is a legal title granting its holder the exclusive right to stop others from using or making his invention. Its further characteristics can be summarized in the following way: "A patent is a certificate delivered by or on behalf of the government confirming that the object of the patent is new, nonobvious, and industrially applicable, and that the patent application contains a sufficiently detailed disclosure of the invention. Patents grant extensive rights. If the object of the patent is a *product*, the patentee has the right to prevent others from making, using, offering for sale, selling, or importing the product for one of these purposes. Owners of a *process* patent have a right to prevent others from using the process, as well as from using, offering for sale, selling, or importing for one of these purposes, at least, the product obtained directly through the application of the process. (...) These rights are enforceable in court. The monopoly rights of patentees are limited in time"[1569].

On the one hand, patents contribute to the speed and the quality of innovation. On the other hand, their innovative efficiency and effectiveness and their ethical value are questioned. "Indeed, the necessity of the patent system cannot be justified beyond doubt from an economic point of view. To see the increase in patent applications as a sign of innovative progress is as meaningful as the increase in the use of prisons as a success in the fight against crime. Unfortunately, there is today an increasing misuse of patent law, with the result that innovation is hindered. Reforms need to re-establish the effective promotion of innovation. For example, innovations that represent interface definitions and standards should be excluded from

---

1568 Scholz et al. 2020.
1569 Sterckx 2006: 250, emphasis in the text.

patentability. The granting of patents on software and software-based business methods must be stopped."[1570]

Due to the two main characteristics of innovation – ground-breaking ideas and concrete impact because of successful application – corporations are among the main actors contributing to innovation because innovation is not only about new ideas but also about efficient and effective application of these ideas. The latter seems to be also implicit when Anita Roddick, founder of The Body Shop, emphasizes the innovative role of business: "There is no power on earth apart from business capable of making the changes we desperately need for the continued survival of the planet"[1571]. As discussed above in subchapter 7.19 Global Injustice, corporations usually go beyond the creation of jobs and payment of taxes in their contributions to society. Business creates value, solutions for societal challenges, and innovation.[1572]

Corporations possess power and influence for driving innovation globally and therefore it can be justified to see them with corresponding responsibilities for contributing to innovation globally.[1573]

8.6.2 Corporations' Ethical Responsibilities for Driving Innovation

Holding corporations responsible for furthering innovation on a global level is legitimate because innovation belongs to the core tasks of a corporation as they enable growth[1574] while at the same time they are never ethically neutral. Change is more complex and cannot be considered positive just for the sake of change. These characteristics of innovation require an ethical assessment of innovations from corporations.[1575] While innovation plays a central role for business, the agency of corporations for innovation and their corresponding responsibility needs to be emphasized. Both justify interpreting corporations as possessing ethical responsibilities for driving innovation globally.

1570   Schindlbeck 2008: 64.
1571   Roddick 2009: 4.
1572   See Dillard / Murray 2013: 199.
1573   See Kirchschlaeger 2015e.
1574   See Brenner / Witte 2011.
1575   See Kirchschlaeger 2013b.

8.6.3 Legitimate Examination of Conventional Instruments of Innovation

One responsibility of corporations linked with innovation is also to examine conventional instruments of innovation continuously from an ethical perspective in their performance and to change them accordingly if necessary. Patents aiming to promote innovation and to disseminate its fruits belong to these conventional instruments.

This examination from an ethical perspective also proves to be legitimate because a patent is considered a means to an end, and not an end in itself. In other words, if patents or parts of the present concept of patents do not serve innovation any more or even block or prevent innovation, corresponding changes are necessary and legitimate.[1576]

Part of this ethical scrutiny needs to focus also on legal instruments of innovation and entails the analysis of their coherence with their own idea and aims, their achievement of objectives, their innovative impact, and their consequences.

8.6.4 The Impact of Patents on Innovation and Their Ethical Significance

While examining patens as conventional instruments of innovation from an ethical perspective,[1577] it becomes obvious that patents play a key-role in improving the speed and the quality of innovation. The inventors get exclusive rights to control commercial exploitation of their inventions for some years – including the use of patent-aggregating companies to capture value from their inventions[1578] – and in return, they disclose a detailed description of their inventions in order to make knowledge available to all. Others can build on the gained knowledge based on these disclosures.

At the same time, doubts arise about the efficiency and effectiveness of patents in providing innovation and about the value of patents from an ethical perspective.[1579] Misalignment of incentives, distortion of priorities, artificially high prices, lack of efficiency because of lobbying and gaming (e.g. anticompetitive agreements), costs for patenting, legal disputes about intellectual property slowing down the innovation-processes, deadweight

---

1576 See Médecins Sans Frontières 2016.
1577 See also Huebner / Spranger 2010.
1578 See Krech et al. 2015.
1579 See Stiglitz 2006; Love / Hubbard 2007: 1519; Ravvin 2008; Kremer / Glennerster 2004.

losses, and limited dissemination of innovations represent some of the phenomena nurturing this skeptical view of patents.[1580] "The patent system allows for the suppression of inventions, as exploitation of patented inventions is not obligatory. (...) The current patent system stimulates the phenomenon of 'inventing around'."[1581]

One of many concrete examples can show the necessity of examination of patents regarding their impact on innovation and their ethical significance: "We tolerate such restrictions in the belief that they might spur innovation, balancing costs against benefits. But the costs of restrictions can outweigh the benefits. It is hard to see how the patent issued by the US government for the healing properties of turmeric, which had been known for hundreds of years, stimulated research. Had the patent been enforced in India, poor people who wanted to use this compound would have had to pay royalties to the United States."[1582]

If one analyzes the impact of patents on markets, it becomes obvious that if multinational corporations find themselves in a leading position in their industry, instead of living up to their responsibility to look for and to foster innovation, they prefer to hold back competitors as long as possible with creative constructions of patent-protection in order not to be obliged to sharing cutting-edge research-findings and -technology with their competitors.

In addition, mature industries or complex technologies suffer from the effect of so-called "patent thicket" because a multitude of patents is involved in each product, which does not facilitate innovation. Instead, it creates massive transaction-costs, barriers, and vertical monopoly, and therefore blocks innovation. In this way, small and medium enterprises are excluded from the patent-game because it is out of their reach or too risky to play.

Furthermore, patents slow the dynamic of research, the spread of technology, and contribute to the absence of technology-transfer.

Patents are also perceived as threats to individual freedom and rights.[1583] They are no longer perceived as being in service to the general interest but provoke doubts that they are designed for the benefit of narrow sections of corporate interest.[1584] Instead of creating and pushing forward innovation,

---

1580 See Pogge 2012.
1581 Sterckx 2006: 262-263.
1582 Stiglitz 2006: 1279.
1583 See Forman 2007: 350.
1584 See Médecins Sans Frontières 2001.

patents seem to fortify monopolies of multinational corporations by preventing competition. The latter is of particular significance for the discourse on innovation as competition also belongs to the conventional instruments of innovation. By avoiding competition, the pricing no longer matches the liberal markets. It results in inflated prices. The poorer humans are, the higher the costs are for this unfair regime. "Their high prices are 'artificial' in the sense that they are enabled by patents. The question is not whether we should subsidize advanced medicines for the poor. Rather, the question is whether we may promote the enforcement of temporary monopolies that drive up the prices at which they can buy such medicines. This is what our governments have done in our name by insisting that innovators must be enabled, even in the less developed countries, to outlaw and suppress the manufacture and sale of generic versions of 'their' product at competitive market prices. In defense of this practice, it has been argued that the manufacture and sale of generic products are moral crimes that any just legal system ought to suppress. But the defenders of this view have not managed to provide a convincing argument to show why the fact that one person has made a new product should give her a natural right to bar others from making a like product out of their own raw materials."[1585]

One could perhaps discuss a positive side effect of this phenomenon if a high percentage of the margin obtained this way by industries ended up in research for innovation. This is not the case though. "Drug companies spend more on advertising and marketing than on research, more on research on lifestyle drugs than on life saving drugs, and almost nothing on diseases that affect developing countries only. This is not surprising. Poor people cannot afford drugs, and drug companies make investments that yield the highest returns."[1586]

Moreover, this legal framework and conditions of the market lead, for example, in the pharmaceutical industry, to an allocation of the small percentage, which is invested in innovation in research on areas where patients can afford the medical products and not in research on medicines and medical treatments, which are most needed and would affect the biggest number of humans.

The initiative "Health Impact Fund" can serve as an exemplary approach for other areas of innovation in order to realize the principles of responsibility, justice, and human rights. For example, robotic surgery has served above as an example for high-tech medical treatment. This medical treat-

---

1585 Pogge 2011: 2; see also Hollis / Pogge 2008.
1586 Stiglitz 2006: 1279.

ment is not affordable to everyone, and therefore humans are discriminated against and excluded from medical treatment and health-care. "The challenge here is to get and use high-tech medical aids but with affordable costs so as not to sharpen the differences between rich and poor."[1587]

The Health Impact Fund is an approach, which meets this challenge. "Financed mainly by governments, the Health Impact Fund (HIF) is a proposed pay-for-performance mechanism that would offer innovators the option – no obligation – to register any new medicine or, under certain conditions, also a traditional medicine or a new use of an existing medicine. By registering a product at the time of marketing approval, the innovator would undertake to make it available, during its first 10 years on the market, wherever it is needed at no more than the lowest feasible cost of production and distribution. The innovator would further commit to allowing, at no charge, generic production and distribution of the product after this decade has ended (if the innovator still has unexpired patents on the product). In exchange, the registrant would receive, during those ten years, annual reward payments based on its product's health impact. (…) The HIF would greatly mitigate the greatest injustice of the present system by limiting the price of any registered medicine to the lowest feasible cost of production and distribution. (…). In addition, the HIF would foster the development of new high-impact medicines against diseases concentrated among the poor. (…) Registrants would be rewarded not for merely selling their products, but for making them effective toward improving global health."[1588] The underlying argument of the approach that alternative incentives for research and development of essential medicines should be triggered by the Health Impact Fund provokes the counterargument that it would demand a cost that is too high for tax-paying citizens of high-income countries to be just, and this cost would be unacceptable from a libertarian point of view.[1589] While agreeing with the starting point of individual autonomy – which can be justified, e.g., from a human rights perspective –, the question arises who is enjoying individual autonomy, and if not, every human should enjoy individual autonomy. While the response to the second question is – from a human rights perspective justified on the fundament of the principle of vulnerability – that all humans have the right to individual autonomy, the response to the first questions is pointing out the reality which looks different: Not every human enjoys individ-

---

1587 Tzafestas 2016: 86.
1588 Pogge 2011: 3-4.
1589 See Sonderholm 2014.

ual autonomy and there are many factors – among others, the phenomena identified by the Health Impact Fund – which are limiting individual autonomy. The third question would be if the cost for tax-paying citizens of high-income countries is really too high, unjust, and unacceptable because, *first*, from a human rights perspective, one could argue that there are duties and responsibilities of every right-holder corresponding to human rights to contribute to the respect, the protection, the implementation, and the realization of human rights of all humans. One could argue that the cost for tax-paying citizens of high-income countries would be part of their contribution to the respect, the protection, the implementation, and the realization of human rights of all humans.

Second, one could present the argument that taxpaying citizens of high-income countries benefit from the success of the pharmaceutical industry based on patents economically (e.g., creation of jobs, taxes, economic growth, etc.) and in terms of their health.

Both moral arguments would lead to the conclusion that the cost of the Health Impact Fund is not too high, unjust, and unacceptable for tax-paying citizens of high-income countries. *Third*, a pragmatic – and therefore of secondary nature – argument could even be introduced that due to global interdependence of markets and economies, it is actually in the particular interest of tax-paying citizens of high-income countries to contribute to global justice.

Another counter-argument is missing evidence that patents are barriers to access.[1590] Looking at the prices of, for example, medical products, limiting access to them significantly and the impact of patents guaranteeing medical products the legal prevention of the manufacture and sale of generic versions of 'their' product at competitive market prices defuses this criticism.

Beyond that, if one looks at which central role small and medium enterprises (SMEs) play for economic systems and especially for innovation, the impact patents do have on small and medium enterprises needs to be taken into consideration as well.

In addition, certain developments in the legal protection of patents seem to go in another direction than their original purpose and innovation. Requirements for patents are novelty ("absolute": worldwide state of the art, or "relative": national state of the art), and non-obviousness. The latter is an abstract and open term that leaves room for differentiation and does

---

1590 See Sonderholm 2009.

not exclude the reality of trivial patents, which damage small and medium enterprises (SMEs) especially and provoke anti-innovative effects.

Finally, the question arises if patents should provide purpose-bound protection or full product protection. Full product protection covers not only purposes (consciously) invented by the inventor but every unknown purpose and effect of a product. If patents are really about innovation, inventions with different economic effects – mechanical or substances (chemical products, biotechnological material, nanotechnological building blocks) – require different legislative solutions, and therefore full product protection does not seem to be adequate if patents should serve innovation. For example, "Swiss-type claims", which claim protection for newly discovered effects of pharmaceutical substances, worsen the situation because they are a wrong form of "differentiation". The protection of specific purpose (effect) of substances cannot be deemed an "exception" – an effect that leads to the extension of the term for full product protection) but the rule must be that only the specific – disclosed – purpose of a substance may be protected by a specific patent. In order to enhance innovation, newly found purposes may be subject to new patents creating an incentive for third parties to develop new fields and banning the risk of monopolizing "essential facilities" (e.g., nanotechnology).

From a global perspective, one can note a growing knowledge- and technology-gap between richer and poorer countries. This reality certainly does not serve innovation. Rather it reduces the sphere of innovation to a small group of humans. While there are no doubts about the essential role patents play for the promotion of innovation, technology-development, and technology-transfer, this anti-innovative global reality to which also patents, among other things, contribute their part (besides finance, local absorptive capacity, local enabling environment, etc.) must be taken into consideration in a critical examination of patents as conventional instruments of innovation. If only so-called "developed countries" can file patents due to their ability to generate innovation and most so-called developing countries lack this ability, and if there is a correlation between GDP per capita and patents,[1591] this exclusion of a part of the world does not serve innovation and demands a change to the patent-system. Innovation is nurtured through the diffusion of knowledge and access to knowledge.

From an ethical perspective, a development that can be identified in the example of the pharmaceutical industry urges, even more, a reconsidera-

---

1591 See Martinot 2000.

tion and adaptation of patents: "Part of the WTO Treaty, the TRIPS Agreement entitles pharmaceutical firms to protect their innovations with product patents, which suppress generic competition, and then to sell their patented medicines at prices far above the cost of production. By pressing less developed countries to institute and enforce stronger patent protections, the wealthier countries enabled their pharmaceutical firms to profit from sales to the more affluent people in the developing world. As a side effect of this success, poor people are now excluded from many advanced medicines which, without TRIPS, would have been immediately available to them as cheap generics. In order to make sure that affluent people in the developing world contribute to the cost of pharmaceutical research and development (R&D), TRIPS causes grave harms and deaths among poor people in the developing world who cannot afford the large mark-ups charged on patented medicines."[1592]

8.6.5 Possibilities for Adaptation of Patents

The critical examination of patents as a conventional instrument of innovation so far does not intend to claim the weakening or the abolishment of patents because both would lead to serious drawbacks (e.g., discouraging investment in the sector). Indeed, it is broadly acknowledged that an effective system for the protection and enforcement of patents promotes innovation. "Without the prospect of an exclusive right to use the invention, and hence a possibility of recouping the money invested in the development of the invention, too little inventing would be done. The patent system offers inventors an indispensable incentive."[1593] Patents also further the disclosure, the trading and sharing of knowledge and the competitiveness of innovative corporations. "The patent system encourages inventors to disclose their inventions instead of keeping them secret. Thanks to the patent system, technological information is disseminated and this promotes technological progress, which in turn fosters economic growth."[1594]

Still, the "paradox of patents" needs to be recognized and considered: "The justification of the patent system is that by slowing down the diffusion of technical progress it ensures that there will be more progress to diffuse (...) Since it is rooted in a contradiction, there can be no such thing as

---

1592 Pogge 2011: 1.
1593 Sterckx 2006: 259.
1594 Sterckx 2006: 259.

an ideally beneficial patent system."[1595] It needs to be taken into account as well that patents do not – from a perspective of distributive justice – reward inventing initiatives because the inventor, who remains without success, or basic researchers also put a lot of effort into their invention and won't receive any reward. Beyond that, the question can be raised if it is just to reward someone – in order to exclude the "free riders" from the completion – by the guarantee of exclusive rights to the determination of the application and use of knowledge. "No link whatsoever exists between the social usefulness of an invention on the one hand and the period of protection (the 'length') and the scope of protection (the 'width') of the patent issued on the other hand. All patents are valid for twenty years irrespective of the usefulness of the invention in question and irrespective of the effort required for the development of the invention."[1596] Finally, patents do create high costs,[1597] and these costs should be balanced with the effect created by them.

The critical examination of patents aims to contribute to keeping the costs of the patents proportional to their positive impact and to strengthen the innovative force of patents. *First,* there is a significant responsibility for jurisprudence, among others, to uphold protection requirements ("inventive step"), to create and clarify limitations and exceptions, and to apply competition law appropriately. Patents should not only create innovation but also progress.[1598]

Second, patent law already knows the possibility of exclusions of protection partially aiming at different approaches of protection (e.g. plant varieties protection) and the possibility of extensions of protection aiming at differentiation of amortization possibilities (e.g. supplementary protection certificate). These possibilities and their application could be extended, for example, with regard to computer programs, "living material" (biotechnology), naturally existing building blocks (e.g. nanotechnology).

Third, countervailing rights to patents must be enforced in order to avoid anti-innovative effects of patents.

Fourth, from a global perspective, concrete measures need to be taken in order to enhance knowledge-, technology- and know-how-transfer and global collaborative research efforts in order to gain an improved spread of

---

1595 Robinson 1958: 87.
1596 Sterckx 2006: 258-259.
1597 See Sterckx 2006: 262-263.
1598 See Sterckx 2006: 261.

innovation and innovations in contextually adapted, efficient, and effective innovative solutions to challenges.

Fifth, ways must be found to reconcile patent-protection as an incentive for innovation with the facilitation of research and innovation through open-sharing of research-findings and knowledge. One concrete element of this balancing could be that results of research and development at universities cannot be patented in order to foster innovation.

Sixth, patent-pools could be a first step and a kind of compromise balancing the interests of the innovator and the beneficiary of the innovation enabling access to scientific data, the diffusion of knowledge, technology, and know-how, and innovative collaboration bringing together different standpoints and perspectives. This mechanism engages several patents of different entities as objects of common research and development by the participating entities, which pay royalties to the holder of the patents as access-fees to the patent-pool.

Seventh, international funds addressing specific industries could be created – following the example of the Health Impact Fund – to generate innovation in areas which have an impact on the lives of many humans and not only on the lives of the few promising future customers, and maybe even to buy patents in order to open the access to common resources.

Eighth, in order to facilitate and promote innovation, patents must be limited to real inventions and should not embrace either elements of nature or minor improvements of existing products.

Ninth, other instruments serving innovation (e.g., alternative incentive-systems, awarding and remuneration, tax-regulation, business-models, educational approaches, global open-share-spaces of knowledge, know-how, technology) should be developed in order to disburden the patents in their role in the creation and promotion of innovation.

Tenth, from an ethical perspective, besides the above-mentioned brief indication of possibilities where an adaptation of patents could start from, criteria determining the legitimacy of the consequences, effects, and the impact of patents and of the adaptations of patents besides their creation, contribution, and promotion of innovation could perhaps enrich the discourse about the innovation of patents. As global inequality is growing, dominating the globe, and oppressing the vast majority of humans, uses, applications, and changes of patents leading to a decrease in global inequality should be included in the focus. According to a report by Oxfam from January 2016, 62 individuals have the same wealth as 3.6 billion people – the bottom half of humanity.[1599] According to the bank Credit Suisse, the richest 1% have now accumulated more wealth than the rest of the world put together.[1600] The Global Agenda Council of the World Economic Forum (WEF) identified the increase in global inequality as the most significant challenge of the year 2015. Al Gore states: "As the world's rich continue to accumulate wealth at record rates, the middle class is struggling. Today, the top 1% of the population receives a quarter of the income in the United States. Over the last twenty-five years, the average income of the top 0.1% has grown twenty times compared to that of the average citizen."[1601] Amina Mohammed, Special Advisor of the UN Secretary General on Post-2015-development-planning and Vice-Chair of the Global Agenda Council on Sustainable Development, explains: "This affects all countries around the world. In developed and developing countries alike, the poorest half of the population often controls less than 10% of its wealth. This is a universal challenge that the whole world must address. While it is true that around the world economic growth is picking up pace, deep challenges remain, including poverty, environmental degradation, persistent unemployment, political instability, violence and conflict. These problems (...) are often closely related to inequality."[1602]

A concrete criterion addressing the issue of global inequality in innovation is the "gap-closing-principle"[1603], which is based on the principles of responsibility, justice, and human rights. Following John Rawls' difference principle ("Social and economic inequalities are to be arranged so that they both are (a) to the greatest benefit of the least advantaged and (b) attached to offices and positions open to all under conditions of fair equality of opportunity"[1604]), the following "gap-closing-principle" should serve – taking into account the consequences, the effects, and the impact of patents – as an ethical point of reference in the reform or revision and the use of patents: *Patents or adaptations of patents are legitimate if they contribute to the realization of human rights of all humans and if they contribute to the closing of the gap between poor and rich.*

The "gap-closing-principle" is based on the Jewish tradition of tithing, which forms a religious and social contribution to Levites, foreigners, wid-

---

1599   See Oxfam 2016.
1600   See Credit Suisse 2015.
1601   Gore 2015.
1602   Mohammed 2015.
1603   See Kirchschlaeger 2016d.
1604   Rawls 1971: 83.

ows, and orphans (see Dtn 12:6; 14:22; 26:12). With tithing, it shares the combination of pursuing one's own self-interest and of contributing to the systematic reduction of one's own advantage in favor of the poorest and this way of the gap between poor and rich. At the same time, the "gap-closing-principle" is a further development of tithing insofar as:

- *First*, it entails a movement away from a charitable nature towards a human rights-based approach because the "gap-closing-principle" relies on the legitimate claim of human rights by all humans;
- *Second*, its human rights-foundation leads to a universality of its horizon which goes beyond the Jewish tradition of tithing as religious and social contributions and which corresponds to a globalized innovation, science, research, technology, and economy, global systems of patents, and global inequality;
- *Third*, the "gap-closing-principle" does not strive for a relative reduction of the difference between poor and rich in the sense of the Jewish tithing (e.g., put in terms of a simplified example, the advantage of the richest grows 50% and they give 10% of it to the poorest, the gap increases only 30%) but for an absolute reduction of the gap between poor and rich (e.g., summarized schematically, the advantage of the richest grows 50%, the growth of the poorest comprises 80% of the initial advantage of the richest so that the absolute gap between poor and rich is diminished by more than 30%).

The "gap-closing-principle" possesses the following advantages:

- Its foundation is the legitimate claims of human rights by all humans and the corresponding negative and positive duties and responsibilities by states and non-state actors to respect and to protect the human rights of all humans, to implement them, and to contribute to their realization.[1605]
- Its focus on the struggle against global inequality and poverty finds its legitimacy in the fact that poverty itself is a massive human rights violation and a constitutive source for other violations of human rights.
- From a pragmatic standpoint, the urgent necessity of overcoming global inequality and poverty is another reason for the focus of the "gap-closing-principle" because of the illegitimate massive differences in in-

---

1605 See Kirchschlaeger 2014b.

come and wealth globally and because 18 million people die annually from poverty-related causes.[1606]

- Secondarily, the "gap-closing-principle" relates to the pragmatic observation of interdependence of globalized innovation, science, research, technology, and economy, global systems of patents, and global inequality and other global challenges they face. More integration in global contexts and the furthering of all serves the particular interests of all participants because it leads to more growth-potential and reduces the probability of political instability, conflicts, violence, terrorism, etc. due to poverty, to a lack of perspectives, aspirations, and economic prospects, to experiences of injustice.
- While maintaining, in the greatest possible way, the economic rationale of pursuing one's own particular interest, the "gap-closing-principle" introduces only a corrective of the *"ad infinitum"* of the pursuit of one's own particular interest. This means the pursuit of one's own particular interest is legitimate and just as long as it reduces the gap between poor and rich. In other words, the maximization of one's own particular interest is legitimate under the condition that the maximization of the interest of the poorest reaches even higher.

8.7 Research

The vision of the melding of human intelligence with data-based systems, in other words, the increasing immediate and direct interaction between human intelligence and data-based systems, will affect the way research is pursued. From an ethical perspective, the individuality of human intelligence and human thoughts and their crucial role for research are at stake. Research projects in this area and other research projects working on or with the aim to develop data-based systems with so-called "general intelligence" should be accompanied by ethics-boards[1607] and put under the monitoring and supervision of an international monitoring agency – the International Data-Based Systems Agency DSA (analogous to the International Atomic Energy Agency [IAEA]) (see above subchapter 8.1 Ethical and Legal Framework for Technological Progress).

Besides that, from an ethical perspective, further specific research, education, and in-service training in ethics on ethical chances and risks of digital

---

1606 See Pogge 2012: 537-559.
1607 See Mannino et al. 2015: 2.

389

transformation and data-based systems (e.g., research concerning the effect of digital transformation and data-based systems on the mental health of humans) are a promising way of meeting these challenges of the near or distant future.

Furthermore, interdisciplinary research that brings research in digital transformation and data-based systems and ethics together, is a further path to pursue.

In addition, further interdisciplinary research should address the ethical, legal, societal, and economic implications of digital transformation and data-based systems.

Moreover, the integration of ethics in research in digital transformation and data-based systems as well as in drafting, designing, developing, and encoding technological systems could help to a certain extent.

Beyond that, the research-based anticipation of future steps should be integrated into the development of precise prevention-measures that can be encoded in technological systems in order to disable the setting of self-given purposes by technological systems – keeping in mind that one deals with self-learning systems which therefore theoretically bear the capability *in se* of also learning themselves how to overcome these prevention measures. Corresponding research could provide relevant insights in that area.

Finally, an urgency exists to address the following gap in the field of digital transformation and data-based systems: "A critical gap in current AI technology is a lack of methodologies to ensure the safety and predictable performance of AI systems."[1608] Particular attention in the research area of data-based systems and digital transformation should be given, from an ethical standpoint, to short-, mid-, and long-term-effects of technological applications on humans (e.g., mental health, physical health, …) and on the ecosystem, the development of human rights-based ways of interaction between technology and humans, the development of secure and independent public testing- and training-environments for digital transformation and data-based systems as well as the development of standards, methods, and tools of evaluation of technologies.

1608 U.S. President National Science and Technology Council Committee on Technology 2016b: 15.

8.8 Education "Empowering" Reason, Not Just Training "Technical Rationality"

An eighth path towards solutions regarding digital transformation and data-based systems from an ethical perspective involves education embracing both the structural and systemic dimension as well as the individual dimension of the concrete actors (for example, teachers, pupils, students).[1609]

From this path, no immediate impact can be expected. Adapting education in the face of digital transformation and data-based systems will only result in mid-term and long-term effects.

Education is of ethical concern because the aims of education present an ethical question. Primarily, education must take care of not losing sight of the essentials as a result of the pursuit of progress. The same ethical principles, norms, and standards are valid in real and virtual reality. This means also that technological applications should only be introduced or used in education if they make sense from an ethical, from a pedagogical, and from a didactic perspective – not just because they represent innovations or because they are sponsored by, or are a gift from, the private sector. Receiving 100 basketballs for free doesn't mean that the school would change its curriculum and fill it with playing basketball, would it? Or at least that is not what should happen although I really like to play Basketball ...

Accordingly, education must address the following questions and answer them not from an economic or technophile point of view but based on purely pedagogical and didactic reasoning – in the "best interest of the pupil and students": Should education be digitalized? If so, how far should digitalization of education go? Should every pupil have his/her own tablet respectively his/her technical device? Or should school be a screen-free oasis? Should school be a place where interpersonal social interaction can be experienced and learned without distraction by screens? Should didactics be digitalized? Should mobile phones be prohibited at school? How should we handle the challenge of having teachers of the 20th century teaching pupils of the 21st century? Should education aim neither for analog nor for digital but rather for using exactly what serves its purpose and leaving the rest out? Should everyone or anyone be equipped from the point of view of justice and equality? Should teachers be empowered in their self-confidence to be teachers for "millennials" but not to be "millennials" themselves? Should education change the way it deals with the fact that education is changing faster and in shorter intervals? "The belief that education

---

1609 See Peters et al. 2018.

can be replaced by a computer program is a myth. Human contact and mentoring make a significant difference in learning outcomes"[1610], states Sebastian Thrun, chairman and co-founder of Udacity.

Education should change how it deals with teachers and/or teachers should change with respect to how technology and technological innovation is perceived. Teachers are not obliged to use technological applications just because they exist, because they are free of charge, because a company links it to a donation in favor of the school, etc. They are obliged to make ethically, pedagogically, and didactically informed and based, rational decisions about whether to use technological applications or not. The criteria of comprehensibility, manageability, and meaningfulness need to be respected. For example, a digital learning assistance system needs to be assessed from an ethical perspective as well.[1611] This could result in the identification of ethical risks such as dependence, of turning the pupils who are using the technology themselves into a product for providing data, of violations of the human right to privacy and data-protection, and so on. For example, Google, Apple, Microsoft offer modern infrastructure, user-friendly design, and powerful functions to schools under economic pressure – almost for free. But "Google Suite", "School Manager", "Microsoft Office 365", and "Windows 10" represent "spies in the classroom"[1612]: They collect as much data as possible from and about children and abuse them economically[1613] while children and their parents erroneously trust the schools and falsely assume that the public education systems are protecting them.

Video conference tools such as "Zoom" collect as much as personal data as possible from the hosts and participants of virtual meetings and sell this data to Facebook and other parties.[1614]

Beyond that, education should adapt to the digital transformation and prepare adequately for the technology-based change, but even more it should fulfill its design responsibility of digital transformation. Schools are a place where digital transformation must be designed, influenced, changed, stopped, etc. Education should involve finding ways to enjoy the ethical opportunities of data-based systems. Education should prepare

---

1610 Bossard 2018: 2.
1611 For an assessment of emotions-sensitive training-systems for humans with autism, see Dziobek et al. 2017.
1612 Fiechter 2019.
1613 See Ehrenhauser 2019.
1614 See Laaff 2020.

against the ethical risks of data-based systems as well.[1615] For example, the present endangerment of the human rights to privacy and to data-protection should be encountered by educational efforts resulting in "privacy literacy": "In our opinion, however, privacy does not have to come to an end. However, it is not a matter of course either, but requires first awareness and then action, that control such things. Especially autonomy as a relevant aspect here must also be maintained and mediated. A digital privacy competence seems to be the central means (privacy literacy), such a one but just not with the technical application of media, but rather with an awareness of their semiotic dimension and the constructive character of what is required in terms of content and communicated, as only then the application in practice is put on a solid foundation and behavior could be related and reflected upon. In sum, the following skills stand for a privacy competence: a) the knowledge of how media communicate and construct privacy semiotically (medial competence), (b) the ability to reflect on why private data should be considered sensitive (ethical competence), (c) the knowledge of who is collecting, processing and disclosing private data and for what purpose (structural competence), (d) the assessment of the consequences that from publication private data could result (risk competence), (e) the knowledge of possible (self-)protection measures and privacy protective communication media (action competence), and (f) the empowerment to reflect on power aspects of digitalization – short big data, big power, and big money (systemic analysis and political knowledge)."[1616]

Moreover, education must take into account the massive reduction of paid professional tasks in the course of digital transformation and the use of data-based systems.

Education should prepare for the digital transformation strengthening the position of humans in the world, empowering them to deal adequately with the rapid change and enhancing the unique competencies of humans, thus distinguishing humans from data-based systems[1617] –, e.g., an attitude grounded in human dignity, human rights, and rights of the child,[1618] ethical reason (*Vernunft*) instead of just technical rationality (*Verstand*), critical thinking, the ability to think in complex systems and/or to interact with complex systems, flexibility, social and interpersonal competence, creativity, arts, moral capability, autonomy, ethical competencies, the capability of

---

1615 See Schandel 2012.
1616 Grimm / Krah 2014: 21-22.
1617 See Brynjolfsson / McAfee 2014: 10-11.
1618 See Bellamy et al. 2007b.

humans to search, discuss, reflect upon, and define their own purposes of life, the capability of humans to devote working-time, spare time, and "societal time" in accordance with their own horizon of meaning. Education should provide a basis for the ability to take a self-confident standpoint in contexts of uncertainty.

Finally, it is the responsibility of education policy, school principals, teachers, and pupils to make schools

- a place where digital transformation and data-based systems are not something given by fate, but objects of human decisions;
- a place where digital transformation and data-based systems are shaped;
- a place of critical thinking about everything – including digital transformation and data-based systems and their place in human and in society's lives;
- a place to be strengthened in saying "yes" and in saying "no" from an ethical perspective to technology-based options;
- a place of empowerment as humans to live up to and continuously form rapidly and constantly changing realities and contexts;
- a place to learn to master uncertainty;
- a place with a clear focus on the unique competencies of humans;
- a place contributing to the present and future respect, protection, implementation, and realization of human dignity and human rights.

8.9 Life With Data-Based Systems

8.9.1 Humans and the Life With Data-Based Systems

"Digital humanism"[1619], "can the digital future be our home?"[1620], ... – doesn't one run the risk of attributing too much meaning, significance, and relevance to data-based systems if one thinks the fundamental ethical basis of peaceful and respectful coexistence of humans around it and/or if we expect data-based systems to provide us with a nest and/or if one attributes an entire separate world to data-based systems? Has humanity ever connotated its normative foundation and/or its embedding with a technology? Shouldn't it be the other way around by keeping alive the distinction

---

1619 See Nida-Ruemelin / Weidenfeld 2019.
1620 Zuboff 2019: 4.

between humans and data-based systems while acknowledging the intense interaction and intertwinement between humans and data-based systems?

The organization, structure, and design of a life with data-based systems lie in the hands of humans. They are responsible for creating something good or right and avoiding what is bad or wrong from an ethical viewpoint. Data-based systems and digital transformation do not happen by themselves – even if they have the ability for self-learning or are even "super-data-based systems". Figuratively speaking or put simply, the first line of code is always written by a human. "However, if one day we should actually put our fate into the decision-making power of digital machines, it would still be our own madness. We cannot get rid of the responsibility for the brooms we called."[1621] This points towards the exclusive responsibility of humans.[1622] It is up to humans to check again and again how they program and train data-based systems, or what they program and train data-based systems to do, to ensure that human dignity and human rights of all humans are respected – especially, e.g., in view of the risk to embed human racial prejudice in data-based systems.[1623] It is down to humans to shape digital transformation and data-based systems in such a way as the realization of existing ethical principles and norms can be adapted and the complexity of ethics be taken into account. It is down to humans to form digital transformation and data-based systems in such a way as ethical opportunities can be used and ethical risks, as well as ethical ambivalence, as well as the "dual use" problem can be mastered. It is down to humans to advance digital transformation and data-based systems in such a way that they serve humans, are used responsibly and fairly, respect all humans in their human dignity, contribute to the respect, protection, implementation, and realization of human rights for all humans, and respect the ecosystem sustainably. It is down to humans to organize and to structure, among others, working with data-based systems assigning work, providing informational support, and evaluating performance to humans in a way that humans "work with intelligent machines not only in an effective way, but also satisfying and meaningful way."[1624]

1621 Stadler 2017.
1622 See Kirchschlaeger 2014a; Posé 2019.
1623 See Misselhorn 2018: 80.
1624 Lee et al. 2015: 9.

8.9.2 Humans Shaping Digital Transformation and Data-Based Systems

While shaping digital transformation and data-based systems, one should keep in mind the uniqueness of this technology-based shift compared to earlier innovation-based eras. It is an intellectual temptation to compare this epoch of change to earlier times of technology-based revolution. For example, Erik Brynjolfsson, and Andrew McAfee compare their second machine age to the Industrial Revolution.[1625] Most of the discourse on digital transformation and data-based systems does the same. On a metaethical level, yielding to this intellectual temptation provokes three fundamental hermeneutic doubts: Why should every innovation-based transformation happen in the same way? There are no reasons why one could automatically assume that. This is, e.g., the underlying assumption of an affirmation like this one: "Computers and other digital advances are doing for mental power – the ability to use our brains to understand and shape our environments – what the steam engine and its descendants did for muscle power. They're allowing us to blow past previous limitations and taking us into new territory. (…) So a vast and unprecedented boost to mental power should be a great boost to humanity, just as earlier boost to physical power so clearly was."[1626] In contrast, theoretically it could also be possible that this technology-based transformation limits humanity or degenerates it. The idea here is to show that there are no reasons why the former should prevail over the latter. Just because it was the case with the Industrial Revolution, this will not automatically repeat itself with the digital transformation and data-based systems. In fact, following such a uniform line of argumentation implies an understanding of human history as linear progress. With history in general and especially in the case of history of science and technology, it can be shown that this is not the case.[1627]

Why should every innovation-based transformation lead to the same pattern of consequences, including benefiting from them if they are positive – and overcoming them if they are negative? "Digitization is going to bring with it some thorny challenges. This in itself should not be too surprising or alarming; even the most beneficial developments have unpleasant consequences that must be managed. The Industrial Revolution was accompanied by soot-filled London skies and horrific exploitation of child labor.

1625   See Brynjolfsson / McAfee 2014: 2-12.
1626   Brynjolfsson / McAfee 2014: 7-8.
1627   See Kuhn 1962; Laudan 1977.

What will be their modern equivalents?"[1628] The argument continues by pointing out that these challenges were met on the occasion of the Industrial Revolution and therefore that will be also the case with the negative consequences of the digital transformation and data-based systems. This seems to be an unfounded line of argumentation because, on the one hand, child labor and environmental pollution are still unacceptable parts of the value-chain of digital transformation and data-based systems as presented above in subchapter 7.19 Global Injustice. On the other, sharing the position that humans were able to get rid of the negative sides of the Industrial Revolution, this does not automatically mean that humans will also be able to liberate themselves from the downsides of digital transformation and data-based systems.

Why should something innovative, of all things, lead to the same method and path and reach similar patterns of result? "It (the second machine age) is an inflection point in the right direction"[1629]. Could it not be possible that all the negative effects listed by Erik Brynjolfsson and Andrew McAfee themselves make it that this innovation-based transformation is actually taking us in the *wrong direction* – namely by destroying humanity and the planet Earth – and that humans need to change that direction immediately? Just because something is new, this does neither mean that it is ethically legitimate nor that it is leading humanity in the right direction.

Beyond that, progress in itself cannot be an end from an ethical perspective. "All progress is progress toward an end, but there can be no progress in the formation, expression, and evaluation of ends themselves, only either their circumscription or proliferation. (…) to treat progress as an end-in-itself is usually to disavow actual ends – whether for equity, for diversity, for increasing gross domestic product, for more reported satisfactions on the happiness index, whatever the end may be – and by so disavowing them so too to relinquish the terms without which any notion of progress at all is finally unintelligible."[1630] Finally, one needs to acknowledge: "The future is a process, not a destination"[1631].

1628 Brynjolfsson / McAfee 2014: 10.
1629 Brynjolfsson / McAfee 2014: 11.
1630 Carrico 2013: 50.
1631 Sterling 2012.

8.9.3 The Responsibility of States and Non-State Actors for Digital Transformation and Data-Based Systems

States and non-state actors (such as companies, religious or worldview-based communities)[1632] carry this responsibility to shape digital transformation and data-based systems, because they can be understood as moral actors.[1633] Because they can be the source of the "freedom to act: ability to deliberately implement certain actions among the possibilities of doing or not doing that are possible in a certain situation", "foresight: ability to focus in advance on expected results and subsequently exercise freedom of action", "ability to survive: ability to rationally evaluate reasons and develop corresponding intentions", "co-concerned: ability to give (the above-mentioned abilities) a moral sense"[1634]. From this list of preconditions, no difference between moral *actors*, such as, e.g. religions, and moral *persons*, such as humans, can be established.

With reference to the ethical instrument of responsibility, it becomes clear that single individuals cannot carry the responsibility that emerges in the context of institutions and organizations.[1635] This becomes obvious in the shadow of the Holocaust where it is not sufficient that, for example, businesses as organizations or the Christian churches as institutions do not take responsibility and admit to their guilt, but blame single employees or believers, and where it is not sufficient "for the churches merely to point to the difference between Christian anti-Semitism and the Nazi variety. If they are to restore their moral integrity and become strong supporters of the new depth of human responsibility to which the experience of the Holocaust calls humankind in the twenty-first century, they must first come to grips with their general failure in moral responsibility toward Hitler's victims, particularly the Jews. Nothing else will suffice."[1636]

Furthermore, it can be established that, for example, religions are not only subjects of legal, but also of moral responsibility, because religions fulfil the demand that goes back to Cicero's legitimation of tyrannicide to violate positive law if the positive law is bad.[1637] Religions as subjects of moral responsibility have this option for a course of action. Additionally,

---

1632 See Kirchschlaeger 2016f; Kirchschlaeger 2017e; Kirchschlaeger 2015c; Kirchschlaeger 2017f.
1633 See Griffin 2008: 32.
1634 Kettner 2001: 149.
1635 See Neuhaeuser 2011: 90.
1636 Pawlikowski 2001: 284.
1637 See Neuhaeuser 2011: 92; Radbruch 1932; Alexy 1986.

state and non-state actors are moral actors, because humans create their communities as moral actors.[1638] State and non-state actors, however, are moral actors and not moral persons, because they are not bearers of human dignity.[1639] Therefore, state and non-state actors are also not bearers of human rights, but only of collective rights for the protection of human rights of all humans as individuals.[1640] Finally, religions, for example, are in so far moral actors as the Divine, God, the God-like or the Transcendent is their guideline or model for acting morally – expressed, for example, for the Jewish-Christian tradition in the following: "Because I am your God who has created you as a humane society, you should and can live and protect this humane society."[1641]

State and non-state actors should not only serve their own particular interests, but rather all humans and society as a whole. This means that states must not only represent national interests but also design and advance digital transformation and data-based systems with a global horizon. As subjects of international law, states have to respect, protect, implement legally binding human rights,[1642] and contribute to their realization.

Companies must not only strive for their own profit, but also have to respect, protect, and implement human rights and contribute to their realization. They have to take on social responsibility and have to decide and act in a just and sustainable manner.[1643] Through their business conduct, they need to "contribute to enabling people to shape their lives better, more successfully and with greater self-determination. The finance sector, which, inevitably, is very oriented on capital, has to respond to the question of how it will contribute to further prosperity and also social justice"[1644]. Companies do not only have to create economic benefit, but also to contribute socially. "Money – just like economy, capital markets and companies – is not an end in itself, to put it simply. It is a means to shape coexistence and has to be handled responsibly"[1645]. The intensity of the reciprocal interdependence in the course of globalization multiplies this power of companies, which is why a failure or partial failure on the part of

---

1638 See Neuhaeuser 2011: 123.
1639 See Neuhaeuser 2011: 181-220.
1640 See Kirchschlaeger 2016f: 152-160.
1641 Zenger 2009: 222.
1642 See Kaelin 2004: 17; Spenlé 2005.
1643 See Kirchschlaeger 2015e.
1644 Haasis 2012: 494.
1645 Neher 2013.

companies to contribute to society as a whole is not sustainable for a society.

In the course of a learning process, there is growth in the awareness of companies of their own power and the associated scope for action, of the interaction of economic and ethical rationality and in the danger of losing sight of ethical rationality. "Market economy lives from entrepreneurial freedom, which needs to be filled not only in the economic sense, but also ethically responsible. Therefore, ethical corporate responsibility is indispensable"[1646]. The importance of corporate social responsibility becomes clear when visualizing the following situation: "A given company relocates to a country with unregulated market conditions, where a lack of ethical and ecological standards allows said company to operate at lower costs. The pressures of competition prompt others to follow this example, catapulting the host countries (which seek to retain capital, and maintain employment rates and tax revenues) into a competition over the lowest possible standard. This triggers a downward spiral that ends with the hypothetical 'worst case scenario' in which profits are privatized and the costs and consequences thereof socialized. On the slopes of an unbalanced global economy, this 'snowball effect' of a one-dimensional pursuit of profit threatens to launch an avalanche of precarious economic conduct"[1647].

Religions prove to be moral actors in various aspects, and therefore must get more involved in the discourse about digital transformation and data-based systems. Religions and morality are closely connected, because religions have their own morality based on their traditions, teachings, beliefs, values, and principles and have discussions and reflections of their own ideas of morality – for example in the Christian tradition in the shape of theological ethics.[1648] This close connection also encompasses that religions, for example, based on their moral competence in a society, take on the role of a public authority for moral questions, critically scrutinize self-evident facts or demand the implementation of norms. There is an interest in their position towards general questions of a peaceful and dignified co-existence.[1649]

The contributions of religions join the choir of the various voices of public discourse[1650] on digital transformation and data-based systems. De-

---

1646 Wiemeyer 2013: 16.
1647 Dierksmeier 2012: 17.
1648 See Schockenhoff 2013.
1649 See Arens 2007: 64.
1650 See Hilpert 2006: 280.

cisive for their power of persuasion is their argumentative radiance and less the reference to authority, in particular outside of the respective religious community. Furthermore, religions can only have an integrative effect on society as a moral actor if their justifications for their positions are rationally accessible and plausible.

Due to their nature as exemplifying morality, shaping morality, giving morality, and founding morality,[1651] religious and worldview-based communities have a special responsibility to contribute to a scientific penetration within the framework of theology, and thus to the criticism and co-shaping of research and science, as well as to social and economic transformation processes such as digital transformation and data-based systems.

Religions, which are addressed by a divine revelation or refer to transcendence, on which base their decisions and actions on, can live morally by striving for what is morally good and right in the world. Religions as moral actors strive to stand at the side of the oppressed, the excluded, and the victims of power abuse and not on the side of the oppressors, the ones doing the excluding, or the ones abusing their power.

When religions live morally in a society, the separation of state and religion needs to be upheld. "On the one hand, it needs to be avoided to mix religion and politics on the level of the respective systems of representation (state - church/religious community). On the other hand, the impression must not be nurtured that religion as social potential is apolitical and has only an individualized and privatized right to exist."[1652] At the same time, the essential functions that religions fulfill as moral actors for a state and a society need to be pointed out: *inter alia*, moral education, conscience formation, contributions to finding an ethical basic consensus in a society, "a contribution to the development of religious policy or a viable definition of the relationship between religious policy and religious law"[1653], and also giving and setting norms. These aspects, however, must not be radicalized to *either* fall into the pattern of the age of Enlightenment and reduce religions to their role as "cultural medium of moralizing through popular education"[1654] *or* religions "claiming this privilege of interpretation for themselves"[1655] and focusing on it. Religion is also not to be considered as a

---

1651 See Kirchschlaeger 2017g.
1652 Heimbach-Steins 2012a: 211.
1653 Heimbach-Steins 2012a: 210.
1654 Luebbe 2001: 128.
1655 Wils 2004: 19.

"drawer in the chest of drawers of culture"[1656] because this limitation to "religious things" does not do justice to the relevance of salvation and the critical questions of humans about everything.

All humans are to be understood as capable of morality. Religions as moral actors live morally. As such, they contribute to the interaction between the law and ethics as "allies in view of the objective to create a society where all can live with each other: a good, sisterly society (...) that takes measure from the human person."[1657]

Religions unite in this duty as moral actors to create a difference for a positive present and future. They also have in common that the boundaries of the field of tension between the pole of the commitment to human rights and the pole of resistance against human rights are not oriented to the boundaries of religious or worldview-based communities, but rather along groups and trends – within religions and within worldview-based communities, as well as across religions and worldview-based communities. "Today Jews, Christians and Muslims must stand together, in defense of humanity, the sanctity of life, religious freedom and the honor of God himself. The real clash of the 21st century will not be between civilizations or religions but within them. It will be between those who accept and those who refuse the separation of religion and power."[1658]

Another aspect is revealed when religions are understood as moral actors who are closely linked, interacting with and constituting for a moral life: Religions have the effect of shaping morals. "For believers, religions in particular have the function to give an ethical sense by transporting a vision of a good life and a fair creation of society."[1659] Here, religions have to be conscious of the epistemic difference between truths of faith and moral truths.[1660]

At the same time, religious moral education tries to master ethical challenges that emerge from the reality in the exchange with the philosophical discourse on those questions, "to justify their options and normative judgements, to introduce them into social discussions and to present them in a way that is accessible and plausible for people of different ideological viewpoints."[1661]

1656 Rosenzweig 1979: 966.
1657 Martini 2001: 17.
1658 Sacks 2015.
1659 Reder 2013: 368.
1660 See Demmer 2000: 12.
1661 Heimbach-Steins 2012b: 12; see Schockenhoff 2015: 56-60.

Apart from shaping morality (and similarly to this), religions as moral actors can also provide morality by supporting state actors – even if they are religiously and worldview-based pluralistic –[1662] and the international community, in particular the UN, as well as non-state actors (e.g., companies, non-governmental organization) with moral principles and ideas of morality. This is to be understood against the background of the "Boeckenfoerde Dilemma". *"The liberal, secular state lives by prerequisites which it cannot guarantee itself. This is the great adventure it has undertaken for freedom's sake"*[1663]. This is related to the fact that states, for example, or the UN can only be regarded as legitimate if they respect and uphold human rights, but they cannot themselves develop morality on which a justification of human rights can be built. For the sake of their own liberality, states and state communities are not even allowed to present people with a morality and may not strive to convince them of a morality.[1664] "For the sake of their own existence and future, modern societies rely on religious groups such as the Christian churches that protect the fundamental values, norms and rights, which are in severe danger to be eroded in the social public from their last anchor in the transcendent sphere and to uphold the religious-cultural inheritance from which in particular secular and non-denominational societies must be able to live."[1665] For example, the secular state benefits when religions "redefine from their inner perspective the relationship of a religious community (a) to a liberal state (b) to other religious communities (c) and to the secular society as a whole."[1666] A secular society also wins if religions contribute to the normative discourse with "an ability for reality and truth that is based on religion (...), (i.e. the one) on which one needs to rely if one is to exist resistant to ideology under conditions of enlightenment"[1667]. Furthermore, religions succeed in introducing the Divine, God, the God-like, or the Transcendent as an authority of final responsibility of humans and placing humans within a larger context.[1668]

All other social actors are winning, if, for example, religions contribute to the public discourse of a society on digital transformation and data-

---

1662 See Palm 2013: 151.
1663 Boeckenfoerde 2006: 112, emphasis in the text; see also Luebbe 1990b: 297-306.
1664 See Graf 2015: 85-86.
1665 Koch 2012: 138.
1666 Habermas 2004.
1667 Luebbe 1990b: 280-281.
1668 See Schroeder 2003: 34.

based systems about their horizons of belief, knowledge, thinking and understanding and the creation of meaning. "Therefore, the liberal state must not only expect secular citizens to take religious fellow citizens they meet in the political public seriously as persons. It may even expect from them that they do not exclude the possibility of recognizing their own suppressed institutions in the contents of religious statements and pronouncements – i.e. potential contents of truth that can be introduced into a public argument, which is free from religion."[1669]

This means at the same time that a secular state will not exclude the existence of a "post-secular society"[1670], where "in public, this constituting area of critical debate between the citizens in a secular society, secular and nonsecular communication takes place simultaneously and where this simultaneousness will create a specific dynamic of development and conflict."[1671] Secularization is not to be misunderstood as an anti-religious reality or a reality without religion, but as "a state of increasing pluralization of religious and non-religious possibilities"[1672]. Secularization also does not mean the decay of a society from a moral point of view.[1673] Also, post-secularity must not be seen from a temporal perspective, but rather from a programmatic one. This program includes contributions from religions to the public discourse[1674] as well as moral contributions.

In viewing religions as moral actors, a secular state has to allow for the duty of tolerance, which is guaranteed by the constitution in the sense of a "respect of the dignity, the personality and differing beliefs and decisions of faith of others and, therefore, reducing one's own excessive demands and expectations of realizing religious beliefs."[1675] This duty of tolerance implies for religions as moral actors the imperative to accept "that the law and political actions are not directly justified and asserted on the basis of religious revelation or ideological position."[1676] The duty of tolerance does not aim at furthering religious or worldview-based indifference. "The political neutralization of religious and worldview-based claims to truth [...] is rather the answer to the question of how peace can be reinstalled and secured under conditions of competing claims to truth, in particular when

---

1669 Habermas 2015: 52.
1670 Habermas 2001b: 39.
1671 Loretan 2011: 423.
1672 Casanova 2015: 19.
1673 See Joas 2015b.
1674 See Holderegger 2015: 73.
1675 Friederich 1993: 350-351.
1676 Hilpert 2006: 280; see also Taylor 2015: 39.

zealots claim them. It is this reason of peace on which the practice of religious tolerance was based on initially."[1677] This demand for tolerance is not a "tolerance of the state that can only be hoped for, but [has] the status of an enforceable legal claim"[1678] in the right to freedom of thought, conscience and religion.[1679] This serves the respect and high regard of "the dignity of belief that wants to be freely taken and lived."[1680] Tolerance will lead to recognizing the respective other precisely in his otherness.[1681] In accordance with this, the secular state demands that religions have to adapt themselves, because they accept the preconditions of the state under the rule of law (*inter alia* human rights), even if they base themselves on a secular morality.[1682] For religions, this can also mean understanding human rights following the Universal Declaration of Human Rights of 1948 as continuous source of global values, outside and within religions,[1683] informing digital transformation and data-based systems.

Religions as moral actors are confronted with the need to justify moral principles, ideas and norms in order to enforce them. With the recourse to their faith, a religious justification of morality succeeds in directly addressing members of the respective religion. The argumentative effect and power of persuasion of such a justification for morality has a unique and particular quality for members of the respective religion. It draws its power from the advantage that, due to its reference to God, for example, and its order of being, its validity can hardly be surpassed in its immediacy and absoluteness. At the same time, it can draw stringent lines of argument and therefore show that the specific morality should be valid.

However, the aspect of belief in particular can also limit a religious justification in its effect, because for non-believers or believers of other faiths, the justification might be difficult to comprehend, since this approach is not purely rational, but only immediately acceptable for those who also share this belief. Therefore, for religious justifications, it needs to be assumed that their relevance might be limited. This is because it might, for example, not be possible to fulfill the principle of generalizability, resulting in an overload in view of a pluralistic circle of recipients.

1677 Luebbe 1990b: 76; see Rawls 1993.
1678 Bielefeldt 1993: 466.
1679 See Kirchschlaeger 2013f.
1680 Bielefeldt 1993: 466.
1681 See Lehmann 2015: 73-78; Schockenhoff 2014b: 465-475.
1682 See Habermas 2011b: 14.
1683 See Kirchschlaeger 2015f.

These thoughts lead to the question of how the term "justification" is to be understood in this context. Because of the reference to transcendence of religious reasons, which provoke the suspicion that they ultimately close themselves off to rational questions and arguments, which allow for proof and conclusions, the term "theological foundation" seems to be adequate to describe this religious path.[1684] A "theological foundation" of morality contains a line of argument, which is based on beliefs or an ideological basis and contains a certain logic in itself. It does not renounce its transcendent reference, but sets a morality in a certain horizon of meaning. This theological horizon of meaning is not only motivating, but the theological tradition of belief lives off altruistic testimony, because as such it also attains a practical plausibility. The conviction is conveyed by practice.

This is why, apart from the theological foundation of morality, a justification of morality is also needed that also makes morality plausible for humans who, for example, do not believe in the love of God or who do not love God.[1685] To simply assume that all people think of the same things as morally good is no longer tenable in today's discourse,[1686] which is shaped by freedom of thought, conscience and religion, as well as tolerance and pluralism, which is understood as a "positive principle that demands from all religious communities to respect and acknowledge each other and to lead a religious dialogue"[1687]. This is because the above-mentioned freedom entails a diverse range of ideas regarding what is good. The respect of the moral self-determination of the individual, understood as responsible self-regulation, is also expressed by this, which makes belief and religious practice in freedom and without coercion possible.[1688] All three aspects naturally have nothing to do with relativism and giving up on religious truth. It is rather a matter of dealing with one's own claim to truth[1689] and of taking the unquestioned self-evidence that what one regards as normal – due to tradition, habit, etc. – can be accepted as an overarching concept of the good life,[1690] and replacing it with an attitude of learning as a "consequence of the provisional nature of the knowledge we have achieved in each case. To be open for new, in the sense of greater and deeper awareness, perception of change and sensibility for new problems connected

---

1684 See Kirchschlaeger 2013a: 153-155.
1685 See Raz 1986.
1686 See Marschuetz 2009: 163-165.
1687 Casanova 2015: 20.
1688 See Raz 1986: 395-399.
1689 See Kirchschlaeger 2010b; Kirchschlaeger 2012b.
1690 See Hilpert 1995.

with the incessant willingness to correct oneself, is the drawback of the contingency of our trying to understand God's will."[1691] The fact that one accepts the need to justify moral principles, ideas, and norms and struggles for an ethical justification proves to be an expression of respect for the moral capability of all humans.[1692] This claim to universality for a moral justification also has an effect on religious morality.[1693] It means that one has recognized that the justification needs to be formulated in such a way that it must be conceivable that all humans, given their effective freedom and autonomy as well as their full equality – within a model of thought and not within a real worldwide referendum – would agree upon these reasons on ethical grounds.

It also means a multi-layered commitment of religious and worldview-based communities for determining and agreeing on objectives, limits, frameworks, principles, and norms for data-based systems and digital transformation. "Ethical regulation of the design and use of AI is a complex but necessary task. The alternative may lead to devaluation of individual rights and social values, rejection of AI-based innovation, and ultimately a missed opportunity to use AI to improve individual wellbeing and social welfare. Humanity learned this lesson the hard way when it did not regulate the impact of the industrial revolution on labor forces, and when it recognized too late the environmental impact of massive industrialization and global consumerism. It has taken a very long time, social unrest, and even revolutions to protect workers' rights and establish sustainability frameworks."[1694] Furthermore, religious and worldview-based communities can take on the important task – as elaborated in subchapter 7.18 Reduction of Paid Jobs – of accompanying humans in the questioning and searching for the meaning of life, the conception of humans and a self-conception, as well as creating space for this discussion.

8.9.4 What World With Data-Based Systems Do We Dream Of?

From an ethical viewpoint, it should be the aim that data-based systems will contribute to solving global problems, to the implementation of justice, responsibility, and human rights for all humans and to the respect of

---

1691 Hilpert 2013: 135-136.
1692 See Pianalto 2012.
1693 See Moehring-Hesse 1997.
1694 Taddeo / Floridi 2018.

nature, and not that a few people and a few companies will get rich and fulfil their own specific interests.

The guiding question should be: What world with data-based systems do we dream of? The guiding questions should not be: Which world brings the biggest profit for a few technology companies? The following paradigmatic example is able to illustrate what this distinction expresses as well as taking away the fear that this is only illusionist theory and unrealistic. "In 2000 a group of computer scientists and engineers at Georgia Tech collaborated on a project called the 'Aware Home'[1695]. It was meant to be a 'living laboratory' for the study of 'ubiquitous computing'. They imagined a 'human-home symbiosis' in which many animate and inanimate processes would be captured by an elaborate network of 'context aware sensors' embedded in the house and by wearable computers worn by the home's occupants. The design called for an 'automated wireless collaboration' between the platform that hosted personal information from the occupants' wearables and a second one that hosted the environmental information from the sensors. There were three working assumptions: *first*, the scientists and engineers understood that the new data systems would produce an entirely new knowledge domain. *Second*, it was assumed that the rights to that new knowledge and the power to use it to improve one's life would belong exclusively to the people who live in the house. *Third*, the team assumed that for all of its digital wizardry, the *Aware Home* would take its place as a modern incarnation of the ancient conventions that understand 'home' as the private sanctuary of those who dwell within its walls."[1696] Digital transformation and data-based systems are also possible by exemplifying and keeping alive justice, responsibility, and human rights. Data-based systems can be part of the better world we are dreaming of without having to give up human rights, human dignity, freedom, autonomy, privacy, or data-protection. The narrative must and can be changed that it would be inherent to digital transformation and data-based systems that they further injustice, irresponsibility and they violate human rights – as this exemplary case shows: Humanity can enjoy the undoubted benefits and opportunities of data-based systems without giving up its humanity. Human rights violations, irresponsibility, and injustice are not a precondition for technological innovation. For example, the narrative must be overcome that search engines would have to technically store the data of the searches: "The reality is that search engines including Google do retain this information for

---

1695 Kidd et al. 1999.
1696 Zuboff 2019: 5-6, emphasis in the text.

some time."[1697] The reality is that it is technically not necessary but beneficial for the providers of search engines. Or, as an example, it is not technically necessary for the provider of email-services (Google, etc.) to scan the private emails in order to target advertisement accordingly.[1698] Or, for example, a social network (Facebook, etc.) can also be run without tracking the users online and without disclosing, sharing, or selling their private information, data, and social behavior.[1699] One does not have to claim that privacy would no longer be a social norm in order to run the technical side of a social network. (It is not without a certain irony that the same person making that claim – Facebook-Founder Mark Zuckerberg – bought the houses around his home to protect his own privacy ...).[1700]

For example, an alternative to such a system of datadeology, datatorship, and datalism could be a revision of digital governance that includes a new classification system for personal data and a distinction between "official data (data authenticated by official bodies), collective data (data that people agree to share with a pre-defined group for collective purposes) and privy data (data that is volunteered by the individual or inferred through their behavior)."[1701] It is questionable, however, whether the sale of one's own personal data is compatible with the human right to privacy and data protection due to the principle of the inalienability of human rights.

One possible solution to make data use ethically acceptable in accordance with the right to privacy and data protection would be the "purpose-driven data use" approach. The "purpose-driven data use" approach starts from the right to privacy and data protection as a prerequisite and respects this right. In automated driving, for example, people must identify themselves with their "personal data" in order to enjoy automated driving at all. But this data is only provided so that mobility providers know that the ride will be paid for and, for example, that they can cover the cost of repairing the vehicle in the event of damage. This data may therefore only be used to enable payment for mobility and, for example, damage – it may neither be used for other purposes nor sold on to third parties. The users also do not have the option of selling this data themselves (e.g. to obtain a discount). To enable the driving process in the first place, the users enter their location and destination. However, this "action data" (data that includes or is

---

1697 Newmann 2009.
1698 See Levy 2011: 172-173.
1699 See Johnson 2010.
1700 See King 2016.
1701 Snower/Twomey/Farell 2020: 6-8.

based on an action) may also only be used to enable mobility – it may neither be used for other purposes nor resold to third parties. There is also no possibility for the users to sell this data themselves (e.g., to gain advantages in automated driving). The individual "action data" may only be retained for the optimization of the individual mobility service. Fully anonymized "action data" may only be kept for the optimization of the collective mobility service with the informed consent of the users – without coercion, without offering advantages. To illustrate this approach in its feasibility, the following analogy serves: when one goes to the doctor, one also shares his/her "personal data" so that he/she knows who he/she has in front of him/her and tells him/her about one's illness ("action data") in order to hopefully experience relief from suffering as well as healing, without either the doctor being allowed to resell this data or the patient being offered to sell this data in order to receive better medical treatment. Furthermore, for the payment as well as the enabling of mobility from A to B, for example, it is irrelevant with whom one starts this journey (whether, for example, with the wife or husband or with the secret lover). The doctor may also keep the patient's file with the medical history strictly confidential – exclusively for the purpose of better treatment of the patient. It is also possible to share completely anonymized data for research purposes if the patient gives informed consent to this sharing.

Human rights-based digital transformation, human rights-based data-based systems HRBDS, and fulfilling the 30 DSA-principles with promising innovative and economically profitable force are possible – let's make it happen.

8.10 One World

Multinational technology corporations create and give wings to the narrative that they operate in a "new" world, in a "separate" world – in the virtual world. In this allegedly "other" world – that they understand to be "their" world – there aren't any laws. It is different from what they call the "old" world where there are democratic institutions, the rule of laws, rights and duties, contracts, market rules, stakeholders and their interests, the sovereignty of the people, and the moral authority of humans. In this "new" world, multinational technology corporations claim for themselves total control and absolute freedom in the name of advancement of technology-based innovation – without any limits, without any quality control, without any checks and balances. This becomes even more relevant in the face of their (not entirely modest) assertions, e.g., that they know everything about all humans (do they really?).

This narrative of a "new" world, a "separate" world, and of a "virtual" world clashes with the position of nation states and the international community recognizing "virtual reality" or a "virtual world" but embedding it in the "real world" and understanding it as part of the same world. As a consequence, the same legal and ethical norms and standards are valid for the "virtual" and for the "real", the same institutions and authorities are in place for a reality without data-based systems as for a reality with data-based systems.

A compromise embraces the construction of a "hybrid" world representing a combination of the "real" and the "virtual", of a reality without data-based systems and a reality with data-based systems. The strengths of this concept of a "hybrid" world lies in the emphasis of the intense interaction and the intertwinement of humans and the world with data-based systems. Its weaknesses consist in the exaggeration of the sphere of influence and the significance of data-based systems, in the blurring of the lines between "real" and "virtual" – between a world without data-based systems and a world with data-based systems as well as in the complete denial of a life without data-based systems that nevertheless still exists, continues to exist, and will always exist. For example, an interpersonal relation between two humans can be a part of life without data-based systems – in the present and in the future.

Acknowledging the epistemic limitation of the viewpoint of a human with all the limitations of anthropocentrism and of human reason in general, from an ethical perspective a life without data-based systems and a life with data-based systems and/or aspects, elements, and spheres of human existence without data-based systems as well as aspects, elements, and spheres of human existence with data-based systems belong to the same *one* world, for which humans possess a responsibility to take care of sustainably, in which humans must strive for intergenerational omni-dynamic social justice, and where humans must respect human rights of all humans. Without or with data-based systems, it is *one* world that lies in our hands.

8.11 Trust

Life with data-based systems should be based on trust in humans, companies and states, which use data-based systems. As has been shortly mentioned above in chapter 4 Critical Review of Terms, we can only trust humans, not data-based systems,[1702] because trust is a relational concept and therefore needs a relationship.[1703] As the possibility to attribute person-hood to data-based systems as elaborated above in chapter 3 Can Ethical Judgment Be Delegated to Technologies? does not exist, a relationship is not possible with a data-based system, and this also rules out trust in data-based systems.

It can be observed that in everyday language the word "trust" is used in wider terms. "In everyday communication we don't only trust concrete people, such as friends, relatives or partners, but we also trust in 'lifeless' things such as technical machines, airplanes, media or institutions"[1704]. This presumed "independence from faces"[1705] of trust can, however, be de-ciphered as "abbreviated phrases"[1706]. "We don't trust the bridge as such, but the engineers who constructed the bridge; we don't trust the car as such, but the engineers and workers who built it; we don't trust the system as such, but the people who fill it; and we don't trust the parliament as such, but the delegates who give it life. But because we don't know these people personally, we put our attention on the establishments where they work or the technical products that they produce and with which we are confronted somewhat more directly."[1707] But this does not seem to be suf-ficient, because it can be observed that we strive to humanize this abstract trust. We are creating "access points", where "face-dependent and face-in-dependent bonds come into contact"[1708]. For example, as representatives of technologies, humans appear to take account of the relationality of trust and thus hope to create trust in the representatives and will have an effect on the technologies through these humans. Without these human repre-sentatives as points of reference, there would be no trust created, because technologies are unable to build relationships and cannot be considered as objects of trust, because a relationship with them is not possible. "Cars can be dependable, but not loyal, because they have no feelings or cannot react to reasons. With regards to lifeless things, we can, therefore, only talk

---

1702 For the opposite position of trust in data-based systems, see Kirkpatrick et al. 2017; for distrust in data-based systems, see Isaac / Bridewell 2017; Winikoff 2018.
1703 See Hartmann 2011: 82-85; Nickel et al. 2010.
1704 Hartmann 2011: 42.
1705 Giddens 1995: 116.
1706 Hartmann 2011: 283.
1707 Hartmann 2011: 283-284.
1708 Giddens 1995: 107.

about loyalty, trust and, I believe, guilt, in a metaphorical sense."[1709] Therefore trust in the humans behind data-based systems should be sought rather than an attempt to, for instance, create a human-machine social interface for trust.[1710]

Connected to this, justice, responsibility, and human rights should be used as criteria when choosing or allocating who will be trusted with the development, production, organization, infrastructure, management, and use of data-based systems. For example, currently the question arises if the company "Huawei", which has at least a close relationship to the Chinese Government, meaning a totalitarian system characterized as a digital dictatorship by its self-image and practice, should be trusted with developing the necessary infrastructure for 5G. As it cannot be ruled out that a government that is about to introduce a country-wide total surveillance of inhabitants on their territory[1711] could use this infrastructure to aim for global surveillance, or rather, it is very plausible that they will do it, since they programmatically declared it, such an infrastructure must not be given to such a company, even if this would be the cheapest option from an economic point of view and the most promising option from a technological standpoint. Otherwise, there would be the danger that human rights, in particular the freedom of humans, would be violated and disrespected by the Chinese dictatorship even outside of Chinese territory.

As trust requires a living relationship, humans, companies, and states using data-based systems must behave in the sense of sustainable relationship building and positive relationship management with humans, with humans working for companies, and with humans working for states. This trust comes from fair and responsible acts, because of the respect, the protection, the implementation, and realization of human rights of all humans.[1712] This trust does not simply come from information and awareness-raising campaigns, from sharing knowledge ("we only need to explain data-based systems to people, and then they will accept it") or from propaganda. Trust needs to be earned.[1713] Rather than explanations, statements, and voluntary commitments – meaning words – we need trustworthy actions and confidence-inspiring behavior of humans, of humans working

---

1709 Scanlon 2008: 161.
1710 See Atkinson / Clark 2013; Schaefer et al. 2016.
1711 See Zuboff 2019: 388-394; Amnesty International Switzerland 2019.
1712 See Hasselbalch 2016.
1713 See Hartmann 2011.

for companies and using data-based systems, and of humans working for states and using data-based systems.

8.12 Sustainable Development

From an ethical standpoint – guided by the principle of responsibility, intergenerational omnidynamic social justice, and human rights – digital transformation and data-based systems should contribute to sustainable development by taking into account the economic, ecological, and social perspectives. Sustainable development aims "to ensure that it meets the needs of the present without compromising the ability of future generations to meet their own needs"[1714]. Sustainable development possesses three pillars of the economic, ecological, and social perspectives, which all need to be respected and taken into account. Sustainable development embraces "(a) justice (with the two different forms, intergenerative and intragenerative, and related issues such as minimum standards of human living conditions, participation rights, risks and precautions, etc.)

(b) focus on the problem of scarce ecological resources (which is reflected, for example, in the formulation of environmental management rules),

(c) safeguarding the productive forces in society; and

(d) societal responsiveness (with recent discourse emphasizing cultural diversity as well as governance issues)"[1715]. Technology-based progress can enhance sustainable development when it includes the economic, ecological, and social standpoint and considers its economic, ecological, and social impact and consequences. Devaki Jain understands the concept of development as "human development"[1716]. Technological progress can contribute to "human development" if it is sustainable.

The concept of sustainable development is expressed by a report to the "Club of Rome" in 1972: "If there is cause for deep concern, there is also cause for hope. Deliberately limiting growth would be difficult, but not impossible. The way to proceed is clear, and the necessary steps, although they are new ones for human society, are well within human capabilities. Man possesses, for a small moment in his history, the most powerful combination of knowledge, tools, and resources the world has ever known. He [she] has all that is physically necessary to create a totally new form of hu-

---

1714 United Nations 1987.
1715 Burger 2007: 17.
1716 Jain 2004: 304.

man society – one that would be built to last for generations. The two missing ingredients are a realistic, long-term goal that can guide humanity to the equilibrium society and the human will to achieve that goal. Without such a goal and a commitment to it, short-term concerns will generate the exponential growth that drives the world system toward the limits of the earth and ultimate collapse. With that goal and that commitment, mankind would be ready now to begin a controlled, orderly transition from growth to global equilibrium."[1717]

The United Nations' Sustainable Development Goals (SDGs) can provide guidance when attempts are being made to contribute to sustainable development through digital transformation and data-based systems. The United Nations' Sustainable Development Goals (SDGs) "are an urgent call for action by all countries – developed and developing – in a global partnership. They recognize that ending poverty and other deprivations must go hand-in-hand with strategies that improve health and education, reduce inequality, and spur economic growth – all while tackling climate change and working to preserve our oceans and forests."[1718] Digital transformation and data-based systems not only have the potential to make a positive difference in the efforts for reaching the United Nations' Sustainable Development Goals (SDGs), the sustainable shaping of digital transformation and data-based systems is a *conditio qua non* for a success story for humanity and the planet Earth in this area.

8.13 "Homo Dignitatis" Instead of "Homo Digitalis"

The idea of "homo digitalis"[1719] is opposed by "homo dignitatis"[1720]. "Homo dignitatis" emphasizes that humans are holders of human dignity, which is protected by human rights. All humans have, hence, human rights, which protect them in the essential elements and areas of human existence necessary for survival and for a life as a human – a life with human dignity. The "super-fundamental right to human dignity"[1721] needs to be defended against data-based systems and in the course of digital trans-

---

1717 Meadows et al. 1972.
1718 United Nations 2015.
1719 See Capurro 2017.
1720 See Kirchschlaeger 2019a.
1721 Hofstetter 2014: 219.

formation.[1722] Understanding humans as "homo dignitatis" instead of trying to digitalize humans and seeing them as digitalizable based on a concept of "homo digitalis" makes a fundamental difference, for example, in building a factory with efficiency in mind or in a more "human-oriented"[1723] way, or in giving data-based societies – instead of knowledge societies[1724] or ubiquitous knowledge societies[1725] – the necessary and empowering vision of humanity, solidarity, and human rights. Data-based societies embrace capabilities to create, generate, produce, provide, share, collect, analyze, process, transform, disseminate, and sometimes use data to build and apply knowledge. "Homo dignitatis" uses these data-reliant processes to serve human and ecological flourishing. "We do not need to take the structural inequalities of the past into the future, which we are creating"[1726].

"Homo dignitatis" avoids the evolution of "homo ignorans" – an indifferent being just reacting and depending on digital and data-based stimuli and more and more receding because "skill opens corners of reality, so to speak, that are inaccessible to the unskilled. To the master woodworker, as not to the novice, a good piece of wood is a field of activity, and invitation to shape and create. (...) If Automania is really on the horizon, then a vast range of such experiences will shortly be out of reach for most people – except those with leisure and money to invest deeply in skilled hobbies."[1727] Instead, "homo dignitatis" celebrates humans as "homo quaerens"[1728] – humans asking questions and experiencing problems – and at the same time as "homo sapiens est homo faber"[1729] by recognizing that human technological, mental, artistic, and intellectual abilities are to be understood in a complementary way.

What concrete impact the emergence and presence of "homo dignitatis" has, will be shown in the following by taking an ethical look at the research project "Moral Machine" of the Massachusetts Institute of Technology (MIT).

Starting from the assumption that machine intelligence will support humans in their ever more complex tasks or will take over completely and

---

1722 See, e.g., in the area of virtual self-presentation, Fricke 2011.
1723 See Menez et al. 2016.
1724 See UNESCO 2005: 27.
1725 See Kaivo-oja / Roth 2015: 4-9.
1726 Bernau 2017; see Helbing 2015m.
1727 Zoller 2017.
1728 See Gerhardt 2019: 49-78.
1729 See Gerhardt 2019: 118-164.

that this greater "autonomy"[1730] may lead to situations where they need to make "autonomous"[1731] decisions, the MIT aims with its project "Moral Machine" "to take the discussion further, by providing a platform for building a crowd-sourced picture of the human opinion on how machines should make decisions when faced with moral dilemmas, and crowd-sourcing assembly and discussion of potential scenarios of moral consequence."[1732] Online, all people are invited to click through scenarios where a self-driving vehicle is facing a moral dilemma and decide whether, for example, an adult or a child, one person or ten persons, etc. should be run over. From an ethical viewpoint, the following questions arise from this research approach: Based on the above in chapter 3 Can Ethical Judgment Be Delegated to Technologies? outlined explanations that machines lack vulnerability, conscience, freedom, responsibility, and autonomy, as well as moral capability, talking of "moral machines", machine "autonomy", or "autonomous" decisions of machines are problematic. Technology cannot have any autonomy without freedom, and without moral capability, machines cannot be thought of as being "moral". Therefore, these terms are inadequate in their usage.

Furthermore, the research project "moral machine" suggests to the participants that they are to make judgments about the life and death of humans, because they are being asked, for example, to decide if a self-driving vehicle should run over an adult or over a child. To believe to have this choice already contains a disrespect for human dignity of all humans, because, to stick with this example, the adult and the child are bearers of human rights. Thus, human life will be illegitimately quantified and evaluated. This would involve "targeting" humans based on their properties and making them victims in these specific situations.[1733]

This option to select whether the self-driving vehicle should run over an adult or a child is based on a misunderstanding about the quality of a moral dilemma. A moral dilemma, with all the various forms, nuances, and facets that it can possess, is characterized in its core by the fact that both available paths are ethically bad or wrong.

Furthermore, the research project does not take into account that – as elaborated above in subchapter 5.1 Ethics Is Not Democracy – a democratic process does not guarantee legitimacy. Ethics as a science is not demo-

---

1730 The research project does not put any quotation marks here.
1731 The research project does not put any quotation marks here.
1732 See Moral Machine n.d.
1733 See Lin 2014.

cratic. It is conceivable that a democratic opinion-forming and decision-making process may also lead to results that are ethically bad or wrong.

Finally, the research project is based on a reductionist understanding of ethics. It lacks a consideration and integration of the complexity of ethics alluded to above in chapter 5 The Complexity of Ethics. Ethics cannot be compressed into rules to be translated into the language of mathematics or algorithms. Even if certain aspects of ethics can be given to machines as rules, *it needs to be considered that some ethical elements cannot be accessed by digital processes*. Ethics also contains, among other elements, doing justice to the concrete, which by far outperforms the regulative because of its uniqueness. Thus, in human beings, the virtue of *epikeia* and conscience in particular, ensures that in a concrete encounter with concrete humans in a concrete situation the limits of principles and norms are perceived and considered with an ethical orientation.

And as regards the moral dilemma that could arise in the case of self-driving vehicles when they need to decide between running over an adult or a child, there would be no easy answer from an ethical perspective by taking into account the human dignity of all humans and human rights (in the sense of that, for example, the adult should be run over and the child should not). Rather, we must demand that more expertise, know-how, creativity, talent and resources (time, money, etc.) should be invested to technically reduce the chances of such a moral dilemma occurring, but obviously along with knowing the limits to human reason and with knowing that human perfection is impossible.

As this example shows: "Homo dignitatis" instead of "homo digitalis" can make a difference. Humans as potential creators and users of data-based systems can decide not to create it, to create it in an ethically legitimate way, not to use it (the example of young people not using Facebook anymore shows the power of humans)[1734], or to use it in an ethically positive way.[1735]

1734 See Stephens 2018.
1735 See Di Lorenzo 2018.

8.14 The COVID-19-Pandemic and Mastering Threats in Times of Data-Based Systems

Many people are dying and have died, or are suffering or have suffered, from the current COVID-19-pandemic and its consequences.[1736] The UN estimates that because of COVID-19, the number of humans affected by hunger will double to 265 million people.[1737]

On the one hand, all humans were made aware of our vulnerability, which is associated with uncertainty. For as humans we never know whether and when a vulnerability turns into an injury and how serious the injury will be. In this respect, all humans are equal. The principle of vulnerability is what makes all humans human.

On the other hand, such a crisis reinforces and increases injustice and inequality, because poor people suffer massively more from a crisis than rich people, and because humans who are otherwise disadvantaged and discriminated against or marginalized are marginalized even more. Targeted political and economic measures are needed to counter this.

In a crisis such as the COVID-19-pandemic, precise and proportionate restrictions may be legitimate. It is crucial that they are lifted immediately if they are no longer necessary from a medical perspective in order to respect the human dignity and freedom of all humans. "In recent years both governments and corporations have been using ever more sophisticated technologies to track, monitor and manipulate people. Yet if we are not careful, the epidemic might nevertheless mark an important watershed in the history of surveillance. Not only because it might normalize the deployment of mass surveillance tools in countries that have so far rejected them, but even more so because it signifies a dramatic transition from 'over the skin' to 'under the skin' surveillance. Hitherto, when your finger touched the screen of your smartphone and clicked on a link, the government wanted to know what exactly your finger was clicking on. But with coronavirus, the focus of interest shifts. Now the government wants to know the temperature of your finger and the blood-pressure under its skin."[1738]

Societies are constantly changing. This is also the case here. Changes are to be expected. This is why the term "new normality" needs to be criticized as problematic, as it carries the risk that, for example, previously unaccept-

---

1736 See Moon et al. 2020.
1737 See World Food Programme 2020.
1738 Harari 2020.

able surveillance methods that violate the human right to privacy and data protection will be declared the "new normality" by some voices. It is important that we as a society continue to take care of human rights and democracy as the normative standards that we have fought for centuries.

Another concern is that attempts could be made to undermine human rights with the "COVID-19 argument". Unfortunately, humanity has experienced such attacks on human rights after 11 September 2001 – for example, attempts to weaken the absolute prohibition on torture. We should be armed and resist such attacks on the dignity and freedom of all humans. "If corporations and governments start harvesting our biometric data *en masse*, they can get to know us far better than we know ourselves, and they can then not just predict our feelings but also manipulate our feelings and sell us anything they want — be it a product or a politician. Biometric monitoring would make Cambridge Analytica's data hacking tactics look like something from the Stone Age. Imagine North Korea in 2030, when every citizen has to wear a biometric bracelet 24 hours a day. If you listen to a speech by the Great Leader and the bracelet picks up the telltale signs of anger, you are done for. (...) My home country of Israel, for example, declared a state of emergency during its 1948 War of Independence, which justified a range of temporary measures from press censorship and land confiscation to special regulations for making pudding (I kid you not). The War of Independence has long been won, but Israel never declared the emergency over, and has failed to abolish many of the 'temporary' measures of 1948 (the emergency pudding decree was mercifully abolished in 2011). Even when infections from coronavirus are down to zero, some data-hungry governments could argue they needed to keep the biometric surveillance systems in place because they fear a second wave of coronavirus, or because there is a new Ebola strain evolving in central Africa, or because... you get the idea."[1739]

At the same time, it would be desirable that we maintain our focus on what is essential – namely to guarantee survival and a life with human dignity for all humans – and that this focus is constantly renewed. For human dignity has neither an age nor a price tag.

In this COVID-19-crisis, we have once again been able and are still able to see how valuable human rights and democracy are. For they protect freedom of expression and information, and include participation and transparency, so that a cover-up or falsification of information cannot result in valuable time being lost, allowing a virus to spread into a global

---

1739 Harari 2020.

pandemic. After the crisis, we should all be all the more resolute in our efforts to promote democracy and to realize the human rights of all humans everywhere in the world – including in political and economic negotiations with dictatorships and even if this should be against our particular political and economic short-term interests.

We should use this caesura to tackle reforms that are urgently needed from an ethical standpoint and make our society and economy fairer and more sustainable. If, for example, an industry is dependent on state aid due to the COVID-19-pandemic, then the opportunity must be seized and a fairer and more sustainable way of creating value must be started with this industry. For example, with the concept of the "Responsible Business Initiative"[1740] in Switzerland (the political initiative received the majority of the popular vote on November 29, 2020 and gained only 8.5 of the required 12 regional majorities across Switzerland's cantons as a majority of both the popular vote and cantonal vote is needed for an initiative to pass), there is still a unique opportunity to make substantial progress in the implementation of human rights on the basis of this conceptual approach holding Swiss companies accountable in Swiss courts for human rights violations in other countries. This conceptual approach of "extraterritorial legislation"[1741] could be also applied in other countries.

The steps of digital transformation and the use of data-based systems taken in the course of the COVID-19-crisis should be consistently examined after the crisis in order to determine what should and should not really be done from an ethical point of view. Just because something is technically feasible, this doesn't mean it should be done – think of the atomic bomb, for example. Surely, it cannot be justified for technical solutions for video conferences to steal our data and violate our self-determination. Something must be done about this. Business models are needed to provide the software for video conferences without violating human rights, without creating injustice and irresponsibility.

Going back to the local is promising if it means doing business more sustainably. At the same time, human rights should lay the foundation for global solidarity, which is necessary to solve the most important issues of the present.

The COVID-19-crisis is causing us to wake up to the fact that we have to make a decision: We cannot claim freedom, justice, and human dignity for ourselves and at the same time violate the human rights of other humans.

1740   See Responsible Business Initiative 2020.
1741   See Deva 2012b; Bernaz 2013; McCorquodale / Simons 2007.

The principle of vulnerability shows – as elaborated above in subchapter 6.4 Human Rights as Ethical Frame of Reference – that the wisest, most prudent, and most rational option for us in terms of pursuing our own interests is to protect all of us with human rights against violations or to provide for compensation – such as access to health care – if a vulnerability should transform into a concrete injury or a violation. For as humans, we never know, for example, whether we will fall ill, when we will fall ill, and how bad it will be – just a cold or a tumor. As humans, we do not know whether we are the ones who have to help or who need help. That is why we should guarantee all humans what is necessary for survival and for a life with dignity in accordance with human rights.

8.15 At Last, The Question of Focus and Priorities

Of course, one does not want to be a spoiled sport. At the same time, applying responsibility, justice, and human rights from an ethical perspective on the understanding of humanity living on planet Earth in a "global village", the following fundamental question arises: Imagine a visitor comes to this village and sees us humans extremely dedicated in pushing forward digital transformation and data-based systems, exploiting nature for and investing endless amounts of time, energy, talent, and resources into this technology-based advancement, while in the same village, humans are starving, humans are dying due to poverty-related causes, and the ecosystem is losing its future due to natural exploitation. This visitor would at least ask us about our focus and our priorities – so shouldn't we be asking ourselves too?

Epilogue I

Once a dog has a collar and a leash, it can be controlled and led. Its freedom is limited, its path ends abruptly, its room for play has clear boundaries, its possibilities are limited, it is under duress. It will be led through life. It will be held back from beautiful things. The dog will be protected from the ugly. Its exploration attempts remain fruitless. Its endeavors end in nothing. The dog's desires have its master in the collar and the leash. Every twitch, every one of its movements is registered and provokes a reaction – noticeable or without pressure on its neck. The tethered dog succumbs to the will that acts on the collar through the leash.

The dog is rewarded and placated with dog biscuits, bones, and other amenities. A tighter collar is perceived as punishment. Other forms of punishment can be added in order to educate the dog, to break its will ... Are we humans like dogs in the course of digital transformation? Are we the dogs of data-based systems?

Do we humans want to hold the leash or carry the collar? We should do everything we can as soon as possible so that we change the reality substantially that the dogs in this imagery are not us, but digital transformation and data-based systems. How do we put a collar on digital transformation, data-based systems and super-data-based systems? How do we put them on a leash? What do we do to ensure that the collar and leash stay in place? *How do we make sure that the dog will not bite anyone?*

This book should not end with leashes and dogs but with the Italian delicacy "panna cotta". Searching for help through the image of "panna cotta" rather than in a pudding is not only a reference to the Italian cuisine but has implications with respect to the content: Differing from a pudding, "panna cotta" is usually served free-standing or free-floating or free-wobbling on a plate. What does "panna cotta" have to do with digital transformation and data-based systems?

I extend the invitation to you to overcome the image of a network and the blurring of the concept of "cloud" and use the image of "panna cotta". Why? The image of a network is not adequate because while living with data-based systems, everyone has an effect on others, even those with whom she or he is not connected. For example, all the people watching a YouTube video still directly influence others who are not connected with them. Beyond that, it is too static to represent the dynamics, the omnipresence, omnipotence, and omniscience as well as the far-reaching nature of data-based systems that goes beyond the nodes of a network.

The idea of network frames human thinking and dominates the way one perceives the world. The idea of the network lets humans believe that, while living with data-based systems, they are nodes acting as individuals, still having everything under control, still deciding with whom they want to connect and by whom they want to be affected as well as still possessing autonomy. It deceives humans into believing that they are still in charge. Contrarily, in the present, humans are part of "panna cotta". Humans affect each other and the "panna cotta", and the "panna cotta" influences all humans. At the moment, in living with data-based systems, this reciprocal impact is not something we can control or determine. It just happens to us. Obviously, a life with data-based systems as "panna cotta" is a threat to human dignity, to individuality of humans, and to the autonomy of humans. Thus, human dignity, the individuality of humans, and the autonomy of humans must be defended in a reality that is not a network but rather a "panna cotta".

This means that we need to free our minds from the illusion of a network making us blind to the challenging threats. We need to face the reality of "panna cotta" in order to stop and prevent being wobbled around and in order to overcome "panna cotta" by taking back our human dignity, our individuality, and our autonomy.

"Panna cotta" is one of my favorite desserts but the dining table is where "panna cotta" belongs ... I trust us as humans – applying a *heuristics of confidence* in humans rather than a "heuristics of fear"[1742] – to make this ethically necessary change in order to enable technological progress while respecting human dignity and human rights of all humans. Applying a *heuristics of confidence* in humans, I trust that the greatest power lies in our idea of a better world ...

1742 See Jonas 1985b: 63-64.

Epilogue II

I dream of a present and a future where technology-based innovation serves the flourishing of all humans and of the planet Earth instead of the greed of a few people and companies, and where technology-based innovation is created, designed, developed, produced, and used with respect to human dignity and human rights of all humans and in a sustainable way.

References

Abney, Keith Yann (2017): "Robots and Space Ethics". In: Lin, Patrick / Abney, Keith / Jenkins, Ryans (Eds.): Robot Ethics 2.0: From Autonomous Cars to Artificial Intelligence. New York: Oxford University Press, 354-368.

Acemoglu, Daron / Restrepo, Pascual (2020): Robots and Jobs: Evidence from US Labor Markets. In: Journal of Political Economy 128(6), 2188-2244.

Achtner, Wolfgang (2010): Willensfreiheit in Theologie und Naturwissenschaften: Ein historisch-systematischer Wegweiser. Darmstadt: Wissenschaftliche Buchgesellschaft.

Adams, Richard / Beth, Kewell / Glenn, Parry (2018): "Blockchain for Good? Digital Ledger Technology and Sustainable Development Goals". In: Filho, Walter Leal / Marans, Robert W. / Callewaert, John (Eds.): Handbook of Sustainability and Social Science Research. Cham: Springer, 127-140.

Adnan, Nadia / Nordin, Shahrina Md / Bin Bahruddin, Mohamad Ariff (2019): "Sustainable Interdependent Networks from Smart Autonomous Vehicle to Intelligent Transportation Networks". In: Amini, M. Hadi / Boroojeni, Kianoosh / Iyengar, S. Sitharama / Pardalos, Panos M. / Blaabjerg, Frede / Madni, Asad M. (Eds.): Sustainable Interdependent Networks II. Studies in Systems, Decision and Control 186. Cham: Springer, 121-134.

Aeberhard, Michael / Rauch, Sebastian / Bahram, Mohammed / Tanzmeister, Georg / Thomas, Julian / Pilat, Yves / Homm, Florian / Huber, Werner / Kaempchen, Nico (2015): "Experience, Results and Lessons Learned from Automated Driving on Germany's Highways." In: IEEE Intelligent Transportation Systems Magazine 7(1), 42-57.

African Charter on Human and Peoples' Rights of 1981 (1981). Online: https://www.achpr.org/public/Document/file/English/banjul_charter.pdf [08.02.2021].

Agar, Nicholas (2016): "Don't Worry about Superintelligence". In: Journal of Evolution and Technology 26 (1 February), 73-82.

Agrawal, Ajay / Gans, Joshua S. / Goldfarb, Avi (2018): Prediction, Judgment and Complexity: A Theory of Decision Making and Artificial Intelligence. Rotman School of Management. Working Paper 3103156. Online: https://ssrn.com/abstract=3103156 [08.02.2021].

Aiolfi, Sergio (2019): "Novartis kooperiert mit Microsoft". In: Neue Zuercher Zeitung, October, 1. Online: https://www.nzz.ch/wirtschaft/novartis-kooperiert-mit-microsoft-ld.1512611 [08.02.2021].

Albert, Anika Christina (2016): "Fremd im vertrauten Quartier. Perspektiven einer kritischen Theologie des Helfens unter den Bedingungen von Alter(n), Demenz und Technik". In: Ethik und Gesellschaft 2, 1-29.

Alessandrini, Adriano / Cattivera, Alessio / Holguin, Carlos / Stam, Daniele (2014): "CityMobil2: Challenges and Opportunities of Fully Automated Mobility". In: Meyer, Gereon / Beiker, Sven (Eds.): Road Vehicle Automation: Lecture Notes in Mobility. Cham: Springer, 169-184.

Aletras, Nikolaos / Tsarapatsanis, Dimitrios / Preoţiuc-Pietro, Daniel / Lampos, Vasileios (2016): "Predicting judicial decisions of the European Court of Human Rights: A natural language processing perspective". In: PeerJ Computer Science 2(e93). Online: https://peerj.com/articles/cs-93/ [08.02.2021].

Alexander, Brian (2003): Rapture: How Biotech Became the New Religion. New York: Basic Books.

Alexy, Robert (1986): Theorie der Grundrechte. Frankfurt am Main: Suhrkamp.

Alexy, Robert (1998): "Die Institutionalisierung der Menschenrechte im demokratischen Verfassungsstaat". In: Gosepath, Stefan / Lohmann, Georg (Eds.): Philosophie der Menschenrechte. Frankfurt am Main: Suhrkamp, 244-264.

Alkim, Tom (2018): "Connected and Automated Driving in The Netherlands – Challenge, Experience and Declaration". In: Meyer, Gereon / Beiker, Sven (Eds.): Road Vehicle Automation 4: Lecture Notes in Mobility. Cham: Springer, 25-31.

Allen, Colin / Wallach, Wendell (2014): "Moral Machines: Contradiction in Terms or Abdication of Human Responsibility?". In: Lin, Patrick / Abney, Keith / Bekey, George A. (Eds.): Robot Ethics: The Ethical and Social Implications of Robotics. Intelligent Robotics and Autonomous Agents. New York: MIT Press, 55-68.

Altmann, Juergen / Asaro, Peter / Sharkey, Noel / Sparrow, Robert (2013): "Armed military robots: editorial". In: Ethics and Information Technology 15, 73-76.

Allen, Mike (2017): "Sean Parker unloads on Facebook: 'God only knows what it's doing to our children's brains'". In: AXIOS, November 9. Online: https://www.axios.com/sean-parker-unloads-on-facebook-god-only-knows-what-its-doing-to-our-childrens-brains-1513306792-f855e7b4-4e99-4d60-8d51-2775559c2671.html [08.02.2021].

Alwang, Jeffrey / Siegel, Paul B. / Jorgenson, Steen L. (2002): "Vulnerability as Viewed from Different Disciplines". In: International Symposium: Sustaining Food Security and Managing Natural Resources in Southeast Asia: Challenges for the 21st Century. January 8–11, Chiang Mai, Thailand. Online: https://studylib.net/doc/18294386/vulnerability-as-viewed-from-different-disciplines [08.02.2021].

American Society of Mechanical Engineers (ASME) (n.d.): Standards. Online: https://www.asme.org/codes-standards [08.02.2021].

Amnesty International (2016): Kinderarbeit für Mobiltelefone und Elektroautos. January 19. Online: https://www.amnesty.ch/de/laender/afrika/demokr-rep-kongo/dok/2016/bericht-kinderarbeit-fuer-mobiltelefone-und-elektroautos [08.02.2021].

Amnesty International (2020a): "Digitale Gesellschaft, Stiftung für Konsumenten-schutz: Überwachungsmassnahmen müssen auch unter Notrecht verhältnismässig sein". Online: https://www.amnesty.ch/de/themen/coronavirus/dok/2020/ueb erwachungsmassnahmen-muessen-auch-unter-notrecht-verhaeltnismaessig [08.02.2021].

Amnesty International (2020b): Human Rights and the Environment: Water Pollution, Water Scarcity and Floods. Submission to the UN Special Rapporteur on Environment and Human Rights. November 13, 2020. Online: https://www.ohc hr.org/Documents/Issues/Environment/EnvironmentWater/Civil%20Society/A mensty%20International.docx [08.02.2021].

Amnesty International Switzerland (2019): "China: Auf dem Weg zur totalen Kontrolle". In: Amnesty. Magazin der Menschenrechte 99, 10-23.

Amnesty International (n.d.): Corporations. Online: https://www.amnesty.org/en/ what-we-do/corporate-accountability/ [08.02.2021].

Ananny, Mike (2016): "Toward an Ethics of Algorithms: Convening, Observation, Probability, and Timeliness". In: Science, Technology, & Human Values 41(1), 93-117.

Anderson, Chris (2008): "The End of Theory: The Data Deluge Makes the Scientific Method Obsolete". In: Wired, June 23. Online: https://www.wired.com/2008/06/ pb-theory/ [08.02.2021].

Anderson, Kenneth / Waxman, Matthew C. (2017): "Debating Autonomous Weapon Systems: Their Ethics, and Their Regulation Under International Law". In: Brownsword, Roger / Scotford, Eloise / Yeung, Karen (Eds.): The Oxford Handbook of Law, Regulation, and Technology. Washington: American University Washington College of Law Research Paper 21. Oxford: Oxford University Press, 1097-1117.

Anderson, Michael / Anderson, Susan (2011): "General Introduction". In: Anderson, Michael / Anderson, Susan (Eds.): Machine Ethics. Cambridge: Cambridge University Press, 1-4.

Andrews, Edmund L. (2008): "Greenspan Concedes Error on Regulation". In: The New York Times, October 23. Online: https://www.nytimes.com/2008/10/24/bu siness/economy/24panel.html [08.02.2021].

Angel, James / McCabe, Douglas M. (2013): "Fairness in Financial Markets: The Case of High Frequency Trading". In: Journal of Business Ethics 112(4), 590-591.

Anrich, Bert / Mayora, Oscar / Bardram, Jakob E. / Troester, Gerhard (2010): "Pervasive healthcare: paving the way for pervasive, user-centered and preventive healthcare model". In: Methods of Information in Medicine 49(1), 67-73.

Antonopolous, Andreas (2016): "Bitcoin Security Model: Trust by Computation". In: Medium, June 3. Online: https://medium.com/@aantonop/bitcoin-security-model-trust-by-computation-d5b93a37da6e [08.02.2021].

Anzenbacher, Arno (1998): Christliche Sozialethik: Einführung und Prinzipien. Paderborn. Ferdinand Schoeningh.

Anzenbacher, Arno (2015): "Moralität, Gewissen und der Wille Gottes: Überlegungen zu Summa theologiae I-II, q. 19". In: ET-Studies 6(2), 273-300.

Apel, Karl-Otto (1986): "Verantwortung heute – nur noch Prinzip der Bewahrung und Selbstbeschränkung oder immer noch der Befreiung und Verwirklichung von Humanität". In: Meyer, Thomas / Miller, Susanne (Eds.): Zukunftsethik und Industriegesellschaft. Zukunftsethik 1. Muenchen: J. Schweitzer, 15-40.

Apel, Karl-Otto (1988): Diskurs und Verantwortung: Das Problem des Überganges zur postkonventionellen Moral. Frankfurt am Main: Suhrkamp.

Appiah, Kwame Anthony (2006): Cosmopolitanism: ethics in a world of strangers. New York: Penguin.

Apple (2020): Apple Watch Series 5. You've never seen a watch like this. Online: https://www.apple.com/apple-watch-series-5/ [08.02.2021].

Apple (2012): Apple-TV-Commercial: 1984 Apple's Macintosh Commercial. Online: https://www.youtube.com/watch?v=VtvjbmoDx-I [08.02.2021].

Arendt, Hannah (1949): "Es gibt nur ein einziges Menschenrecht". In: Die Wandlung 4, 754-770.

Arendt, Hannah (1958): The human condition. Chicago: University of Chicago Press.

Arendt, Hannah (2001): Vita activa oder vom tätigen Leben. Muenchen: Piper.

Arendt, Rieke (2016): Völkerrechtliche Probleme beim Einsatz autonomer Waffensysteme, Menschenrechtszentrum der Universitaet Potsdam 41. Berlin: BWV Berliner Wissenschafts-Verlag.

Arens, Edmund (2007): "Was ist Religion? Analytische Differenzierungen – theoretische Zugänge – theologische Reflexion". In: Durst, Michael / Muenk, Hans J. (Eds.): Religion und Gesellschaft, Freiburg im Uechtland: Paulusverlag, 35-93.

Aristoteles (1983): Nikomachische Ethik. Dirlmeier, Franz (Ed.). Stuttgart: Reclam.

Arkin, Ronald C. (1998): Behavior-Based Robotics. Cambridge: MIT Press.

Arkin, Ronald C. (2009): Governing Lethal Behavior in Autonomous Robots. New York: Chapman and Hall / CRC.

Arkin, Ronald C. (2018): "Lethal Autonomous Systems and the Plight of the Noncombatant". In: AISB Quarterly: Newsletter of the Society for the Study of Artificial Intelligence and Simulation of Behaviour 137, 1-14.

Armand, Jean-Louis (2012): "The bringing together of technology, sustainability and ethics". In: Sustainability Science 7(2), 113-116.

Armstrong, Stuart (2014): Smarter Than Us: The Rise of Machine Intelligence. Berkeley: MIRI.

Arnaldi, Simone / Bianchi, Luca (2016): Responsibility in Science and Technology: Elements of a Social Theory. Wiesbaden: Springer.

Article 36 (2015): "Killing by Machine: Key Issues for Understanding Meaningful Human Control". Online: http://www.article36.org/weapons/autonomous-weapons/killing-by-machine-key-issues-for-understanding-meaningful-human-control/ [08.02.2021].

Asad, Ullah / Wang, Aimin / Mansoora, Ahmed (2018): "Smart Automation, Customer Experience and Customer Engagement in Electric Vehicles". In: Sustainability 10(5), 1-11.

Asaro, Peter M. (2006): "What Should We Want From a Robot Ethic?". In: International Review of Information Ethics 6(12), 9-16.

Asaro, Peter M. (2008): "How just could a robot war be?". In: Briggle, Adam / Waelbers, Katinka / Brey, Philip A. E. (Eds.): Current Issues in Computing And Philosophy. IOS Press: Amsterdam, 50-64.

Asaro, Peter M. (2012): "On banning autonomous weapon systems: human rights, automation, and the dehumanization of lethal decision-making". In: International Review of the Red Cross 94(886), 687-709.

Asaro, Peter M. (2019): "Algorithms of Violence: Criticial Social Perspectives on Autonomous Weapons". In: Social Research 86(2), 537-555.

Asimov, Isaac (1982): Meine Freunde, die Roboter. Bibliothek der Science Fiction Literatur. Muenchen: Heyne.

Assheuer, Thomas (2019): "Die neue Sklavenhaltergesellschaft". In: Die Zeit, December 6. Online: https://www.zeit.de/2018/51/crispr-china-biotechnologie-geno mveraenderung-ethik-gentechnik [08.02.2021].

Association for Computing Machinery's Committee on Professional Ethics (2017): "2018 ACM Code of Ethics and Professional Conduct: Draft 3". Association for Computing Machinery Committee on Professional Ethics. Online: https://ethics .acm.org/2018-code-draft-3/ [08.02.2021].

Association for Computing Machinery US Public Policy Council (2017): Statement on Algorithmic Transparency and Accountability. January 12. Online: https://w ww.acm.org/binaries/content/assets/public-policy/2017_usacm_statement_algori thms.pdf [08.02.2021].

Aste, Tomaso (2016): "The Fair Cost of Bitcoin Proof of Work". In: SSRN Electronic Journal, June 27. Online: https://papers.ssrn.com/sol3/papers.cfm?abstract_id= 2801048 [08.02.2021].

Aste, Tomaso / Tasca, Paolo / Di Matteo, Tiziana (2018): "Blockchain Technologies: The Foreseeable Impact on Society and Industry". In: Computer 9(50), 18-28.

Atkinson, David. J. / Clark, Micah H. (2013): "Autonomous agents and human interpersonal trust: Can we engineer a human-machine social interface for trust?". In: Trust and Autonomous Systems – Papers from the AAAI Spring Symposium. Online: https://www.aaai.org/ocs/index.php/SSS/SSS13/paper/viewFile/5739/600 4 [08.02.2021].

Atzori, Marcella (2015): Blockchain Technology and Decentralized Governance: Is the State Still Necessary?. Online: https://static.nzz.ch/files/9/3/1/blockchain+Is+t he+State+Still+Necessary_1.18689931.pdf [08.02.2021].

Auer, Alfons (1982): "Darf der Mensch, was er kann?". In: Busch, Alois J. / Splett, Joerg (Eds.): Wissenschaft – Technik – Humanität. Frankfurt am Main: Verlag Josef Knecht, 11-35.

Australian Human Rights Commission (2019): "Human Rights and Technology". Discussion Paper. Online: https://tech.humanrights.gov.au/?_ga=2.211445781.16 41337062.1609843370-1930064430.1609843370 [08.02.2021].

Austrian Council on Robotics and Artificial Intelligence (2018): "Die Zukunft Österreichs mit Robotik und Künstlicher Intelligenz: White Paper". Online: https://www.acrai.at/wp-content/uploads/2019/04/ACRAI_whitebook_online_2018.pdf [08.02.2021].

Austrian Gene Technology Act 1994 (2015): Online: https://www.ecolex.org/details/legislation/genetic-technology-act-lex-faoc089381/ [08.02.2021].

Austrian Federal Act on Civil Liability for Damage Caused by Radioactivity (1999): Online: https://www.oecd-nea.org/law/legislation/austria/AUSTRIA-AtomicLiab ilityAct.pdf [08.02.2021].

Axhausen, Kay W. (2016): „Autonome Fahrzeuge: Erste Überlegungen: Lecture in the occasion of the Summer-Academy of the Swiss Study Foundation on the topic: Automatization of Mobility". September 6. Online: https://www.research-collection.ethz.ch/bitstream/handle/20.500.11850/119702/v600.pdf?sequence=2 &isAllowed=y [08.02.2021].

Bachelet, Michelle (2019): "Human rights in the digital age – Can they make a difference?". Keynote speech by Michelle Bachelet, UN High Commissioner for Human Rights. Japan Society, New York, October 17. United Nations. Online: https://www.ohchr.org/EN/NewsEvents/Pages/DisplayNews.aspx?NewsID=2515 8&LangID=E [08.02.2021].

Bachinger, Leo Matteo / Fuchs, Walter (2013): "Rechtliche Herausforderungen des Technikeinsatzes in der Altenpflege: eine rechtssoziologische Perspektive auf Ambient Assisted Living". In: SWS-Rundschau 53(1), 73-94.

Bacon, Francis (1990): Neues Organon (Novum Organon) 1. Krohn, Wolfgang (Ed.). Hamburg: Felix Meiner.

Bacon, Francis (2000): The Instauratio Magna: Last Writings. Rees, Graham (Ed.). The Oxford Francis Bacon 13. Oxford: Oxford Clarendon Press.

Bacon, Francis (2003): The Advancement of Learning. Kiernan, Michael (Ed.). The Oxford Francis Bacon 4. Oxford: Oxford Clarendon Press.

Bacon, Francis (2004): The Instauratio Magna Part II: Novum Organum and Associated Texts. Rees, Graham / Wakely, Maria (Eds.). The Oxford Francis Bacon 11. Oxford: Oxford Clarendon Press.

Bacon, Francis (2007): The Instauratio Magna Part III: Historia naturalis et experimentalis: Historia ventorum and Historia vitæ & mortis. Rees, Graham / Wakely, Maria (Eds.). The Oxford Francis Bacon 12. Oxford: Oxford Clarendon Press.

Bahnsen, Ulrich (2018): "Darf er, was er kann?". In: Die Zeit, November 29. Online: https://www.zeit.de/autoren/B/Ulrich_Bahnsen/index.xml [08.02.2021].

Baier, Kurt (1974): Der Standpunkt der Moral: Eine rationale Grundlegung der Ethik. Duesseldorf: Patmos.

Bainbridge, Lisanne (1983): Ironies of automation. In: Automatica 19(6), 775-779.

Bajari, Patrick / Chernozhukov, Victor / Hortaçsu, Ali / Suzuki, Junichi (2019): "The Impact of Big Data on Firm Performance: An Empirical Investigation". In: AEA Papers and Proceedings, American Economic Association 109, 33-37.

Barlow, John Perry (1996): "A Declaration of the Independence of Cyberspace". In: Electronic Frontier Foundation, February 8. Online: https://projects.eff.org/~bar low/Declaration-Final.html [08.02.2021].

Barnes, Michael (2002): Theology and the Dialogue of Religions. Cambridge Studies in Christian Doctrine. Cambridge: Cambridge University Press.

Barocas, Solon / Selbst, Andrew D. (2016): "Big data's disparate impact". In: California Law Review 104, 671-729. Online: http://www.californialawreview.org/w p-content/uploads/2016/06/2Barocas-Selbst.pdf [08.02.2021].

Bartlett, Albert (2007): Dr. Albert Bartlett on Compounding. Online: https://www. peakprosperity.com/dr_albert_bartlett/ [08.02.2021].

Bartoletti, Ivana (2018): "Women must act now, or male-designed robots will take over our lives". In: The Guardian, March 13. Online: https://www.theguardian.c om/commentisfree/2018/mar/13/women-robots-ai-male-artificial-intelligence-aut omation [08.02.2021].

Bashir, Qasim (2000): "Technology vs. morality". In: Surgical Neurology 54(1), 92.

Bassi, Eleonora (2019): "European Drones Regulation: Today's Legal Challenges". In: Institute of Electrical and Electronics Engineers (IEEE) (Ed.): International Conference on Unmanned Aircraft Systems (ICUAS). Atlanta: Institute of Electrical and Electronics Engineers (IEEE), 443-450.

Basu, Rounaq / Andrea, Araldo / Arun, Prakash Akkinepally / Bat Hen Nahmias, Biran / Kalaki, Basak / Ravi, Seshadri / Neeraj, Deshmukh / Nishant, Kumar / Lima Azevedo, Carlos / Moshe, Ben-Akiva (2018): "Automated Mobility-on-Demand vs. Mass Transit: A Multi-Modal Activity-Driven Agent-Based Simulation Approach". In: Transportation Research Record: Journal of the Transportation Research Board 2672(8), 608-618.

Bathaee, Yavar (2018): "The Artificial Intelligence Black Box and the Failure of Intent and Causation". In: Harvard Journal of Law & Technology 31(2), 889-938.

Battaglia, Fiorella (2016): "Vorstellungen über die 'Natur des Menschen' in Technik-Debatten". In: Manzeschke, Arne / Karsch, Fabian (Eds.): Roboter, Computer und Hybride. Was ereignet sich zwischen Menschen und Maschinen?. TTN-Studien 5. Baden-Baden: Nomos Verlagsgesellschaft, 67-87.

Baudrillard, Jean (1993): "Xeros and Infinity". In: Baudrillard, Jean: The Transparency of Evil: Essays on Extreme Phenomena. London: Verso, 51-59.

Bauer, Emmanuel J. (Ed.) (2007): Freiheit in philosophischer, neurowissenschaftlicher und psychotherapeutischer Perspektive. Muenchen: Wilhelm Fink.

Bauernhansl, Thomas (Ed.) (2015): Technische Assistenzsysteme in der Pflege. Stuttgart: Verein zur Förderung Produktionstechnischer Forschung.

Baumann-Hoelzle, Ruth (1999): "Autonomie und Freiheit in der Medizin-Ethik". Freiburg im Breisgau / Muenchen: Karl Alber.

Bavelier, Daphne / Green, C. Shawn / Han, Doug Hyun / Renshaw, Perry / Merzenich, Michael M. / Gentile, Douglas A. (2011): "Brains on video games". In: Nature Reviews Neuroscience 12(12), 763-768.

Bavitz, Christopher / Hessekiel, Kira (2018): Algorithms and Justice: Examining the Role of the State in the Development and Deployment of Algorithmic Technologies. Berkman Klein Center for Internet and Society. Online: https://cyber.h arvard.edu/story/2018-07/algorithms-and-justice [08.02.2021].

Bayertz, Kurt (1995): "Eine kurze Geschichte der Herkunft der Verantwortung". In: Bayertz, Kurt: Verantwortung. Prinzip oder Problem? Darmstadt: WBG, 3-71.

Bayertz, Kurt (2009): "Hat der Mensch eine 'Natur'? Und ist sie wertvoll?". In: Weiss, Martin G. (Ed.): Bios und Zoe. Die menschliche Natur im Zeitalter ihrer technischen Reproduzierbarkeit. Frankfurt am Main: Suhrkamp, 191-218.

Bayertz, Kurt (2010): "Art. Verantwortung". In: Sandkuehler, Hans Joerg (Ed.): Enzyklopädie Philosophie 3 (Q-Z). Hamburg: Felix Meiner, 2861-2862.

Beard, Jack M. (2014): "Autonomous Weapons and Human Responsibilities". In: Georgetown Journal of International Law 45, 617-681.

Beck, Susanne (2012): "Roboter und Cyborgs – erobern sie unsere Welt?". In: Beck, Susanne (Ed.): Jenseits von Mensch und Maschine. Ethische und rechtliche Fragen zum Umgang mit Robotern, Künstlicher Intelligenz und Cyborgs. Robotik und Recht 1. Baden-Baden: Nomos Verlagsgesellschaft, 9-21.

Beck, Susanne / Grzegorzek, Marcin / Lichtenthaeler, Christina / Macke, Jakob / Muhl, Claudia / Reiser, Ulrich / Scholz, Ingo / Seibel, Benjamin / Urban, Iris (2013): "Mit Robotern gegen den Pflegenotstand". In: Stiftung Neue Verantwortung 4(13), 1-10.

Beer, Stafford (1973): Fanfare for Effective Freedom: Cybernetic Praxis in Government. The Polytechnic: Brighton.

Bellamy, Carol / Zermatten, Jean / Kirchschlaeger, Peter G. / Kirchschlaeger, Thomas (Eds.) (2007): Realizing the Rights of the Child. Swiss Human Rights Book 2. Zurich: Rueffer & Rub.

Benanti, Paolo (2018): Le Macchine Sapienti: Intelligenze artificiali e decisioni umane. Bologna: Marietti.

Bendel, Oliver (2015): "Die Industrie 4.0 aus ethischer Sicht". In: Zeitschrift HMD Praxis der Wirtschaftsinformatik 52, 739-748.

Bendel, Oliver (2016): "Die Datenbrille aus Sicht der Informationsethik". In: Informatik-Spektrum 39(1), 21-29.

Benedek, Jávor (2006): "Institutional protection of succeeding generations – Ombudsman for Future Generations in Hungary". In: Tremmel, Joerg Chet (Ed.): Handbook of Intergenerational Justice. Cheltenham: Edward Elgar Publishing, 282-298.

Benedek, Wolfgang (2008): "Internet Governance and human rights". In: Benedek, Wolfgang / Bauer, Veronika / Kettemann, Matthias C. (Eds.): Internet governance and the information society: global perspectives and European dimensions. Utrecht: Eleven, 31-49.

Benedek, Wolfgang / Kettemann, Matthias C. (2013): Freedom of Expression and the Internet. Strasbourg: Council of Europe.

Bengler, Klaus / Dietmayer, Klaus / Farber, Berthold / Maurer, Markus / Stiller, Christoph / Winner, Hermann (2014): "Three Decades of Driver Assistance Systems: Review and Future Perspectives". In: IEEE Intelligent Transportation Systems Magazine 6(4), 6-22.

Bensinger, Greg (2020): "Google Gives Cover to Trump's Lies". In: The New York Times, March 21. Online: https://www.nytimes.com/2020/03/21/opinion/google-covid-trump.html [08.02.2021].

Bentham, Jeremy (2007): An Introduction to the Principles of Morals and Legislation. Dover Philosophical Classics. New York: Dover.

Berendt, Bettina / Dettmar, Gebhard / Esslinger, Bernhard / Gramm, Andreas / Grillenberger, Andreas / Hug, Alexander / Witten, Helmut (2015): "Datenschutz im 21. Jahrhundert – Ist Schutz der Privatsphäre (noch) möglich?". In: Gallenbacher, Jens (Ed.): Informatik allgemeinbildend begreifen. Bonn: Gesellschaft für Informatik, 33-42.

Berković, Mirza / Kosovac, Amel (2020): "Predictive Model of Personalization of Services of Automated Mobility Based on the Records of User Movement in Mobile Networks". In: Karabegović, Isak (Ed.): New Technologies: Development and Application III. Lecture Notes in Networks and Systems 128. Cham: Springer, 581-595.

Bernau, Varinia (2017) Joy Boulamwini: "Haben Algorithmen Vorurteile?". In: Wirtschaftswoche, September 1, 54-57.

Bernaz, Nadia (2013): "Enhancing Corporate Accountability for Human Rights Violations: Is Extraterritoriality the Magic Potion?". In: Journal of Business Ethics 117, 493-511.

Bertarelli, Ernesto (2002): "Science Between Goals and Limits". In: 32nd ISC-Symposium at the University of St. Gallen (Ed.): Pushing Limits – Questioning Goals. St Gallen: ISC-Symposium, 47-50.

Besson, Samantha (2015): "Human Rights and Constitutional Law". In: Cruft, Rowan / Liao, S. Matthew / Renzo, Massimo (Eds.): Philosophical Foundations of Human Rights. Oxford: Oxford University Press, 279-299.

Betschon, Stefan (2015): "Automatisierung. Ein neues Maschinenzeitalter". In: Neue Zuercher Zeitung, August 21. Online: https://www.nzz.ch/gesellschaft/leb ensart/gesellschaft/ein-neues-maschinenzeitalter-1.18599135 [08.02.2021].

Betts, Jennifer / Sezer, Sakir (2014): "Ethics and Privacy in National Security and Critical Infrastructure Protection". In: IEEE International Symposium on Ethics in Science, Technology and Engineering, Chicago, 1-7. Online: https://ieeexplor e.ieee.org/abstract/document/6893417/similar#similar [08.02.2021].

Bhargava, Vikram / Kim, Tae Wan (2017): "Autonomous Vehicles and Moral Uncertainty". In: Lin, Patrick / Jenkins, Ryan / Abney, Keith (Eds.): Robot ethics 2.0: From autonomous cars to artificial intelligence. New York: Oxford University Press, 5-19.

Bieber, Christoph (2013): Die Veränderung politischer Kommunikation im Internetzeitalter: Medien und Demokratie und die These von der Postdemokratie. In: Jahrbuch für Christliche Sozialwissenschaften 54, 155-180.

Bielefeldt, Heiner (1993): "Zur Doppeldeutigkeit der staatlichen 'Neutralität'". In: Schwartlaender, Johannes (Ed.): Freiheit der Religion: Christentum und Islam unter dem Anspruch der Menschenrechte. Mainz: Matthias-Gruenewald-Verlag, 464-466.

Bieri, Matthias / Dickow, Marcel (2014): "Letale autonome Waffensysteme als Herausforderung". In: CSS Analysen zur Sicherheitspolitik 164, 1-4.

Birnbacher, Dieter (2006): "Responsibility for future generations". In: Tremmel, Joerg Chet (Ed.): Handbook of Intergenerational Justice. Cheltenham: Edward Elgar Publishing, 23-38.

Birnbacher, Dieter (2009): "Wieweit lassen sich moralische Normen mit der 'Natur des Menschen' begründen?" In: Weiss, Martin G. (Ed.): Bios und Zoe. Die menschliche Natur im Zeitalter ihrer technischen Reproduzierbarkeit. Frankfurt am Main: Suhrkamp, 219-239.

Birnie, Patricia / Boyle, Alan / Redgwell, Catherine (1992): International Law and the Environment. New York: Oxford University Press.

Birrer, Frans A. J. (2005): "Data mining to combat terrorism and the roots of privacy concerns". In: Ethics and Information Technology 7(4), 211-220.

Bishop, Christopher M. (2006): Pattern Recognition and Machine Learning. Information Science and Statistics 1. New York: Springer.

Bleecker, Julian (2009): Design Function. A Short Essay on Design, Science, Fact, and Fiction. Online: http://blog.nearfuturelaboratory.com/2009/03/17/design-fiction-a-short-essay-on-design-science-fact-and-fiction/ [08.02.2021].

Bleich, Erik (2013): "Freedom of Expression versus Racist Hate Speech: Explaining Differences Between High Court Regulations in the US and Europe". In: Journal of Ethnic and Migration Studies 40(2), 2-37.

Bloch, Ernst (1959): Das Prinzip Hoffnung: Kapitel 1-32. Werkausgabe 5. Frankfurt am Main: Suhrkamp.

Bloch, Walter (2011): Willensfreiheit? Neue Argumente in einem alten Streit. Hodos – Wege bildungsbezogener Ethikforschung in Philosophie und Theologie 11. Frankfurt am Main: Peter Lang.

Bloching, Bjoern / Luck, Lars / Ramge, Thomas (2012): Data Unser: Wie Kundendaten die Wirtschaft verändern. Muenchen: Redline.

Blumenberg, Hans (2015): "Technik und Wahrheit". Schmitz, Alexander / Stiegler, Bernd (Eds.). Blumenberg, Hans: Schriften zur Technik. Berlin: Suhrkamp, 42-50.

Bobbert, Monika / Scherzinger, Gregor (Eds.) (2019): Gute Begutachtung?: Ethische Perspektiven der Evaluation von Ethikkommissionen zur medizinischen Forschung am Menschen. Wiesbaden: Springer.

Boddington, Paula (2017): Towards a Code of Ethics for Artificial Intelligence. Cham: Springer.

Bode, Ingvild / Huelss, Hendrik (2018): "Autonomous weapons systems and changing norms in international relations". In: Review of International Studies 44(3), 393-413.

Boden, Margaret A. (2016): AI: Its Nature and Future. Oxford: Oxford University Press.

Boeckenfoerde, Ernst-Wolfgang (2006): "Die Entstehung des Staates als Vorgang der Säkularisation". In: Boeckenfoerde, Ernst-Wolfgang: Recht, Staat, Freiheit. Studien zur Rechtsphilosophie, Staatstheorie und Verfassungsgeschichte. 4. Auflage. Frankfurt am Main: Suhrkamp, 92-114.

Boesch, Patrick M. / Ciari, Francesco / Axhausen, Kay W. (2016): "Autonomous Vehicle Fleet Sizes Required to Serve Different Levels of Demand". In: Transportation Research Record: Journal of the Transportation Research Board 2542(1), 111-119.

Bołtuć, Piotr (2017): "Church-Turing Lovers". In: Lin, Patrick / Abney, Keith / Jenkins, Ryans (Eds.): Robot Ethics 2.0: From Autonomous Cars to Artificial Intelligence. New York: Oxford University Press, 214-228.

Bond, Robert M. / Fariss, Christopher J. / Jones, Jason / Kramer, Adam D. (2012): "A 61-Million-Person Experiment in Social Influence and Political Mobilization". In: Nature 489(7415), 295-298.

Bondolfi, Alberto (2009): "Justice et droit". In: Causse, Jean-Daniel / Mueller, Denis (Eds.): Introdcution à l'éthique. Penser, croire, agir. Le Champ Éthique 51. Geneva: Éditions Labor et Fides, 481-509.

Bonhoeffer, Dietrich (1992): Ethik. Werke 6. Guetersloh: Guetersloher Verlagshaus.

Bonnefon, Jean-François / Shariff, Azim / Rahwan, Iyad (2016): "The social dilemma of autonomous vehicles". In: Science 352(6293), 1573-1576.

Borenstein, Jason / Howard, Ayanna / Wagner, Alan R. (2017): "Pediatric Robotics and Ethics. The Robot is Ready to See You Now, But Should it Be Trusted?". In: Lin, Patrick / Jenkins, Ryan / Abney, Keith (Eds.): Robot ethics 2.0: From autonomous cars to artificial intelligence. New York: Oxford University Press, 127-141.

Borgman, Albert (1992): Crossing the Postmodern Divide. Chicago: University of Chicago.

Borgmann, Albert (1995): "The Moral Significance of Material Culture". In: Feenberg, Andrew / Hannay, Alistair (Eds.): Technology and the Politics of Knowledge. Bloomington: Indiana University Press, 85-93.

Bossard, Carl (2018): "Digital first! Reflexion second". In: Luzerner Zeitung, March 9. Online: https://www.luzernerzeitung.ch/schweiz/digital-first-reflexion-second-ld.81789 [08.02.2021].

Bostrom, Nick (2005): "In defense of posthuman dignity". In: Bioethics 19(3), 202-214.

Bostrom, Nick (2006): "How long before superintelligence?". In: Linguistic and Philosophical Investigations 5(1), 11-30.

Bostrom, Nick (2008a): "Why I Want to be a Posthuman When I Grow Up". In: Gordijn, Bert / Chadwick, Ruth (Eds.): Medical Enhancement and Posthumanity. Doldrecht: Springer 107-137.

Bostrom, Nick (2008b): "Dignity and Enhancement". In: Schulman, Alan (Ed.): Human Dignity and Bioethics: Essays Commissioned by the President's Council on Bioethics. Washington: US President's Council on Bioethics, 173-207.

Bostrom, Nick (2009): "The Future of Humanity". In: Olsen, Jan-Kyrre Berg / Selinger, Evan / Riis, Soren (Eds.): New Waves in Philosophy of Technology. New York: Palgrave McMillan, 186-216.

Bostrom, Nick (2012): "The Superintelligent Will: Motivation and Instrumental Rationality in Advanced Artificial Agents". In: Minds and Machines 22(2), 71-85.

Bostrom, Nick (2013): "Existential Risk Prevention as Global Priority". In: Global Policy 4(1), 15-31.

Bostrom, Nick (2014): Superintelligence: Paths, Dangers, Strategies. New York: Oxford University Press.

Bostrom, Nick / Sandberg, Anders (2008): Whole Brain Emulation: A Roadmap. Oxford: Future of Humanity Institute.

Bostrom, Nick / Yudkowsky, Eliezer (2014): "The ethics of artificial intelligence". In: Ramsey, William, M. / Frankish, Keith (Eds.): The Cambridge Handbook of Artificial Intelligence. Cambridge: Cambridge University Press, 316-334.

Bourg, Dominique (2006): "The French Constitutional Charter for the environment: an effective instrument?". In: Tremmel, Joerg Chet (Ed.): Handbook of Intergenerational Justice. Cheltenham: Edward Elgar Publishing, 230-243.

Boutellier, Roman / Heinzen, Mareike / Raus, Marta (2010): "Paradigms, Science, and Technology: The Case of E-Customs". In: Becker, S. Ann / Niebuhr, Robert E. (Eds.): Cases on Technology Innovation: Entrepreneurial Successes and Pitfalls. New York: Business Science Reference, 134-155.

Bowles, Nellie (2018): "Early Facebook and Google Employees Form Coalition to Fight What They Built". In: The New York Times, February 4. Online: https://www.nytimes.com/2018/02/04/technology/early-facebook-google-employees-fight-tech.html [08.02.2021].

Braidotti, Rosi (2014): Posthumanismus. Leben jenseits des Menschen. Frankfurt am Main: Campus.

Braun, Hans (2009): "Verantwortung". In: Die Neue Ordnung 63(4), 244-252.

Braendle, Claudia / Grunwald, Armin (2019): "Autonomes Fahren aus Sicht der Maschinenethik". In: Rath, Matthias / Krotz, Friedrich / Karmasin, Matthias (Eds.): Maschinenethik. Wiesbaden: Springer, 281-300.

Brayne, Sarah / Rosenblat, Alex / Boyd, Danah (2015): "Predictive policing. Data & civil rights: A new era of policing and justice". In: Data & Civil Rights. Online: https://datacivilrights.org/pubs/2015-1027/Predictive_Policing.pdf [08.02.2021].

Breazal, Cynthia (2002): Designing Sociable Robots. Cambridge: MIT Press.

Breiding, James R. / Christen, Markus / Helbing, Dirk (2015): "Lost Robustness". In: Helbing, Dirk: Thinking Ahead – Essays on Big Data, Digital Revolution, and Participatory Market Society. Cham: Springer, 27-37.

Brenner, Walter / Witte, Christoph (2011): Business Innovation: CIOs im Wettbe werb der Ideen. Frankfurt am Main: Frankfurter Allgemeine Buch.

Brey, Philip A. E. (2014): "From Moral Agents to Moral Factors: The Structural Ethics Approach". In: Kroes, Peter / Verbeek, Peter-Paul (Eds.): The Moral Status of Technical Artefacts. Philosophy of Engineering and Technology 17. Dordrecht: Springer, 124-142.

Brey, Philip A. E. / Soraker, Johnny (2009): Philosophy of Computing and Information Technology. Amsterdam: Elsevier.

Broad, William J. (2014): "Billionaires With Big Ideas Are Privatizing American Science". In: The New York Times, March 15. Online: https://www.nytimes.com /2014/03/16/science/billionaires-with-big-ideas-are-privatizing-american-science. html [08.02.2021].

Brodmerkel, Sven (2017): "Dynamic pricing: Retailers using artificial intelligence to predict top price you'll pay". In: ABC, June 27. Online: http://www.abc.net.a u/news/2017-06-27/dynamic-pricing-retailers-using-artificial-intelligence/863834 0 [08.02.2021].

Broeckling, Ulrich (2015): "Heldendämmerung? Der Drohnenkrieg und die Zukunft des militärischen Heroismus". In: BEHEMOTH, A Journal on Civilisation 8(2), 97-107.

Brooks, David (2013): "The Philosophy of Data". In: The New York Times, February 4. Online: https://www.nytimes.com/2013/02/05/opinion/brooks-the-philoso phy-of-data.html [08.02.2021].

Brooks, Rodney (2017): "The Seven Deadly Sins of AI Predictions". In: MIT Technology Review, October 6. Online: https://www.technologyreview.com/s/60904 8/the-seven-deadly-sins-of-ai-predictions/ [08.02.2021].

Brost, Marc / Hamann, Goetz (2018): "Ein autonom fahrendes Auto erkennt bei Nacht kein Wildschwein". In: Die Zeit, July 26. Online: https://www.zeit.de/201 8/31/kuenstliche-intelligenz-autonomes-fahren-wolfgang-wahlster-interview [08.02.2021]

Broussard, Meredith (2019): "Artificial Unintelligence: How Computers Misunderstand the World". In: The Information Society 35(5), 1-3.

Brown Weiss, Edith (1989): In Fairness to Future Generations: International Law, Common Patrimony, and Intergenerational Equity. Tokyo: United Nations University / Transnational Publishing.

Brown, Jennings (2017): "Former Facebook Exec: 'You Don't Realize It But You Are Being Programmed'". In: Gizmodo, November 12. Online: https://gizmodo. com/former-facebook-exec-you-don-t-realize-it-but-you-are-1821181133 [08.02.2021].

Brugger, Walter (1992): "Stufen der Begründung von Menschenrechten". In: Der Staat 31(1), 19-31.

Brundage, Miles / Future of Humanity Institute, University of Oxford / Centre for the Study of Existential Risk / University of Cambridge / Centre for a New American Security / Electronic Frontier Foundation / Open AI (2018): "The Malicious Use of Artificial Intelligence: Forecasting, Prevention, and Mitigation". In: arXiv. Online: https://arxiv.org/ftp/arxiv/papers/1802/1802.07228.pdf [08.02.2021].

Brynjolfsson, Erik / McAffee, Andrew (2011): Race Against the Machine: How the Digital Revolution is Accelerating Innovation, Driving Productivity, and Irreversibly Transforming Employment and the Economy. Lexington: Digital Frontier Press.

Brynjolfsson, Erik / McAfee, Andrew (2014): The Second Machine Age: Work, Progress, and Prosperity in a Time of Brilliant Technologies. New York / London: W. W. Norton & Company.

Bryson, Joanna (2010): "Robots Should Be Slaves". In: Wilks, Yorick (Ed.): Close Engagements with Artificial Companions: Key Social, Psychological, Ethical and Design Issues. Amsterdam: John Benjamins Publishing, 63-74.

Buchanan, Allen (2015): "Why International Legal Human Rights?". In: Cruft, Rowan / Liao, S. Matthew / Renzo, Massimo (Eds.): Philosophical Foundations of Human Rights. Oxford: Oxford University Press, 244-262.

Buchholz, Rogene A. / Rosenthal, Sandra B. (2002): "Technology and Business: Rethinking the Ethical Dilemma". In: Journal of Business Ethics 41(1), 45-50.

Buchwald, Sabine (2019): "Sind die Forscher am von Facebook finanzierten Ethik-Institut wirklich frei?". In: Sueddeutsche Zeitung, December 13. Online: https://www.sueddeutsche.de/muenchen/muenchen-tu-finanzierung-facebook-1.472356 6 [08.02.2021].

Budde, Jannica / Oevel, Gudrun (2016): "Innovationsmanagement an Hochschulen: Massnahmen zur Unterstützung der Digitalisierung von Studium und Lehre". In: Mayr, Heinrich C. / Pinzger, Martin (Eds.): INFORMATIK 2016. Series of the Gesellschaft für Informatik (GI). Bonn: Koellen Druck + Verlag GmbH, 947-960.

Buehl, Walter L. (1998): Verantwortung für soziale Systeme: Grundzüge einer globalen Gesellschaftsordnung. Stuttgart: Cotta'sche Buchhandlung.

Buiter, Wilhelm H. (2009): Lessons from the global financial crisis for regulators and supervisors. European Institute, London School of Economics and Political Science, CEPR and NBER. Discussion Paper 635. Online: http://www.lse.ac.uk/f mg/workingPapers/discussionPapers/fmgdps/DP635.pdf [08.02.2021].

Buolamwini, Joy / Gebru, Timnit (2018): "Gender Shades: Intersectional Accuracy Disparities in Commercial Gender Classification". In: Proceedings of Machine Learning Research 81, 1-15.

Burger, Paul (2007): "Nachhaltigkeitstheorie als Gesellschaftstheorie. Ein philosophisches Plädoyer". In: Kaufmann-Hayoz, Ruth / Burger, Paul / Stoffel, Martine (Eds.): Nachhaltigkeitsforschung – Perspektiven der Sozial- und Geisteswissenschaften, Bern: Schweizerische Akademie der Geistes- und Sozialwissenschaften, 13-34.

Burgess, Matt (2016): "Holding AI to account: Will algorithms ever be free of bias if they are created by humans?". In: WIRED, January 11. Online: https://www.wired.co.uk/article/creating-transparent-ai-algorithms-machine-learning [08.02.2021].

Burkert, Andreas (2017): "Die Ethik und die Gefahren der künstlichen Intelligenz". In: ATZ – Automobiltechnische Zeitschrift 119, 8-13.

Burrell, Jenna (2016): "How the machine 'thinks': Understanding opacity in machine learning algorithms". In: Big Data & Society 3(1), 1-12.

Burridge, Brian (2003): "UAVs and the dawn of post-modern warfare: a perspective on recent operations". In: RUSI Journal 148(5), 18-23.

Burt, Andrew / Shirrell, Stuart / Leong, Brenda / Wang, Xiangnong Georg (2018): "Beyond Explainability: A Practical Guide to Managing Risk in Machine Learning Models". In: The Future of Privacy Forum. Online: https://fpf.org/wp-content/uploads/2018/06/Beyond-Explainability.pdf [08.02.2021].

Buschauer, Regine (2014): "Autos und Information". In: POP. Kultur und Kritik 3, 19-23.

Butler, Judith (2004): Le pouvoir des mots. Politique du performatif. Paris: Éditions Amsterdam.

Bynum, Terrell Ward (2004): "Ethics and the Information Revolution". In: Spinello, Richard A. / Tavani, Herman T. (Eds.): Readings in Cyberethics. Massachusetts: Jones and Bartlett Publishers, 13-29.

Cachelin, Joël Luc (2017): Internetgott: Die Religion des Silicon Valley. Bern: Staempfli.

Cadwalladr, Carole (2018): "I Made Steve Bannon's Psychological Warfare Tool: meet the data war whistleblower". In: The Guardian, March 18. Online: https://www.theguardian.com/news/2018/mar/17/data-war-whistleblower-christopher-wylie-faceook-nix-bannon-trump [08.02.2021].

Callicott, Baird (1989): In Defense of the Land Ethic: Essays in Environmental Philosophy. Albany: State University Press of New York Press.

Calvo, Patrici (2020): "The ethics of Smart City (EoSC): moral implications of hyperconnectivity, algorithmization and the datafication of urban digital society". In: Ethics and Information Technology 22, 141-149.

Cambridge Dictionary (n.d.): Digital. Online: https://dictionary.cambridge.org/dictionary/english/digital [08.02.2021].

Campaign to Stop Killer Robots (2020): "Who wants to Ban Fully Autonomous Weapons?". Online: stopkillerrobots.org [08.02.2021].

Čapek, Karel (2017): W.U.R. Werstands universal Robots. Intelligent Robotics and Autonomous Agents. Translated by Otto Pick. Berlin: Contumax-Verlag.

Capurro, Rafael (2017): Homo Digitalis. Beiträge zur Ontologie, Anthropologie und Ethik der digitalen Technik. Wiesbaden: Springer.

Carnevale, Antonio (2016): "Will robots know us better than we know ourselves?". In: Robotics and Autonomous Systems 86 (Supplement C), 144-151.

Carrico, Dale (2013): "Futorological Discourses and Posthuman Terrain". In: Existenz. An International Journal in Philosophy, Religion, Politics, and Arts 8(2), 47-63.

Carroll, Archie B. (1991). "The pyramid of corporate social responsibility: Toward the moral management of organizational stakeholders". In: Business Horizons 34(4), 39-48.

Carroll, Archie B. (1999): "Corporate Social Responsibility. Evolution of a Definitional Construct". In: Business and Society 38(3), 268-295.

Carvalho, Ashwin / Lefévre, Stéphanie / Schildbach, Georg / Kong, Jason / Borrelli, Francesco (2015): "Automated driving: The role of forecasts and uncertainty – A control perspective". In: European Journal of Control 24, 14-32.

Casanova, José (2015): "Der säkulare Staat, religiöser Pluralismus und Liberalismus". In: Schwarz, Gerhard / Sitter-Liver, Beat / Holderegger, Adrian / Tag, Brigitte (Eds.): Religion, Liberalität und Rechtsstaat: Ein offenes Spannungsverhältnis. Zuerich: Verlag Neue Zuercher Zeitung, 19-25.

Casner, Stephen M. / Hutchins, Edwin L. / Norman, Don (2016): "The challenges of partially automated driving". In: Communications of the ACM 59(5), 70-77.

Cass, Kelly (2015): "Autonomous Weapons and Accountability: Seeking Solutions in the Law of War". In: Loyola of Los Angeles Law Review 48, 1017-1067.

Cassirer, Ernst (1985): "Form und Technik". In: Cassirer, Ernst: Symbol, Technik, Sprache. Hamburg: Felix Meiner, 39-91.

Castelvecchi, Davide (2016): "Can We Open the Black Box of AI?". In: Nature 538(7623), 20-23.

Catton, William/Dunlap, Riley (1980): "A New Ecological Paradigm for Post-Exuberant Sociology". In: American Behavioral Scientist 24(1), 15-47.

Cellarius, Mathias (2017): "Artificial Intelligence and the Right to Informational Self-determination". In: The OECD Forum. Online: https://www.oecd-forum.or g/users/75927-mathias-cellarius/posts/28608-artificial-intelligence-and-the-right-t o-informational-self-determination [08.02.2021].

Center of Human Rights Education (ZMRB) (n.d.): International Human Rights Forum Lucerne (IHRF). Online: www.ihrf.ch [08.02.2021].

Cernea, Mihail-Valentin (2018): "The Ethical Troubles of Future Warfare. On the Prohibition of Autonomous Weapon Systems". In: Annals of the University of Bucharest – Philosophy Series 66(2), 67-89.

Chalmers, David (2010): "The Singularity: A Philosophical Analysis". In: Journal of Consciousness Studies 17(9-10), 7-65.

Chandler, Geoffrey (2000): "Foreword". In: Frankental, Peter / House, Frances (Eds.): Human Rights – Is It Any of Your Business?. London: Amnesty International / The Prince of Wales Business Leaders Forum, 5.

Chapman, Audrey R. (2009): "Towards an Understanding of the Right to Enjoy the Benefits of Scientific Progress and Its Applications". In: Journal of Human Rights 8(1), 1-36.

Charter of Fundamental Digital Rights of the European Union (n.d.): Revised version of 2018. Online: https://digitalcharta.eu/ [08.02.2021].

Cheok, Adrian David / Karunanayaka, Kasun / Zhang, Emma Yann (2017): "Lovotics: Human - Robot Love and Sex Relationships". In: Lin, Patrick / Abney, Keith / Jenkins, Ryans (Eds.): Robot Ethics 2.0: From Autonomous Cars to Artificial Intelligence. New York: Oxford University Press, 193-213.

Childs, James M. Jr. (2015): "Beyond the Boundaries of Current Human Nature: Some Theological and Ethical Reflections on Transhumanism". In: Dialog, 54(1), 8-19.

Chorost, Michael (2005): Rebuilt. How Becoming Part Machine Made Me More Human. New York: Houghton Mifflin.

Chouldechova, Alexandra (2016): "Fair prediction with disparate impact: A study of bias in recidivism prediction instruments". In: Big Data 5(2), 153-163.

Chow, Marvin (2017): "AI and machine learning get us one step closer to relevance at scale". In: Think with Google, September. Online: https://www.thinkwithgoogle.com/marketing-resources/ai-personalized-marketing/ [08.02.2021].

Christin, Angèle / Rosenblat, Alex / Boyd, Danah (2015): Courts and Predictive Algorithms. Presentation at the Data & Civil Rights: A New Era of Policing and Justice Conference. Washington, October 27. Online: http://www.law.nyu.edu/sites/default/files/upload_documents/Angele%20Christin.pdf [08.02.2021].

Citron, Danielle K. / Pasquale, Frank A. (2014): "The scored society: Due process for automated predictions". In: Washington Law Review 89(8), 1-35.

Clark, Andy (1999): "An Embodied Cognitive Science?". In: Trends in Cognitive Sciences 3(9), 345-351.

Clarke, Cris / Tooker, Lauren (2017): "Social finance meets financial innovation: contemporary experiments in payments, money and debt". In: Theory, Culture & Society 35(3), 3-11.

Clever, Peter / Ramb, Christina (2010): "Freiheit ohne Verantwortung verkommt. Die Finanz- und Wirtschaftskrise – Folgen für unternehmerisches Handeln und die gesellschaftliche Verantwortung von Unternehmen". In: Heimbach-Steins, Marianne (Ed.): Weltwirtschaft und Gemeinwohl. Eine Zwischenbilanz der Wirtschaftskrise. Muenster: Aschendorff, 53-63.

Clifford, Catherine (2018) Elon Musk: "Mark my words – A.I. is far more dangerous than nukes". In: CNBC, March 13. Online: https://www.cnbc.com/2018/03/13/elon-musk-at-sxsw-a-i-is-more-dangerous-than-nuclear-weapons.html [08.02.2021].

Clynes, Manfred E. / Kline, Nathan S. (1995): "Cyborgs and Space". In: Gray, Chris Hables (Ed.): The Cyborg Handbook. New York: Routledge, 29-34.

CNN Money (2010): "Facebook broadcasts engagement ring purchase". In: CNN Money, December 14. Online: https://money.cnn.com/galleries/2010/technology/1012/gallery.5_data_breaches/3.html [08.02.2021].

Coeckelbergh, Mark (2012): Growing Moral Relations: Critique of Moral Status Ascription. New York: Palgrave Macmillan.

Coeckelbergh, Mark (2013): Human Being @ Risk: Enhancement, Technology, and the Evaluation of Vulnerability Transformations. Cham: Springer.

Coeckelbergh, Mark (2017): New Romantic Cyborgs: Romanticism, Information Technology, and the End of Machine. Cambridge: MIT Press.

Coeckelbergh, Mark (2020): AI Ethics. The MIT Press Essential Knowledge. Cambridge: MIT Press.

Coeckelbergh, Mark / Wackers, Ger (2007): "Imagination, distributed responsibility, and vulnerability: The case of Snorre A". In: Science and Engineering Ethics 13(2), 235-248.

Contratto, Franca (2017): "Technologie und Finanzmarktregulierung: Narrative von Interdependenz und Co-Evolution". In: Weber, Rolf H. / Stoffel, Walter A. / Chenaux, Jean-Luc / Sethe, Rolf (Eds.): Aktuelle Herausforderungen des Gesellschafts- und Finanzmarktrechts: Festschrift für Hans Caspar von der Crone zum 60. Geburtstag. Zuerich: Schulthess, 421-440.

Cooper, Rick / Davis, Michael / Van Vliet, Ben (2016): "The Mysterious Ethics of High-Frequency Trading". In: Business Ethics Quarterly 26(1), 1-22.

Corillon, Carol (1989): "The Role of Science and Scientists in Human Rights". In: The Annals of American Academy of Political and Social Science 506(1), 129-140.

Council of Europe (2018a): Discrimination, Artificial Intelligence and Algorithmic Decision-Making. Online: https://rm.coe.int/discrimination-artificial-intelligence-and-algorithmic-decision-making/1680925d73 [08.02.2021].

Council of Europe (2018b): Algorithms and human rights – Study on the human rights dimensions of automated data processing techniques and possible regulatory implications. Online: https://rm.coe.int/algorithms-and-human-rights-en-rev/16807956b5 [08.02.2021].

Council of Europe (2018c): Recommendation CM/Rec(2018)7 of the Committee of Ministers: Guidelines to respect, protect and fulfil the rights of the child in the digital environment. Online: https://edoc.coe.int/en/children-and-the-internet/7921-guidelines-to-respect-protect-and-fulfil-the-rights-of-the-child-in-the-digital-environment-recommendation-cmrec20187-of-the-committee-of-ministers.html [08.02.2021].

Council of Europe (2019a): Consultative Committee of the Convention for the Protection of Individuals with regard to the Processing of Personal Data (Convention 108): Guidelines on Artificial Intelligence and Data Protection. Online: https://rm.coe.int/guidelines-on-artificial-intelligence-and-data-protection/168091f9d8 [08.02.2021].

Council of Europe (2019b): Committee of Ministers: Declaration on the manipulative capabilities of algorithmic processes. Online: https://search.coe.int/cm/pages/result_details.aspx?ObjectId=090000168092dd4b [08.02.2021].

Council of Europe (2019c): European Ethical Charter on the use of artificial intelligence (AI) in judicial systems and their environment. Online: https://rm.coe.int/ethical-charter-en-for-publication-4-december-2018/16808f699c [08.02.2021].

Council of Europe (2003): Additional Protocol to the Council of Europe Convention on Cybercrime concerning the criminalization of acts of a racist and xenophobic nature committed through computer systems of January 28, 2003. Online: https://www.coe.int/en/web/conventions/full-list/-/conventions/treaty/189?desktop=true [08.02.2021].

Council of Europe: European Commission against Racism and Intolerance (ECRI) (2014): Annual Report. Online: https://www.coe.int/en/web/european-commission-against-racism-and-intolerance/annual-reports [08.02.2021].

Counts, Laura (2018): "Minority homebuyers face widespread statistical lending discrimination, study finds". In: Newsroom, November 13. Online: https://newsroom.haas.berkeley.edu/minority-homebuyers-face-widespread-statistical-lending-discrimination-study-finds/ [08.02.2021].

Cowen, Tyler (2013): Average is over: Powering America Beyond the Age of the Great Stagnation. New York: Dutton.

Crawford, Kate (2016): "Artificial intelligence's white guy problem". In: The New York Times, June 25. Online: https://www.nytimes.com/2016/06/26/opinion/sunday/artificial-intelligences-white-guy-problem.html?_r=0 [08.02.2021].

Crawford, Kate / Calo, Ryan (2016): "There is a Blind Spot in AI Research". In: Nature 538, 311-313.

Credit Suisse (2015): Global Wealth Report 2015. Online: https://www.credit-suisse.com/media/assets/corporate/docs/about-us/research/publications/global-wealth-report-2015.pdf [08.02.2021].

Crichton, Danny (2018): "Liquid democracy uses blockchain to fix politics, and now you can vote for it". In: Tech Crunch, February 24. Online: https://techcrunch.com/2018/02/24/liquid-democracy-uses-blockchain/ [08.02.2021].

Crouch, Colin (2008): Postdemokratie. Frankfurt am Main: Suhrkamp.

Cunningham, Lilian (2011): "Google's Eric Schmidt Expounds on His Senate Testimony". In: The Washington Post, September 30. Online: https://www.washingtonpost.com/national/on-leadership/googles-eric-schmidt-expounds-on-his-senate-testimony/2011/09/30/gIQAPyVgCL_story.html [08.02.2021].

Czarnecki, Krzysztof / Salay, Rick (2018): "Towards a Framework to Manage Perceptual Uncertainty for Safe Automated Driving". In: Gallina, Barbara / Skavhaug, Amund / Schoitsch, Erwin / Bitsch, Friedemann (Eds.): Computer Safety, Reliability, and Security. SAFECOMP. Lecture Notes in Computer Science 11094. Cham: Springer, 439-445.

Dabrock, Peter (2017): "Wenn Autos Menschen fahren. Warum die wirklichen ethischen Herausforderungen des autonomen Fahrens jenseits der Trolley-Probleme lauern". In: Zeitschrift für evangelische Ethik 61, 83-88.

Daniels, Jessie (2009): Cyber Racism. White Supremacy Online and the New Attack on Civil Rights. Lanham: Rowman & Littlefield Publishers.

Danish Ministry of Finance, Agency for Digitalisation (n.d.): Denmark's National Strategy for Artificial Intelligence. Online: https://en.digst.dk/policy-and-strategy/denmark-s-national-strategy-for-artificial-intelligence/ [08.02.2021].

Darling, Kate (2017): "'Who's Jonny?' Anthropomorphic Framing in Human-Robot Interaction, Integration, and Policy". In: Lin, Patrick / Abney, Keith / Jenkins, Ryans (Eds.): Robot Ethics 2.0: From Autonomous Cars to Artificial Intelligence. New York: Oxford University Press, 173-191.

Davis, Ernest (2015): "Ethical Guidelines for A Superintelligence". In: Artificial Intelligence 220, 121-124.

Davis, Michael / Kumiega, Andrew / Van Vliet, Ben (2013): "Ethics, Finance, and Automation: A Preliminary Survey of Problems in High Frequency Trading". In: Science and Engineering Ethics 19(3), 1-8.

De Jesus, Ayn (2018): "Augmented Reality Shopping and Artificial Intelligence – Near-Term Applications". In: Emerj, April 20. Online: https://www.techemergence.com/augmented-reality-shopping-and-artificial-intelligence/ [08.02.2021].

De Melo-Martín, Immaculada (2010): "The Two Cultures: An introduction and assessment". In: Technology in Society 32(1), 5-9.

De Saint-Exupéry, Antoine (1948): Citadelle. Paris: Gallimard.

De Soto, Hernando (2003): The Mystery of Capital. Why Capitalism Triumphs in the West and Fails Everywhere Else. New York: Basic Books.

De Soto, Hernando / Cheneval, Francis (2006): Realizing Property Rights. Swiss Human Rights Book 1. Zurich: Rueffer and Rub.

De Vries, Katja (2010): "Identity, profiling algorithms and a world of ambient intelligence". In: Ethics and Information Technology 12(1), 71-85.

Decker, Michael (2013): "Mein Roboter handelt moralischer als ich? Ethische Aspekte einer Technikfolgenabschätzung der Robotik". In: Bogner, Alexander (Ed.): Ethisierung der Technik – Technisierung der Ethik: Der Ethik-Boom im Lichte der Wissenschafts- und Technikforschung. Wissenschafts- und Technikforschung 11. Baden-Baden: Nomos Verlagsgesellschaft, 215-231.

Decker, Michael (2019a): "Autonome Systeme und ethische Reflexion". In: Thimm, Caja / Bächle, Thomas Christian (Eds.): Freund oder Feind?. Wiesbaden: Springer, 135-158.

Decker, Michael (2019b): "Ethische Fragen bei autonomen Systemen". In: Mueller, Oliver / Liggieri, Kevin (Eds.): Mensch-Maschine-Interaktion. Stuttgart: J.B. Metzler, 309-315.

DeepMind (n.d.): Exploring the real-world impacts of AI. Online: https://deepmind.com/about/ethics-and-society#fellows [08.02.2021].

Deleuze, Gilles (1992): "Postscript on the societies of control". In: October 59, 3-7.

Delmas-Marty, Mireille (2013): "Foreword: The Internet: disrupting, revealing and producing rules". In: Massit-Folléa, Françoise / Méadel, Cécile / Monnoyer-Smith, Laurence (Eds.): Normative Experience in Internet Politics. Paris: Presses des Mines, 11-18.

Demiridi, Elissavet / Kopelias, Pantelis / Nathanail, Efithia / Skabardonis, Alexander (2019): "Connected and Autonomous Vehicles – Legal Issues in Greece, Europe and USA". In: Nathanail, Eftihia / Karakikes, Ioannis D. (Eds.): Data Analytics: Paving the Way to Sustainable Urban Mobility. Advances in Intelligent Systems and Computing 879. Cham: Springer, 756-763.

Demmer, Klaus (2000): Shaping the Moral Life: An Approach to Moral Theology. Washington: Georgetown University Press.

Demmer, Klaus (2010): Bedrängte Freiheit. Die Lehre von der Mitwirkung – neu bedacht. Studien zur Theologischen Ethik 127. Freiburg im Uechtland: Herder.

Demuth, Yves (2018) Cathy O'Neil: "Die unheimliche Macht der Algorithmen". In: Beobachter, April 26. Online: https://www.beobachter.ch/digital/multimedia /big-data-die-unheimliche-macht-der-algorithmen [08.02.2021].

Dengler, Katharina / Matthes, Britta (2015): Folgen der Digitalisierung für die Arbeitswelt: Substituierbarkeitspotenziale von Berufen in Deutschland. Forschungsbericht 11. Institut für Arbeitsmarkt und Berufsforschung: Nuremberg.

Der Grosse Herder (1935): "Verantwortung". In: Nachschlagewerk für Wissen und Leben 12. 4. Auflage. Freiburg im Breisgau: Herder, 153-154.

Derrick, Dominic / Chhawri, Sumeet / Eustice, Ryan M. / Ma, Di / Weimerskirch, André (2016): "Risk Assessment for Cooperative Automated Driving". In: Association for Computing Machinery (Ed.): CPS-SPC '16: Proceedings of the 2nd ACM Workshop on Cyber-Physical Systems Security and Privacy. Vienna: Association for Computing Machinery, 47-58.

Deva, Surya (2007): "Globalisation and its Impact on the Realisation of Human Rights: Indian Perspective on a Global Canvas". In: Kumar, C. Raj / Chockalingam, Kumaravelu (Eds.): Human rights, Justice and Constitutional Empowerment. New Delhi: Oxford University Press, 237-263.

Deva, Surya (2012a): "Guiding Principles on Business and Human Rights: Implications for Companies". In: European Company Law 9(2), 101-109.

Deva, Surya (2012b): "Corporate Human Rights Violations: A Case for Extraterritorial Regulation". In: Luetge, Christoph (Ed.): Handbook of the Philosophical Foundations of Business Ethics. New York: Springer, 1077-1090.

Deva, Surya (2012c): Regulating Corporate Human Rights Violations: Humanizing Business. New York: Routledge.

Di Giovanna, James (2017): "Artificial Identity". In: Lin, Patrick / Abney, Keith / Jenkins, Ryans (Eds.): Robot Ethics 2.0: From Autonomous Cars to Artificial Intelligence. New York: Oxford University Press, 307-321.

Di Lorenzo, Giovanni (2018): "Übernehmen Sie Verantwortung!" In: Die Zeit, February 8, 63-64. Online: https://www.zeit.de/2018/07/studenten-leben-verantw ortung-universitaet-idealismus [08.02.2021].

Dickow, Marcel (2015): Robotik – ein Game-Changer für Militär und Sicherheitspolitik?. SWP-Studie 14. Berlin: Stiftung Wissenschaft und Politik – Deutsches Institut für Internationale Politik und Sicherheit.

Dickow, Marcel / Linnenkamp, Hilmar (2012): "Kampfdrohnen – Killing Drones: Ein Plädoyer gegen die fliegenden Automaten". In: SWP-Aktuell 75, 1-8.

Die Zeit (2020): "Social Media: Friedrich Merz weist Kritik an Medien-Äusserung zurück". In: Die Zeit, February 17. Online: https://www.zeit.de/kultur/2020-02/f riedrich-merz-social-media-klassische-medien-berichterstattung-djv [08.02.2021].

Dierksmeier, Claus (2006): "John Rawls on the rights of future generations". In: Tremmel, Joerg Chet (Ed.): Handbook of Intergenerational Justice. Cheltenham: Edward Elgar Publishing, 72-85.

Dierksmeier, Claus (2012): "How should we do Business? Global Ethics in the Age of Globality". In: Tenth Global Ethic Lecture. Online: https://www.weltethos.or g/1-pdf/20-aktivitaeten/eng/we-reden-eng/speech_Dierksmeier_eng.pdf [08.02.2021].

Dierksmeier, Claus / Seele, Peter (2018): "Cryptocurrencies and Business Ethics". In: Journal of Business Ethics 152(1), 1-14.

Digital Health & AI Research Collaborative (I-DAIR) (n.d.): Homepage. Online: https://graduateinstitute.ch/I-DAIR [08.02.2021].

Dignum, Virginia (2019): Responsible Artificial Intelligence: How to Develop and Use AI in a Responsible Way. Cham: Springer.

Dillard, Jesse (2013): "Human Rights within an Ethic of Accountability". In: Haynes, Kathryn / Murray, Alan / Dillard, Jesse (Eds.): Corporate Social Responsibility. A research handbook. London: Routledge, 196-220.

Dillard, Jesse / Murray, Allan (2013): "Deciphering the Domain of Corporate Social Responsibility". In: Haynes, Kathryn / Dillard, Jesse / Murray, Allan (Eds.): Corporate Social Responsibility. A research handbook. London: Routledge, 10-27.

Dittmann, Frank (2016): "Mensch und Roboter – ein ungleiches Paar". In: Manzeschke, Arne / Karsch, Fabian (Eds.): Roboter, Computer und Hybride. Was ereignet sich zwischen Menschen und Maschinen?. TTN-Studien 5. Baden-Baden: Nomos Verlagsgesellschaft, 17-46.

Dix, Alexander (2016): "Datenschutz im Zeitalter von Big Data. Wie steht es um den Schutz der Privatsphäre?". In: Stadtforschung und Statistik: Zeitschrift des Verbandes Deutscher Städtestatistiker 29(1), 59-64.

Donders, Yvonne (2015): "Balancing Interests: Limitations to the Right to Enjoy the Benefits of Scientific Progress and Its Applications". In: European Journal of Human Rights 4, 486-503.

Doorn, Neelke / van de Poel, Ibo (2012): "Editors' Overview: Moral Responsibility in Technology and Engineering". In: Science and Engineering Ethics 18(1), 1-11.

Doshi-Velez, Finale / Kortz, Mason (2017): "Accountability of AI Under the Law: The Role of Explanation". Berkman Klein Center Working Group on Explanation and the Law, Berkman Klein Center for Internet & Society working paper. In: arXiv. Online: https://arxiv.org/ftp/arxiv/papers/1711/1711.01134.pdf [08.02.2021].

Dove, Edward S. / Townend, David / Meslin, Eric M. / Bobrow, Martin / Littler, Katherine / Dianne, Nicol / de Vries, Jantina / Junker, Anne / Garattini, Chiara / Bovenberg, Jasper / Shabani, Mahsa / Lévesque, Emmanuelle / Knoppers, Bartha M. (2016): "Ethics review for international data-intensive research". In: Science 351(6280), 1399-1400.

Dreyfus, Hubert L. (1972): What Computers Can't Do: The Limits of Artificial Intelligence. New York: MIT Press.

Dreyfus, Hubert L. / Dreyfus, Stuart E. (1986): Mind Over Machine: The Power of Human Intuition and Expertise in the Era of the Computer. New York: Free Press.

Droesser, Christoph (2018): "Eine Überdosis Facebook". In: Die Zeit, May 3, 31-32. Online: https://www.zeit.de/2018/19/medienverhalten-facebook-twitter-youtube-silicon-valley-manipulation-alternativen [08.02.2021].

Druga, Stefania / Williams, Randi (2017): "Kids, AI Devices, and Intelligent Toys". In: MIT Media Lab, June 6. Online: https://www.media.mit.edu/posts/kids-ai-de vices/ [08.02.2021].

Duerrenmatt, Friedrich (1962): Die Physiker. Zuerich: Arche.

Duewell, Marcus (2010): "Menschenwürde als Grundlage der Menschenrechte". In: Debus, Tessa / Kreide, Regina / Krennerich, Michael / Malowitz, Karsten / Poll-mann, Arnd / Zwingel, Susanne (Eds.): Zeitschrift für Menschenrechte 4, 64-79.

Duewell, Marcus / Neumann, Josef J. (Eds.) (2005): Wie viel Ethik verträgt die Medizin?. Paderborn: Mentis.

Duttge, Gunnar (2016): "Das Recht auf Nichtwissen in einer informationell ver-netzten Gesundheitsversorgung". In: Medizinrecht 34(9), 664-669.

Dutton, Ian R. (1990): "Engineering code of ethics". In: IEEE Potentials 9(4), 30-31. Online: https://ieeexplore.ieee.org/document/65865 [08.02.2021].

Deutsche Welle (DW) (2020): "'No time to wait' for tax reforms, says German fi-nance minister". Online: https://www.dw.com/en/no-time-to-wait-for-tax-reform s-says-german-finance-minister/a-52475061 [08.02.2021].

Dziobek, Isabel / Lucke, Ulrike / Manzeschke, Arne (2017): "Emotions-sensitive Trainingssysteme für Menschen mit Autismus". In: Eibl, Maximilian / Gaedke, Martin (Eds.): INFORMATIK 2017. Bonn: Gesellschaft für Informatik, 369-380.

Edwards, Douglas (2011): I'm Feeling Lucky. Boston: Houghton Mifflin Harcourt.

Eggers, Dave (2013): The Circle. New York: Penguin Random House.

Eggers, William D. (2014): "Social by the numbers: An interview with Sandy Pent-land". In: Deloitte Review 15. Online: https://www2.deloitte.com/us/en/insights /deloitte-review/issue-15/sandy-pentland-mit-interview.html. [08.02.2021].

Ehrenhauser, Astrid / Knuth, Hannah (2019): "Wer darf mitmachen?". In: Die Zeit, August 8, 55-56. Online: https://www.zeit.de/2019/33/digitalisierung-schule-it-ko nzerne-kooperation [08.02.2021].

Eichhorst, Werner / Hinte, Holger / Rinne, Ulf / Tobsch, Verena (2016): Digital-isierung und Arbeitsmarkt: Aktuelle Entwicklungen und sozialpolitische Herausforderungen. Institut zur Zukunft der Arbeit 85. Bonn: Institut zur Zukunft der Arbeit.

Eiholzer, Stefan (2019): "Schnelleres Digitalisieren: Google Books spannt mit Schweizer Bibliotheken zusammen". In: Swiss National Radio Television SRF News. Online: https://www.srf.ch/news/schweiz/schnelleres-digitalisieren-google -books-spannt-mit-schweizer-bibliotheken-zusammen [08.02.2021].

Eimler, Sabrina / Geisler, Stefan / Mischewski, Philipp (2018): "Ethik im autonomen Fahrzeug: Zum menschlichen Verhalten in drohenden Unfallsituationen". In: Dachselt, Raimund / Weber, Gerhard (Eds.): Mensch und Computer. Bonn: Gesellschaft für Informatik, 709-716.

Ekmekçi, Asli (2014): "An Examination of the Relationship Between Companies' Corporate Social Responsibility (CSR): Acitivites and Consumers' Purchase Behavior". In: Yueksel Mermod, Asli / Idowu, Samuel O. (Eds.): Corporate Social Responsibility in the Global Business World. Heidelberg: Springer, 49-73.

Elder, Alexis (2017): "Robot Friends for Autistic Children. Monopoly Money or Counterfeit Currency?". In: Lin, Patrick / Abney, Keith / Jenkins, Ryans (Eds.): Robot Ethics 2.0: From Autonomous Cars to Artificial Intelligence. New York: Oxford University Press, 113-126.

Electronic Privacy Information Centre (n.d.): Homepage. Online: https://www.epic.org/ [08.02.2021].

El-Hitami, Hannah (2017): "Kalte Logik der Algorithmen". In: Amnesty International Switzerland, Magazin der Menschenrechte, June, 28-29.

Eliasson, Jan (2015): "Deputy Secretary-General, Marking Fiftieth Anniversary of Anti-Racism Convention, Urges Internet to Be Used as Powerful Tool in Fight against Racial Discrimination". United Nations, December 2. Online: https://www.un.org/press/en/2015/dsgsm921.doc.htm [08.02.2021].

Elliot, Robert (1992): "Intrinsic value, environmental obligation, and naturalness". In: The Monist 75, 138-160.

Ellul, Jacques (1964): The Technological Society. New York: Vintage Books.

Elsbernd, Astrid / Lehmeyer, Sonja / Schilling, Ulrike (2014): Technikgestützte Pflege: Grundlagen, Perspektiven und Entwicklungen. Online: https://hses.bsz-bw.de/frontdoor/deliver/index/docId/84/file/Grundlagenartikel_Technik_und_Pflege AE08.pdf [08.02.2021].

Elstner, Steffen / Feld, Lars P. / Schmidt, Christoph M. (2016): "Bedingt abwehrbereit – Deutschland im digitalen Wandel". In: Wirtschaftspolitische Blaetter 2, 287-308.

Emunds, Bernhard (2014): Politische Wirtschaftsethik globaler Finanzmärkte. Wiesbaden: Springer.

Enderle, Georges (2002): "Veränderungen der Ökonomie im Kontext von Globalisierungsprozessen". In: Virt, Guenter (Ed.): Der Globalisierungsprozess: Facetten einer Dynamik aus ethischer und theologischer Perspektive. Freiburg im Breisgau: Herder, 19-40.

Enderle, Georges (2015a): "Ethical innovation in business and economy – a challenge that cannot be postponed". In: Enderle, Georges / Murphy, Patrick E. (Eds.): Ethical Innovation in Business and the Economy. Cheltenham: Edward Elgar Publishing, 1-22.

Enderle, Georges (2015b): "The Theme of the Sixth World Congress of the International Society of Business, Economics, and Ethics in 2016 in Shanghai, China: 'Ethics, Innovation, and Well-Being in Business and the Economy'". In: ISBEE, July 22. Online: http://isbee.org/the-theme-of-the-sixth-world-congress-of-the-int ernational-society-of-business-economics-and-ethics-in-2016-in-shanghai-china-et hics-innovation-and-well-being-in-business-and-the-econom/ [08.02.2021].

Engel Bromwich, Jonah / Victor, Daniel / Isaac, Mike (2016): "Police Use Surveillance Tool to Scan Social Media, A.C.L.U. Says". In: The New York Times, October 11. Online: https://www.nytimes.com/2016/10/12/technology/aclu-faceboo k-twitter-instagram-geofeedia.html [08.02.2021].

Engineering and Physical Sciences Research Council (2011): EPSRC Principles of Robotics 2011. Online: https://www.epsrc.ac.uk/research/ourportfolio/themes/e ngineering/activities/principlesofrobotics/ [08.02.2021].

Engineering and Physical Sciences Research Council (2010): Principles of robotics. Online: https://epsrc.ukri.org/research/ourportfolio/themes/engineering/activitie s/principlesofrobotics/ [08.02.2021].

Englert, Matthias / Siebert, Sandra / Ziegler, Martin (2014): "Logical Limitations to Machine Ethics with Consequences to Lethal Autonomous Weapons". In: arXiv. Online: https://arxiv.org/abs/1411.2842 [08.02.2021].

Etienne, Hubert (2020): "When AI Ethics Goes Astray: A Case Study of Autonomous Vehicles". In: Social Science Computer Review 28, 608-618.

Etzioni, Amitai / Etzioni, Oren (2017): "Pros and Cons of Autonomous Weapons Systems". In: Military Review (May-June), 72-80.

European Commission (2018): Knowledge for Policy. Dual-Use Technologies. Online: https://ec.europa.eu/knowledge4policy/foresight/topic/changing-security-pa radigm/artificial-intelligence-quantum-cryptography_en [08.02.2021].

European Commission (n.d.): Artificial Intelligence. Online: https://ec.europa.eu/d igital-single-market/en/artificial-intelligence [08.02.2021].

European Digital Rights (EDRi) (2014): The Charter of Digital Rights. Online: https://edri.org/wp-content/uploads/2014/06/EDRi_DigitalRightsCharter_web.p df [08.02.2021].

European Group on Ethics in Science and New Technologies (2009): Ethics of information and communication technologies. Online: https://op.europa.eu/en/p ublication-detail/-/publication/c35a8ab5-a21d-41ff-b654-8cd6d41f6794/language- en/format-PDF/source-77404276 [08.02.2021].

European Group on Ethics in Science and New Technologies (2014): Ethics of Security and Surveillance Technologies. Online: https://op.europa.eu/en/publicati on-detail/-/publication/6f1b3ce0-2810-4926-b185-54fc3225c969 [08.02.2021].

European Group on Ethics in Science and New Technologies (2015): The ethical implications of new health technologies and citizen participation. Online: https: //op.europa.eu/en/publication-detail/-/publication/e86c21fa-ef2f-11e5-8529-01aa7 5ed71a1/language-en/format-PDF/source-77404221 [08.02.2021].

European Group on Ethics in Science and New Technologies (2018a): Statement on Artificial Intelligence, Robotics and 'Autonomous' Systems. Online: http://ec.europa.eu/research/ege/pdf/ege_ai_statement_2018.pdf [08.02.2021].

European Group on Ethics in Science and New Technologies (2018b): Future of Work, Future of Society. Online: https://ec.europa.eu/info/sites/info/files/researc h_and_innovation/ege/ege_future-of-work_opinion_122018.pdf [08.02.2021].

European Parliament (2017a): "Rise of the robots: Mady Delvaux on why their use should be regulated". In: European Parliament, February 15. Online: https://ww w.europarl.europa.eu/news/en/headlines/economy/20170109STO57505/rise-of-t he-robots-mady-delvaux-on-why-their-use-should-be-regulated [08.02.2021].

European Parliament (2017b): "Robots and artificial intelligence: MEPs call for EU-wide liability rules". In: European Parliament, February 16. Online: https:// www.europarl.europa.eu/news/en/press-room/20170210IPR61808/robots-and-art ificial-intelligence-meps-call-for-eu-wide-liability-rules [08.02.2021].

European Standard (1992): Manipulating industrial robots: Safety. EN775/1992. Brussels: European Comitee for Standardization. Online: https://standards.iteh.a i/catalog/standards/cen/0f2ba937-d2ff-48ce-adc4-ef36fcd95371/en-775-1992 [08.02.2021].

Evans, David (2014): "Economic Aspects of Bitcoin and Other Decentralized Public-Ledger Currency Platforms". In: Coase-Sandor Institute for Law & Economics Research Paper No. 685. Online: https://papers.ssrn.com/sol3/Delivery.cf m/SSRN_ID2438085_code249436.pdf?abstractid=2424516&mirid=1 [08.02.2021].

Ewers, Michael (2010): "Vom Konzept zur klinischen Realität – Desiderata und Perspektiven in der Forschung über die technikintensive häusliche Versorgung in Deutschland". In: Pflege & Gesellschaft 4, 314-328.

Fairness, Accountability, and Transparency in Machine Learning (FAT/ML) (2016): Principles for Accountable Algorithms and a Social Impact Statement for Algorithms. Online: www.fatml.org/resources/principles-for-accountable-algorithms [08.02.2021].

Falenczyk, Tanya (2019): "Per Rechtsklick". In: Die Zeit, August 14. Online: https:/ /www.zeit.de/2019/34/rechte-propaganda-junge-identitaere-youtube [08.02.2021].

Farooq, Omer / Khan, Salman Ahmed / Khalid, Sadaf (2014): "Financial Ethics: A Review of 2010 Flash Crash". In: International Journal of Computer and Information Engineering 8(6), 1652-1654.

Feige, Edgar L. (1989): Taxing all Transactions: The Automated Payment Transactions (APT) Tax System. Buenos Aires: International Institute of Public Finance Conference on Public Finance and Steady Economic Growth.

Ferguson, Andrew Guthrie (2014): "Big Data and Predictive Reasonable Suspicion". In: University of Pennsylvania Law Review 163(2/1), 327-373.

Ferkiss, Victor (1969): Technological Man: The Myth and the Reality. New York: Braziller.

Ferrarese, Estelle (2009): "'Gabba-Gabba, We Accept you, One of us': Vulnerability and Power in the Relationship of Recognition". In: Constellations 16(4), 604-614.

Ferraris, Maurizio (2019): "Chinesische Briefe 3: China ist das Reich des neuen Kapitals". In: Neue Zuercher Zeitung, February 12. Online: https://www.nzz.ch/feuilleton/ferraris-chinesische-briefe-3-china-daten-sind-gold-wert-ld.1458857?reduced=true [08.02.2021].

Ferrell, O. C. (2017): "Broadening marketing's contribution to data privacy". In: Journal of the Academy of Marketing Science 45(2), 160-163.

Fichter, Adrienne (2019): "Der Spion im Schulzimmer". In: Die Republik, July 2. Online: https://www.republik.ch/2019/07/02/der-spion-im-schulzimmer [08.02.2021].

Fiedler, Christoph (2002): Meinungsfreiheit in einer vernetzten Welt. Staatliche Inhaltskontrolle, gesetzliche Providerhaftung und die Inhaltsneutralität des Internets. Law and Economics of International Telecommunications 48. Baden-Baden: Nomos Verlagsgesellschaft.

Fields, A. Belden / Narr, Wolf-Dieter (1992): "Human Rights as Holistic Concept". In: Human Rights Quarterly 14(1), 1-20.

Filipović, Alexander (2015): "Die Datafizierung der Welt. Eine ethische Vermessung des digitalen Wandels". In: Communicatio Socialis 48(1), 6-15.

Finanzen.ch (2014): "Finma ermittelt gegen UBS-Banker". In: Finanzen.ch, November 12. Online: https://www.finanzen.ch/nachrichten/aktien/finma-ermittelt-gegen-ubs-banker-1000371702 [08.02.2021].

Finanzen.ch (2018): "Roche will digitaler Vorreiter sein – Kein Kontakt zu Trump-Anwalt". In: Finanzen.ch, May, 18. Online: https://www.finanzen.ch/nachrichten/aktien/roche-will-digitaler-vorreiter-sein-kein-kontakt-zu-trump-anwalt-1024857354 [08.02.2021].

Fine, Arthur (2001): "The Natural Ontological Attitude". In: Papineau, David (Ed.): Oxford Readings in The Philosophy of Science. New York: Oxford University Press, 21-44.

Fink, Helmut / Rosenzweig, Rainer (Eds.) (2006): Freier Wille – frommer Wunsch? Gehirn und Willensfreiheit. Paderborn: Mentis.

Finn, Rachel L. / Wright, David (2016): "Privacy, data protection and ethics for civil drone practice. A survey of industry, regulators and civil society organisations". In: Computer Law & Security Review 32(4), 577-586.

Flaiz, Bettina / Meiler, Manuela (2014): "Dementia Care Mapping (DCM) und das Heidelberger Instrument zur Erfassung der Lebensqualität Demenzkranker (H.I.L.D.E) – eine pflegewissenschaftliche Betrachtung und Diskussion". In: Pflege & Gesellschaft 15, 235-367.

Fleischer, Margot (2012): Menschliche Freiheit – ein vielfältiges Phänomen: Perspektiven von Aristoteles, Augustin, Kant, Fichte, Sartre und Jonas. Freiburg im Breisgau: Karl Alber.

Floridi, Luciano (2011): "On the Morality of Artificial Agents". In: Anderson, Michael / Anderson, Susan Leigh (Eds.): Machine Ethics. Cambridge: Cambridge University Press, 184-212.

Floridi, Luciano (2014): "Artificial Agents and Their Moral Nature". In: Kroes, Peter / Verbeek, Peter-Paul (Eds.): The Moral Status of Technical Artefacts. Philosophy of Engineering and Technology 17. Dordrecht: Springer, 185-212.

Floridi, Luciano (2015a): "Hyperhistory and the Philosophy of Information Policies". In: Floridi, Luciano (Ed.): The Onlife Manifesto: Being Human in a Hyperconnected Era. Cham: Springer, 36-49.

Floridi, Luciano (2015b): Die 4. Revolution: Wie die Infosphäre unser Leben verändert. Frankfurt am Main: Suhrkamp.

Floridi, Luciano / Sanders, Jeff W. (2004a): "On the Morality of Artificial Agents". In: Minds and Machines 14(3), 349-379.

Floridi, Luciano / Sanders, Jeff W. (2004b): "The Foundationalist Debate in Computer Ethics". In: Spinello, Richard A. / Tavani, Herman T. (Eds.): Readings in Cyberethics. Massachusetts: Jones and Bartlett Publishers, 81-95.

Floridi, Luciano (2012): "Big Data and Their Epistemological Challenge". In: Philosophy & Technology 25(4), 435-437.

Fofiu, Adela (2013): Apocalypse on the net. Extreme Threat and the Majority-Minority Relationship on the Romanian Internet. European University Studies 451, Series 22 Sociology. Frankfurt am Main: Peter Lang.

Foot, Philippa (2002): The Problem of Abortion and the Doctrine of Double Effect, in: Foot, Philippa: Virtues and Vices and Other Essays in Moral Philosophy. Oxford: Oxford University Press, 19-32.

Ford, Martin (2009): The Lights in the Tunnel: Automation, Accelerating Technology and the Economy of the Future. United States: Acculant Publishing.

Ford, Martin (2015): Rise of the Robots: Technology and the Threat of a Jobless Future. New York: Basic Books.

Forman, Lisa (2007): "Trade Rules, Intellectual Property, and the Right to Health". In: Ethics & International Affairs 21(3), 337-357.

Fortmann-Roe, Scott (2012): Understanding the Bias-Variance Tradeoff. Online: http://scott.fortmann-roe.com/docs/BiasVariance.html [08.02.2021].

Foucault, Michael (1984): "What is Enlightenment?". In: Rabinow, Paul (Ed.): The Foucault Reader. New York: Pantheon Books, 32-50.

Foy, James (2014): "Autonomous Weapon Systems: Taking the Human Out of International Humanitarian Law". In: Dalhousie Journal of Legal Studies 23, 47-70.

Fraedrich, Eva / Beiker, Sven / Lenz, Barbara (2015): "Transition pathways to fully automated driving and its implications for the sociotechnical system of automobility". In: European Journal of Futures Research 3(11), 1-11.

Franke, Ulrike Esther / Leveringhaus, Alexander (2015): "Militärische Robotik". In: Jaeger, Thomas (Ed.): Handbuch Sicherheitsgefahren. Globale Gesellschaft und internationale Beziehungen. Wiesbaden: Springer, 297-311.

Franssen, Maarten (2014): "The Good, the Bad, the Ugly … and the Poor: Instrumental and Non-instrumental Value of Artefacts". In: Kroes, Peter / Verbeek, Peter-Paul (Eds.): The Moral Status of Technical Artefacts. Philosophy of Engineering and Technology 17. Dordrecht: Springer, 213-234.

Frebel, Lisa (2015): "Roboter gegen das Vergessen? Technische Assistenz bei Altersdemenz im Spielfilm aus medizinethischer Sicht". In: Weber, Karsten / Frommeld, Debora / Manzeschke, Arne / Fingerau, Heiner (Eds.): Technisierung des Alltags. Beitrag für ein gutes Leben? Stuttgart: Franz Steiner, 99-116.

Frehe, Volker / Teuteberg, Frank / Ickerott, Ingmar (2016): "IKT als Enabler für soziale Innovationen in Smart Rural Areas – Das Alter im ländlichen Raum hat Zukunft". In: Nissen, Volker / Stelzer, Dirk / Strassburger, Steffen / Fischer, Daniel (Eds.): Multikonferenz Wirtschaftsinformatik (MKWI) 2016. Technische Universität Ilmenau, 09.-11. März 2016, Ilmenau: Universitätsverlag, 631-642.

Frey, Carl Benedikt / Osborne, Michael A. (2013): The future of employment: How susceptible are jobs to computerisation?. Oxford Martin School 7. Online: http://www.oxfordmartin.ox.ac.uk/downloads/academic/The_Future_of_Employment.pdf [08.02.2021].

Freyth, Antje (2020): Veränderungsbereitschaft stärken. Impulse und Übungen für Mitarbeiter und Führungskräfte. Cham: Springer.

Frezzo, Mark (2015): The Sociology of Human Rights: An Introduction. Cambridge: Polity Press.

Fricke, Ernst (2011): "Achtung der Menschenwürde als ständige Herausforderung. Virtualität und Inszenierung – auch ein Rechtsproblem?". In: Communicatio Socialis 44(4), 455-461.

Friederich, Ueli (1993): Kirchen und Glaubensgemeinschaften im pluralistischen Staat: Zur Bedeutung der Religionsfreiheit im schweizerischen Staatskirchenrecht. Bern: Staempfli.

Friedman, Batya / Nissenbaum, Helen (1996): "Bias in computer systems". In: ACM Transactions on Information Systems 14(3), 330-347.

Friesacher, Heiner (2014): "Pflege und Technik – eine kritische Analyse". In: Pflege & Gesellschaft 15, 293-313.

Fritsche, Wolfgang / Zerling Lutz (2002): Umwelt und Mensch – Langzeitfolgen und Schlussfolgerungen für die Zukunft. Stuttgart: Hirzel.

Fritzsche, K. Peter (2016): Menschenrechte: Eine Einführung mit Dokumenten. Paderborn: Ferdinand Schoeningh.

Fritzsche, K. Peter / Kirchschläger, Peter G. / Kirchschläger, Thomas (2017): Grundlagen der Menschenrechtsbildung: Theoretische Überlegungen und Praxisorientierungen. Schwalbach: Wochenschau.

Fry, Hannah (2018): Hello World. Being Human in the Age of Algorithms. New York: Independent Publishers Since 1923.

Fuchs, Christian (2014): Digital Labour and Karl Marx. New York: Routledge.

Fuchs, Michael (2021): "Digitalisierung als Herausforderung für Anthropologie und Ethik". In: Ulshoefer, Gotlind / Kirchschlaeger, Peter G. / Huppenbauer, Markus (Eds.): Digitalisierung aus theologischer und ethischer Perspektive. Konzeptionen – Anfragen – Impulse. Zuerich: Pano (in print).

Fukuyama, Francis (2002): Our posthuman future. Consequences of the Biotechnology Revolution. New York: Farrar, Straus and Giroux.

Future of Life Institute (2015): Autonomous Weapons: An Open Letter from AI & Robotics Researchers. Online: https://futureoflife.org/open-letter-autonomous-weapons/ [08.02.2021].

Future of Life Institute (2017): Asilomar AI Principles. Online: https://futureoflife.org/ai-principles/ [08.02.2021].

Future of Life Institute (n.d.): Lethal Autonomous Weapons Systems. Online: https://futureoflife.org/lethal-autonomous-weapons-systems/?cn-reloaded=1 [08.02.2021].

Gabriel, Ingeborg / Kirchschlaeger, Peter G. / Sturn, Michael (Eds.) (2017): Eine Wirtschaft, die Leben fördert. Wirtschafts- und unternehmensethische Reflexionen im Anschluss an Papst Franziskus. Ostfildern: Matthias-Gruenewald-Verlag.

Gagliardone, Iginio (2015): Countering Online Hate Speech. Paris: UNESCO.

Gandia, Rodrigo Marçal / Braga, Ricardo / Antonialli, Fabio / Cavazza, Bruna Habib / Yutaka Sugano, Joel / Castro, Cleber / Luiz Zambalde, André / Neto, Arthur Miranda / Nicolai, Isabelle (2017): The quintuple helix model and the future of mobility: The case of autonomous vehicles. Presentation at the 25th International Colloquium of Gerpisa - R/Evolutions. New technologies and services in the automotive industry. Paris, June. Online: https://pdfs.semanticscholar.org/25d6/6e9ed72fb933b3330645e6f44c895bbf2c47.pdf [08.02.2021].

Gariup, Deane (2011): "Der harzige Weg zum Frauenstimmrecht". In: POLITHINK.ch, February 7. Online: https://swisspolithink.wordpress.com/2011/02/07/der-harzige-weg-zum-frauenstimmrecht/ [11.15.2020].

Geert, Bernard (1970): The Moral Rules: A New Rational Foundation for Morality. New York: Harper & Row.

Geiss, Robin (2015): The International Law-Dimension of Autonomous Weapon Systems. Friedrich-Ebert-Stiftung. Online: http://library.fes.de/pdf-files/id/ipa/11673.pdf [08.02.2021].

Gerding, Jonas (2019): "Ein Rohstoff und sein Preis". In: Die Zeit, July 18. Online: https://www.zeit.de/2019/30/kobalt-kongo-rohstoff-elektroautos-smartphones-bergbau [08.02.2021].

Gerhardt, Volker (2019): Humanität. Über den Geist der Menschheit. Muenchen: C. H. Beck.

German Federal Ministry of Justice and Consumer Protection (2015): Gemeinsam gegen Hassbotschaften – Task Force stellt Ergebnisse vor. Online: http://www.bmjv.de/SharedDocs/Artikel/DE/2015/12152015_ErgebnisrundeTaskForce.html [08.02.2021].

German Federal Ministry of Labour and Social Affairs (2017): Weissbuch: Arbeiten 4.0. Arbeit weiter denken 48. Online: https://www.bmas.de/SharedDocs/Downl oads/DE/PDF-Publikationen/a883-weissbuch.pdf?__blob=publicationFile [08.02.2021].

Gertz, Nolen (2016): "Autonomy online: Jacques Ellul and the Facebook emotional manipulation study". In: Research Ethics 12(1), 55-61.

Gesang, Bernward (2007): Perfektionierung des Menschen. Berlin: De Gruyter.

Geser, Hans (2011): "Waffensysteme als ,derivierte' Akteure: Kampfroboter im asymmetrischen Krieg": In: Technikfolgenabschätzung – Theorie und Praxis 20(1), 52-59.

Gibbs, Samuel (2017). "Elon Musk Leads 116 Experts Calling for Outright Ban of Killer Robots". In: The Guardian, August 20. Online: https://www.theguardian.c om/technology/2017/aug/20/elon-musk-killer-robots-experts-outright-ban-lethal-autonomous-weapons-war [08.02.2021].

Giddens, Anthony (1995): Die Konsequenzen der Moderne. Frankfurt am Main: Suhrkamp.

Giers, Joachim (1957): "Zum Begriff der iustitia socialis: Ergebnisse der theologischen Diskussion seit dem Erscheinen der Enzyklika 'Quadragesimo anno' 1931". In: Muenchener Theologische Zeitschrift 7, 61-74.

Gigerenzer, Gerd / Schlegel-Matthies, Kirsten / Wagner, Gert G. (2016): Digitale Welt und Gesundheit. EHealth und mHealth-Chancen und Risiken der Digitalisierung im Gesundheitsbereich. Berlin: Sachverständigenrat für Verbraucherfragen beim Bundesministerium der Justiz und für Verbraucherschutz.

Gladden, Matthew E. (2015): "Cryptocurrency with a Conscience: Using Artificial Intelligence to Develop Money that Advances Human Ethical Values." In: Annales. Ethics in Economic Life 18(4), 85-98.

Glatzel, Norbert (2000): "'Soziale Gerechtigkeit' – ein umstrittener Begriff". In: Nothelle-Wildfeuer, Ursula / Glatzel, Norbert (Eds.): Christliche Sozialethik im Dialog: Zur Zukunftsfähigkeit von Wirtschaft, Politik und Gesellschaft. Festschrift für Lothar Roos zum 65. Geburtstag. Grafschaft: Vektor, 139-150.

Gobry, Pascal-Emmanuel (2011): "Eric Schmidt To World Leaders at eG8: Don't Regulate Us, Or Else". In: Business Insider, May 24. Online: https://static4.busin essinsider.com/eric-schmidt-google-eg8-2011-5 [08.02.2021].

Goebel, Randy / Chander, Ajay / Holzinger, Katharina / Lecue, Freddy / Akata, Zeynep / Stumpf, Simone / Kieseberg, Peter / Holzinger, Andreas (2018): "Explainable AI: The new 42?". In: Holzinger, Andreas / Kieseberg, Peter / Tjoa, A Min / Weippl, Edgar (Eds.): 2nd International Cross-Domain Conference for Machine Learning and Knowledge Extraction, Hamburg, August 27-30. Lecture Notes in Computer Science. Heidelberg: Springer, 295-303.

Gogoll, Jan / Mueller, Julian F. (2017): "Autonomous Cars: In Favor of a Mandatory Ethics Setting". In: Science and Engineering Ethics 23(3), 681-700.

Goldstein, Steve (2018): "Here's the staggering amount banks have been fined since the financial crisis". In: Market Watch, February 24. Online: https://www.marke twatch.com/story/banks-have-been-fined-a-staggering-243-billion-since-the-finan cial-crisis-2018-02-20 [08.02.2021].

Good, Irving John (1966): "Speculations Concerning the First Ultraintelligent Machine". In: Advances in Computers 6, 31-88.

Goodall, Noah J. (2014): "Machine Ethics and Automated Vehicles". In: Meyer, Gereon / Beiker, Sven (Eds.): Road Vehicle Automation. Lecture Notes in Mobility. Cham: Springer, 93-102.

Goodfellow, Ian / Bengio, Yoshua / Courville, Aaron (2017): Deep Learning. Adaptive Computation and Machine Learning. Cambridge: MIT Press.

Google (2011): "Google Management Discusses Q3 (2011): Results – Earnings Call Transcript About Alphabet Inc. (GOOG)". In: Seeking Alpha, October 14. Online: https://seekingalpha.com/article/299518-google-management-discusses-q3-2 011-results-earnings-call-transcript [08.02.2021].

Gordon, Robert J. (2016): The Rise and Fall of American Growth: The U.S. Standard of Living since the Civil war. Princeton: Princeton University Press.

Gore, Al (2015): "Introduction". In: World Economic Forum (WEF) (Ed.): Top 10 Trends of 2015. Online: http://reports.weforum.org/outlook-global-agenda-2015/ top-10-trends-of-2015/ [08.02.2021].

Gosepath, Stefan (2010): "Gerechtigkeit". In: Sandkuehler, Hans Joerg (Ed.): Enzyklopädie Philosophie 1. Hamburg: Felix Meiner, 835-839.

Gosseries, Axel (2008): "Theories of intergenerational justice: A synopsis". In: Surveys and Perspectives Integrating Environment and Society 1(1), 61-71.

Gould, Carol C. (2015): "A Social Ontology of Human Rights". In: Cruft, Rowan / Liao, S. Matthew / Renzo, Massimo (Eds.): Philosophical Foundations of Human Rights. Oxford: Oxford University Press, 177-195.

Graef, Inge / Husovec, Martin / van den Boom, Jasper (2019): Spill-Overs in Data Governance: The Relationship Between the GDPR's Right to Data Portability and EU Sector-Specific Data Access Regimes. TILEC Discussion Paper No. DP 2019-005. Online: https://papers.ssrn.com/sol3/papers.cfm?abstract_id=3369509 [08.02.2021].

Graf, Friedrich Willhelm (2015): "Der freiheitliche Rechtsstaat und die Religion". In: Schwarz, Gerhard / Sitter-Liver, Beat / Holderegger, Adrian / Tag, Brigitte (Eds.): Religion, Liberalität und Rechtsstaat: Ein offenes Spannungsverhältnis. Zuerich: Verlag Neue Zuercher Zeitung, 79-86.

Grahle, Alexander / Song, Young-Woo / Brueske, K. / Bender, Beate / Goehlich, Dietmar (2020): "Autonomous shuttles for urban mobility on demand applications – ecosystem dependent requirement elicitation". In: International Conference in Engineering Design (Ed.): Proceedings of the Design Society: International Conference on Engineering Design. Cambridge: Cambridge University Press, 887-896.

Grassie, William J. (2012): "Is Transhumanism Scientifically Plausible? Posthuman Predictions and the Human Predicament". In: Tirosh-Samuelson, Hava / Mossman, Kenneth L. (Eds.): Building Better Humans? Frankfurt am Main: Peter Lang, 465-480.

Grassie, William J. (2017): "Foreword". In: Trothen, Tracy J. / Mercer, Calvin (Eds.): Religion and Human Enhancement: Death, Values, and Morality. Palgrave Studies in the Future of Humanity and its Successors. Cham: Palgrave Macmillan, v-viii.

Graves, Mark (2017): "Shared Moral and Spiritual Development Among Human Persons and Artificially Intelligent Agents". In: Theology and Science 15(3), 333-351.

Gray, Alex (2017): "These are the world's 10 biggest corporate giants". In: World Economic Forum (WEF), January 16. Online: https://www.weforum.org/agenda/2017/01/worlds-biggest-corporate-giants/ [08.02.2021].

Green, Nancy / Rubinelli, Sara / Scott, Donia / Visser, Adriaan (2013): "Introduction: Health communication meets artificial intelligence". In: Patient Education and Counseling 92, 139-141.

Greenblatt, Jeffery B. / Shaheen, Susan (2015): "Automated Vehicles, On-Demand Mobility, and Environmental Impacts". In: Current Sustainable / Renewable Energy Reports 2, 74-81.

Greene, Kate (2009): "TR10: Reality Mining". In: MIT Technology Review, February 19. Online: https://www.technologyreview.com/2009/02/19/215785/tr10-reality-mining-2/ [08.02.2021].

Grefe, Christian (2018): "Der Stromhunger wächst". In: Die Zeit, February 1. Online: https://www.zeit.de/2018/06/digitalisierung-klimaschutz-nachhaltigkeit-strombedarf [08.02.2021].

Grewe, Torsten (2015): "Subjektive Sicherheit in altersgerechten Assistenzsystemen". In: Weber, Karsten / Frommeld, Debora / Manzeschke, Arne / Fingerau, Heiner (Eds.): Technisierung des Alltags. Beitrag für ein gutes Leben?, Stuttgart: Franz Steiner, 151-178.

Griffin, James (2001): "First Steps in an Account of Human Rights". In: European Journal of Philosophy 9(3), 306-327.

Griffin, James (2008): On Human Rights. Oxford: Oxford University Press.

Griffin, James (2015): "The Relativity and Ethnocentricity of Human Rights". In: Cruft, Rowan / Liao, S. Matthew / Renzo, Massimo (Eds.): Philosophical Foundations of Human Rights. Oxford: Oxford University Press, 555-569.

Grimal, Francis / Sundaram, Jae (2018): "Combat Drones: Hives, Swarms, and Autonomous Action?". In: Journal of Conflict & Security Law 23(1), 105-135.

Grimm, Jacob / Grimm, Wilhelm (1956): "Verantwortung". In: Wörterbuch 12(1). Muenchen: Deutscher Taschenbuch Verlag, columns 79-82.

Grimm, Petra / Keber, Tobias O. / Zoellner, Oliver (2015): Anonymität und Transparenz in der digitalen Gesellschaft. Stuttgart: Franz Steiner.

459

Grimm, Petra / Krah, Hans (2014): Ende der Privatheit? Eine Sicht der Medien- und Kommunikationswissenschaft. Institut für Digitale Ethik. Online: https://www.zbw-mediatalk.eu/wp-content/uploads/2016/08/Ende_der_Privatheit_Grimm_Krah.pdf [08.02.2021].

Grimm, Ruediger / Braeunlich, Katharina (2015): "Vertrauen und Privatheit". In: Datenschutz und Datensicherheit-DuD 39(5), 289-294.

Gringsjord, Salendra / Govindarajulu, Naveen Sundar (2018): "Artificial Intelligence". In: The Stanford Encyclopedia of Philosophy Archive. Online: https://plato.stanford.edu/archives/fall2018/entries/artificial-intelligence/ [08.02.2021].

Grobner, Cornelia (2018): "Das Paradoxon der digitalen Freiheit". In: Die Presse, August 25. Online: https://www.diepresse.com/5485360/das-paradoxon-der-digitalen-freiheit [08.02.2021].

Gross, Grant (2014): "The future of artificial intelligence: Will computers take your job?". In: Computerworld, October 7. Online: https://www.computerworld.com/article/2692377/the-future-of-artificial-intelligence-will-computers-take-your-job.html [08.02.2021].

Gruber, Malte C. (2013): "Gefährdungshaftung für informationstechnologische Risiken: Verantwortungszurechnung im 'Tanz der Agenzien'". In: Kritische Justiz 46(4), 356-371.

Gruber, Malte C. (2014): "Vermittler, Störer, Rechtsverletzer: Zur Hybridhaftung im Internet". In: Zeitschrift für Geistiges Eigentum 3, 302-324.

Grunwald, Armin (2018): "Ethik-Dilemma – Wie schlimm?" In: ATZ – Automobiltechnische Zeitschrift 120(74), 3.

Grut, Chantal (2013): "The Challenge of Autonomous Lethal Robotics to International Humanitarian Law". In: Journal of Conflict & Security Law 18(1), 5-23.

Guarini, Marcello / Bello, Paul (2012): "Robotic warfare: some challenges in moving from noncivilian to civilian theaters". In: Lin, Patrick / Abney, Keith / Bekey, George A. (Eds.): Robot Ethics: The Ethical and Social Implications of Robotics. Intelligent Robotics and Autonomous Agents. New York: MIT Press, 129-144.

Guckes, Barbara (2003): Ist Freiheit eine Illusion? Eine metaphysische Untersuchung. Paderborn: Mentis.

Guersenzvaig, Ariel (2018): "Autonomous Weapon Systems. Failing the Principle of Discrimination". In: IEEE Technology and Society Magazine, 55-61.

Guetlein, Mike (2005): "Lethal Autonomous Weapons – Ethical and Doctrinal Implications". In: Joint Military Operations Department. Online: https://apps.dtic.mil/dtic/tr/fulltext/u2/a464896.pdf [08.02.2021].

Gunkel, David J. (2018): "The Other Question: Can and Should Robots Have Rights?". In: Ethics and Information Technology 20(2), 87-99.

Gunkel, David J. (2021): "Lingua Ex Machina 2.0: The Theological Origins and Destinations of Machine Translation". In: Ulshoefer, Gotlind / Kirchschlaeger, Peter G. / Huppenbauer, Markus (Eds.): Digitalisierung aus theologischer und ethischer Perspektive. Konzeptionen – Anfragen – Impulse. Zuerich: Pano (in print).

Gurbuz, Ali Osman / Gokmen, Mehpare Karahan / Aybars, Asli (2014): "Do Institutional Investors Prefer to Invest in Socially Responsible Companies? An Empirical Analysis in Turkey". In: Corporate Social Responsibility in the Global Business World. Berlin: Springer, 311-324.

Gurdus, Lizzy (2019): "Tim Cook: Apple's greatest contribution will be 'about health'". In: CNBC, January 8. Online: https://www.cnbc.com/2019/01/08/tim-cook-teases-new-apple-services-tied-to-health-care.html [08.02.2021].

Gurkaynak, Gonenc / Yilmaz, Gonenc / Haksever, Gunes (2016): "Stifling Artificial Intelligence: Human Perils". In: Computer Law & Security Review 32(5), 749-758.

Gurney, Jeffrey K. (2017): "Imputing Driverhood. Applying a Reasonable Driver Standard to Accidents Caused by Autonomous Vehicles". In: Lin, Patrick / Abney, Keith / Jenkins, Ryan (Eds.): Robot Ethics 2.0: From Autonomous Cars to Artificial Intelligence. New York: Oxford University Press, 51-65.

Gut, Walter (2008): "Eine Sternstunde der Menschheit: Die Allgemeine Erklärung der Menschenrechte von 1948". In: Schweizerische Kirchenzeitung 176(49), 816-819.

Guthrie, Clifton F. (2013): "Smart Technology and the Ethical Life". In: Ethics & Behavior 23(4), 324-337.

Haas, Michael Carl / Fischer, Sophie-Charlotte (2017): "The evolution of targeted killing practices: Autonomous weapons, future conflict, and the international order". In: Contemporary Security Policy 38(2), 281-306.

Haasis, Heinrich (2012): "Werte, Werteorientierung und Wertewandel. Die Rolle der Finanzwirtschaft und ihrer Akteure nach der Finanzkrise". In: Brun-Hagen, Hennerkes / George, Augustin (Eds.): Wertewandel mitgestalten. Guthandeln in Gesellschaft und Wirtschaft. Freiburg im Breisgau: Herder, 493-513.

Habermas, Juergen (1998): "Konzeptionen der Moderne, Ein Rückblick auf zwei Traditionen". In: Habermas, Juergen: Die postnationale Konstellation: Politische Essays. Frankfurt am Main: Suhrkamp, 195-231.

Habermas, Juergen (1999a): "Richtigkeit versus Wahrheit". In: Habermas, Juergen: Wahrheit und Rechtfertigung. Frankfurt am Main: Suhrkamp, 271-318.

Habermas, Juergen (1999b): "Zur Legitimation durch Menschenrechte". In: Brunkhorst, Hauke / Niesen, Peter (Eds.): Das Recht der Republik. Frankfurt am Main: Suhrkamp, 386-403.

Habermas, Juergen (2001a): Die Zukunft der menschlichen Natur. Auf dem Weg zu einer liberalen Eugenik? Frankfurt am Main: Suhrkamp.

Habermas, Juergen (2001b): "Glauben und Wissen". In: Börsenverein des Deutschen Buchhandels (Ed.): Friedenspreis des Deutschen Buchhandels 2001: Jürgen Habermas. Frankfurt am Main: Suhrkamp, 37-54.

Habermas, Juergen (2004): "Intoleranz und Diskriminierung". In: Mattioli, Aram / Ries, Markus / Rudolph, Enno (Eds.): Intoleranz im Zeitalter der Revolutionen – Europa 1770 - 1848. Kultur – Philosophie – Geschichte 1. Zuerich: Orell Fuessli, 43-56.

Habermas, Juergen (2008): "Vorwort". In: Sandel, Michael J.: Plädoyer gegen die Perfektion. Ethik im Zeitalter der genetischen Technik. Berlin: Berlin University Press, 7-14.

Habermas, Juergen (2011a): "'The Political'. The Rational Meaning of Questionable Inheritance of Political Theology". In: Mendieta, Eduardo / VanAntwerpen, Jonathan (Eds.): The Power of Religion in the Public Sphere. New York: Columbia University Press, 15-33.

Habermas, Juergen (2011b): "Das Konzept der Menschenwürde und die realistische Utopie der Menschenrechte". In: Habermas, Juergen: Zur Verfassung Europas: Ein Essay. Berlin: Suhrkamp, 13-38.

Habermas, Juergen (2015): "Wie viel Religion verträgt der liberale Staat?". In: Schwarz, Gerhard / Sitter-Liver, Beat / Holderegger, Adrian / Tag, Brigitte (Eds.): Religion, Liberalität und Rechtsstaat: Ein offenes Spannungsverhältnis. Zuerich: Verlag Neue Zuercher Zeitung.

Haerle, Wilfried (2011): Ethik. Berlin: De Gruyter.

Haibach, Holger / Zeidler, Stephan (2005): "Internet-Zensur auf dem Vormarsch". In: Die Politische Meinung Nr. 428, 49-53.

Hamann, Nikolaus (2014): "Ethische Aspekte geistigen Eigentums". In: Mitteilungen der VOEB 67(1), 88-108.

Hammarberg, Thomas (2008): Viewpoint of the Council of Europe Commissioner for Human Rights. October 6. Online: http://www.coe.int/t/commissioner/View points/081006_en.asp [08.02.2021].

Hammond, Daniel N. (2015): "Autonomous Weapons and the Problem of State Accountability." In: Chicago Journal of International Law 15(2), 652-687.

Hanson, F. Allan (2014): "Which Came First, the Doer or the Deed?". In: Kroes, Peter / Verbeek, Peter-Paul (Eds.): The Moral Status of Technical Artefacts. Philosophy of Engineering and Technology 17. Dordrecht: Springer, 55-73.

Hao, Karen (2020): "KI: Das 'Greenwashing' muss ein Ende haben". In: heise online. Online: https://www.heise.de/tr/artikel/KI-Das-Greenwashing-muss-ein-Ende-haben-4647795.html [08.02.2021].

Harari, Yuval Noah (2017): Homo Deus: A Brief History of Tomorrow. London: Harvill Secker.

Harari, Yuval Noah (2020): "The World after Coronavirus". In: Financial Times, March 20. Online: https://www.ft.com/content/19d90308-6858-11ea-a3c9-1fe6fe dcca75 [08.02.2021].

Haraway, Donna (1991): "A Cyborg Manifesto. Science, Technology, and Socialist-Feminism in the Late Twentieth Century". In: Haraway, Donna: Simians, Cyborgs and Women: The Reinvention of Nature. New York: Routledge, 149-181.

Hare, Richard Mervyn (1992): Moralisches Denken: Seine Ebenen, seine Methode, sein Witz. Frankfurt am Main: Suhrkamp.

Hartmann, Martin (2011): Die Praxis des Vertrauens. Frankfurt am Main: Suhrkamp.

Hasselbalch, Gry / Tranberg, Penille (2016): Data Ethics: The New Competitive Advantage. Tel Aviv: Publishare / Spintype.

Hauptman, Allyson (2013): "Autonomous Weapons and the Law of Armed Conflict". In: Military Law Review 218, 170-195.

Hausmanninger, Thomas / Capurro, Rafael (Eds.) (2002): Netzethik. Grundlegungsfragen der Internetethik. Schriftenreihe des International Center for Information Ethics (ICIE) 1. Muenchen: Fink.

Haux, Reinhold (2010): "Medical Informatics: past, present, future". In: International Journal of Medical Informatics 79(9), 599-610.

Haux, Reinhold / Marschollek, Michael / Wolf, Klaus-Hendrik (2016): "Über assistierende Gesundheitstechnologien und neue Formen kooperativer Gesundheitsversorgung durch Menschen und Maschinen". In: Manzeschke, Arne / Karsch, Fabian (Eds.): Roboter, Computer und Hybride. Was ereignet sich zwischen Menschen und Maschinen?, TTN-Studien Bd. 5. Baden-Baden: Nomos Verlagsgesellschaft, 131-143.

Hayes, Tom (2011): "America Needs a Department of 'Creative Destruction'". In: Huffpost, October 27. Online: https://www.huffpost.com/entry/america-needs-a-departmen_b_1033573 [08.02.2021].

Heesen, Jessica (2014): "Mensch und Technik. Ethische Aspekte einer Handlungspartnerschaft zwischen Personen und Robotern". In: Hilgendorf, Eric (Ed.): Robotik im Kontext von Recht und Moral. Robotik und Recht 3. Baden-Baden: Nomos Verlagsgesellschaft, 251-269.

Heidbrink, Ludger (2003): Kritik der Verantwortung: Zu den Grenzen verantwortlichen Handelns in komplexen Kontexten. Weilerswist: Velbrueck.

Heilinger, Jan-Christoph (2010): Anthropologie und Ethik des Enhancements. Berlin: De Gruyter.

Heilinger, Jan-Christoph / Mueller, Oliver (2016): "Der Cyborg. Anthropologische und ethische Überlegungen". In: Manzeschke, Arne / Karsch, Fabian (Eds.): Roboter, Computer und Hybride. Was ereignet sich zwischen Menschen und Maschinen?. TTN-Studien 5. Baden-Baden: Nomos Verlagsgesellschaft, 47-66.

Heimbach-Steins, Marianne (2012a): Religionsfreiheit. Ein Menschenrecht unter Druck. Paderborn: Ferdinand Schoeningh.

Heimbach-Steins, Marianne (2012b): "Christliche Sozialethik – im Gespräch mit der Bibel". In: Heimbach-Steins, Marianne / Steins, Georg (Eds.): Bibelhermeneutik und Christliche Sozialethik. Stuttgart: Wilhelm Kohlhammer, 11-36.

Heinrich, Christian (2018): "Digitaler Hausbesuch". In: Die Zeit, April 26, 35-36. Online: https://www.zeit.de/2018/18/telemedizin-digitalisierung-internet-telefon-aerzte-patienten-versorgung [08.02.2021].

Heinrichs, Dirk / Cyganski, Rita (2015): "Automated Driving: How It Could Enter Our Cities and How This Might Affect Our Mobility Decisions". In: The Planning Review 51(2), 74-79.

Helbing, Dirk (2015a): "Introduction – Have We Opened Pandora's Box?" In: Helbing, Dirk: Thinking Ahead – Essays on Big Data, Digital Revolution, and Participatory Market Society. Cham: Springer, 1-26.

Helbing, Dirk (2015b): "Big Data – A Powerful New Resource of the Twenty-first Century". In: Helbing, Dirk: Thinking Ahead – Essays on Big Data, Digital Revolution, and Participatory Market Society. Cham: Springer, 75-81.

Helbing, Dirk (2015c): "How and Why Our Conventional Economic Thinking Causes Global Crises". In: Helbing, Dirk: Thinking Ahead – Essays on Big Data, Digital Revolution, and Participatory Market Society. Cham: Springer, 39-52.

Helbing, Dirk (2015d): "'Networked Minds' Require a Fundamentally New Kind of Economics". In: Helbing, Dirk: Thinking Ahead – Essays on Big Data, Digital Revolution, and Participatory Market Society. Cham: Springer, 53-56.

Helbing, Dirk (2015e): "A New Kind of Economy is Born. Social Decision-Makers Beat the 'Homo Economicus'". In: Helbing, Dirk: Thinking Ahead – Essays on Big Data, Digital Revolution, and Participatory Market Society. Cham: Springer, 57-65.

Helbing, Dirk (2015f): "Global Networks Must be Redesigned". In: Helbing, Dirk: Thinking Ahead – Essays on Big Data, Digital Revolution, and Participatory Market Society. Cham: Springer, 67-73.

Helbing, Dirk (2015g): "Societal, Economic, Ethical and Legal Challenges of the Digital Revolution". In: Jusletter IT, 21 May, 1-23.

Helbing, Dirk (2015h): "From Technology-Driven Society to Socially Oriented Technology: The Future of Information Society – Alternatives to Surveillance". In: Helbing, Dirk: Thinking Ahead – Essays on Big Data, Digital Revolution, and Participatory Market Society. Cham: Springer, 95-102.

Helbing, Dirk (2015i): "Big Data, Privacy, and Trusted Web: What Needs to Be Done". In: Helbing, Dirk: Thinking Ahead – Essays on Big Data, Digital Revolution, and Participatory Market Society. Cham: Springer, 115-176.

Helbing, Dirk (2015j): "What the Digital Revolution Means for Us". In: Helbing, Dirk: Thinking Ahead – Essays on Big Data, Digital Revolution, and Participatory Market Society. Cham: Springer, 177-187.

Helbing, Dirk (2015k): "Creating ('Making') a Planetary Nervous System as Citizen Web". In: Helbing, Dirk: Thinking Ahead – Essays on Big Data, Digital Revolution, and Participatory Market Society. Cham: Springer, 187-194.

Helbing, Dirk (2015l): "Google as God? Opportunities and Risks of the Information Age". In: Helbing, Dirk: Thinking Ahead – Essays on Big Data, Digital Revolution, and Participatory Market Society. Cham: Springer, 83-93.

Helbing, Dirk (2015m): "Big Data Society: Age of Reputation or Age of Discrimination?". In: Dirk Helbing: Thinking Ahead – Essays on Big Data, Digital Revolution, and Participatory Market Society. Cham: Springer, 103-114.

Helbing, Dirk (2018): "Facebook & Co.: How to Stop Surveillance Capitalism". In: The Globalist, April 26. Online: https://www.theglobalist.com/capitalism-democracy-technology-surveillance-privacy/ [08.02.2021].

Helft, Miguel (2012): "Larry Page on Google". In: Fortune, December 11. Online: https://fortune.com/2012/12/11/fortune-exclusive-larry-page-on-google/ [08.02.2021].

Heller, Ágnes (2016): Von der Utopie zur Dystopie: Was können wir uns wünschen?. Wien: Edition Konturen.

Hennchen, Esther (2014): "Royal Dutch Shell in Nigeria: Where Do Responsibilities End?". In: Journal of Business Ethics 129(1), 1-25.

Henne, Melissa / Friedhof, Sonja / Kopp, Stefan (2016): Übertragung ethischer Bewertungen in das Design und die Ausgestaltung technischer Assistenzsysteme. Presentation at the Conference: Zukunft Lebensräume, 20.04.2016 - 21.04.2016 in Frankfurt am Main. Berlin: VDE-Verlag. Online: https://www.vde-verlag.de/p roceedings-en/454212065.html [08.02.2021].

Henschke, Adam (2017): "The Internet of Things and Dual Layers of Concern". In: Lin, Patrick / Jenkins, Ryan / Abney, Keith (Eds.): Robot ethics 2.0: From Autonomous Cars to Artificial Intelligence. New York: Oxford University Press, 229-243.

Herbst, Tobias (2016): "Rechtliche und ethische Probleme des Umgangs mit Proben und Daten bei grossen Biobanken". In: Datenschutz und Datensicherheit-DuD 40(6), 371-375.

Herrmann, Andreas / Brenner, Walter (2018): Die autonome Revolution: Wie selbstfahrende Autos unsere Welt erobern. Frankfurt am Main: Frankfurter Allgemeine Buch.

Herrmann, Christian / Rohlfs, Ingo (2011): "DigiTheo – Deutsche Theologie digital". In: Bibliotheksdienst 45(3/4), 259-273.

Hersch, Jeanne (1992): Im Schnittpunkt der Zeit. Zuerich: Benzinger.

Herzberg, Stephan (2019): "Die menschliche Natur und das gute Leben. Eine aristotelische Kritik des Transhumanismus". In: ET-Studies 10(2), 207-228.

Herzog, Roman (2016): "Geleitwort". In: Schliesky, Ute / Schulz, Soenke E. / Gottberg, Friedrich / Kuhlmann, Florian: Demokratie im digitalen Zeitalter, DIVSI-Perspektiven 5. Baden-Baden: Nomos Verlagsgesellschaft, 5-8.

Hessler, Martina (2016): "Zur Persistenz der Argumente im Automatisierungsdiskurs". In: Aus Politik und Zeitgeschichte 66(18-19), 17-24. Online: https://ww w.bpb.de/apuz/225690/zur-persistenz-der-argumente-im-automatisierungsdiskur s [08.02.2021].

Hetzer, Dirk / Muehleisen, Maciej / Kousaridas, Apostolos / Alonso-Zarate, Jesus (2019): "5G Connected and Automated Driving: Use Cases and Technologies in Cross-border Environments". In: Institute of Electrical and Electronics Engineers IEEE (Ed.): 2019 European Conference on Networks and Communications (EuCNC), Valencia, June 18-21, 78-82.

Heuser, Jean (2015): "Die unheimliche Mission von Mr. Google". In: Die Zeit, May 21, 21-23.

Heuser, Jean (2018): "Peter Thiel gründete PayPal und war Facebooks erster Investor – jetzt verliert er den Glauben an das Silicon Valley". In: Die Zeit, December 19, 21-22. Online: https://www.zeit.de/2018/53/peter-thiel-gruender-pay pal-facebook-silicon-valley [08.02.2021].

Heuser, Uwe Jean / Nezik, Ann-Kathrin (2019): "Der Facebook-Fluch". In: Die Zeit, December 18, 23. Online: https://time.com/5669537/brad-smith-microsoft-big-tech/ [08.02.2021].

Hevelke, Alexander / Nida-Rümelin, Julia (2016): "Selbstfahrende Autos und Trolley Probleme: Zum Aufrechnen von Menschenleben im Falle unausweichlicher Unfälle". In: Sturma, Dieter / Honnefelder, Ludger / Fuchs, Michael (Eds.): Jahrbuch für Wissenschaft und Ethik 19(1), Berlin: De Gruyter, 5-24.

Heylighen, Francis (2015): "Return to Eden? Promises and Perils on the Road to a Global Superintelligence". In: Goertzl, Ben / Goertzl, Ted (Eds.): The End of the Beginning: Life, Society and Economy on the Brink of the Singularity. Los Angeles: Humanity+ Press, 243-305.

Heyns, Christof (2013): Report of the Special Rapporteur on Extra-Judicial, Summary or Arbitrary Executions. United Nations. Online: http://www.ohchr.org/Documents/HRBodies/HRCouncil/RegularSession/Session23/A-HRC-23-47_en.pdf [08.02.2021].

Heyns, Christof (2014): Autonomous weapons systems and human rights law. Presentation made at the informal expert meeting organized by the state parties to the Convention on Certain Conventional Weapons, May 13-16, Geneva, Switzerland. Online: https://www.unog.ch/80256EDD006B8954/(httpAssets)/DDB079530E4FFDDBC1257CF3003FFE4D/$file/Heyns_LAWS_otherlegal_2014.pdf [08.02.2021].

Hielscher, Volker / Nock, Lukas / Kirchen-Peters, Sabine / Blass, Kerstin (2013): Zwischen Kosten, Zeit und Anspruch: Das alltägliche Dilemma sozialer Dienstleistungsarbeit. Wiesbaden: Springer.

High-Level Expert Group on Artificial Intelligence HLEG AI of the European Commission (2019): Ethics Guidelines for Trustworthy Artificial Intelligence. Online: https://ec.europa.eu/digital-single-market/en/high-level-expert-group-artificial-intelligence [08.02.2021].

High-Level Expert Group on Artificial Intelligence HLEG AI of the European Commission (2020): Robotics and Artificial Intelligence (Unit A.1). Online: https://ec.europa.eu/digital-single-market/en/high-level-expert-group-artificial-intelligence [08.02.2021].

Hilgendorf, Eric (2012): "Können Roboter schuldhaft handeln? Zur Übertragbarkeit unseres normativen Grundvokabulars auf Maschinen". In: Beck, Susanne (Ed.): Jenseits von Mensch und Maschine: Ethische und rechtliche Fragen zum Umgang mit Robotern, Künstlicher Intelligenz und Cyborgs. Robotik und Recht 1. Baden-Baden: Nomos Verlagsgesellschaft, 119-132.

Hilgendorf, Eric (2017): "Dilemma-Problem gelöst. Ergebnisse der Ethikkommission zum automatisierten Fahren". In: ATZelektronik 12, 46-49.

Hilgendorf, Eric (2020): "Automatisiertes Fahren als Herausforderung für Ethik und Rechtswissenschaft". In: Rath, Matthias / Krotz, Friedrich / Karmasin, Matthias (Eds.): Maschinenethik. Wiesbaden: Springer, 1-18.

Hilpert, Konrad (1995): "Das Recht, anders zu sein". In: ETHICA 3, 339-363.

Hilpert, Konrad (2006): "Abschied von der Toleranz? Kultur und Religion in der offenen Gesellschaft". In: Hilpert, Konrad / Bohrmann, Thomas (Eds.): Solidarische Gesellschaft. Christliche Sozialethik als Auftrag zur Weltgestaltung im Konkreten. Regensburg: Friedrich Pustet, 271-282.

Hilpert, Konrad (2013): "Christlicher Ethos und Erkenntniszuwachs. Methodologische Vergewisserung über die Notwendigkeit des Lernens in theologischer Ethik". In: Goertz, Stephan / Hein, Rudolf B. / Kloecker, Katharina (Eds.): Fluchtpunkt Fundamentalismus? Gegenwartsdiagnosen katholischer Moral. Freiburg im Breisgau: Herder, 123-139.

Hilty, Reto / Henning-Bodewig, Frauke (2014): "Vorwort und Einführung in die Thematik". In: Hilty, Reto M. / Henning-Bodewig, Frauke (Eds.): Corporate Social Responsibility – Verbindliche Standards des Wettbewerbsrechts? MPI Studies on Intellectual Property and Competition Law 21. Berlin: Springer, 3-5.

Hinds, Rebecca (2018): "How Natural Language Processing is shaping the Future of Communication". In: MarTechSeries, February 5. Online: https://martechseries.com/mts-insights/guest-authors/how-natural-language-processing-is-shaping-the-future-of-communication/ [08.02.2021].

Hoeffe, Otfried (1991): "Transzendentale Interessen: Zur Anthropologie der Menschenrechte". In: Kerber, Walter (Ed.): Menschenrechte und kulturelle Identität. Muenchen: Kindt, 15-36.

Hoeffe, Otfried (1994): "Wann ist eine Forschungsethik kritisch? Plädoyer für eine judikative Kritik". In: Baumgartner, Hans Michael / Becker, Werner (Eds.): Grenzen der Ethik. Ethik der Wissenschaften 9, Paderborn: Wilhelm Fink / Ferdinand Schoeningh, 41-56.

Hoefling, Wolfram (2014): "Gewissens- und religionsfreiheitlich fundierte Profilierung kirchlicher Gesundheitseinrichtungen?". In: Bormann, Franz-Josef / Wetzstein, Verena (Eds.): Gewissen: Dimensionen eines Grundbegriffs medizinischer Ethik. Berlin: De Gruyter, 89-99.

Hoernle, Tatjana (2011): "Zur Konkretisierung des Begriffs 'Menschenwürde'". In: Joerden, Jan C. / Hilgendorf, Eric / Petrillo, Natalia / Thiele, Felix (Eds.): Menschenwürde und moderne Medizintechnik. Baden-Baden: Nomos Verlagsgesellschaft, 57-76.

Hoffmann, Christian / Luch, Anika / Schulz, Soenke / Borchers, Kim Corinna (2015): Die digitale Dimension der Grundrechte. Das Grundgesetz im digitalen Zeitalter. Baden-Baden: Nomos Verlagsgesellschaft.

Hoffmann, Gerd E. (1979): Computer, Macht und Menschenwürde. Frankfurt am Main: Fischer.

Hoffmann-Riem, Wolfgang (2001): "Art. 5". In: Wassermann, Rudolf (Ed.): Alternativkommentar zum Grundgesetz für die Bundesrepublik Deutschland. Neuwied: Hermann Luchterhand.

Hoffmaster, Barry (2006): "What Does Vulnerability Mean?" In: Hastings Center Report 36(2), 38-45.

Hofheinz, Marco (2008): Gezeugt, nicht gemacht. In-vitro-Fertilisation in theologischer Perspektive. Muenster: LIT-Verlag.

Hofstetter, Yvonne (2014): Sie wissen alles. Wie intelligente Maschinen in unser Leben eindringen und warum wir für unsere Freiheit kämpfen müssen. Muenchen: C. Bertelsmann.

Hofstetter, Yvonne (2017): "EMANZIPIERT EUCH! Menschwerdung im digitalen Zeitalter". In: Spiess, Brigitte / Fabisch, Nicole (Eds.): CSR und neue Arbeitswelten: Perspektivwechsel in Zeiten von Nachhaltigkeit, Digitalisierung und Industrie 4.0. Management-Reihe Corporate Social Responsibility. Berlin: Springer, 73-90.

Hogan, Linda (2004): "Conscience in the Documents of Vatican 2". In: Curran, Charles E. (Ed.): Conscience. Readings in Moral Theology 14. New York: Paulist Press, 82-88.

Holder, Martin Friedrich / Rosenberger, Philipp / Bert, Felix / Winner, Hermann (2018): Data-driven Derivation of Requirements for a Lidar Sensor Model. Universitäts- und Landesbibliothek Darmstadt: Darmstadt.

Holderegger, Adrian (2006): "Verantwortung". In: Wils, Jean-Pierre / Huebenthal, Christoph (Eds.): Lexikon der Ethik. Paderborn: Ferdinand Schoeningh, 394-403.

Holderegger, Adrian (2015): "Religion – Säkularisierung – Postsäkularität: Marginalien zu umstrittenen Begriffen". In: Schwarz, Gerhard / Sitter-Liver, Beat / Holderegger, Adrian / Tag, Brigitte (Eds.): Religion, Liberalität und Rechtsstaat: Ein offenes Spannungsverhältnis. Zuerich: Verlag Neue Zuercher Zeitung, 65-77.

Holderegger, Adrian / Sitter-Liver, Beat / Hess, Christian W. / Rager, Guenther (Eds.) (2007): Hirnforschung und Menschenbild: Beiträge zur interdisziplinären Verständigung. Basel: Schwabe / Academic Press Fribourg.

Holderegger, Adrian / Weichlein, Siegfried / Zurbuchen, Simone (Eds.) (2011): Humanismus: Sein kritisches Potential für Gegenwart und Zukunft. Basel: Schwabe.

Hollis, Aidan / Pogge, Thomas (2008): The Health Impact Fund: Making new medicines available for all. New Haven: Incentives for Global Health.

Holstein, Tobias / Dodig-Crnkovic, Gordana / Pelliccione, Patrizio (2018): "Ethical and Social Aspects of Self-Driving Cars, Computers and Society". In: arXiv. Online: https://arxiv.org/abs/1802.04103 [08.02.2021].

Holzhey, Helmut (1975): "Soll man sich des Gewissens wegen ein Gewissen machen? (Vorwort)". In: Holzhey, Helmut (Ed.): Gewissen?. Philosophie aktuell 4. Basel: Schwabe, 7-10.

Honecker, Martin (1990): Einführung in die Theologische Ethik: Grundlagen und Grundbegriffe. Berlin: De Gruyter.

Hong, Paul (2017): "Using Machine Learning to Boost Click-Through Rate for your Ads". In: Linkedin, August 27. Online: https://www.linkedin.com/pulse/using-machine-learning-boost-click-through-rate-your-ads-tay/ [08.02.2021].

Honnefelder, Ludger (1982): "Praktische Vernunft und Gewissen". In: Hertz, Anselm / Korff, Wilhelm / Rendtorff, Trutz / Ringeling, Hermann (Eds.): Handbuch der Christlichen Ethik 3. Freiburg im Breisgau: Herder, 19-43.

Honnefelder, Ludger (1993): "Vernunft und Gewissen: Gibt es eine philosophische Begründung für die Normativität des Gewissens?". In: Hoever, Gerhard / Honnefelder, Ludger (Eds.): Der Streit um das Gewissen. Paderborn: Schoeningh.

Honnefelder, Ludger (2012): "Theologische und metaphysische Menschenrechtsbegründungen". In: Pollmann, Arnd / Lohmann, Georg (Eds.): Menschenrechte. Ein interdisziplinäres Handbuch. Stuttgart: J.B. Metzler, 171-178.

Honnefelder, Ludger (Eds.) (1998): Der Streit um das Gewissen. Paderborn: Ferdinand Schoeningh.

Honneth, Axel (2011): Das Recht der Freiheit: Grundriss einer demokratischen Sittlichkeit. Berlin: Suhrkamp.

Hood, Joel (2015): "The Equilibrium of Violence: Accountability in the Age of Autonomous Weapons Systems". In: International Law & Management Review 11, 12-40.

Hopkins, Debbie / Schwanen, Tim (2018): "Automated Mobility Transitions: Governing Processes in the UK". In: Sustainability 10(4), 1-19.

Hoppe, Thomas (2002): "Soziale Gerechtigkeit – ein zentrales Anliegen der katholischen Soziallehre". In: Rauscher, Anton (Ed.): Soziale Gerechtigkeit. Koeln: J.P. Bachem, 31-56.

Horizon 2020 Commission Expert Group to advise on specific ethical issues raised by driverless mobility (2020): Ethics of Connected and Automated Vehicles: recommendations on road safety, privacy, fairness, explainability and responsibility. Luxembourg: European Union.

House of Commons of the United Kingdom – Science and Technology Committee (2017): Algorithms in Decision-Making. Fourth Report of Session 2017-19, HC351, May 23. Online: https://publications.parliament.uk/pa/cm201719/cmsel ect/cmsctech/351/351.pdf [08.02.2021].

Howard, Don / Riek, Laurel (2015): A Code of Ethics for the Human-Robot Interaction Profession. Presentation at the Conference "We Robot 2014: Risks & Opportunities". Miami, April 4-5. Online: http://robots.law.miami.edu/2014/wp-co ntent/uploads/2014/03/a-code-of-ethics-for-the-human-robot-interaction-professi on-riek-howard.pdf [08.02.2021].

Hubbard, Patrick F. (2011): "'Do Androids Dream?' Personhood and Intelligent Artefacts". In: Temple Law Review 83, 405-441.

Huber, Wolfgang (2015): "Human Rights and Globalization". In: Graeb, Wilhelm / Charbonnier, Lars (Eds.): Religion and Human Rights: Global Challenges from Intercultural Perspectives. Berlin: De Gruyter, 7-23.

Hubig, Christoph (2007): Die Kunst des Möglichen II, Grundlinien einer dialektischen Philosophie der Technik 2: Ethik der Technik als provisorische Moral. Bielefeld: Transcript-Verlag.

Hubig, Christoph (2008): "Der technisch aufgerüstete Mensch – Auswirkungen auf unser Menschenbild". In: Rossnagel, Alexander / Sommerlatte, Tom / Winand, Udo (Eds.): Digitale Visionen. Berlin: Springer, 165-176.

Hubig, Christoph (2011): "Technikethik". In: Stoecker, Ralf / Neuhaeuser, Christian / Raters, Marie-Luise (Eds.): Handbuch Angewandte Ethik. Stuttgart: J. B. Metzler, 170-175.

Hubig, Christoph (2018): "Mensch-Maschine-Interaktion in hybriden Systemen". In: Hubig, Christoph / Koslowski, Jana / Koslowski, Peter (Eds.): Maschinen, die unsere Brüder werden: Mensch-Maschine-Interaktion in hybriden Systemen. Muenchen: Paderborn, 9-17.

Huebner, Dietmar / Spranger, Tade Matthias (2010): "Patente". In: Fuchs, Michael / Heinemann, Thomas / Heinrichs, Bert / Huebner, Dietmar / Kipper, Jens / Rottlaender, Kathrin / Runkel, Thomas / Spranger, Tade Matthias / Vermeulen, Verena / Voelker-Albert, Moritz (Eds.): Forschungsethik: Eine Einführung. Stuttgart: J. B. Metzler, 136-155.

Huebner, Dietmar / White, Lucie / Ahlers, Markus (2020): "Ethische Aspekte von Crash Algorithmen für autonome Fahrzeuge: Rechte, Ansprüche und die Konstitutivität von Verkehrsregeln". In: Oppermann, Bernd / Stender-Vorwachs, Jutta (Eds.): Autonomes Fahren. Muenchen: C.H. Beck, 61-74.

Huebsch, Stefan (1995): Philosophie des Gewissens: Beiträge zur Rehabilitierung des philosophischen Gewissensbegriffs. Neue Studien zur Philosophie 10. Goettingen: Vandenhoeck and Ruprecht.

Huelsken-Giesler, Manfred (2014): "Technikkompetenzen in der Pflege – Anforderungen im Kontext der Etablierung Neuer Technologien in der Gesundheitsversorgung". In: Pflege & Gesellschaft 15, 330-352.

Huelsken-Giesler, Manfred (2015): "Technische Assistenzsysteme in der Pflege in pragmatischer Perspektive der Pflegewissenschaft". In: Weber, Karsten / Frommeld, Debora / Manzeschke, Arne / Fingerau, Heiner (Eds.): Technisierung des Alltags. Beitrag für ein gutes Leben?. Stuttgart: Franz Steiner, 117-130.

Hueper, Melanie (2004): Zensur und neue Kommunikationstechnologien. Aachen: Shaker.

Human Rights Watch (n.d.): Killer Robot. Online: https://www.hrw.org/topic/arms/killer-robots [08.02.2021].

Humanity Plus (2009): Transhumanist Declaration. Online: https://humanityplus.org/philosophy/transhumanist-declaration/ [08.02.2021].

Hunt, Paul (2008): Promotion and protection of human rights: human rights questions, including alternative approaches for improving the effective enjoyment of human rights and fundamental freedoms: The right to health. Report of the Special Rapporteur on the right of everyone to the enjoyment of the highest attainable standard of physical and mental health. UN Human Rights Council. Sixty-third Session. A/63/263. United Nations. Online: https://undocs.org/A/63/263 [08.02.2021].

Hunter, Richard S. (2002): World Without Secrets: Business, Crime, and Privacy in the Age of Ubiquitous Computing. New York: John Wiley & Sons.

Huriet, Claude (2009): "Ethics Committees". In: Have, Henk A. M. J. ten / Jean, Michele S. (Eds.): The UNESCO Universal Declaration on Bioethics and Human Rights: Background, principles and application. Ethics Series. Paris: UNESCO Publishing, 265-270.

Hurlburt, George F. / Miller, Keith W. / Voas, Jeffrey M. (2008): "An Ethical Analysis of Automation, Risk, and the Financial Crisis of 2008". In: IEEE Reliability Society 2008 Annual Technology Report. Online: https://rs.ieee.org/images/files/Publications/2008/2008-02.pdf [08.02.2021].

Hurst, Samia / Belser, Eva Maria / Burton-Jeangros, Claudine / Mahon, Pascal / Hummel, Cornelia / Monteverde, Settimio / Krones, Tanja / Dagron, Stéphanie / Bensimon, Cécile / Schaffert, Bianca / Trechsel, Alexander / Chiapperino, Luca / Kloetzer, Laure / Zittoun, Tania / Jox, Ralf / Fischer, Marion / Dalle Ave, Anne / Kirchschlaeger, Peter G. / Moon, Suerie (2020): "Continued Confinement of Those Most Vulnerable to COVID-19". In: Kennedy Institute of Ethics Journal 30(3/4), 401-418. Online: https://kiej.georgetown.edu/continued-confinement-covid-19-special-issue/ [08.02.2021].

Hurtz, Simon (2020): "Neues Jahr, neuer Skandal?". In: Die Sueddeutsche Zeitung, January 7. Online: https://www.sueddeutsche.de/digital/cambridge-analytica-facebook-brittany-kaiser-1.4747594 [08.02.2021].

Hutson, Matthew (2017): "Artificial intelligence prevails at predicting Supreme Court decisions". In: Science Magazine, May 2. Online: http://www.sciencemag.org/news/2017/05/artificial-intelligence-prevails-predicting-supreme-court-decisions [08.02.2021].

Huxley, Aldous (1932): Brave New World. London: Vintage Classics.

Huxley, Julian (1967): Religion without Revelation. London: Watts.

International Committee of the Red Cross (ICRC) (1977): Protocol Additional to the Geneva Conventions of 12 August 1949, and relating to the Protection of Victims of International Armed Conflicts (Protocol I), 8 June 1977. Online: https://ihl-databases.icrc.org/ihl/INTRO/470 [08.02.2021].

Idowu, Samuel / Yuksel Mermod, Asli (2014): "Investing Peacefully. A Global Overview of Socially Responsible Investing". In: Yüksel Mermod, Asli / Idowu, Samuel O. (Eds.): Corporate Social Responsibility in the Global Business World, Springer: Cham, 325-355.

Institute of Electrical and Electronic Engineers (IEEE) (n.d.): Ethically Aligned Design Version 2. Institute of Electrical and Electronics Engineers IEEE. Online: https://standards.ieee.org/industry-connections/ec/ead-v1.html [08.02.2021].

Institute of Electrical and Electronic Engineers (IEEE) Standards Association (n.d.): The IEEE Global Initiative on Ethics of Autonomous and Intelligent Systems. Online: https://standards.ieee.org/industry-connections/ec/autonomous-systems.html [08.02.2021].

Ihde, Don (1990): Technology and the Lifeworld: From Garden to Earth. Bloomington: Indiana University Press.

Idhe, Don (2011) "Smart: Amsterdam urinals and autonomic computing". In: Hildebrandt, Mireille / Rouvroy, Antoinette (Eds.): The Philosophy of Law Meets the Philosophy of Technology: Autonomic Computing and Transformations of Human Agency. Routledge: London, 12-26.

International Monetary Fund (IMF) (2018): "Money, Transformed. The future of currency in a digital world". In: Finance & Development 55(2), June 2018. Online: https://www.imf.org/external/pubs/ft/fandd/2018/06/pdf/fd0618.pdf [08.02.2021].

Institut für Innovation und Technik (Ed.) (2011): Facetten des Demographischen Wandels. Neue Sichtweisen auf einen gesellschaftlichen Veränderungsprozess. Berlin: IIT.

Institute for Ethics in Artificial Intelligence (n.d.): Homepage. Online: https://ieai.mcts.tum.de/ [08.02.2021].

Intel (2017): Artificial Intelligence: The Public Policy Opportunity. Online: https://blogs.intel.com/policy/files/2017/10/Intel-Artificial-Intelligence-Public-Policy-White-Paper-2017.pdf [08.02.2021].

International Atomic Energy Agency (IAEA) (n.d.): Homepage. Online: https://www.iaea.org./ [08.02.2021].

International Conference of Data Protection and Privacy Commissioners (ICDPP) (2018): Declaration on Ethics and Data Protection in Artificial Intelligence. Online: https://edps.europa.eu/sites/edp/files/publication/icdppc-40th_ai-declaration_adopted_en_0.pdf [08.02.2021].

Internet Governance Forum (IGF) (2014): The Global Multistakeholder for Dialogue on Internet Governance Issues. Online: http://intgovforum.org/cms/2014/IGFBrochure.pdf [08.02.2021].

Internet Governance Forum (IGF) (2019): Best Practice Forum on Internet of Things, Big Data, Artificial Intelligence. Online: https://www.intgovforum.org/multilingual/filedepot_download/8398/1915 [08.02.2021].

Introna, Lucas D. (2014): "Towards a Post-human Intra-actional Account of Socio-material Agency (and Morality)". In: Kroes, Peter / Verbeek, Peter-Paul (Eds.): The Moral Status of Technical Artefacts. Philosophy of Engineering and Technology 17. Dordrecht: Springer, 31-53.

Ionita, Silviu (2017): "Autonomous vehicles: from paradigms to technology". In: IOP Conference Series: Materials Science and Engineering 252(1). Online: https://iopscience.iop.org/article/10.1088/1757-899X/252/1/012098/meta [08.02.2021].

Irrgang, Bernhard (2005): Posthumanes Menschsein? Künstliche Intelligenz, Cyberspace, Roboter, Cyborgs und Designer-Mensch – Anthropologie des künstlichen Menschen im 21. Jahrhundert. Wiesbaden: Franz Steiner.

Isaac, Alistair M. C. / Bridewell, Will (2017): "White Lies on Silver Tongues. Why Robots Need to Deceive (and How)". In: Lin, Patrick / Abney, Keith / Jenkins, Ryans (Eds.): Robot Ethics 2.0: From Autonomous Cars to Artificial Intelligence. New York: Oxford University Press, 157-172.

Isler, Thomas (2019): "Wer die falschen Filme schaut, kann keine Flugtickets mehr kaufen: Wie China den totalen Überwachungsstaat errichtet". In: Neue Zuercher Zeitung am Sonntag, June 30, 18-19. Online: https://nzzas.nzz.ch/hintergrund/ein-ueberwachungsstaat-wie-bei-george-orwell-nein-nein-das-ist-viel-konsequenter-und-intensiver-als-bei-orwell-ld.1492616?reduced=true [08.02.2021].

ISO (2020): "Information technology – Electronic discovery – Part 3: Code of practice for electronic discovery". Online: https://www.iso.org/standard/78648.html [08.02.2021].

Issenberg, Sasha (2013): The Victory Lab: The Secret Science of Winning Campaigns. New York: Crown.

International Transport Forum (ITF) (2018): Safer Roads with Automated Vehicles?. Online: https://www.itf-oecd.org/sites/default/files/docs/safer-roads-automated-vehicles.pdf [08.02.2021].

Information Technology Industry Council (ITIC) (2017): AI Policy Principles. Online: www.itic.org/resources/AI-Policy-Principles-FullReport2.pdf [08.02.2021].

Iversen, Gudmund R. / Gergen, Mary (1997): Statistics: The Conceptual Approach. Springer Undergraduate Textbooks in Statistics. New York: Springer.

Jacobs Henderson, Jennifer (2013): "The Boundaries of Free Speech in Social Media". In: Stewart, Daxton R. (Ed.): Social Media and the Law. A Guidebook for Communication Students and Professionals. New York: Routledge, 1-22.

Jagtiani, Julapa / Lemieux, Catharine (2019): The roles of alternative data and machine learning in Fintech lending: Evidence from the LendingClub Consumer Platform. Federal Reserve Bank of Philadelphia Working Paper 18-15. Online: https://www.philadelphiafed.org/-/media/frbp/assets/working-papers/2018/wp18-15r.pdf?la=en [08.02.2021].

Jahangir, Asma (2008): "Religionsfreiheit und Meinungsfreiheit". In: Bielefeldt, Heiner (Ed.): Jahrbuch Menschenrechte 2009. Wien: Boehlau, 117-122.

Jain, Devaki (2004): "Human Rights and Development". In: Kirchschlaeger, Peter G. / Kirchschlaeger, Thomas / Belliger, Andrea / Krieger, David (Eds.): Menschenrechte und Wirtschaft im Spannungsfeld zwischen State und Nonstate Actors. Internationales Menschenrechtsforum Luzern (IHRF) II. Bern: Staempfli, 297-311.

Jain, Sarthak (2017): "NanoNets: How to use deep learning when you have limited data: Part 2: Building object detection models with almost no hardware". In: Medium, January 30. Online: https://medium.com/nanonets/nanonets-how-to-use-deep-learning-when-you-have-limited-data-f68c0b512cab [08.02.2021].

Jansen, Philip / Broadhead, Stearns / Rodrigues, Rowena / Wright, David / Brey, Philp / Fox, Alice / Wang, Ning (2018): State-of-the-Art Review, Draft of the D4.1 deliverable submitted to the European Commission on April 13, 2018. A report for the SIENNA Project, an EU H2020 research and innovation program under grant agreement No. 741716. Online: https://ec.europa.eu/research/participants/documents/downloadPublic?documentIds=080166e5b9f93f94&appId=PPGMS [08.02.2021].

Jarzebski, Sebastian (2014): "Regulierung durch Algorithmen?". Online: https://regierungsforschung.de/regulierung-durch-algorithmen/ [08.02.2021].

Jaspers, Karl (1931): Die geistige Situation der Zeit. Berlin: De Gruyter.

Jaume-Palasi, Lorena / Spielkamp, Matthias (2017): Ethik und algorithmische Prozesse zur Entscheidungsfindung oder -vorbereitung. AlgorithmWatch Working Papers 4. Online: https://algorithmwatch.org/wp-content/uploads/2017/06/A lgorithmWatch_Arbeitspapier_4_Ethik_und_Algorithmen.pdf [08.02.2021].

Javers, Eamon (2020): "Facebook and Twitter decline Pelosi request to delete Trump video". In: CNBC, February 7. Online: https://www.cnbc.com/2020/02/0 7/facebook-and-twitter-decline-pelosi-request-to-delete-trump-video.html [08.02.2021].

Jedok, Kim / Young-Jun, Moon / Suh, In-Soo (2015): "Smart Mobility Strategy in Korea on Sustainability, Safety and Efficiency Toward 2025". In: IEEE Intelligent Transportation Systems Magazine 7(4), 58-67.

Jenkins, Holman W. (2010): "Google and the Search for the Future". In: Wall Street Journal, August 14. Online: https://www.wsj.com/articles/SB10001424052 7487049011045754232940995272l2 [08.02.2021].

Jennings, Bruce (2010): "Enlightenment and enchantment: Technology and ethical limits". In: Technology in Society 32(1), 25-30.

Jensen, Bjornar / Koch, Markus (2015): Mensch und Maschine: Roboter auf dem Vormarsch? Folgen der Automatisierung für den Schweizer Arbeitsmarkt. Deloitte: Zuerich. Online: https://www2.deloitte.com/content/dam/Deloitte/ch/Do cuments/innovation/ch-de-innovation-automation-report.pdf [08.02.2021].

Jessen, Jens (2013): "Transhumanismus. Die Besten sind Bestien". In: Die Zeit, May 23. Online: https://www.zeit.de/2013/22/klonen-optimierter-mensch [08.02.2021].

Jessen, Jens (2014): "Der neue Mensch". In: Die Zeit, December 17. Online: https:// www.zeit.de/2014/52/jahresrueckblick-2014-social-freezing-gendertheorie-sterbe hilfe [08.02.2021].

Joas, Hans (2011): Die Sakralität der Person: Eine neue Genealogie der Menschenrechte. Berlin: Suhrkamp.

Joas, Hans (2015a): Sind die Menschenrechte westlich?. Muenchen: Koesel-Verlag, 71-80.

Joas, Hans (2015b): "Führt Säkularisierung zum Moralverfall? Einige empirisch gestützte Überlegungen". In: Schwarz, Gerhard / Sitter-Liver, Beat / Holderegger, Adrian / Tag, Brigitte (Eds.): Religion, Liberalität und Rechtsstaat: Ein offenes Spannungsverhältnis. Zuerich: Verlag Neue Zuercher Zeitung, 105-120.

Joh, Elizabeth E. (2017): "The undue influence of surveillance technology companies on policing". In: New York University Law Review Online 92(19), 19-47. Online: https://www.nyulawreview.org/wp-content/uploads/2017/08/NYULawR eviewOnline-92-Joh_0.pdf [08.02.2021].

Johannes Reiter (1991): "Die Frage nach dem Gewissen". In: Seidel, Walter (Ed.): Befreiende Moral: Handeln aus christlicher Verantwortung. Wuerzburg: Echter, 11-31.

Johansson, Henrik (2013): High Frequency Trading. Market abuse and how to reestablish confidence in the market?. Master thesis within Economics. Joenkoeping International Business School. Online: http://www.diva-portal.org/smash/get/diva2:627869/FULLTEXT01.pdf [08.02.2021].

Johnson, Bobbie (2010): "Privacy No Longer a Social Norm, Says Facebook Founder". In: The Guardian, January 10. Online: https://www.theguardian.com/technology/2010/jan/11/facebook-privacy [08.02.2021].

Johnson, Deborah (2006a): "Computer Systems: Moral Entities but not Moral Agents". In: Ethics and Information Technology 8(4), 195-204.

Johnson, Deborah (2011): "Computer Systems: Moral Entities but not Moral Agents". In: Anderson, Michael / Anderson, Susan Leigh (Eds.): Machine Ethics. Cambridge: Cambridge University Press, 168-183.

Johnson, Deborah / Noorman, Merel (2014): "Artefactual Agency and Artefactual Moral Agency". In: Kroes, Peter / Verbeek, Peter-Paul (Eds.): The Moral Status of Technical Artefacts. Philosophy of Engineering and Technology 17. Dordrecht: Springer, 143-158.

Johnson, Jeffrey Alan (2006b): "Technology and pragmatism: From value neutrality to value criticality". In: SSRN Scholarly Paper. Online: http://papers.ssrn.com/abstract=2154654 [08.02.2021].

Jonas, Hans (1984): "Warum wir heute eine Ethik der Selbstbeschränkung brauchen". In: Stoecker, Elisabeth (Ed.): Grenzen der Ethik. Ethik der Wissenschaften 1. Paderborn: Wilhelm Fink / Ferdinand Schoeningh, 75-86.

Jonas, Hans (1985a): Technik, Medizin und Ethik. Zur Praxis des Prinzips der Verantwortung. Frankfurt am Main: Suhrkamp.

Jonas, Hans (1985b): Das Prinzip Verantwortung: Versuch einer Ethik für die technologische Zivilisation. 4. Auflage. Frankfurt am Main: Insel.

Jones, Charles (1999): Global Justice: Defending Cosmopolitanism. Oxford: Oxford University Press.

Jones, Emily (2018): "A Posthuman-Xenofeminist Analysis of the Discourse on Autonomous Weapons Systems and Other Killing Machines". In: Australian Feminist Law Journal 44(1), 93-118.

Jonietz, David / Bucher, Dominik (2018): "Continuous Trajectory Pattern Mining for Mobility Behaviour Change Detection". In: Kiefer, Peter / Huang, Haosheng / van de Weghe, Nico / Raubal, Martin (Eds.): Progress in Location Based Services. Lecture Notes in Geoinformation and Cartography. Cham: Springer, 211-230.

Japanese Society for Artificial Intelligence (JSAI) (2017): The Japanese Society for Artificial Intelligence Ethical Guidelines. Online: http://ai-elsi.org/wp-content/uploads/2017/05/JSAI-Ethical-Guidelines-1.pdf [08.02.2021].

Joy, Bill (2000): "Why the Future Doesn't Need Us". In: Wired, April 1. Online: https://www.wired.com/2000/04/joy-2/ [08.02.2021].

Kaelin, Walter (2004). "What Are Human Rights?". In: Kaelin, Walter / Mueller, Lars / Wyttenbach, Judith (Eds.): The face of human rights. Baden: Lars Mueller Publishers, 14-37.

Kaeser, Eduard (2019): "Magie und Technik: Warum Handys unser Voodoo sind". In: Neue Zuercher Zeitung am Sonntag, February 9, 49-50. Online: https://nzzas .nzz.ch/wissen/wie-unser-glaube-an-magische-kraefte-unsere-beziehung-zu-mode rner-technik-praegt-ld.1458439?reduced=true [08.02.2021].

Kahl, Anne / Puig Larrauri, Helena (2013): "Technology for Peacebuilding, Stability". In: International Journal of Security & Development 2(3), 1-15.

Kahn, Leonard (2017): "Military Robots and the Likelihood of Armed Combat". In: Lin, Patrick / Abney, Keith / Jenkins, Ryans (Eds.): Robot Ethics 2.0: From Autonomous Cars to Artificial Intelligence. New York: Oxford University Press, 274-287.

Kainz, Georg Markus (2016): "'Datenschutz ist Menschenrecht' – Privatsphäre und das Recht auf Informationsfreiheit". In: Russmann, Uta / Beinsteiner, Andreas / Ortner, Heike (Eds.): Grenzenlose Enthüllungen. Medien zwischen Öffnung und Schliessung. Innsbruck: Innsbruck University Press, 111-124.

Kaivo-oja, Jari / Roth, Steffen (2015): The Technological Future of Work and Robotics. Kiel and Hamburg: ZBW – Deutsche Zentralbibliothek für Wirtschaftswissenschaften, Leibniz-Informationszentrum Wirtschaft.

Kane, Edward J. (2008): Regulation and Supervision: An Ethical Perspective. NBER Working Paper 13895. Online: https://www.nber.org/papers/w13895 [08.02.2021].

Kant, Immanuel (1784): "Beantwortung der Frage: Was ist Aufklärung?". In: Berlinische Monatsschrift 12, 481-494.

Kant, Immanuel (1974): Grundlegung zur Metaphysik der Sitten. Weischedel, Wilhelm (Ed.). Werkausgabe 7. Frankfurt am Main: Suhrkamp.

Kant, Immanuel (1990): Eine Vorlesung über Ethik. Gerhardt, Gerd (Ed.). Frankfurt am Main: Frankfurter Fischer Taschenbuch Verlag.

Kant, Immanuel (1995a): Kritik der reinen Vernunft 2. Weischedel, Wilhelm (Ed.). Werkausgabe 4. Frankfurt am Main: Suhrkamp.

Kant, Immanuel (1995b): "Über Pädagogik". In: Kant, Immanuel: Schriften zur Anthropologie, Geschichtsphilosophie, Politik und Pädagogik 2. Weischedel, Wilhelm (Ed.). Werkausgabe 12. Frankfurt am Main: Suhrkamp, 691-761.

Kant, Immanuel (1997): Die Metaphysik der Sitten. Weischedel, Wilhelm (Ed.). Werkausgabe 8. Frankfurt am Main: Suhrkamp.

Kaplan, Andreas / Haenlein, Michael (2018): "Siri, Siri in my Hand, who's the Fairest in the Land? On the Interpretations, Illustrations and Implications of Artificial Intelligence". In: Business Horizons 62(1), 15-25.

Karsch, Fabian / Roche, Matthias (2016): "Die Vermessung des Selbst. Digitale Selbstvermessung zwischen Empowerment, Medikalisierung und neuer Technosozialität". In: Manzeschke, Arne / Karsch, Fabian (Eds.): Roboter, Computer und Hybride. Was ereignet sich zwischen Menschen und Maschinen? TTN-Studien 5. Baden-Baden: Nomos Verlagsgesellschaft, 145-160.

Kastan, Benjamin (2013): "Autonomous Weapons Systems: A Coming Legal 'Singularity'?". In: Journal of Law, Technology & Policy 45(1), 46-82.

Katz, Eric (1992): The call of the wild. In: Environmental Ethics 14, 265-273.

Kaufmann, Stefan (2010): "Der 'digitale Soldat'. Eine Figur an der Front der Informationsgesellschaft". In: Apelt, Maja (Ed.): Forschungsthema: Militär. Wiesbaden: Springer, 271-294.

Kavanagh, Camino (2019): New Tech, New Threats, and New Governance Challenges: An Opportunity to Craft Smarter Responses? Washington: Carnegie Endowment for International Peace. Online: https://carnegieendowment.org/files/ WP_Camino_Kavanagh___New_Tech_New_Threats1.pdf [08.02.2021].

Kaye, David (2018): Promotion and protection of human rights: human rights questions, including alternative approaches for improving the effective enjoyment of human rights and fundamental freedoms. Promotion and protection of the right to freedom of opinion and expression. Report of the Special Rapporteur on the promotion and protection of the right to freedom of opinion and expression. UN Human Rights Council. Seventy-third Session. A/73/348. United Nations. Online: https://digitallibrary.un.org/record/1643488/files/A_73_348-EN .pdf [08.02.2021].

Kedmey, Dan (2015): "Here's What Really Makes Microsoft's Cortana So Amazing". In: Time, July 20. Online: https://time.com/3960670/windows-10-cortana/ [08.02.2021].

Keen, Andrew (2015): Das digitale Debakel. Muenchen: Deutsche Verlags-Anstalt (DVA).

Keenan, James F. (2010): A History of Catholic Moral Theology in the Twentieth Century: From Confessing Sins to Liberating Conscience. New York: Continuum.

Kehl, Danielle / Guo, Priscilla / Kessler, Samuel (2017): Algorithms in the Criminal Justice System: Assessing the Use of Risk Assessment in Sentencing. Responsive Communities Initiative, Berkman Klein Center for Internet & Society, Harvard Law School. Online: https://dash.harvard.edu/bitstream/handle/1/33746041/201 7-07_responsivecommunities_2.pdf [08.02.2021].

Kelleher, John D. / Tierney, Brendan (2018): Data Science. Cambridge: MIT Press.

Kellermann, Paul (2014): "Werden Roboter uns das Grundeinkommen bringen?". In: Der Standard, November 13. Online: https://www.derstandard.at/story/2000 008033740/werden-roboter-uns-das-grundeinkommen-bringen [08.02.2021].

Kelley, Scott B. / Lane, Bradley / DeCicco, John (2019): "Pumping the Brakes on Robot Cars: Current Urban Traveler Willingness to Consider Driverless Vehicles". In: Sustainability 11(18), 1-15.

Kerqueno, Raphaël (2018): "It's Always Sunny in Silicon Valley: How Big Tech Dominates Digital Lobbying". Transparency International EU. Online: https://tr ansparency.eu/sunny-silicon-vallley/ [08.02.2021].

Kernaghan, Kenneth (2014): "Digital dilemmas: Values, ethics and information technology". In: Canadian Public Administration 57(2), 295-317.

Kersten, Jens (2013): "Personalisierte Medizin". In: Zeitschrift für Evangelische Ethik 57(1), 23-33.

Kersten, Jens (2016): "Die maschinelle Person – Neue Regeln für den Maschinenpark". In: Manzeschke, Arne / Karsch, Fabian (Eds.): Roboter, Computer und Hybride. Was ereignet sich zwischen Menschen und Maschinen?. TTN-Studien 5. Baden-Baden: Nomos Verlagsgesellschaft, 89-105.

Kettner, Matthias (2001): "Moralische Verantwortung in individueller und kollektiver Form". In: Wieland, Josef (Ed.): Die moralische Verantwortung kollektiver Akteure. Heidelberg: Physica-Verlag, 146-170.

Keynes, John Maynard (1936): The General Theory of Employment, Interest and Money. Cambridge: Macmillian Cambridge University Press.

Kharpal, Arjun (2017): "Stephen Hawking says A.I. could be 'worst event in the history of our civilization'". In: CNBC, November 6. Online: https://www.cnbc.com/2017/11/06/stephen-hawking-ai-could-be-worst-event-in-civilization.html [08.02.2021].

Kidd, Cory D. / Orr, Robert / Abowd, Gregory D. / Atkeson, Christopher G. / Essa, Irfan A. / MacIntyre, Blair / Mynatt, Elizabeth / Starner, Thad E. / Newstetter, Wendy (1999): "The Aware Home: A Living Laboratory for Ubiquitous Computing Research". In: Streitz, Norbert A. / Hartkopf, Volker / Siegel, Jane / Konomi, Shin'ichi (Eds.): Proceedings of the Second International Workshop on Cooperative Buildings, Integrating Information, Organization, and Architecture, CoBuild '99, Pittsburgh on October 1-2, 1999. London: Springer, 191-198.

Kim, Gunoo (2017): "Robot Ethics vs. Robot Law: Apart and Together". In: Studies in Legal Philosophy 20(2), 7-44.

King, Hope (2016): "Mark Zuckerberg to tear down and rebuild four houses surrounding his home". In: CNN Business, May 25. Online: https://money.cnn.com/2016/05/25/technology/mark-zuckerberg-palo-alto-house/index.html [08.02.2021].

Kipke, Roland (2011): Besser werden. Eine ethische Untersuchung zu Selbstformung und Neuro-Enhancement. Paderborn: Mentis.

Kirchschlaeger, Peter G. (2007a): "Brauchen die Menschenrechte eine (moralische) Begründung?". In: Kirchschlaeger, Peter G. / Kirchschlaeger, Thomas / Belliger, Andrea / Krieger, David (Eds.): Menschenrechte und Kinder. Internationales Menschenrechtsforum Luzern (IHRF) 4. Bern: Staempfli, 55-64.

Kirchschlaeger, Peter G. (2010a): "Human Rights Education for a Sustainable Future: The Relationship between Human Rights Education and Education for Sustainable Development". In: Waldron, Fionnuala / Ruane, Brian (Eds.): Human Rights Education: Reflections on Theory and Practice. Dublin: The Liffexy Press, 67-85.

Kirchschlaeger, Peter G. (2010b): Nur ich bin die Wahrheit: Der Absolutheitsanspruch des johanneischen Christus und das Gespräch zwischen den Religionen. Herders Biblische Studien 63. Freiburg im Breisgau: Herder.

Kirchschlaeger, Peter G. (2011): "Das ethische Charakteristikum der Universalisierung im Zusammenhang des Universalitätsanspruchs der Menschenrechte". In: Ast, Stephan / Mathis, Klaus / Haenni, Julia / Zabel, Benno (Eds.): Gleichheit und Universalität. Archiv für Rechts- und Sozialphilosophie 128. Stuttgart: Franz Steiner, 301-312.

Kirchschlaeger, Peter G. (2012a): "Evolution of the International Environment Law and Position of Child from a Philosophical Perspective". In: Institut international des Droits de l'Enfant (Ed.): Changement Climatique: Impacts sur les enfants et leurs droits. Sion: Institut international des Droits de l'Enfant, 73-87.

Kirchschlaeger, Peter G. (2012b): "Ich bin der Weg, die Wahrheit und das Leben (Joh 14,6). Der Wahrheitsanspruch des joh Christus und Wahrheit in anderen Religionen". In: Bibel und Liturgie 85(2), 123-147.

Kirchschlaeger, Peter G. (2013a): Wie können Menschenrechte begründet werden? Ein für religiöse und säkulare Menschenrechtskonzeptionen anschlussfähiger Ansatz. ReligionsRecht im Dialog 15. Muenster: LIT-Verlag.

Kirchschlaeger, Peter G. (2013b). "Human Rights as an Ethical Basis for Science". In: Journal of Law, Information and Science 22(2), 1-17.

Kirchschlaeger, Peter G. (2013c): "Gerechtigkeit und ihre christlich-sozialethische Relevanz". In: Zeitschrift für katholische Theologie 135(4), 433-456.

Kirchschlaeger, Peter G. (2013d): "Die Multidimensionalität der Menschenrechte – Chance oder Gefahr für den universellen Menschenrechtsschutz?". In: MenschenRechtsMagazin 18(2), 77-95.

Kirchschlaeger, Peter G. (2013e): "Menschenrechte und Politik". In: Yousefi, Hamid Reza (Ed.): Menschenrechte im Weltkontext: Geschichten – Erscheinungsformen – Neuere Entwicklungen. Heidelberg: Springer, 255-260.

Kirchschlaeger, Peter G. (2013f): "Religionsfreiheit – ein Menschenrecht im Konflikt". In: Freiburger Zeitschrift für Philosophie und Theologie 60(2), 353-374.

Kirchschlaeger, Peter G. (2014a): "Verantwortung aus christlich-sozialethischer Perspektive". In: ETHICA 22(1), 29-54.

Kirchschlaeger, Peter G. (2014b): "Human Rights and Corresponding Duties and Duty Bearers". In: International Journal of Human Rights and Constitutional Studies 2(4), 309-321.

Kirchschlaeger, Peter G. (2014c): "Ethics and Human Rights". In: Ancilla Juris 9, 59-98.

Kirchschlaeger, Peter G. (2014d): "The Relation between Democracy and Human Rights". In: Grinin, Leonid E. / Ilyin, Ilya V. / Korotayev, Andrey V. (Eds.): Globalistics and Globalization Studies: Aspects & Dimensions of Global Views, Yearbook. Volgograd: Uchitel Publishing House, 112-125.

Kirchschlaeger, Peter G. (2015a): "Das Prinzip der Verletzbarkeit als Begründungsweg der Menschenrechte". In: Freiburger Zeitschrift für Philosophie und Theologie 62(1), 121-141.

Kirchschlaeger, Peter G. (2015b): "Wie kann eine humanitäre Intervention begründet werden?". In: Manzeschke, Arne / Reuters, Lars (Eds.): Proceedings from The Ethics of War and Peace. 51st Annual Conference of the Societas Ethica, Maribor, Slovenia, August 21-24. Linkoeping: Linkoeping University Electronic Press, 77-95.

Kirchschlaeger, Peter G. (2015c): "Multinationale Konzerne und Menschenrechte". In: ETHICA 23(3), 261-280.

Kirchschlaeger, Peter G. (2015d): "Adaptation – A Model for Bringing Human Rights and Religions Together". In: Acta Academica 47(2), 163-191.

Kirchschlaeger, Peter G. (2015e): "CSR zwischen Greenwashing und ethischer Reflexion – Menschenrechte als ethischer Referenzrahmen für Corporate Social Responsibility (CSR)". In: Zeitschrift für Wirtschafts- und Unternehmensethik 16(3), 264-287.

Kirchschlaeger, Peter G. (2015f): "Menschenrechte als kontinuierliche Quelle von Wertegeneralisierung". In: Jahrbuch für Christliche Sozialwissenschaften 56, 227-250.

Kirchschlaeger, Peter G. (2016a): "Zensur zum Schutz vor Rassismus versus Informationsfreiheit – ein Spannungsfeld im Internet". In: Communicatio Socialis 49(4), 354-366.

Kirchschlaeger, Peter G. (2016b): "Digitalisierung und Robotisierung der Gesellschaft aus ethischer Perspektive". In: feinschwarz.net, March 30. Online: http://www.feinschwarz.net/digitalisierung-und-robotisierung-der-gesellschaft-aus-theologisch-ethischer-perspektive/ [08.02.2021].

Kirchschlaeger, Peter G. (2016c): "KonsumActors – mehr Macht beim Einkauf als an der Urne? Konsumethische Überlegungen zur Verantwortung beim Einkaufen". In: ETHICA 24(2), 133-157.

Kirchschlaeger, Peter G. (2016d): "Globale Gerechtigkeit aus einer finanzethischen Perspektive". In: Freiburger Zeitschrift für Philosophie und Theologie 63(2), 534-552.

Kirchschlaeger, Peter G. (2016e): "How Can We Justify Human Rights?". In: International Journal of Human Rights and Constitutional Studies 4(4), 313-329.

Kirchschlaeger, Peter G. (2016f): Menschenrechte und Religionen. Nichtstaatliche Akteure und ihr Verhältnis zu den Menschenrechten. Gesellschaft – Ethik – Religion 7. Paderborn: Ferdinand Schoeningh.

Kirchschlaeger, Peter G. (2016g): "The Interplay of the Legal and the Moral Dimension of Human Rights for the Implementation of Human Rights". In: International Journal of Human Rights and Constitutional Studies 4(1), 31-44.

Kirchschlaeger, Peter G. (2016h): "To What Extent Should the State Protect Human Beings from Themselves? An Analysis from a Human Rights Perspective". In: Mathis, Klaus / Tor, Avishalom (Eds.): 'Nudging' – Possibilities, Limitations and Applications in European Law and Economics. Cham: Springer, 59-67.

Kirchschlaeger, Peter G. (2016i): "Missachtung der Menschenwürde als Schlüsselerfahrung". In: Kraemer, Klaus / Vellguth, Klaus (Eds.): Menschenwürde. Diskurse zur Universalität und Unveräusserlichkeit. Theologie der Einen Welt 8. Freiburg im Breisgau: Herder, 193-206.

Kirchschlaeger, Peter G. (2017a): "Roboter und Ethik". In: Aktuelle Juristische Praxis 26(2), 240-249.

Kirchschlaeger, Peter G. (2017b): "Automatisierung der Mobilität – theologisch-ethische Überlegungen". In: feinschwarz.net, January 13. Online: http://www.feinschwarz.net/automatisierung-der-mobilitaet-theologisch-ethische-ueberlegungen/ [08.02.2021].

Kirchschlaeger, Peter G. (2017c): "Die Rede von 'moral technologies': Eine Kritik aus theologisch-ethischer Sicht". In: feinschwarz.net, March 20. Online: https://www.feinschwarz.net/die-rede-von-moral-technologies/ [08.02.2021].

Kirchschlaeger, Peter G. (2017d). "Gewissen aus moraltheologischer Sicht". In: Zeitschrift für katholische Theologie 139(2), 152-177.

Kirchschlaeger, Peter G. (2017f): "Wirtschaft und Menschenrechte". In: Gabriel, Ingeborg / Kirchschlaeger, Peter G. / Sturn, Michael (Eds.): Eine Wirtschaft, die Leben fördert. Wirtschafts- und unternehmensethische Reflexionen im Anschluss an Papst Franziskus. Ostfildern: Matthias-Gruenewald-Verlag, 241-264.

Kirchschlaeger, Peter G. (2017g): "Religionen als moralische Akteure". In: Bergold, Ralph / Sautermeister, Jochen / Schroeder, André (Eds.): Dem Wandel eine menschliche Gestalt geben. Sozialethische Perspektiven für die Gesellschaft von morgen. Festschrift zur Neueröffnung und zum 70-jährigen Bestehen des Katholisch-Sozialen Instituts. Freiburg im Breisgau: Herder, 133-158.

Kirchschlaeger, Peter G. (2018): "Die Menschenrechte als hermeneutischer Schlüssel zu ethischen Grundfragen des 21. Jahrhunderts: Begründung und Ausblick". In: Zeitschrift für katholische Theologie 140, 361-379.

Kirchschlaeger, Peter G. (2019a): "Homo Dignitatis – ethische Orientierung im Zeitalter digitaler Transformation". In: Psychologie in Österreich 4, 274-284.

Kirchschlaeger, Peter G. (2019b): "Digital Transformation of Society and Economy Ethical Considerations from a Human Rights Perspective". In: International Journal of Human Rights and Constitutional Studies 6(4), 301-321.

Kirchschlaeger, Peter G. (2019c): "Bedingungsloses Grundeinkommen – eine menschenrechtsethische Betrachtung". In: Hladschik, Patricia / Steinert, Fiona (Eds.): Menschenrechten Gestalt und Wirksamkeit verleihen: Making Human Rights Work. Festschrift für Hannes Tretter und Manfred Nowak. Wien: NWV, 551-563.

Kirchschlaeger, Peter G. (2020a): "The Correlation between Ethics and Technology". In: Isetti, Giulia / Innerhofer, Elisa / Pechlaner, Harald / de Rachewiltz, Michael (Eds.): Religion in the Age of Digitalization: From New Media to Spiritual Machines. Routledge: London, 165-180.

Kirchschlaeger, Peter G. (2020b): "Omni-dynamische soziale Gerechtigkeit und ihre Bedeutung für medienethische Überlegungen". In: Ulshoefer, Gotlind / Wilhelm, Monika (Eds.): Theologische Medienethik im digitalen Zeitalter. Ethik – Grundlagen und Handlungsfelder 14. Stuttgart: Wilhelm Kohlhammer, 237-254.

Kirchschlaeger, Peter G. (2020c): "Artificial Intelligence and the Complexity of Ethics". In: Asian Horizons 14(3), 587-600.

Kirchschlaeger, Peter G. (2020d): "Human Dignity and Human Rights: Fostering and Protecting Pluralism and Particularity". In: Interdisciplinary Journal for Religion and Transformation in Contemporary Society 6(1), 90-106.

Kirchschlaeger, Peter G. (2020e): "Kollektive versus individuelle Religionsfreiheit – was ist gerecht?". In: Freiburger Zeitschrift für Philosophie und Theologie 67(1), 52-66.

References

Kirchschlaeger, Peter G. (2020f): Wie sähe die Welt ohne UNO aus? 75 Jahre UN-Charta. In: feinschwarz.net, October 22. Online: https://www.feinschwarz.net/7 5-jahre-un-charta/ [08.02.2021].

Kirchschlaeger, Peter G. (2021): "Ethics of Blockchain Technology". In: Ulshoefer, Gotlind / Kirchschlaeger, Peter G. / Huppenbauer, Markus (Eds.): Digitalisierung aus theologischer und ethischer Perspektive. Konzeptionen – Anfragen – Impulse. Zuerich: Pano (in print).

Kirchschlaeger, Peter G. (Ed.) (2017e): Die Verantwortung von nichtstaatlichen Akteuren gegenüber den Menschenrechten. Religionsrechtliche Studien 4. Zuerich: TVZ.

Kirchschlaeger, Peter G. / Belliger, Andréa / Krieger, David J. (Eds.) (2003): Stammzellenforschung. SCIENCE & SOCIETY 1. Zuerich: Seismo-Verlag.

Kirchschlaeger, Peter G. / Belliger, Andréa / Krieger, David J. (Eds.) (2005): Forschung am Menschen. SCIENCE & SOCIETY 2. Zuerich: Seismo-Verlag.

Kirchschlaeger, Peter G. / Kirchschlaeger, Thomas / Belliger, Andrea / Krieger, David (Eds.) (2005): Menschenrechte und Wirtschaft im Spannungsfeld zwischen State und Nonstate Actors. Internationales Menschenrechtsforum Luzern (IHRF) 2. Bern: Staempfli.

Kirchschlaeger, Peter G. / Kirchschlaeger, Thomas (2007): "Rights of the Child and Human Rights". In: Bellamy, Carol / Zermatten, Jean / Kirchschlaeger, Peter G. / Kirchschlaeger, Thomas (Eds.): Realizing the Rights of the Child. Swiss Human Rights Book 2. Zuerich: Rueffer & Rub, 23-27.

Kirchschlaeger, Peter G. / Kirchschlaeger, Thomas (Eds.) (2010): Human Rights and Pervasive Computing. International Human Rights Forum (IHRF) 7. Bern: Staempfli.

Kirkpatrick, David (2011): The Facebook Effect: The Inside Story of the Company That Is Connecting the World. New York: Simon & Schuster.

Kirkpatrick, Jesse / Hahn, Erin N. / Haufler, Amy J. (2017): "Trust and Human-Robot Interaction". In: Lin, Patrick / Abney, Keith / Jenkins, Ryans (Eds.): Robot Ethics 2.0: From Autonomous Cars to Artificial Intelligence. New York: Oxford University Press, 142-156.

Kirschbaum, Markus (2015): "Highly automated driving for commercial vehicles". In: Pfeffer, Peter (Eds.): 6th International Munich Chassis Symposium 2015. Proceedings. Wiesbaden: Springer, 5-15.

Kitchin, Rob (2016): "The ethics of smart cities and urban science". In: Philosophical transactions. Series A, Mathematical, physical, and engineering sciences, 374(2083). Online: https://www.ncbi.nlm.nih.gov/pmc/articles/PMC5124065/#i dm140704258514688title [08.02.2021].

Klaus, Tim / Elzweig, Brian (2017): "The market impact of HFT systems and potential regulation". In: Law and Financial Markets Review 11(1), 13-19.

Klein, Eckart (1997): Menschenrechte: Stille Revolution des Völkerrechts und Auswirkungen auf die innerstaatliche Rechtsanwendung. Baden-Baden: Nomos Verlagsgesellschaft.

482

Klincewicz, Michal (2015): "Autonomous Weapons Systems, the Frame Problem and Computer Security". In: Journal of Military Ethics 14(2), 162-176.

Klincewicz, Michał (2017): "Challenges to Engineering Moral Reasoners". In: Lin, Patrick / Jenkins, Ryan / Abney, Keith (Eds.): Robot ethics 2.0: From Autonomous Cars to Artificial Intelligence. New York: Oxford University Press, 244-257.

Klumpp, Dieter (2014): "Aufhaltsamer Abstieg zur Heteronomie in einer Softwarewelt?". In: Coy, Wolfgang / Garstka, Hansjuergen (Eds.): Wovon – für wen – wozu? Systemdenken wider die Diktatur der Daten. Wilhelm Steinmueller zum Gedächtnis. Berlin: Helmholtz Zentrum für Kulturtechnik, 145-160.

Kneser, Jakob / Dietsche, Pina (2015): Das Ende des Zufalls. Documentary. Online: https://www.3sat.de/wissen/wissenschaftsdoku/das-ende-des-zufalls-100.html?mode=play&obj=71022 [08.02.2021].

Knight, Victoria / van de Steene, Steven (2017): "The Capacity and Capability of Digital Innovation in Prisons: Towards Smart Prisons". In: Advancing Corrections 4(8), 88-101.

Knight, Will (2017a): "The Dark Secret at the Heart of AI". In: MIT Technology Review, April 11. Online: https://www.technologyreview.com/s/604087/the-dark-secret-at-the-heart-of-ai/ [08.02.2021].

Knight, Will (2017b): "The Financial World Wants to Open AI's Black Boxes". In: MIT Technology Review, April 13. Online: https://www.technologyreview.com/s/604122/the-financial-world-wants-to-open-ais-black-boxes/ [08.02.2021].

Ko, Insok (2017): "Can Artificial Intelligence Be an Autonomous Entity?". In: Korean Journal of Philosophy 133, 163-187.

Kobrin, Stephen. J. (2009): "Private Political Authority and Public Responsibility: Transnational Politics, Transnational Firms, and Human Rights". In: Business Ethics Quarterly 19(3), 349-374.

Koch, Kurt (2012): "'Ihr seid mehr wert als viele Spatzen': Zum Beitrag der christlichen Ökumene bei der Revitalisierung menschlicher Werte". In: Hennerkes, Brun-Hagen / Augustin, George (Eds.): Wertewandel mitgestalten: Gut handeln in Gesellschaft und Wirtschaft. Freiburg im Breisgau: Herder, 119-148.

Koch, Sabine / Marschollek, Michael / Wolf, Klaus-Hendrik (2009): "On health-enabling and ambient-assistive technologies. What has been achieved and where do we have to go?" In: Methods of Information in Medicine 48(1), 29-37.

Koertner, Ulrich H. J. (2010): "Der machbare Mensch? Ethische Bewertungen und implizite Menschenbilder aus theologischer Sicht". In: Boehlemann, Peter / Hattenbach, Almut / Klinnert, Lars / Markus, Peter (Eds.): Der machbare Mensch? Moderne Hirnforschung, biomedizinisches Enhancement und christliches Menschenbild. Berlin: LIT-Verlag, 115-133.

Koespsell, David R. (2000): The Ontology of Cyberspace. Philosophy, Law, and the Future of Intellectual Property. Open Court: Chicago.

Koeszegi, Sabine (2019): "Künstliche Intelligenz: 'Wenige wissen, wie manipulierbar sie werden'". In: Die Presse, August 24. Online: https://www.diepresse.com/5678566/kunstliche-intelligenz-bdquowenige-wissen-wie-manipulierbar-sie-werd enldquo [08.02.2021].

Kohlberg, Lawrence (1981): Essays on Moral Development, Vol. I: The Philosophy of Moral Development, Harper & Row: San Francisco.

Kohlberg, Lawrence (1984): Essays on Moral Development, Vol. II: The Psychology of Moral Development, Harper & Row: San Francisco.

Koller, Peter (1990): "Die Begründung von Rechten". In: Koller, Peter / Varga, Csaba / Weinberger, Ota (Eds.): Theoretische Grundlagen der Rechtspolitik. Ungarisch-Österreichisches Symposium der internationalen Vereinigung für Rechts- und Sozialphilosophie. Archiv für Rechts- und Sozialphilosophie 54. Stuttgart: Franz Steiner, 74-84.

Koller, Peter (2005): Zum Verhältnis von Domestischer und Globaler (Un)Gerechtigkeit. Lecture at the Conference 'The Diversitiy of Human Rights: Constitution and Human Rights'. Dubrovnik: Inter University Centre, 3-10 September (manuscript kindly provided by the author).

Responsible Business Initiative (2020): Homepage. Online: https://konzern-initiativ e.ch/ [08.02.2021].

Koreng, Ansgar (2010): Zensur im Internet. Der verfassungsrechtliche Schutz der digitalen Massenkommunikation. Leipzig: Nomos Verlagsgesellschaft.

Korff, Wilhelm (1989): "Zur naturrechtlichen Grundlegung der katholischen Soziallehre". In: Baadte, Guenter / Rauscher, Anton (Eds.): Christliche Gesellschaftslehre: Eine Ortsbestimmung. Graz: Styria, 11-52.

Korff, Wilhelm / Wilhelms, Guenter (2001): "Verantwortung". In: Lexikon für Theologie und Kirche 10, Freiburg im Breisgau: Herder, 597-600.

Kos, Barbara / Krawczyk, Grzegorz / Tomanek, Robert (2020): "The Paradigm of Sustainable Transport and Mobility in Modern Transport Policy – A Case Study of the Mobility of the Creative Class in Poland". In: Sładkowski, Aleksander (Ed.): Ecology in Transport: Problems and Solutions. Lecture Notes in Networks and Systems. Cham: Springer, 381-439.

Kosack, Stephen / Fung, Archon (2014): "Does transparency improve governance?". In: Annual Review of Political Science 17(1), 65-87. Online: https://www.annual reviews.org/doi/pdf/10.1146/annurev-polisci-032210-144356 [08.02.2021].

Kosinski, Michael / Stillwell, David / Graepel, Thore (2013): "Private traits and attributes are predictable from digital records of human behavior". In: PNAS, March 11. Online: http://www.pnas.org/content/pnas/early/2013/03/06/1218772 110.full.pdf [08.02.2021].

Kottow, Miguel H. (2004): "Vulnerability: What kind of principle is it?". In: Medicine, Health Care and Philosophy 7(3), 281-287.

Kraemer, Felicitas / van Overveld, Kees / Peterson, Martin (2011): "Is there an ethics of algorithms?". In: Ethics and Information Technology 13(3), 251-260.

Kramer, Adam / Guillory, Jamie / Hancock, Jeffrey (2014): "Experimental Evidence of Massive-Scale Emotional Contagion Through Social Networks". In: Proceedings of the National Academy of Sciences of the United States of America 111(24), 8788-8790.

Kramer, Rolf (1992): Soziale Gerechtigkeit – Inhalt und Grenzen. Sozialwissenschaftliche Schriften 18. Berlin: Duncker & Humblot.

Kranich-Stroetz, Christiane (2008): Selbstbewusstsein und Gewissen: Zur Rekonstruktion der Individualitätskonzeption bei Peter Abaelard. Subjekt – Zeit – Geschichte 2. Muenster: LIT-Verlag.

Krech, Carol Anne / Ruether, Frauke / Gassmann, Oliver (2015): "Profiting From Invention: Business Models of Patent Aggregating Companies". In: International Journal of Innovation Management 19(3), 1-26.

Kremer, Michael / Glennerster, Rachel (2004): Strong Medicine: Creating Incentives for Pharmaceutical Research on Neglected Diseases. Princeton: Princeton University Press.

Krenn, Brigitte (2016): "Multiuse Tool and Ethical Agent". In: Trappl, Robert (Ed.): A Construction Manual for Ethical Systems. Cham: Springer, 11-29.

Krieger, Bernhard / Grubmueller, Verena / Schaefer, Claudia (2014): "Ethische Herausforderungen bei der sozialwissenschaftlichen Analyse von Social-Media-Inhalten". In: SWS-Rundschau 54(2), 201-216.

Krings, Bettina-Johanna / Boehle, Knud / Decker, Michael / Nierling, Linda / Schneider, Christoph (2014): "Serviceroboter in Pflegearrangements". In: Decker, Michael / Fleischer, Torsten / Schippl, Jens / Weinberger, Nora (Eds.): Zukünftige Themen der Innovations- und Technikanalyse: Lessons learned und ausgewählte Ergebnisse. Karlsruhe: KIT Scientific Publishing, 63-121.

Krishnan, Armin (2009a): Killer Robots: The Legality and Ethicality of Autonomous Weapons. London: Routledge.

Krishnan, Armin (2009b): "Automating War: The Need for Regulation". In: Contemporary Security Policy 30(1), 172-193.

Kroes, Peter / Verbeek, Peter-Paul (Eds.) (2014): The Moral Status of Technical Artefacts. Philosophy of Engineering and Technology 17. Dordrecht: Springer.

Kroes, Peter (2009): "Technical Artifacts, Engineering Practice, and Emergence". In: Krohs, Ulrich / Kroes, Peter (Eds.): Functions in Biological and Artificial Worlds. Comparative Philosophical Perspectives. Cambridge: MIT Press, 277-292.

Krugman, Paul (2013): "The Conscience of a Liberal". In: The New York Times, December 28. Online: https://krugman.blogs.nytimes.com/2013/12/28/bitcoin-is-evil/ [08.02.2021].

Kshetri, Nir (2014): "Big Data's Impact on Privacy, Security and Consumer Welfare". In: Telecommunications Policy 38(1), 1134-1145.

Kugler, Logan (2018): "Why Cryptocurrencies Use So Much Energy – and What to Do About It". In: Communications of the ACM 61(7), 15-17.

Kuhn, Thomas S. (1962): The Structure of Scientific Revolutions. Chicago: University of Chicago Press.

Kurzweil, Ray (1999): The Age of Spiritual Machines: When Computers Exceed Human Intelligence. New York: Viking.

Kurzweil, Ray (2001): The law of accelerating returns. Kurzweil Accelerating Intelligence. Online: https://www.kurzweilai.net/the-law-of-accelerating-returns [08.02.2021].

Kurzweil, Ray (2005): The Singularity is Near: When Humans Transcend Biology. New York: Viking.

Kyriakidis, Miltos / Happee, Riender / de Winter, Joost (2015): "Public opinion on automated driving: Results of an international questionnaire among 5000 respondents". In: Transportation Research Part F: Traffic Psychology and Behaviour 32, 127-140.

La Mettrie, Julien Offray (2009): Die Maschine Mensch. Becker, Claudia (Ed.). Philosophische Bibliothek 407. Hamburg: Felix Meiner.

La Pointe, Cara / Fishbane, Lara (2018): "The Blockchain Ethical Design Framework". In: Innovations 12(3), 50-71.

La Rue, Frank (2011): Report of the Special Rapporteur on the Promotion and Protection of the Right to Freedom of Opinion and Expression. UN Human Rights Council. U.N. Doc. A/HRC, 17/27. May 16. Online: http://www2.ohchr.org/english/bodies/hrcouncil/docs/17session/a.hrc.17.27_en.pdf [08.02.2021].

Laaff, Meike (2020): "Ok, Zoomer". In: Die Zeit, March 31. Online: https://www.zeit.de/digital/2020-03/videokonferenzen-zoom-app-homeoffice-quarantaene-coronavirus/komplettansicht [08.02.2021].

LaBossiere, Michael (2017): "Testing the Moral Status of Artificial Beings; Or 'I'm Going to Ask You Some Questions…'". In: Lin, Patrick / Abney, Keith / Jenkins, Ryans (Eds.): Robot Ethics 2.0: From Autonomous Cars to Artificial Intelligence. New York: Oxford University Press, 293-306.

Ladwig, Bernd (2007): "Das Recht auf Leben – nicht nur für Personen". In: Deutsche Zeitschrift für Philosophie 55(1), 17-39.

Laidlaw, Emily B. (2015): Regulating Speech in Cyberspace. Gatekeepers, Human Rights and Corporate Responsibility. Cambridge: Cambridge University Press.

Land, Molly (2013): "Toward an International Law of the Internet". In: Harvard International Law Journal 54(2), 393-458.

Landini, Sara (2020): "Ethical Issues, Cybersecurity and Automated Vehicles". In: Marano, Pierpaolo / Noussia, Kyriaki (Eds.): InsurTech: A Legal and Regulatory View. AIDA Europe Research Series on Insurance Law and Regulation 1. Cham: Springer, 291-312.

Langan, John (1982): "Human Rights in Roman Catholicism". In: Swidler, Arlene (Ed.): Human Rights in Religious Traditions. New York: The Pilgrim Press, 25-39.

Lanier, Jaron (2018): Zehn Gründe, warum du deine Social Media Accounts sofort löschen musst. Hamburg: Hoffmann und Campe.

Lanzing, Marjolein (2019): "Strongly Recommended: Revisiting Decisional Privacy to Judge Hypernudging in Self-Tracking Technologies". In: Philosophy & Technology 32(3), 549-568.

Latour, Bruno (1992): "Where Are the Missing Masses? The Sociology of a Few Mundane Artifacts". In: Bijker, Wiebe E. / Law, John (Eds.): Shaping Technology / Building Society. Cambridge: MIT Press, 151-180.

Latour, Bruno (1994): "On Technical Mediation – Philosophy, Sociology, Genealogy". In: Common Knowledge 3(2), 29-64.

Laudan, Larry (1977): Progress and Its Problems: Towards a Theory of Scientific Growth. Berkeley: University of California Press.

Lauricella, Tom / McKay, Peter A. (2010): "Dow Takes a Harrowing 1,010.14-point Trip". In: The Wall Street Journal, May 7. Online: https://www.wsj.com/articles/ SB10001424052748704370704575227754131412596 [08.02.2021].

Lazarus, Jessica R. / Shaheen, Susan A. / Young, Stanley E. / Fagnant, Daniel (2018): "Shared Automated Mobility and Public Transport". In: Meyer, Gereon / Beiker, Sven (Eds.): Road Vehicle Automation 4. Lecture Notes in Mobility. Cham: Springer, 141-161.

Lazer, David / Baum, Matthew / Benkler, Yochai / Berinsky, Adam / Greenhill, Kelly / Menczer, Filippo / Metzger, Miriam / Nyhan, Brendan / Pennycook, Gordon / Rothschild, David / Schudson, Michael / Sloman, Steven / Sunstein, Cass R. / Thorson, Emily / Watts, Duncan / Zittrain, Jonathan (2018): "The Science of Fake News". In: Science 359, 1094-1096.

Le Cun, Yann / Bengio, Yoshua / Hinton, Geoffrey (2015): "Deep learning". In: Nature 521(7553), 436-444.

Lee, Kai-Fu (2018): AI Superpowers. China, Silicon Valley, and the New World Order. Boston: Houghton Mifflin Harcourt.

Lee, Lisa M. (2017): "Ethics and Subsequent Use of Electronic Health Record Data". In: Journal of Biomedical Informatics 71, 143-146.

Lee, Min Kyung / Kusbit, Daniel / Metsky, Evan / Dabbish, Laura (2015): Working with Machines: The Impact of Algorithmic and Data-Driven Management on Human Workers. Seoul: Economy Record.

Lee, Timothy B. (2018): "Fully driverless Waymo taxis are due out this year, alarming critics". In: Ars Technica, October 1. Online: https://arstechnica.com/cars/20 18/10/waymo-wont-have-to-prove-its-driverless-taxis-are-safe-before-2018-launch/ [08.02.2021].

Lehmann, Karl (2015): Toleranz und Religionsfreiheit: Geschichte und Gegenwart in Europa. Freiburg im Breisgau: Herder.

Lehmann-Maldonado, Stephan (2016) Joël Luc Cachelin: "Du sollst online sein! Interview mit Joël Luc Cachelin". In: UBS Magazin, October 2016, 6-13.

Leibowitz, Jon (2009): "Introductory Remarks for FTC Privacy Roundtable". Online: https://www.ftc.gov/public-statements/2009/12/introductory-remarks-ftc-privacy-roundtable [08.02.2021].

Lele, Ajey (2019): "Debating Lethal Autonomous Weapon Systems". In: Journal of Defense Studies 13(1), 51-70.

Lenartowicz, Marta (2017): "Creatures of the semiosphere: A problematic third party in the 'humans plus technology' cognitive architecture of the future global superintelligence". In: Technological Forecasting and Social Change 144, 35-42.

Lenk, Hans / Maring, Matthias (2001): "Responsibility and Technology". In: Auhagen, Ann Elisabeth / Bierhoff, Hans-Werner (Eds.): Responsibility: The many faces of a social phenomenon. London: Routledge, 93-107.

Lepping, Joachim / Palzkill, Matthias (2016): "Die Chance der digitalen Souveränität". In: Wittpahl, Volker (Eds.): Digitalisierung. Bildung, Technik, Innovation. Berlin: Springer, 17-25.

Leutheusser-Schnarrenberger, Sabine (2015): "Vom Vergessen und Erinnern". In: Datenschutz und Datensicherheit - DuD 39(9), 586-588.

Levy, Frank / Murnane, Richard (2004): The New Division of Labor. Princeton: Princeton University Press.

Levy, Steven (2011): In the Plex: How Google Thinks, Works, and Shapes Our Lives. New York: Simon & Schuster Publishing.

Lewis, John (2015): "The Case for Regulating Fully Autonomous Weapons". In: The Yale Law Journal 124, 1309-1325.

Lewis, Paul (2017): "'Our minds can be hijacked': the tech insiders who fear a smartphone dystopia". In: The Guardian, October 6. Online: https://www.theguardian.com/technology/2017/oct/05/smartphone-addiction-silicon-valley-dystopia [08.02.2021].

Leys, Nathan (2018): "Autonomous Weapon Systems and International Crises". In: Strategic Studies Quarterly 12(1), 48-73.

Li, Yeti / Burns, Catherine / Hu, Rui (2015): "Understanding Automated Financial Trading Using work Domain Analysis". In: Proceedings of the Human Factors and Ergonomics Society Annual Meeting 59(1), 165-169.

Liessmann, Konrad Paul (2016): "Neue Menschen! Bilden, optimieren, perfektionieren". In: Liessmann, Konrad Paul (Ed.): Neue Menschen! Bilden, optimieren, perfektionieren. Philosophicum Lech 19. Wien: Zsolnay, 7-26.

Liessmann, Konrad Paul (2019): "In der Ich-Falle". In: Die Presse, September 28. Online: https://www.diepresse.com/1458209/in-der-ich-falle [08.02.2021].

Lim, Hazel Si Min Lim / Taeihagh, Araz (2019): "Algorithmic Decision-Making in AVs: Understanding Ethical and Technical Concerns for Smart Cities". In: Sustainability 11(20), 1-28.

Lin, Patrick (2014): "The Robot Car of Tomorrow May Just Be Programmed to Hit You". In: Wired, June 5. Online: https://www.wired.com/2014/05/the-robot-car-of-tomorrow-might-just-be-programmed-to-hit-you/ [08.02.2021].

Lin, Patrick / Bekey, George / Abney, Keith (2008): Autonomous Military Robotics: Risk, Ethics, and Design. Ballston: US Department of Navy, Office of Naval Research.

Lin, Patrick / Jenkins, Ryan / Abney, Keith (2017): "Moral and Legal Responsibility". In: Lin, Patrick / Jenkins, Ryan / Abney, Keith (Eds.): Robot ethics 2.0: From Autonomous Cars to Artificial Intelligence. New York: Oxford University Press, 1-3.

Linke, Anna F. (2015): "Autonomie bei technischen Assistenzsystemen. Ein Trade-Off zwischen Privatheit, Unabhängigkeit und Sicherheit". In: Weber, Karsten / Frommeld, Debora / Manzeschke, Arne / Fingerau, Heiner (Eds.): Technisierung des Alltags. Beitrag für ein gutes Leben?. Stuttgart: Franz Steiner, 179-193.

Lippert, John / Gruley, Bryan / Inoue, Kae / Coppola, Gabrielle (2018): "Toyota's vision of autonomous cars is not exactly driverless". In: Bloomberg Business Week, September 19. Online: https://www.bloomberg.com/news/features/2018-09-19/toyota-s-vision-of-autonomous-cars-is-not-exactly-driverless [08.02.2021].

Liu, Hin-Yan (2012): "Categorization and legality of autonomous and remote weapons systems". In: International Review of the Red Cross 94(886), 627-652.

LobbyControl (2020): "Big Tech: Google, Amazon & Co. üben undurchsichtig Einfluss aus". In: LobbyControl, September 24. Online: https://www.lobbycontrol.de/2020/09/big-tech-google-amazon-co-ueben-undurchsichtigen-einfluss-aus/ [08.02.2021].

Locke, John (2006): Versuch über den menschlichen Verstand. Hamburg: Felix Meiner.

Loh, Janina (2018): Trans- und Posthumanismus zur Einführung. Hamburg: Junius.

Loh, Wulf / Loh, Janina (2017): "Autonomy and Responsibility in Hybrid Systems". In: Lin, Patrick / Abney, Keith / Jenkins, Ryans (Eds.): Robot Ethics 2.0: From Autonomous Cars to Artificial Intelligence. New York: Oxford University Press, 35-50.

Lohmann, Georg (2000): "Die unterschiedlichen Menschenrechte". In: Fritzsche, K. Peter / Lohmann, Georg (Eds.): Menschenrechte zwischen Anspruch und Wirklichkeit. Wuerzburg: Ergon, 9-23.

Lohmann, Georg (2004): "Menschenrechte in Theorie und Praxis". In: Kirchschlaeger, Peter G. / Kirchschlaeger, Thomas / Belliger, Andrea / Krieger, David (Eds.): Menschenrechte und Terrorismus. Internationales Menschenrechtsforum Luzern (IHRF) 1. Bern: Staempfli, 305-309.

Lohmann, Georg (2008a): "Zu einer relativen Begründung der Universalisierung der Menschenrechte". In: Nooke, Guenter / Lohmann, Georg / Wahlers, Gerhard (Eds.): Gelten Menschenrechte universal? Begründungen und Infragestellungen. Freiburg im Breisgau: Herder, 218-228.

Lohmann, Georg (2008b): "Zur Verständigung über die Universalität der Menschenrechte. Eine Einführung". In: Nooke, Guenter / Lohmann, Georg / Wahlers, Gerhard (Eds.): Gelten Menschenrechte universal? Begründungen und Infragestellungen. Freiburg im Breisgau: Herder, 47-60.

Lohmann, Georg / Pollmann, Arnd / Mahler, Claudia / Weiss, Norman / Gosepath, Stefan (2005): Die Menschenrechte: Unteilbar und gleichgewichtig? Potsdam Studien zu Grund- und Menschenrechten 11. Potsdam: Universitaetsverlag Potsdam.

Lohmann, Melinda Florina (2016): "Liability Issues Concerning Self-Driving Vehicles". In: European Journal of Risk Regulation EJRR 7(2), 335-340.

Lohmann, Melinda (2018): "Rise and Regulation of Algorithms". In: Berkeley Global Society (BGS) Perspectives, November 1. Online: https://berkeleylawsoci ety.com/en/perspectives/rise-and-regulation-of-algorithms [08.02.2021].

Loretan, Adrian (2011): "Kirche und Staat in der Schweiz im Horizont einer globalisierten Gesellschaft". In: Loretan, Adrian (Ed.): Religionsfreiheit im Kontext der Grundrechte: Religionsrechtliche Studien, 2. Zuerich: TVZ, 414-442.

Love, James / Hubbard, Tim (2007): "The Big Idea: Prizes to Stimulate R&D for New Medicines". In: Chicago-Kent Law Review 82(3), 1519-1554.

Luca, Michael / Wu, Timothy / Couvidat, Sebastian / Frank, Daniel / Seltzer, William (2015): Does Google Content Degrade Google Search?: Experimental Evidence. Harvard Business School Working Paper 16-035. Online: http://nrs.ha rvard.edu/urn-3:HUL.InstRepos:23492375 [08.02.2021].

Lucchi, Nicola (2016): The Impact of Science and Technology on the Rights of the Individual. Law, Governance and Technology 26. Cham: Springer.

Ludwig, Wolfram / Wolf, Klaus-Hendrik / Duwenkamp, Christopher / Gusew, Nathalie / Hellrung, Nils / Marschollek, Michael / Von Bargen, Tobias / Wagner, Markus / Haux, Reinold (2010): "Health information systems for home telehealth services – a nomenclature for sensor-enhanced transinstitutional information system architectures". In: Informatics for Health and Social Care 35(3-4), 211-225.

Luebbe, Hermann (1990a): Der Lebenssinn der Industriegesellschaft: Über die moralische Verfassung der wissenschaftlich-technischen Zivilisation. Berlin: Springer.

Luebbe, Hermann (1990b): Religion nach der Aufklärung. Graz: Styria.

Luebbe, Herrmann (2001): "Religion und Ethik: Sind sie austauschbar?". In: Luebbe, Herrmann: Aufklärung anlasshalber. Philosophische Essays zu Politik, Religion und Moral. Graefelfing: Resch, 125-129.

Luetge, Christoph (2017): "The German Ethics Code for Automated and Connected Driving". In: Philosophy & Technology 30, 547-558.

Luetge, Christoph / Kriebitz, Alexander / Raphael, Max (2019): "Ethische und rechtliche Herausforderungen des autonomen Fahrens". In: Mainzer, Klaus (Ed.): Philosophisches Handbuch Künstliche Intelligenz. Cham: Springer, 1-18.

Lugano, Giuseppe (2017): "Virtual assistants and self-driving cars". In: Institute of Electrical and Electronic Engineers (IEEE) (Ed.): 15th International Conference on ITS Telecommunications. Warsaw, May 29-31. Online: https://ieeexplore.ieee .org/document/7972192 [08.02.2021].

Lyotard, Jean-Francois (1988): Le Postmoderne expliqué aux enfants. Correspondence 1982-1985. Paris: Galilée.

Macdonald, Kate (2011): "Re-thinking 'Spheres of Responsibility': Business Responsibility for Indirect Harm". In: Journal of Business Ethics 99(4), 549-563.

Mackworth, Alan K. (2011): "Architectures and Ethics for Robots: Constraint Satisfaction as a Unitary Design Framework". In: Anderson, Michael / Anderson, Susan Leigh (Eds.): Machine Ethics. Cambridge: Cambridge University Press, 335-360.

Mackworth, Norman H. (1950): Researches on the measurement of human performance. Medical Research Council. Special Report Series 268. London: H. M. Stationery Office.

Madrigal, Alexis (2019): "The Coalition Out to Kill Tech as We Know It". In: The Atlantic, June 4. Online: https://www.theatlantic.com/technology/archive/2019/06/how-politicians-and-scholars-turned-against-big-tech/591052/ [08.02.2021].

Mancini, Anna (2005): Internet Justice. Philosophy of Law for the Virtual World. Dover: Buenos Books America.

Mangold, Patrizia (2016) Angela Merkel: "Daten sind die Rohstoffe des 21. Jahrhunderts". In: Frankfurter Allgemeine Zeitung, March 3. Online: https://www.faz.net/aktuell/wirtschaft/cebit/angela-merkel-fordert-mehr-modernisierte-digitale-technologien-14120493.html [08.02.2021].

Mannino, Adriano / Althaus, David / Erhardt, Jonathan / Gloor, Lukas / Hutter, Adrian / Metzinger, Thomas (2015): "Künstliche Intelligenz: Chancen und Risiken". In: Diskussionspapiere der Stiftung für effektiven Altruismus 2, 1-17.

Manzscheke, Arne (2014): "Digitales Operieren und Ethik". In: Niederlag, Wolfgang / Lemke, Heinz U. / Strauss, Gero / Feussner, Hubertus (Eds.): Der digitale Operationssaal. Berlin: De Gruyter, 227-249.

Manzeschke, Arne (2015): "Angewandte Ethik organisieren: MEESTAR – ein Modell zur ethischen Deliberation in sozio-technischen Arrangements". In: Maring, Matthias (Ed.): Vom Praktischwerden der Ethik in interdisziplinärer Sicht: Ansätze und Beispiele der Institutionalisierung, Konkretisierung und Implementierung der Ethik. Zentrum für Technik- und Wirtschaftsethik 7. Karlsruhe: KIT Scientific Publishing, 315-330.

Manzeschke, Arne (2019): "Roboter in der Pflege: Von Menschen, Maschinen und anderen hilfreichen Wesen". In: Ethik Journal 5(1), 1-11. Online: https://www.ethikjournal.de/fileadmin/user_upload/ethikjournal/Texte_Ausgabe_1_11_2019/Manzeschke_1.Nov_FINAL.pdf [08.02.2021].

Manzeschke, Arne / Assadi, Galia / Karsch, Fabian / Viehoever, Willy (2016): "Funktionale Emotionen und emotionale Funktionalität. Über die neue Rolle von Emotionen und Emotionalität in der Mensch-Technik-Interaktion". In: Manzeschke, Arne / Karsch, Fabian (Eds.): Roboter, Computer und Hybride. Was ereignet sich zwischen Menschen und Maschinen?. TTN-Studien 5. Baden-Baden: Nomos Verlagsgesellschaft, 109-129.

Manzeschke, Arne / Brink, Alexander (2020): "Ethik der Digitalisierung in der Automobilbranche am Beispiel selbstfahrender Autos". In: Walter, Franz (Ed.): Handbuch Industrie 4.0: Recht, Technik und Gesellschaft. Heidelberg: Springer, 713-718.

Manzeschke, Arne / Karsch, Fabian (2016): "Einleitung". In: Manzeschke, Arne / Karsch, Fabian (Eds.): Roboter, Computer und Hybride. Was ereignet sich zwischen Menschen und Maschinen? TTN-Studien 5, Baden-Baden: Nomos Verlagsgesellschaft, 7-14.

Manzeschke, Arne / Weber, Karsten / Rother, Elisabeth / Fangerau, Heiner (2013): Ethische Fragen im Bereich Altersgerechter Assistenzsysteme: Ergebnisse der Studie. Ludwigsfelde: Druckerei Thiel Gruppe.

Marauhn, Thilo (2014): An Analysis of the Potential Impact of Lethal Autonomous Weapons Systems on Responsibility and Accountability for Violations of International Law. Presentation on the occasion of the CCW expert meeting on lethal autonomous systems, Geneva, May 13-16. Online: https://www.unog.ch/8 0256EDD006B8954/(httpAssets)/35FEA015C2466A57C1257CE4004BCA51/$file /Marauhn_MX_Laws_SpeakingNotes_2014.pdf [08.02.2021].

Marchant, Gary E. / Allenby, Braden / Arkin, Ronald / Barrett, Edward T. / Borenstein, Jason / Gaudet, Lyn M. / Kittrie, Orde F. / Lin, Patrick / Lucas, George R. / O'Meara, Richard / Silberman, Jared (2011): "International Governance of Autonomous Military Robots". In: The Columbia Science and Technology Law Review 7, 272-315.

Marcuse, Herbert (1964): One-Dimensional Man. Studies in the ideology of advanced industrial society. Boston: Beacon Press.

Mărcuț, Mirela (2020): The Governance of Digital Policies. Towards a New Competence in the European Union. Cham: Springer.

Margalit, Avishai (1998): The Decent Society. Cambridge: Harvard University Press.

Maritain, Jacques (1948): "Introduction". In: UNESCO (Ed.): Human Rights: Comments and interpretations. UNESCO/PHS/3 (rev.). Paris: UNESCO, I-IX.

Marketers Media (2018): Global Smart Homes Market 2018 by Evolving Technologies, Projections & Estimations, Business Competitors, Cost Structure, Key Companies and Forecast to 2023. Online: https://marketersmedia.com/global-s mart-homes-market-2018-by-evolving-technology-projections-estimations-busine ss-competitors-cost-structure-key-companies-and-forecast-to-2023/302165 [08.02.2021].

Marr, Bernhard (2018): "How AI and machine learning are transforming law firms and the legal sector". In: Forbes, May 23. Online: https://www.forbes.com/sites/ bernardmarr/2018/05/23/how-ai-and-machine-learning-are-transforming-law-fir ms-and-the-legal-sector/#7587475832c3 [08.02.2021].

Marschollek, Michel / Becker, Clemens (2013): "Assistierende Gesundheitstechnologien in der geriatrischen Sturzforschung. Auf dem Weg zur Evidenz". In: Zeitschrift für Gerontologie und Geriatrie 46(8), 704-705.

Marschuetz, Gerhard (2009): Theologisch ethisch nachdenken 1: Grundlagen. Wuerzburg: Echter.

Marsh, Sarah (2017): "Girls suffer under pressure of online 'perfection', poll finds". In: The Guardian, August 23. Online: https://www.theguardian.com/society/201 7/aug/23/girls-suffer-under-pressure-of-online-perfection-poll-finds [08.02.2021].

Marten, Rainer (1975): "Versuch über die philosophische Bestimmung des Gewissens". In: Holzhey, Helmut (Ed.): Gewissen? Philosophie aktuell 4. Basel: Schwabe, 119-133.

Martinesco, Andrea / Netto, Mariana / Miranda Neto, Arthur / Etgens, Victor H. (2019): "A Note on Accidents Involving Autonomous Vehicles: Interdependence of Event Data Recorder, Human-Vehicle Cooperation and Legal Aspects". In: IFAC-PapersOnLine 51(34), 407-410.

Martínez-Díaz, Margarita / Soriguera, Francesc / Pérez, Ignacio (2018): "Autonomous driving: a bird's eye view". In: IET Intelligent Transport Systems 13(4), 563-579.

Martini, Carlo Maria (2001): Damit Leben stimmig wird. Orientierungen. Muenchen: Neue Stadt.

Martinot, Eric (2000): Ten cases of technology transfer. Washington, D.C.: World Bank Group. Online: http://documents.worldbank.org/curated/en/78361148067 3964102/Ten-cases-of-technology-transfer [08.02.2021].

Martinsen, Renate (2004): Staat und Gewissen im technischen Zeitalter: Prolegomena einer politologischen Aufklärung. Weilerswist: Velbrueck.

Martin-Shields, Charles (2013): "Inter-ethnic Cooperation Revisited: Why Mobile Phones Can Help Prevent Discrete Events of Violence, Using the Kenyan Case Study". In: International Journal of Security and Development 2(58), 1-13.

Massit-Folléa, Françoise (2013): "Standards, Agreements, and Normative Collissions in Internet Governance". In: Massit-Folléa, Françoise / Méadel, Cécile / Monnoyer-Smith, Laurence (Eds.): Normative Experience in Internet Politics. Paris: Presses des Mines, 67-89.

Mateescu, Alexandra / Brunton, Douglad / Rosenblat, Alex / Patton, Desmond / Gold, Zachary / Boyd, Danah (2015): "Social Media Surveillance and Law Enforcement". In: Data & Civil rights: A new era of policing and justice. Online: https://datasociety.net/wp-content/uploads/2015/10/Social_Media_Surveillance_ and_Law_Enforcement.pdf [08.02.2021].

Mathias, Paul (2007): "The last frontier? L'Internet au-delà de tout territoire". In: Cités 3(31), 93-103.

Mathieu, Nadine / Loehnhardt, Benjamin / Gruetz, Romanus / Weil, Philipp / Krawczak, Michael (2013): "Ethische und rechtliche Implikationen der Speicherung humaner Genomdaten". In: Medizinische Genetik 25(2), 278-283.

Mathis, Klaus / Tor, Avishalom (Eds.) (2016): 'Nudging' – Possibilities, Limitations and Applications in European Law and Economics. Cham: Springer.

Mathis, Leonie (2019): 'Sexroboter': Repräsentanten, funktionale Dienstleister und beziehungsstiftende Spielzeuge. Masters Seminar Paper (Supervisor: Peter G. Kirchschlaeger), Faculty of Humanities and Social Sciences: Philosophy, University of Lucerne.

Mathwig, Frank (2000): Technikethik – Ethiktechnik: Was leistet Angewandte Ethik?. Forum Systematik 3. Stuttgart: Wilhelm Kohlhammer.

Matthias, Andreas (2004): "The responsibility gap: ascribing responsibility for the actions of learning automata". In: Ethics Information Technology 6, 175-183.

Matzner, Tobias (2019): "Autonome Trolleys und andere Probleme. Konfigurationen Künstlicher Intelligenz in ethischen Debatten über selbstfahrende Kraftfahrzeuge". In: Zeitschrift für Medienwissenschaft 21(11), 46-55.

MaxAudience (2016): "Millennials check their phones 157 times a day!" Online: https://www.facebook.com/maxaudiencemarketing/posts/millennials-check-thei r-phones-157-times-a-day/1072911816083584/ [08.02.2021].

Maxwell, Maltz (2015): Psycho-Cybernetics: Updated and Expanded. New York: Tarcher Perigee.

Mayer-Tasch, Peter Cornelius (2006): Mitte und Mass: Leitbild des Humanismus von den Ursprüngen bis zur Gegenwart. Baden-Baden: Nomos Verlagsgesellschaft.

McCarthy, John / Minsky, Marvin L. / Rochester, Nathaniel/ Shannon, Claude E. (1995): "A Proposal for the Dartmouth Summer Research Project on Artificial Intelligence: August 31, 1955". In: AI Magazine 27(4), 12-14.

McCorquodale, Robert (2009): "Corporate Social Responsibility and International Human Rights Law". In: Journal of Business Ethics 87, 385-400.

McCorquodale, Robert / Simons, Penelope (2007): "Responsibility Beyond Borders: State Responsibility for Extraterritorial Violations by Corporations of International Human Rights Law". In: Modern Law Review 70, 598-625.

McDonald, Aleecia M. / Cranor, Lorrie Faith (2008): "The Cost of Reading Privacy Policies". In: Journal of Policy for the Information Society 4(3), 540-565.

McDonald, Shannon Sanders / Rodier, Caroline (2015): "Envisioning Automated Vehicles within the Built Environment: 2020, 2035, and 2050". In: Meyer, Gereon / Beiker, Sven (Eds.): Road Vehicle Automation 2. Lecture Notes in Mobility. Cham: Springer, 225-233.

McFarland, Tim / McCormack, Tim (2014): "Mind the Gap: Can Developers of Autonomous Weapons Systems be Liable for War Crimes?". In: International Law Studies 90, 361-385.

McGee, Ellen / Maguire, Gerald (2001): "Implantable Brain Chips: Ethical and Policy Issues". In: Journal of Medical Ethics 24(2), 1-8.

McKinnnon, Rebecca (2012): Consent of the Networked: The Worldwide Struggle For Internet Freedom. New York: Basic Books.

McKinsey Global Institute (2017): Jobs lost, jobs gained: What the future of work will mean for jobs, skills, and wages. Online: https://www.mckinsey.com/~/media/McKinsey/Industries/Public%20and%20Social%20Sector/Our%20Insights/What%20the%20future%20of%20work%20will%20mean%20for%20jobs%20skills%20and%20wages/MGI-Jobs-Lost-Jobs-Gained-Executive-summary-December-6-2017.pdf. [08.02.2021].

McLaren, Bruce (2011): "Computational Models of Ethical Reasoning: Challenges, Initial Steps, and Future Directions". In: Anderson, Michael / Anderson, Susan Leigh (Eds.): Machine Ethics. Cambridge: Cambridge University Press, 297-315.

McNamara, Steven (2016): "The Law and Ethics of High-Frequency Trading". In: Minnesota Journal of Law, Science & Technology 17(1), 71-152.

Meacharm, Darian / Studley, Matthew (2017): "Could a Robot Care? It's All in the Movement". In: Lin, Patrick / Abney, Keith / Jenkins, Ryans (Eds.): Robot Ethics 2.0: From Autonomous Cars to Artificial Intelligence. New York: Oxford University Press, 97-112.

Meadows, Donella / Meadows, Dennis / Randers, Jørgen / Behrens, William W. III (1972): The limits to growth. New York: Universe books.

Médecins Sans Frontières (2001): A Matter of Life and Death: The Role of Patents in Access to Essential Medicines. Geneva: Médecins Sans Frontières.

Médecins Sans Frontières (2016): Patent Opposition Database. Online: https://www .patentoppositions.org/en/about [08.02.2021].

Mehta, Krishen / Shubert, Esther / Dayle Siu, Erika (2020): Tax Justice and Global Inequality. London: Zed Books Ltd.

Meissner, Anne (2017): "Technisierung der professionellen Pflege. Einfluss. Wirkung. Veränderung". In: Hagemann, Tim (Ed.): Gestaltung des Sozial- und Gesundheitswesen im Zeitalter von Digitalisierung und technischer Assistenz. Forschung und Entwicklung in der Sozialwirtschaft 11. Baden-Baden: Nomos Verlagsgesellschaft, 153-172.

Meixner, Werner (2016): Die Gefahr der totalen Vernetzung. TU Muenchen, Institut für Informatik, April 25. Online: http://wwwmayr.in.tum.de/personen/meix ner/GefahrTotalerVernetzung_Mannheim.pdf [08.02.2021].

Meixner, Werner (2017): Vernetzte Smarte Diktatur oder Ethische Reformation?. Technische Universität Muenchen, Institut für Informatik, July. Online: http:// wwwmayr.in.tum.de/personen/meixner/SmarteDiktaturOderEthischeReformati on.pdf [08.02.2021].

Menez, Raphael / Pfeiffer, Sabine / Oestreicher, Elke (2016): Leitbilder von Mensch und Technik im Diskurs zur Zukunft der Fabrik und Computer Integrated Manufacturing (CIM). Universitaet Hohenheim, Lehrstuhl für Soziologie. Working Paper 01-2016. Online: http://docplayer.org/32557644-Leitbilder-von-mensch-und-technik-im-diskurs-zur-zukun8-der-fabrik-und-computer-integrated-manufacturing-cim.html [08.02.2021].

Menke, Christoph / Pollmann, Arnd (2007): Philosophie der Menschenrechte zur Einführung. Hamburg: Junius.

Mensching, Christian (2014): Hassrede im Internet. Grundrechtsvergleich und re-gulatorische Konsequenzen. Schriften zum Internationalen Recht 196. Berlin: Duncker & Humblot.

Merat, Natasha / Jamson, Hamish A. (2009): "Is Drivers' Situation Awareness Influ-enced by a Fully Automated Driving Scenario?". In: de Waard, Dick / Godthelp, Hans / Kooi, Frank / Brookhuis, Karel (Eds.): Human Factors, Security and Safe-ty. Human Factors and Ergonomics Society Europe Chapter Conference, Soesterberg, the Netherlands. Maastricht: Shaker Publishing, 15-17.

Merkel, Miriam (2018): Mein Kopf gehört mir. Eine Reise durch die schöne neue Welt des Brainhacking. Muenchen: Piper.

Mertes, Michael (2010): "Menschenrechtsschutz im Cyberspace". In: Die Politische Meinung 492, 10-14.

Mertz, Marcel / Jannes, Marc / Schlomann, Anna / Manderscheid, Enza / Rietz, Christian / Woopen, Christiane (2016): Digitale Selbstbestimmung. Cologne: Cologne center for ethics, rights, economics, and social sciences of health. On-line: https://kups.ub.uni-koeln.de/6891/1/ceres_Digitale_Selbstbestimmung.pdf [08.02.2021].

Metzinger, Thomas (2019): "Nehmt der Industrie die Ethik weg!". In: Tagesspiegel, April 8. Online: https://www.tagesspiegel.de/politik/eu-ethikrichtlinien-fuer-kue nstliche-intelligenz-nehmt-der-industrie-die-ethik-weg/24195388.html [08.02.2021].

Metzler, Marco (2016) Martin Ford: "Automatisierung wird die ganze Arbeitswelt erfassen". In: Neue Zuercher Zeitung, February 19. Online: https://nzzas.nzz.ch/ wirtschaft/martin-ford-automatisierung-wird-die-ganze-arbeitswelt-erfassen-ld.14 5015?reduced=true [08.02.2021].

Meyer, Gereon (2019): "European Roadmaps, Programs, and Projects for Innovation in Connected and Automated Road Transport". In: Meyer, Gereon / Beiker, Sven (Eds.): Road Vehicle Automation 5. Lecture Notes in Mobility. Cham: Springer, 27-39.

Meyer, Matthias (2015): "Die Digitalisierung als sozialethische Herausforderung". In: Kirche und Gesellschaft 16(424), 6-7.

Meyer, Michelle N. (2014b): "Misjudgements will drive social trials underground". In: Nature 511, 265.

Meyer, Sibylle (2016): Technische Unterstützung im Alter – was ist möglich, was ist sinnvoll? Expertise zum Siebten Altenbericht der Bundesregierung. Berlin: Deutsches Zentrum für Altersfragen.

Meyer, Stephan (2014a): "Der Einsatz von Robotern zur Gefahrenabwehr". In: Hilgendorf, Eric (Ed.): Robotik im Kontext von Recht und Moral. Robotik und Recht 3, 211-237.

Meyer, Wolfgang / Huffziger, Anne (2015): "Einsatz technischer Assistenzsysteme in ambulanten Wohngemeinschaften. Ein Mehrwert für Bewohner, Mitarbeiter und Unternehmen". In: Becher, Berthold / Hoelscher, Martin (Eds.): Wohnen und die Pflege von Senioren. Neue Versorgungsarrangements, neue Geschäftsmodelle. Hannover: Vincentz Network, 284-294.

Michels-Riess, Birgit / Johnigk, Ulrich (2017): "Altenhilfe integriert smarte Technik". In: Heilberufe / Das Pflegemagazin 68(9), 44-45.

Mieth, Dietmar (1992): "Gewissen". In: Wils, Jean-Pierre / Mieth, Dietmar (Eds.): Grundbegriffe der christlichen Ethik. Paderborn: Ferdinand Schoeningh, 225-242.

Mikkelae, Julius (2015): Should I Cyborg? A study into public opinion on Human Enhancement Technologies. Oerebro: Oerebro University School of Business.

Millar, Jason (2017): "Ethics Settings for Autonomous Vehicles". In: Lin, Patrick / Abney, Keith / Jenkins, Ryans (Eds.): Robot Ethics 2.0: From Autonomous Cars to Artificial Intelligence. New York: Oxford University Press, 20-35.

Miller, David (1992): Distributive Justice: What the People Think. In: Ethics 102(April), 555-593.

Miller, Paul D. (2012) Bruce Sterling: "Bruce Sterling: Notes From the Near Future". In: Origin Magazine, May 10.

Miller, Seumas (2018): Dual Use Science and Technology, Ethics and Weapons of Mass Destruction. Cham: Springer.

Misselhorn, Catrin (2018): Grundfragen der Maschinenethik. Stuttgart: Reclam.

Misselhorn, Catrin (2019): Roboterethik. Konrad-Adenauer-Stiftung. Analysen & Argumente 340, February. Online: https://www.kas.de/documents/252038/4521 287/AA340_Roboterethik.pdf/34379c53-23dc-bfb0-239f-4b0fcc6a8947?version=1. 0&t=1549957355653 [08.02.2021].

MIT Connection Science (2018): The Technology of Innovation. Online: https://co nnection.mit.edu/ [08.02.2021].

Mitcham, Carl (2014): "Agency in Humans and in Artifacts: A Contested Discourse". In: Kroes, Peter / Verbeek, Peter-Paul (Eds.): The Moral Status of Technical Artefacts. Philosophy of Engineering and Technology 17. Dordrecht: Springer, 11-29.

Mittelstadt, Brent Daniel / Wachter, Sandra / Allo, Patrick / Taddeo, Mariarosaria / Floridi, Luciano (2016): "The ethics of algorithms: Mapping the debate". In: Big Data & Society 3(2), 1-21.

Mittler, Elmar (2014): "Nachhaltige Infrastruktur für die Literatur- und Informationsversorgung: Im digitalen Zeitalter ein überholtes Paradigma – oder so wichtig wie noch nie?". In: Bibliothek, Forschung und Praxis 38(3), 344-364.

Mladenović, Milos N. / Abbas, Montasir / McPherson, Tristram (2014): "Development of socially sustainable traffic-control principles for self-driving vehicles: The ethics of anthropocentric design". In: Institute of Electrical and Electronic Engineers (IEEE) (Ed.): IEEE International Symposium on Ethics in Science, Technology and Engineering, 1-8. Online: https://ieeexplore.ieee.org/document/ 6893448 [08.02.2021].

Mladenović, Milos N. / McPherson, Tristram (2016): "Engineering Social Justice into Traffic Control for Self-Driving Vehicles?". In: Science and Engineering Ethics 22, 1131-1149.

Moeckli, Andreas (2019): "Roche-Präsident über Digitalisierung: 'Ich halte nichts von Angstmacherei'". In: Luzerner Zeitung, February 11. Online: https://www.l uzernerzeitung.ch/wirtschaft/roche-praesident-ueber-digitalisierung-ich-halte-nic hts-von-angstmacherei-ld.1092784 [08.02.2021].

Moehring-Hesse, Matthias (1997): Theozentrik, Sittlichkeit und Moralität christlicher Glaubenspraxis. Theologische Reflexionen. Studien zur Theologischen Ethik 75. Freiburg im Uechtland: Herder.

Mohammed, Amina (2015): "Deepening income inequality". In: World Economic Forum (WEF) (Ed.): Top 10 Trends of 2015. Online: http://reports.weforum.org/ outlook-global-agenda-2015/top-10-trends-of-2015/1-deepening-income-inequalit y/ [08.02.2021].

Montag, Ali (2018): "Nobel-winning economist: Authorities will bring down 'hammer' on bitcoin". In: CNBC, July 9. Online: https://www.cnbc.com/2018/07/09/ nobel-prize-winning-economist-joseph-stiglitz-criticizes-bitcoin.html [08.02.2021].

Montreal Declaration (2018): For a Responsible Development of AI. Online: https:/ /www.montrealdeclaration-responsibleai.com/the-declaration [08.02.2021].

Montreal Protocol on Substances that Deplete the Ozone Layer (1987): About Montreal Protocol. UN Environment Programme (UNEP). Online: https://www .unep.org/ozonaction/who-we-are/about-montreal-protocol [08.02.2021].

Moor, James H. (1985): "What is Computer Ethics?". In: Metaphilosophy 16(4), 266-275.

Moor, James H. (1995): "Is Ethics Computable?". In: Metaphilosophy 26(1/2), 1-21.

Moor, James H. (2006): "The Nature, Importance, and Difficulty of Machine Ethics". In: IEEE Intelligent Systems 21(4), 18-21.

Moral Machine (n.d.): Homepage. Online: https://www.moralmachine.net/ [08.02.2021].

Moravec, Hans (1988): Mind Children: The Future of Robot and Human Intelligence. Cambridge: Harvard University Press.

Morgan Stanley (2018): "Power Play: What Impact Will Cryptocurrencies Have on Global Utilities?". Online: https://www.morganstanley.com/ideas/cryptocurrencies-global-utilities [08.02.2021].

Morozov, Evgeny (2013): To Save Everything, Click Here. London: Penguin Books.

Morsink, Johannes (2010): "The Universal Declaration and the Conscience of Humanity". In: Huhle, Rainer (Ed.): Human Rights and History: A Challenge for Education. Foundation Remembrance, Responsibility and Future. Berlin: Stiftung Erinnerung, Verantwortung und Zukunft, 25-36.

Mousave, Seyed Sajad / Schukat, Michael / Howley, Enda (2018): "Deep reinforcement learning: An overview". In: arXiv. Online: https://arxiv.org/abs/1806.08894 [08.02.2021].

Moyn, Samuel (2010): The Last Utopia: Human Rights in History. Cambridge: Harvard University Press.

Mueller, Joerg Paul (2005): "Menschenrechte als Grundlage einer globalen wirtschaftlichen und politischen Ordnung". In: Kirchschlaeger, Peter G. / Kirchschlaeger, Thomas / Belliger, Andrea / Krieger, David (Eds.): Menschenrechte und Wirtschaft im Spannungsfeld zwischen State und Nonstate Actors. Internationales Menschenrechtsforum Luzern (IHRF) 2. Bern: Staempfli, 185-196.

Mueller, Julian F. / Gogoll, Jan (2020): "Should Manual Driving be (Eventually) Outlawed?". In: Science and Engineering Ethics 26, 1549-1567.

Mueller, Vincent C. (2014): "Autonomous killer robots are probably good news". In: Frontiers in Artificial Intelligence and Applications 273, 297-305.

Mueller, Vincent C. / Bostrom, Nick (2014): "Future Progress in artificial intelligence: A poll among experts". In: AI Matters 1(1), 9-11.

Mueller, Vincent C. / Bostrom, Nick (2016): "Future progress in artificial intelligence: A survey of expert opinion". In: Mueller, Vincent C. (Ed.): Fundamental Issues of Artificial Intelligence. Synthese Library. Berlin: Springer, 553-571.

Mueller-Dott, Christoph (2019): "KI und Ethik – Wenn autonome Fahrzeuge Fehler machen". In: ATZelektronik 14(11), 16-19.

Muggah, Robert / Diniz, Gustavo (2013): "Digitally Enhanced Violence Prevention in the Americas". In: International Journal of Security and Development 2(57), 1-23.

Mukerji, Nikil / Nida-Ruemelin, Julian (2014): "Towards a Moderate Stance on Human Enhancement". In: Humana.mente – Journal of Philosophical Studies 7(26), 17-33.

Mullins, Brody / Nicas, Jack (2017): "Paying Professors: Inside Google's Academic Influence Campaign". In: The Wall Street Journal, July 14. Online: https://www.wsj.com/articles/paying-professors-inside-googles-academic-influence-campaign-1499785286 [08.02.2021].

Murray, Shanahan (2015): The Technological Singularity. Cambridge: MIT Press.

Musgrave, Alan (2001): "NOA's Ark – Fine for Realism". In: Papineau, David (Ed.): Oxford Readings in The Philosophy of Science. New York: Oxford University Press, 45-60.

Nadella, Satya (2016): "The Partnership of the Future: Microsoft's CEO explores how humans and A.I. can work together to solve society's greatest challenges". In: Slate, June 28. Online: http://www.slate.com/articles/technology/future_tens e/2016/06/microsoft_ceo_satya_nadella_humans_and_a_i_can_work_together_t o_solve_society.html [08.02.2021].

Nakamura, Lisa (2013): Cybertypes: Race, Ethnicity, and Identity on the Internet. New York: Routledge.

National Society of Professional Engineers (NSPE) (n.d.): Code of Ethics. Online: https://www.nspe.org/resources/ethics/code-ethics [08.02.2021].

Nature (2016): "Digital intuition". In: Nature, January 27. Online: http://www.natu re.com/news/digital-intuition-1.19230 [08.02.2021].

Neher, Peter (2013): "Zwischen Wirtschaftlichkeit und Menschlichkeit". In: Kirche und Gesellschaft 41(405), 3-16.

Nemitz, Paul Friedrich (2018): "Constitutional Democracy and Technology in the Age of Artificial Intelligence". In: Philosophical Transactions of the Royal Society 376(2133). Online: https://royalsocietypublishing.org/doi/10.1098/rsta.2018.0 089 [08.02.2021].

Neue Zuercher Zeitung (2011): "Der lange Weg zum Frauenstimmrecht". In: Neue Zuercher Zeitung, February 4. Online: https://www.nzz.ch/frauenstimmrecht-1.9350588?reduced=true [11.15.2020].

Neuhaeuser, Christian (2011): Unternehmen als moralische Akteure. Berlin: Suhrkamp.

Neuhaeuser, Christian (2012): "Künstliche Intelligenz und ihr moralischer Standpunkt". In: Beck, Susanne (Ed.): Jenseits von Mensch und Maschine: Ethische und rechtliche Fragen zum Umgang mit Robotern, Künstlicher Intelligenz und Cyborgs. Robotik und Recht 1. Baden-Baden: Nomos Verlagsgesellschaft, 23-42.

Neuhaeuser, Christian (2014): "Roboter und moralische Verantwortung". In: Hilgendorf, Eric (Ed.): Robotik im Kontext von Recht und Moral. Robotik und Recht 3. Baden-Baden: Nomos Verlagsgesellschaft, 269-286.

Neuman, Gerald (2003): "Human Rights and Constitutional Rights". In: Stanford Law Review 55(5), 1863-1900.

Neuss, Robert (2001): Usability Engineering als Ansatz zum Multimodalen Mensch-Maschine-Dialog. Muenchen: Technische Universitaet.

Nevejans, Nathalie (2016): European Civil Law Rules in Robotics. Study for the JURI Committee, European Parliament. Strasbourg: European Parliament. Online: https://www.europarl.europa.eu/RegData/etudes/STUD/2016/571379/IPOL _STU(2016)571379_EN.pdf [08.02.2021].

Newell, Sue / Marabelli, Marco (2015): "Strategic opportunities (and challenges) of algorithmic decision-making: A call for action on the long-term societal effects of 'datification'". In: The Journal of Strategic Information Systems 24(1), 3-14.

Newmann, Jared (2009): "Google's Schmidt Roasted for Privacy Comments". In: PC World, December 11. Online: https://www.pcworld.com/article/184446/goo gles_schmidt_roasted_for_privacy_comments.html [08.02.2021].

Newton, Michael A. (2015): "Back to the Future: Reflections on the Advent of Autonomous Weapons Systems". In: Journal of International Law 47, 5-23.

Nezik, Ann-Kathrin (2019): "Regelt das!". In: Die Zeit, September 19, 24. Online: https://www.zeit.de/2019/39/digitalunternehmen-facebook-apple-google-digitalis ierung-regelung [08.02.2021].

Nickel, James W. (2015): "Personal Deserts and Human Rights". In: Cruft, Rowan / Liao, S. Matthew / Renzo, Massimo (Eds.): Philosophical Foundations of Human Rights. Oxford: Oxford University Press, 153-165.

Nickel, Philip J. / Frank, Lily E. (2020): "Trust in medicine". In: Simon, Judith (Ed.): Routledge Handbook of Trust and Philosophy. London: Routledge Taylor & Francis Group, 367-377.

Nickel, Philip J./ Franssen, Maarten P. M. / Kroes, Peter A. (2010): "Can we make sense of the notion of trustworthy technology?". In: Knowledge, Technology & Policy 23(3-4), 429-444.

Nida-Ruemelin, Julian (2005): Über menschliche Freiheit. Stuttgart: Reclam.

Nida-Ruemelin, Julian (2011): Verantwortung. Stuttgart: Reclam.

Nida-Ruemelin, Julian (2018): "Vorwort von Julian Nida-Rümelin". In: Nida-Ruemelin, Julian / Weidenfeld, Nathalie (Eds.): Digitaler Humanismus: Eine Ethik für das Zeitalter der Künstlichen Intelligenz. Muenchen: Piper, 9-11.

Nida-Ruemelin, Julian / Weidenfeld, Nathalie (Eds.) (2018): Digitaler Humanismus: Eine Ethik für das Zeitalter der Künstlichen Intelligenz. Muenchen: Piper.

Nienaber, Andre (2017): "Versorgungskonzepte und technische Assistenz". In: Hagemann, Tim (Ed.): Gestaltung des Sozial- und Gesundheitswesen im Zeitalter von Digitalisierung und technischer Assistenz. Forschung und Entwicklung in der Sozialwirtschaft 11. Baden-Baden: Nomos Verlagsgesellschaft, 169-182.

Nienhaus, Lisa (2019): "Operation Grössenwahn". In: Die Zeit, June 27. Online: https://www.zeit.de/2019/27/digitalwaehrung-facebook-visa-mastercard-geld-not enbanken/komplettansicht [08.02.2021].

Noble, Safiya (2018): Algorithms of Oppression. New York: New York University Press.

Nodder, Chris (2013): Evil by Design: Interaction Design to Lead Us into Temptation. Indianapolis: John Wiley & Sons.

Noichl, Franz (1993): Gewissen und Ideologie: Zur Möglichkeit der Rekonstruktion eines unbedingten Sollens. Freiburger theologische Studien 152. Freiburg im Breisgau: Herder.

Norwawi, Norita Md / Alwi, Najwa Hayaati Mohd / Ismail, Roesnita / Wahid, Fauziah / Alkaenay, Nader M. (2014): "Promoting Islamic Ethics on Privacy in Digital Social Network For User Data Protection and Trust". In: Ulūm Islāmiyyah Journal 13, 115-127.

Nosthoff, Anna-Verena / Maschewski, Felix (2019): Die Gesellschaft der Wearables. Digitale Verführung und soziale Kontrolle. Berlin: Nicolai Publishing & Intelligence GmbH.

Nothelle-Wildfeuer, Ursula (1999): Soziale Gerechtigkeit und Zivilgesellschaft. Paderborn: Ferdinand Schoeningh.

Nothelle-Wildfeuer, Ursula (2008): "Die Sozialprinzipien der Katholischen Soziallehre". In: Rauscher, Anton (Ed.): Handbuch der Katholischen Soziallehre. Berlin: Duncker & Humblot, 143-163.

Novet, Jordan (2018): "Facebook forms a special ethics team to prevent bias in its A.I. software". In: CNBC, May 3. Online: https://www.cnbc.com/2018/05/03/facebook-ethics-team-prevents-bias-in-ai-software.html [08.02.2021].

Nowak, Manfred (2002): Einführung in das internationale Menschenrechtssystem. Wien: NWV.

Nussbaum, Martha C. (1993): "Menschliches Tun und soziale Gerechtigkeit. Zur Verteidigung des aristotelischen Essentialismus". In: Brumlik, Micha / Brunkhorst, Hauke (Eds.): Gemeinschaft und Gerechtigkeit. Frankfurt am Main: Suhrkamp, 324-363.

Nussbaum, Martha C. (1995): "Human Capabilities, Female Human Beings". In: Nussbaum, Martha C. / Glover, Jonathan (Eds.): Women, culture, and development: A study of human capabilities. Oxford: Oxford University Press, 61-104.

Nussbaum, Martha C. (2002): Capabilities and Human Rights. In: De Greiff, Pablo/Ciaran, Cronin P. (Eds.): Global Justice and Transnational Politics: Essays on the Moral and Political Challenges of Globalization. Cambridge: MIT Press, 117–149.

Nussbaum, Martha C. (2006): Frontiers of Justice. Disability, Nationality, Species Membership. Cambridge: Harvard University Press.

Nyholm, Sven / Smids, Jilles (2020): "Automated cars meet human drivers: responsible human-robot coordination and the ethics of mixed traffic". In: Ethics and Information Technology 22, 335-344.

O'Connor, Tom (2016): "The Value of Competent Human Advisers". In: CFA Institute Magazine 27(2), 22.

O'Neil, Cathy (2016): Weapons of Math Destruction: How Big Data Increases Inequality and Threatens Democracy. New York: Broadway Books.

Odiot, Alice / Gallet, Audrey (2012): Sambia: Wer profitiert vom Kupfer?. Online: https://www.youtube.com/watch?v=_D2N4QwGOQU [08.02.2021].

OECD (2015): Data-Driven Innovation: Big Data for Growth and Well-Being. Online: https://read.oecd.org/10.1787/9789264229358-en?format=pdf [08.02.2021].

OECD (2016): The Internet of Things: Seizing the Benefits and Addressing the Challenges. Background report for Ministerial Panel 2.2. Directorate for Science, Technology and Innovation Committee on Digital Economy Policy. May 24. Online: http://www.oecd.org/officialdocuments/publicdisplaydocumentpdf/?cote=DSTI/ICCP/CISP%282015%293/FINAL&docLanguage=En [08.02.2021].

OECD (2019a): Artificial Intelligence in Society. Online: https://read.oecd.org/10.1787/eedfee77-en?format=pdf [08.02.2021].

OECD (2019b): OECD Principles on Artificial Intelligence. Online: https://www.oecd.org/going-digital/ai/principles/ [08.02.2021].

OECD (2019c): Recommendation of the Council on Artificial Intelligence. OECD Legal Instruments. OECD/LEGAL/0449. Online: https://legalinstruments.oecd.org/api/print?ids=648&lang=en [08.02.2021].

OECD (2020): OECD presents analysis showing significant impact of proposed international tax reforms. February 13. Online: https://www.oecd.org/tax/oecd-presents-analysis-showing-significant-impact-of-proposed-international-tax-reforms.htm [08.02.2021].

OECD (n.d.): What is BEPS? Inclusive Framework on Base Erosion and Profit Shifting. Online: http://www.oecd.org/tax/beps/about/#mission-impact [08.02.2021].

Oehler, Andreas (2015): Digitale Welt und Finanzen. Zahlungsdienste und Finanzberatung unter einer Digitalen Agenda. Sachverständigenrat für Verbraucherfragen. Berlin: Sachverständigenrat für Verbraucherfragen beim Bundesministerium der Justiz und für Verbraucherschutz. Online: https://www.svr-verbraucherfragen.de/dokumente/digitale-welt-und-finanzen-ergebnisse-und-handlungsempfehlungen/ [08.02.2021].

Oerder, Katharina (2016): "Mitbestimmung 4.0. Der Wandel der Arbeitswelt als Chance für mehr Beteiligung". In: WISO Direkt 24, 1-4.

Office of the UN High Commissioner for Human Rights (n.d.): The Right to Privacy in the Digital Age. Online: https://www.ohchr.org/en/issues/digitalage/pages/digitalageindex.aspx [08.02.2021].

Office of the UN High Commissioner for Human Rights (2000): Business and Human Rights: A Progress Report. Online: https://www.ohchr.org/Documents/Publications/BusinessHRen.pdf [08.02.2021].

Ohly, Lukas (2019a): Ethik der Robotik und der Künstlichen Intelligenz. Theologisch-Philosophische Beiträge zu Gegenwartsfragen 22. Berlin: Peter Lang.

Ohly, Lukas (2019b): "Was heisst hier autonom? Über die moralische Autorenschaft selbstfahrender Autos". In: Zeitschrift für Evangelische Ethik 63(4), 294-300.

Ong-Van-Cung, Kim Sang (2010): "Reconaissance et vulnérabilité: Honneth et Butler". In: Archives de Philosophie 73(1), 119-141.

Opitz, Peter J. (2002): Menschenrechte und internationaler Menschenrechtsschutz im 20. Jahrhundert: Geschichte und Dokumente. Muenchen: Wilhelm Fink.

On-Road Automated Driving (ORAD) Committee, Society of Automotive Engineers SAE International (2016): "Taxonomy and definitions for terms related to driving automation systems for on-road motor vehicles". Online: https://saemob ilus.sae.org/content/j3016_201609 [08.02.2021].

OSCE (2013): Guidelines on Human Rights Education for Health Workers. Online: https://www.osce.org/odihr/105053 [08.02.2021].

Organization of American States (OAS) (1988): Protocol of San Salvador. Online: http://www.oas.org/juridico/english/Treaties/a-52.html [08.02.2021].

Ortega y Gasset, José (1949): Betrachtungen über die Technik. Stuttgart: Deutsche Verlags-Anstalt.

Orwell, Georges (1949): Nineteen Eighty-Four. London: Ullstein.

Ott, Konrad (2005): "Technikethik". In: Nida-Ruemelin, Julian (Ed.): Angewandte Ethik: Die Bereichsethiken und ihre theoretische Fundierung: Ein Handbuch. Stuttgart: Alfred Kroener, 569-590.

Oxfam (2016): An Economy for the 1%. How privilege and power in the economy drive extreme inequality and how this can be stopped. Online: https://www.oxfa m.org/en/research/economy-1 [08.02.2021].

Pagallo, Ugo (2014): "The Legal Challenges of the Information Revolution and the Principle of 'Privacy by Design'". In: Luppicini, Rocci (Ed.): Evolving Issues Surrounding Technoethics and Society in the Digital Age. Pennsylvania: Hershey, 128-148.

Partnership on AI (PAI) (2016): Tenets. Online: www.partnershiponai.org/tenets/ [08.02.2021].

Parfit, Derek (1984): Reasons and Persons, Oxford: Clarendon Press.

Palazzani, Laura (2017): Dalla bio-etica alla tecno-etica: nuove sfide al diritto. Torino: Giappichelli.

Palm, Julian (2013): Berechtigung und Aktualität des Böckenförde-Diktums. Eine Überprüfung vor dem Hintergrund der religiös-weltanschaulichen Neutralität des Staates: Möglichkeiten des Staates zur Pflege seiner Voraussetzungen durch Werteerziehung in der öffentlichen Schule. Frankfurt am Main: Peter Lang.

Panek, Paul / Dangl, Hannes / Hlauschek, Walter / Mayer, Peter / Wagner, Peter / Werner, Franz / Zagler, Wolfgang (2014): "Ein ambientes Assistenzsystem im Alltagseinsatz – Erfahrungen und Ausblick". In: Kempter, Guido / Ritter, Walter (Eds.): Conference: uday XII, At FH Vorarlberg, Dornbirn, Volume: Assistenztechnik für betreutes Wohnen, Beiträge zum Usability Day XII, Lengerich: Pabst Science Publisher, 68-77.

Papa, Enrica / Ferreira, Antonio (2018): "Sustainable Accessibility and the Implementation of Automated Vehicles: Identifying Critical Decisions". In: Urban Science 2(5), 1-14.

Papacharissi, Zizi (2002): "The virtual sphere: the internet as a public sphere". In: Media & Society 4, 9-27.

Pappenberger, Manfred (2013): "Schattenkriege im 21. Jahrhundert. Die Automatisierung des Krieges durch Drohnen und Roboterwaffen". In: Forum Pazifismus 2, 38-44.

503

Pawlikowski, John T. (2001): "The Holocaust: Its Challenges for Understanding Human Responsibility". In: Bank, Judith H. / Pawolikowski, John T. (Eds.): Ethics in the Shadow of the Holocaust: Christian and Jewish Perspectives. Chicago: Sheed & Ward, 261-289.

Pech, Timo / Gabriel, Matthias / Jaehn, Benjamin / Kuehnert, David / Reisdorf, Pierre / Wanielik, Gerd (2016): "Prototyping Framework for Cooperative Interaction of Automated Vehicles and Vulnerable Road Users". In: Schulze, Tim / Mueller, Beate / Meyer, Gereon (Eds.): Advanced Microsystems for Automotive Applications 2016. Lecture Notes in Mobility. Cham: Springer, 43-53.

Pentland, Alex (2007): "On The Collective Nature of Human Intelligence". In: Journal of Adaptive Behavior 15(2), 189-198.

Pentland, Alex (2008): Honest Signals: How they shape our world. Cambridge: MIT Press.

Pentland, Alex (2009): "Society's Nervous System: A Key to Effective Government, Energy Efficiency, and Public Health". In: MIT Faculty Newsletter 21(5). Online: http://web.mit.edu/fnl/volume/215/pentland.html [08.02.2021].

Pentland, Alex (2014a): Social Physics: How Social Networks can make us smarter. New York: Penguin.

Pentland, Alex (2014b): Social Physics: How Good Ideas Spread: The Lessons from a new Science. New York: Penguin.

Pentland, Alex (2014c): Alex Pentland's response to Javier Livas. Online: https://twitter.com/alex_pentland/status/460086689956761600 [08.02.2021].

Pereira, Andre Maia / Anany, Hossam / Přibyl, Ondrej / Přikryl, Jan (2017): "Automated vehicles in smart urban environment: A review". In: Institute of Electrical and Electronic Engineers (IEEE) (Ed.): 2017 Smart City Symposium Prague (SCSP). Prague, May, 25-26. Online: https://ieeexplore.ieee.org/document/7973864 [08.02.2021].

Pereira, Luís Monz / Saptawijaya, Ari (2016): Programming Machine Ethics. Studies in Applied Philosophy, Epistemology and Rational Ethics. Cham: Springer.

Perret, Fabienne / Arnold, Tobias / Fischer, Remo / de Haan, Peter / Haefeli, Ueli (2018): Automatisiertes Fahren in der Schweiz: Das Steuer aus der Hand geben?. Online: https://www.ebp.ch/sites/default/files/2020-02/3996_Automatisiertes-Fahren-in-der-Schweiz_OA.pdf [08.02.2021].

Perry, Michael J. (2005): "The Morality of Human Rights: A Nonreligious Ground?". In: Emory Law Journal 54, 97-150.

Peters, Michael A. / Jandrić, Petar / Hayes, Sarah (2018): "The curious promise of educationalising technological unemployment: What can places of learning really do about the future of work?". In: Educational Philosophy and Theory 51(3), 242-254.

Peters, Ted (2011): "Progress and provolution: Will transhumanism leave sin behind?". In: Cole-Turner, Ronald (Ed.): Transhumanism and Transcendence: Christian Hope in an Age of Technological Enhancement. Washington: Georgetown University Press, 63-86.

Peters, Ted (2015): "Theologians Testing Transhumanism". In: Theology and Science 13(2), 130-149.

Petersen, Steve (2017): "Superintelligence as Superethical". In: Lin, Patrick / Jenkins, Ryan / Abney, Keith (Eds.): Robot ethics 2.0: From autonomous cars to artificial intelligence. New York: Oxford University Press, 322-337.

Peterson, Bela (2014): "The vision of automated driving: What is it good for? Answers from society with economical and organizational perspectives". In: IEEE (Ed.): 11th European Radar Conference, 420-426. Online: https://ieeexplore.ieee.org/document/6991297 [08.02.2021].

Peterson, Martin (2009): An Introduction to Decision Theory. Stockholm: Cambridge University Press.

Pfeifer, Rolf / Scheier, Christian (1999): Understanding Intelligence. Cambridge: MIT Press.

Pianalto, Matthew (2012): "Moral Courage and Facing Others". In: International Journal of Philosophical Studies 20(2), 165-184.

Piater, Justus (2020): Künstliche Intelligenz: Grundlagen, Erfolge, Herausforderungen. Keynote at the Annual Meeting of the "Innsbrucker Kreis von Moraltheolog*innen und Sozialethiker*innen" 2020 (manuscript kindly provided by the author).

Pichai, Sundar (2018): AI at Google: Our Principles. Online: https://www.blog.google/technology/ai/ai-principles/ [08.02.2021].

Pieper, Annemarie (1994): Einführung in die Ethik. Tuebingen: UTB.

Piepgras, Ilka (2019) Olivia Sudjic: "Je mehr ich poste, desto schlechter fühle ich mich". In: Die Zeit, November 6. Online: https://www.zeit.de/zeit-magazin/2019/46/olivia-sudjic-roman-internet-psyche-menschen [08.02.2021].

Pinker, Steven (2007): The language instinct: How the mind creates language. New York: Brilliance Publishing.

Pitts, Chip (2015): For a Treaty on Business & Human Rights. Online: https://international.nd.edu/assets/133586/remarks_pro_treaty_by_chip_pitts.pdf [08.02.2021].

Platon (1989): Der Staat: Über das Gerechte. Apelt, Otto / Bormann, Karl (Eds.). Philosophische Bibliothek 80. Hamburg: Felix Meiner.

Plummer, Libby (2017): "This is how Netflix's top-secret recommendation system works". In: Wired, August 22. Online: https://www.wired.co.uk/article/how-do-netflixs-algorithms-work-machine-learning-helps-to-predict-what-viewers-will-like [08.02.2021].

Pogge, Thomas (1999): "Menschenrechte als moralische Ansprüche an globale Institutionen". In: Gosepath, Stefan / Lohmann, Georg (Eds.): Philosophie der Menschenrechte. Frankfurt am Main: Suhrkamp, 378-400.

Pogge, Thomas (2002): World Poverty and Human Rights. Cambridge: John Wiley & Sons Publishing.

Pogge, Thomas (2011): The Health Impact Fund: More justice and efficiency in global health. Development Policy Centre Discussion Paper 7, Crawford School of Public Policy. Canberra: The Australian National University.

Pogge, Thomas (2012): "The Health Impact Fund: Enhancing Justice and Efficiency in Global Health. The 2011 Mahbub ul Haq Memorial Lecture of the Human Development and Capability Association". In: Journal of Human Development and Capabilities 13(4), 537-559.

Pogge, Thomas / Mehta, Krishen (2016): Global Tax Fairness. Oxford: Oxford University Press.

Polrot, Simon (2017): "'Blockchain': State of the Art and Prospective". January 31. Online: https://medium.com/@si-monpolrot/blockchain-state-of-the-art-and-pros pective-4777e329df14 [08.02.2021].

Portmess, Lisa / Tower, Sara (2014): "Data barns, ambient intelligence and cloud computing: The tacit epistemology and linguistic representation of Big Data". In: Ethics and Information Technology 17(1), 1-9.

Posé, Ulf (2019): "Digitale Ethik: Digitalisierung und künstliche Intelligenz – wie behalten wir das ethisch im Griff?" In: Ökologisches Wirtschaften 2, 12-13.

Postman, Neil (1985): Amusing Ourselves to Death: Public Discourse in the Age of Show Business. New York: Penguin Random House.

Prainsack, Barbara / Buyx, Alena (2017): Solidarity in Biomedicine and Beyond. Cambridge: Cambridge University Press.

Prensky, Marc (2001): "Digital Natives, Digital Immigrants, Part II: Do They Really Think Differently?". In: On the Horizon 9(6), 1-9.

PricewaterhouseCoopers (2016): "The Un(der)banked is FinTech's Largest Opportunity". In: DeNovo Q2 2016 FinTech ReCap and Funding ReView, 1-48.

PricewaterhouseCoopers United States (2017): Making sense of bitcoin, cryptocurrency and blockchain. Online: https://www.pwc.com/us/en/industries/financial-services/fintech/bitcoin-blockchain-cryptocurrency.html [08.02.2021].

Price, Antoinette. (2018): "First international standards committee for entire AI ecosystem". In: IE e-tech, Issue 3. Online: https://iecetech.org/Technical-Commit tees/2018-03/First-International-Standards-committee-for-entire-AI-ecosystem [08.02.2021].

Prodhan, Georgina (2017): "European parliament calls for robot law, rejects robot tax". In: Reuters, February 16. Online: https://www.reuters.com/article/us-europ e-robots-lawmaking/european-parliament-calls-for-robot-law-rejects-robot-tax-id USKBN15V2KM [08.02.2021].

Project Baseline (n.d.): Homepage. Online: https://www.projectbaseline.com/ [08.02.2021].

Przybylski, Andrew / Murayama, Kou / de Haan, Cody R. / Gladwell, Valerie (2013): "Motivational, Emotional, and Behavioral Correlates of Fear of Missing Out". In: Computers in Human Behavior 29(3), 1841-1848.

Pugh, Jeffrey C. (2017): "The Disappearing Human: Gnostic Dreams in a Transhumanist World". In: Religions 8(5), 81-91.

Rabossi, Eduardo (1990): "La teoria de los derechos umanos naturalizada". In: Revista del Centro de Estudio Constitucionales 5(Enero-marzo), 159-175.

Radbruch, Gustav (1932): Rechtsphilosophie. Leipzig: Quelle & Mayer.

Radin, Margaret Jane (2012): Boilerplate: The Fine Print, Vanishing Rights, and the Rule of Law. Princeton: Princeton University Press.

Radlmayr, Jonas / Gold, Christian / Lorenz, Lutz / Mehdi, Farid / Bengler, Klaus (2014): "How Traffic Situations and Non-Driving Related Tasks Affect the Take-Over Quality in Highly Automated Driving". In: Proceedings of Human Factors and Ergonomics Society Annual Meeting 58(1), 2063-2067.

Rainey, Stephen / Goujon, Phillipe (2011): "Toward a normative ethics for technology development". In: Journal of Information, Communication and Ethics in Society 9(3), 157-179.

Raisaro, Jean Louis / Ayday, Erman / Hubaux, Jean-Pierre (2014): "Patient privacy in the genomic era". In: Praxis 103(10), 579-586.

Ramge, Thomas (2019): Mensch und Maschine. Wie künstliche Intelligenz und Roboter unser Leben verändern. Stuttgart: Reclam.

Rammert, Werner (2003): Die Zukunft der künstlichen Intelligenz: verkörpert – verteilt – hybrid. Technical University Technology Studies Working Papers 4. Fak. VI Planen, Bauen, Umwelt, Institut für Soziologie Fachgebiet Techniksoziologie. Berlin: Technische Universitaet Berlin.

Rammert, Werner (2004): "Technik als verteilte Aktion: Wie technisches Wirken als Agentur in hybriden Aktionszusammenhängen gedeutet werden kann". In: Kornwachs, Klaus (Ed.): Technik – System – Verantwortung. Berlin: Technische Universitaet Berlin, 219-231.

Randolph, John / Masters, Gilbert M. (2018): "Whole Community Energy, Mobility, and Land Use". In: Randolph, John / Masters, Gilbert M. (Eds.): Energy for Sustainability. Washington: Island Press, 461-494.

Rath, Johannes / Ischi, Monique / Perkins, Dana (2014): "Evolution of Different Dual-use Concepts in International and National Law and Its Implications on Research Ethics and Governance". In: Science and engineering ethics 20(3), 769-790.

Rauterberg, Hanno (2012): "Die Diktatur der Einfachheit". In: Die Zeit, August 9. Online: https://www.zeit.de/2012/33/Apple-Design-Ideologiekritik [08.02.2021].

Rauterberg, Hanno (2019): "Malende Maschinen". In: Die Zeit, December 14, 57-58. Online: https://www.zeit.de/2019/52/kuenstliche-intelligenz-kunst-algorit hmen [08.02.2021].

Ravvin, Michael (2008): "Incentivizing Access and Innovation for Essential Medicines: A Survey of the Problem and Proposed Solutions". In: Public Health Ethics 1(2), 110-123.

Rawls, John (1971): A Theory of Justice. Cambridge: Harvard University Press.

Rawls, John (1993): Political Liberalism. New York: Columbia University Press.

Rawls, John (1999): The Law of Peoples. Cambridge: Harvard University Press.

Raz, Joseph (1986): The Morality of Freedom. Oxford: Clarendon Press.

Raz, Joseph (2015): "Human Rights in the Emerging World Order". In: Cruft, Rowan / Liao, S. Matthew / Renzo, Massimo (Eds.): Philosophical Foundations of Human Rights. Oxford: Oxford University Press, 217-231.

Reder, Michael (2013): Religion in säkularer Gesellschaft. Über die neue Aufmerksamkeit für Religion in der politischen Philosophie. Freiburg im Breisgau: Karl Alber.

Reeder, John P. (2015): "On Grounding Human Rights: Variations on Themes by Little". In: Twiss, Sumner B. / Simion, Marian G. / Petersen, Rodney L. (Eds.): Religion and Public Policy: Human Rights, Conflict, and Ethics. New York: Cambridge University Press, 96-119.

Reiijers, Wessel / Coeckelbergh, Mark (2018): "The Blockchain as a Narrative Technology: Investigating the Social Ontology and Normative Configurations of Cryptocurrencies". In: Philosophy & Technology 31(1), 103-130.

Remele, Kurt (2009): "Gerechtigkeit lehren, gerecht leben: Katholische Sozialethik und Soziallehre als institutionalisierte Gesellschaftsreflexion und praktisches Handeln". In: Salzburger Theologische Zeitschrift 13, 192-205.

Remmers, Hartmut (2016): Ethische Implikationen der Nutzung altersgerechter technischer Assistenzsysteme: Expertise zum Siebten Altenbericht der Bundesregierung. Berlin: Deutsches Zentrum für Altersfragen.

Renda, Andrea (2019): "Artificial Intelligence: Ethics, governance, and policy challenges: Report of a CEPS Task Force". In: CEPS Centre for European Policy Studies. Online: https://www.ceps.eu/download/publication/?id=10869&pdf=AI_TFR.pdf [08.02.2021].

Richter, Wolfgang (2013): "Rüstungskontrolle für Kampfdrohnen". In: SWP-Aktuell 29, 1-8.

Rietz, Helga (2017): "Autonome Fahrzeuge brauchen keine Ethik-Software". In: Neue Zuercher Zeitung, August 30. Online: https://www.nzz.ch/meinung/autonome-fahrzeuge-brauchen-keine-ethik-software-ld.1308201?reduced=true [08.02.2021].

Righetti, Ludovic / Quang Cuong, Pham / Madhavan, Radhamadhavan / Chatila, Raja (2018): "Lethal Autonomous Weapon Systems: Ethical, Legal, and Societal Issues". In: IEEE Robotics & Automation Magazine 25(1), 123-126.

Rippe, Klaus Peter (2004): "Von der Robo-Roach zum RoboCop. Cyborg-Technologie aus ethischer Sicht". In: Vierteljahresschrift der Naturforschenden Gesellschaft in Zuerich 149(1), 23-28.

Robinson, Joan (1958): The Accumulation of Capital. London: Macmillan.

Robolaw (2014): Guidelines for regulating robotics. Online: http://www.robolaw.eu/ [08.02.2021].

Roddick, Anita (2009): The Body Shop International. Living Our Values, Values Report 2009. London: The Body Shop International.

Rodrigues, Paulo (2019): "Anthropologie chrétienne et transhumanisme". In: ET-Studies 10(2), 229-248.

Roemelt, Josef (2011): Das Geschenk der Freiheit: Christlicher Glaube und moralische Verantwortung. Innsbruck: Tyrolia.

Roff, Heather M. (2014): "The Strategic Robot Problem: Lethal Autonomous Weapons in War". In: Journal of Military Ethics 13(3), 211-227.

Roff, Heather M. (2015): "Lethal Autonomous Weapons and Jus Ad Bellum Proportionality: 47 Case Western Reserve". In: Journal of International Law 47(1), 37-52.

Rogers, Jay Logan (2014): "Legal Jugement Day for the Rise of the Machines: A National Approach to Regulating Fully Autonomous Weapons". In: Arizona Law Review 56(4), 1257-1272.

Rolston, Holmes III. (1986): Philosophy Gone Wild: Essays in Environmental Ethics. Amherst: Prometheus.

Romar, Daniel (2015): On the moral agency for high frequency trading systems and their role in distributed morality. Student Thesis. Umea: Umea Universiteit.

Romm, Tony (2020): "Tech giants led by Amazon, Facebook and Google spent nearly half a billion on lobbying over the past decade, new data shows". In: The Washington Post, January 22. Online: https://www.washingtonpost.com/techno logy/2020/01/22/amazon-facebook-google-lobbying-2019/ [08.02.2021].

Rorty, Richard (1996): "Menschenrechte, Rationalität und Gefühl". In: Shute, Stephen / Hurley, Susan (Eds.): Die Idee der Menschenrechte. Frankfurt am Main: Suhrkamp, 144-170.

Rosenfeld, Michel (2012): "Hate Speech in Constitutional Jurisprudence". In: Herz, Michael (Ed.): The Content and Context of Hate Speech, Cambridge: Cambridge University Press, 242-289.

Rosenzweig, Franz (1979): Der Mensch und sein Werk: Briefe und Tagebücher 1: Gesammelte Schriften. Rosenzweig, Rachel / Rosenzweig, Edith / Casper, Bernhard (Eds.). Den Haag: Martinus Nijhoff Publishers.

Roth, Gerhard (2003): Aus Sicht des Gehirns. Frankfurt am Main: Suhrkamp.

Rotman, David (2013): "How Technology is Destroying Jobs". In: MIT Technology Review 16(4), 28-35. Online: https://www.technologyreview.com/s/515926/how-technology-is-destroying-jobs/ [08.02.2021].

Rudin, Cynthia (2019): "Stop explaining black box machine learning models for high stakes decisions and use interpretable models instead". In: Nature Machine Intelligence 1(May), 206-215.

Rueegger, Heinz (2016): "Ethische Fragen zur Technikanwendung im Kontext der Betreuung und Pflege alter Menschen". In: Angewandte GERONTOLOGIE Appliquée, 15-17.

Runggaldier, Edmund (2003): "Deutung menschlicher Grunderfahrungen im Hinblick auf unser Selbst". In: Rager, Guenter / Quitterer, Josef / Runggaldier, Edmund (Eds.): Unser Selbst – Identität im Wandel neuronaler Prozesse. Paderborn: Ferdinand Schoeningh, 143-221.

Runkel, Thomas (2010): Enhancement und Identität. Die Idee einer biomedizinischen Verbesserung des Menschen als normative Herausforderung. Tuebingen: Mohr Siebeck.

Russel, Stuart J. / Norvig, Peter (2009): Artificial Intelligence: A Modern Approach. London: Pearson Education.

Russell, Stuart / Dewey, Daniel / Tegmark, Max (2015): "Research Priorities for Robust and Beneficial Artificial Intelligence". In: AI Magazine 36(4), 105-114.

Russell, Stuart / Dewey, Daniel / Temark, Max (2013): "Research priorities for robust and beneficial artificial intelligence". Boston: Future of Life Institute.

Russell, Stuart J. (2015): "Will They Make Us Better People?". In: Edge. Online: https://www.edge.org/response-detail/26157 [08.02.2021].

Rutkin, Aviva (2016): "Blockchain grid to let neighbours trade solar power in Australia". In: NewScientist, August 18. Online: https://www.newscientist.com/artic le/2101667-blockchain-grid-to-let-neighbours-trade-solar-power-in-australia/ [08.02.2021].

Ryan, Mark (2020): "The Future of Transportation: Ethical, Legal, Social and Economic Impacts of Self-driving Vehicles in the Year 2025". In: Science and Engineering Ethics 26, 1185-1208.

Sabaliauskaite, Giedre / Cui, Jin / Liew, Lin Shen / Zhou, Fengjun (2018): "Integrated Safety and Cybersecurity Risk Analysis of Cooperative Intelligent Transport Systems". In: IEEE (Ed.): Joint 10th International Conference on Soft Computing and Intelligent Systems (SCIS) and 19th International Symposium on Advanced Intelligent Systems (ISIS)". Toyama: IEEE, 723-728.

Sachs, Jeffrey D. (2019): "Roundtable: AI and the future of Global Affairs". In: Ethics & International Affairs 33(2), 159-167.

Sacks, Jonathan (2015): "Sword Into Plowshares". In: The Wall Street Journal Review, October 3, C1-C2. Online: https://www.wsj.com/articles/swords-to-plowsh ares-unlikely-any-time-soon-1444422562 RonaldLethal Autonomous Systems [08.02.2021].

Salmon, Wesley C. (1983): Logik. Stuttgart: Reclam.

Samek, Wojciech / Wiegand, Thomas / Mueller, Klaus-Robert (2017): "Explainable Artificial Intelligence: Understanding, Visualizing and Interpreting Deep Learning Models". In: arXiv. Online: https://arxiv.org/abs/1708.08296 [08.02.2021].

Sample, Ian (2017): "'Big Tech Firms' AI Hiring Frenzy Leads to Brain Drain at UK Universities". In: The Guardian, November 2. Online: https://www.theguardian. com/science/2017/nov/02/big-tech-firms-google-ai-hiring-frenzy-brain-drain-uk-u niversities [08.02.2021].

Sandel, Michael (2007): The Case Against Perfection: Ethics in the Age of Genetic Engineering. Cambridge: Harvard University Press.

Sandkuehler, Hans-Joerg (2010): "Menschenrechte". In: Sandkuehler, Hans-Joerg (Ed.): Enzyklopädie Philosophie 2. Hamburg: Felix Meiner, 1530-1553.

Sandler, Ronald L. (2014): Ethics and Emerging Technologies. New York: Palgrave Macmillan.

Santoni de Sio, Filippo (2016): Ethics and Self-driving Cars: A White Paper on Responsible Innovation in Automated Driving Systems. Online: https://repository. tudelft.nl/islandora/object/uuid:851eb5fb-0271-47df-9ab4-b9edb75b58e1?collecti on=research [08.02.2021].

Santoni de Sio, Filippo / van den Hoven, Jeroen (2018): "Meaningful Human Control over Autonomous Systems: A Philosophical Account". In: Frontiers in Robotics and AI 5, 1-14.

Santos de Carvalho, Juliana (2018): "A 'Male' Future?: An Analysis on the Gendered Discourses Regarding Lethal Autonomous Weapons". In: Amsterdam Law Forum 10(2), 41-61.

Sartre, Jean-Paul (1943): Das Sein und das Nichts: Versuch einer phänomenologischen Ontologie. Hamburg: Rowohlt.

Sassòli, Marco (2014): "Autonomous Weapons and International Humanitarian Law: Advantages, Open Technical Questions and Legal Issues to be Clarified". In: International Law Studies Naval War College 90, 308-340.

Savov, Vlad (2018): "Google's selfish Ledger is an unsettling vision of Silicon Valley social engineering". In: The Verge, May 17. Online: https://www.theverge.co m/2018/5/17/17344250/google-x-selfish-ledger-video-data-privacy [08.02.2021].

Savulescu, Julian / Kahane, Guy (2009): "The Moral Obligation to Create Children With the Best Chance of the Best Life". In: Bioethics 23(5), 274-290.

Saxon, Dan (2014): "A Human Touch: Autonomous Weapons, Directive 3000.09, and the 'Appropriate Levels of Human Judgment over the Use of Force'". In: Georgetown Journal of International Affairs 15(2), 100-109.

Scanlon, Thomas M. (2008): Moral Dimensions. Permissibility, Meaning, Blame. Cambridge: Harvard University Press.

Schaar, Peter (2016): "Schutz der Privatsphäre im Gesundheitswesen. Zu den rechtlichen Grenzen der Überwachung in der Medizin". In: Zeitschrift für medizinische Ethik 62(1), 31-39.

Schaefer, Kristin / Chen, Jessie / Szalma, James / Hancock, Peter (2016): "A Meta-Analysis of Factors Influencing the Development of Trust in Automation: Implications for Understanding Autonomy in Future Systems". In: The Journal of the Human Factors and Ergonomics Society 58, 1-62.

Schaeffner, Vanessa (2020): "Wenn Ethik zum Programm wird: Eine risikoethische Analyse moralischer Dilemmata des autonomen Fahrens". In: Zeitschrift für Ethik und Moralphilosophie 4, 27-49.

Scharre, Paul (2016): Autonomous Weapons and Operational Risk: Ethical Autonomy Project. Online: https://s3.amazonaws.com/files.cnas.org/documents/CNAS _Autonomous-weapons-operational-risk.pdf [08.02.2021].

Scharre, Paul (2018): Army of None: Autonomous Weapons and the Future of War. New York: W.W Norton & CO.

Scharre, Paul (2019): "Killer Apps: The Real Dangers of an AI Arms Race". In: Foreign Affairs 98, 135-144.

Schaudel, Dieter (2012): "Ethik und/oder/wegen Automatisierung?!". In: at – Automatisierungstechnik 60(1), 4-9.

Schaupp, Walter (2014): "Zwischen personal beliefs und professional duties: Weltanschaulich-religiöser Pluralismus als neue Herausforderung für das ärztliche Gewissen". In: Bormann, Franz-Josef / Wetzstein, Verena (Eds.): Gewissen: Dimensionen eines Grundbegriffs medizinischer Ethik. Berlin: De Gruyter, 3-23.

Scheck, Justin / Shifflett, Shane (2018): "How dirty money disappears into the black hole of cryptocurrency". In: The Wall Street Journal, September 28. Online: https://www.wsj.com/articles/how-dirty-money-disappears-into-the-black-hole-of-cryptocurrency-1538149743 [08.02.2021].

Schell, Bernadette H. (2014): Internet Censorship: A Reference Handbook. Santa Barbara: ABC-CLIO.

Schildmann, Jan / Marckmann, Georg / Vollmann, Jochen (2013): "Personalisierte Medizin. Medizinische, ethische, rechtliche und ökonomische Analysen". In: Ethik in der Medizin 25(3), 169-172.

Schindlbeck, Corinne (2008): "Ein übergrosser Teil der Patente ist rein taktisch und nicht innovativ". In: Markt&Technik, June 24, 62-64.

Schleidgen, Sebastian / Marckmann, Georg (2013): "Alter Wein in neuen Schläuchen? Ethische Implikationen der Individualisierten Medizin". In: Ethik in der Medizin 25(3), 223-231.

Schloegl-Flierl, Kerstin (2016): "Die Tugend der Epikie im Spannungsfeld von Recht und Ethik". In: Chittilappilly, Paul-Chummar (Ed.): Horizonte gegenwärtiger Ethik. Festschrift Josef Schuster. Freiburg im Breisgau: Herder, 29-39.

Schmidhuber, Juergen (2006): "Gödel Machines: Fully Self-Referential Optimal Universal Self-Improvers". In: Goertzel, Ben / Pennachin, Cassio (Eds): Artificial General Intelligence. Cognitive Technologies. Berlin: Springer, 119-226.

Schmidt, Eric (2015): "Eric Schmidt on How to Build a Better Web". In: The New York Times, December 7. Online: http://www.nytimes.com/2015/12/07/opinion/eric-schmidt-on-how-to-build-a-better-web.html?_r=1 [08.02.2021].

Schmidt, Eric / Cohen, Jared (2013): Die Vernetzung der Welt. Reinbek: Rowohlt.

Schmidt, Eric / Cohen, Jared (2014): The New Digital Age: Transforming Nations, Businesses, and Our Lives. New York: Vintage Books.

Schmidt, Hermann (1941): Denkschrift zur Gründung eines Institutes für Regelungstechnik. Berlin: Schnelle.

Schmitt, Hanspeter (2008): Sozialität und Gewissen. Anthropologische und theologisch-ethische Sondierung der klassischen Gewissenslehre. Studien der Moraltheologie 40. Wien: LIT-Verlag.

Schneider, Friedrich / Dreer, Elisabeth (2017): Grundeinkommen in Österreich?. Linz: Linz Johannes Kepler Universitaet.

Schockenhoff, Eberhard (2013): "Vom Ethos der Moraltheologie". In: Sautermeister, Jochen (Ed.): Verantwortung und Integrität heute: Theologische Ethik unter dem Anspruch der Redlichkeit. Freiburg im Breisgau: Herder, 58-68.

Schockenhoff, Eberhard (2014a): Grundlegung der Ethik: Ein theologischer Entwurf. Freiburg im Breisgau: Herder.

Schockenhoff, Eberhard (2014b): "Glaube und Toleranz. Überlegungen zu ihrem schwierigen Verhältnis". In: Schloegl-Flierl, Kerstin / Prueller-Jagenteufel, Gunter M. (Eds.): Aus Liebe zu Gott – im Dienst der Menschen: Spirituelle, pastorale und ökumenische Dimensionen der Moraltheologie. Festschrift Herbert Schloegel. Muenster: Aschendorff, 465-475.

Schockenhoff, Eberhard (2015): "Aufgaben und gegenwärtige Herausforderungen der Moraltheologie". In: Amesbury, Richard / Ammann, Christoph (Eds.): Was ist theologische Ethik? Beiträge zu ihrem Selbstverständnis und Profil. Zuerich: Institut fuer Sozialethik der Universitaet Zuerich, 49-73.

Schoenauer, Hermann / Horneber, Markus (2011): "Ethisch vertretbarer Technikeinsatz in der Sozial- und Gesundheitswirtschaft". In: Rueter, Georg / Da-Cruz, Patrick / Schwegel, Philipp (Eds.): Gesundheitsökonomie und Wirtschaftspolitik. Festschrift Peter Oberender. Stuttgart: Lucius & Lucius, 431-444.

Schoenheit, Ingo (2014): Corporate Social Responsibility and Consumers. Berlin: Springer.

Schoenherr-Mann, Hans-Martin (2010): Die Macht der Verantwortung. Freiburg im Breisgau: Karl Alber.

Schoernig, Niklas (2010): "Die Automatisierung des Krieges". In: HSFK-Standpunkt 5, 1-12.

Scholz, Olaf / Calvino, Nadia / Gualtieri, Roberto / Le Maire, Bruno (2020): "Ein gerechtes internationales Steuersystem". In: Die Welt, February 22. Online: https://www.welt.de/print/die_welt/debatte/article206059379/Gastkommentar-Ein-gerechtes-internationales-Steuersystem.html [08.02.2021].

Scholz, Roland W. / Bartelsman, Eric J. / Diefenbach, Sarah / Franke, Lude / Grunwald, Arnim / Helbing, Dirk / Hill, Richard / Hilty, Lorenz / Hoejer, Mattias / Klauser, Stefan / Montag, Christian / Parycek, Peter / Prote, Jan Philipp / Renn, Ortwin / Reichel, André / Schuh, Guenther / Steiner, Gerald / Viale Pereira, Gabriela (2018): "Unintended Side Effects of the Digital Transition: European Scientists Message from a Proposition-Based Expert Round Table". In: Sustainability 10(6), 1-48.

Scholz, Volker / Kempf, Marius (2016): "Autonomes Fahren: Autos im moralischen Dilemma?". In: Proff, Heike / Fojcik, Thomas Martin (Eds.): Nationale und internationale Trends in der Mobilität. Wiesbaden: Springer, 217-230.

Schreurs, Miranda A. / Steuwer, Sibyl D. (2015): "Autonomous Driving – Political, Legal, Social, and Sustainability Dimensions". In: Maurer, Markus / Gerdes, Christan J. / Lenz, Barbara / Winner, Hermann (Eds.): Autonomes Fahren. Technische, rechtliche und gesellschaftliche Aspekte. Berlin: Springer, 151-173.

Schroeder, Bernd (2003): "Religion und Ethik". In: Nissen, Ulrich / Andersen, Svend / Reuter, Lars (Eds.): The Sources of Public Morality – On the ethics and religion debate: Proceedings of the annual conference of the Societas Ethica in Berlin. Muenster: LIT-Verlag, 15-35.

Schroeder, Doris / Gefenas, Eugenijus (2009): "Vulnerability: Too Vague and Too Broad?". In: Cambridge Quarterly of Healthcare Ethics 18(2), 113-121.

Schueller, Bruno (1980): Die Begründung sittlicher Urteile. Typen ethischer Argumentation in der katholischen Moraltheologie. Duesseldorf: Patmos-Verlag.

Schulz, Peter J. / Rubinelli, Sara (2010): "Internet-enhanced health communication". In: Social Semiotics 20(1), 3-7.

Schulz, Soehnke E. (2016): "Ausblick". In: Schliesky, Ute / Schulz, Soenke E. / Gottberg, Friedrich / Kuhlmann, Florian (Eds.): Demokratie im digitalen Zeitalter, DIVSI-Perspektiven 5. Baden-Baden: Nomos Verlagsgesellschaft, 136-137.

Schulz, Wolfgang H. / Wieker, Horst / Arnegger, Bettina (2019): "Cooperative, Connected and Automated Mobility". In: Kruessel, Peter (Ed.): Future Telco. Cham: Springer, 219-229.

Schulzke, Marcus (2011): "Robots as Weapons in Just Wars". In: Philosophy and Technology 24(3), 293-306.

Schulzke, Marcus (2013): "Autonomous Weapons and Distributed Responsibility". In: Philosophy and Technology, 26(2), 203-219.

Schumann, Florian (2018): "In der Chat-Therapie". In: Die Zeit, May 17. Online: https://www.zeit.de/2018/21/psychotherapie-therapieplatz-online-hilfe-wartezeit [08.02.2021].

Schumann, Florian (2019): "Strahlendes Experiment". In: Die Zeit, January 17, 34. Online: https://www.zeit.de/2019/04/mobilfunknetz-5g-datenuebertragung-gesu ndheitsgefahr-strahlenbelastung [08.02.2021].

Schumpeter, Joseph A. (1972): Kapitalismus, Sozialismus und Demokratie. Bern: Francke.

Schumpeter, Joseph A. (1991): The Economics and Sociology of Capitalism. Princeton: Princeton University Press.

Schumpeter, Joseph A. (2008): Capitalism, Socialism and Democracy. New York: Harper Perennial Modern Classics.

Schuster, Johannes / Kerber, Walter (2016): "Gewissen". In: Brugger, Walter (Ed.): Philosophisches Wörterbuch. Freiburg im Breisgrau: Herder, 144-146.

Schuurman, Egbert (2010): "Responsible Ethics for Global Technology". In: Axiomathes 20(1), 107-127.

Schwab, Katharine (2018): "The Exploitation, Injustice, and Waste Powering Our AI". In: Fast Company, September 18. Online: https://www.fastcompany.com/9 0237802/the-exploitation-injustice-and-waste-powering-our-ai [08.02.2021].

Schwartz, Paul M. (1989): "The Computer in German and American Constitutional Law: Towards an American Right of Informational Self-Determination". In: American Journal of Comparative Law 37, 675-702.

Schweighofer, Johannes (2016): "Zur Befreiung des Menschen von mühevoller Arbeit und Plage durch Maschinen, Roboter und Computer – Auswirkungen der Digitalisierung auf die Arbeitsmärkte". In: Wirtschaft und Gesellschaft 42(2), 219-255.

Schweitzer, Doris (2017): "Die digitale Person: Die Anrufung des Subjekts im Recht auf Vergessenwerden". In: Österreichische Zeitschrift für Soziologie 42(3), 237-257.

Schweizer, Daniel (2015): Dirty Gold War – Dreckiges Gold. Arte Doku. Online: https://www.youtube.com/watch?v=WoK8cmdarIU [08.02.2021].

Schweizerische Nationalkommission Justitia et Pax (1998): Machbares Leben? Ethik in der Medizin. Zuerich: NZN Buchverlag.

Searle, John R. (1980): "Minds, Brains, and Programs". In: Behavioral and Brain Sciences 3(3), 417-457.

Securities & Exchange Commission / The Commodity Futures Trading Commission (2010): Findings Regarding the Market Events of May 6, 2010. Report of the Staffs of the CFTC and SEC to the Joint Advisory Committee on Emerging Regulatory Issues. Online: https://www.sec.gov/news/studies/2010/marketevents-report.pdf [08.02.2021].

Seele, Peter (2016): "Digitally unified reporting how XBRL-based real-time transparency helps in combining integrated sustainability reporting and performance control". In: Journal of Cleaner Production 136 (Part A), 65-77.

Seele, Peter (2018): "Let Us Not Forget: Crypto Means Secret. Cryptocurrencies as Enabler of Unethical and Illegal Business and the Question of Regulation". In: Humanist Management Journal 3, 133-139.

Segal, Adam (2017): "Teaching Morality to Machines". In: Council on Foreign Relations, November 14. Online: https://www.cfr.org/blog/teaching-morality-machines [08.02.2021].

Sen, Amartya (1999): Development as Freedom. New York: Alfred A. Knopf.

Sen, Amartya (2004): "Elements of a Theory of Human Rights". In: Philosophy & Public Affairs 32(4), 315-356.

Seseri, Rudina (2018): "The Problem with Explainable AI". In: Tech Crunch, June 14. Online: https://techcrunch.com/2018/06/14/the-problem-with-explainable-ai/ [08.02.2021].

Sevini, Filippo / Colpo, Pascal / Lequarré, Anne-Sophie / Charatsis, Christos / Barrero, Josefa / Michel, Quentin / Janssens, Willem Alfons Marc / Novau, Xavier Arnes (2018): Emerging Dual-Use Technologies and Global Supply Chain Compliance. Presentation at the IAEA Symposium on International Safeguards 2018. Vienna, January: Online: https://www.researchgate.net/profile/F-Sevini/publication/330258872_EMERGING_DUAL-USE_TECHNOLOGIES_AND_GLOBAL_SUPPLY_CHAIN_COMPLIANCE/links/5c35f8d7458515a4c718cf94/EMERGING-DUAL-USE-TECHNOLOGIES-AND-GLOBAL-SUPPLY-CHAIN-COMPLIANCE.pdf [08.02.2021].

Shanahan, Murray (2015): The Technological Singularity. Cambridge: MIT Press.

Shannon, Claude E. (1950): "XXII. Programming a computer for playing chess". In: The London, Edinburgh and Dublin Philosophical Magazine and Journal of Science 41(314), 256-275.

Sharkey, Amanda (2018): "Autonomous weapons systems, killer robots and human dignity". In: Ethics and Information Technology 21, 75-87.

Sharkey, Noel E. (2007): "Automated killers and the computing profession". In: Computer 40(11), 122-124.

Sharkey, Noel E. (2012): "Killing made easy". In: Lin, Patrick / Abney, Keith / Bekey, George A. (Eds.): Robot Ethics: The Ethical and Social Implications of Robotics. Intelligent Robotics and Autonomous Agents. New York: MIT Press, 111-128.

Sharkey, Noel E. (2011): "The automation and proliferation of military drones and the protection of civilians". In: Law Innovation Technology 3, 229-240.

Sharon, Tamar (2016): "The Googlization of health research". In: Personalized Medicine 13(6), 563-574.

Sharon, Tamar (2018): "When digital health meets digital capitalism, how many common goods are at stake?". In: Big Data & Society (July-December), 1-12.

Shaver, Lea (2015): "The Right to Science: Ensuring that Everyone Benefits from Scientific and Technological Progress". In: European Journal of Human Rights 4, 411-430.

Shaw, Gienna (2019): "Hackers Tap Deep Learning and AI for Nefarious Purposes". In: Health Tech Magazine, May 24. Online: https://healthtechmagazine.net/article/2019/05/hackers-tap-deep-learning-and-ai-nefarious-purposes [08.02.2021].

Shead, Sam (2019): "Google Announced An AI Advisory Council, But The Mysterious AI Ethics Board Remains A Secret". In: Forbes, March 27. Online: https://www.forbes.com/sites/samshead/2019/03/27/google-announced-an-ai-council-but-the-mysterious-ai-ethics-board-remains-a-secret/#34ba580e614a [08.02.2021].

Shelton Dinah (1991): "Human Rights, Environmental Rights, and the Right to Environment". In: Stanford Journal of International Law 28, 103-138.

Shetty, Salil (2015): "Corporations have rights. Now we need a global treaty on their responsibilities". In: The Guardian, January 21. Online: https://www.theguardian.com/global-development-professionals-network/2015/jan/21/corporations-abuse-rights-international-law [08.02.2021].

Shibasaki, Fumikazu (2005): "Technology and ethics". In: Philosophy & Criticism 31(18), 487-498.

Shift Project (2019): "Lean ICT: Towards digital sobriety". Online: https://theshiftproject.org/wp-content/uploads/2019/03/Lean-ICT-Report_The-Shift-Project_2019.pdf [08.02.2021].

Shoham, Shlomo / Lamay, Nira (2006): "Commission for Future Generations in the Knesset: lessons learnt". In: Tremmel, Joerg Chet (Ed.): Handbook of Intergenerational Justice. Cheltenham: Edward Elgar Publishing, 244-281.

Shooman, Yasemin (2014): "... weil ihre Kultur so ist". Narrative des antimuslimischen Rassismus. Bielefeld: Transcript.

Silva, Daniel / Cunha, Liliana / Barros, Carla / Baylina, Pilar (2019): "Preparing the Future Scenario of Automated Vehicles: Recommendations Drawn from the Analysis of the Work Activity of Road Transport Workers". In: Cotrim, Teresa / Serranheira, Florentino / Sousa, Paulo / Hignett, Sue / Albolino, Sara / Tartaglia, Riccardo (Eds.): Health and Social Care Systems of the Future: Demographic Changes, Digital Age and Human Factors. HEPS 2019: Advances in Intelligent Systems and Computing 1012. Cham: Springer, 301-310.

Simon, Judith (2015): "Distributed Epistemic Responsibility in a Hyperconnected Era". In: Floridi, Luciano (Ed.): The Onlife Manifesto. Being Human in a Hyperconnected Era. Cham: Springer, 135-151.

Simonite, Tom (2018): "Probing the dark side of Google's ad-targeting system". In: MIT Technology Review, 6 July. Online: https://www.technologyreview.com/s/5 39021/probing-the-dark-side-of-googles-ad-targeting-system/ [08.02.2021].

Singer, Peter (2004): "One Community". In: Singer, Peter: One World: The Ethics of Globalization. New Haven: Yale University Press, 150-193.

Singer, Peter (2009): Wired for War: The Robotics Revolution and Conflict in the 21st Century. New York: Penguin Press.

Singularity 2030 (n.d.): Homepage. Online: https://singularity2030.ch/ [08.02.2021].

Smith, Adam (2004): Theorie der ethischen Gefühle. Hamburg: Felix Meiner.

Smith, Brad / Browne, Carol Ann (2019): Tools and Weapons: The Promise and the Peril of the Digital Age. New York: Penguin Press.

Smith, Dave (2015): "GOOGLE CHAIRMAN: 'The Internet Will Disappear'". In: Business Insider, January 25. Online: https://www.businessinsider.com/google-c hief-eric-schmidt-the-internet-will-disappear-2015-1?r=US&IR=T [08.02.2021].

Smith, Noah (2013): "The End Of Labor: How to Protect Workers From the Rise of Robots". In: The Atlantic, January 14. Online: https://www.theatlantic.com/b usiness/archive/2013/01/the-end-of-labor-how-to-protect-workers-from-the-rise-of -robots/267135/ [08.02.2021].

Snower, Dennis J./Twomey, Paul/Farrell, Maria (2020): "Revisiting Digital Governance". In: Social Macroeconomics Working Paper Series of the Blavatnik School of Governance, Oxford University (30 September 2020). Online: https:// www.bsg.ox.ac.uk/sites/default/files/2020-10/SM-WP-2020-003%20Revisiting%2 0digital%20governance.pdf [08.02.2021].

Soares, Nate / Fallenstein, Benya (2017): "Agent Foundations for Aligning Machine Intelligence with Human Interests: A Technical Research Agenda". In: Callaghan, Victor / Miller, James / Yampolskiy, Roman / Armstrong, Stuart (Eds.): The Technological Singularity: Managing the Journey. Berlin: Springer, 103-125.

Soeiro, Diana (2020): "Smart Cities, Well-Being and Good Business: The 2030 Agenda and the Role of Knowledge in the Era of Industry 4.0". In: Matos, Florinda / Vairinhos, Valter / Salavisa, Leif Edvinsson / Massaro, Maurizio (Eds.): Knowledge, People, and Digital Transformation. Contributions to Management Science. Cham: Springer, 55-67.

Sohangir, Sahar / Wang, Dingding / Pomerantes, Anna / Koshgoftaar, Taghi M. (2018): "Big data: Deep learning for financial sentiment analysis". In: Journal of Big Data (5)1. Online: https://journalofbigdata.springeropen.com/articles/10.118 6/s40537-017-0111-6 [08.02.2021].

Sokolin, Lex / Low, Matthew James (2018): "Machine Intelligence and Augmented Finance: How Artificial Intelligence Creates $1 Trillion Dollar of Change in the Front, Middle and Back Office". In: Autonomous Research LLP. Online: https:// next.autonomous.com/augmented-finance-machine-intelligence [08.02.2021].

Solomonoff, Ray (1985): "The Time Scale of Artificial Intelligence: Reflections on Social Effects". In: Human Systems Management 5, 149-153.

Son, Hugh (2017): "JPMorgan software does in seconds what took lawyers 360,000 hours". In: Bloomberg, February 28. Online https://www.bloomberg.com/news/articles/2017-02-28/jpmorgan-marshals-an-army-of-developers-to-automate-high-finance [08.02.2021].

Sonderholm, Jorn (2009): "A Reform Proposal in Need of Reform: A Critique of Thomas Pogge's Proposal for How to Incentivize Research and Development of Essential Drugs". In: Public Health Ethics 3(2), 1-11.

Sonderholm, Jorn (2014): "A critique of an argument against patent rights for essential medicines". In: Ethics & Global Politics 7(3), 119-136.

Sorensen, Roy (2003): A Brief History of the Paradox. Philosophy and Labyrinths of Mind. Oxford: Oxford University Press.

Sorgner, Stefan Lorenz (2016): Transhumanismus. "Die gefährlichste Idee der Welt"!? Freiburg im Breisgau. Herder.

South African Government (1996): Constitution of the Republic of South Africa. Online: https://www.gov.za/documents/constitution-republic-south-africa-1996 [08.02.2021].

Sovacool, Benjamin / Griffiths, Steve (2020): "Culture and low-carbon energy transitions". In: Nature Sustainability, 1-9.

Spahn, Andreas (2013): "Freie Fahrt für freie Maschinen – Zur Ethik des vernetzten Autos". In: ATZagenda 2, 34-37.

Sparrow, Robert (2009): "Building a Better WarBot: Ethical Issues in the Design of Unmanned Systems for Military Applications". In: Science and Engineering Ethics 15, 169-187.

Sparrow, Robert (2017): "Killer Robots". In: Journal of Applied Philosophy 24(1), 62-77.

Sparrow, Robert / Howard, Mark (2020): "Make way for the wealthy? Autonomous vehicles, markets in mobility, and social justice". In: Mobilities 15(4), 514-526.

Spenlé, Christoph A. (2005): "Neue Entwicklungen im Völkerrecht: Zur Umsetzung des internationalen Paktes über wirtschaftliche, soziale und kulturelle Rechte von 1966 (UNO-Pakt I)". In: Kirchschlaeger, Peter G. / Kirchschlaeger, Thomas / Belliger, Andrea / Krieger, David (Eds.): Menschenrechte und Wirtschaft im Spannungsfeld zwischen State und Nonstate Actors. Internationales Menschenrechtsforum Luzern (IHRF) 2. Bern: Staempfli, 197-224.

Sperling, Daniel / van der Meer, Ellen / Pike, Susan (2018): "Vehicle Automation: Our Best Shot at a Transportation Do-Over?". In: Sperling, Daniel (Eds.): Three Revolutions. Washington: Island Press, 77-108.

Sperling, Joshua / Young, Stanley E. / Beck, John M. / Garikapati, Venu / Hou, Yi / Duvall, Andrew L. (2019): "Exploring Energy-Efficient and Sustainable Urban Mobility Strategies: An Initial Framework to Curate Data/Models, Measure Performance, and Diffuse Innovation: Preprint". In: National Renewable Energy Laboratory. U.S. Department of Energy. Office of Scientific and Technical Information. Online: https://www.osti.gov/biblio/1557548 [08.02.2021].

Spice, Byron (2017): "Carnegie Mellon Artificial Intelligence Beats Top Poker Pros". In: Carnegie Mellon University, January 31. Online: https://www.cmu.ed u/news/stories/archives/2017/january/AI-beats-poker-pros.html [08.02.2021].

Spiekermann, Sarah (2019): Digitale Ethik: Ein Wertesystem für das 21. Jahrhundert. Muenchen: Droemer.

Spielkamp, Matthias (2019a): "Wenn Algorithmen über den Job entscheiden". In: Die Presse, July 20. Online: https://www.diepresse.com/5662249/wenn-algorith men-uber-den-job-entscheiden?from=rss [08.02.2021].

Spielkamp, Matthias (2019b): Automating Society: Taking Stock of Automated Decision-Making in the EU. Berlin: Bertelsmannstiftung Studies.

Spieser, Kevin / Treleaven, Kyle. / Zhang, Rick / Frazzoli, Emilio / Morton, Daniel / Pavone, Marco (2014): "Toward a Systematic Approach to the Design and Evaluation of Automated Mobility-on-Demand Systems: A Case Study in Singapore." In: Meyer Gereon / Beiker, Sven (Eds.): Road Vehicle Automation. Lecture Notes in Mobility. Cham: Springer, 229-245.

Spinello, Richard A. (2002): Regulating Cyberspace. The Policies and Technologies of Control. Westport: Greenwood Publishing Group.

Spinello, Richard A. (2011): Cyberethics. Morality and Law in Cyberspace. Sudbury: Jones & Bartlett Learning.

Swiss National Radio Television SRF (2018): Facebook erhält Höchststrafe im Datenskandal. October 25. Online: https://www.srf.ch/news/international/camb ridge-analytica-skandal-facebook-erhaelt-hoechststrafe-im-datenskandal [08.02.2021].

Srivastava, Lara (2010): "Mobile Phones and the Evolution of Social Behaviour". In: Behaviour & Information Technology 24(2), 111-129.

Staab, Philipp / Nachtwey, Oliver (2016): "Die Digitalisierung der Dienstleistungsarbeit". In: Politik und Zeitgeschichte 18-19, 24-31.

Stadler, Wilfried (2017): "Über autonomes Fahren und Denken". In: Furche-Kolumne 218, 29. Online: https://www.wilfried-stadler.com/218 [08.02.2021].

Stadler, Wilfried (2019): Nice to Have. Gedanken zu Gesinnungs- und Verantwortungsethik in der Finanzwirtschaft. EthicsImpulse at the Institute of Social Ethics ISE of the University of Lucerne on October 30, 2019 (manuscript kindly provided by the author).

Stalinsky, Steven (2018): "The cryptocurrency-terrorism connection is too big to ignore". In: The Washington Post, December 17. Online: https://www.washington post.com/opinions/the-cryptocurrency-terrorism-connection-is-too-big-to-ignore/ 2018/12/17/69ed6ab4-fe4b-11e8-83c0-b06139e540e5_story.html?noredirect=on& utm_term=.d54c66c1e78a [08.02.2021].

Staszkiewicz, Piotr (2015): "High Frequency Trading Readiness in Central Europe". In: Journal on Business Review 4(2), 61-67.

Steil, Jochen J. (2019): "Roboterlernen ohne Grenzen? Lernende Roboter und ethische Fragen". In: Woopen, Christiane / Jannes, Marc (Eds.): Roboter in der Gesellschaft. Studies on Health and Society 2. Berlin: Springer, 15-33.

Steinbuch, Karl (1963): Automat und Mensch. Berlin: Springer.

Steiner, Jutta (2015): "Blockchain Can Bring Transparency to Supply Chains. The Business of Fashion". In: The Business of Fashion, June 19. Online: http://www.businessoffashion.com/articles/opinion/op-ed-blockchain-can-bring-transparency-to-supply-chains [08.02.2021].

Stephens, Lara (2018): "Alt und Pummelig". In: Die Zeit, May 2. Online: https://www.zeit.de/2018/19/facebook-jugendliche-nutzungsverhalten-soziale-medien [08.02.2021].

Sterckx, Sigrid (2006): "The Moral Justifiability of Patents". In: Ethical Perspectives 13(2), 249-265.

Sterling, Greg (2014): "Google Co-Founder Sergey Brin: I Wish I Could Forget The Right To Be Forgotten". In: Search Engine Land, May 28. Online: https://searchengineland.com/google-co-founder-brin-wish-forget-right-forgotten-192648 [08.02.2021].

Stiglitz, Joseph E. (1994): The Role of the State in Financial Markets. Proceedings of the World Bank Annual Conference on Development Economics. Washington: The International Bank for Reconstruction and Development.

Stiglitz, Joseph E. (2006): "Scrooge and Intellectual Property Rights". In: British Medical Journal (BMJ) 333, 1279-1280.

Stiglitz, Joseph E. (2015): The Great Divide. Unequal Societies and What We Can Do About Them. New York: W. W. Norton & Company.

Stocker, Adam / Shaheen, Susan (2018): "Shared Automated Mobility: Early Exploration and Potential Impacts". In: Meyer, Gereon / Beiker, Sven (Eds.): Road Vehicle Automation 4. Lecture Notes in Mobility. Cham: Springer, 125-139.

Stoeber, Rudolf (2011): "Meinungsfreiheit: zu wichtig, um sie durch Generalverbote zu schützen". In: Publizistik 56, 127-132.

Storino, John R. / Steffen, Justin C. / Gordon, Matthew T. (2017): "Decrypting the Ethical Implications of Blockchain Technology". In: Legaltech News, November 13. Online: https://www.law.com/legaltechnews/sites/legaltechnews/2017/11/13/decrypting-the-ethical-implications-of-blockchain-technology/?slreturn=20210021143635 [08.02.2021].

Streit, Guenther (1993): Computer und Informatisierung der Gesellschaft. Sozialethische Überlegungen zur dritten Phase der Industriellen Revolution. Erfahrung und Theologie. Schriften zur Praktischen Theologie 22. Frankfurt am Main: Peter Lang, 183-191.

Strumpf, Dan / Wenxin, Fan (2017): "Who Wants to Supply China's Surveillance State? The West". In: The Wall Street Journal, November 1. Online: https://www.wsj.com/articles/who-wants-to-supply-chinas-surveillance-state-the-west-1509540111 [08.02.2021].

Sturma, Dieter (2003): "Autonomie: Über Personen, Künstliche Intelligenz und Robotik". In: Christaller, Thomas / Wehner, Josef (Eds.): Autonome Maschinen. Wiesbaden: Westdeutscher Verlag, 38-55.

Sudmann, Lena (2015): Schnittstelle Mensch – Maschine: Die Prothese. Diploma thesis, Theatre, Film and Media studies, University of Vienna. Online: http://oth es.univie.ac.at/37151/ [08.02.2021].

Sullins, John P. (2006): "When Is a Robot a Moral Agent". In: International Review of Information Ethics 6(12), 23-30.

Sullins, John P. (2010): "Rights and Computer Ethics". In: Floridi, Luciano (Ed.): The Cambridge Handbook of Information and Computer Ethics. Cambridge: Cambridge University Press, 116-133.

Sullins, John P. (2013): "An Ethical Analysis of the Case for Robotic Weapons Arms Control". In: Podins, Karls / Stinissen, Jan / Maybaum, Markus (Eds.): 5th International Conference on Cyber Conflict. Tallinn: NATO CCD COE Publications, 1-20.

Summers, Lawrence / Summers, Victoria P. (1989): "When Financial Markets Work Too Well: A Cautious Case for a Securities Transactions Tax". In: Journal of Financial Services Research 3(2-3), 261-286.

Susskind, Richard / Susskind, Daniel (2015): The Future of the Professions. How Technology Will Transform the Work of Human Experts. New York: Oxford University Press.

Swan, Melanie (2015): Blockchain. Blueprint for a New Economy. Sebastopol: O'Reilly Media.

Swan, Melanie / de Filippi, Primavera (2015): "Toward A Philosophy of Blockchain: A Symposium Introduction". In: Metaphilosophy 48(5), 603-619.

Sweeney, Latanya (2013): "Discrimination in online ad delivery". In: arXiv. Online: https://arxiv.org/abs/1301.6822 [08.02.2021].

Swiss Federal Council (2020): "Leitlinien Künstliche Intelligenz für den Bund. Orientierungsrahmen für den Umgang mit künstlicher Intelligenz in der Bundesverwaltung". Bern: Swiss Federal Council.

Swiss Federal Office for the Environment (FOEN) (2020): Bundesrat entscheidet über weiteres Vorgehen im Bereich Mobilfunk und 5G. Online: https://www.ba fu.admin.ch/bafu/de/home/themen/elektrosmog/dossiers/bericht-arbeitsgruppe-mobilfunk-und-strahlung.html [08.02.2021].

Swiss Financial Market Supervisory Authority FINMA (2013): Annual Report 2013. Online: https://www.finma.ch/en/~/media/finma/dokumente/dokumente ncenter/myfinma/finma-publikationen/geschaeftsbericht/jb13_d_finma.pdf?la=e n [08.02.2021].

Swiss Learning Health System (n.d.): About the Project. Online: https://www.slhs.c h/en/about-the-project [08.02.2021].

Taddeo, Mariarosaria / Floridi, Luciano (2018): "How AI can be a force for good". In: Science 361(6404), 751-752.

Taddeo, Mariarosaria / Floridi, Luciano (2015): "The Debate on the Moral Responsibilities of Online Service Providers". In: Science and Engineering Ethics 22, 1-29.

Taddy, Matt (2019): "The Technological Elements of Artificial Intelligence". In: Agrawal, Ajay / Gans, Joshua / Goldfarb, Avi (Eds.): The Economics of Artificial Intelligence: An Agenda. Chicago: University of Chicago Press, 61-87.

Taiebat, Morteza / Brown, Austin L. / Safford, Hannah R. / Qu, Shen / Xu, Ming (2018): "A Review on Energy, Environmental, and Sustainability Implications of Connected and Automated Vehicles". In: Environmental Science Technology 52(20), 11449-11465.

Talbot, Brian / Jenkins, Ryan / Purves, Duncan (2017a): "When Robots Should Do the Wrong Thing". In: Lin, Patrick / Jenkins, Ryan / Abney, Keith (Eds.): Robot ethics 2.0: From Autonomous Cars to Artificial Intelligence. New York: Oxford University Press, 258-273.

Talbot, David / Kim, Levin / Goldstein, Elena / Sherman, Jenna (2017b): "Charting a roadmap to ensure AI benefits all". In: Medium, November 30. Online: https://medium.com/berkman-klein-center/charting-a-roadmap-to-ensure-artificial-inte lligence-ai-benefits-all-e322f23f8b59 [08.02.2021].

Taleb, Nassim Nicholas (2010): The Black Swan: The Impact of the Highly Improbable: The Impact of the Highly Improbable With a New Section: 'on Robustness and Fragility'. New York: Random House.

Taparelli, Luigi (1855): Saggio teoretico di diritto naturale appoggiato sul fatto 1. Roma: La Civiltà cattolica.

Tasioulas, John (2015): "On the Foundations of Human Rights". In: Cruft, Rowan / Liao, S. Matthew / Renzo, Massimo (Eds.): Philosophical Foundations of Human Rights. Oxford: Oxford University Press, 45-70.

Tavani, Herman T. (2004): Ethics and Technology: Ethical Issues in an Age of Information and Communication Technology. New York: John Wiley and Sons.

Tax Justice Network-Africa (2005): Tax Us If You Can: Why Africa should stand up for Tax Justice. London: Tax Justice Network. Online: https://www.taxjustice.ne t/cms/upload/pdf/tuiyc_-_eng_-_web_file.pdf [08.02.2021].

Taylor, Charles (2015): "Für eine grundlegende Neubestimmung des Säkularismus". In: Schwarz, Gerhard / Sitter-Liver, Beat / Holderegger, Adrian (Eds.): Religion, Liberalität und Rechtsstaat: Ein offenes Spannungsverhältnis. Zuerich: Verlag Neue Zuercher Zeitung, 27-45.

Taylor, Kate / Goggin, Benjamin (2019): "49 of the biggest scandals in Uber's history". In: Business Insider, May 10. Online: https://www.businessinsider.com/uber -company-scandals-and-controversies-2017-11?r=US&IR=T [08.02.2021].

Teichtweiter, Georg (1976): "Moral – wieder gefragt?". In: Hirschmann, Johannes (Ed.): Der Christ in der Welt 5(7a/b). Aschaffenburg: Paul Pattloch, 102-123.

Teller, Astro (2012): "Speed of Dreams". In: Think with Google. Online: https://ww w.thinkwithgoogle.com/marketing-resources/speed-of-dreams-astro-teller/ [08.02.2021].

Tezuka, Osamu (2009): "Ten Principles of Robot Law". In: Schodt, Frederik L. (Ed.): Inside the Robot Kingdom. Japan, Mechatronics, and the Coming Robotopia. Online: http://www.realtechsupport.org/UB/MC/JapaneseRobots_le cture_2009.pdf [08.02.2021].

The Economist (2019): "The rise of the financial machines". In: The Economist, October 3. Online: https://www.economist.com/leaders/2019/10/03/the-rise-of-th e-financial-machines [08.02.2021].

The Seasteading Institute (2017): The Floating Island Project: French Polynesia. Online: https://www.seasteading.org/floating-city-project/ [08.02.2021].

the world unplugged (2019): Homepage. Online: https://theworldunplugged.word press.com/ [08.02.2021].

Thierer, Adam (2014): Permissionless Innovation: The Continuing Case for Comprehensive Technological Freedom. Washington: Mercatus Center at George Mason University.

Thimm, Caja / Bächle, Thomas Christian (2018): "Autonomie der Technologie und autonome Systeme als ethische Herausforderung". In: Rath, Matthias / Krotz, Friedrich / Karmasin, Matthias (Eds.): Maschinenethik. Wiesbaden: Springer, 73-87.

Thomas Aquinas (1937): Summa Theologica 6. Katholischer Akademikerverband (Ed.). Übersetzt von Dominikanern und Benediktinern Deutschlands und Österreichs. Salzburg: Anton Pustet.

Thomas, Bradan T. (2015): "Autonomous Weapon Systems: The Anatomy of Autonomy and the Legality of Lethality". In: Houston Journal of International Law 37, 235-261.

Thomopoulos, Nikolas / Givoni, Moshe (2015): "The autonomous car – a blessing or a curse for the future of low carbon mobility? An exploration of likely vs. desirable outcomes". In: European Journal of Futures Research 3(14). Online: https://eujournalfuturesresearch.springeropen.com/articles/10.1007/s40309-015-0071-z [08.02.2021].

Thompson, Derek (2010): "Google's CEO: 'The Laws Are Written by Lobbyists'". In: The Atlantic, October 1. Online: https://www.theatlantic.com/technology/ar chive/2010/10/googles-ceo-the-laws-are-written-by-lobbyists/63908/ [08.02.2021].

Thompson, Janna (2010): "What is Intergenerational Justice?". In: Future Justice, 5-20. Online: http://www.futureleaders.com.au/book_chapters/pdf/Future_Justic e/Janna_Thompson.pdf. [08.02.2021].

Thompson, Nicholas / Vogelstein, Fred (2018): "Inside the Two Years That Shook Facebook – and the World". In: Wired, December 2. Online: https://www.wired. com/story/inside-facebook-mark-zuckerberg-2-years-of-hell/ [08.02.2021].

Thomson, Judith Jarvis (1985): "The Trolley Problem". In: Yale Law Journal 94, 1395-1415.

Thuerkauf, Max (1980): Technomanie – die Todeskrankheit des Materialismus: Ursachen und Konsequenzen der technologischen Masslosigkeiten unserer Zeit. Schaffhausen: Novalis.

Thun-Hohenstein, Christoph (2017): "Sense and Sensibility in the Digital Age: Let Us Wake Up and Take Action! Introductory Essay". In: Thun-Hohenstein, Christoph (Ed.): Vienna Biennale 2017. Wien: Verlag für Moderne Kunst, 16-30.

Tingyang, Zhao (2020): Alles unter dem Himmel. Vergangenheit und Zukunft der Weltordnung. Berlin: Suhrkamp.

Tiqqun, Ronald Voullié (2007): Kybernetik und Revolte. Zuerich: Diaphanes.

Tirosh-Samuelson, Hava (2017): "Technological Transcendence: A Critique of Transhumanism". In: Trothen, Tracy J. / Mercer, Calvin (Eds.): Religion and Human Enhancement. Death, Values, and Morality, Palgrave Studies in the Future of Humanity and its Successors. London: Palgrave Macmillan, 267-283.

Tobin, James (1978). "A proposal for international monetary reform". In: Eastern Economic Journal 4(3-4), 153-159.

Tomasi, Silvano M. (2013): "Annual Meeting of the High Contracting Parties to the Convention on Prohibitions or Restrictions on the Use of Certain Conventional Weapons Which May Be Deemed to Be Excessively Injurious or to Have Indiscriminate Effects, 10 October 1980". In: United Nations (Ed.), Treaty Series 1342. Geneva: UN.

Tomuschat, Christian (2003): Human rights: Between idealism and realism. Oxford: Oxford University Press.

Topol, Sarah A. (2017): "Der Frieden braucht neue Formen". In: Greenpeace Magazin 2, 21-33.

Torrance, Steve (2008): "Ethics and consciousness in artificial agents". In: AI & Society 22, 495-521.

Torrance, Steve (2011): "Machine Ethics and the Idea of a More-Than-Human-World". In: Anderson, Michael / Anderson, Susan Leigh (Eds.): Machine Ethics. Cambridge: Cambridge University Press, 115-137.

Toscano, Christopher P. (2015): "Friend of Humans: An Argument for Developing Autonomous Weapons Systems". In: Journal of National Security and Policy 8, 189-246.

Tracy, David (1981): The Analogical Imagination: Christian Theology and Culture of Pluralism. New York: Crossroad.

Trappl, Robert (2016): "Robots' Ethical Systems: From Asimov's Laws to Principlism, from Assistive Robots to Self-Driving Cars". In: Trappl, Robert (Ed.): A Construction Manual for Ethical Systems: Requirements, Methods, Implementations. Cham: Springer, 1-8.

Tremmel, Joerg Chet (2006): "Establishing intergenerational justice in national constitutions". In: Tremmel, Joerg Chet (Ed.): Handbook of Intergenerational Justice. Cheltenham: Edward Elgar Publishing, 187-214.

Tripathi, Salil (2005): "Social human rights and international economical policy". In: Kirchschlaeger, Peter G. / Kirchschlaeger, Thomas / Belliger, Andrea / Krieger, David (Eds.): Menschenrechte und Wirtschaft im Spannungsfeld zwischen State und Nonstate Actors. Internationales Menschenrechtsforum Luzern (IHRF) 2. Bern: Staempfli, 151-169.

Trotter Cockburn, Catherine (1702): A Defence of Mr. Lock's [sic.] Essay of Human Understanding. London: William Turner & John Nutt.

Tucker, Patrick / One, Defense (2014): "Can the Military Really Teach Robots Right from Wrong?". In: The Atlantic, May 14. Online: https://www.theatlantic.com/technology/archive/2014/05/the-military-wants-to-teach-robots-right-from-wrong/370855/ [08.02.2021].

Tufekci, Zeynep (2019): "Think You're Discreet Online? Think Again". In: The New York Times, April 21. Online: https://www.nytimes.com/2019/04/21/opinion/computational-inference.html [08.02.2021].

Tuffley, David (2015): "Job survival in the age of robots and intelligent machines". In: The Conversation, January 1. Online: https://theconversation.com/job-survival-in-the-age-of-robots-and-intelligent-machines-33906 [08.02.2021].

Tugendhat, Ernst (1999): "Die Kontroverse um die Menschenrechte". In: Gosepath, Stefan / Lohmann, Georg (Eds.): Philosophie der Menschenrechte. Frankfurt am Main: Suhrkamp, 48-61.

Turing, Alan M. (2009): "Computing Machinery and Intelligence". In: Epstein, Robert / Roberts, Gary / Beber, Grace (Eds.): Parsing the Turing Test: Philosophical and Methodological Issues in the Quest for the Thinking Computer. Springer: Berlin, 23-65.

Turkle, Sherry (2007): "Authenticity in the age of digital companions". In: Interaction Studies 50(8/3), 501-517.

Turner, Bryan S. (2006): Vulnerability and Human Rights. Pennsylvania: Pennsylvania State University Press.

Tussyadiah, Iis P. / Zach, Florian J. / Wang, Jianxi (2017): "Attitudes Toward Autonomous on Demand Mobility System: The Case of Self-Driving Taxi". In: Schegg, Roland / Stangl, Brigitte (Eds.): Information and Communication Technologies in Tourism 2017. Cham: Springer, 755-766.

Tutt, Andrew (2016): "An FDA for algorithms". In: SSRN Scholarly Paper. Online: http://www.datascienceassn.org/sites/default/files/An%20FDA%20for%20Algorithms.pdf [08.02.2021].

Tzafestas, Spyros G. (2016): Roboethics: A Navigating Overview. Intelligent Systems, Control and Automation: Science and Engineering. Cham: Springer.

Uenver, Halit (2015): Globale Vernetzung, Kommunikation und Kultur – Konflikt oder Konvergenz? Dissertation, Universitaet Ulm.

The Public Voice Coalition (2018): "Universal Guidelines on Artificial Intelligence (UGAI)". In: The Public Voice Coalition. Online: https://thepublicvoice.org/ai-universal-guidelines/ [08.02.2021].

Ullrich, Stefan (2014): "Informationelle Mü(n)digkeit". In: Datenschutz und Datensicherheit - DuD 38(10), 696-700.

Ulpian, Domitius (2005): Corpus Iuris Civilis: Digesten 1. Knuetel, Rolf / Kupisch, Berthold / Seiler, Hans Hermann / Behrends, Okko (Eds.). Heidelberg: C. F. Mueller.

UN Committee on Economic, Social and Cultural Rights (2000): General Comment No. 14: The Right to the Highest Attainable Standard of Health, 11 August 2000. Online: https://digitallibrary.un.org/record/425041 [08.02.2021].

UN Committee on the Elimination of Racial Discrimination (CERD) (2013): International Convention on the Elimination of all Forms of Racial Discrimination. General recommendation No. 35: Combating racist hate speech. Online: http://docstore.ohchr.org/SelfServices/FilesHandler.ashx?enc=6QkG1d%2fPPRiCAqhK b7yhssyNNtgI51ma08CMa6o7Bglz8iG4SuOjovEP%2bcqr8joDoVEbW%2bQ1 MoWdOTNEV99v6FZp9aSSA1nZya6gtpTo2JUBMI0%2boOmjAwk%2b2xJW% 2bC8e [08.02.2021].

UN Human Rights Committee (1983): General Comment No. 11: Prohibition of propaganda for war and inciting national, racial or religious hatred (Art. 20). July 29. Online: https://www.ohchr.org/Documents/Issues/Opinion/CCPRGeneral CommentNo11.pdf [08.02.2021].

UN Human Rights Committee (1988): General Comment No. 16: Article 17 (The right to respect of privacy, family, home and correspondence, and protection of honour and reputation). Online: https://tbinternet.ohchr.org/Treaties/CCPR/Sh ared%20Documents/1_Global/INT_CCPR_GEC_6624_E.doc [08.02.2021].

UN Human Rights Council (2019): New and emerging digital technologies and human rights. Online: https://www.ohchr.org/EN/HRBodies/HRC/AdvisoryCo mmittee/Pages/DigitalTechnologiesandHR.aspx [08.02.2021].

UN Special Rapporteur on Freedom of Opinion and Expression (2011): International Mechanisms for Promoting Freedom of Expression. Joint Declaration on Freedom of Expression on the Internet, June 1. Online: www.osce.org/fom/7830 9 [08.02.2021].

UNESCO (2005): Towards knowledge societies: UNESCO world report. Online: https://unesdoc.unesco.org/ark:/48223/pf0000141843 [08.02.2021].

UNESCO (2018): The UNESCO Courier: Many Voices, One World. A lexicon for artificial intelligence. Online: https://en.unesco.org/courier/2018-3/lexicon-artificial-intelligence [08.02.2021].

UNESCO (2019): Steering AI and Advanced ICTs for Knowledge Societies: A Rights, Openness, Access, and Multi-stakeholder Perspective. Online: https://un esdoc.unesco.org/ark:/48223/pf0000372132 [08.02.2021].

UNESCO (2020): Elaboration of a Recommendation on the ethics of artificial intelligence. Online: https://en.unesco.org/artificial-intelligence/ethics [08.02.2021].

UNESCO COMEST (2017): Report of COMEST on Robotics Ethics. World Commission on the Ethics of Scientific Knowledge and Technology (COMEST). Online: http://unesdoc.unesco.org/images/0025/002539/253952E.pdf [08.02.2021].

Ungerer, Aria (2019): "Als Vater war er gleichermassen grossartig und furchtbar". In: Die Zeit Magazin, October 16. Online: https://www.zeit.de/zeit-magazin/201 9/43/aria-ungerer-tomi-ungerer-tochter-literatur [08.02.2021].

UNI Global Union (2017): "Top 10 Principles for Ethical Artificial Intelligence". Online: www.thefutureworldofwork.org/media/35420/uni_ethical_ai.pdf [08.02.2021].

UNICEF (2017): The State of the World's Children: Children in a Digital World. https://www.unicef.org/publications/index_101992.html [08.02.2021].

Universal Declaration of Human Rights of 1948 (1948). United Nations. Online: https://www.un.org/en/universal-declaration-human-rights/ [08.02.2021].

United Nations (1950): French Delegate to the Sixth Commission on Human Rights 1950. Summary Record of the 165th meeting: Draft International covenant on human rights. Economic and Social Council. Commission on Human Rights. Sixth Session. E/CN.4/SR.165. Paris: United Nations.

United Nations (1987): Report of the World Commission on Environment and Development: Our Common Future. New York: Oxford University Press.

United Nations Declaration on the Rights of Indigenous Peoples of 2007 (2007). Online: https://www.un.org/development/desa/indigenouspeoples/declaration-on-the-rights-of-indigenous-peoples.html [08.02.2021].

United Nations (2011): Guiding Principles on Business and Human Rights: Implementing the United Nations 'Protect, Respect and Remedy' Framework. Promotion and Protection of all Human Rights, Civil, Political, Economic, Social and Cultural Rights Including the Right to Development. Report of the Special Representative of the UN Secretary-General on the Issue of Human Rights and Transnational Corporations and Other Business Enterprises, John Ruggie. Human Rights Council, Seventeenth Session, A/HRC/17/31. United Nations. Online: https://undocs.org/en/A/HRC/17/31 [08.02.2021].

United Nations (2012): "Countries must boost measures to combat Internet racism – UN independent expert". In: UN News, November 5. Online: https://news.un.org/en/story/2012/11/424852-countries-must-boost-measures-combat-internet-racism-un-independent-expert [08.02.2021].

United Nations (2015): UN Sustainable Development Goals. Online: https://sustainabledevelopment.un.org/?menu=1300 [08.02.2021].

United Nations (2019): Moving Together to build a healthier World. High-level Meeting at the UN General Assembly. Political Declaration on Universal Health Coverage, September 23, para. 5. United Nations. Online: https://www.un.org/pga/73/wp-content/uploads/sites/53/2019/07/FINAL-draft-UHC-Political-Declaration.pdf [08.02.2021].

UN Secretary-General's High-level Panel on Digital Cooperation (2019): The Age of Digital Interdependence. Report of the UN Secretary-General's High-level Panel on Digital Cooperation, June 2019. Online: http://www.un.org/en/pdfs/DigitalCooperation-report-for%20web.pdf [08.02.2021].

Urban, Tim (2015): "The AI Revolution: The Road to Superintelligence". In: Wait but Why: New post every sometimes, January 22. Online: https://waitbutwhy.com/2015/01/artificial-intelligence-revolution-1.html [08.02.2021].

U.S. Department of Health and Human Services: National Toxicology Program (2018): Cell Phone Radio Frequency Radiation. Online: https://ntp.niehs.nih.gov/whatwestudy/topics/cellphones/index.html [08.02.2021].

U.S. President National Science and Technology Council Committee on Technology (2016a): Preparing for the Future of Artificial Intelligence. October 12. Online: https://obamawhitehouse.archives.gov/sites/default/files/whitchouse_files/microsites/ostp/NSTC/preparing_for_the_future_of_ai.pdf [08.02.2021].

U.S. President National Science and Technology Council Committee on Technology (2016b): The national artificial intelligence research and development strategic plan. October 13. Online: https://www.nitrd.gov/PUBS/national_ai_rd_strategic_plan.pdf [08.02.2021].

University of Washington (2006): The History of Artificial Intelligence. University of Washington. History of Computing Course (CSEP 590A). Online: https://courses.cs.washington.edu/courses/csep590/06au/projects/history-ai.pdf [08.02.2021].

Vallor, Shannon / Bekey, George A. (2017): "Artificial Intelligence and the Ethics of Self-Learning". In: Lin, Patrick / Jenkins, Ryan / Abney, Keith (Eds.): Robot Ethics 2.0 from Autonomous cars to Artificial Intelligence. New York: Oxford University Press, 338-353.

Van Eeten, Michel (2017): "Patching Security Governance: An Empirical View of Emergent Governance Mechanisms for Cybersecurity". In: Digital Policy, Regulation and Governance 19(6), 429-448.

Van Est, Rinie / Stemerding, Dirk (2012): Making *Perfect* Life. European Governance Challenges in 21st Century Bioengineering. STOA Science and Technology Options Assessment. Brussels: European Union.

Van Opstal, Rocus / Timmerhuis, Jacqueline (2006): "The role of CPB in Dutch economic policy". In: Tremmel, Joerg Chet (Ed.): Handbook of Intergenerational Justice. Cheltenham: Edward Elgar Publishing, 299-316.

Van Vliet, Benjamin Edward (2012): Systematic Finance: Essays on Ethics, Methodology and Quality Control in High Frequency Trading. Chicago: Illinois Institute of Technology.

Van Wynsberghe, Aimee (2015): Healthcare Robots: Ethics, Design and Implementation. Farnham: Ashgate.

Vance, Ashlee (2010) Andrew Orlowski: "Merely Human? That's So Yesterday". In: The New York Times, June 12. Online: https://www.nytimes.com/2010/06/13/business/13sing.html [08.02.2021].

Varian, Hal (2014a): "Beyond Big Data". In: Business Economics 49(1), 27-31.

Varian, Hal (2014b): "Big Data: New Tricks for Econometrics". In: Journal of Economic Perspectives 28(2), 3-28.

Varian, Hal (2018): Artificial Intelligence, Economics and Industrial Organization. NBER Working Paper 24839. Online: https://www.nber.org/papers/w24839 [08.02.2021].

Veith, Werner (2014): "Gerechtigkeit". In: Heimbach-Steins, Marianne (Ed.): Christliche Sozialethik: Ein Lehrbuch 1. Studienliteratur. Regensburg: Friedrich Pustet, 315-326.

Verbeek, Peter-Paul (2005): What Things Do: Philosophical Reflections on Technology, Agency, and Design. Pennsylvania: Penn State University Press.

Verbeek, Peter-Paul (2011a): Moralizing Technology: Understanding and Designing the Morality of Things. Chicago: Chicago University Press.

Verbeek, Peter-Paul (2011b): "Subject to Technology: on autonomic computing and human autonomy". In: Rouvroy, Antoinette / Hildebrandt, Mireille (Eds.): Law, Human Agency, and Autonomic Computing: The Philosophy of Law meets the Philosophy of Technology. London: Routledge, 27-45.

Verbeek, Peter-Paul (2014): "Some Misunderstandings About the Moral Significance of Technology". In: Kroes, Peter / Verbeek, Peter-Paul (Eds.): The Moral Status of Technical Artefacts. Philosophy of Engineering and Technology 17. Dordrecht: Springer, 75-88.

Verbeek, Peter-Paul (2015a): "Designing the Public Sphere: Information Technologies and the Politics of Mediation". In: Floridi, Luciano (Ed.): The Onlife Manifesto: Being Human in a Hyperconnected Era. Cham: Springer, 208-219.

Veruggio, Gianmarco / Operto, Fiorella (2008): "Roboethics: Social and Ethical Implications of Robotics". In: Siciliano, Bruno / Katib, Oussama (Eds.): Springer Handbook of Robotics. Berlin: Springer, 1499-1524.

Viehl, Alexander / Gleich, Udo / Post, Hendrik / ASSUME Partners (2017): "Affordable Safe and Secure Mobility Evolution". In: Watzenig, Daniel / Horn, Martin (Eds.): Automated Driving. Cham: Springer, 583-588.

Villani, Cédric (2018): For a Meaningful Artificial Intelligence: Towards a French and European Strategy. Online: https://www.aiforhumanity.fr/pdfs/MissionVilla ni_Report_ENG-VF.pdf [08.02.2021].

Villhauer, Bernd (2016): "Finanzmarktkriminalität und Ethik". In: Zoche, Peter / Kaufmann, Stefan / Arnold, Harald (Eds.): Grenzenlose Sicherheit?: Gesellschaftliche Dimensionen der Sicherheitsforschung. Berlin: LIT-Verlag, 235-250.

Virt, Guenter (2007): Damit Menschsein Zukunft hat: Theologische Ethik im Einsatz für eine humane Gesellschaft. Marschuetz, Gerhard / Prueller-Jagenteufel, Gunter M. (Eds.). Wuerzburg: Echter.

Voegeli, Vogeli (2016): "Credit Suisse, CIA-funded palantir to target rogue bankers". In: Bloomberg, March 22. Online: https://www.bloomberg.com/news/ articles/2016-03-22/credit-suisse-cia-funded-palantir-build-joint-compliance-firm [08.02.2021].

Vogel, Johan (2019): "Spielregeln für Giganten". In: Die Zeit, July 25. Online: https://www.zeit.de/2019/31/datenschutz-internetkonzerne-kontrolle-eu-wettber werbsrecht [08.02.2021].

Vogel, Kenneth (2017): "Google Critic Ousted From Think Tank Funded by the Tech Giant". In: The New York Times, August 30. Online: https://www.nytimes. com/2017/08/30/us/politics/eric-schmidt-google-new-america.html [08.02.2021].

Vogt, Markus (2005): "Natürliche Ressourcen und intergenerationelle Gerechtigkeit". In: Heimbach-Steins, Marianne (Ed.): Christliche Sozialethik: Ein Lehrbuch 2. Studienliteratur. Regensburg: Friedrich Pustet, 137-162.

Von Cranach, Xaver (2019): "Er hat einen Traum". In: Die Zeit, October 30. Online: https://www.zeit.de/2019/45/raj-chetty-big-data-soziale-ungleichheit-oekono mie [08.02.2021].

Wachter, Sandra / Mittelstadt, Bernt / Russell, Chris (2017): "Counterfactual explanations without opening the black box: Automated decisions and the GDPR". In: Harvard Journal of Law & Technology 31(2), 841-887.

Wagner, Markus (2014): "The Dehumanization of International Humanitarian Law: Legal, Ethical, and Political Implications of Autonomous Weapon Systems". In: Vanderbilt Journal of Transnational Law 47, 1371-1424.

Waid, Bill (2018): "AI-enabled personalization: The new frontier in dynamic pricing". In: Forbes, July 9. Online: https://www.forbes.com/sites/forbestechcouncil/2018/07/09/ai-enabled-personalization-the-new-frontier-in-dynamic-pricing/#71e470b86c1b [08.02.2021].

Wakefield, Jane (2019): "Google's ethics board shut down". In: BBC News, April 5. Online: https://www.bbc.com/news/technology-47825833 [08.02.2021].

Walker, Francesco / Verwey, Willem / Martens, Marieke (2018): "Gaze Behaviour as a Measure of Trust in Automated Vehicles". In: Van Nes, Nicole / Voegelé, Charlotte (Eds.): Proceedings of the 6th Humanist Conference, The Hague, Netherlands, June 13-14. Online: https://www.humanist-vce.eu/fileadmin/contributeurs/humanist/TheHague2018/29-walker.pdf [08.02.2021].

Walker-Smith, Bryant (2013): "Automated vehicles are probably legal in the United States". In: Texas A&M Law Review 1(3), 411-521.

Wallace-Wells, Benjamin (2015): "As Jeopardy! Robot Watson Grows Up, How Afraid of It Should We Be?". In: New York Magazine, May 20. Online: https://nymag.com/intelligencer/2015/05/jeopardy-robot-watson.html [08.02.2021].

Wallach, Wendell (2015): A Dangerous Master: How to Keep Technology from Slipping Beyond Our Control. New York: Basic Books.

Wallach, Wendell (2017): "Toward a ban on lethal autonomous weapons: surmounting the obstacles". In: Communications of the ACM 60(5), 28-34.

Wallach, Wendell / Allen, Collin (2009): Moral Machines: Teaching Robots Right from Wrong. Oxford: Oxford University Press.

Wallach, Wendell / Allen, Collin / Smit, Iva (2008): "Machine Morality: Bottom-up and Top-down Approaches for Modeling Human Moral Faculties". In: AI & Society 22(4), 565-582.

Walsh, James Igoe (2015): "Political Accountability and autonomous weapons". In: Research & Politics 2(4), 1-6.

Wandschneider, Dieter (1993): "'Neuer 'Ethikbedarf'. Technische Machbarkeit und Massentechnisierung als philosophisch-ethisches Problem". In: Daecke, Sigurd Martin / Henning, Klaus (Eds.): Verantwortung in der Technik: Ethische Aspekte der Ingenieurwissenschaften. Mannheim: BI Wissenschaftsverlag, 47-65.

Wang, Zhangjing / Yu, Wu / Qingqing, Niu (2020): "Multi-Sensor Fusion in Automated Driving: A Survey". In: IEEE Access 8, 2847-2868.

Wardrop, Murray (2010): "'Young will have to change names to escape cyber past' warns Google". In: Telegraph, August 18. Online: https://www.telegraph.co.uk/technology/google/7951269/Young-will-have-to-change-names-to-escape-cyber-past-warns-Googles-Eric-Schmidt.html [08.02.2021].

Warwick, Kevin (2002): I, Cyborg. London: Century.

Waters, Richard (2014a): "Google's Larry Page resists secrecy but accepts privacy concerns". In: Financial Times, May 30. Online: https://www.ft.com/content/f3b 127ea-e708-11e3-88be-00144feabdc0 [08.02.2021].

Waters, Richard (2014b): "FT interview with Google co-founder and CEO Larry Page". In: Financial Times, October 31. Online: https://www.ft.com/content/317 3f19e-5fbc-11e4-8c27-00144feabdc0 [08.02.2021].

Watzenig, Daniel / Horn, Martin (Eds.) (2016): Automated Driving: Safer and More Efficient Future Driving. Cham: Springer.

Weber, Karsten (2014). "Normative Herausforderungen an Technik für die Pflege im Alter. Hauswirtschaft und Wissenschaft". In: Europäische Zeitschrift für Haushaltsökonomie, Haushaltstechnik und Sozialmanagement 62, 116-121.

Weber, Karsten (2015): "MEESTAR: Ein Modell zur ethischen Evaluierung soziotechnischer Arrangements in der Pflege- und Gesundheitsversorgung". In: Weber, Karsten / Frommeld, Debora / Manzeschke, Arne / Fangerau, Heiner (Eds.): Technisierung des Alltags – Beitrag für ein gutes Leben?. Stuttgart: Franz Steiner, 247-262.

Weber, Karsten / Wackerbarth, Alena (2015): "Partizipative Gestaltung verlässlicher Assistenzsysteme für die Pflege alter und hochbetagter Menschen". In: Cunningham, Douglas / Hofstedt, Petra / Meer, Klaus / Schmitt, Ingo (Eds.): Informatik 2015. Bonn: Gesellschaft für Informatik, 1247-1249.

Weber, Sebastian / Hanke, John (2015): "Reality as Virtual Playground". In: Making Games, January 22. Online: https://www.makinggames.biz/feature/reality-as-a-virtual-playground 7286.html [08.02.2021].

Wegmann, Fabian (2014): Autonomie unbemannter Waffensysteme: das CCW-Expertentreffen zum Thema 'lethal autonomous weapons systems' und der gegenwärtige Stand der Technik. IFSH IFAR Working Paper 19. Online: http://edoc.v ifapol.de/opus/volltexte/2014/5677/pdf/IFAR_WP_19.pdf [08.02.2021].

Wegner, Jochen (2018): "Künstliche Intelligenzen überlegen nicht, was sie nach Feierabend machen". In: Die Zeit, April 17, 29-30. Online: https://www.zeit.de/wissen/2019-04/computerlinguistik-kuenstliche-intelligenz-sprachverarbeitung-richard-socher [08.02.2021].

WeGovNow (2020): Towards #WeGovernment: Collective and participative approaches for addressing local policy challenges. Online: https://wegovnow.eu// [08.02.2021].

Weichert, Thilo (2014): "Big Data, Gesundheit und der Datenschutz". In: Datenschutz und Datensicherheit - DuD 38(12), 831-838.

Weinberger, David (2018): "Optimization over explanation: Maximizing the benefits of machine learning without sacrificing its intelligence". In: Medium, January 28. Online: https://medium.com/@dweinberger/optimization-over-explanation-maximizing-the-benefits-we-want-from-machine-learning-without-347ccd9f 3a66 [08.02.2021].

Weiser, Mark (1999): "The Computer for the 21st Century". In: Scientific American 265(3), 94-105.

Weiss, Norman (2007): "Menschenrechtsschutz". In: Volger, Helmut (Ed.): Grundlagen und Strukturen der Vereinten Nationen. Muenchen: De Gruyter Oldenbourg, 163-188.

Weizenbaum, Joseph (1976): Computer Power and Human Reason: From Judgment to Calculation. New York: W. H. Freeman and Company.

Weizenbaum, Joseph (1987): "Not Without Us". In: ETC: A Review of General Semantics 44(1), 42-48.

Welzer, Harald (2019): "Fröhliche Unbedarftheit in Sachen Wirklichkeit". In: Die Zeit, August 14. Online: https://www.zeit.de/2019/34/digitalisierung-kuenstliche-intelligenz-algorithmen-denken-dummheit [08.02.2021].

Wertheim, Margaret (1999): The Pearly Gates of Cyberspace: A History of Space from Dante to the Internet. New York: W.W. Norton.

Wettstein, Florian (2010): "The Duty to Protect: Corporate Complicity, Political Responsibility, and Human Rights Advocacy". In: Journal of Business Ethics 96(1), 33-47.

Wettstein, Florian (2012a): "Human Rights as a Critique of Instrumental CSR: Corporate Responsibility Beyond the Business Case". In: Notizie di Politeia 28(106), 18-33.

Wettstein, Florian (2012b): "CSR and the Debate on Business and Human Rights: Bridging the Great Divide". In: Business Ethics Quarterly 22(4), 739-770.

Wettstein, Florian (2012c): "Human Rights as Ethical Imperatives for Business: The UN Global Compact's Human Rights Principles". In: Lawrence, Joanne T. / Beamish, Paul W. (Eds.): Globally Responsible Leadership: Managing According to the UN global compact. Thousand Oaks: Sage Publications, 73-88.

Wetz, Franz Josef (1998): Die Würde des Menschen ist antastbar: Eine Provokation. Stuttgart: Klett-Cotta.

Weyer, Johannes (2015): "Creating Order in Hybrid Systems: Reflexions on the Interaction of Man and Smart Machines". Working Paper 7. Dortmund: Technische Universitaet Dortmund. Online: https://www.ssoar.info/ssoar/bitstream/handle/document/10974/ssoar-2005-weyer_et_al-creating_order_in_hybrid_systems.pdf?sequence=1&isAllowed=y&lnkname=ssoar-2005-weyer_et_al-creating_order_in_hybrid_systems.pdf [08.02.2021].

White, Trevor N. / Baum, Seth D. (2017): "Liability for Present and Future Robotics Technology". In: Lin, Patrick / Abney, Keith / Jenkins, Ryans (Eds.): Robot Ethics 2.0: From Autonomous Cars to Artificial Intelligence. New York: Oxford University Press, 66-79.

Wiemeyer, Joachim (2013): "Unternehmensethik aus christlich-sozialethischer Sicht". In: Kirche und Gesellschaft 41(403), 3-16.

Wiener, Nobert (1988): The Human Use of Human Beings: Cybernetics and Society. Cambridge: Da Capo Press.

Wiener, Norbert (1948): Cybernetics: Or Control and Communication in the Animal and the Machine. Massachusetts: MIT Press.

Wildhaber, Isabelle / Lohmann, Melinda F. / Kasper, Gabriel (2019): "Diskriminierung durch Algorithmen – Überlegungen zum schweizerischen Recht am Beispiel von prädiktiver Analytik am Arbeitsplatz". In: Zeitschrift für Schweizerisches Recht 138(1), 459-489.

Wilhelms, Guenter (2018): "Wie die Digitalisierung das Verhältnis des Menschen zu seiner Arbeit verändert: Versuch einer Kritik". In: Amosinternational 12, 3-9.

Wilk, Asher (2019): "Teaching AI, Ethics, Law and Policy, Computers and Society". In: arXiv. Online: https://arxiv.org/ftp/arxiv/papers/1904/1904.12470.pdf [08.02.2021].

Willoweit, Dietmar (1992): "Die Veräusserung der Freiheit. Über den Unterschied von Rechtsdenken und Menschenrechtsdenken". In: Bielefeldt, Heiner / Brugger, Winfried / Dicke, Klaus (Eds.): Würde und Recht des Menschen. Festschrift Johannes Schwartlaender. Wuerzburg: Koenigshausen & Neumann, 255-268.

Wils, Jean-Pierre (2004): "Sakrale Gewalt. Elemente einer Urgeschichte der Transzendenz". In: Wils, Jean-Pierre (Ed.): Die Moral der Religion. Kritische Sichtungen und konstruktive Vorschläge. Paderborn: Ferdinand Schoeningh, 9-51.

Wils, Jean-Pierre / Mieth, Dietmar (1989): "Vorwort der Herausgeber". In: Wils, Jean-Pierre / Mieth, Dietmar (Eds.): Ethik ohne Chance? Erkundungen im technologischen Zeitalter. Tuebingen: Attempto, VII-XII.

Winfield, Alan F. T. / Jirotka, Marina (2017): "The Case for an Ethical Black Box". In: Gao, Yang / Fallah, Saber / Jin, Yaochu / Lekakou, Constantina (Eds.): Towards Autonomous Robotic Systems. Proceedings of TAROS 2017, Cham: Springer, 262-273.

Winikoff, Michael (2018): "Towards Trusting Autonomous Systems". In: El Fallah Segrouchni, Amal / Ricci, Alessandro / Trao, Son (Eds.): Engineering Multi-Agent Systems. Cham: Springer, 3-20.

Winkler, Eva C. / Ose, Dominik / Glimm, Hanno / Tanner, Klaus / Von Kalle, Christof (2013): "Personalisierte Medizin und Informed Consent. Klinische und ethische Erwägungen im Rahmen der Entwicklung einer Best Practice Leitlinie für die biobankbasierte Ganzgenomforschung in der Onkologie". In: Ethik in der Medizin 25(3), 195-203.

Winner, Hermann / Wachenfeld, Walter / Junietz, Phillip (2018): "Validation and Introduction of Automated Driving". In: Winner, Hermann / Prokop, Gunter / Maurer, Markus (Eds.): Automotive Systems Engineering II. Cham: Springer, 177-196.

Winner, Langdon (1980): "Do Artifacts Have Politics?" In: Daedalus 109(1), 121-136.

Winston, Patrick Henry (1992): Artificial Intelligence. Reading: Addison-Wesley Publishing. Online: https://courses.csail.mit.edu/6.034f/ai3/rest.pdf [08.02.2021].

Winter, Clemens (2005): Robotik in der Medizin. Eine strafrechtliche Untersuchung. Recht & Medizin 74. Frankfurt am Main: Peter Lang.

Winter, Sabrina (2020): "Undurchsichtige Lobbyarbeit der US-Techkonzerne aufgedeckt. Verstösse gegen EU-Transparenzregeln". In: Der Spiegel, September 28. Online: https://www.spiegel.de/netzwelt/netzpolitik/facebook-google-amazo n-apple-microsoft-undurchsichtige-lobbyarbeit-aufgedeckt-a-432bb716-0844-4a1 a-95c0-6bfec6e733c5 [08.02.2021].

Witschen, Dieter (1999): "Menschenrechte – Menschenpflichten: Anmerkungen zu einer Korrelation". In: Theologie und Glaube 42, 191-202.

Witschen, Dieter (2002): Christliche Ethik der Menschenrechte: Systematische Studien. Studien der Moraltheologie 28. Muenster: LIT-Verlag.

Witt, Elke (2015): "Digitale Spiegelbilder – Ethische Aspekte grosser Datensammlungen". In: Bundesgesundheitsblatt – Gesundheitsforschung – Gesundheitsschutz 58(8), 853-858.

Woelm, Erik (2018): "Warum mein Auto nie allein schuld sein wird". In: Rath, Matthias / Krotz, Friedrich / Karmasin, Matthias (Eds.): Maschinenethik. Wiesbaden: Springer, 173-191.

Wodak, Ruth (2016): Politik mit der Angst: Zur Wirkung rechtspopulistischer Diskurse. Horn: Edition Konturen.

Wohlfart, Guenter (2002): "Alte Geschichten zum wuwei". In: Eberfeld, Rolf / Wohlfart, Guenter (Eds.): Komparative Ethik: Das gute Leben zwischen den Kulturen. Koeln: Edition Chora.

Woisetschlaeger, David M. (2016): "Consumer Perceptions of Automated Driving Technologies: An Examination of Use Cases and Branding Strategies". In: Maurer, Markus / Gerdes, Christian J. / Lenz, Barbara / Winner, Hermann (Eds.): Autonomous Driving. Berlin: Springer, 687-706.

Wolbert, Werner (2003): "Menschenwürde, Menschenrechte und Theologie". In: Salzburger Theologische Zeitschrift 7(2), 161-179.

Wolbert, Werner (2008): Gewissen und Verantwortung: Gesammelte Studien. Studien zur Theologischen Ethik 118. Freiburg im Breisgau: Herder.

Wolf, Clark (2003): "Intergenerational Justice". In: Frey, Raymond G. / Wellman, Christopher Heath (Eds.): A Companion to Applied Ethics. Malden: Wiley Blackwell Publishing, 279-294.

Wolf, Ingo (2015): "Wechselwirkung Mensch und autonomer Agent". In: Maurer, Markus / Gerdes, Christan J. / Lenz, Barbara / Winner, Hermann (Eds.): Autonomes Fahren. Technische, rechtliche und gesellschaftliche Aspekte. Berlin: Springer, 103-125.

Wolf, Jean-Claude (1993): Utilitarismus, Pragmatismus und kollektive Verantwortung. Freiburg im Breisgau: Herder.

Wolfangel, Eva (2019): "Die Angst der Maschine". In: Die Zeit, August 8, 27-28. Online: https://www.zeit.de/2019/33/robotik-kuenstliche-intelligenz-emotionen-angst [08.02.2021]

Woodward, Alan (2012): "Viewpoint: Changing the way the internet is governed is risky". In: BBC, June 14. Online: http://www.bbc.com/news/technology-184405 58 [08.02.2021].

World Food Programme (2020): "COVID-19 will double number of people facing food crises unless swift action is taken". In: World Food Programme News. Online: https://www.wfp.org/news/covid-19-will-double-number-people-facing-food-crises-unless-swift-action-taken [08.02.2021].

World Government Summit (2017): The future of money. Back to the future – the internet of money. Online: https://www.worldgovernmentsummit.org/api/publications/document?id=23747dc4-e97c-6578-b2f8-ff0000a7ddb6 [08.02.2021].

World Health Organization (n.d.): Dual Use Research of Concern (DURC). Online: https://www.who.int/csr/durc/en/ [08.02.2021].

World Summit on the Information Society (2003): Declaration of Principles, Building the Information Society: a global challenge in the new Millennium. December 12, 2003. Document WSIS-03/GENEVA/DOC/4-E. Online: https://www.itu.int/net/wsis/docs/geneva/official/dop.html [08.02.2021].

Worstall, Tim (2012): "That Robot Economy And The Rentier Class". In: Forbes, December 10. Online: https://www.forbes.com/sites/timworstall/2012/12/10/that-robot-economy-and-the-rentier-class/#4e678294763f [08.02.2021].

Wrobel, Stefan / Voss, Hans / Koehler, Joachim / Beyer, Uwe / Auer, Soeren (2015): "Big Data, Big Opportunities". In: Informatik-Spektrum 38(5), 370-378.

Wyllie, Doug (2013): "How 'big data' is helping law enforcement". In: Police One, August 20. Online: https://www.policeone.com/police-products/software/Data-Information-Sharing-Software/articles/6396543-How-Big-Data-is-helping-law-enforcement/ [08.02.2021].

Yampolski, Roman V. (2013): "Artificial Intelligence Safety Engineering: Why Machine Ethics Is a Wrong Approach". In: Mueller, Vincent C. (Ed.): Philosophy and Theory of Artificial Intelligence. Cham: Springer, 289-296.

Yampolskiy, Roman V. (2018): "Could an artificial intelligence be considered a person under the law?". In: Science, October 7. Online: https://www.pbs.org/newshour/science/could-an-artificial-intelligence-be-considered-a-person-under-the-law [08.02.2021].

Yang, Xifan (2018): "Europa ist abgemeldet". In: Die Zeit, September 20. Online: https://www.zeit.de/2018/39/weltkonferenz-kuenstliche-intelligenz-shanghai-technologie-china-usa [08.02.2021].

Yarrow, Jay (2013): "Google CEO Larry Page Wants a Totally Separate World Where Tech Companies Can Conduct Experiments On People". In: Business Insider, May 16. Online: https://www.businessinsider.com/google-ceo-larry-page-wants-a-place-for-experiments-2013-5?r=US&IR=T [08.02.2021].

Yehya, Naief (2005): Homo cyborg: Il corpo postumano tra realtà e fantascienza. Milano: Elèuthera.

Yeung, Karen (2017): "'Hypernudge': Big data as a mode of regulation by design". In: Information, Communication & Society 20(1), 118-136.

Yom-Tov, Elad / Horvitz, Eric J. / White Ryen, William / De Choudhury, Munmun / Counts, Scott J. (2016): User behavior monitoring on a computerized device. US9427185. Online: https://www.freshpatents.com/-dt20141225ptan20140377727.php [08.02.2021]

Young, Simon (2006): Designer Evolution: A Transhumanist Manifesto. New York: Amherst.

Zenger, Erich (2009): "Du sollst keine anderen Götter haben neben mir: Der biblische Dekalog als Verfassungsurkunde einer humanen Gesellschaft". In: Nacke, Bernhard (Ed.): Orientierung und Innovation: Beiträge der Kirche für Staat und Gesellschaft. Freiburg im Breisgau: Herder, 207-222.

Zentrum für Digitalen Fortschritt D 64 (n.d.): Der Einfluss künstlicher Intelligenz auf Freiheit, Gerechtigkeit und Solidarität. Online: d-64.org [08.02.2021].

Zhenji, Lua / Happee, Riender / Cabrall, Christopher D. D. / Kyriakidis, Miltos / de Winter, Joost C.F. (2016): "Human factors of transitions in automated driving: A general framework and literature survey". In: Transportation Research Part F: Traffic Psychology and Behaviour 43, 183-198.

Zhou, Yijia / Huang, Jiaqi / Li, Guiqin / Chen, Feng / Gao, Zhiyuan (2019): "Autonomous Driving Ethics Case Study for Engineering Ethics Education". In: Association for Computing Machinery (Ed.): Proceedings of the 2019 International Conference on Modern Educational Technology. New York: Association for Computing Machinery, 106-110.

Ziegler, Sven (2016): "Robotik in der Pflege von Personen mit Demenz". In: Burzan, Nicole / Hitzler, Ronald / Kirschner, Heiko (Eds.): Materiale Analysen. Erlebniswelten. Wiesbaden: Springer, 53-69.

Ziemer, Laura (2001): "Application to Tibet of the principles on human rights and the environment". In: Harvard Human Rights Journal 14, 233-275.

Zimmer, Oliver: "Mythos Fortschritt: Jene, die sich auf ihn berufen, beanspruchen oftmals bloss das Deutungsmonopol über die Gegenwart". In: Neue Zuercher Zeitung, February 9, 43. Online: https://www.nzz.ch/feuilleton/mythos-fortschritt-es-geht-staendig-und-nur-um-deutungshoheit-ld.1457501?reduced=true [08.02.2021]

Zimmerli, Walther C. (1993): "Wandelt sich Verantwortung mit technischem Wandel?". In: Lenk, Hans / Rophl, Guenther (Eds.): Technik und Ethik. Stuttgart: Reclam, 92-111.

Zimmermann, Klaus F. (2015b): Nur noch Roboter und Selbstausbeutung? Über die Herausforderungen und Chancen der neuen Welt der Arbeit. IZA-Standpunkte 80. Bonn: Institute of Labor Economics IZA.

Zimmermann, Markus (2015a): "Grenzverschiebungen – Zur Natur des Menschen in bioethischen Diskursen". In: Bogner, Daniel / Muegge, Cornelia (Eds.): Natur des Menschen. Brauchen die Menschenrechte ein Menschenbild? Studien zur Theologischen Ethik 144. Freiburg im Uechtland: Academic Press, 175-195.

Zlotowski, Jakub / Proudfoot, Diane / Yogeeswaran, Kumar / Bartneck, Christoph (2014): "Anthropomorphism: Opportunities and challenges in human-robot interaction". In: International Journal of Social Robotics 7(3), 347-360.

Zoglauer, Thomas (2006): "Klone, Chimären und Cyborgs: Hybridwesen zwischen Natur und Technik". In: Erwägen – Wissen – Ethik 17, 611-612.

Zoller, David (2017): "Skilled Perception, Authenticity, and the Case Against Automation". In: Lin, Patrick / Abney, Keith / Jenkins, Ryans (Eds.): Robot Ethics 2.0: From Autonomous Cars to Artificial Intelligence. New York: Oxford University Press, 97-188.

Zuboff, Shoshana (2019): The Age of Surveillance Capitalism. The Fight for a Human Future at the New Frontier of Power. London: PublicAffairs.